Individual Differences in Children and Adolescents

Individual Differences in Children and Adolescents

Donald H. Saklofske
Sybil B. G. Eysenck
Editors

With a new introduction by the editors

Transaction Publishers

New Brunswick (U.S.A.) and London (U.K.)

New material this edition copyright © 1998 by Transaction Publishers, New Brunswick, New Jersey 08903. Originally published in 1988 by Hodder and Stoughton.

Library of Congress Catalog Number: 97-4510
ISBN: 1-56000-981-0
Printed in the United States of America

Library of Congress Cataloging-in-Publication Data

Individual differences in children and adolescents / edited by Donald H. Saklofske and Sybil B.G. Eysenck ; with a new introduction by the editors.
    p. cm.
Originally published: London : Hodder and Stoughton, 1988.
Includes bibliographical references (p.   ) and index.
ISBN 1-56000-981-0 (pbk. : alk. paper)
    1. Individual differences in children. 2. Individual differences in adolescence.
I. Saklofske, Donald H. II. Eysenck, Sybil B. G. (Sybil Bianca Giuletta)
BF723.I56I53   1997
155.4'182—dc21   97-4510
                                                     CIP

This book is dedicated to:

My parents, Harold and Fran,
and the memory of Denny – DHS

My husband, Hans – SBGE

Contents

Introduction to the Transaction Edition

We are especially pleased that "Individual Differences in Children and Adolescents" has been republished by Transaction Publishers, Rutgers University. First published in the United Kingdom in 1988, the book remained relatively unknown in the United States and Canada. The publication of our book in North America will certainly increase its accessibility on this side of the Atlantic Ocean.

Individual differences are a central theme in both the discipline and practice of psychology as well as other areas of the social and behavioral sciences. When this book was first published, our purpose was to assemble a growing body of literature on individual differences that reflected more than a "western" perspective. At that time there was little access to the kinds of research and applied issues that were being addressed in certain parts of the world, largely due to political restraints regarding the dissemination of information in scholarly journals or at scientific and professional meetings. As well, there was, and still is, somewhat of a tendency for scientific journals to be less willing to publish articles that don't fit with mainstream topics in psychology or which do not have direct relevance to western views surrounding the social issues of the day. Therefore, some of this exciting and important research on individual differences that we were aware of was not likely to be published or heard at major conferences. For all of these reasons, we undertook the task of assembling a unique collection of papers that would offer an international perspective on individual differences, with respect to both research and practical findings, especially in relation to children and adolescents. Such papers would also shed light not only on topics of concern and specific findings from these countries, but also on the methodologies employed in conducting particular research investigations.

We sought out authors who were recognized for their research contributions to the study of individual differences. Finding highly regarded authors from Australia, Canada, the United States, the United Kingdom and other 'western' countries was difficult only because there are so many psychologists and others who are researching especially important topics. The task was even harder as we sought authors from countries where fewer links had been established or were even permitted. We were fortunate to receive contributions from authors in eastern Europe, Africa, and Asia. We did not restrict the topics of authors but rather gave them free rein to write about their specific individual differences research programs or summarize relevant work that was occurring in their country.

We feel that many of the papers first published in this book some nine years ago are still of relevance and interest to an examination of individual differences in children and adolescents. Thus, we are including the complete collection of original papers as they were published in 1988. We decided not to ask any of the authors to change their papers although we recognize that some information in a few of the chapters may be a bit dated. However, we wished to preserve the integrity of the original publication which we trust will be of interest to anyone wanting to gain further insight into the study of individual differences within and outside of North America and Europe.

Today, there is a much more open and free exchange of ideas amongst psychologists throughout the world. As well, restrictions on travel are not as limiting as they were during the east-west split. Psychology associations exist in a great many countries, international psychology meetings attract large numbers of psychologists from all corners of the globe, and of course, there is e-mail and so many other ways of exchanging information quickly and widely. Associations such as the International Society for the Study of Individual Differences and its journal, *Personality and Individual Differences,* are now well established and boast a very international membership and readership respectively. We hope that our book will contribute to the growing body of information about individual differences that is now readily shared amongst psychologists from all countries.

We again thank all of the authors for their chapters and hope they will be pleased by this new publication of their original work. We are especially indebted to Irving Horowitz of Transaction Publishers for his encouragement to republish our book and make it available in North America. Thanks also to Charles Knight of Hodder and Stoughton Ltd. for assisting in the transfer of our book to Transaction Publishers. We thank The University of Saskatchewan for providing a publication grant and Dr. Michael Owen who was instrumental in ensuring the republication of this book. We gratefully recognize Professor Hans Eysenck who believed that we had produced a good book which should be more accessible to interested readers. This book belongs to all of you.

D.H.S. and S.B.G.E
January 1997

Contributors

Adriana Bäban, Psychologist, Institute of Hygiene and Public Health, Cluj-Napoca, Romania

I. Bango, Ministry of Education, Aszód, Hungary

Jeffrey P. Braden, PhD, University of Florida, Gainsville, Florida, USA

L. Bujdos, Ministry of Education, Aszód, Hungary

S. Channon, MPhil, Institute of Psychiatry, London, England

Aurelia Coaşan, Dr, Psychologist, Institute of Hygiene and Public Health, Cluj-Napoca, Romania

Clyde V. Collard, PhD, California State University, Turlock, California, USA

Irene Daum, Dipl Psych, Institute of Psychiatry, London, England

D. Derevenco, MD, Dr Med Sc, Institute of Hygiene and Public Health, Cluj-Napoca, Romania

Evangelos C. Dimitriou, MD, Medical School, University of Thessaloniki, Thessaloniki, Greece

E. Eisenriegler, MSc, University of Dusseldorf, Dusseldorf, Germany

John M. Elliott, PhD, National University of Singapore, Singapore

S.B.G. Eysenck, PhD, Institute of Psychiatry, London, England

H.J. Eysenck, PhD, DSc, Institute of Psychiatry, London, England

Antanas Goštautas, CandSc, Z. Januškevičius Institute for Cardiovascular Research, Kaunas, Lithuania, USSR

Loreta Grinevičeine, Z. Januškevičius Institute for Cardiovascular Research, Kaunas, Lithuania, USSR

Yuri L. Hanin, DSc, Research Institute of Physical Culture, Leningrad, USSR

Franz-Josef Hehl, PhD, University of Dusseldorf, Dusseldorf, Germany

Julia A. Hickman, PhD, University of Texas, Austin, Texas, USA

Dennis Hunt, PhD, University of Saskatchewan, Saskatoon, Saskatchewan, Canada

Saburo Iwawaki, PhD, Hyogo University of Education, Yashirocho, Katogun, Hyogo, Japan

Robert N. Jamison, PhD, Vanderbilt University, Nashville, Tennessee, USA

R. Jokiel, MSc, University of Dusseldorf, Dusseldorf, Germany

Bèla Kozèki, PhD, DSc, Institute for Psychology of the Hungarian Academy of Sciences, Budapest, Hungary

Philip de Lacey, PhD, University of Wollongong, Wollongong, New South Wales, Australia

Hyun Soo Lee, MA, MPhil, Chung-Ang University, Seoul, Korea

Foo Yee Long, MA, Woodbridge Hospital, Singapore

Rob McGee, PhD, Medical School, University of Otago, Dunedin, New Zealand

J. McLeod, PhD, University of Saskatchewan, Saskatoon, Saskatchewan, Canada

Malka Margalit, PhD, Tel Aviv University, Ramat Aviv, Tel Aviv, Israel

Terrie E. Moffitt, PhD, University of Wisconsin, Madison, Wisconsin, USA

Jethro A. Opolot, PhD, Makerere University, Kampala, Uganda

Arūnas Pakula, MSc, Z. Janušzkevičius Institute for Cardiovascular Research, Kaunas, Lithuania

K.M.H. Perera, MBBS, PhD, Ruhuna University, Galle, Sri Lanka

José Luis Porrata, MA, Clínica Dr Eugenio Fernándes García, Hato Rey, Puerto Rico

Lea Pulkkinen, PhD, University of Jyväskylä, Jyväskylä, Finland

Bikkar S. Randhawa, PhD, University of Saskatchewan, Saskatoon, Saskatchewan, Canada

Egon Reitz, MA, Wiesbaden Polytechnic, Wiesbaden, Germany

Cecil R. Reynolds, PhD, Texas A&M, University College Station, Texas, USA

D.H. Saklofske, PhD, University of Saskatchewan, Saskatoon, Saskatchewan, Canada

Ezio Sanavio, University of Padova, Padova, Italy

N. Seisdedos, PhD, TEA Ediciones SA, Madrid, Spain

David Share, PhD, University of Queensland, Brisbane, Queensland, Australia

Phil A. Silva, PhD, Medical School, University of Otago, Dunedin, New Zealand

Krishna K. Singh, MA, MPhil, Fulbourn Hospital, Cambridge, England

Pero Šipka, PhD, Military Academy of the Army, Belgrade, Yugoslavia

K. Sipos, MD, PhD, Ministry of Education, Aszód, Hungary

M. Sipos, Institute for Psychology of the Hungarian Academy of Sciences, Budapest, Hungary

Jennifer J. Vasterling, BA, Vanderbilt University, Nashville, Tennessee, USA

Sheila Williams, BSc, Medical School, University of Otago, Dunedin, New Zealand

Victor L. Willson, PhD, Texas A&M University, College Station, Texas, USA

M. Zakar, Ministry of Education, Aszód, Hungary

Foreword

It is universally agreed that science is international. Hitler's absurd notion that relativity theory was Jewish, and should therefore be banned, and Stalin's equally absurd proposition that it was bourgeois, and could therefore not be tolerated, are rightly regarded as abuses of the scientific spirit. Yet in psychology, practice limps behind theory. It is well known that American psychologists hardly ever read anything not written in English, and British, Canadian and Australian psychologists share this weakness. German, Scandinavian, Russian, Japanese or Spanish work only makes an impact when it is written in English, and published in American or British journals. This does not suggest that the international ideal is really widely accepted; it is more honoured in the breach than the observance!

In this book, the editors have attempted to make more widely known work done in many different countries. All the contributions are written in English, but they stem from a great variety of sources. Among the countries represented are Germany, Greece, Japan, Korea, Romania, Hungary, Singapore, Israel, Uganda, Sri Lanka, Puerto Rico, Finland, Lithuania, Italy, Spain, Yugoslavia and the USSR – as well as, to prevent the accusation of inverse exclusion, the USA, Canada, the United Kingdom, Australia and New Zealand. The common theme is that of individual differences in children and adolescents, a topic on which research is being carried out in many countries throughout the world, and it seemed desirable to bring together a reasonably representative sample of workers in this field from all the countries mentioned. Similarities and dissimilarities in approach and execution should be of considerable interest in overcoming the common insularity of workers in any one country.

The contributions are too numerous, and too diverse, to be discussed in this foreword. What is evident is that similar problems have been attacked in many different countries, and that methodologies, theories and approaches generally are sufficiently similar to allow comparison from one country to another. Perhaps there does, after all, exist some kind of international consensus about the topic that should be researched, the methods that should be used, and the theories that are most acceptable at present. Whether this is so or not, the reader must be the best judge. Whatever the topic he or she may be working on, however, it is almost certain that the reader will find something of interest in this volume, learn something not previously known, and get some feeling of the international nature of the field in general. There are of course differences in conceptions, standards and ways of approaching the field, but these only add to the interest of the endeavour. This book makes an important and unusual contribution, and may hopefully serve to further the ideal of internationalism in psychology.

H.J. Eysenck, PhD, DSc
Institute of Psychiatry, University of London

Editors' preface

The importance of, and renewed enthusiasm for, the study of individual differences is reflected in several recent books and the publication of the journal *Personality and Individual Differences*, beginning in 1980. As well, the International Society for the Study of Individual Differences (ISSID) was founded in 1983 to further promote communication among the international research community. Cross-cultural studies of the Junior Eysenck Personality Questionnaire gave rise to extensive correspondence between the second editor of this book and many psychologists engaged in clinical or research work with children and adolescents in a number of countries and cultures. Together with our association with ISSID and our individual work with colleagues from abroad, it became obvious that some extremely interesting individual difference research with younger age groups was being undertaken in far off countries which is rarely reported on in the Western psychological literature. While there is some commonality of interest in certain key areas such as delinquency, there is also considerable variation in the range of cognitive, personality and social characteristics examined and in the methods of study.

What we have tried to do in this book is to bring together some of these research studies in other countries and to provide an indication as to the general state of child and adolescent psychology internationally. Further, we hope to offer a relative balance between contemporary issues and international perspectives. We believe that such a collection of original research and descriptive overviews will serve as a useful reference source to anyone interested in the study of individual differences in children and adolescents.

Clearly, the task of preparing such a book seemed difficult but tempting. The difficulties were greater than we had anticipated. Since 'international perspectives' suggests contributions from all countries, we have to state quite categorically that there is absolutely no claim to completeness in our choice of countries, nor any attempt to justify which authors were approached to contribute. By and large the situation was that we contacted psychologists who had cooperated in Junior EPQ cross-cultural studies and who were, therefore, known to be working with children or adolescents, and were probably experimentally minded, since they were concerning themselves with personality testing. From there, other psychologists who were known or recommended to us were invited to contribute a chapter to our book, and so gradually we compiled a list of some 25 contributors' abstracts.

What we now offer in the following chapters is, therefore, inevitably confined to those authors who felt able to make a contribution from whatever country or culture they lived in. There is a wide difference in style of writing, topic and material covered, and conventionality of presentation between the countries. We welcome this difference and have consciously put few editorial constraints on the various styles, beyond the obvious need for concepts and language to be clearly understandable, and references to be comprehensive. We have tried to leave chapters in their original form so that the atmosphere is as authentic as possible, while obviously making linguistic editorial suggestions where authors had difficulties with the English language.

We hope that what we have achieved is a selective overview of what is happening in the field of individual differences in children and adolescents, in some widely different countries and cultures. Whether we have managed to gather a sufficiently international, though not representative, sample of chapters is up to the reader to judge.

We would like to thank all the authors who have written the following chapters and salute those, in particular, who attempted the task in a totally foreign tongue. We, the editors, at any rate, are confident that this venture has been worthwhile, having gained a great deal of new information about the field and having enjoyed the work we put into the compiling of this book.

D.H.S. and S.B.G.E.

1 Thinking, planning and personality

P. de Lacey, D. Hunt & Bikkar S. Randhawa

Introduction

The idea of personality is epistemologically fundamental: it is, in essence, 'the quality, character or fact of being a person as distinct from being a thing' (*Oxford English Dictionary*, p. 727). Personality is thus almost the ultimate subsuming category in the human conceptual structure; it is closely aligned with the most basic questions, pondered since ancient times, concerning the nature of man and the universe. Small wonder that the concept, and its component parts, have turned out to be pervasive in scope and evasive to both enquiry and analysis. In the seventeenth century, Locke had recognised within his interpretation of the notion of personality, this pervasiveness in encompassing cognitive, conative and affective domains of mental life, when he described it as 'those ideas which our powers of understanding provide, occurring in patterns of volition and in patterns of those actions to which they lead when we are at liberty' (Axtell, 1968, p. 240). In modern technical usage, however, the term personality has become restricted principally to refer to the affective domain, akin to a traditional use of 'disposition', which is defined as a 'natural tendency or bent of mind, especially in relation to moral or social qualities; mental constitution or temperament: turn of mind (possibly of astrological origin)' (*Oxford English Dictionary*, p. 493). Thus Lindzey, Hall & Manosevitz (1973) have come to describe personality as 'social skill or adroitness', or 'the most outstanding impression which (a person) creates in others' (p. 7). It is with the bearing of personality characteristics upon cognition that this chapter is essentially concerned.

Theoretical bases

Throughout the present century, many of the attempts that have been made on a theoretical plane to elaborate the structure of the construct of personality have not met with consistent success. One theory for which substantial empirical validity has been demonstrated is that of Eysenck (1967). In his search for the major dimensions of human personality, he identified three factors: Extraversion (EX), Neuroticism (N), and Psychoticism (P). The EX factor, say Eysenck & Eysenck (1975), 'may resemble' (p. 9) a picture described by Jung; that is, that the extravert is sociable, shuns solitude, takes chances, tends to be impulsive, aggressive and sometimes unreliable, and in most of these respects contrasts with the introvert. The high N-factor scorer is characteristically anxious, moody and often depressed, may sleep badly, have psychosomatic disorders and may show strong emotional reactions. The P factor is the most recent addition by Eysenck to his major personality dimensions. High P-factor scores are typical of people who are solitary, lacking in feeling or empathy, insensitive, tending to be cruel and hostile, liking unusual things, disregarding danger and liking to upset others. Individuals of this bent indulge in sensation seeking, are poor socialisers and seldom feel guilt. Eysenck describes non-institutionalised, high P-factor scorers as 'tough-minded'.

As well as identifying these three major basic personality dimensions, Eysenck has suggested the existence of three *traits*: Impulsiveness (I), Venturesomeness (V), and Empathy (E), which represent a second level of his hierarchy of personality characteristics (Eysenck & Eysenck, 1978). Another postulated personality characteristic is 'faking good', or dissimulation, measured by a Lie (L) scale. Initially, this was considered merely to indicate the reliability of a subject's responses on the other scales, but has since been regarded as measuring 'some stable personality factor which may possibly reveal some degree of social naivete' (Eysenck & Eysenck, 1975). All of these factors, both domains and traits, have demonstrated a high degree of consistency and factorial validity across several national settings (Eysenck & Eysenck, 1977; Eysenck & Eysenck, 1978; Eysenck & Saklofske, 1983). This consistency was also found in a study by Randhawa, de Lacey & Saklofske (1986), who cautioned against an uncritical use of Eysenck's measures across cultures, while noting the demands which mainstream cultural expectations tend, perforce, to impose upon minority cultures and subcultures in an industrialised country.

Efforts to develop a theoretical basis for the more clearly defined notion of cognitive functioning have been carried somewhat further. Building on the earlier psychometric and Piagetian approaches, both Sternberg (1982) and Randhawa (1985) have emphasised a universality of intellectual processes, in some contrast to others, such as Berry (1984) who have questioned the usefulness of comparing intellectual functioning across cultures in a quantitative manner. Most cognitive researchers, however, have acknowledged the considerable influence of culture and environment in the realisation of cognitive potential. Luria, employing recent neurological findings, extended the attempts of Berlyne (1960) and Hebb (1949) to link the formerly somewhat separate enquiries of psychology and neurophysiology. Moruzzi & Magoun (1949), and Lindsley (1958) had described a Reticular Formation (RF), a small network of neurones in the brain stem, serving as a kind of general alarm, by responding to any sensory stimulus with facilitating impulses, arousing the cortex over a wide area. The RF thus awakens the organism to action, maintaining it in an aroused condition until the cortex regains control of the situation by sending inhibiting impulses back to regulate the amount of activity in the RF. Luria (1966) and Das (1985) also referred to the RF, which Luria considered to be the main structure in the first of three interrelated functional blocks in the central nervous system, providing respectively for arousal, processing and planning functions, and all operating at three hierarchical zones, described as the primary, secondary and tertiary projection areas. These three cognitive functions – arousal, processing and planning – are of especial interest to the present authors, and will be referred to later in this chapter.

The personality–intelligence relationship enigma

There are surprisingly few data of substance on any relationship between personality characteristics and cognitive functions. But the possibility of this relationship has long been a source of interest and speculation. The absent-minded professor and the mad genius have epitomised a category of stereotypes which might be derived from the effects of pressures of social conformity and preoccupation as much as from any real link between personality type and level of cognitive functioning. Yet, at a less empirical, logical or observational level, it might be argued that intelligence, or sophistication of cognitive functioning, and some personality characteristics should show a degree of relationship. Teachers notice among their charges that some children who are, for example, lively and distractible, though not to the point of formal hyperactivity, seem to lack the persistence necessary to achieve at a high level. On the other hand, markedly introverted children with an excess of anxiety and an apparent unwillingness to try, may not demonstrate high levels of achievement and this behavioural tendency could be mistakenly interpreted by less observant teachers as sullen obstinacy. Yet, there may be many lively, confident, extraverted children who do well.

More formal enquiries, however, have found relatively little association between personality characteristics and level of cognitive functioning, inasmuch as these dimensions have been defined in ways that might reveal any relationship. In a recent study in Australia, Randhawa, de Lacey & Saklofske (1986) reported some sex, race and age differences among aboriginal and white children on several personality characteristics. This has been corroborated in a further study by Hunt, de Lacey & Randhawa (1986). They concluded that there are probably cultural and subcultural differences in personality dimensions and traits across the groups being studied, and that the differences found may be associated with some cognitive differences. Earlier, Eysenck (1970) had proposed that personality and intelligence are not correlated; and Saklofske (1985) has recently supported this hypothesis in a formal study. Saklofske used the Junior Eysenck Personality Questionnaire (JEPQ) to measure the personality dimensions, and some standardised intelligence tests – part of the Woodcock–Johnson Psycho-Educational Battery, and the Kauffman Assessment Battery for Children. Saklofske found only one significant relationship: a negative correlation between Psychoticism and Sequential Processing. His analyses suggested to him that Eysenck was correct: 'that personality and intelligence are uncorrelated' (p. 433). But an earlier study, to which Saklofske did not refer (no doubt because it was not directly based on the Eysenckian theory with which he was concerned) might have suggested otherwise. Hunt & Randhawa (1980) compared above-normal-intelligence and below-normal-intelligence children on measures from the Children's Personality Questionnaire of Porter & Cattell (1959). A discriminant analysis of their results suggested that high-intelligent children 'tended towards being excitable, assertive, enthusiastic, venturesome and forthright, whereas the low group tended towards being phlegmatic, obedient, sober, shy and shrewd' (Hunt & Randhawa, 1980, p. 902). It seems very likely that some of Eysenck's personality variables, such as the traits of Venturesomeness and Empathy, and the dimensions of Extraversion and Psychoticism, are represented in the Porter and Cattell measures. A likely link between the findings in this earlier study and one recently conducted by the present authors will be discussed later in this chapter.

Are personality and intelligence unrelated? Might not the problems of identifying a relationship be based on a lack of consistency of the manifestations of both personality and cognition; and might this very inconsistency be a function of the definitions of the (elusive, remember) characteristics, rather than an unequivocal lack of a relationship between them? In part to answer this question, but also to illuminate other manifestations of personality and cognition, especially across ethnic and cultural boundaries, the authors carried out an extensive study in Canada and Australia, among a variety of children.

Thinking, problem-solving, planning and personality

The research in the study we are about to describe is part of a long-term enquiry into Australian children's mental processes, both cognitive and affective, and of their school achievement and social development. The section of the work described here is related to a rather broader set of measures of Eysenckian personality characteristics than Saklofske (1985) used in his study, and extends work on cognition conducted by Leasak, Hunt & Randhawa (1982) and Hunt & Randhawa (1980, 1983) based on Luria's model of functional processing units.

Cognitive functioning is seen here, not only in terms of intelligence, but also in terms of the dynamic process of thinking, which includes considering various possibilities, making inferences and planning ahead, to solve well-structured problems.

One such class of problems is the 'river-crossing' task of which the 'missionaries-cannibals' problem is an example. This problem is well structured in the sense that its knowledge base is provided to the children attempting it, an algorithm is available (though not necessarily known to the subjects) for the completion of the task required in the solution, and an end state is known to the subject. Most of the previous research on solving this problem has been carried out with adults, with the main aim of obtaining simulated computer models of the cognitive processes involved (Atwood & Polson, 1976; Greeno, 1974; Jeffries, Polson, Razran & Atwood, 1977; Reed, Ernst & Banerji, 1974; Simon & Reed, 1976; Thomas, 1974). But constructing a computer program which may be typical of the processes followed by most people in solving a well-structured problem does not demonstrate that subjects would necessarily think that way. As Das (1985) suggests, creative cognitive gambling may be more typical of problem-solving behaviour. Again, no study so far has examined directly the effect of the mode of presentation or task complexity on the problem outcome, using children of different age groups; nor has the relationship between success on this task and measured intelligence and personality variables been investigated.

An Australian study

As the first phase in the enquiry, the authors carried out a series of studies largely to discover any relationship between various areas of cognitive functioning and Eysenck's personality dimensions and traits. The main study among these was carried out in Australia among primary-school children (Years kindergarten to 6) and high-school children (Years 7 to 12). The sample consisted of 96 pupils in Year 6 (mean chronological age 135 months) and 61 pupils in Year 8 (mean chronological age 165 months) from four schools situated in rural and urban New South Wales.

The children were given several tests to measure certain cognitive abilities and some personality characteristics. These tests are described in another report (Hunt, de Lacey & Randhawa, 1987); here we are concerned with three of them: two personality measures, a measure of verbal intelligence and a problem-solving task known as the River-Crossing Problem.

Personality was measured by the Junior Eysenck Personality Questionnaire (JEPQ) which gives measures of Neuroticism (N), Psychoticism (P), Social Desirability (L) and Extraversion (EX); and the children's version of the IVE Scale which gives a measure of Impulsivity (I), Venturesomeness (V) and Empathy (E). The JEPQ consists of 81 statements and the IVE 77 statements to which the student answers 'yes' or 'no'. These tests were administered orally with the children following the written statements in order to minimize reading difficulties.

Intelligence was measured by the Peabody Picture Vocabulary Test (PPVT). This test gives a verbal intelligence estimate by measuring hearing vocabulary and has been found to be a reliable measure with Australian children (Taylor, de Lacey & Nurcombe, 1972).

The standard river-crossing problem consists of transporting a number of travellers by boat across a river from the left to the right bank. The task is restricted by not allowing certain combinations of travellers and restricting the number of people in the boat. For the purpose of the present study, two forms of the river-crossing problem were used, each designed to be presented in two contrasting formats – either on an Apple 2e micro-computer, or by a hands-on presentation involving the movement by the student of a model boat and model men. The first form involved three blue and three green men and the second form involved two blue and two green men. In each case the restrictions were such that at no time were the blue men to outnumber the green men on either bank and there could be only one or two men in the boat at one time. All subjects were tested individually with an equal number of children for each mode of presentation. Each child completed the problem at each level of difficulty, with the levels of difficulty counter-balanced across the design. The computer programme returned the child to the original position if an illegal move was made and the experimenter asked the child to say why such a particular move was illegal. The same procedure was followed in the presentation mode. Move-by-move protocols were recorded by the researchers in both modes. If the subject did not complete the task in either 30 moves or 15 minutes, the task was aborted and the student was considered as being unsuccessful at the task. The number of legal moves, illegal moves, backward moves and time taken to complete the task were recorded.

A full analysis of the results are reported elsewhere (Hunt, de Lacey & Randhawa, 1986). For the present purposes, we are concerned only with the measures of verbal intelligence (PPVT), problem solving (the river-crossing test) and the two personality tests (JEPQ and the IVE).

The results of the Hunt, de Lacey & Randhawa study (1987) showed that there was a significant difference in verbal intelligence between those who were successful on the river-crossing problem and those who were not ($r = .21$; $p = .01$); however, there were no personality differences between those who were successful and those who were not, except for the trait of empathy which is discussed below. This would indicate that verbal intelligence and personality are as Eysenck suggests, independent. An examination of those who did not succeed on the task, however, showed that there was a significant relationship between scores on certain personality variables and measures of performance on the river-crossing problem such as the number of legal and illegal moves made, the average time it took them to make a move, and the number of backward moves, they made on the way. From Table 1.1, it can be seen that there was a significant negative correlation between the time taken per move and Impulsiveness ($r = -.27$), a significant positive correlation between the number of backward or retraced moves and Venturesomeness ($r = .36$) and Extraversion ($r = .42$), a significant positive correlation between illegal moves and Psychoticism ($r = .30$) and a positive correlation between legal moves and Extraversion ($r = .44$). It could be argued that tendencies towards impulsiveness, venturesomeness, extraversion and psychoticism in the successful group were mediated by the group's higher verbal intelligence and used to advantage, while in the unsuccessful group these personality characteristics were not used to advantage because of the lower verbal intelligence of the group. Another way to interpret these correlations would be to extend the definition of intelligence to include, as already stated, making inferences, planning and problem solving. If this is done, then intelligence and personality are not independent. It is the restriction of the breadth of what is considered to be intelligent behaviour that gives rise to the independence of intelligence and personality. In spite of these explanations, the

Table 1.1 Product moment correlations for successful and unsuccessful groups between personality and river-crossing variables

Variable	Successful (N=105)	Unsuccessful (n=52)
Time	n.s.	I($-.27$)*
Backward moves	n.s.	V(.36)*,EX(.42)***
Illegal moves	n.s.	P(.30)**
Legal moves	n.s.	EX(.44)**

*$p<.05$; **$p<.01$; ***$p<.001$

Table 1.2   Product moment correlations for the total group (N=160) between verbal intelligence and personality variables

Variables	Extraversion	Venturesomeness	Lie Scale
Verbal intelligence	.14*	.24**	−.24**
Extraversion		.46**	−.04
Venturesomeness			−.15

*p<.05; **p<.001

Hunt *et al.* (1986) study did, in fact, as seen in Table 1.2, show a significant positive correlation between verbal intelligence and Extraversion ($r = .14$; $p < .05$), and between verbal intelligence and Venturesomeness ($r = .24$; $p < .001$). There was also a negative correlation ($r = -.24$; $p = .001$) between intelligence and the Lie Scale in agreement with trends found by Eysenck (1971) and Saklofske (1985), suggesting that children displaying dissimulation, or social naivete, tend not to be among the smartest. These results suggest that intelligence and personality, however they might be defined, are not unrelated.

The interesting effect of empathy

In previous research in this area, the empathy measure has proved to be rather unstable, raising questions about its validity. In the Hunt, de Lacey & Randhawa (1986) study, however, empathy turned out to be relatively stable. Empathy is a recent term, dating only from the beginning of the century. It is 'the power of entering into the experience of, or understanding, objects or emotions outside ourselves' (*Oxford English Dictionary*, p. 329); and this meaning can be seen to be consistent with the questions in the Empathy Scale, for example 'Would you feel sorry for a lonely stranger in a group?'; and 'Does it affect you very much when one of your friends seems upset?'. In the present study, the empathy variable seems to be important for success in the computer mode but not necessarily so in the hands-on mode. Although empathy has been shown to be the least valid of the Eysenck traits, it is interesting to note that it is the only personality variable which differentiates between those who were successful on the task and those who were not ($p < .05$). In a discriminant analysis of these data, Empathy was also the variable that discriminated the most between those who were successful and those who were not. However, in the multivariate analysis this difference was shown to be in the computer mode only. It could be argued that, as the empathy score is a measure of the extent to which a person is able to relate to, and is affected by, other people's actions, those who score high in this area find that, when attempting the problem, they are able to become more involved in the problem situation, e.g. men being attacked and crossing a river to escape, which in turn could have affected the degree of attention shown to the problem-situation details. Certainly this was reflected in some of the comments made by the students such as: 'It's not fair he gets eaten' or 'Couldn't he stay and help him?' Such comments reflect an active involvement of those students in the specifics of the situation. Apparently this is easier to do in the computer mode than the hands-on mode.

If we consider that problem solving is a component of intelligence as Sternberg (1984) suggests, and that empathy implies attention and arousal as part of Luria's Block 1 of cognitive functioning, then the relationship we have found between empathy and intelligence is understandable, and questions the conclusion of Eysenck, supported by Saklofske, that personality and intelligence are uncorrelated.

The mutability of personality characteristics

In the context of some initial evidence of the relationship between personality measures and cognitive measures, and the fact that cognitive interventions have been found to be effective and durable, it is tempting to propose the possibility of mutability of personality structure due to intervention, acculturation, and dramatic and sudden changes within a culture or across cultures. It is not uncommon to find that once docile and law-abiding adolescents in many present-day situations volunteer to be members of suicide squads. Similarly, in times of economic depression or high unemployment, crime and juvenile delinquency rates soar, while in times of war or reconstruction after a natural disaster they plummet. Commitment to a cause, so it seems, alters the manifested personality repertoire of individuals, groups and societies. Represented in behavioural schemes of once emphatic, rational, and introverted individuals, under the changed circumstances, these become apparent manifestations characteristic of psychotic, cruel and irrational tendencies. Is not this to be expected? For if this were not possible, then what is the utility of psychotherapy or medical intervention for the treatment of mental disorders?

There is a speculative hint in the Randhawa, de Lacey & Saklofske (1986) study that, both in personality traits and dimensions, the Aboriginal children, as they progressed through school, from primary to secondary, became more similar to the Anglocelt Australians. Stability of traits, once a sought-after characteristic resulting from attempts at measurement of difficult and complex human qualities, may not be the ideal psychologists should be pursuing. Is the trait notion still alive and well or is it vanishing in importance?

As it has been argued that personality characteristics are mutable, and as the research reported here indicates that affective and cognitive processes may be more closely related than hitherto believed, there may be implications for educational and psychological practice. Since it appears that the two processes are interdependent, attempts to improve or enhance one may be more effective when this interdependence is recognised in practice. As with many new findings in psychology or education, an intuitive though previously unclearly-defined belief in the interdependence of affect and cognition, as part of the 'whole man', can be seen historically from ancient times in the curriculum of the Greek city state schools, and in the trivium and quadrivium of ancient Roman schools, and later in the prescription for school studies of educational philosophers like Pestalozzi and Herbart. Today, it can be seen in the practice of counsellors, and some teachers, when they try to help children to feel positive and competent about their capacity to manage their school work, at least sufficiently to attain worthwhile goals. But intuition can be a mischievous guide – while it can lead to a great many productive policies and practices, its misguidance is equally legion. Only research like the enquiries reported here can confirm the validity of the suggestions that intuition may direct us to.

Conclusion

The degree of any relationship between personality variables and intelligence can now be seen most likely to depend upon how these two rather global human attributes are defined. On the one hand, Eysenck (1986) has recently emphasised that 'there is a central core to IQ tests which is quite independent of reasoning judgement, problem-solving learning, comprehension and memory' (p. 76). If this is true, cognition and personality may in fact (though not necessarily) be independent. However, on the other hand, Sternberg (1984), in his triarchic theory of intelligence, has offered a multiple-faceted definition of intelligence, which would suggest that a relationship between intelligence and personality is quite possible, or even likely. In general, the more the components of intelligence and personality are distinguished and refined, the more it seems that significant correlations between them are likely to appear.

The significant relationship found between the river crossing score and verbal intelligence is not surprising. Presumably, a substantial level of verbal intelligence is a requirement for all problem situations. It is necessary, in such situations, to articulate concepts, and the bearing of one concept upon another; and also to interpret and convey both the context and the content of these concepts, by means of words, which must be selected with discrimination and precision.

It is barely a century since cognitive and affective aberrations were widely considered to be inevitable parts of a general malady, the victims of which were often consigned to be restrained in institutions for the possessed and the insane. From the early decades of the century, however, with the gradual unfolding of the nature of some of the characteristics of intellectual handicap on one hand, and emotional disturbance on the other, the possibility of substantial interaction between them has tended to become neglected. Where such a possibility has been investigated, the enquiry has been made on rather a global scale, and an interaction has not generally been found. As some researchers like Hansen (1986) are beginning to realise, the time is ripe for a re-examination of this problem. The study reported here has helped re-open the question of the existence of such an interaction, and has produced some evidence that there probably is a widespread relationship between personality and intelligence, and that the relationship may be stronger than hitherto suspected. Further investigations will extend the illumination of this question.

References

ATWOOD, M. & POLSON, P. (1976) A process model for water-jug problems. *Cognitive Psychology*, **8**, 191–216.

AXTELL, J.L. (1968) *The educational writings of John Locke*, Cambridge: Cambridge University Press.

BERLYNE, D. (1960) *Conflict, arousal and curiosity*, New York: McGraw Hill.

BERRY, J.W. (1984) Towards a universal psychology of cognitive competence. *International Journal of Psychology*, **19**, 335–61.

DAS, J.P. (1985) *Cognitive assesssment: the measurement of attention, coding and planning*. Edmonton, Alberta: University of Alberta, Centre for Mental Retardation.

EYSENCK, H.J. (1967) *Biological basis for personality*, Springfield, Ill.: Thomas.

EYSENCK, H.J. (1970) *The structure of human personality*, London: Methuen.

EYSENCK, H.J. (1971) Relationship between intelligence and personality. *Perceptual and Motor Skills*, **32**, 637–8.

EYSENCK, H.J. (1986) Intelligence and reaction time: the contribution of Arthur Jensen. In S. Modgil & C. Modgil (eds.), *Arthur Jensen: consensus and controversy*, Bartombe, U.K.: Falmer Press.

EYSENCK, H.J. & EYSENCK, S.B.G. (1975) *Manual of the Eysenck Personality Questionnaire*, London: Hodder & Stoughton.

EYSENCK, S.B.G. & EYSENCK, H.J. (1977) The place of impulsiveness in a dimensional system of personality description. *British Journal of Social and Clinical Psychology*, **16**, 57–68.

EYSENCK, S.B.G. & EYSENCK, H.J. (1978) Impulsiveness and venturesomeness: their position in a dimensional system of personality description. *Psychological Reports*, **43**, 1247–55.

EYSENCK, S.B.G. & SAKLOFSKE, D.H. (1983) A comparison of response of Canadian and English children on the Junior Eysenck Personality questionnaire. *Canadian Journal of Behavioural Science*, **15**, 121–30.

GREENO, J.H. (1974) Hobbits and Orcs: Acquisition of a sequential concept. *Cognitive Psychology*, **6**, 270–92.

HANSEN, R. (1986) They have a feel for thinking. *Human Intelligence*, **7** (2), 3.

HEBB, D.O. (1949) *The organisation of behaviour*, New York: Wiley.

HUNT, D., DE LACEY, P.R. & RANDHAWA, B.S. (1987) Problem solving, planning and personality. *International Journal of Psychology*, **22**, 97–110.

HUNT, D. & RANDHAWA, B.S. (1980) Personality factors and ability groups. *Perceptual and Motor Skills*, **50**, 902.

HUNT, D. & RANDHAWA, B.S. (1983) Cognitive processes and achievement. *Alberta Journal of Educational Research*, **29**, 206–15.

JEFFRIES, R., POLSON, P.Q., RAZRAN, L. & ATWOOD, M.E. (1977) A process model for missionaries-cannibals and other river-crossing problems. *Cognitive Psychology*, **9**, 412–40.

LEASACK, J., HUNT, D. & RANDHAWA, B.S. (1982) Cognitive processing, intervention and achievement. *Alberta Journal of Educational Research*, **28**, 257–66.

LINDSLEY, D.B. (1958) The reticular system: perceptive discrimination. In H.H. Jasper, L.D. Proctor, R.S. Knighton, W.C. Noshay, and R.T. Costello, *The reticular formation and the brain*, (513–34), Boston: Little-Brown.

LINDZEY, G., HALL, C.S. & MANOSEVITZ, M. (eds.). (1973) *Theories of personality: primary sources and research*, New York: Wiley.

LURIA, A.R. (1966) *The human brain and psychological processes*, New York: Harper & Row.

MORUZZI, G. & MAGOUN, H.W. (1949) Brainstem reticular formation and activation of the E.E.G. *E.E.G. Clinical Neurology*, **1**, 455–73.

Oxford English Dictionary, (1933), Oxford: Clarendon Press.

PORTER, R.B. & CATTELL, R.B. (1959) *Handbook for the Children's Personality Questionnaire*, Champaign, IL: Institute for Personality and Ability Testing.

RANDHAWA, B.S. (1985) Cultural relativism and determinism: intelligent behaviour. In M.E. Poole, P.R. de Lacey & B.S. Randhawa (eds.), *Australia in transition: culture and life possibilities*, Sydney: Harcourt, Brace & Jovanovich.

RANDHAWA, B.S., DE LACEY, P.R. & SAKLOFSKE, D.H. (1986) Personality and behavioural measures: Gender, age, and race contrasts in an Australian setting. *International Journal of Psychology*, **21**, 389–402.

REED, S.K., ERNST, G.W. & BANERJI, R. (1974) The role of analogy in transfer between similar problem states. *Cognitive Psychology*, **8**, 165–90.

SAKLOFSKE, D.H. (1985) The relationship between Eysenck's major personality dimensions and simultaneous and sequential processing in children. *Personality and Individual Differences*, **6**, 429–33.

SIMON, H.A. & REED, S.K. (1976) Modelling strategy shifts in a problem-solving task. *Cognitive Psychology*, **8**, 86–97.

STERNBERG, R.J. (1982) *Handbook of human intelligence*, Cambridge: Cambridge University Press.

STERNBERG, R.J. (1984) What should intelligence tests test? Implications of a triarchic theory of intelligence for intelligence testing. *Educational Researcher*, **13** (1), 5–15.

TAYLOR, L.J., DE LACEY, P.R. & NURCOMBE, B. (1972) An assessment of the reliability of the Peabody Picture Vocabulary Test. *Australian Psychologist*, **7**, 167–9.

THOMAS, J.C. (1974) An analysis of behaviour in the Hobbits-Orcs problem. *Cognitive Psychology*, **6**, 257–69.

2 Individual differences from the perspective of computer-guided psycho-educational diagnosis

J. McLeod

> . . . however modest and precise may seem the conduct of [theoretical researchers'] own actual investigation, it nearly always terminates with and justifies itself by a number of sweeping conclusions; and these latter will be found essentially to imply some assumed general function or process, such as 'memory', 'association', 'attention', . . . etc., and at the same time that this function is adequately represented by the laboratory test. To take for instance the speed of mental association, there is hardly a psychologist of note who has not at some time or other made wide reaching assertions . . .; the more practically minded . . . content themselves with demonstrating the details of its actual conduct.
>
> . . . The general fact is that our limited intellects can only hope to deal with the infinite complexity of Nature after analyzing it down into its bare unaesthetic elements.
>
> *Charles Spearman, 1904*

Individual differences have always been a self-evident 'given' to educators and psychologists whose work has been concerned with children who have special educational needs. Indeed, one might mischievously observe that by the time many educationists had 'discovered' individual differences, special educators had moved on to the re-discovery of individual similarities, as exemplified by the movement toward mainstreaming and normalization.

However, psycho-educational diagnosis is primarily a process of uncovering and exploring clinically relevant and significant deviations in behaviour and performance and it is obvious that the computer, with its ability to make searches of data, to carry out analyses of the data and to apply a vast inventory of rules, quickly and accurately, offers the prospect of revolutionary help to the diagnostician. But experience with an ongoing research project in Canada whose ultimate goal is to produce an 'expert system' for psycho-educational diagnosis of learning difficulties has led the author to question whether the potential extent of the revolution, as it relates to mental measurement and the perspective in which individual differences are generally viewed, might not be greater than is presently realised.

The beginnings of the study of individual differences

Until the middle of the nineteenth century, psychologists (whose work was virtually a sub-category of philosophy) thought in terms of 'the mind', and were largely concerned with the structure of, or analysis of mental processes within, that monolithic concept in terms of ideas and images linked by the laws of association. Intra-human variability in intelligence had not even become a topic for psychological study, 'intelligence' having the connotation of something possessed by human beings which distinguishes them from lower species. In the literature of nineteenth-century novelists such as Dickens and Trollope, to say that one person 'had more intelligence' than another would be interpreted as meaning that the first person had received some news which the second had not; a Victorian listener would not have concluded that the first person was 'cleverer' than the second. And, insofar as anyone had considered the academic aptitudes of children, the English educational system of 'payment-by-results' whereby elementary schools were reimbursed according to the number of students who successfully completed each grade suggests that, in that country at any rate, there was an implicit assumption that all children except idiots and imbeciles had the potential to master the grade curriculum. Special schools for the mentally retarded did not begin to appear until the end of the nineteenth century. The reaction time experiment, which might be considered to have been the first vehicle for the study of individual differences, was invented by Helmholtz (Woodworth, 1951, p. 299), originally for the purpose of determining the speed of sensory nerve transmission *in man*, not for the purpose of studying the *variability* of transmission speed in men.

But there had been significant work in the field of individual differences in the second half of the nineteenth century, which stemmed from the study of the 'Personal Equation', i.e. reaction time. It is probably no accident that Galton, in his seminal paper 'Classification of Men According to Their Natural Gifts' (1869) relies heavily on the work of Quetelet, the then Astronomer Royal of Belgium, who had developed the 'Law of Deviation from an Average'. Half a century earlier, Maskelyne, the British Astronomer Royal, had fired an assistant for habitually 'incorrectly' recording the time of transit of a star across the reference grid in the telescope. This episode led to interest by astronomers into the unreliability of human observers, and to the discovery that individuals differed in their reaction times. Galton's massive collection of anthropometric data, and more particularly his mathematical treatment of that data, set the stage which has effectively provided a scenario for the interpretation of individual differences until the present; i.e. standard scores, standard deviations, the normal curve of probability. It is now taken for granted that evaluation of individual performance is made by assessing the deviation of an individual's test score from the population mean in standard deviation units; that the reliability of an individual evaluation is assessed in terms of the probability with which the obtained score deviates from a hypothetical true score, etc. Galton's (1869) dictum that the 'law of deviation from the average is perfectly general in its application' has been faithfully observed in the subsequent history of mental assessment.

The limitations of 'range of confidence' for individual assessment

In survey-type research, or in research which is concerned with comparing the characteristics of identifiable groups, such an approach has proved indispensible. Whether or not it has been quite so useful in psychological evaluation of the individual is open to question. Educational and clinical psychologists have been exhorted by their more mathematically sophisticated colleagues to express a child's measured IQ as a range, e.g. between 91 and 109 in the case of a student whose obtained IQ is 100, in order to emphasize that the observed IQ is subject to error of measurement. However, it is not always helpful to proceed clinically on the hypothesis that the child might be somewhere between low average intelligence and high average. And the ambiguity gets worse as more test data are accumulated. Consider, for example, a child with a measured IQ of 100 and an Educational Quotient of 90, assuming means of 100 and standard deviations of 15, and assuming both the IQ and the educational assessment to have reliabilities of 0.91. The test information tells us that we may conclude with 95% certainty that the child's IQ is somewhere between 91 and 109 and that her/his true Educational Quotient lies between 81 and 99. Error variance compounds, so the observed discrepancy between the scores, 10, is subject to an error of plus or minus 13 for 95% certainty, i.e. her/his educational underachievement is between 23 points and −3, somewhere between marginal overachievement and serious underachievement. In making multiple score comparisons, observed differences soon drown in their compounded unreliabilities, which immediately presents a problem when attempting to develop rules for a computer-based diagnostic expert system if one approaches the task along conventional psychometric lines.

The traditional approach has led us to think in terms of performance as 'low' or 'high' in comparison with some point of reference. The point of reference is the population norm when evaluating the individual's general status, and the individual's overall average level of performance when evaluating intra-individual differences. Thus, for example, in demonstrating the virtually infinite number of possible individual diagnoses, McLeod (1983) presented a diagnostic model (Figure 2.1), observing that if only a 'high', 'average' or 'low' assessment were to be made in each of the twelve modules of the diagnostic portion of the model, over 20 000 different diagnostic patterns would emerge. From the perspective of 1987 (four years is a long time in computer-guided diagnosis!) this seems an oversimplification of the diagnostic process, but illustrates the same perspective of individual differences which characterizes some programs that purport to produce individual intelligence test reports on the basis of juggling subtest scores and score discrepancies. In effect, such programs produce a summary of research relating to combinations and permutations of subtest score discrepancies. Following scientific tradition, mental measurement has invoked the law of parsimony, by attempting to describe the infinite variety of human diversity in terms of variability of performance over a limited number of conceptualized traits or elements. Perhaps factor analysis is the most extreme example of the process, where the end-products literally represent the 'lowest common factor' of the many tests (which themselves represent a sampling of individuals' behaviour). Occam would be satisfied with the condensation of the description of behaviour into elements of functional or conceptual uniformity (Spearman's phrases), but the clinician is liable to lose valuable information. The consolidation of behaviour into abstract elements, and then working in terms of those elements, inevitably loses something of the depth and richness of individual variability.

Diagnosis: a hierarchy of specific decisions

In developing a computer-guided diagnostic system, it soon became apparent that neither the modular representation of the diagnostic process exemplified by Figure 2.1, or its flowchart equivalent (Figure 2.2) was entirely appropriate.

At the same time, computer programmers must clone the human diagnostician; there must be no abrogation or contortion of sound diagnostic practice simply for the convenience of programming. However, one of the vicarious benefits of computerizing diagnostic methodology is that the diagnostician is compelled to examine his/her diagnostic behaviour in detail. When one considers the diagnostic process, it becomes clear that psycho-educational diagnosis consists of a sequence of progressively analytic or discriminating assessments, arranged in hierarchical order. This overall representation of the diagnostic process is depicted in Figure 2.3.

Assessment proceeds from the gross to the highly specific until there is no detectable difference between the subject's performance in a pertinent prerequisite skill and the threshold of tolerable performance. It is from this point (or these points) that remediation must begin. Thus, if a child is referred for diagnosis because someone believes he is underachieving, but ability and achievement testing shows his performance to be within acceptable limits for his age and ability, then that is the end of the diagnostic process – but probably not the end of diplomatic dialogue with the person who made the referral! On the other hand, if general achievement is markedly below what is acceptable, then the need for more detailed achievement testing is indicated. If arithmetic skills are found to be acceptable, but reading is

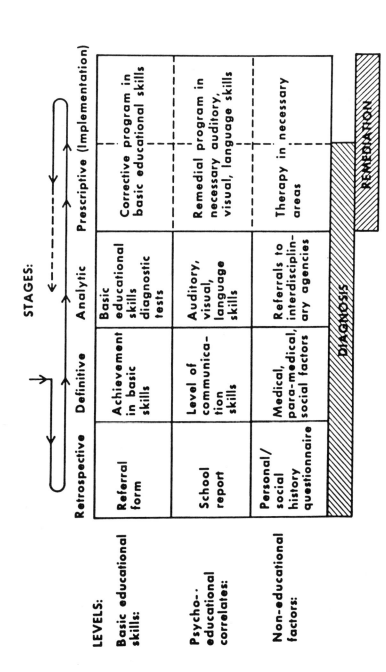

DIAGNOSTIC STRATEGY

Figure 2.1 The diagnostic model (modular version)

deficient, arithmetic diagnosis is terminated and deeper probing into the correlates of reading skills is indicated. If it is found that the child is unable to decode words involving consonantal blends, the diagnostician will proceed deeper along this particular strand of the diagnostic hierarchy and examine ability to read single consonants and, if satisfactory, this represents the starting point – or at least one of the starting points – in the prescriptive/remedial process.

The beginning of the diagnostic process is illustrated diagrammatically in Figure 2.4. For a student who has been referred on account of suspected learning disability, the first* decision point in the diagnostic procedural hierarchy ascertains whether or not there is a discrepancy between expected and actual achievement (where expectancy may be based on either the student's age or ability level). If there is, then more indepth diagnosis is indicated; if no discrepancy is detected, then a different subsequent procedure is indicated. But, it could be argued, are we not back in the realm of 'significance of score differences' which was criticized above? Reference to Figure 2.4 (which is itself an abbreviated representation of this section of the system) shows that the subsequent action indicated is to *check* on the empirical observation by requesting feedback, i.e. there is a move from the traditional probabilistic treatment of the data to one which might be termed a 'threshold' approach. In this particular example, the referring agency either confirms that perhaps there really is no problem, or maintains that – in spite of the test results – there is a problem. If the feedback is that the test results are accepted, then the case is terminated. On the other hand, if the referring agency disagrees with the test results, then retesting with alternative instruments is indicated. The threshold approach is distinguished from the probabilistic approach in that the 'IF . . . THEN . . .' decisions are binary. That is, subject to confirmation through checks and feedback at subsequent decision points, diagnostic action (including the prescription of remediation) proceeds on the assumption that the answer to the question asked at each decision point is unequivocally 'Yes' or 'No'. Reverting to the example of the student with measured IQ 100 and Achievement Quotient 90, a ten point discrepancy between ability and achievement will be accepted, plus or minus zero, as the best estimate of the student's degree of underachievement which the diagnostician has to work with, until there is substantial evidence to the contrary.

The availability of the computer has made it possible to examine not only combinations of assessments of an individual's status on conceptual elements such as intelligence, introversion, self-concept, etc., but of relatively specific behaviours. For example, a social history is obtained in the early stages of the diagnostic process, partly by means of a *home questionnaire* in the case of our own system. A *school report* is also obtained. Each item in the home questionnaire is cross-classified with other relevant items within the questionnaire itself, in the school report, and with other potential sources of comparable information throughout the hierarchical trees illustrated in Figures 2.3–2.12.† Thus, if the child's parents report that s/he is incapable of remembering a short message such as a telephone number, an immediate search is instituted throughout the entire system for information about immediate auditory memory and related factors such as tasks involving auditory perception and acuity, sequencing ability, etc., noting whether the information is confirmatory, contradictory or absent. If absent, the system will recommend that the omission be rectified by, say, administering the WISC Digit Span, Coding and Picture Arrangement

---

* The 'testing for discrepancy' is not the first decision which the diagnostician has to make. An earlier hierarchy must exist for the decision as to which tests to use. What grade level? What area of achievement? What are the diagnostician's competencies?, etc. These are some of the questions that have to be answered by the diagnostician, maybe subconsciously, before diagnosis can begin.

† See Appendix A for Figures 2.5–2.12.

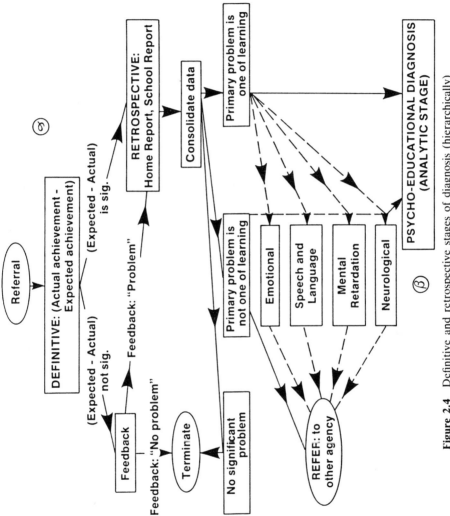

Figure 2.4 Definitive and retrospective stages of diagnosis (hierarchically)

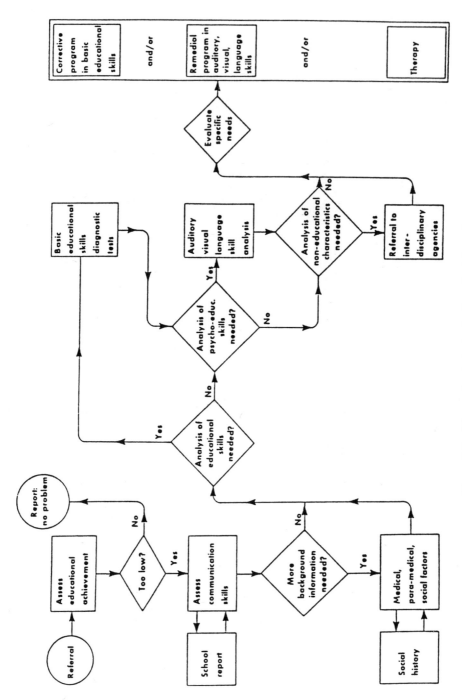

Figure 2.2   Diagnostic strategies in flow chart format

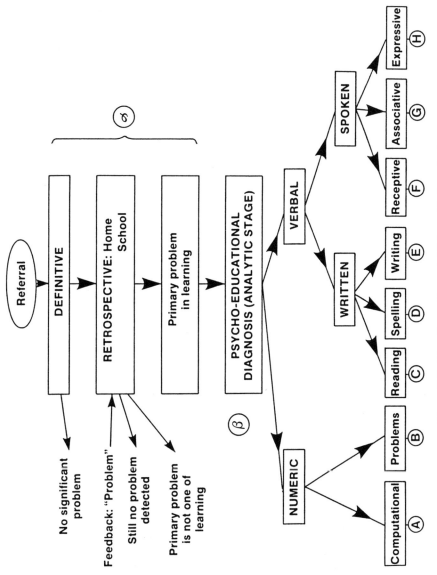

Figure 2.3 The diagnostic model (hierarchical version)

subtests, obtaining a missing school report, etc. Attempting to construct the multiple, and interlocking, hierarchies that comprise the total diagnostic process immediately enhances one's awareness that the extent of differences between individuals with special educational needs is far more complex than is indicated by simply observing their distribution along some continuum of performance on designated tests.

Following on from the bottom section of Figure 2.3, Figures 2.5–2.12 (Appendix A) illustrate the sort of progressive hierarchical psycho-educational diagnostic model which is emerging, and which is being operationalized. It should be emphasized that this model is not different in substance from the original modular representation (Figure 2.1). It represents the same strategy, but is expressed in a different format.

Implications for mental measurement

In the rudimentary stages of developing an expert diagnostic system, it is unavoidable that the decision rules be based largely on heuristics, i.e. the opinions of experienced human diagnosticians. As the system itself 'gains experience', it is anticipated that it will be able to generate its own decision-making rules. However, whatever the basis for the decision rules, the 'successive approximation' approach seems inevitably preferable to psychometrically-based decision rules, if only on logistical grounds. In order to be able to determine whether a child's performance on different tests are comparable, it is necessary that not only the reliability of every test, but every test's intercorrelation with every other test in the system, must be stored in memory – and at every grade level. It is not a major problem to store test reliabilities, as these are available from the technical data provided for any reputable test. Intercorrelations between all possible pairs of tests, including validity coefficients, however, even at the relatively uncomplicated level of comparing ability and achievement, do not necessarily exist. If they do exist, can one be sufficiently confident in their validity that they may be generalized to the population from which individual diagnostic cases are drawn?

Very few assessment instruments have been co-normed, i.e. normed on the same standardization sample, and it is a dubious practice to make important decisions about an individual on the seductive basis of applying sophisticated mathematics to compare her/his scores on tests which have been normed on different populations, perhaps decades apart. If the intertest correlations do not exist, then an impossibly massive and unrealistic task is indicated; hitech has not yet come up with a method of providing validity coefficients without testing children.

Some early expert systems employed estimates of confidence ('certainty factors'), which represent the opinions of experts, quantitatively expressed, as to the validity of particular data or decisions. The compounding of decisions based on these certainty factors involves a quasi-mathematical treatment somewhat similar to that for combining probabilistic errors. But this is a further step from reality, because while the compounding of probabilistic errors is ultimately based in empirical data or mathematical premises, certainty factors rest only on guesses – albeit the guesses of human experts. Finally, no matter how the psychometric characteristics of a test are handled, all existing validity co-efficients and other intercorrelations are rendered obsolete immediately a test is revised, e.g. the WRAT or the Stanford–Binet – and, with them, a computerized system which is based upon them.

The identification of underachievers

A practical example of the shift from the apparent precision of the conventionally psychometric to what might seem to be a far less elegant, almost trial-and-error approach may be cited from a not unrelated context, i.e. the identification, essentially for administrative purposes, of educational underachievers. In the euphoria which accompanied the then 'new testing' movement in the early part of the present century, pioneers such as E. L. Thorndike (Thorndike & Gates, 1929) and Burt (1937) proposed that each student's 'Accomplishment Quotient' (i.e. Achievement Quotient divided by IQ) ought to equal unity, and that the degree to which it fell short of 1.00 could be interpreted as a reflection of the competence of the teacher! Experience of remedial educators showed that what had appeared to be the self-evident validity of the proposition that 'achievement ought to be in line with ability' was oversimplistic when considered in a psychometric context, because requiring that all students' Achievement Quotients should be equal to their IQs failed to take into account the phenomenon of statistical regression. Several formulae were proposed by Bond & Tinker (1967), Harris (1970), Myklebust (1968), and others, but these were artificial and arbitrary. Others (e.g. Cone & Wilson, 1981; McLeod, 1979; Willson, 1984; summarized by Reynolds 1984) have produced more respectable mathematically-based formulae designed to determine whether the magnitude of ability/achievement discrepancies might be large enough to be considered as constituting educational underachievement. However, no matter how elegant or mathematically pure the formula, the arbitrary decision remains as to what the critical value of the discrepancy must be before it may legitimately be regarded as significant. Before the advent of the computer, the only practical procedure was to produce a formula which reduces description of the total pattern of scores to the basic parameters of means and standard deviations and, by manipulating these parameters, along with test reliabilities and intercorrelations, to determine a critical cutoff discrepancy, which *ought* to identify the specified number of students, if the underlying mathematical and psychometric assumptions were satisfied, and to accept all students whose discrepancy exceeded the critical value.

McLeod (1978) produced one such formula and employed it to identify the most serious underachievers in a number of school districts.* As school district superintendents have the task of providing the resources, both human and financial, to implement remedial programs, they are naturally interested in identifying a known number of underachievers, and so the cutoff discrepancy was fixed at such a value as would identify the prescribed number. In practice, the formula always identified the requested number of students – almost. But with the fast, obedient computer, it is possible to rank all students according to the extent to which their actual achievement falls short of prediction and then simply count off from the most extreme underachievers until the required number has been located, i.e. by progressive approximation until the required conditions have been satisfied. This is less elegant and less impressive than the application of a complex formula, but it does provide pinpoint accuracy. And the identified underachievers are exactly the same underachievers as would have been identified by a perfect formula, because the extent of an individual's underachievement is assessed in both cases from the level which is obtained by means of the equation which – as Galton (1869) showed a century ago – takes regression into account.

Summation

The examples of diagnostic decision-making thus far have been the relatively straightforward decisions to be made at the Definitive Stage (Figure 2.1), which lend themselves most readily to psychometric treatment. However, as diagnosis proceeds through the crucial Analytic Stage, a further problem is encountered, i.e. the integration of data from standardized tests whose reliability is known and is

---

* See Appendix B.

20   *J. McLeod*

usually high, with more informal, even qualitative, data from teachers, parents and psychologists. This problem becomes particularly pertinent when diagnostic data have to be incorporated into a computer-based system; short-term unequivocal decisions, with consistent inbuilt checks to prevent straying too far down the wrong paths seems to be the most promising way to go.

It is clear that diagnostic decision-making at the Analytic Stage of diagnosis must rely on a hierarchy of such decisions, and that the complexity of that hierarchy reflects the incredible multidimensional range of individual differences of children with special educational needs. But, in charting a course through the labyrinth of hierarchies, instead of proceeding primarily by probabilistic decisions, with inevitable accumulation of error, decisions which are made at every stage are subject to immediate feedback as to whether the recommended procedure led to acceptable consequences and, if not, decisions are amended and adjustments are made to recommendations based on those decisions. Ultimate understanding of the individual is therefore conceptualized, not in terms of a central tendency surrounded by a grey zone of uncertainty, but as an understanding which is arrived at by a process of successive approximation.

Appendix A

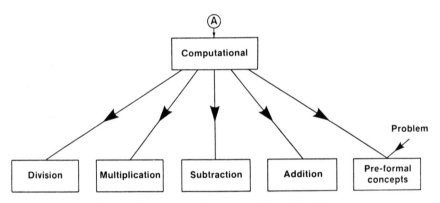

Figure 2.5 Diagnosis of computational difficulties

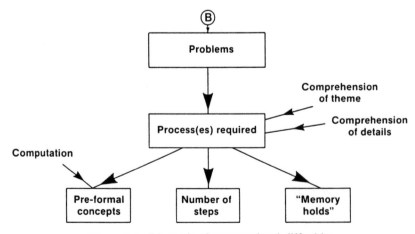

Figure 2.6 Diagnosis of computational difficulties

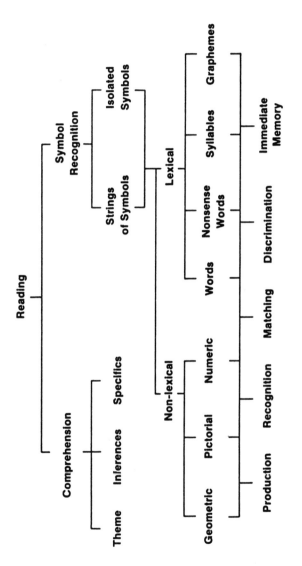

Figure 2.7 Reading skills

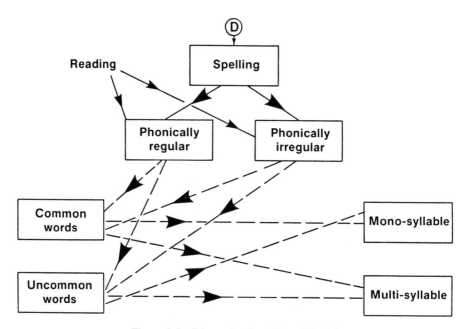

Figure 2.8   Diagnosis of spelling difficulties

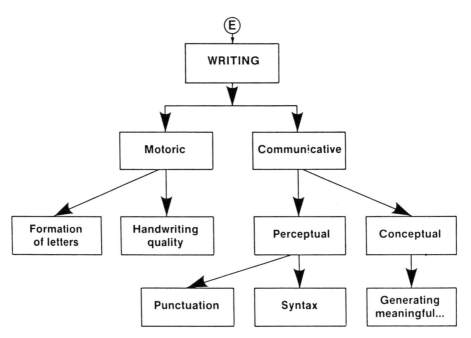

Figure 2.9   Diagnosis of writing difficulties

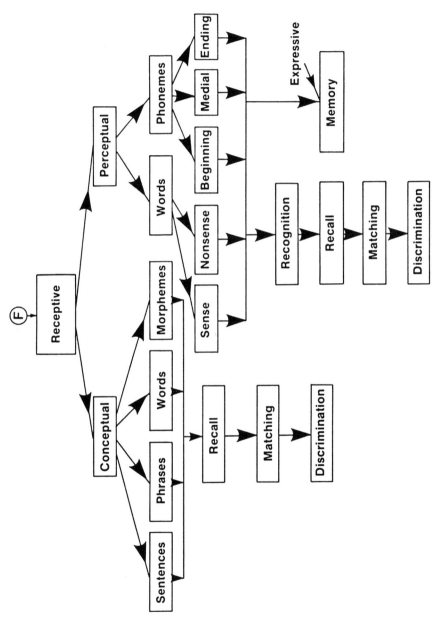

Figure 2.10   Diagnosis of receptive speed difficulties

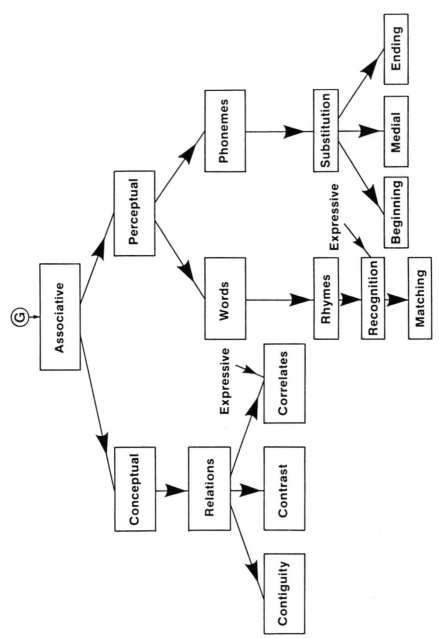

Figure 2.11 Diagnosis of associative speech difficulties

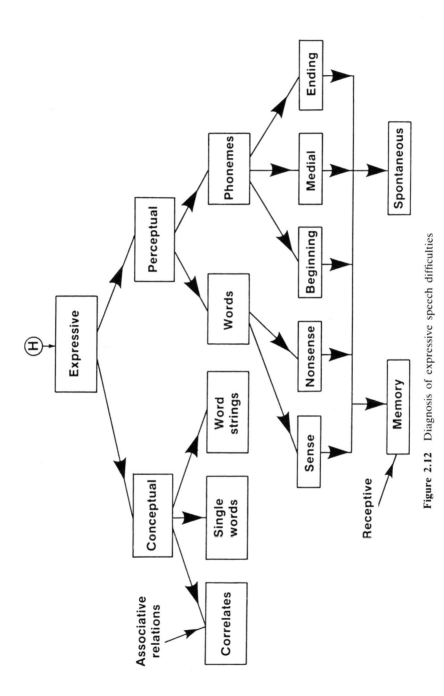

Figure 2.12 Diagnosis of expressive speech difficulties

Appendix B

Evaluating significant underachievement (McLeod, 1978)

Predicted Educational Quotient,

$$\hat{E}Q = r.SD(E).(IQ - 100)/SD(I) + 100$$

where:

r = product-moment correlation between IQ and EQ
SD(E) = standard deviation of the EQ distribution
SD(I) = standard deviation of the IQ distribution

Standard error of the difference between an individual's IQ and EQ,

$$SE(diff.) = SD(E) 2 - rr(E) - rr(I) - r$$

where:

rr(E) = reliability of educational achievement test
rr(I) = reliability of intelligence test

References

BOND, G. & TINKER, M.A. (1967) *Reading difficulties: their diagnosis and remediation*, New York: Appleton-Century-Crofts.

BURT, C. (1937) *The backward child*, London: University of London Press.

CONE, T. & WILSON, L. (1981) Quantifying a severe discrepancy: a critical analysis. *Learning Disability Quarterly*, **4**, 359–71.

GALTON, F. (1869) *Hereditary genius; an inquiry into its laws and consequences*, D. Appleton and Co. (Chapter 3 reprinted in Jenkins, J.J. & Paterson, D.G. (1961) *Studies in individual differences*, New York: Appleton-Century-Crofts.

HARRIS, A.J. (1970) *How to increase reading ability*, New York: Mackay.

MCLEOD, J. (1978) *Psychometric identification of children with learning disabilities*, Saskatoon: University of Saskatchewan Institute of Child Guidance and Development. (2nd edition, revised 1981).

MCLEOD, J. (1979) Educational underachievement: toward a defensible definition. *Journal of Learning Disabilities*, **12**, 42–50.

MCLEOD, J. (1983) La non-fiabilite psychometrique et ses implications dans une politique pour les enfants doues. *Revue Canadienne de Psycho-education*, **12**, 2, 118–31.

MYKLEBUST, H.R. (1968) Learning disabilities: definition and overview. In H. R. Myklebust (ed.) *Progress in learning disabilities*, New York: Grune and Stratton.

REYNOLDS, C.R. (1984) Critical measurement areas in learning disabilities. *Journal of Special Education*, **18**, (4), 451–76.

SPEARMAN, C. (1904) 'General intelligence,' objectively determined and measured. *American Journal of Psychology*, **15**, 201–92.

THORNDIKE, E.L. & GATES, A.I. (1929) *Elementary principles of education*, New York: Macmillan.

WILLSON, V.L. (1984) Derivation of reliability of regression estimate of true score difference. In C. R. Reynolds (1984).

WOODWORTH, R.S. (1951) *Experimental psychology*, London: Methuen.

3 A two-dimensional model as a framework for interindividual differences in social behaviour

Lea Pulkkinen

Interindividual differences in conflict behaviour

Since the employment of the factor analytical model for the purpose of reducing the great number of variables describing personality to fewer more general concepts, several personality psychological investigations have shown that a large proportion of the common variance of social and emotional behaviour can be described in terms of two orthogonal dimensions. The researchers have given diverse names to the two main dimensions. One of the dimensions has depicted differences in social activity/passivity (Extraversion/Introversion, Eysenck, 1960), the other one differences in emotional stability or lability (Neuroticism/Stability).

A two-dimensional model as a framework for differences in situation-specific behaviour

The present author (Pitkänen, 1969) was interested in the variations of individual behaviour in situations which may elicit aggression. According to my findings, a small proportion of individuals, even children, behave aggressively in threatening situations. Most people react in other ways. Nonaggressive ways of coping with threatening situations were little known or studied in the 1960s when prosocial behaviour had not yet become a focus of study. For outlining various behavioural alternatives, I developed a two-dimensional model to depict differences in behaviour in a threatening situation. The two dimensions of Social Activity/Passivity and Strong/Weak Control of Behaviour, were used to define four patterns of behaviour (Pitkänen, 1969, 104–7).

(1) *Uncontrolled expression of impulses* (high activity and weak control). The goal of action in a threatening situation is to eliminate a noxious stimulus immediately. This is done by delivering noxious stimuli to another organism, for which reason the response is defined as aggressive.

This pattern of behaviour was expected to be related to a child's general activity and either parental indifference toward the child's way of expressing impulses (lack of guidance) or to the direct or vicarious reinforcement of aggressive behaviour.

(2) *Controlled expression of impulses* (high activity and strong control). Activation aroused by aggression stimuli is kept under cognitive control and displayed in neutral forms. An individual's behaviour is motivated by a desire to behave in a socially acceptable manner, in accordance with prevailing norms. Therefore s/he considers alternative ways of coping with threatening situations. The behavioural aspect manifests itself as efforts towards the peaceful settlement of controversies and attempts to influence the other person's behaviour. Aggressive behaviour occurs only in situations in which aggression is not strongly incompatible with socially acceptable behaviour.

It was supposed that this pattern of behaviour may require a certain level of cognitive capacity. A prerequisite for it is also reinforcement of socially acceptable behaviour and prosocial models.

(3) *Uncontrolled inhibition of impulses* (high passivity and weak control). In threatening stimulus situations an individual's responses are characterized by avoidance behaviour. He has no response habits enabling him to eliminate the threat nonaggressively. Activation aroused by the stimulus is bound to emotions, fear of the threatening stimulus, and anxiety about an inability to defend. S/he tries to eliminate the threat by conciliatory gestures such as crying or withdrawal, and to control the anger instigated by the stimulus by negative labelling, which manifests itself as verbal descriptions of emotions, intentions of revenge, and generalized hostile attitudes. If aggression is aroused, e.g. because of continuous accumulation, it is assumed to have an indirect manifestation.

This pattern of behaviour may be due to lack of personal resources (physical or cognitive weakness) or discouragement of active coping efforts.

(4) *Controlled inhibition of impulses* (high passivity and strong control). Avoidance behaviour here differs from uncontrolled inhibition of impulses in that an individual tends to block awareness of his emotional state by cognitive appraisal of the situation. The appraisal process may even distort reality, in which case it can be called defensive. Action is motivated by the need for approval, a consequence of strong dependency on authority figures. Aggressive behaviour would threaten this relationship, and therefore an individual tends to submit and adjust. In order to succeed in adjustment and to be able to avoid anxiety aroused by the recognized impulse towards aggression, the individual makes efficient use of the cognitive processes. This pattern of behaviour was thought to be learned as a result of the same childhood experiences which develop dependency, and of nonaggressive identification models.

It was assumed that in an individual's behaviour there occur variations due to transient external and internal stimuli and social learning. Nevertheless, the assumption was made that interindividual differences in behaviour toward threatening stimuli may be described in terms of the four patterns of behaviour defined above.

Empirical evidence conforming to the two-dimensional model

The four patterns emerged in eight-year-old children's behaviour which was measured by peer nominations and teacher ratings on 38 variables (e.g. Who might hurt another child when angry? Who tries to act reasonably even in annoying situations?; Pitkänen, 1969; Pulkkinen, 1983) and 16 scales from two personality inventories, the Junior Eysenck Personality Inventory (Eysenck, 1965) and the Personality Inventory for the Lower Forms of the Primary School (KTK 1) modified from Cattell and Coan's (1959) personality questionnaire (see Pitkänen, 1969). The subjects (196 boys and 173 girls) were drawn from 12 classes of second-grade pupils attending the elementary schools in Jyväskylä.

The first two factors explained a considerable proportion of the common variance (see Pitkänen, 1969). The factors were bipolar. One of them was spanned by Aggressive vs. Submissive behaviour, the other by Constructive vs. Anxious behaviour. Their compositions were as follows.

Variables for rated aggression, disobedience, the teacher's concern for the child's future because of ensuing symptoms of antisocial behaviour and the inventory scales for Impulsive Extraversion and Restlessness formed a cluster of variables which corresponded to the hypothesis on uncontrolled expression of impulses. Opposite to this were variables for controlled inhibition of impulses, i.e. for unaggressive behaviour (never quarrels, leaves quarrelling company, peaceable), passivity, and the inventory scales for Altruism, Dependency, Femininity, and Submissiveness.

One end of the other factor consisted of variables for controlled activity both in a threatening situation (negotiating, reasonable behaviour) and in general (school success, leadership qualities, and social activity), and the teacher's prediction of the child's successful development in later life. At the other end of the factor were variables for weak control of behaviour (lacking concentration) and passivity (too withdrawn). In accordance with the hypothesis, the cluster also comprised variables for socially helpless behaviour (is afraid of other children, easily starts crying, would not be chosen as a leader), and the inventory scale for Emotionality together with the Lie scale.

Six extreme groups were formed on the basis of the factor scores to represent uncontrolled expression of impulses (Aggressive), uncontrolled inhibition of impulses (Anxious), a combination of these two (Uncontrolled), controlled expression of impulses (Constructive), controlled inhibition of impulses (Submissive), and a combination of these latter two (Controlled). School success was lowest in the Anxious children, and, correspondingly, their results in achievement tests for vocabulary, reading, and arithmetic problems were the poorest (Table 3.1). The Aggressive children were, however, more careless in their work as shown by the school report and the high number of mistakes in the test for reading. Controlled children had the highest scores in all cognitive achievements.

The study of social background of the extreme groups revealed that the Anxious children came from homes of lower socioeconomic status than the Controlled and Constructive children. The mothers of the Aggressive and Uncontrolled children were most often working outside the home, while the mothers of the Submissive children stayed at home the most often. Passive children (Anxious and Submissive) were more often youngest or only children in the family and the Aggressive children who were more often first-born or middle children.

The results confirmed the hypotheses of the differences between the patterns of behaviour obtained. Aggressive children were uncontrolled in their social behaviour as well as in their cognitive performances, and the way they expressed their impulses was, compared with the other groups, less controlled by the mothers who were working full-time outside home. The Submissive children, on the other hand, had the mothers at home and they were often youngest or only children. In these conditions, the control of the mother over the child may become strong and high dependency between the child and mother may develop. Constructive children who had good social skills came from homes of higher socio-economic status than the socially helpless, Anxious children, and their cognitive performances exceeded those of the latter. Control of behaviour was related to cognitive capacity. Aggressive children did not have the poorest capacity, but a follow-up study six years later

Table 3.1 Means of the scores for school achievement in extreme groups (10 boys in each)

	Aggress.	Uncontr	Anxious	Constr.	Contr.	Submiss.	F
School report (scale 4–10)							
Mark averages, all subjects	7.08	6.93	6.67	7.89	8.28	7.35	***
Mark averages, theoretical subjects	7.04	6.98	6.72	8.24	8.58	7.50	***
Carefulness	6.79	6.99	7.69	8.79	9.39	8.69	***
Achievement Test							
Vocabulary	31.9	27.5	26.3	35.1	39.6	32.6	***
Reading: Result	26.0	25.0	23.2	32.7	35.7	27.0	**
Reading: Mistakes	10.1	8.8	6.7	6.1	2.8	3.6	*
Arithmetic problems	15.1	15.1	12.2	16.2	19.8	15.9	**

***The effect of grouping significant; one-way-analysis of variance, ($p < .001$), ** $p < .01$, * $p < .05$.

In all variables the means of the Aggressive and Uncontrolled differed from the means of the Constructive and Controlled significantly, among others.

(Pulkkinen, 1977) showed that their school reports were weaker than those of the others; aggressive and impulsive children may become under-achievers.

The stability of the control of behaviour

The follow-up study at the age of 14 by using peer nominations, teacher ratings, and semi-structured interviews of children and their parents confirmed the hypotheses on interindividual differences. Continuity in the quality of the control of behaviour was rather high; 48.4% of the children who belonged to the extreme groups for weak control of behaviour at the age of eight were identified as correspondingly extreme cases six years later. For strong control, continuity was lower (30%). Stability correlations of peer nominations on aggression concerning 189 boys and 162 girls (Pitkänen–Pulkkinen, 1981) were significant (.37 for both girls and boys), but they were even higher for anxiety (.42 for girls, .48 for boys). Strong control of behaviour did not manifest the same stability although correlations were higher for boys than girls in both submissiveness (.22 for girls and .29 for boys) and constructiveness (.11 for girls, .29 for boys).

The significance of the differentiation between weak and strong control of behaviour was demonstrated by the results at the age of 26. When the criminal registers of the eight-year-old subjects were searched 18 years later, in 1986, it was observed that convictions were overrepresented in the extreme groups for weak control of behaviour. For instance, 9 out of 10 extremely aggressive boys at the age of 8 had committed offences by the age of 26, but none of the ten Submissive boys had done so. No one from the extreme groups for strong control of behaviour (N = 30) became a 'chronic offender' with a criminal 'career', but 6 out of 8 male (and 1 out of 2 female) 'chronic offenders' had belonged to the extreme groups for weak control of behaviour at the age of 8 (N = 30). Two male (1 female) 'chronic offenders' came from the large non-extreme group (N = 136 for males, N = 113 for females).

Convictions were highly concentrated. Although about half of males and 20% of females were found in the official criminal register or local police registers, only 4.1% of males (N = 8) and 1.2% of females (N = 2) accounted for half of all convictions in the sample by the age of 26 (Pulkkinen, 1987). These 'chronic offenders' had committed offences on a regular basis since the age of 18, while other offenders had the peak of offences at the age of 17 to 19 and then a sharp decline.

The results showed that a criminal career in early adulthood was related to weak control of behaviour in childhood. Also in late adolescence, at the age of 20, offenders and non-offenders differed in their personality ratings in childhood such that offenders had been more aggressive. Especially adolescents who had committed several different types of offences (violence, larceny, and alcohol-related offences) differed from the rest (Pulkkinen, 1983). The adolescents who committed several types of offences were becoming 'chronic offenders'.

Continuity in the styles of life

The predictive power of interindividual differences in behaviour in threatening situations was also seen in correlations between peer nominations at the age of 8 and various measures used at the age of 26. For example, aggression at the age of 8 correlated significantly ($p < .01$) with Psychoticism (P) and Extraversion (E) from the Eysenck Personality Questionnaire (Eysenck & Eysenck, 1975), while constructiveness correlated ($p < .001$) negatively with Neuroticism (N). Orientation toward schooling and occupational career and activity in the use of leisure time correlated with constructiveness. Anxiety in childhood correlated with passivity. Both aggression and anxiety in childhood were related to the feelings and fears of personal failure in early adulthood.

Continuity in social behaviour from the age of 8 to 20 has been condensed by calculating correlations between the factor scores (Pulkkinen, 1982). According to these previous results, aggressive behaviour in childhood predicted stronger orientation toward peers than parents in puberty, experiments with tobacco and alcohol, and spending leisure time in the streets. Peer-orientation was a precursor for the style of life called 'Reveller' at the age of 20 which refers to pleasure-seeking behaviour, for instance, drinking, spending time in bars and restaurants, and indifference toward conventional norms (see Table 3.2). The opposite to Aggression, Submissive behaviour, predicted high dependency on the parents and home, lack of friends, abstinence, conformity to norms, and the style of life called 'Loner'.

Anxious behaviour in childhood predicted negativistic attitudes toward school and life in general in puberty. It was a precursor for a style of life called 'Loser' in late adolescence. The Losers were afraid of the future and they lived day by day. They had interrupted schooling and experienced unemployment. The opposite to Anxiety, Constructive behaviour, predicted responsibility and orientation toward schooling and career, characteristic of the style of life called 'Striver'.

At the age of 26, five dimensions for the styles of life were extracted from questionnaire data and criminal records: excessive substance use, married (vs. single), long schooling, criminality, and self-confidence. Table 3.2 shows that criminality was predicted by the development from Anxious behaviour via Negativism to the style of life of Loser. In addition, Aggressive behaviour predicted criminality as well as the style of life of Reveller, but orientation toward peers in puberty did not predict it. Instead, excessive substance use was related to development from Aggressive behaviour via peer-orientation to the style of life of Reveller. Long schooling, on the other hand, was characteristic of people whose development proceeded from Constructive behaviour via Responsibility to the style of life of Striver. Marriage at the age of 26 was more typical of those who had been peer-oriented and manifested the style of life of Reveller in late adolescence more than of those who had been home-oriented and lonely. Self-confidence was most characteristic of those who expressed the style of life of Striver in late adolescence.

Conclusions

The results of the Jyväskylä Longitudinal Study of Social Behaviour confirmed the hypotheses on the nature and significance of interindividual differences in conflict behaviour. The context for the definition of interindividual differences (responses to threatening stimuli) might sound limited, but the results showed high generalizability and predictability of the patterns of behaviour to social behaviour and orientation to life.

The reasons for interindividual differences were attached to socialization experiences and activity level as a temperament characteristic in the original hypotheses. A bulk of data was obtained to confirm the significance of socialization experiences (Pulkkinen, 1982, 1984), but the role of the child's temperament as a precursor for social development remained open in the longitudinal study.

Interindividual differences in temperament

Problem and method

The nature of temperament variation was studied separately in a cross-sectional study with preschool children representing several age cohorts (Pulkkinen, Ahonen, Hirvikallio, Näkkilä, Pakarinen, Stranden & Vaalamo, 1983). There are several traditions with little mutual interaction in the study of interindividual differences in temperament. The tradition which was a focus of interest in the present study is based on the classic conception of four temperaments. According to Eysenck & Eysenck (1969), the view of classic temperaments (Sanguine, Melancholic, Choleric

Table 3.2 Significant relationships between factor scores from the age 8 to 26

	Factor scores: Age 26				
Factor scores	Substance use	Married	Long schooling	Criminality	Self-confidence
Age 8					
(a1) Aggressive	***			***	
(vs. Submissive)				***	
(b1) Anxious					
(vs. Constructive)	**		***		
Age 14					
(a2) Peer-oriented	**	***			
(vs. Home-oriented)					
(b2) Negativism				***	
(vs. Responsibility)			***		
Age 20					
(a3) Reveller	***	***		***	
(vs. Loner)			**		
(b3) Loser	*			***	
(vs. Striver)			***		**

(a) Continuity from a1 to a3 significant (see Pulkkinen, 1982).
(b) Continuity from b1 to b3 significant.
* $p < .05$; ** $p < .01$; *** $p < .001$.

and Phlegmatic) as unrelated, separate categories was changed when Wundt at the beginning of this century presented a two-dimensional system of temperaments in which temperaments vary dimensionally in strength and quality.

The four classic categories of temperament were popular in the beginning of this century, for instance in the Soviet Union because of Pavlov's work. Nowadays they are missing from the scientific description of interindividual differences even in the Soviet Union, where Pavlov has been criticized after his death for taking the four Greek categories for granted and for trying to find explanations for them in the higher nervous system (Nebylitsyn & Gray, 1972). However, the long history of the four types brought about the question of their descriptive value. It was hypothesized that the classic categories are still valuable in a description of individual differences in a two-dimensional framework. The physiological or other constitutional reasons for individual variation in temperament were not considered in the present investigation.

The subjects, 231 children (half girls and half boys) aged 1.5 to 7.5 years, were drawn from day care centers. Temperament ratings of the subjects were made by 38 teachers by using the scale called SACHOMEPH (*sa*nguine, *cho*leric, *me*lancholic, *ph*legmatic). The scale consists of 52 characteristics which were chosen on the basis of the analyses of classic temperaments and factor analytic studies of personality. The characters include, for instance, 'gets easily excited', 'impulsive' and 'adaptable'. The correlations between independent teacher ratings were generally high; most correlations were .60 or above.

Two-factor structure of temperament
The structure of temperament ratings was studied by analysing the development of factors when the number of varimax-rotated factors was increased. The first and

second factors were strongly bipolar. The first factor was interpreted to characterize a Choleric vs. Phlegmatic temperament. The highest positive loadings were found in items for a choleric temperament: aggressive, selfish, impatient, obstinate, loses temper easily, and capricious, while the highest negative loadings were in items depicting a phlegmatic temperament: good-natured, adaptable, calm, and deliberate.

The second factor was interpreted as describing a Melancholic vs. Sanguine temperament. The highest positive loadings characterized a melancholic temperament: withdrawn, is left out in a group of children, introverted, insecure, shy, slow-to-warm-up, submissive, slow tempo, and difficulties in making friends. The highest negative loadings were in the items for a sanguine temperament: lively confident, energetic, gets easily excited, dominating, and merry.

When the variables were plotted on a plane on the basis of the factor loadings it could be seen that the Choleric and Sanguine temperaments shared the variance of characteristics for social activity and the Melancholic and Phlegmatic temperaments for social passivity. The Choleric and Melancholic temperaments, on the other hand, shared characteristics for emotionality and distraction (e.g. gets hurt, cries easily, and unable to concentrate), and the Sanguine and Phlegmatic temperaments those for stability (e.g. adaptable and trusting).

The sex of the subjects did not explain the variation in the temperaments. The stability of the two-factor structure was studied by extracting the two-factor solutions for each of the six age cohorts and by comparing the factor structures in pairs using the method of a symmetric transformation analysis (Sänkiaho, 1974). The stability of the structures turned out to be very high. There were, however, some variables which did not adjust to the two-factor structure. They were related to prosocial behaviour, for instance popular, friendly, helpful, and empathic. When a third factor was extracted it consisted of these variables for prosocial behaviour, while the first two temperament factors remained unchanged. However at an older age, the third factor was stronger, and more clearly bipolar as regards social adjustment versus social difficulties, than at a younger age.

The explorative factor analytical results were confirmed by using LISREL-factor models (Leskinen and Pulkkinen, 1985). The results showed that instead of interpreting the temperament factors as two bipolar dimensions, the factors should be interpreted as four independent and in pairs negatively correlating factors (Table 3.3). The negative correlations between opposite temperaments were high ($-.77$ and $-.90$) showing exclusiveness of temperaments. Other correlations between the temperament factors showed that, at the younger age, the Choleric and Sanguine temperaments correlated positively, expressing the existence of a component of general activity. At the older age, the quality of activity differentiated. The correlations showed also that in girls the Melancholic and Phlegmatic temperaments correlated positively expressing the existence of a component for general passivity. It did not exist in boys.

The fifth factor emerged for prosocial behaviour (friendly, popular, helpful, empathic) in all groups. It correlated negatively with the Choleric temperament and positively with the Phlegmatic temperament, and at the older age, also with the Sanguine temperament. The negative correlation between prosocial behaviour and the Choleric temperament increased with age only in boys. Thus, prosocial activity differentiated from less cooperative activity more clearly in boys than in girls.

Reasons for interindividual differences
The younger age group (72 children) was studied more intensively some months later. The aim was to study to what extent interindividual differences seemed to emerge as a result of socialization and to what extent they seemed to be inherent. The children were presented a subtest 'Speech' from the Illinois Test of Psycholingusitic Abilities (ITPA) modified for Finland by Kuusinen & Blåfield

Table 3.3   Correlations between temperament factors: LISREL

Aged 2.5 to 5 years[1]		Boys				
		Choleric	Phlegm.	Melanch.	Sanguine	Prosocial
	Choleric	1	−90	0*	35	−63
	Phlegmatic	−84	1	0*	−24	84
Girls	Melancholic	0*	30	1	−77	0*
	Sanguine	48	−40	−84	1	0*
	Prosocial	−69	84	0*	0*	1
Aged 5 to 7.5 years		Boys				
	Choleric	1	−90	0*	0*	−84
	Phlegmatic	−84	1	0*	0*	84
Girls	Melancholic	0*	30	1	−77	0*
	Sanguine	0*	0*	−84	1	39
	Prosocial	−69	84	0*	39	1

* Fixed as zero (a significant correlation did not exist).
[1] The subjects from the age of 1.5 to 2.4 were omitted because of the skewed distributions of teacher ratings for prosocial characteristics; especially in boys the number of zero ratings was high at this age.

(1974), and other structured methods devised for the present study of social behaviour (Pulkkinen *et al.*, 1983), for instance, a doll play and a test for mood labelling, and an interview of understanding one's own and other's feelings (Pitkänen-Pulkkinen, 1977). The children's behaviour was also observed in the day care center, and their mothers were also interviewed at home.

In the doll play, the material consisted of a doll family with three children: a daughter, a son, and a child without an indicated sex. The subjects were first allowed to play freely with the dolls. Later a semistructured and a structured play was arranged. The child's behaviour was scored on the following scales: level of organization of the play, perception of the situation, proposals for a solution to the situation, role taking, and empathy. The test for moods labelling consisted of four drawings of facial expressions: joy, grief, anger, and fear. The subjects were asked to explain how the child in the picture felt. The responses were scored from 0 to 5 (5 = adequate adjective; 4 = adequate verb; 3 = insufficient expression; 2 = inadequate feeling; 1 = no response as to feelings; 0 = no response).

The results showed that prosocial behaviour correlated with the chronological and psycholinguistic age as well as with all test variables (Table 3.4). In contrast, there were no significant correlations between the temperament factors and test variables. The independence of the temperament factors from age and cognitive performances confirmed the conception that interindividual differences in temperament are not learned with age as prosocial behaviour is. The correlations with the mother interview showed, without revealing exactly what the causal relationships are, that a child's choleric temperament may become accentuated in certain conditions (inconsistency between the parents) and also result in certain child rearing methods, such as giving up with an obstinate child. Melancholic children, on the other hand, may suffer more than other children from changes and an irregular rhythm of life. Interestingly, parental indifference (an equivalent of giving up) and inconsistency were factors correlating with aggression at the age of 14, while unstable life conditions correlated with anxiety in the Jyväskylä Longitudinal Study of Social Behaviour (Pitkänen-Pulkkinen, 1980).

Table 3.4 Specimens of correlations between the factor scores for temperaments, test scores, and variables for child rearing; N = 72

	Choleric/ Phlegmatic	Melancholic/ Sanguine	Prosocial behaviour
Psycholinguistic age (ITPA: speech)	−10	07	50***
Chronological age	00	14	42***
Sex of the subjects (F=2, M=1)	−04	11	26*
Doll play: Proposals for activity	10	08	46***
Empathy	13	17	49***
Level of organization	20	−07	23*
Perception of social situations	12	−10	43***
Perception of causal relationships	13	−15	46***
Role taking	07	04	36**
Mood labeling: Sad	08	03	53***
Joyful	04	14	45***
Angry	02	15	52***
Fearful	03	09	22
Observation:			
Concentration in test	02	−06	43***
Social flexibility	18	06	33**
Mother interview:			
Parents read books to the child daily	00	17	27*
The child is included in household activities	15	−07	26*
The child's health: problems	−03	−10	−26*
Child rearing methods: giving up	38***	05	−07
Low consistency between the parents	37***	07	03
Mother is irritated because of the child's character	23*	−04	15
The child is reluctant to leave the parents	−24*	04	−18
Many playmates of different ages	00	−23*	18
Mother works in shifts (vs. regular working hours)	−13	32**	−11
Changes in family structure	−17	33**	10
The child's stay in day care center: irregular	−05	24*	05
Mother's occupational status low	−07	22	07

* $p < .05$; ** $p < .01$; *** $p < .001$.

Discussion

There was some resemblance between the four temperament categories labelled by using classic concepts and the three categories extracted in the New York Longitudinal Study (Thomas & Chess, 1977), but an overlapping was not clear. A combination of a choleric and melancholic temperament may have an equivalent in a 'difficult child', whereas a combination of a melancholic and phlegmatic temperament may have an equivalent in a 'slow-to-warm-up child', and that of a phlegmatic and sanguine temperament in an 'easy child'. The two-dimensional description of temperament variation was, however, more relevant to the present material. Of course, the use of the classic concepts could have been avoided by introducing other concepts, but because the aim of the present investigation was to study the descriptive value of the classic concepts they were used here after finding a sufficient overlapping with them.

The presence of the third dimension which depicted prosocial behaviour was interesting. Prosocial behaviour emerges gradually during preschool years as shown in a separate study with 4- to 6-year-old children (Pulkkinen, Hänninen, Kakko, Mikkola, Mursula, Palu, Pensas & Viljakainen, 1980). Various test scores showed that moral judgment, inhibition of impulses, and understanding one's own and other's feelings and reactions increase strongly between the ages of 4 and 5, and cognitive role-taking, helping, and control of behaviour between the ages of 5 and 6. Test indicators which expressed prosocial development correlated with the teacher rating on constructiveness in behaviour. Ratings on aggression, on the other hand, correlated negatively with affective role-taking, helping, and understanding constructive solutions in a conflict situation.

The results of the longitudinal, temperament, and early prosocial development studies might be combined to show that from a very early age temperament differences are discernible, but quite soon a socially important dimension for interindividual differences emerges. It depicts prosocial behaviour, the opposite of which emerges more clearly in boys' than in girls' behaviour by the age of 7 (the start of compulsory education in Finland). At a later age, in adolescence and adulthood, anti-social behaviour differentiates from prosocial behaviour very clearly. Early prosocial behaviour is first related positively to the phlegmatic temperament and later to the sanguine temperament, but negatively to the choleric temperament. It means that a choleric child is at risk of not developing prosocial skills which are more easily adopted by a phlegmatic or sanguine child. Child-rearing practices respond to a child's temperament, and a choleric child easily gets treated in ways which increase defiance and destructive behaviour.

In the two-dimensional model of the Jyväskylä Longitudinal Study, aggression (uncontrolled expression of impulses) quite probably depicted children who had a choleric temperament, but unsuccessful home environment in terms of 'goodness of fit' (Lerner & Lerner, 1983). Because prosocial characteristics were shared by the two types of controlled behaviour it is obvious that the two-dimensional model for social behaviour represents a combination of temperament qualities and socialization experiences. At the age of eight, when the longitudinal study was started, the temperament qualities are already mixed with other influences in a way which predicts later development.

References

CATTÈLL, R.B. & COAN, R.W. (1959) The development of an early school personality questionnaire. *Journal of Experimental Education*, **28**, 143–52.

EYSENCK, H.J. (1960) *The structure of human personality*, London: Methuen.

EYSENCK, H.J. & EYSENCK, S.B.G. (1969) *Personality structure and measurement*, London: Routledge and Kegan Paul.

EYSENCK, H.J. & EYSENCK, S.B.G. (1975) *Manual of the Eysenck Personality Questionnaire (junior and adult)*, London: Hodder & Stoughton.

EYSENCK, S.B.G. (1965) A new scale for personality measurements in children. *British Journal of Educational Psychology*, **35**, 362–7.

KUUSINEN, J. & BLÅFIELD, L. (1974) The Illinois Test of Psycholinguistic Abilities (In Finn.). University of Jyväskylä, Finland: Institute for Educational Research. Bulletin, Nr. 234.

LERNER, J.V. & LERNER, R.M. (1983) Temperament and adaptation across life: theoretical and empirical issues. In P.B. Baltes & O.G. Brim, Jr. (eds.) *Life-span development and behavior*, (vol. 5) New York: Academic Press.

LESKINEN, E. & PULKKINEN, L. (1985) The use of exploratory and confirmatory factor analysis in the study of the structure of children's temperament. (Finn.) *Reports from the Department of Psychology, University of Jyväskylä, Finland*. Whole Nr. 272.

NEBYLITSYN, V.D. & GRAY, J.A. (1972) *Biological bases of individual behavior*, New York: Academic Press.

PITKÄNEN, L. (1969) A descriptive model of aggression and nonaggression with applications to children's behaviour. *Jyväskylä Studies in Education, Psychology and Social Research*. University of Jyväskylä, Finland. Whole Nr. 19.

PITKÄNEN-PULKKINEN, L. (1977) Effects of stimulation programmes on the development of self-control. In C.F.M. van Lieshout & D.J. Ingram (eds.) *Stimulation of social development in school.* Sets & Zeitlinger, 176–90.

PITKÄNEN-PULKKINEN, L. (1980) The child in the family. *Nordisk Psykologi,* **32**, 147–57.

PITKÄNEN-PULKKINEN, L. (1981) Long-term studies on the characteristics of aggressive and non-aggressive juveniles. In P.F. Brain & D. Benton (eds.) *Multidisciplinary approaches to aggression research,* Amsterdam: Elsevier/North-Holland.

PULKKINEN, L. (1977) *Psychology of upbringing,* (Finn.). Jyväskylä: Gummerus.

Pulkkinen, L. (1982) Self-control and continuity from childhood to late adolescence. In P. B. Baltes & O.G. Brim, Jr. (eds.) *Life-span development and behavior,* (vol. 4) New York: Academic Press, 63–103.

PULKKINEN, L. (1983) Finland: The search for alternatives to aggression. In A.P. Goldstein & M.H. Segall (eds.) *Aggression in global perspective,* New York: Pergamon Press, 104–44.

PULKKINEN, L. (1984) *Youth and home ecology,* (Finn.) Helsinki: Otava.

PULKKINEN, L. (1987) Delinquent development: Theoretical and empirical considerations. In M. Rutter (ed.) *Risk and protective factors in psychosocial development.* (In preparation).

PULKKINEN, L., AHONEN, S., HIRVIKALLIO, M., NÄKKILÄ, K., PAKARINEN, T., STRANDEN, P. & VAALAMO, P. (1983) Interindividual differences in social behaviour as a function of temperament and socialization. A paper presented in the symposium on 'Interindividual differences in social development: the role of socialization and temperament.' Seventh ISSBD Meetings, Munich.

PULKKINEN, L., HÄNNINEN, M., KAKKO, S., MIKKOLA, P., MURSULA, S., PALU, S., PENSAS, R.-L. & VILJAKAINEN, J. (1980) Early development of prosocial behaviour. (Finn.) *Reports from the Department of Psychology, University of Jyväskylä, Finland.* Whole Nr. 230.

SÄNKIAHO, R. (1974) Methodological tricks and how they are performed. (Finn.) *Institute for Educational Research, University of Jyväskylä, Finland.* Whole Nr. 220.

THOMAS, A. & CHESS, S. (1977) *Temperament and development.* New York: Brunner/Mazel.

Personality correlates of delinquent behaviour in juveniles and adolescents: evidence from German studies

4

I. Daum & E. Reitz

Juvenile delinquency and personality: theoretical considerations

Statistics on criminal acts in the Federal Republic of Germany in 1985 (Bundeskriminalamt, 1986) revealed a worrying picture. Of nearly 28% of all suspects, those involved in delinquency were children (4.6%), juveniles (14–16 years, 11.4%) and adolescents (18–21 years, 11.8%). Boys participated three times more often in crimes than girls. A particularly high involvement of young delinquents was found for crimes such as theft, robbery, bodily harm, blackmail, handling stolen goods and arson as well as drug offences. Many of these crimes that are typical of juvenile delinquency have a common element of a planning and decision phase that precedes the delinquent act. The question therefore arises, which factors influence this process of decision-making and lead the adolescent into crime.

No theory will claim that there is one single cause leading to the development of delinquent behaviour. But a number of factors can be identified that influence the development of anti-social behaviour in childhood and adolescence. An interactive model seems to be appropriate in which both environment and person-specific factors are considered. Sociological theories have put forward evidence on the contribution of variables like low social class, broken home family or low level of education (Göppinger, 1976), but they cannot explain differences within groups of individuals to which these criteria apply. The importance of person-specific factors in the development of anti-social behaviour will be addressed in the present contribution.

Linking personality traits to the development of delinquency does not mean that individuals are 'diagnosed' and therefore stigmatised. If the question is approached from a different angle, personality research might explain why the majority of young people from lower social classes, broken homes and of low education do not become delinquent. It is therefore of interest to assess which personality traits protect an individual from becoming delinquent in an environment that favours anti-social behaviour.

A further misinterpretation of research on personality and delinquency is that the identification of 'delinquent personality types' implies that there is no possibility of changing the individual's anti-social behaviour. However, knowledge about the susceptibility of different individuals to different educational techniques (cf Gray, 1970) might be used in rehabilitation and therapy programmes. It is argued that there is a lot to be gained for both society and the juvenile offender from findings relating to personality correlates of anti-social behaviour.

Research into the relationship between personality and delinquency has suffered from a lack of psychological theories. For this and other reasons, Eysenck's theory (1964, 1970, 1977) has played a major role in the generation of theory-guided hypotheses and their empirical testing. His theory is based on the assumption that

Acknowledgement The authors wish to thank Ms Brigitte Daum, Institute for Public International Law, Göttingen, FRG, for her assistance in preparing this manuscript.

social responsibility and social behaviour are learned by Pavlovian conditioning. Individuals with an introverted personality form conditioned responses more readily and more strongly than extraverts due to lower susceptibility to inhibition and higher levels of arousal. Neurotic tendencies intensify emotional reactions. As a consequence, socialisation fails in individuals who are both extraverted and neurotic which results in various forms of anti-social behaviour. A further important personality dimension in Eysenck's theory is psychoticism, defined by items relating to anti-social conduct (Eysenck & Eysenck, 1971). In short, delinquents should score high on scales that measure extraversion, neuroticism and psychoticism. Regarding extraversion, the impulsivity component which relates to a desire for stimulation and a willingness to take risks seems to be of particular relevance, especially in the evaluation of juvenile delinquency (Eysenck, 1970; Schwenkmezger, 1983). Reviews on the empirical evidence for Eysenck's theory, mainly based on Anglo-American studies, are given by Passingham (1972) and Wilson (1981).

An interesting extension to Eysenck's theory is offered by Gray (1970, 1981). Gray hypothesised that introverts are characterised by a heightened susceptibility to fear or warnings of punishment. If delinquents are seen as individuals taking rewards without considering the consequences, this behaviour pattern could be interpreted as lack of fear of punishment. The predictions regarding anti-social behaviour remain the same as Eysenck's: greater susceptibility to punishment in the introvert should lead to the stronger formation of social behaviour. Neuroticism is thought to intensify the degree of sensitivity to punishment or reward.

The aim of the present chapter is to provide a review on the evidence for a relationship between juvenile delinquency and personality obtained from German studies, the results of which might help to clarify whether personality differences between adolescent delinquents and non-delinquents might be the consequence of factors like stigmatisation and incarceration or whether they existed prior to 'official' registration and therefore might have played a role in the development of delinquent behaviour.

Empirical studies

Studies using the Freiburger Persönlichkeitsinventar (FPI)

One of the most frequently used personality inventories in German-speaking countries is the Freiburger Persönlichkeitsinventar (FPI, Fahrenberg, Selg & Hampel, 1978; Fahrenberg, Hampel & Selg, 1984). The items are combined to form nine trait scales which are labelled nervousness, aggressiveness, depression, excitability, sociability, stability, dominance, inhibition and openness. Additionally, there are three higher-order scales which are extraversion, emotional instability (neuroticism) and masculinity. The extraversion and neuroticism scales resemble those described in the dimensional system of Eysenck & Eysenck (1971). A review of the investigations carried out in prisoner groups is given by Steller & Hunze (1984). A summary of the studies with adolescents will be presented in temporal order.

Lukats, Luthe & Barth (1973) subdivided a group of juvenile delinquents (no information on age) according to whether they had committed crimes which expressed a tendency to attack and damage or whether the delinquent acts were predominantly 'asthenic' in character. The first group scored high on nervousness, excitability and emotional lability whereas the latter deviated from norm values on the depression factor.

In a large-scale investigation on the relationship between personality variables and self-reported delinquency. Walter, Merschmann & Höhner (1975) studied a group of students (mean age 17.6 years). Self-reported delinquency was positively correlated with aggressiveness, dominance, openness and extraversion across all social classes. However, subjects who had very high or very low scores on the FPI profile did not differ in the amount or nature of admitted delinquent acts. The authors concluded on the basis of these results that there was no clear evidence that traits measured by the FPI predisposed an individual to anti-social behaviour.

Lösel & Wüstendörfer (1976) administered a short version of the FPI and a self-report scale on delinquent activity to a sample of juvenile prisoners, a sample of correctional inmates and a sample of pupils. The mean age of the subjects was 17.2 years. The groups differed significantly on the aggressiveness, depression, excitability, dominance and emotional instability scales with higher values associated with increasing delinquency. The traits that discriminated between the three different groups were positively related to self-report delinquency within the whole sample as well as within the different subsamples. Additionally, extraversion was positively related to delinquent activity in the delinquent group and the pupil group. Hormuth, Lamm, Michelitsch, Scheuermann, Trommsdorff & Vögele (1977) studied groups of incarcerated and released delinquents, a group of factory workers and a group of army recruits. The groups were matched according to age (17–24 years old) and social class. Army recruits were chosen because they had to stay in their barracks most of the time during their training and therefore were thought to provide information on the effect of institutionalisation on responses to personality questionnaires. The authors also used a measure of motor inhibition to assess impulse control or 'delay capacity'.

Delinquents showed lower impulse control and proved to be significantly higher than non-delinquents on the nervousness, aggressiveness, depression, excitability, openness, extraversion and neuroticism scales. There was a significant correlation between excitability and the impulse control task. The institutionalisation factor was not significant. It remains questionable, however, whether army recruits were an institutionalised group comparable to prison inmates. When administering the FPI to 13–19-year-old boys of a remand home institution, Klein & Sturzebecher (1979) obtained similar results. The boys showed significantly increased scores on the nervousness, aggressiveness, depression, excitability, sociability and dominance scales as well as on the extraversion and neuroticism scales when the scores were compared to handbook scores. Kury (1980) administered the FPI to adolescent delinquents within one week after imprisonment on remand. The adolescents described themselves as more aggressive, excitable, anxious and depressed, but also as more extraverted and emotionally labile than expected on the basis of handbook norms.

Steller (1983) investigated whether the time still to be spent in prison might have an effect on the responses to the FPI. A group of 16–24-year-old prisoners scored significantly higher than norm values on the nervousness, depression, excitability, sociability, dominance, extraversion and emotional lability scales and lower on the inhibition scale. Time already spent in detention correlated only with the inhibition scale. A general trend emerged that subjects who had been in prison for a considerable amount of time tended to describe themselves more positively than subjects who had been in detention for a short period of time which Steller attributed to differences in social comparison processes. Time still to be spent in detention was significantly correlated with the depression scale ($-.20$).

A carefully controlled study by Villow-Feldkamp & Kury (1983) presented data on personality differences between incarcerated and self-reported delinquents without official record and non-delinquents matched for age (14–25 years), social class and level of education. Both delinquent groups differed from the non-delinquents on the nervousness, depression, aggressiveness, excitability, dominance as well as on the extraversion and emotional instability scales. Imprisoned delinquents scored significantly higher on the depression and stability scales when compared to the self-reported delinquents. The authors concluded that there was evidence for a relationship between personality traits and delinquency. They added that the cause of the deviations from norm values were due to the fact that many delinquents grew up in problem families.

Remschmidt, Höhner & Walter (1984) reported that young adults who had been registered as delinquent in a study on self-reported 'hidden' crimes during childhood, scored significantly higher on the extraversion scale than non-delinquents. Subjects who were registered before being 14 years of age resembled the non-delinquents, whereas those who were repeatedly registered as delinquent after the age of 14 were more depressed, dominant and emotionally labile than non-delinquents. Steller & Hunze (1984) reported that adolescent prisoners (mean age 19.5 years) scored significantly above the norm on the nervousness, depression, excitability, sociability, extraversion and emotional lability scales. Self-description on the FPI scales and time served in detention were unrelated.

In summing up the results of the comparison between delinquent and non-delinquent adolescents using the FPI for assessing personality traits, it can be said that delinquents describe themselves as higher on the depression, nervousness, aggressiveness, excitability, sociability, and dominance scales. Juvenile delinquents also score consistently higher on the extraversion and emotional lability scales, which is – interestingly – not always the case for adult delinquents (cf Steller & Hunze, 1984). The personality differences as assessed by the FPI confirm Eysenck's hypothesis of a combination of increased extraversion and neuroticism in delinquent adolescents. The results appear to be independent of the time already spent in detention or sentences still to be served. The general picture obtained from studies on self-reported 'hidden' crimes is quite clear: incarcerated juveniles resemble self-reported delinquents who have no official record and both differ from non-delinquent adolescents on a number of personality traits. A problem for the evaluation of FPI results in juvenile delinquents is however posed by the fact that the factor structure of the FPI could not always be replicated in samples of incarcerated adolescents (cf Hesener & Hilse, 1983 but also Villow-Feldkamp & Kury, 1983).

Studies using other personality questionnaires

Baltes, Wender & Steigerwald (1968) administered the MMPI to a group of delinquent male adolescents (ages 14–21 years) who were in an educational institution at the time of testing and a group of age-matched, non-delinquent pupils. Discriminant analyses revealed a satisfactory discrimination between groups with discrimination increasing if intelligence was used as an additional predictor. No further analyses as to the predictive value of the individual scales were made.

Witte & Witte (1974) compared three groups of male adolescents (ages 16–18) of different socio-economic levels with a group of male delinquents of the same age. The instrument used was a German version of the 16 PF (Cattell & Nesselroade, 1965). Delinquents were found to be more naive, simple and direct than the other groups and tended to describe themselves as more unreliable and less in control and having less willpower than adolescents of the two groups of medium and lower social class. The groups did not differ on ratings concerning emotional stability or extraverson.

Seitz & Pate (1983) compared a gorup of 14–16-year-old convicted delinquents with a group of unregistered juveniles on an age-adapted version of a personality questionnaire for children and self-reported delinquency. The convicted juveniles scored higher on the 'masculinity' and 'dependence on adults' scales and lower on the 'preparedness for social activity' scale. They showed a tendency for higher scores on the 'extravert-active temperament' scale. High rates of self-reported delinquency were related to assertiveness, emotionality and low scores on 'open-optimistic activity', but not to 'self-sufficient isolation' (sociability).

The results of these studies are difficult to evaluate as they were not so much designed to test hypotheses as to examine some correlates of delinquency through the use of personality questionnaires. Several studies added evidence to Eysenck's theory (Seitz & Pate, 1983); others did not (Witte & Witte, 1974).

Attitudes and values

The main characteristics of juvenile delinquents are thought to be impulsivity and impatience, the inability to plan the future and to delay gratification and reward (Lösel, 1975; Landau, 1976). Lösel (1975) established a positive correlation between self-ratings on risk-taking behaviour and self-reported delinquency in a group of pupils who had no criminal records. Schwenkmezger (1983) showed that adolescent delinquents and controls differed on some measures of risk-taking, but not on others. Risk-taking correlated with impulsivity and sensation-seeking, but not with extraversion. The author concluded that impulsive decision strategies might favour delinquent behaviour with individual differences contributing to decision making as well as situational variables.

Hasenpusch & Hommers (1975) tested the hypothesis of a lack of willingness to delay gratification in adolescent delinquents. The 56 items of the list administered in the study contained items such as the preference of 3 packets of cigarettes today compared with 5 packets in three weeks time. Subjects were rewarded for their participation in the study by choosing to receive a small number of stamps upon submission of the questionnaire or a larger number after some days. The results revealed a tendency for the older prisoners (over 21 years old) to prefer to have the reward stamps immediately rather than after some days. The reverse was true for prisoners under 21. The study was however limited because no comparison was made with a non-delinquent group.

In a study on future time perspective and value systems, Dillig (1982) compared a group of juvenile and young adult offenders (age 15 to 24) from 7 different institutions in Germany with a group of non-delinquent adolescents matched for age, educational level and family background. Subjects had to rate the desirability and the subjective probability of future events such as having a harmonious family life or a good job. In general, the delinquents' appreciation of future events was greater than peers' and the expectation of achieving goals was more optimistic in the 'private' sphere but less optimistic regarding employment. Dillig's results largely agree with those of a study by Margraf & Stiksrud (1978). Juvenile prisoners and juvenile non-delinquents (average age for both: 18.7 years), detention officers and age-matched adults in various other professions were compared regarding their value preferences on items such as friendship, job or nature. The results indicated that subjects of the same age were highly similar in their preference ratings (.831 for adults and .684 for adolescents). As the criminal adolescents expressed preferences that mirrored those of a non-delinquent age-matched sample, a typical specific 'criminal value system' could not be confirmed.

Attitudes which are thought to influence social behaviour are self-esteem and esteem for one's parents. American studies demonstrated a less positive self-image in delinquents as compared to controls and therefore positive self-esteem was thought to be an 'insulator' against delinquency (Reckless, Dinitz & Murray, 1956). German studies, however, could not always confirm this hypothesis. Deusinger (1973) found that a group of male juvenile delinquents (aged 15 to 24 years) had a very positive self-image (assessed by adjective lists) which was highly correlated with the self-ratings of a non-delinquent group of the same age (.96). The self-ratings of delinquents were however not correlated with their ratings of the 'typical juvenile delinquent' (.021). These results contradict Reckless's hypothesis that a positive self-image acts as a protection against delinquency. In another study, Trautner & Schuster

(1975) investigated institutionalised delinquents and non-delinquent controls (15–19 years old) subdivided into two different social classes. The subjects had to rate themselves, father and mother on an 80 item adjective rating scale. Additionally, the lie scale from the EPI was administered. There were no differences between delinquents and non-delinquents in self-esteem for the middle class subjects. Delinquents from the lower class had a much more positive self-image than non-delinquents which is in direct contrast to Reckless's theory and findings by Lösel (1983) who reported that officially registered delinquent juveniles had lower self-esteem than comparison groups. Esteem for parents was not different between delinquents and non-delinquents within the same social class. Thus the assumption that high esteem for parents would act as a protection against becoming delinquent could also not be confirmed. Both groups did not differ on the lie score, so one can discount the possibility that delinquents tried specifically to make a good impression.

Lösel, Toman & Wüstendörfer (1976) investigated whether parental rejection and low control favoured the development of delinquency. The study was based on the model that a post-punishment increase of previously forbidden acts might occur (Stapf, Herrmann, Stapf & Stäcker 1972) in children who experienced strict child rearing practices, so high strictness scores might then be expected in juvenile delinquents. A sample of 104 juvenile delinquents were compared to 100 non-delinquents of the same age (16–18 years) and social class on their ratings on short versions of the Marburg scales on perceived parental behaviour (Herrmann, Stapf & Krohne 1971). The results confirmed the hypothesis of greater paternal strictness and revealed either very high or very low support ratings among the delinquents. Göppinger (1976) confirmed these results with an older sample of young adult offenders (20–30 years old). Remschmidt, Höhner & Walter (1984) also reported a relationship between increasing delinquency and high parental strictness and low support. However, these findings are difficult to interpret because they rely on the memory of the subjects and greater parental strictness might be the consequence as well as the cause of anti-social behaviour of a child. Personality factors as well as environmental factors may therefore provide an explanation for the association between methods of education and delinquency.

In conclusion, there was little support from German studies for Reckless's hypothesis that a positive self-image and high esteem for parents would act as an 'insulator' against delinquency. The general findings suggest that delinquents have a positive self-image and appreciate the same values as non-delinquents of the same age. There was also some evidence for the hypothesis that inconsistent parental child rearing methods that involved high strictness and low support, might play a role in the development of delinquent behaviour.

Drug offences and personality

Drug takers constitute a rather special subgroup of delinquents. The investigation of the personality of drug offenders within the context of delinquency seems to be of importance as it has been shown that drug abuse might lead to cognitive disturbances which might result in anti-social behaviour (cf Stübing, 1970).

Lennertz (1970) compared the self-description of male juvenile non-hospitalised hash-smokers (mean age 18.9 years) with the self-ratings of pupils aged 15 to 19 years on various personality scales. The two groups did not differ on extraversion or neuroticism, but the hash-smokers described themselves as lower on rigidity and intolerance of ambiguity.

Rüdiger & Täschner (1974) subdivided pupils and students aged 14–20 years into three different groups: a group of habitual drug takers who received medical treatment because of drug dependence, 'occasionals' who were acquainted with drugs and 'non-consumers' who had never taken drugs. The adolescents completed

'Problemfragen für Jugendliche' (Süllwold, Roth & Berg, 1967) which assesses emotional and social problems in areas such as school, home, health or 'myself' (emotional stability). Drug users reported a higher incidence of family problems and a lack of communication, but also more neurotic tendencies such as feeling low, insecurity and daydreaming. Rüdiger & Täschner interpreted their results in accordance with Ausubel's theory (1968) that juvenile adjustment problems such as drug addiction or juvenile delinquency are due to the fact that personality traits have not matured as a result of inadequate methods of education.

Hobi (1973) pointed out that cannabis consumption was correlated with the FPI scales of nervousness, inhibition and emotional instability. Based on these results, Spille & Guski (1975) administered the FPI to a group of 14–31-year-old subjects divided into non-drug users, cannabis users and a group that used cannabis and other hallucinogens. Long-term use of cannabis in subjects with a low level of education (pupils, trainees) was associated with depression and nervousness while the use of mescaline in older subjects was related to lower sociability and lower emotional instability. Use of LSD was correlated with higher emotional instability. The authors concluded that the prediction of drug-related variables by FPI scales and demographic variables was better than the prediction of personality by drug variables, so that factors like neuroticism might precede the long-term use of drugs.

The latter hypothesis received more support from the results of a study by Sieber & Bentler (1982) carried out in Switzerland. The study was designed to investigate whether personality traits indicative of maladjustment preceded the use of illegal drugs. More than six thousand 19-year-old adolescents completed the FPI and a questionnaire relating to the consumption of various drugs such as cannabis, stimulants, opiates, analgesics, tobacco and alcohol. A sample of 841 subjects also completed the same questionnaire three years after the initial ratings. A highly significant correlation between the personality traits and the future consumption of legal and illegal drugs emerged, and remained significant even when the effect of drug consumption at the age of 19 was partialled out. The use of analgesics and cigarettes was predicted by the dominance and excitability scales whereas the consumption of alcohol and cannabis correlated positively with aggression, excitability and sociability. The authors concluded that personality traits contributed a small, but significant amount to the prediction of drug use. In a further study carried out in Switzerland, Hornung, Schmidtchen & Scholl-Schaaf (1983) investigated the personality structure of a representative sample of 15–25-year-old subjects subdivided into different groups based on the amount of interest in drugs and drug consumption. Extraversion turned out to be positively correlated with drug consumption, neuroticism was higher in the group that was interested in drugs as compared to those who were not interested or drug consumers. Nervousness and openness were also related to drug consumption.

In general, the pattern emerging from the investigation of the personality of drug users mirrors the pattern found for delinquents: neuroticism and to a lesser extent extraversion seem to be critical factors related to the consumption of illegal drugs. More evidence is, however, needed from longitudinal or follow-up studies such as that carried out by Sieber & Bentler (1982).

Methodological problems

A number of methodological problems arise with the interpretation of findings that are based on questionnaire studies. These issues will be discussed with reference to the German studies described above.

It has often been stated that questionnaire studies are not very valid because the incarcerated subjects might either try to manipulate their responses in a way that they might gain some special advantages within the prison or try to score high on those responses that are socially desirable. The studies that employed scales to control for these tendencies (e.g. the lie scale of the EPI or EPQ), could not confirm this hypothesis. Trautner & Schuster (1975) found no differences between delinquents and non-delinquents on the EPI lie scale. Hesener & Hilse (1983) compared the FPI results of two groups of incarcerated adolescent delinquents who either had to give their names when filling in the questionnaire or completed the questionnaire anonymously. The only group difference was found for the aggressiveness scale. The results of a similar study by Kury (1983) however revealed that juvenile delinquents tended to falsify the aggressiveness, nervousness, excitability and openness scores if they expected that the results would be added to their files. When the sample of Hesener & Hilse's study was subdivided on the basis of a median-split on the openness scale, the more honest subjects scored significantly higher on the nervousness, aggressiveness, depression, excitability, dominance, extraversion and emotional instability scales. These results point to the relevance of the openness score when FPI results of juvenile delinquents are evaluated. In other words, dissimulation would work against Eysenck's theory of high extraversion and neuroticism scores in delinquent samples.

Another question is whether the increased or decreased personality trait scores that are found in juvenile delinquents played a role in the development of delinquency or whether they are a consequence of conviction and incarceration. After all, life in prison includes deprivation from the outside social world, lack of privacy, loss of autonomy and a loss of heterosexual contact, all of which can lead to identity problems (Hohmeier, 1969). Adolescents in institutions might therefore not be representative of the general population of juvenile delinquents. Those in prisons might also be those who either have committed more serious crimes or those who are more easily caught and convicted. This leads to the problem of finding adequate comparison groups. The comparison groups used in the studies described above consisted usually of non-delinquent pupils or trainees matched for sex, age and social class. But often nothing is known about the delinquency rate in these groups, so the 'real' differences between delinquents and non-delinquents cannot be concluded from studies in which the delinquency rate in the comparison group is unknown. There are also problems in comparing the scores of delinquents with handbook norms (cf Steller, 1983).

However, the results of studies on self-reported 'hidden' crimes indicated that personality traits of delinquents differed in a specific way from the personality of non-delinquents, irrespective of whether the delinquent sample was incarcerated or not (e.g. Villow-Feldkamp & Kury, 1983). In addition, adolescents who had only spent a few days in detention showed deviations from FPI norms that were typical for juvenile delinquents although effects of incarceration could hardly have had a prominent effect at that stage (Kury, 1980). Longitudinal studies, although there are only few, also confirmed that there is a net effect of personality on the development of anti-social behaviour (e.g. Sieber & Bentler, 1982).

Finally, a less obvious problem has to be considered: since a large number of scales are frequently administered (e.g. in case of the FPI), a certain number of significant results might occur by chance when correlations are calculated or when groups are compared. In order to avoid this kind of 'artificial' significance produced by the large number of statistical tests, the level of significance in a study should be adjusted depending on the number of comparisons made.

Conclusions

The results from German studies of the personality traits of delinquents permit the conclusion that Eysenck's theory regarding the relationship between increased extraversion and neuroticism and delinquency was largely confirmed. There is evidence from studies on self-reported crimes that deviations from norm values on these scales existed prior to official conviction and therefore were not only 'produced' by incarceration. The behaviour patterns associated with these personality traits might therefore play a causal role, in interaction with environmental factors, in the development of anti-social behaviour. But a much greater number of prospective studies is needed before firm conclusions about causes and effects can be made.

When drug offences were investigated, the major results from the studies on general juvenile delinquency were replicated. Extraversion and emotional lability discriminated (among other traits like nervousness or openness) between drug users and non-users. Extraversion was found to increase with increasing consumption, but decreased again in a group of heavy users (cf Hornung *et al.*, 1983) which might be attributed to drug effects or a greater retreat from reality. Neuroticism was more prevalent in drug users compared to non-consumers, but was highest in a group interested in drugs. High neuroticism scores might therefore be indicative of the individual who is at risk for drug consumption. These differential findings point to the fact that there might not be a linear relationship between personality traits and various forms of anti-social and delinquent behaviour, including drug use.

There was also evidence for differences in family interaction processes and parenting factors between delinquents and non-delinquents. Various studies revealed that delinquents were subjected to a home environment that was characterised by great strictness, very high or very low support and inconsistencies regarding the consequences of their behaviours. According to psychological learning theory, these parenting behaviours would, in general, not favour the establishment of socialised behaviour. High strictness might lead to a post-punishment increase of previously forbidden acts, as hypothesised by Stapf *et al.* (1972). As personality is related to an individual's susceptibility to punishment or reward, extraverts in particular would be less likely to learn to inhibit anti-social and delinquent behaviour under the conditions delinquents appear to have been subjected to in childhood and adolescence. Strong conditioning, however, can lead to the inhibition of criminal tendencies even in an environment or under living conditions that favour delinquent behaviour. Whether conditioning of socialised behaviour and social responsibility succeeds, depends on the conditionability of an individual (e.g. personality) as well as on the quality and intensity of external conditioning stimuli (e.g. socialisation). Well-established conditioned behaviour could be thought to help coping with tension, conflicts and aggressiveness and therefore lead to a more stable personality that is resistant to delinquent behaviour. Non-delinquents would therefore have low neuroticism scores, whereas high neuroticism would be related to delinquent behaviour tendencies (cf Reitz, 1981). In general, the present discussion is in agreement with an interactional model in which both environment and personality contribute to the development of anti-social behaviour.

Many unanswered questions emerge when the research evidence on the problem of juvenile delinquency is reviewed. One major question relates to the definition of delinquency. Even if it is difficult to define delinquency on the level of behaviour (Lösel, 1977), there is a need to clarify to what forms of anti-social behaviour 'delinquency' refers. Future studies should investigate whether different crimes are correlated with different patterns of personality traits. This strategy has been adopted in recent studies (e.g. Amelang & Rodel, 1970; McGurk & McEwan, 1983) but is still neglected in the German literature on juvenile delinquency. Does a picture different from the present one emerge if only severe and repeated criminal acts are considered? Do adolescents who frequently engage in crime but are never caught differ from those who are caught and convicted? Is there a linear relationship between degree of delinquency and certain personality traits? These important questions (cf Kaiser, 1976) still remain to be answered.

In future questionnaire studies, a German version of the P scale (e.g. Eysenck, 1982) should be incorporated if theory-guided hypotheses are to be tested. It would be of interest to consider the impulsivity and sociability items of the extraversion scale separately if incarcerated delinquents and comparison groups are analysed, as sociability might be influenced strongly by the restrictive prison environment and with increasing duration of imprisonment (Häcker, Schwenkmezger & Utz, 1976). Although it is not easy to measure 'susceptibility to punishment' or 'susceptibility to reward', hypotheses drawn from Gray's reinterpretation of Eysenck's theory (Gray, 1981) are well worth testing in juvenile prisoner samples.

Gray's hypotheses are of particular importance within the context of rehabilitation. Personality theory predicts that introverted delinquents respond to signals of punishment or non-reward whereas extraverts respond better to signals of reward. Rehabilitation methods should therefore include considerations about the personality of the adolescent delinquent who is to be treated. The findings of the German studies in which the FPI was employed point to a further problem. Many juvenile delinquents scored high on the 'clinical' FPI scales (e.g. nervousness, depression). These results imply that there is possibly a greater need for psychological treatment than realised so far.

Finally, it has to be stressed again that the findings of a relationship between certain personality traits and juvenile anti-social behaviour do not imply that changes in the adolescents' behaviour patterns are impossible. On the contrary, personality theory can be of considerable help in bringing about these changes by providing information on how to plan individual personality-geared rehabilitation and therapy programmes from which both the juvenile offender and society might profit. Future rehabilitation outcome studies will tell whether this approach is an adequate one.

References

AMELANG, M. & RODEL, G. (1970) Persönlichkeits- und Einstellungskorrelate krimineller Verhaltensweisen. *Psychologische Rundschau*, **21**, 157–79.

AUSUBEL, D.P. 1968) *Das Jugendalter, Fakten-Probleme-Theorien*, München: Juventa-Verlag.

BALTES, P.B., WENDER, K. & STEIGERWALD, F. (1968) Diskriminanzanalytische Untersuchungen mit dem MMPI Saarbrücken zum Problem der Delinquenz männlicher Jugendlicher. *Zeitschrift für experimentelle und angewandte Psychologie*, **15**, 404–18.

Bundeskriminalamt (1986) *Polizeiliche Kriminalstatistik 1985*. Wiesbaden: Bundeskriminalamt.

CATTELL, R.B. & NESSELROADE, J. (1965) Untersuchung der interkulturellen Konstanz der Persönlichkeitsfaktoren im 16 PF-Test. *Psychologische Beiträge*, **8**, 502–15.

DEUSINGER, I. (1973) Untersuchungen zum Selbstkonzept von Strafgefangenen. *Psychologische Rundschau*, **24**, 100–13.

DILLIG, P. (1982) Zukunftsperspektive junger Strafgefangener und PEERs sowie daraus ableitbare Resozialisierungsziele/-maßnahmen. *Zeitschrift für klinische Psychologie*, **11**, 16–32.

EYSENCK, H.J. (1964) *Crime and personality*, London: Routledge & Kegan Paul.

EYSENCK, H.J. (1970) *Crime and personality*, London: Paladin.

EYSENCK, H.J. (1977) *Kriminalität und Persönlichkeit*. Wien: Europaverlag.

EYSENCK, H.J. & EYSENCK, S.B.G. (1976) *Psychoticism as a dimension of personality*, London: Hodder & Stoughton.

EYSENCK, S.B.G. (1982) A cross-cultural study of personality: Germany and England. *Zeitschrift für differentielle und diagnostische Psychologie*, **3**, 293–300.

EYSENCK, S.B.G. & EYSENCK, H.J. (1971) A comparative study of criminals and matched controls on three dimensions of personality. *British Journal of Social and Clinical Psychology*, **10**, 362–6.

FAHRENBERG, J., HAMPEL, R. & SELG, H. (1984) *Das Freiburger Persönlichkeitsinventar FPI*, Göttingen: Hogrefe.

FAHRENBERG, J., SELG, H. & HAMPEL, R. (1978) *Das Freiburger Persönlichkeitsinventar FPI*, Göttingen: Hogrefe.

GÖPPINGER, H. (1976) *Kriminologie*, München: Beck.

GRAY, J.A. (1970) The psychophysiological basis of introversion–extraversion. *Behaviour Research and Therapy*, **8**, 249–66.

GRAY, J.A. (1981) A critique of Eysenck's theory of personality. In: Eysenck, H.J. (ed.) *A model for personality*, Berlin: Springer, 246–76.

HÄCKER, H., SCHWENKMEZGER, P. & UTZ, H. (1976) Zur Persönlichkeitsstruktur von Strafgefangenen. Einige kritische Anmerkungen zu einer Untersuchung von Deusinger. *Psychologische Beiträge*, **18**, 224–32.

HASENPUSCH, B. & HOMMERS, W. (1975) Ein Beitrag zur Messung des Spannungsbogens von jugendlichen Delinquenten. *Zeitschrift für experimentelle und angewandte Psychologie*, **22**, 600–12.

HERRMANN, T., STAPF, A. & KROHNE, H.W. (1971) Die Marburger Skalen zur Erfassung des elterlichen Erziehungsstils. *Diagnostica*, **17**, 118–31.

HESENER, B. & HILSE, J. (1983) Empirische Ergebnisse zur Anwendbarkeit des FPI bei inhaftierten Jugendlichen. *Monatsschrift für Kriminologie und Strafrechtsreform*, **66**, 75–7.

HOBI, V. (1973) *Das Drogenproblem bei Jugendlichen*, Bern: Huber.

HOHMEIER, J. (1969) Die soziale Situation des Strafgefangenen: Deprivationen der Haft und ihre Folgen. *Monatsschrift für Kriminologie und Strafrechtsreform*, **52**, 292–304.

HORMUTH, S., LAMM, H., MICHELITSCH, I., SCHEUERMANN, H., TROMMSDORFF, G. & VÖGELE, I. (1977) Impulskontrolle und einige Persönlichkeitscharacteristika bei delinquenten und nichtdelinquenten Jugendlichen. *Psychologische Beiträge*, **19**, 340–54.

HORNUNG, R., SCHMIDTCHEN, G. & SCHOLL-SCHAAF, M. (1983) *Drogen in Zürich: Ergebnisse einer repräsentativen Motivstudie*, Bern: Huber.

KAISER, G. (1976) Die Frage nach der Persönlichkeit des Rechtsbrechers heute. *Zeitschrift für Sozialpsychologie*, **7**, 198–201.

KLEIN, W. & STURZEBECHER, K. (1979) Das Freiburger Persönlichkeitsinventar FPI bei Jugendlichen in Heimerziehung. *Diagnostica*, **25**, 170–80.

KURY, H. (1980) Prognose und Behandlung von jungen Rechtsbrechern. In: Forschungsgruppe Kriminologie (eds.) *Empirische Kriminologie*, Freiburg: Eigenverlag, 371–95.

KURY, H. (1983) Verfälschungstendenzen bei Persönlichkeitsfragebogen im Strafvollzug. *Monatsschrift für Kriminologie und Strafrechtsreform*, **66**, 72–4.

LANDAU, S.F. (1976) Delinquency, institutionalization and time orientation. *Journal of Consulting and Clinical Psychology*, **44**, 745–59.

LENNERTZ, E. (1970) Zur Frage der anti-sozialen Persönlichkeit jugendlicher Haschisch-Raucher. *Zeitschrift für Sozialpsychologie*, **1**, 48–56.

LÖSEL, F. (1975) *Handlungskontrolle und Jugenddelinquenz. Persönlichkeitspsychologische Erklärungsansatze delinquenten Verhaltens – theoretische Integration und empirische Prüfung*, Stuttgart: Enke.

LÖSEL, F. (1977) Auf dem Weg zu veränderten Junktoren zwischen Paradigmen sozialer Abweichung. *Zeitschrift für Sozialpsychologie*, **8**, 276–9.

LÖSEL, F. (1983) Entwicklungsstörungen sozialen Verhaltens – Zusammenhänge zwischen Umweltmerkmalen, Erfahrungsdifferenzen, Persönlichkeitsdispositionen und Jugenddelinquenz. *Deutsche Forschungen zur Kriminalitätsentstehung und Kriminalitätskontrolle*, **6**, 595–615.

LÖSEL, F., TOMAN, W. & WÜSTENDÖRFER, W. (1976) Eine Untersuchung zum perzipierten elterlichen Erziehungsstil bei jugendlichen Delinquenten. *Zeitschrift für experimentelle und angewandte Psychologie*, **23**, 45–61.

LÖSEL, F. & WÜSTENDÖRFER, W. (1976) Persönlichkeitskorrelate delinquenten Verhaltens oder offizieller Delinquenz. *Zeitschrift für Sozialpsychologie*, **7**, 177–91.

LUKATS, E., LUTHE, R. & BARTH, E. (1973) Voraussetzungen und vorläufige Ergebnisse einer Reihenuntersuchung jugendlicher und heranwachsender Straftäter. *Monatsschrift für Kriminologie und Strafrechtsreform*, **56**, 28–33.

MARGRAF, J. & STIKSRUD, H.A. (1978) Werthierarchien jugendlicher Häftlinge aus entwicklungspsychologischer Perspective. *Monatsschrift für Kriminologie und Strafrechtsreform*, **61**, 376–86.

McGURK, B.J. & McEWAN, A.W. (1983) Personality types and recidivism among Borstal trainees. *Personality and Individual Differences*, **2**, 165–70.

PASSINGHAM, R.E. (1972) Crime and personality: a review of Eysenck's theory. In: V.D. Nebylitsyn & J.A. Gray (eds.) *Biological bases of individual behaviour*, New York: Academic Press, 342–71.

RECKLESS, W.C., DINITZ, S. & MURRAY, E. (1956) Self-concept as an insulator against delinquency. *American Sociological Review*, **21**, 744–6.

REITZ, E. (1981) Kriminalistik-Kriminologie. In: K.H. Amff (ed.) *Polizeihandbuch*, Lübeck: Schmidt-Römhild, 1–6.

REMSCHMIDT, H., HÖHNER, G. & WALTER, R. (1984) Kinderdelinquenz und Frühkriminalität. *Kriminologische Gegenwartsfragen*, **16**, 87–105.

RÜDIGER, D. & TÄSCHNER, H. (1974) Untersuchungen zur Problemstruktur jugendlicher Rauschmittelkonsumenten. *Zeitschrift für experimentelle und angewandte Psychologie*, **21**, 146–61.

SCHWENKMEZGER, P. (1983) Risikoverhalten, Risikobereitschaft und Delinquenz: Theoretische Grundlagen und differentialdiagnostische Untersuchungen. *Zeitschrift für differentielle und diagnostische Psychologie*, **4**, 223–39.

SEITZ, W. & PATER, A. (1983) Beziehung von Persönlichkeitsmerkmalen zu offiziell registrierter und selbstberichteter Delinquenz bei männlichen Jugendlichen. *Deutsche Forschungen zur Kriminalitätsentstehung und Kriminalitätskontrolle*, **6**, 532–65.

SIEBER, M. & BENTLER, P.M. (1982) Zusammenhänge zwischen Persönlichkeitsmerkmalen und späterem Konsum legaler und illegaler Drogen bei jungen Männern. Eine Längsschnittuntersuchung. *Zeitschrift für experimentelle und angewandte Psychologie*, **29**, 649–68.

SPILLE, D. & GUSKI, R. (1975) Langfristiger Drogenkonsum und Persönlichkeitsmerkmale. *Zeitschrift für Sozialpsychologie*, **6**, 31–42.

STAPF, K.H., HERRMANN, T., STAPF, A. & STÄCKER, K.H. (1972) *Psychologie des elterlichen Erziehungsstils*, Stuttgart: Klett.

STELLER, M. (1983) Haftdauereinflüsse auf Selbstbeschreibungen von Delinquenten: Bezugsgruppeneffekte? *Zeitschrift für experimentelle und angewandte Psychologie*, **30**, 474–99.

STELLER, M. & HUNZE, D. (1984) Zur Persönlichkeitsbeschreibung von Delinquenten im Freiburger Persönlichkeitsinventar (FPI) – eine Sekundäranalyse empirischer Untersuchungen. *Zeitschrift für differentielle und diagnostische Psychologie*, **5**, 87–109.

STÜBING, G. (1970) Haschisch und Marihuana. *Das öffentliche Gesundheitswesen*, **8**, 379–86.

SÜLLWOLD, F., ROTH, H. & BERG, M. (1967) *Problemfragen für Jugendliche*, Göttingen: Verlag für Psychologie.

TRAUTNER, H.M. & SCHUSTER, B. (1975) Zur Bedeutung des Selbstbilds und des perzipierten Elternbilds für das Delinquenzproblem. *Archiv für Psychologie*, **127**, 116–30.

VILLOW-FELDKAMP, H. & KURY, H. (1983) Delinquenz und Persönlichkeit – Zusammenhänge bei Jugendlichen auf der Basis von Dunkelfeldergebnissen. *Monatsschrift für Kriminologie und Strafrechtsreform*, **66**, 113–17.

WALTER, R., MERSCHMANN, W. & HÖHNER, G. (1975) Unregistrierte Delinquenz Strafunmündiger und Persönlichkeitsmerkmale im FPI. *Monatsschrift für Kriminologie und Strafrechtsreform*, **58**, 339–57.

WILSON, G.D. (1981) Personality and social behavior. In: Eysenck, H.J. (ed.) *A model for personality*, Berlin: Springer, 210–45.

WITTE, H. & WITTE, E.H. (1974) Persönlichkeitsmerkmale und -idealvorstellungen von Jugendlichen verschiedener sozialer Schichten und einer Gruppe jugendlicher Delinquenten. *Zeitschrift für Sozialpsychologie*, **5**, 219–32.

5 The negative function of nonverbal communication in anorexic families: a family experiment

F.-J. Hehl, E. Eisenriegler, R. Jokiel &
S. Channon

Introduction

Watzlawick, Beavin & Jackson (1969) and Watzlawick & Weakland (1980) proposed that every communication contains both a content and a relational component. The content component is primarily 'digital' and mediated by language, whilst the relational component is predominantly 'analogue', i.e. conveyed by nonverbal or paralinguistic means (Watzlawick, Weakland & Fisch, 1974).

Minuchin, Rosman & Baker (1981) demonstrated that it is the relational component which is disturbed above all in anorexic families. They used the construct 'enmeshment' in this context to refer to an extreme degree of emotional closeness between the family members. They stated that in an extremely enmeshed and self-preoccupied family, changes in one family member or in the relationship between members have an effect on the whole system. The boundaries of the subsystems are very unclearly formed, and easily transgressed. The interpersonal differentiation for the individual in the enmeshed family is therefore very sketchy. They consider that this extreme degree of emotional closeness might prevent the problem from being properly resolved, i.e. an effective communication with respect to the content component. Kendon (1967) found that the participants in a discussion avert their gaze when the temperature of the emotional affect rises. According to Argyle & Dean (1965), frequent or prolonged gaze avoidance produces uneasiness in the recipient during discussions of personal relevance.

A further construct which Minuchin *et al.* (1981) believe to be present in psychosomatic families is 'conflict non-resolution'. They observed that many psychosomatic families do not admit to having any problems at all. The family members see no need to have differing opinions on any subject, and place great value on agreement and harmony. Other families do in fact frequently display their differences of opinion, but since they continually interrupt one another and never stay on a single theme for long, they manage to exhaust any controversial issue before it has properly emerged.

Wirkan, Faleide & Blakar (1978) were able to show something similar. According to their description, the communication in psychosomatic families is characterised by lack of clarity, pseudo-agreement, conflict avoidance and passivity. Gutezeit (1981) was able to demonstrate dependency on parents in patients with anorexia. According to Gensicke (1979), the balance of interaction has been lost in anorexic families. The disturbance in the content component of psychosomatic and especially anorexic families is present in all these studies. Attempts to solve problems are made either by not perceiving them as such, or by avoiding the issue.

In connection with family studies of psychosomatically ill children from 'enmeshed' families, Wirsching & Stierlin (1982) noted the similarities between the descriptions given respectively by Minuchin, Rosman & Baker (1978) of 'enmeshed' families, and by Jackson & Yacom (1966) of 'restricted' families or of families with 'anxious cohesion' given by Tichener, Riskin & Emerson (1967). In such families, Wirsching

& Stierlin (1982) look upon the conflict avoidance, which leads all the members to know everything about each other, and the fact that the children's attempts to become independent lead to family crises, as important causes of psychosomatic illnesses in young people.

The 'enmeshment' and 'conflict avoidance' displayed by anorexic families can therefore be put together in the following way: The 'enmeshment' represents the primary disturbance in the relational component; and the 'conflict avoidance' represents the attempt which this generates to find a solution to the problems despite the disturbance in the relational component, without destroying the family.

If we return now to Watzlawick *et al.*'s (1974) suppositions that the relational component is mediated primarily by nonverbal and paralinguistic means, and the content component primarily by speech, then we can consider whether the content component of the problem-solving process in anorexia nervosa could be improved by attempting to eliminate the primary disturbance in the nonverbal relational component. Further justification for this formulation appears to be provided by Rosenthal's (1979) findings that adding nonverbal communication channels (the relational component) had a negative effect on the decoding of messages in psychiatric patients, but a positive effect in normal controls. McGhee (1973) and Meiselman (1973) also found that psychiatric patients were less able than normal controls to decode a message if auditory and visual signals were presented at the same time, compared to when only one of the two channels was functioning.

Our hypotheses can be formulated in the following way:

(1) Limiting the problem-solving processes in a healthy family to the auditory communication channel impairs the healthy relational component and reduces the effectiveness of the content component (solving the problem) of the message.

(2) Limiting the problem-solving processes in an anorexic family to the auditory communication channel partially eliminates the damaged relational component and increases the effectiveness of the content component (solving the problem) of the message.

Method

In order to be able to test the hypotheses specified above, more aspects of the communication processes need to be operationalised. We therefore endeavoured both to portray the individual segments of the problem-solving processes which best depicted the normal processes in these families (high external validity), and at the same time to test them as stringently as possible (high internal validity).

In particular the following parts of the communication process had to be operationalised: (i) the content component (the problem); (ii) the different communication channels (auditory versus auditory + visual); (iii) the verbal and nonverbal messages.

(i) Operationalisation of the content of the communication

First of all it is worth clarifying here which events and aspects can be looked upon as problematic in families with adolescent members. Eighteen short stories were finally produced describing typical family situations which generally lead to conflicts in this type of family. Since the development of autonomy in the children appears to be a critical stage for these families according to Wirsching & Stierlin (1982), all the stories deal with these children's struggles with their parents regarding autonomy. The eighteen short stories have the following themes:

(1) Reading versus domestic chores
(2) Allocation of spare time depending on school performance
(3) Career interests versus time for the family
(4) Mother's worries about the daughter's party invitation
(5) A bicycle trip – to tell or not to tell?
(6) Varying opinions on the son's appearance
(7) The family meal together is put at risk
(8) A parental row – a family row
(9) Risking a row over a boyfriend
(10) Suitable clothing
(11) Who sees to the Christmas presents?
(12) A secret diary has been read
(13) Pocket money problems
(14) The contraceptive pill
(15) A school function
(16) Recuperation after an illness
(17) Parental suggestions about diet for an overweight teenager
(18) Personal needs versus family interests

The following story (No. 10: Suitable clothing) is an example of the kind of scenarios we used: 'Helga prefers to dress herself casually and comfortably. She has frequent clashes over this with her mother, who thinks that Helga neglects her outward appearance. When she and Helga want to do a bit of shopping she insists that Helga dresses herself according to her mother's taste.'

Each family member was required to adopt an attitude towards the conflicts being acted out independently of the others, and to tick one of the two possible hypothetical solutions on an answer sheet. One of the possible solutions leaned in the direction of granting autonomy, and the other in the direction of attempting to obstruct it. Afterwards each member of the family, (still acting independently), had to tick in the relevant place whether the conflict described had arisen in their own family or not.

Ten of the eighteen stories were selected for each respective family by the experimenter using two criteria. At least one member of the family had to have selected a different solution to the other family members (conflict). If differing solutions had been selected in less than 10 stories, those which were classified as relevant to at least two family members were taken.

(ii) Operationalising the differentiation of the communication channels

The 'natural' audiovisual channel was set up with the four family members sitting in a semi-circle so as to be able to see and hear each other. The restricted, exclusively auditory channel was set up with the family members sitting in a third of a circle with partition walls between the chairs so that the individual members could not see each other.

(iii) Operationalising the verbal and nonverbal messages

All the interactions were videotaped. With the aid of two directional microphones the verbal messages and reactions could be clearly documented. Six judges who had successfully completed training made retrospective judgements of the videotaped interaction 'statements'. A 'statement' was defined as any verbalisation made by a family member whose beginning and ending was defined by the remark of another. An observation unit was a statement with more than three words. A statement could consist of several observation units. This descriptive coding system was developed following Olson & Ryder (1975) and Gottman (1977). Each individual category was operationally defined and illustrated with an example. The system employs the following categories:

Verbal communication
(I)   *Verbalisations during the course of conversation*
01   Beginning conversation
02   Leading back to the theme
03   General comments to come up with a solution
04   A successful interruption
05   An attempted interruption
06   An individual speaks in the plural case
07   Metacommunication
08   Reading aloud, e.g. repeating the story

(II)   *Opinions*
09   Disclosing one's own view
10   Repeating one's own view
11   Opinions drawn from one's own experience
12   Interpreting others' opinions, feelings and ways of behaving
13   Vague remarks
14   Finishing off another family member's sentence

(III)   *Comments referring to solutions*
15   Father adopts mother's viewpoint
16   Father adopts the child's viewpoint
17   Mother adopts father's viewpoint
18   Mother adopts the child's viewpoint
19   The child adopts father's viewpoint
20   The child adopts mother's viewpoint
21   Father adopts his own viewpoint
22   Mother adopts her own viewpoint
23   The child adopts her own viewpoint
24   The father's/mother's/child's autonomy is acknowledged
25   Autonomy is not acknowledged
26   Digressions from the theme

(IV)   *Questions*
27   Questions about the procedure
28   Questions about the content
29   Questions about the outcome
30   Rhetorical questions

(V)   *Feedback*
31   Direct agreement
32   Qualified agreement
33   Rejection
34   Praise, e.g. support
35   Disapproval
36   Criticism of the patient
37   Self-critical comments

Nonverbal communication
(I)   *Head*

38   Smiling
39   Nodding
40   Turning towards someone during a statement of opinion
41   Shaking the head
42   Looking away during a statement of opinion (looking at the sheet of paper or in the air)

(II)   *Voice*
43   Laughter
44   Reducing the volume
45   Crying
46   Raising the volume

(III)   *Body*
47   Reducing the distance
48   Bending forwards
49   Increasing the distance
50   Folding the arms

The target families
The medical findings and diagnoses were based on the judgements of hospital doctors or GPs who were asked with the families' consent and filled in a medical history questionnaire designed by us. Three selection criteria were applied to both the anorexic families and to the healthy families. They had to comprise at least the three members, father, mother and daughter; there could also be an additional child over 12 years old. At the time of the study, one daughter had to be between 13 and 17 years old. We restricted ourselves to juvenile anorexia on account of the themes of the stories to be discussed; at this stage the themes referred to the crisis of autonomy. The family had to belong to the middle classes (determined by the parents' professions and education and the children's education).

    Additional criteria were required for the anorexic families. The 13–17-year-old daughter had to meet the criteria for anorexia defined by Feighner, Robins, Guze, Woodruff, Winokur & Munoz (1972) (see also Steinhausen, 1979). The families had not (yet) received family therapy. For the healthy families, the children had to have no psychosomatic illness and none of the family members should be suffering from a chronic medical illness.

Study design
A factorial design was used with two independent variables, which each had two levels, namely factor 1: Psychosomatic disturbance (yes/no); and factor 2: Communication channel (audiovisual/auditory only). The design of the study is shown in Table 5.1.

    All the families discussed five conflicts in the audiovisual condition and five in the auditory condition. Three of the anorexic families and three of the healthy families started in the audiovisual condition, and the remaining three families in each case started in the auditory condition. The verbal and nonverbal messages and reactions of the family members during the problem-solving process comprised the dependent variables.

Data analysis
In view of the hypotheses described above, the interaction between the first and second factors was of primary interest. Since the first factor (communication channel) had to be tested as a repeated measure, the following inferential statistics were employed. An analysis of variance was performed for the second factor using the

Table 5.1 Design of the study

| | | Factor | | |
		auditory	audiovisual	
Factor	ill	3 families ――――――➤		6
		◄―――――― 3 families		
2	healthy	3 families ――――――➤		6
		◄―――――― 3 families		
	Total	6 families	6 families	12

difference scores obtained from the first factor. Since not all the dependent variables could be assumed to be normally distributed, the non-parametric analysis of variance described by Kruskal & Wallis (1952) was used. If a significant result emerged for the first factor, an interaction effect between the first and the second factor would be ensured.

Results

In the following we only present the significant interactions between factor 1 and factor 2. We did not expect to find many above-chance interactions for two reasons. Firstly, the two samples were extremely small, and some of the dependent variables appeared too rarely. Secondly, the main effects of one or the other of the variables might have been so influential that there was hardly any room for the interaction to exert any effect. Nevertheless we took this first study of the hypotheses in question to initially examine whether there was any effect in the predicted direction. This should then ideally be tested out in a follow-up study using bigger sample sizes and a reduced coding system. The dependent variables were next averaged over all the family members. Then all the variables were analysed for the father alone, then for the mother, and finally for the anorexic daughter. These results are reported in Figures 5.1–5.4.

For the 'total family', the effects of the interaction appear to be due to the fact that for the anorexic families in the 'normal' conversation condition compared to the restricted condition, a higher mean proportion of their conversation fell into the categories of 'vague comments', 'father adopts the child's viewpoint', and 'autonomy is not granted'. For the healthy families, the proportion of conversation falling into the same categories was less in the normal speech condition than for the restricted condition (see Figure 5.1).

The proportion in the normal condition was less for the psychosomatically disturbed families than for the restricted condition in the categories 'qualified agreement' and 'laughter'. For the healthy families, the effect of communication modality operated in the reverse direction.

The interactions between factor 1 and factor 2 for the fathers are shown in Figure 5.2.

A = anorexic families;
H = healthy families;
A + V = audiovisual;
A = auditory alone;
p = the probability of the interaction

(a) Vague comments (13)

	A + V		A	
	x̄	SD	x̄	SD
A	2.55	(0.55)	1.45	(0.65)
H	1.60	(0.45)	1.65	(0.50)

p < .047

(b) Father adopts child's viewpoint (16)

	A + V		A	
	x̄	SD	x̄	SD
A	0.55	(0.20)	1.45	(0.15)
H	0.25	(0.25)	0.65	(0.45)

p < .008

(c) Autonomy is not granted (25)

	A + V		A	
	x̄	SD	x̄	SD
A	1.70	(0.40)	1.30	(0.55)
H	1.30	(0.35)	1.95	(1.30)

p < .047

(d) Qualified agreement (32)

	A + V		A	
	x̄	SD	x̄	SD
A	0.75	(0.10)	1.00	(0.55)
H	0.75	(0.60)	0.65	(0.55)

p < .047

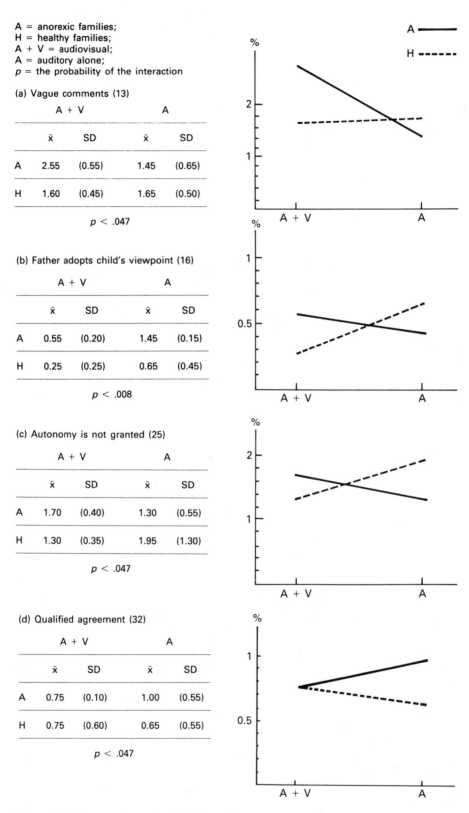

Figure 5.1 Means and standard deviations for the interactions between factor 1 and factor 2 for the *total family*

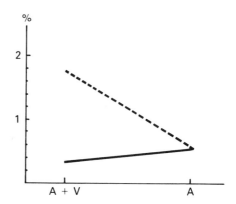

(e) Laughter (43)

	A + V		A	
	x̄	SD	x̄	SD
A	0.35	(0.20)	0.50	(0.45)
H	1.75	(0.85)	1.50	(0.15)

$p < .032$

Figure 5.1 continued

The interaction appeared to operate in the following way for the fathers. In the psychosomatically disturbed families, the proportion of conversation which fell into the categories 'vague remarks' and 'repetition of own viewpoint' was greater in the normal conversation condition than in the restricted condition, whilst for the fathers from healthy families it was less. These on the other hand showed a higher proportion of 'laughter', 'qualified agreement' and 'attempted interruptions' in the normal condition than in the restricted condition, whilst the effect of communication modality on the fathers from the psychosomatic families was the opposite for these categories.

The interactions between factor 1 and factor 2 for the mothers are shown in Figure 5.3.

For the mothers, the interaction effects showed up in the categories 'laughter', 'digressions from the theme' and 'questions about the theme'. Once again the proportion of these results for the total interaction process was higher in the normal conversation condition compared to the restricted condition for the mothers from healthy families, whilst the anorexic family mothers were the opposite. On the other hand, for the mothers from anorexic families in the normal conversation condition compared to the restricted condition, the proportion was greater in the category 'vague remarks', and the reverse for the healthy mothers.

The interactions between factor 1 and factor 2 for the children are shown in Figure 5.4.

The interaction effect for the children was shown in the behaviour 'metacommunication'. For the children from healthy families the proportion in this category was greater in the normal conversation condition compared to the restricted one, and the opposite for the children from anorexic families.

Discussion

Since we only looked at the interactions between anorexia (yes/no) and communication channel (auditory/audiovisual) and a very specific hypothesis about the effects of the two factors was tested out, we might have expected no clearcut results, especially in view of the small sample size. All the same, 14 of the 15 significant interactions were in the direction of the proposed hypothesis. The healthy families showed a greater tendency to avoid conflict during problem-solving if the communication channel was restricted. By comparison, the effect of restricted communication on the anorexic families was advantageous. Looking at the interactions of all the family members in the auditory alone communication, the number of vague remarks decreased markedly; the fathers less often adopted the child's viewpoint; autonomy

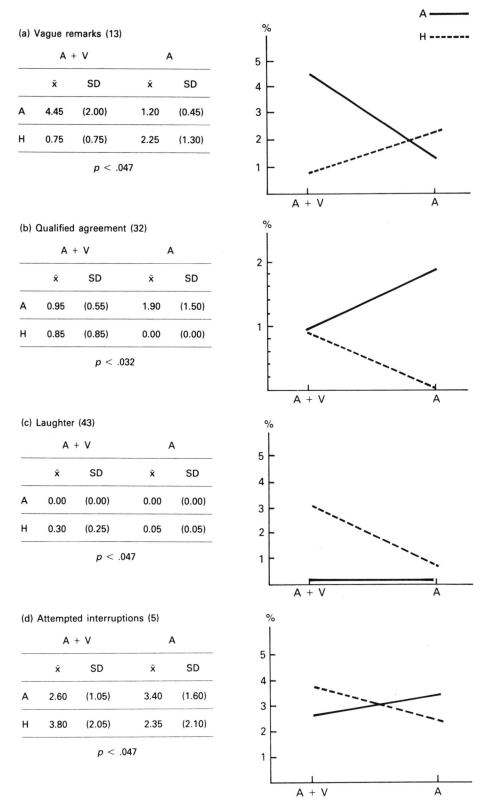

(a) Vague remarks (13)

	A + V		A	
	x̄	SD	x̄	SD
A	4.45	(2.00)	1.20	(0.45)
H	0.75	(0.75)	2.25	(1.30)

$p < .047$

(b) Qualified agreement (32)

	A + V		A	
	x̄	SD	x̄	SD
A	0.95	(0.55)	1.90	(1.50)
H	0.85	(0.85)	0.00	(0.00)

$p < .032$

(c) Laughter (43)

	A + V		A	
	x̄	SD	x̄	SD
A	0.00	(0.00)	0.00	(0.00)
H	0.30	(0.25)	0.05	(0.05)

$p < .047$

(d) Attempted interruptions (5)

	A + V		A	
	x̄	SD	x̄	SD
A	2.60	(1.05)	3.40	(1.60)
H	3.80	(2.05)	2.35	(2.10)

$p < .047$

Figure 5.2   Means and standard deviations for the interactions between factor 1 and factor 2
for the *fathers*

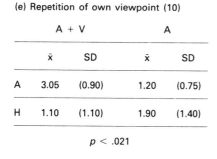

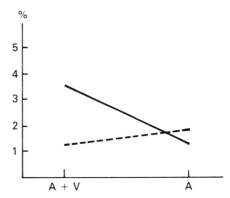

(e) Repetition of own viewpoint (10)

	A + V		A	
	$\bar{x}$	SD	$\bar{x}$	SD
A	3.05	(0.90)	1.20	(0.75)
H	1.10	(1.10)	1.90	(1.40)
	$p < .021$			

Figure 5.2 continued

was more frequently granted; qualifications were more often made in giving agreements; and the amount of laughter was also increased. The converse was found in the healthy families.

Additionally, for the fathers alone in the auditory condition, the fathers from anorexic families attempted to interrupt the other family members, and repeated their own viewpoints significantly less often. The mothers of anorexics also showed particular tendencies when the problem could only be negotiated with words. They put more frequent questions about the themes of the stories and digressed from the problem less often, but in comparison to the healthy ones they digressed more. (This was the only significant interaction which did not clearly support the hypothesis.) The anorexics themselves displayed significantly more frequent metacommunication in the auditory condition than the healthy ones or than in the 'natural' conversation condition. Altogether, 14 of the 15 variables clearly showed that in the verbal alone condition, the anorexic families tend to resolve conflicts such as autonomy. In healthy families it was precisely the converse: they permitted their members less autonomy and tended to avoid conflict when they could see each other.

Palazzoli (1982) assumed that the emotional relationship of the parents is disturbed in anorexic families. This disturbed relationship between the parents appears to constitute the cause of the enmeshment in the family. Minuchin *et al.* (1981) considered that any major dysfunction in the marital system has an impact on the entire family and affects all its members. The children would also be used as scapegoats in the situation or be drawn into an alliance with one of the partners.

According to Watzlawick (1980), a disturbance in the process may be manifested in the nonverbal interaction. If these nonverbal messages are removed from the interaction, it appears that the content component of the problem-solving relational is improved in anorexic families. The signs of enmeshment seem to decrease, and the autonomy of the individual family member is strengthened. Should the enmeshment itself be an important constituent in the process which brings about anorexia nervosa, then therapy which attempts to improve communication in families such as these through verbal means alone without the members seeing each other might have an initial impact on the enmeshment.

Similar, albeit less rigorous therapeutic principles were proposed by Minuchin *et al.* (1978) and Petzold (1979) when they attempted to define rules for confrontations to detach an individual family member from the enmeshment. The fundamental point of Petzold's confrontational therapy was Lasegue's claim that the isolation of the patient from her family is called for during the treatment. According to Petzold (1979), the first therapeutic task with an anorexic family is to change the context in which the family operates. He attempts this by direct confrontation with any two of the family members. Hehl & Weber (1983) were able to demonstrate in a single case study that a confrontation of this nature can be successful, particularly from

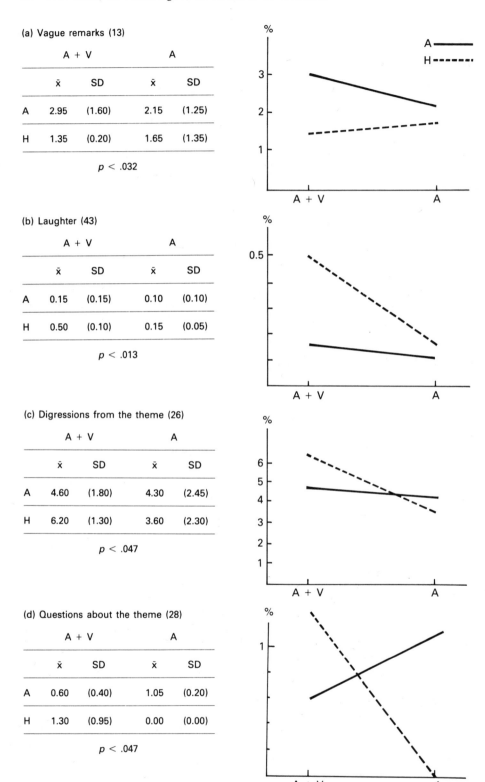

(a) Vague remarks (13)

	A + V		A	
	x̄	SD	x̄	SD
A	2.95	(1.60)	2.15	(1.25)
H	1.35	(0.20)	1.65	(1.35)

p < .032

(b) Laughter (43)

	A + V		A	
	x̄	SD	x̄	SD
A	0.15	(0.15)	0.10	(0.10)
H	0.50	(0.10)	0.15	(0.05)

p < .013

(c) Digressions from the theme (26)

	A + V		A	
	x̄	SD	x̄	SD
A	4.60	(1.80)	4.30	(2.45)
H	6.20	(1.30)	3.60	(2.30)

p < .047

(d) Questions about the theme (28)

	A + V		A	
	x̄	SD	x̄	SD
A	0.60	(0.40)	1.05	(0.20)
H	1.30	(0.95)	0.00	(0.00)

p < .047

Figure 5.3 Means and standard deviations for the interactions between factor 1 and factor 2 for the *mothers*

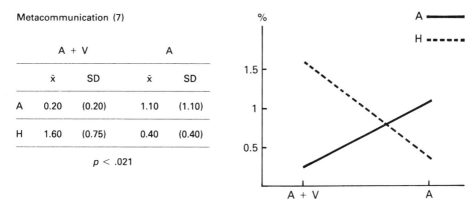

Figure 5.4   Means and standard deviations for the interactions between factor 1 and factor 2 for the *children*

the point of view of bringing about greater autonomy for all the family members.

The results of this study also supply a plausible explanation for the finding that anorexic families are very resistant to change if all the family members participate in the therapy. From the apparently enmeshed relational component which shows up non-verbally, the problem-solving process which is usually tackled in family therapy does not make sense. The enmeshment which operates at a nonverbal level obstructs every attempt at therapy. However, if one does wish to work with these therapeutic principles, one must ensure that nonverbal communication is made impossible or made subject to different rules.

Clearly the findings from this study can only be tentatively interpreted, since they are based on small sample sizes on a single occasion. Further work is needed to explore these preliminary results in more detail, and to establish whether the improvement shown by anorexic families in the restricted communication condition reflects a stable characteristic which can be made use of in therapy. Watzlawick *et al.* (1974) emphasised the importance of both nonverbal and paralinguistic processes in mediating the relational component of a communication, and this study has addressed itself only to the nonverbal aspects. The paralinguistic aspects also need to be explored since devices such as refusing to speak could obviously have a very powerful effect on communication. We are currently examining the role of paralinguistic factors in anorexic families by employing a condition in which verbal communication takes place by written rather than spoken means.

If the current findings are substantiated by further studies, they might be applied to changing the family context in the therapeutic setting in several ways. Family members could be asked to communicate without seeing each other, e.g. separated by partitions or in different rooms connected by telephone. At the moment we are engaged in a single case study testing out this approach. Another possibility would be to confront anorexics with one parent, not in the 'normal' arrangement where they sit opposite one another, but back to back (see also Hehl, 1986). All the other family members should sit (as near as possible to the therapist) so that the two who are confronting each other cannot see them either, or can barely see them. Planned telephone calls from hospitalised anorexics to a parent could also be used. In this way the patient could maintain contact with the normal environment – particularly her parents – and at the same time use this to dissolve the restriction or enmeshment with the parents and negotiate the central problem of establishing her own autonomy.

Summary

The hypothesis was tested that nonverbal communication (facial and body movements) has an important role for the members of anorexic families in both lack of conflict resolution and restricting the autonomy of the individual. Therefore the verbal problem-solving behaviour and the nonverbal communication of six anorexic and six families without psychosomatic problems were compared in selected conflict situations. The experimental manipulation was that all the families had to solve five conflict situations under normal conditions (sitting in a semi-circle) and five in a condition where they were separated from each other by partition walls, but could still talk to each other. The results gave considerable support to the hypothesis that anorexic families do very badly under normal circumstances at resolving conflicts. However, if they cannot see each other and can only talk to each other, they resolve conflicts better. In healthy families the converse is the case.

References

ARGYLE, M. & DEAN, J. (1965) Eye contact distance and affiliation. *Sociometrie*, **28**, 289–304.

FEIGHNER, J.P., ROBINS, E., GUZE, S.B., WOODRUFF, R.A., WINOKUR, G. & MUNOZ, R. (1972) Diagnostic criteria for use in psychiatric research. *Arch. Gen. Psychiatr.*, **26**, 57–63.

GENSICKE, P. (1979) Anorexia nervosa: a deficiency of family socialisation? *Zeitschr. f. Psychosom. Med. u. Psychoanal.*, **25**, 201–15.

GOTTMAN, J.M. (1977) *Couples and Interaction Scoring System (CISS) – Coder Coordinators Manual*, Department of Psychology, Univ. of Illinois.

GUTEZEIT, G. (1981) Ergebnisse psychodiagnostischer Untersuchungen bei weiblichen und mannlichen Patienten mit Anorexia nervosa. In: H.C. Steinhausen (ed.) *Psychosomatische Storungen und Krankheiten bei Kindern und Jugendlichen*, Stuttgart: Kohlhammer, 178–92.

HEHL, F.-J. (1986) *Versuch einer systemischen Betrachtung der Genese und Therapie von Magersucht*, Vortrag auf einem Symposium über Jugendfragen der Stadt Köln.

HEHL, F.-J. AND WEBER, A. (1983) *Eine Einzelfallanalyse zur Konfrontationstherapie bei Anorexia nervosa*. Vortrag auf dem 12. Kongress für Angewandte Psychologie, Düsseldorf.

JACKSON, D.D. & YACOM, I. (1966) Family research on the problems of ulcerative colitis. *Arch. Gen. Psychiat.* **15**, 410–18.

KENDON, A. (1967) Functions of gaze direction in social interaction. *Acta Psychol.* **26**, 22–63.

KRUSKAL, W.H. & WALLIS, W.A. (1952) Use of ranks in one-criterion variance analysis. *J. Amer. Statist. Ass.* **47**, 582–621.

McGHEE, A. (1973) Psychological studies of schizophrenia. In: B. Maher (ed.) *Contemporary abnormal psychology*, Harmondsworth, England: Penguin, 120–33.

MEISELMAN, K.C. (1973) Broadening dual modality cue utilisation in chronic nonparanoid schizophrenics. *J. Cons. and Clin. Psychol.* **41**, 447–53.

MINUCHIN, S., ROSMAN, B.L. & BAKER, L. (1978) *Psychosomatic families. Anorexia nervosa in context*, Cambridge: Harvard University Press.

MINUCHIN, S., ROSMAN, B.L. & BAKER, L. (1981) *Psychosomatische Krankheiten in der Familie*, Stuttgart: Klett.

OLSON, D.H. & RYDER, R.G. (1975) *Marital and Family Interaction Coding System (MFICS)*, Minnesota: University Press.

PALAZZOLI, S. (1982) *Magersucht*, Stuttgart: Klett.

PETZOLD, E. (1979) *Familienkonfrontationstherapie bei Anorexia nervosa*, Göttingen: Vandenhoeck & Ruprecht.

ROSENTHAL, R. (1979) Measuring sensitivity to nonverbal communication: the Pons Test. In: A. Wolfgang (ed.): *Nonverbal behaviour – applications and cultural implications*, New York: Academic Press.

STEINHAUSEN, H.C. (1979) Anorexia nervosa – eine aktuelle Literaturübersicht. Teil 1: Diagnostische Aspekte. *Zeitschr. Kinder-Jugendpsychiatr.*, **7**, 149–69.

TICHENER, J.L., RISKIN, J. & EMERSON, R. (1967) The family in psychosomatic process. In: G. Handel (ed.) *The psychosocial interior of the family*. Chicago: Allen & Unwin.

WATZLAWICK, P., BEAVIN, J. & JACKSON, D.D. (1969) *Menschliche Kommunikation*, Bern: Huber.

WATZLAWICK, P., WEAKLAND, J.H. & FISCH, R. (1974) *Lösungen*, Bern: Huber.

WATZLAWICK, P. & WEAKLAND, J.H. (eds.) (1980) *Interaktion*, Bern: Huber.

WIRKAN, R., FALEIDE, A. & BLAKAR, R.M. (1978) Communication in the family of the asthmatic child. *Acta Psychiatr. Scand.* **57**, 11–26.

WIRSCHING, M. & STIERLIN, H. (1982) *Krankheit und Familie*, Stuttgart: Klett-Cotta.

6 Research on individual differences in children and adolescents: a Greek perspective

E.C. Dimitriou

Introduction

In Greece, social and psychiatric services for children and adolescents are not yet well developed. In a country with a population of about 10 million, in 1982 there were less than 300 psychologists and only 25 child psychiatrists, while there was one doctor for 487 inhabitants and 6.7 general psychiatrists for 100 000 people (Tsiantis, Mardikian-Gezerian, Sipitanou & Tata-Stamboulopoulou, 1982a).

The existing paedopsychiatric services are concentrated in Athens, Piraeus and Thessaloniki. Hence almost all studies concerning psychological problems of children and adolescents refer to these areas, which represent approximately half of the entire population. This part of the population is also the most active and wealthy one.

With these limitations in mind we will try to describe the existing situation in Greece with regard to child and adolescent mental health and to refer to some differences that may exist between individuals and various groups of subjects.

The Greek social environment

Greece is a country in transition. The rapid changes in every aspect of life that are leading Greece from the group of developing countries to that of developed ones is also endangering the process of continuous adaptation of the Greek people. The per capita gross national income at constant prices (1970) has risen from US$329 in 1950 to US$1445 in 1982 (HRMC, 1976; GMNE, 1985). Nevertheless, in spite of the considerable increase of the per capita income, a study that was carried out in the Greater Athens area and based on a representative sample of 984 households with 1251 children aged 0–5 years, found that 56% of the children were living under poor and unsatisfactory conditions (Deligeorgis, 1978).

The percentage of those living in urban areas has increased from 37% in 1951 to 58% in 1981 (NSSG, 1956; 1984). Divorce rates have risen from 0.41 to 0.69 per 1000 people between 1965 and 1980 (ONSG, 1971; 1984). Men and women are getting married at a younger age. In 1956 19.2% of bridegrooms were 20–24 years of age, while in 1980 the percentage rose to 28.1%. In 1956 12.6% of the brides were 15–19 years of age, while in 1980 the percentage rose to 29.6% (NSSG, 1958; 1984).

Passenger cars per 1000 inhabitants have increased from 25.8 to 108.2 between 1970 and 1983 (NSSG, 1985). Telephones per 1000 inhabitants have increased from 186.7 to 335.5 between 1973 and 1983 (NSSG, 1985).

Thousands of Greeks returning from their temporary migration to Western Europe bring home customs and ideas acquired abroad. New ideas and habits are also imported to Greece by the tide of ever increasing numbers of tourists.

Through all these changes, the Western culture and way of living has invaded every Greek town and village. Next to the traditional Greek 'taverna' and 'psistaria' (a shop serving various dishes of broiled or baked meat) you find pizzarias, pubs and discos. The plain Greek coffee-house has given over its place to richly furnished cafeterias and Greek coffee to 'espresso', instant coffee and the like. The traditional

Greek alcoholic drinks 'ouzo' and 'retsina' have been pushed aside by the more 'civilized' and certainly more expensive whisky, campari, vodka and the like.

Drug addiction and alcoholism are on the increase. Cheap hashish has been replaced by heroin and more recently by cocaine. Criminality is running high and people in large cities are afraid of walking alone in the streets at night. Installing safety locks on the doors has become a thriving business.

The Greek family environment

Not too long ago the Greek traditional family setting was mainly of the extended type, i.e. three to four generations living together in the same house. Close groups were also established. These 'in-groups' were defined as groups of people concerned with each other, members of the family (not necessarily all), friends and friends of friends with whom one could establish interdependence (Vassiliou, 1969; Vassiliou & Vassiliou, 1970; 1973).

The extended type of family and the 'in-group' system used to provide security but also meant that each member of the group had to obey certain rules. The atmosphere within these settings was one of trust, loyalty, honesty and humanity. 'Philotimo' was the most important shared value.

'Philotimo' is one of the highest Greek values. Literally it means 'love of honour' but its meaning is actually much wider and includes pride, self-respect, ambition and emulation. 'Philotimo' safeguards relationships from becoming exploitative and dictates that one reciprocates generosity with more generosity, that one should be ready to sacrifice everything to help the other, to whom in turn 'philotimo' dictates *not* to accept the sacrifice unless it is absolutely necessary for his survival (Vassiliou & Vassiliou, 1984).

But today things have changed. Most Greek families are of the nuclear type, consisting of parents and unmarried children. The average number of members of the Greek household has dropped from 4.29 in 1920 and 4.11 in 1951 to 3.12 in 1981 (NSSG, 1985). The need to belong to an 'in-group' system has diminished (Vassiliou & Vassiliou, 1984) probably due to the considerable increase of per capita income and the improvement of social services, such as schools, hospitals and communication networks. Relationships have been diverted from a person-to-person basis to that of a person-to-services one. Today, man feels more self-sufficient and self-confident but also more lonely.

It was indicated elsewhere that the Greek feels excessively safe in his own house but rather unsafe outside it. He does not easily trust other people, although he seriously considers their opinion of himself. Because of this he tries to show himself in the best light, sometimes to an exaggerated degree (Dimitriou, 1977). This tendency may also explain the aforementioned 'philotimo'.

The Greek family is still patriarchically structured and the role of each family member is quite distinct. There are traditional rules defining the rights and obligations of each member and usually there are close ties among the various members of the family. Interaction between family members follows a linear pattern and not a collateral one as in other Mediterranean countries, such as Italy (Papajohn, 1979).

The father is the master of the house and his main duty is to provide security and to earn the family's bread. He keeps the family's savings. Even in cases where the mother is working, she has to pass all her earnings to him and to ask afterwards for her personal expenses. The same holds true for the working children. Instead of paying their share in the house expenses, they also have to pass all their earnings to their father and to ask him for pocket-money.

The father decides on all financial matters. Sometimes things are different, especially when the mother has received a substantial dowry from her parents and the management of the dowry has not passed to her husband. Such mothers tend to be overdemanding and overbearing, especially when the father's job is not so profitable. This obviously influences family dynamics, confusing the parental role and thus affecting the normal rearing of the children (Dimitriou & Didangelos, 1987).

The mother is the one who has the responsibility for the house and children. The mother–child relationship is most important in the Greek family setting and it is respected and helped by all other members of the family (Ierodiakonou, 1985). The mother will take care of the children's health and accompany them to the doctor. She will supervise and help them do their homework. She will choose the children whom her child is going to play with. She will try to find brides for her sons and bridegrooms for her daughters.

In the Greek family setting, boys and girls are treated differently. The boy, especially if he is the only boy in the family, is the pride of the family (Vassiliou & Vassiliou, 1970; Dimitriou, Ierodiakonou & Kokantzis, 1978; Ierodiakonou, 1985; Dimitriou & Didangelos, 1987). The boy is expected to fulfil the ambitions of the parents and to take over the father's protective role. The 'best' of the family is reserved for the son. He will be taken to the doctor more promptly when he is sick (Dimitriou *et al.*, 1978; Tsiantis, Yannopoulou-Kavouridi, Xypolita-Tsantili, Tsanira, Kallias & Pitsouni, 1982), will have more pocket-money, and will receive better education than the girl of the family, although it appears that this aspect is changing. In the academic year 1957–8 out of a total of 21 594 university students the male/female ratio was 3:1 (NSSG, 1959). In the academic year 1981–2 out of a total of 94 746 university students the male/female ratio dropped to 1:3 (NSSG, 1985). This is probably due to the fact that many Greek families now only have one child, which, when this is a girl, gives her the same opportunities to go to university as the boys.

The boy is allowed and sometimes pushed to have sexual relationships at an early age, something forbidden for the girl. On the other hand, he is obliged not to get married before all his sisters get married too, and to help the family to provide a suitable dowry to all of them. The girl is the 'weak' member of the family and is 'protected' by all the male members of the family in a suffocating manner. Most times her ambitions end with a 'good' and 'rich' marriage.

Child rearing practices determine the environment where the child grows up. The proportion of Greek children that were breast-fed during the first month of their lives dropped from 90% in 1968 (Vassiliou & Vassiliou, 1970) to 65% in 1980 (Matsaniotis, Lagos, Nikolaidou, Roma, Papagrigoriou-Theodoridou & Karpathios, 1980) or even to 33% (Fytanides, 1980). Greek mothers tend to wean their children rather hastily and only 30% of the children are shifted gradually from breast-feeding to cup and spoon. The less educated the mother is, the more harsh she is in weaning her child (Vassiliou & Vassiliou, 1970).

Toilet training starts early in Greece. It usually begins before the ninth month and is completed around the twentieth month of the child's life (Vassiliou & Vassiliou, 1970). Verbal and corporal punishment is frequently used to facilitate the process of toilet training.

It seems that punishment is rather common in child rearing practices (Agathonos-Marouli, Stathakopoulou, Adam & Nakou, 1982). In a fairly representative sample of 165 Athenian mothers, it was found that 82% of them were frequently using verbal and/or corporal punishment. Corporal punishment was used on approximately 50% of the children. Quite a few mothers (20%) admitted that they very seldom used positive reinforcement (Zarnari, 1979).

Mothers are more permissive and overprotective toward boys than girls. Boys are praised for their good manners and initiatives, girls for learning to be good housewives (Vassiliou & Vassiliou, 1970; Zarnari, 1979).

Sexual education programmes do not exist in Greece and parents are rarely prepared to handle such a delicate subject. In a study by Zarnari (1979), 58% of mothers admitted that they had given inaccurate answers to their children in questions regarding sexual matters. In the study of Vassiliou & Vassiliou (1970), the percentage was 50% and sometimes children were punished for asking questions on sexual matters.

The existing educational programmes in Greece seem to generate a lot of anxiety in the Greek family setting and to promote individualism over collective effort, hindering the child's anticipation for social cooperation and trust (Ierodiakonou, 1979; Vassiliou & Vassiliou, 1982). Parents, and especially mothers, are actively involved in their childrens' studies, pushing them hard for higher academic achievements. Every parent's dream is that his child, especially if a boy, should go to university, and since the odds of entering the university are about 1 in 7, the pressure put upon the child is obvious.

From the very beginning of high school studies the children have to attend extra classes, plus the classes for foreign languages, thus making their lives almost unbearable and leaving no time for rest and play. It is not surprising then that quite a few freshmen university students show a 'burned out syndrome' having difficulties in following a less structured programme of study.

From what has been said it is apparent that quite a few children grow up in a rather stressful environment and many of their emotional problems may be attributed to it.

Special problems of Greek children and adolescents

Substance use and abuse

It is now largely accepted that drug use and abuse, especially among adolescents, has become a major problem for every country. The proportion of those adolescents who smoke, drink, consume coffee and use various drugs is increasing every year.

In a study carried out in the Thessaloniki area in the 1982–3 academic year, the proportion of those high-school male students, who consumed large quantities of coffee and alcohol, and were heavy smokers was 7.4%, 11.2% and 20.7% respectively. Two years later in the same area the proportion of students of the same age and sex jumped to 14.2%, 21.6% and 24.2% respectively. The corresponding proportions for female students went up from 8.5%, 0.8% and 5.4% to 13.4%, 5.0% and 13.4% respectively (Peonides & Achladas, 1984; Peonides, Achladas & Syrmou, 1985).

The study by Peonides *et al.* (1985) showed that male adolescents consume many more cigarettes and alcoholic beverages than female adolescents do, while girls consume common analgesics more frequently than boys do (6.1% vs. 2.2%). No difference was found between boys and girls regarding the consumption of coffee.

In another study carried out in the Thessaloniki area, in a sample of 1354 male and 905 female high-school students aged 15–18 years, it was found that 40.7% of boys and 20.7% of girls were cigarette smokers. Of the smoking boys 36.8% consumed more than ten cigarettes daily, while of the smoking girls only 11.8% consumed more than ten cigarettes daily. At the age of 15 years, 20% of the boys and 7% of the girls were smoking, while at the age of 18 the percentage rose to 48% for boys and 29% for girls (Kargopoulos, Antoniadou-Melissa & Vloutis, 1977).

A study of 502 elementary school pupils aged 12 years from the island of Corfu found that more children from rural areas smoke, or had some time tried smoking, than those from the town of Corfu (28% vs. 12%), and that boys smoke more than girls (22% vs. 11%). Also, children living in the town of Corfu consume more beer than children living in rural areas, while the latter consume more wine than those children living in the town of Corfu. Children from rural areas were found to consume more coffee than the children of the town of Corfu (Martinos, Monopolis,

Galanopoulou, Moraitis, Kouvari, Varonos & Tselikas, 1975; Monopolis, Galanopoulou, Martinos, Moraitis, Kouvari, Kafouros & Varonos, 1975).

In a study carried out in a Greek provincial town concerning 405 boys and 495 girls aged 14–19 years, it was found that only 1.5% of boys and 2% of girls had sometime made use of narcotics (Diminas, 1979). Another study carried out in Athens, concerning 639 male and 1361 female students aged 17–20 years showed that 8.3% of males and 2.2% of females had sometime made use of narcotics (Papageorgiou, 1982).

From the research of Peonides & Achladas (1984) and Peonides *et al.* (1985) it was shown that the proportion of those male and female students who had tried various drugs (mostly hashish), at least once, rose in a two year period from 4.8% and 1.1% to 6.4% and 3.3% respectively. Working students, both male and female, had made greater use of narcotics in comparison to non working students (Table 6.1). The study by Peonides *et al.* (1985) also reported that those who had tried narcotics consumed much more coffee, cigarettes, alcohol and common analgesics than those who had not tried narcotics (Table 6.2).

It seems that the proportion of Greek adolescents who consume coffee, tobacco and alcohol is increasing year after year, and that more boys than girls are using these substances systematically. The finding that quite a few children from the island of Corfu consume alcoholic beverages probably also applies to other wine producing areas of the country but not to the whole of Greece.

The use of narcotics by adolescents is on the increase although it has not yet become a serious problem. Hashish and heroin are the two most frequently used drugs. Again, the use of these drugs is more common among boys than girls, and among working adolescents than non working ones.

Table 6.1 The use of narcotics by high-school students aged 18 years (approx.)

	Ordinary students (668)	
	male (310)	female (358)
Sometimes tried narcotics..%	6.4	3.3
Taking narcotics %	2.2	0.2
	Working students (463)	
	male (324)	female (139)
Sometimes tried narcotics %	13.0	3.6
Taking narcotics %	5.2	1.4

Adapted with permission. *Hellen Iatr.*, 1985, **51**, 215–22.

Juvenile delinquency

It is largely accepted that a very small proportion of juvenile delinquents come to psychiatric attention or are referred to juvenile courts. Thus understanding the Greek juvenile delinquent is quite difficult.

Official statistics show that juvenile criminality is on the increase. In 1971 the number of juveniles, aged 13 to 17, that were finally sentenced by juvenile courts in Greece was 452, while those juveniles for whom reformative or corrective measures were taken were 2678 (NSSG, 1977). In 1983 these figures jumped to 1135 and 6915

Table 6.2 Consumption of coffee, tobacco, alcohol and common analgesics with regard to the use of narcotics by adolescents aged 18 years (approx.)

Degree of consumption	Coffee	Tobacco	Alcohol	Analgesics
Male (62) that have made use of narcotics				
None %	10	5	—	52
Small %	34	8	31	26
Large %	56	87	69	22
Male (572) that have not made use of narcotics				
None %	18	48	12	78
Small %	65	16	74	21
Large %	17	36	14	1
Female (17) that have made use of narcotics				
None %	—	—	6	30
Small %	53	29	53	29
Large %	47	71	41	41
Female (480) that have not made use of narcotics				
None %	15	51	17	57
Small %	71	29	80	39
Large %	14	20	3	4

Adapted with permission. *Hellen Iatr*, 1985, **51**, 215–22.

respectively (NSSG, 1985). Almost all of those who were finally sentenced were boys, 419 out of 452 in 1971 and 1104 out of 1135 in 1983. The juvenile male and female population is approximately the same (NSSG, 1985).

Many Greek studies have indicated that more than 85% of juvenile offenders, referred to various agencies, are boys (Papatheophilou & Harvati-Fenton, 1964; Ierodiakonou, 1968; Tsaousis & Koppe-Crueger, 1974; Kotsopoulos & Loutsi, 1977). Girls are referred to juvenile courts because of complaints made against them regarding their behaviour. Most of these girls are referred to the authorities by their parents, who seek harsh preventive measures for them in order to 'correct' their behaviour (Kotsopoulos & Loutsi, 1977).

The most common charges brought against juvenile offenders are traffic offences, mostly driving motorcycles without a driver's licence (in Greece driving motorcycles is allowed at the age of 18), and it almost exclusively refers to boys (Kotsopoulos & Loutsi, 1977). The second most common charge (and first in earlier studies) is dishonesty, mainly theft (Papatheophilou & Harvati-Fenton, 1964; Ierodiakonou, 1968; Tsaousis & Koppe-Crueger, 1974; Kotsopoulos & Loutsi, 1977).

The most common complaint of parents referring their children to juvenile courts for 'protective measures' is the girl's promiscuity or the boy's disobedience to parents, and aggressive behaviour (Kotsopoulos & Loutsi, 1977). No confirmed cases of drug or alcohol abuse have been recorded. A considerable proportion of the referred children and adolescents are to some degree mentally retarded (Papatheophilou & Harvati-Fenton, 1964; Kotsopoulos & Kalogeropoulou, 1974). None of these children have been found to belong to a juvenile gang (Ierodiakonou, 1968; Tsaousis & Koppe-Crueger, 1974).

Almost half of the juvenile delinquents come from a disturbed or broken home environment (Papatheophilou & Harvati-Fenton, 1964; Ierodiakonou, 1968; Kotsopolous & Kalogeropoulou, 1974). In the study of Kotsopoulos and Loutsi (1977) the large majority (83.3%) of those charged with offences came from nuclear families, while only 28.4% of those referred by their parents for 'protective measures' to be taken were members of a nuclear family. A study of a large representative sample of 1784 children from all over Greece, aged 13 to 14 years, indicated that children who receive either a very large or a very small amount of general information at home tend to show a greater degree of antisocial behaviour (Paritsis & Lyketsos, 1982). Another study based on the same material (Paritsis, Pallis, Lyketsos & Phylaktou, 1985) showed that more boys than girls express antisocial behaviour (23.1% vs. 8.3%). The antisocial behaviour was positively correlated with (1) bad physical health of the child, (2) increased time of watching TV, (3) decreased time of study, (4) aggressive behaviour towards children of the same age and (5) a large family.

In summary, juvenile delinquency in Greece is increasing, most adolescent delinquents are boys, a large proportion of them are to some degree mentally retarded and come from a disturbed home environment.

Emotional problems

A study that was carried out in the Greater Athens area, comprising 1245 randomly selected children 0–5 years of age, indicated that boys show more psychopathology than girls (13.6% vs. 9.7%). Physical problems, such as neonatal clinical history, hearing problems, infections and heart problems were positively correlated with higher psychopathology (Paritsis, Pallis, Vlachonicolis, Phylactou & Deligeorgis, 1986). Other factors affecting the incidence of psychological problems in pre-school children were found to be divorce of parents and the mother's low level of education (Paritsis, Pallis, Vlachonicolis, Phylactou & Deligeorgis, 1984b).

In a representative sample of 1783 Greek children aged 13–14 years, it was found that more girls than boys exhibit psychopathological problems (11.5% vs. 9.8%). Also, children living in urban areas exhibit more psychopathology (13.2%) than children living in semi-urban (8.1%) and rural (9.7%) areas. However, in an earlier study in the Athens area, comprising 793 children aged 6–12 years, it was found that boys showed more psychopathology than girls did. Neuroses accounted for 11% of the cases and psychoses for 0.25% (Chassapis, Papageorgiou & Cassimos, 1973b). Another study also conducted in the Greater Athens area (Papatheophilou, Bada, Micheloyiannakis, Makaronis & Pantelakis, 1981), on a sample of 603 children aged 6–8 years, indicated that more boys than girls were considered disturbed by their parents (49.19% vs. 39.02%) and by their teachers (35.08% vs. 17.8%).

In comparison to English children, Greek children were found to have higher scores on emotionality (neuroticism) and the social desirability scale (lie scale), and lower scores on extraversion on the Eysenck Personality Inventory (Paritsis, Pallis, Lyketsos, Saraphidou, Phylactou & Vrachni, 1984a). The same differences in personality have been found between Greek and English adults using the Eysenck Personality Questionnaire (Dimitriou, 1977).

An extensive study that was carried out in the Thessaloniki area, regarding the special problems and personality of adolescents showed that boys who work during the day and attend high-school classes in the evening, differ from the ordinary high-school students as regards their personality. They show higher scores on P (tough-mindedness), on E (extraversion) and on L (social desirability) on the Eysenck Personality Questionnaire. Girls who work during the day and attend high-school classes in the evening differ from the regular high-school girls in that they show higher scores on E and L (Achladas, 1982).

In summary, emotional problems are quite common among Greek children. It appears that in those aged less than 13 years, boys more frequently show psychological problems than girls, while in those above 13 the lead is taken by the girls. Also, children living in urban areas show more psychopathology than those living in rural areas. As regards their personality, Greek children appear to be less extraverted and to have more neurotic tendencies than English children of the same age. Adolescents, who work during the day and attend high-school classes in the evening, differ from ordinary high-school adolescents in that they are more extraverted and try to show more socially acceptable behaviour.

Self-destructive behaviour

In Greece, self-poisoning in children and adolescents (accidental or intentional) seems to be on the increase (Avrilionis, Zantopoulos & Pektasides, 1979; Vlachos, Koutselinis, Poulos, Kentarchou, Smyrnakis & Papadatos, 1979; Pallis, Coutsoumari-Haughton & Koutsoulieris, 1980), while suicides are decreasing (Bazas, Tjemos, Stefanis & Trichopoulos, 1978). A more recent study (Pallis, Paritsis & Phylactou, 1984) showed that during the last ten years, while suicides in girls are decreasing they have increased considerably in boys (more than three times).

Two studies on attempted suicide in children (Malaka-Zafiriou, Dimitriou, Drosou-Agakidou, Giangou & Cassimos, 1980; Tsiantis, Yannopoulou-Kavouridis & Xypolita-Tsantili, 1981) concerning 22 and 21 consecutive cases respectively, showed that the majority of the attempters were girls (76%) suffering from adjustment reaction or depressive neurosis. Almost all of them came from a disturbed family environment. The main areas of conflict were sexual relationships and pressure for higher academic achievements.

In summary, self-destructive behaviour in children and adolescents is now being investigated in Greece, but more work is needed for a better understanding of the problem and for effective measures to be taken.

Sexuality

In an extensive study in the Athens area, 784 subjects were randomly selected from a population of 4000 male high-school students. It was found that 80% of them had started masturbation at the age of 14, and that 40–50% of them continued to practise masturbation as their main sexual outlet at the age of 17–18 years. The proportion of those who had full sexual relationships varied between 1% at the age of 14 years to 38% at the age of 18 years. Boys from higher socioeconomic classes masturbated less frequently, while they had heterosexual relationships more frequently (Chassapis, Cassimos & Papageorgiou, 1973a).

In another sample of 395 female and 334 male students, aged 18–24 years, it was found that 17% of the female and 54% of the male students had started their sexual relationships before the age of 18 years. Abortions were reported by 19% of the female students at the age of 19, while at the age of 22 the percentage rose to 33% (Zavitsianos, Roukas, Kadas, Mavrou, Danezis & Trichopoulos, 1980).

A study of 82 male and 48 female senior medical students showed that their median age when they first had intercourse was 18 and 19 years respectively. Their median age at the time they had started masturbation was 13 years for males and 15 years for females. In all, 99% of male and 77% of female students had masturbated at some time in their lives. Of those female students who had full sexual relationships, 63.5% had had at least one abortion (Manos, 1983).

As previously mentioned, sexual education programmes do not exist in Greece. Greek children learn from each other about masturbation and sex, and girls hear nothing about how to avoid pregnancy. Research on the subject is scarce. Greek boys start masturbation before the age of 14 and many of them continue to practise masturbation well after the age of 18. Girls start masturbation a little later. Boys start having full sexual relationships usually after the age of 18, while girls again start a little later.

Abortion is a Greek social problem. Although illegal, it is very easy and relatively cheap for a girl in Greece to have an abortion. It is estimated that most Greek women have two to three abortions during their sexual life. The above-mentioned studies indicate that a large number of girls have their first abortion at a relatively young age and before getting married.

The battered child syndrome
We have already mentioned that in Greece corporal punishment is still somewhat socially accepted. Nevertheless, very few battered children are referred for protection to the authorities or for medical attention. Boys and girls seem to be equally affected and 75% of them have had a sibling who has also been mistreated. One-third of the children are referred to the authorities by neighbours (Marouli, 1977). In another study concerning 50 battered children it was found that most of them were unwanted, they were born prematurely and were boys (Nakou, Adam, Agathonos & Stathakopoulou, 1982).

Research on the battered child syndrome in Greece is rare, probably because corporal punishment is to some degree socially accepted. There is now an extensive research programme going on at the Institute of Child Health in Athens. It is hoped that it will throw sufficient light on this interesting subject.

Emigration
During the last thirty years approximately one-fifth of the Greek population have temporarily emigrated, mostly to Western Europe. Between 1968–77 some 755 000 Greeks had emigrated, while at the same time 237 000 emigrants had returned home (NSSG, 1985).

This tide of emigrants created a lot of problems, mainly to their children, who were left behind to be looked after by their grandparents or other relatives. Many of these children were found to show psychosomatic and psychological disturbances such as stuttering, enuresis, aggressiveness, phobias, nightmares, etc. Children living in urban areas showed such psychopathology in as many as 54% of cases in contrast to 12% of those children living in rural areas (Madianou, 1978).

Kantarakias, Ierodiakonou & Bikos (1981) studied 52 preschool children of emigrants, mostly from rural areas, who had been left in Greece to be looked after by their grandparents or other relatives. These children showed much more psychosomatic disturbances in comparison to a control group. Those children who were separated from their mothers before the age of three months, showed greater loss of weight, loss of vitality, constipation and had suffered more frequently from various physical illnesses. Those children who were separated from their mothers after the age of two years, showed greater sleep disturbances, irritability, restlessness, apathy and had suffered more frequently from various physical illnesses in comparison to the control group.

In summary, emigration is a major problem for Greece. It affects not only those who emigrate but also those who are left behind and especially the emigrants' children, who show various disturbances to a greater extent than children of non-emigrant families. These disturbances are mostly of a developmental and psychosomatic type.

Conclusions

Greece is still a country of contrasts. The new mingles with the old. Although in many respects Greece could be classified among the developed countries, there are quite a few aspects of social and cultural life that keep Greece still bound to developing ones. The patriarchal structure of the family still exists but with somewhat faded colours. The extended family is vanishing. Boys are still advantaged in terms of privileges but girls are catching up. Drug abuse and delinquency are on the increase but they have not yet become serious problems. Nevertheless, it appears that it is only a matter of time before Greece becomes fully Westernized.

References

ACHLADAS, C. (1982) *Specific problems and personality traits of the working student.* M.D. Thesis. University of Thessaloniki Medical School (in Greek).

AGATHONOS-MAROULI, H., STATHAKOPOULOU, N., ADAM, H. & NAKOU, S. (1982) Child abuse and neglect in Greece. Sociomedical aspects. *Child Abuse and Neglect Journal*, **6**, 307–11.

AVRILIONIS, F., ZANTOPOULOS, D. & PEKTASIDES, D. (1979) A paediatric department in the Corinthos hospital: patient turnover and nursing conditions. *Paediatriki*, **42**, 193–206 (in Greek).

BAZAS, T., TJEMOS, J., STEFANIS, K. & TRICHOPOULOS, D. (1978) Incidence, seasonal variation and demographic characteristics of suicide in Greece. *Materia Medica Greca*, **6**, 38–46 (in Greek).

CHASSAPIS, J., CASSIMOS, C. & PAPAGEORGIOU, K. (1973a) Sexual development of 784 male high-school pupils aged 12–18 years. *Archives of the Greek Paediatric Society*, **36**, 452–62 (in Greek).

CHASSAPIS, J., PAPAGEORGIOU, K. & CASSIMOS, C. (1973b) Psychological problems in 793 elementary school children. *Paediatric Clinic of Thessaloniki University Annals*, **2**, 257–65 (in Greek).

DELIGEORGIS, D. (1978) *Socioeconomical characteristics and health problems in children 0–5 years of age in the Greater Athens area.* Assistant professorship thesis. University of Athens (in Greek).

DIMINAS, D. (1979) *Research on the problems and way of life of adolescents.* Katerini (in Greek).

DIMITRIOU, E.C. (1977) *The Eysenck Personality Questionnaire (EPQ) in the study of the Greek personality and its use in clinical practice.* Assistant professorship thesis. University of Thessaloniki Medical School (in Greek).

DIMITRIOU, E.C. & DIDANGELOS, P.A. (1987) Family therapy in childhood disorders: a Greek experience. *American Journal of Family Therapy* (in press).

DIMITRIOU, E.C., IERODIAKONOU, C.S. & KOKANTZIS, N. (1978) Family attitude towards the mentally suffering child in Greece: sociopsychological aspects. In *Issues in Mental Health*, Center for Mental Health Publications No. 56, Athens, 67–75.

FYTANIDES, K.G. (1980) A study of breast feeding practices in Nikea-Korydallos area. *Paediatriki*, **43**, 412–20 (in Greek).

GMNE, Greek Ministry of National Economics (1985) *Provisional national accounts of Greece 1984*, Athens.

HRMC, Hellenic Republic, Ministry of Coordination (1976) *National accounts of Greece 1958–75*, Athens.

IERODIAKONOU, C.S. (1968) *A psychiatric study of antisocial behaviour of children and adolescents.* Assistant professorship thesis. University of Thessaloniki Medical School (in Greek).

IERODIAKONOU, C.S. (1979) *Children's mental health and the Greek family: preventive aspects.* Paper read at the World Congress on Mental Health for Children and Families. 8–13 July 1979, Salzburg, Austria.

IERODIAKONOU, C.S. (1985) Psychosomatic manifestations in the context of Greek culture. *Dynamic Psychotherapy*, **3**, 88–94.

KANTARAKIAS, S., IERODIAKONOU, C.S. & BIKOS, C. (1981) Psychosomatic and emotional disturbances in infants of emigrant parents. *Mediterranean Journal of Social Psychiatry*, **2**, 116–22.

KARGOPOULOS, V., ANTONIADOU-MELISSA, A. & VLOUTIS, A. (1977) Research on smoking in adolescence. *Paediatriki*, **40**, 184–96 (in Greek).

KOTSOPOULOS, S. & KALOGEROPOULOU, E. (1974) Delinquent behaviour in girls: facts and prevention. *Helleniki Iatriki*, **43**, 247–58 (in Greek).

KOTSOPOULOS, S. AND LOUTSI, Z. (1977) Trends of juvenile delinquency in Greece. *International Journal of Offender Therapy and Comparative Criminology*, **21**, 270–8.

MADIANOU, D. (1978) Sociopsychological sequelae of emigration on children of emigrants that were left home. *Review of Social Researches*, **33–4**, 504–8 (in Greek).

MALAKA-ZAFIRIOU, K., DIMITRIOU, E.C., DROSOU-AGAKIDOU, V., GIANGOU, K. & CASSIMOS, C. (1980) Attempted suicide in children. *Archives of Paediatric Society of Northern Greece* 27–32 (in Greek).

MANOS, N. (1983) Sexual life, problems and attitudes of the prospective Greek physician. *Archives of Sexual Behavior*, **12**, 435–43.

MAROULI, E. (1977) A retrospective study of the battered child syndrome. *Review of Social Researches*, **2–3**, 275–84 (in Greek).

MARTINOS, A., MONOPOLIS, S., GALANOPOULOU, P., MORAITIS, I., KOUVARI, M., VARONOS, D. & TSELLIKAS, E. (1975) Consumption of beer and wine by elementary school pupils in the island of Corfu. *Paediatriki*, **38**, 268–75 (in Greek).

MATSANIOTIS, N., LAGOS, P., NIKOLAIDOU, P., PAPAGRIGORIOU-THEODORIDOU, M. & KARPATHIOS, T. (1980) Maternal suckling. 18th Panhellenic Paediatric Congress. Nicosia, Cyprus 1980. *Paediatriki (Abstracts)*, **I**, 33 (in Greek).

MONOPOLIS, S., GALANOPOULOU, P., MARTINOS, A., MORAITIS, I., KOUVARI, M., KAFOUROS, K. & VARONOS, D. (1975) Smoking and coffee consumption by elementary school pupils in the island of Corfu. *Paediatriki*, **38**, 169–84 (in Greek).

NAKOU, S., ADAM, H., AGATHONOS, H. & STATHAKOPOULOU, N. (1982) Health status of abused and neglected children and their siblings. *Child Abuse and Neglect Journal*, **6**, 279–84.

NSSG, National Statistical Service of Greece (1956) *Statistical Yearbook of Greece 1985*, Athens.

NSSG, National Statistical Service of Greece (1958) *Statistical Yearbook of Greece 1957*, Athens.

NSSG, National Statistical Service of Greece (1959) *Statistical Yearbook of Greece 1958*, Athens.

NSSG, National Statistical Service of Greece (1977) *Statistical Yearbook of Greece 1976*, Athens.

NSSG, National Statistical Service of Greece (1984) *Statistical Yearbook of Greece 1983*, Athens.

NSSG, National Statistical Service of Greece (1985) *Statistical Yearbook of Greece 1984*, Athens.

ONSG, Office National de Statistique de Grèce (1971) *Mouvement naturel de la population de la Grèce 1965*, Athens.

ONSG, Office National de Statistique de Grèce (1984) *Mouvement naturel de la population de la Grèce 1981*, Athens.

PALLIS, D., COUTSOUMARI-HAUGHTON, I. & KOUTSOULIERIS, E. (1980) Self-poisoning of children in Greece: an increasing problem. *Materia Medica Greca*, **8**, 311–16 (in Greek).

PALLIS, D., PARITSIS, N. & PHYLACTOU, C. (1984) *Suicides in children and adults, demographic factors of increased danger in Greece*. Paper read at the 10th Annual Panhellenic Medical Congress. 2–4 May 1984, Athens (in Greek).

PAPAGEORGIOU, J. (1982) *Greek students and narcotics: research, conclusions, propositions*, Athens (in Greek).

PAPAJOHN, P. (1979) Intergenerational value orientation and psychopathology in Greek-American families. *International Journal of Family Therapy*, **1**, 107–32.

PAPATHEOPHILOU, R. & HARVATI-FENTON, N. (1964) Some observations on child criminality in Greece. *Enchephalos*, **2**, 3–12 (in Greek).

PAPATHEOPHILOU, R., BADA, K., MICHELOYIANNAKIS, J., MAKARONIS, G. & PANTELAKIS, S. (1981) Psychiatric disorders in 6 to 8 year old children in the greater Athens area. *Bibliotheca Psychiatrica*, No. 160. Karger, Basel, 92–100.

PARITSIS, N. & LYKETSOS, G. (1982) *Relationship between the experiences of the family and the child's behaviour at school*. Paper read at the 20th Panhellenic Paediatric Congress. Chalkidiki, 5–6 June 1982, Greece (in Greek).

PARITSIS, N., PALLIS, D., LYKETSOS, G. & PHYLAKTOU, C. (1985) *School delinquency: incidence and aetiological factors*. Paper read at the 11th Annual Medical Congress, 8–11 May, 1985, Athens (in Greek).

PARITSIS, N., PALLIS, D., LYKETSOS, G., SARAPHIDOU, E., PHYLACTOU, C. & VRACHNI, F. (1984a) *Psychological problems in adolescent students of a representative sample from the schools of Greece*. Paper read at the 10th Annual Panhellenic Medical Congress, 2–6 May 1984, Athens (in Greek).

PARITSIS, N., PALLIS, D., VLACHONICOLIS, J. PHYLACTOU, C. & DELIGEORGIS, D. (1984b) *An epidemiological study of factors affecting the incidence of psychological problems in pre-school children*. Paper read at the 22nd Panhellenic Paediatric Congress, 9–10 June 1984, Corfu (in Greek).

PARITSIS, N., PALLIS, D., VLACHONICOLIS, J., PHYLACTOU, C. & DELIGEORGIS, D. (1986) *Epidemiological study of the relationship between psychological problems and somatic factors in pre-school children.* Paper read at the 16th European Conference on Psychosomatic Research, 6–11 September 1986, Athens.

PEONIDES, A. & ACHLADAS, C. (1984) Coffee, cigarette and alcohol consumption and the use of common analgesic drugs and narcotics by high-school pupils. *Paediatriki*, **47**, 124–9 (in Greek).

PEONIDES, A., ACHLADAS, C. & SYRMOU, H. (1985) Coffee, cigarette and alcohol consumption and the use of narcotics by ordinary and working high-school pupils. *Helleniki Iatriki*, **51**, 215–22 (in Greek).

TSAOUSIS, D. & KOPPE-CRUEGER, E. (1974) *The criminality of juveniles in the area of Athens*, National Center for Social Research, Athens (in Greek).

TSIANTIS, J., MARDIKIAN-GEZERIAN, B., SIPITANOU, A. & TATA-STAMBOULOPOULOU, L. (1982a) Child mental health and psychosocial development in Greece. *Paediatriki*, **45**, 321–408 (in Greek).

TSIANTIS, J. YANNOPOULOU-KAVOURIDIS, S. & XYPOLITA-TSANTILI, D. (1981) Suicidal attempts in children and adolescents. *Paediatriki*, **44**, 99–110 (in Greek).

TSIANTIS, J., YANNOPOULOU-KAVOURIDIS, S., XYPOLITA-TSANTILI, D., TSANIRA, E., KALLIAS, F. & PITSOUNI, D. (1982) Experiences and observations from the function of a department of child psychiatry in a general paediatric hospital. *Paediatriki*, **45**, 81–91 (in Greek).

VASSILIOU, G. (1969) Aspects of parent adolescent transaction in the Greek family. In *Adolescence: Psychological perspectives.* G. Kaplan & S. Lebovici (eds.), Basic Books, New York.

VASSILIOU, G. & VASSILIOU, V. (1970) On aspects of child rearing in Greece. In *The Child in his Family* E. Anthony & C. Koupernik (eds.), John Wiley, New York.

VASSILIOU, G. AND VASSILIOU, V. (1982) Promoting psychosocial functioning and preventing malfunctioning. *Paediatrician*, **11**, 90–8.

VASSILIOU, G. AND VASSILIOU, V. (1984) On group therapy developments in context: a hellenic view. *International Journal of Group Psychotherapy*, **34**, 377–85.

VASSILIOU, V. AND VASSILIOU, G. (1973) The implicative meaning of the Greek concept of 'philotimo'. *Journal of Cross-Cultural Psychology*, **4**, 323–41.

VLACHOS, P., KOUTSELINIS, A., POULOS, L., KENTARCHOU, P., SMYRNAKIS, Z. & PAPADATOS, K. (1979) A preliminary study of the incidence of self-poisoning in Greece. *Materia Medica Greca*, **7**, 239–43 (in Greek).

ZARNARI, O. (1979) Child socialization in the Greek urban family. *Eklogi*, **49**, 3–10 (in Greek).

ZAVITSIANOS, X., ROUKAS, K., KADAS, K., MAVROU, K., DANEZIS, J. & TRICHOPOULOS, K. (1980) Incidence of sexual relations and abortions in students. *Hippocrates*, **8**, 153–9 (in Greek).

7 Motivational and personality structures in education – individual differences in Hungarian school-aged children

B. Kozéki

Life is ever seeking for particularity and variation, and how poor indeed a monotone humanity would be!

M. Babits (20th century Hungarian poet)

Without knowing about individual differences, education cannot be what it should be: the improvement of personality. The analysis of individual differences has become a central issue in contemporary education and educational psychology.

The problem: to become aware of the individual differences

'Since individual differences research has made little development over the last eighty years it is not surprising that educational practice is similarly stunted in the area of individual variation.' (Riding, 1983, p. 166). A number of reasons for this situation are described by Riding (1983) and H.J. Eysenck (1983). The final conclusion of Riding (1983) is that 'Whatever the reason for the neglect of individual differences research, if it continues it will prevent psychology from being a mature science and do much to rob it of the ability to make an effective contribution to the real world of education' (p. 166). Therefore, we have tried to identify specific patterns, into which the individual personality traits can be classified and also the ways in which educators may become aware of these individual differences.

Dimensional models of motivation and personality – methods

Dimensions of motivation

Our analysis is focused on the motivational structures that have developed during the individual's life, which are interconnected with the basic temperamental traits that characterize the children and are inherited or present from the beginning of their lives. We have published details of our extensive research conducted partly in Hungary and also in the form of several international comparisons (among others Kozéki, 1980, 1984; Kozéki & Entwistle, 1983, 1984; Entwistle & Kozéki, 1985). The following is a brief summary of the findings.

The model of motivation in education, developed from a comprehensive series of interviews, questionnaires and tests conducted in central Europe (Kozéki, 1980), draws attention to the importance of three domains of motivation – (A) affective, (B) cognitive, and (C) moral.

(A) The *affective domain* is dependent on relationships with parents, teachers and peers, and reflects, in terms of the child's motivation, respectively warmth, identification and sociability.

(B) The *cognitive domain* describes motives derived from the rewards associated with developing independence, competence and interest.

(C) The *moral domain* includes the motives for trust, compliance and responsibility (see Figure 7.1).

The repeated analyses of pupils' interviews, together with discussions with parents and teachers gradually established that these motives within the three domains represented a parsimonious, but full, description of motives most closely related to the individual motivational structures of school-aged children. Using questionnaires, we came to the same conclusions, namely children who had high scores on dimension 'A' have good social relations, those on 'B' were active and the children with high scores on 'C' strived for self-control. Statistical analyses showed that the main motives could be condensed into six factors, equally divided between the affective (A), cognitive (B), and moral (C) domains as follows: warmth (A1), sociability (A2), competence (B1), interest (B2), responsibility (C1), compliance (C2). Similar factors have been identified in Britain (Kozéki & Entwistle, 1984).

Using the test scores for individual children it was possible to identify the dominant patterns in terms of the three domains. Using a simple division into high (+), medium (o), and low (−) scores in each domain, 27 possible combinations are theoretically possible. The extreme combinations of '+' and '−' (+++, ++−, +−+, −++, +−−, −+−, −−+, −−−) just because of their extremity, highlight the traits of each structure in question and its difference from other structures, and therefore we refer to such patterns in this paper.

The 'A' motive dominated structures are as follows:

+−+   (usually A1+, C2+, the 'B' motives are weak): this type of pupil considers it most important to establish a warm reciprocal relationship with others, to earn respect, liking and praise. The child is warm, compliant, anxious to please parents and teachers making efforts to avoid failure but rather a passive follower.

+−−:   the strong affiliative motive is not supported by moral motives, the pupil may want to solve everything by relying on personal relationships and so become over-dependent, even hypocritical.

'B' dominant motivational structures:

++−   (usually A2+, B2+, moral motives are weak): He is strongly motivated towards competence, the supporting strength of affiliation indicates the need for applause. He is sociable but not warm: the need is to be popular, the pupil is interested, sociable, seeking challenge and competition.

−+−:   if the affiliative needs diminish, there is likely to be an accompanying increase in rivalry, ruthlessness or aggression.

'C' dominant motivational structures:

−++   (usually B1+, C1+, the emotional needs are not strong): the pupil is independent-minded, emotionally independent of others: the strong moral motives imply not only interest in academic work and self-improvement, but also in doing it well, living up to what is expected, although he is responsible rather than compliant. His/her slogan is: 'if something is worth doing it's worth doing well'.

−−+:   where the moral strength loses cognitive support the person may be seen as having iron discipline and may be over-demanding on self or others, in the extreme even fanatic.

The +++ pattern includes the advantageous traits of all the three motivational domains; '−−−' structure is its opposite, without specific dominant motives and actually none of the motives are strong enough.

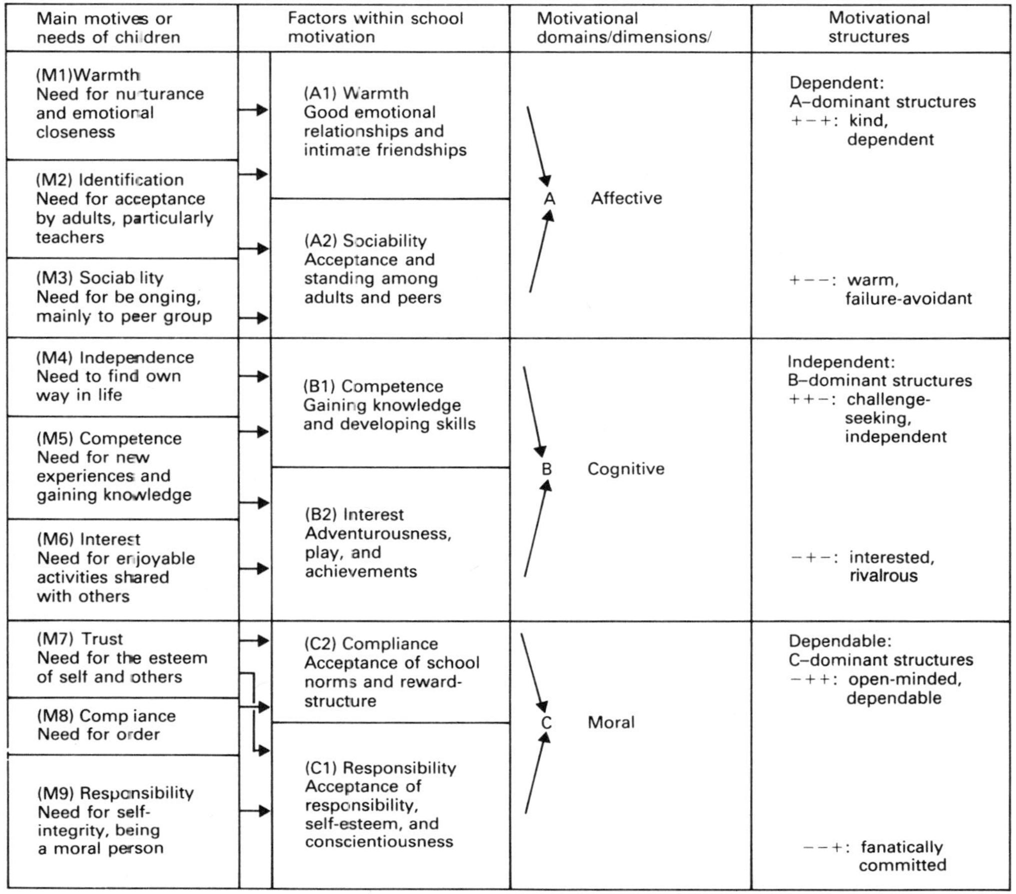

Main motives or needs of children	Factors within school motivation	Motivational domains/dimensions/	Motivational structures
(M1) Warmth — Need for nurturance and emotional closeness	(A1) Warmth — Good emotional relationships and intimate friendships	A Affective	Dependent: A-dominant structures + − +: kind, dependent
(M2) Identification — Need for acceptance by adults, particularly teachers	(A2) Sociability — Acceptance and standing among adults and peers		+ − −: warm, failure-avoidant
(M3) Sociability — Need for be ongoing, mainly to peer group			
(M4) Independence — Need to find own way in life	(B1) Competence — Gaining knowledge and developing skills	B Cognitive	Independent: B-dominant structures + +: challenge-seeking, independent
(M5) Competence — Need for new experiences and gaining knowledge	(B2) Interest — Adventurousness, play, and achievements		− + −: interested, rivalrous
(M6) Interest — Need for enjoyable activities shared with others			
(M7) Trust — Need for the esteem of self and others	(C2) Compliance — Acceptance of school norms and reward-structure	C Moral	Dependable: C-dominant structures − + +: open-minded, dependable
(M8) Compliance — Need for order	(C1) Responsibility — Acceptance of responsibility, self-esteem, and conscientiousness		− − +: fanatically committed
(M9) Responsibility — Need for self-integrity, being a moral person			

Figure 7.1 Relationship between motives, factors, domains, structures and styles

The dimensions of temperament

When analyzing motivation in education, our basic assumption was that these motives and motivational structures develop in the course of child-rearing and education. However, genetic factors have an unquestionable role in the development of the personality. Since we have been thinking in terms of a dimensional approach and have looked for simple procedures applicable in schools, it is a natural consequence that we investigate these factors in relation to the well-known Eysenck-type dimensions.

For this purpose, and in the same way as the motivational dimensions and subscales were formed, we carefully standardised, in cooperation with the original authors, the Hungarian version of the Junior Eysenck Personality Questionnaire (Eysenck & Eysenck, 1975; Eysenck, Kozéki & Kálmánchey, 1980) and that of the Junior Impulsivity, Venturesomeness, Empathy Questionnaire (Eysenck, Easting & Pearson, 1983; Kozéki & Eysenck, 1985).

Variables of motivation, temperament and academic achievement

Finally data measured over 14 dimensions were available from our surveys (marked with letters described hereinafter much in the same fashion as the characteristic motivational styles were marked with combinations of signs '+' and '−').

Motivational variables:

(1) A1: *Warmth*, good emotional relationship and intimate friendships;
(2) A2: *Sociability*, acceptance and standing among adults and peers;
(3) B1: *Competence*, gaining knowledge and developing skills;
(4) B2: *Interest*, adventurousness, liking for play and rivalry;
(5) C1: *Responsibility*, need for self-integrity, being a moral person;
(6) C2: *Compliance*, need for order, acceptance of social norms.

Variables of temperament

 (7) P: *Psychoticism*, toughmindedness, sensation-seeking;
 (8) E: *Extraversion*, the outgoing, sociable, uninhibited dimension;
 (9) N: *Neuroticism*, the dimension of tension, worry, irritability;
(10) L: *'Lie'*, social desirability, conformity;
(11) i: *Impulsivity*, acting on the spur of the moment;
(12) v: *Venturesomeness*, risk-taking, liking for challenge;
(13) e: *Empathy*, experiencing the other's emotion as one's own.

Achievement variable:
(14) a: index of school *attainment Motivational Structures:*
+ − +:   kind, dependent;
+ − −:   warm, failure-avoidant;
+ + −:   challenge-seeking, independent;
− + −:   interested, rivalry dominated:
− + +:   open-minded, dependable;
− − +:   fanatically committed

We conducted our surveys in normal school classes; 968 pupils aged 13 to 15 were involved. About the same number of boys and girls were interviewed but we did not group the sample according to sex and age, otherwise the sample components would have been too small. We were also looking for pupils with extreme individual personality structures who represent a minor, so called deviant sample of 158 pupils which was also analyzed. The latter sample contains children educated in special schools as boarders, who had problems in fitting into the normal school environment. This minor sample composition we call 'deviant', while the major sample are referred to as 'normal' hereinafter.

Motivational and personality structures in education

Relationship between the motives and temperament traits

The first important result is that both the Hungarian versions of the Eysenck tests in Hungary, and the foreign language versions of the Hungarian motivational questionnaires abroad worked very well and similar findings were identified in various countries, along with some national features originating in the child-rearing and educational differences.

The deviant sample indicated significantly higher values in the 'N' and 'i' temperament characteristics. A fraction of the total sample prone to criminality had higher 'E', 'N', 'P' and lower 'L' scores. Their 'B' and 'C' motives and schoolwork results indicated much lower scores.

As regards the correlation matrices, in the normal sample the correlation of 'N' with 'i' as well as 'E' with 'v' was high. 'L' correlated positively and 'P' and 'i' negatively with all motivational variables. The positive correlation of 'E' with the motive 'B2' ('Interest') the negative relation of 'N' with 'A2' ('Sociability') and 'B2' ('Interest') and the negative correlation of 'P' with 'C1' ('Responsibility') were all high. The deviant sample differs from this on 'N' in not showing a relation with any of the motives, while 'e' had a positive correlation with all motives. The positive correlation between 'P' and 'i' and the negative relation of 'P' with 'L' were high.

We factor analysed the six motivational and seven temperamental variables and obtained three factors. The first one included the motivational components and 'L'. The second factor incorporated 'N' and 'P' with high factor loadings and 'e' with an inverted sign. The third factor included 'E' together with 'v' and 'i'. In the deviant sample a separate 'N' factor was added to the 'P', 'E' and motivational one.

Analysing our samples from many aspects, the variables 'L', 'i', 'v' and 'e' always had their specific modifying role, but we feel that the decisive role of the 'A', 'B' and 'C' motivational and 'E', 'N', 'P' temperamental dimensions, has unambigously been shown in this study.

Relations between the motivational and temperamental structures

We studied the temperamental and performance factor values in each motivational structure. With the aid of such data we were able to plot the position of groups with different motivational structures, derived from members of the normal and deviant samples, in the space defined by the temperamental dimensions 'P', 'E' and 'N' (Figure 7.2). All the temperamental and performance factor indices in the different motivational structures are illustrated in Figure 7.3.

'E', 'N', 'P' and motivation

Investigating the 'E', 'N', 'P' defined temperamental and 'A', 'B', 'C' dominated motivational types with regard to success, we note three stages: (I) 'E−, N−, P−', (tenderminded phlegmatic) with '+++', '+−+', '−++' normal and '+−+', '−++' deviant motivational types being successful: (II) the 'P−' temperamental types

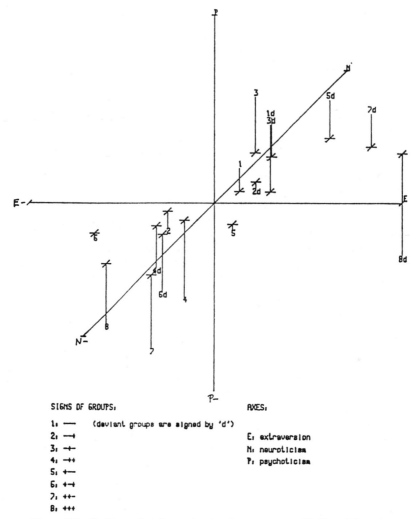

Figure 7.2   Position of eight motivational structures on E, N and P scales

(tenderminded, sanguine, choleric, melancholic) with normal '++−', '+−−' and deviant motivational styles being moderately successful: (III) the temperamental types high on 'P', primarily 'E', 'N' and 'P', with the toughminded choleric, the normal '−−−', '−+−' and the residual deviant groups being unsuccessful.

Based on our findings we may draw the conclusion that 'B' and 'C' motivational and 'E−, N−, P−' temperamental types may be successful in all educational situations: the 'A, C' and the 'A, B' motivational styles and 'E−, N' as well as 'E, N−' with low 'P' engender success if their suitable educational style is met: finally those children who have only one strong positive motive and belong to temperamental type 'E, N' (especially with higher 'P') can only achieve success if their suitable educational style is provided with permanent and consistent strengthening and particular care and control. Finally, if none of the motivational areas have appropriately strong motives and if 'E, N' are associated with high 'P', or 'E−, N' as well as the 'E−, N−' types are extreme, then there is a very, remote possibility of getting good results.

Figure 7.3 shows the means (z-transformed) of school achievement and the seven personality dimensions in eight motivational structures.

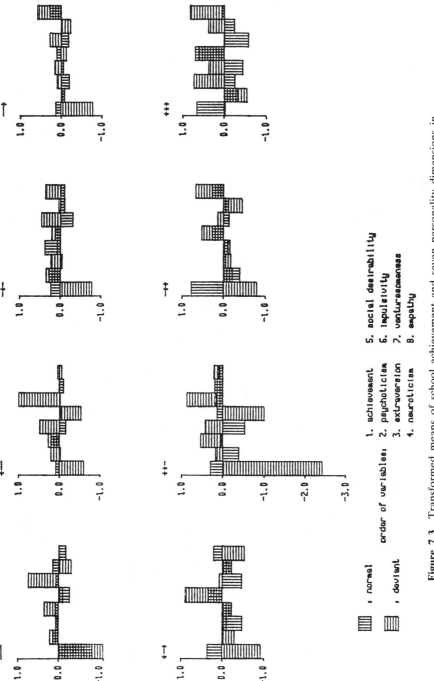

Figure 7.3 Transformed means of school achievement and seven personality dimensions in eight motivational structures

Based on the dominant role of motives 'A', 'B' and 'C', it is worth-while analyzing the motivational styles in pairs because they show one of the obvious ways of development towards improved structures (Kozéki, 1985: in fact, the other way is the development within the same temperamental structure). In the dependent styles ('+ − +', '+ − −') 'P' is low. 'N' is below the average. They are different for 'E': the '+ − +' type being phlegmatic, performing tasks in a tranquil manner: the '+ − −' sanguine type progresses well in the beginning but, relying only on interpersonal relations, he/she may lack independence. The independent types ('+ + −', '− + −') are distinguished by 'N': the '− + −' type is tense and irritable, so it is important that it can be transformed to style '+ + −' by subjecting 'P' and 'N' to self-control which requires primarily an understanding and firm environment. The two autonomous types are the most uniform ('− + +', '− − +'), both are 'E−, N−': even the deviant groups are close to the normal ones and all the four categories show low 'P', 'i' and high 'e' values. This fact proves, on the one hand, that the 'E−, N−' types adapt themselves best to the objective of education, therefore they are more successful in progressing and, on the other hand, emphasizes the importance of the 'C' motivation and motives in education.

'E', 'N', 'P' and motivation in education

Using dimensions 'E', 'N' and 'P', Wakefield (1979) endeavoured to describe categories for education, and it is worth comparing these with our motivational types formed for a similar purpose.

The '− − −' motivational types of children have unsatisfied emotions, they are opposing, inhibited in independence, neurotic, lacking moral motivation and have no self-control. Their characteristics agree with Wakefield's (1979) statement about the temperamental group called 'PN': 'These students have emotional and behavioural problems in combination' (p. 69).

The '− − +' types of pupils differ in their strong control, therefore they are not so much motivated to be in opposition: in general, all their motives are around zero value but this is more a stressed, ambivalent state than repose. Based on its position and description, the normal '− − +' may be identified as Wakefield's 'E−', and the deviant '− − +' as his 'E+N' type. The pupils of the first type 'respond well to schoolwork when presented as a serious undertaking' (p. 64) while the latter type pupils are anxious and overreactive.

The pupils in '− + −' are also negativistic, no self-control has been developed in their personality and their anxiety has no preventive effect. Both the normal and deviant pupils score high on the 'N' and 'P' dimensions, but the deviant children are also more extraverted. Therefore the normal types correspond to 'P+N', and the deviant to 'E+P': they are 'continually agitated, sensation seeking without concern for consequences', as well as 'extremely impulsive . . . often violently' (p. 68). Both types are close to type 'P' students, who, as Wakefield also says, are likely to be very original and creative but very hard to work with.

The '+ − −' motivational type is motivated by warmth and love and exclusively by that. This way, or under the effect of compliance these pupils become warm sanguine type 'E' which is indicated by the normal '+ − −' or the uncertain, overprotective parents' behaviour may initiate their opposition, such as type 'E+PN', similar to our deviant '+ − −' group.

The '− + +' is autonomous, a readily adapting, constructive type, both the deviant and normal groups are more introverted, with low values on 'N' and 'P'. The normal group is more introverted and recalls Wakefield's group 'E$_o$': 'they are fairly well adjusted and perform up to their capacity in school' (p. 62). The deviant pupils are more like the description of type 'E−': they are more inhibited but also diligent and do their best to perform their tasks well.

Both versions of '+−+' are in the tenderminded phlegmatic zone: they are perhaps close to the '−++' types because Wakefield's 'E−' classification also applies to them, they are motivated to do schoolwork, are alert and cooperative and work diligently.

The '++−' type of pupils have been educated in a flexible, good emotional atmosphere, without moral requirements: they are primarily motivated to be successful, which may turn to an egocentric rivalry. Therefore the normal and deviant versions are entirely different. The normal tenderminded pupils are sanguine and 'E+' in Wakefield's category, while the deviant toughminded and choleric pupils are in a category similar to Wakefield's 'E+PN'.

The '+++' is the other contradictory category. The pupils in the normal sample are tenderminded phlegmatic, well adjusted, cooperative, diligent, called 'E$_o$': the deviant pupils, '+++', are very placid but have very high values on 'E' and 'N', corresponding to Wakefield's 'E+N' category that incorporates a complicated and inconsistent characterization: 'These children are outgoing and uninhibited as well as anxious and overreactive' (p. 66).

Summarizing the projections of Figure 7.3 we see that as the motivational types are ordered according to their values and directions of development from the end points 'A−', 'B−', C−' into directions progressing to 'A', 'B', 'C', the categories at risk from an adaptational point of view in the temperamental fields group around 'E', 'P', 'N', while the readily adaptable categories are around 'E−', 'N−' and 'P−'. More exactly, the autonomous motivational styles and those dominated by two strong motives are not far from the intersectional points of the temperamental dimensions. All analyses we have attempted up to now also prove that the 'P−', 'E−' and 'N−' temperaments and motivational factors 'A', 'B' and 'C' basically determine the adaptation. The other factors have important modifying roles. 'L', for example, influences success in a positive direction. In addition, 'L' is mostly incident upon '+−+', 'i' upon '+−−', 'v' upon '++−' and 'e' is upon '−++', therefore these traits may probably be developed or suppressed in similar ways.

To design teaching on the basis of personality theory

The Wizard of Oz − the important role of coping with individual differences in education
Covington (1984) says:

> L. Frank Baum's charming fantasy, *The Wizard of Oz*, presents a penetrating allegory of mankind's quest for self-acceptance. The cowardly lion, the most beloved member of that intrepid band of adventurers, sought acceptance by reason of brave deeds. The scarecrow, sensing the inadequacy of straw and cloth, sought to fill the void with brains and in so doing to become worthy by reason and brilliance. Finally, the tin woodsman quested for a heart and the approval of others through acts of kindness. (p. 77)

It is obvious that the basic need of man is to accept himself and have himself accepted; the logical consequence of this is that his dynamic traits are subordinated to this aim. There are three paths very similar to the above-mentioned citation in our motivational researches: (A) the 'A' dominated (dependent) children are motivated primarily by the expectation of good social relations with the people they love and like, just as the tin woodsman seeks approval of others through acts of kindness; (B) pupils who have 'B' dominant motives are like an ambitious scarecrow whose dream is to become worthy by reason and brilliance and they seek excitement and excellence in play and study as well; (C) finally, the little lion seeks acceptance and mainly self-acceptance by brave deeds and virtue; the 'C' dominated children would like to have a valuable personality in moral terms, by taking responsibility. It is true all three paths have their potential dead-ends that appear more in the form of educational tasks, such as: (A) the anxiety dominated overdependent little tin woodsman who always needs somebody to oil him: (B) the rivalry dominated, priggish scarecrow who wants to overcome and suppress everybody with his brilliance: (C) the fanaticism dominated lion who is only a coward, since he does only what others expect him to do.

In the same fashion these three ways have been outlined in other temperament investigations as well: (a) the sanguine child, like the little tin woodsman, who would like to have good relations with everybody, 'the good old fatty' as he is called in the literature: (b) the restless choleric scarecrow who always wants to prove himself: (c) the controlled phlegmatic lion who simply carries out what he had started. True, these paths also have extreme 'branch' versions: (a) children who have high 'P' scores are demanding, adherent, unreliable sanguines: (b) the violent choleric child who – having the Robin Hood syndrome – wants to fight with everybody: (c) the really cowardly lion, the tamed choleric who at most says he is phlegmatic because he endeavours to suppress his tensions in much the same way as he does his anxiety and alienation (the '– – +' types typically changed places around the point of origin within the field defined by 'E' and 'N', between the contacting corners of the choleric and phlegmatic fields).

We identified three basic types, the dependent, independent and autonomous styles. It is the duty of psychology researchers and teachers to help (like Wizards of Oz) each child to be accepted, preserving his/her own personality: remaining kind, ambitious and fair; with defencelessness, rivalry and fanaticism turned to positive values or removed.

Suitably combined reinforcing patterns help in developing balanced individual personality traits in children. The personality structures may be developed in two directions. Children may either develop along the main 'motivational lines' (i.e. within the 'Dependent' – 'Independent' and 'Autonomous' structures) and, on the other hand the less valuable motivational structures can be transformed to more desirable ones positioned in the same temperamental field by strengthening the 'ancillary' motive developed beside the dominant one. For instance, the 'Dependent' '+ – –' type may be turned into the more acceptable '+ – +' type in the 'Dependent' line by applying a consistently demanding educational technique and satisfying the needs for dependability. This line is worth following when the 'A1' motive is very strong. But if this '+ – –' type is 'sanguine' then, particularly if his/her 'A2' motive is sufficiently dominant, we can build upon that and can develop the also typically 'sanguine' but more desirable '+ + –' structure in the child.

The important role of individual differences was recognized long ago but this recognition has often been eclipsed. By the turn of the century it was 'rehabilitated' in scientific research. Then it was forgotten for a long period. By the 1970s it was again becoming clear that the relationships between personality and school attainment were mediated by individual difference variables, but the interest of educational psychologists subsequently shifted to the possibility of interactions between student characteristics and instructional methods in affecting outcome of learning. This is an important improvement but it cannot push to the background the investigation of the relatively permanent personality traits, since the interactional approach cannot omit knowledge of individual differences and the extensive application of this knowledge.

The educational (teaching) methods assumed to be ideal keep changing according to the development of theory and practice; what remains, however, unaltered is that school children have different temperaments and if properly motivated, they become more efficient and successful.

References

COVINGTON, M.V. (1984) The motive of self-worth. In: R. Ames and G. Ames (eds.) *Student motivation 1*, Academic Press. Inc., 77–113.

ENTWISTLE, N.J. & KOZÉKI, B. (1985) Relationships between school motivation: approaches to studying, and attainment, among British and Hungarian adolescents. *British Journal of Educational Psychology*, **55**, 124–37.

EYSENCK, H.J. (1983) Human learning and individual differences: the genetic dimension. *Educational Psychology*, **3**, 3–4, 169–88.

EYSENCK, H.J. & EYSENCK, S.B.G. (1975) *Manual of the EPQ* London: Hodder & Stoughton: San Diego: Educational and Industrial Testing Service, 47.

EYSENCK, S.B.G., EASTING, G. & PEARSON, P.R. (1983) Age norms for Impulsiveness, Venturesomeness and Empathy in children. *Personality and Individual Differences*, **5**, 315–21.

EYSENCK, S.B.G., KOZÉKI, B. & KÁLMÁNCHEY, M. (1980) Cross-cultural comparisons of personality: Hungarian children and English children. *Personality and Individual Differences*, **1**, 1, 347–53.

KOZÉKI, B. (1980) *A Motiválás és Motiváció összefüggéseinek pedagógiai pszichológiai vizsgálata* (Educational psychological analysis of the relationships between motivating and motivation), Budapest, Akadémiai Kiadó.

KOZÉKI, B. (1980a) Assessing the motivation of Hungarian and American Students. *The High School Journal*, **64**, 1, 5–7.

KOZÉKI, B. (1984) Die Struktur der Lernmotivation. *Zeitschrift für Psychologie*, **192**, 4, 403–24.

KOZÉKI, B. (1985) Motives and motivational styles in education. In N.J. Entwistle (ed.) *New directions in educational psychology*. The Falmer Press, Lewes, Sussex, 189–98.

KOZÉKI, B. & ENTWISTLE, N.J. (1983) Describing and utilizing motivational styles in education. *British Journal of Educational Studies*, **31**, 184–97.

KOZÉKI, B. & ENTWISTLE, N.J. (1984) Identifying dimensions of school motivation in Britain and Hungary. *British Journal of Educational Psychology*, **54**, 306–19.

KOZÉKI, B. & EYSENCK, S.B.G. (1985) Magyar és angol iskoláskorúak összehasonlitó vizsgálata az impulzivitás – kockázatvállalás – empátia kérdöiv magyar változata. (Hungarian and English comparative studies. The Hungarian versions of the impulsivity – venturesomeness – empathy scale), *Pszichológia*, **5**, 579–600.

RIDING, R.J. (1983) The current status of individual differences in educational research. *Educational Psychology*, **3**, nos. 3–4, 165–8.

WAKEFIELD, J.A. (1979) *Using personality to individualize instruction*. Edits, San Diego: California, 60–71.

Some psychological characteristics of institutionalized delinquent teenage boys in Hungary

8

K. Sipos, L. Bujdos, I. Bangó, M. Zakar & M. Sipos

The Rehabilitation Institute of Aszód in Hungary was opened in August 1894 on the basis of the 5th Act of the 1878 Criminal Law. This is the date when institutionalized rehabilitation of adolescents in Hungary began. Until 1950, the main authority of the Institute was the Ministry of Justice, but it is now under the direction of the Ministry of Education. By this changeover, the government indicated that the rehabilitation of delinquent adolescents was a pedagogical task. Until 1962 the aim of the Institute had been to rehabilitate delinquent boys between the ages of 12 and 20 years, but in 1962 the lower age limit for 'punishments' was raised from 12 to 14. The boys spend an average of one year in the Institute and are then released by the decision of the criminal court.

The history of the Institute is characterized by the fact that from its beginnings, 'family-like' groups were formed to aid the rehabilitation process. Here boys receive education as well as work experience. The new pedagogical programme established in 1984, aims to place younger boys, casual thieves, multiple criminals, robbers and those manifesting personality disturbances in the most suitable units of the Institute. The Institute has created specialized units for newly admitted boys with marked signs of neurosis and/or adaptational troubles, for addicts, for psychiatric patients and for especially difficult boys or 'tough guys'. Before assigning a new boy to a group, he must go through psychological, psychopedagogical, and if needed, psychiatric examinations. The decisive factors in choosing the most suitable group are based on the boy's personality and educational capability.

Most of our subjects are treated in family-like groups of 10–15 members. Leaders of the units or 'families' are assisted in their everyday work by psychologists, social workers and physicians. As the boys have generally fallen behind in their school studies, small classes have been formed which creates the opportunity for them to learn the material of two terms in only one term. They can also obtain qualification in up to ten industrial and agricultural professions.

To date, follow-up data indicates that 65% of the boys leaving the Institute adapt relatively easily to society. Approximately 20% of our pupils will probably commit crimes again. There is no reliable information about 10–15% of the boys after they had left the Institute.

Several recent trends regarding the characteristics of delinquents in Hungary have been observed. Since the so called 'gipsy explosion' of the 1970s, the proportion of gipsy children among our pupils became much greater, being approximately 70% at this time. The way of committing crimes has also changed: the proportion of boys committing crimes alone has decreased from 70–80% to 20–25%, while the proportion of collective crimes has increased from 20–25% to more than 60%. The remaining 10–15% of crimes are committed by young gangs.

By the 1980s, it would appear that the number of the pupils with personality disturbances has increased. Eighty-seven per cent of the Aszód boys smoke regularly and alcohol and glue sniffing has increased in frequency among delinquents. The proportion of drug addicts has reached such a level and degree that their treatment is undertaken in the hospital wing of the Institute.

The present investigation

All our pupils were examined with psychological tests in the 1984/85 academic year and from 1985/86 this task was accomplished with the help of a computerized test battery (Computest Programs, 1983). As stated before, these results assist in the placement of boys in the group most suitable for them and where their personal and pedagogical needs can then be determined and met.

Our test battery employs many of the scales which are considered in the international literature to be suitable for the rapid and reliable diagnosis of antisocial behaviour and various personality disturbances. As well, this makes possible international and nationwide comparisons.

Method

Subjects

The purpose of the present study was to examine the data of those delinquent boys at Aszód between 1 October 1984 and 15 October 1986 who had completed our standard test battery. A special interest in smoking behaviour was also included in this study as a large proportion of delinquent boys do smoke cigarettes. Of the 276 boys, the average age was 16.03 years (SD=1.02). In general they have finished less than 7 of the 8 elementary grades. The average length of residence in boarding schools before coming to Aszód is 31.88 months (SD=54.6) but it should be noted that half of these boys grew up in boarding schools. The average number of escapes from Aszód before the psychological examinations was 0.78 (SD=1.68) suggesting that many of the boys run away or leave Aszód without permission at least once.

The pupils (N=145) of the Gardonyi Geza Technical School No. 201 in Dunakeszi were selected as a comparison group. They had a mean age of 16.24 years (SD=.99). Those pupils were chosen who, on the basis of their school achievements, behaviour including smoking and drinking as well as their family history of mental illness, alcoholism, suicide and crime required much more 'attention' than usual and were most highly at risk of dropping out of school.

In order to compare the Aszód and technical school boys to a 'normal' Hungarian sample, descriptive and normative data obtained for young adults (Sipos, Zsembery, Vura, Sipos & Jakabházy, 1987) and 15-year-old school boys (Kozéki, 1984) were used. Finally, correlations between selected personality variables were compared for Hungarian, Canadian and British samples.

Instruments

When choosing the measuring instruments for this study, an effort was made to employ those tests which have proven to be most suitable for describing various components of personality, including anxiety. In order to measure our pupils' physical achievements (e.g. running performance) in connection with personality factors, scales measuring anxiety before competition and attitude toward regular running were employed. It was also deemed important to obtain measures of toughmindedness – impulsivity and extraversion – venturesomeness for our samples. Because of the very high incidence of smoking, the connection between various pupil personality factors and the degree of smoking was analyzed. Some of our preliminary data, as well as Parkes's results (1984) seemed to contradict Spielberger & Jacobs's (1982) conclusion that smokers, as compared to non-smokers, 'are more extraverted, neurotic and tense' and may be characterized by increased antisocial tendencies.

Consequently, the following measures were obtained for all subjects:

The State-Trait Anxiety Inventory (STAI) Spielberger, 1970. This inventory has been extensively used in various clinical situations throughout the world (Spielberger &

Diaz-Guerrero, 1976, 1983, 1986). A Hungarian version (Sipos, 1978, Sipos & Sipos, 1983) of the STAI has been developed and was administered in the present study.

The Multicomponent Anxiety/IV (MCA/IV) scale and the Impulsiveness-Monotony Avoidance-Detachment (IMD) scale (Schalling, 1978). These scales have been employed in studies of personality and psychopathy to test the hypothesis that psychopathic patients do not experience anxiety. The MCA/IV measures 'Somatic Anxiety' and 'Muscle Tension' and the level of 'Psychic Anxiety'.

The IMD scale measures two characteristic subgroups of psychopaths: 'impulsive' and 'detachment' individuals. In Schalling's view, a person is impulsive if s/he scores high on the Impulsivity, Monotony Avoidance (IMD) and Somatic Anxiety (MCA/IV) scales. Those subjects who comprise the detachment subgroup of psychopaths have high Detachment (IMD) scores and high scores on Eysenck's Psychoticism factor at the same time.

The standardization of the MCA/IV and IMD scales in Hungary has been ongoing for several years (Sipos, Vura, Istvánfi, Sipos, 1986; Sipos *et al.*, 1987) One of the most important parts of the psychological description of the pupils in Aszód is based on these measures and Schalling's (1978) description of personality and psychopathy.

The Hungarian Junior Eysenck Personality Questionnaire (HJEPQ) (Eysenck, G. Kálmánchey & Kozéki, 1981). This questionnaire is extensively used in Hungary, as in other parts of the world. It appears to be a useful measure in studies of antisocial personality and delinquency (e.g. Saklofske & Eysenck, 1980).

The Eysenck Impulsiveness-Venturesomeness-Empathy Questionnaire (HEIVEQ) (Eysenck & Eysenck, 1978). Hungarian norms for HEIVEQ have been published for secondary school pupils (Sipos *et al.*, 1986) and for healthy adult men (Sipos *et al.*, 1987). At Aszód, the HEIVEQ is administered to obtain a second measure of Impulsivity. Further, it was of interest to investigate the relationship of venturesomeness and empathy to other personality factors and antisocial behaviour following Eysenck (1981) and Saklofske & Eysenck (1983).

The Sport Competition Anxiety Test (SCAT) (Martens, 1977). This is a psychometric scale which was adapted for use in Hungary by Vura, Sipos & Sipos (1982, 1983) and was standardized for elementary and secondary school pupils (Sipos *et al.*, 1986). Together with the *Commitment to Running Scale (CRS)* (Carmack & Martens, 1979) these instruments are used at Aszód to compare the 'healthy' personality factors of our pupils to youths of the same age, on the one hand, and to assess the impact of 'running therapy' (Sachs & Buffone, 1984) as part of the standard program at our institute, on the other hand. Running therapy, provided three times each week for at least 20 minutes, is believed to decrease emotional difficulties such as depression and aggression. Of interest here was the attitude towards running and running performance among antisocial teenagers in rehabilitation settings compared with other children and adolescents (Sipos *et al.*, 1986, 1987; Vura, 1986; Vura *et al.*, 1982, 1983).

In summary, we obtained measures of Extraversion (E), Neuroticism (N), Psychoticism (P), and Dissimulation or Lie-factor (L), Impulsivity (Imp), Venturesomeness (Ven) and Empathy (Emp) according to Eysenck & Eysenck (1978) and Eysenck (1981). As well, Schalling's (1978) measures of impulsivity, monotony avoidance and detachment were completed by all subjects. Previous studies (Sipos, 1978, Sipos & Sipos, 1983) have demonstrated the necessity of measuring various anxiety factors in investigations of deviant behaviour. Thus anxiety is assessed from the perspective of Spielberger's State-Trait Anxiety Model (1966), situation specific anxiety (Martens, 1977, Spielberger, 1980) and Schalling's (1978) description of anxiety factors associated with psychopathy. Also administered was a Sport Competition Anxiety Test and a Commitment to Running Scale.

Results

Personality measures
Descriptive statistics for the delinquent sample of Aszód (N=276), the sample of technical schoolboys (N=145) and the Hungarian norm samples of adult men (N=335) and secondary school boys, aged 15, (N=160) are shown in Table 8.1. As well the *t*-test values were calculated in order to compare the Rehabilitation Institute of Aszód boys with the technical school boys on the one hand, and technical school boys and the Hungarian normative samples, on the other hand. The *t*-value of 1.98 was significant at the $p = .05$ level, the $p < .01$ level is indicated by the *t*-value of at least 2.61 and the $p < .001$ level begins at $t = 3.37$.

The sample of antisocial boys as well as the technical school boys were characterized by a significantly greater degree of anxiety compared to the Hungarian standardization values. At the same time, the difference in anxiety between the anti-social boys and the technical school boys is highly significant. The delinquent boys' State Anxiety, Trait Anxiety, 'Psychic Anxiety', 'Somatic Anxiety' and 'Muscle Tension Anxiety' exceeded significantly, the corresponding mean values of the technical school group. The difference between the SCAT means shows that the pupils in Aszód, followed by the 'problem children' of the technical school are more anxious before competition compared to healthy adult men.

The Aszód boys held the most favourable attitude towards running (CRS). There was no significant difference between the technical school group and the adult male Hungarian standardization group on the CRS.

Turning to the HJEPQ factors, the present results, were not in line with those described in other investigations that compared antisocial and normal population. Although delinquent boys were highest on N, they were not more extraverted and toughminded and their L scores were not lower compared with Kozéki's (1984) secondary school boys. Delinquent boys and technical school boys did not differ statistically on the P factor. At the same time, the latter group was more extraverted and had lower L scores than the antisocial boys and the Hungarian normative group. Moreover, the P or toughmindedness scores of 'problem children' in the technical school exceeded the Hungarian norms. Thus higher scores on Eysenck's dimensions of extraversion and toughmindedness and low scores on the Lie Scale were most characteristic of the 'problem children' attending technical school. This may suggest that institutionalization can affect either personality ratings or produce changes in personality.

The HEIVEQ data indicated that the most impulsive subjects were the pupils of Aszód, followed by the technical school boys while the least impulsive individuals in this study are healthy adult men. In contrast to impulsiveness and risk taking, venturesomeness was significantly less characteristic of the antisocial teenagers than of the two comparison groups. Venturesomeness is discriminated from Impulsivity by Saklofske & Eysenck (1983) in the following way:

> We regard one of the main differences between Impulsiveness and Venturesomeness to be the recognition of risk . . . Those subjects scoring high on Venturesomeness perceive danger or risk and decide to take the chance whereas those scoring high on Impulsiveness do not evaluate a situation in terms of risk and may be expected to act truly 'on impulse'. (Saklofske & Eysenck, 1983, p. 151)

Another unexpected result occurred for the Empathy measure, in which the boys in Aszód were more empathic than the technical school group. However this difference is so small that measurement error can not be ruled out in accounting for differences on this factor.

The IMD Impulsivity factor separates only the two adolescent groups from healthy adults and therefore seems less sensitive a measure of impulsivity than that provided by the HEIVEQ. Another unexpected result is that Monotony Avoidance is less

Table 8.1 Means and standard deviations of psychological measures for delinquent boys, for technical school boys and Hungarian norms, Sipos *et al.* (1987) and Kozéki (1984)*

Psychological tests		Delinquent boys	Technical school boys		Hungarian norms	
		N=276	N=145	df=419	N=335	df=478/303°
STAI-H, A-State	M	42.26	35.63	t=7.66	32.45	t=4.76
	SD	8.77	7.77		6.21	
A-Trait	M	45.36	39.2	t=9.18	35.94	t=5.42
	SD	6.52	6.59		5.81	
MCA/IV Psychic Anxiety	M	20.39	17.82	t=5.06	15.82	t=5.24
	SD	5.19	4.45		3.55	
Somatic Anxiety	M	19.13	14.81	t=8.28	12.08	t=8.78
	SD	5.38	4.48		2.31	
Muscle tension	M	16.39	13.69	t=6.04	11.58	t=8.51
	SD	4.74	3.53		1.88	
SCAT-H	M	20.9	19.45	t=3.17	18.48	t=2.20
	SD	4.33	4.68		4.32	
CRS-H	M	41.29	39.09	t=2.47	38.66	t=0.47
	SD	8.12	9.71		9.1	
HJEPQ N-factor	M	11.69	7.68	t=8.58	8.94*	t=2.31
	SD	4.57	4.53		4.97	
E-factor	M	16.11	17.93	t=5.39	16.41*	t=4.33
	SD	3.52	2.81		3.27	
P-factor	M	3.29	3.73	t=1.62	3.01*	t=2.30
	SD	2.36	3.14		2.3	
L-factor	M	9.51	6.38	t=6.62	9.9*	t=6.88
	SD	5.07	3.56		5.14	
HEIVEQ Impulsiveness	M	11.21	9.33	t=4.40	6.01	t=9.40
	SD	4.22	4.06		3.31	
Venturesomeness	M	10.16	11.15	t=3.10	11.19	t=0.14
	SD	3.22	2.88		2.87	
Empathy	M	11.87	11.1	t=2.81	11.82	t=2.61
	SD	2.75	2.5		2.88	
IMD Impulsivity	M	22.59	22.83	t=0.55	21.41	t=3.64
	SD	4.1	4.56		3.62	
Monotony avoidance	M	26.92	29.23	t=4.78	29.22	t=0.03
	SD	4.85	4.43		3.81	
Detachment	M	23.72	20.65	t=7.63	19.89	t=1.87
	SD	3.97	3.83		4.19	

*Kozéki (1984) HJEPQ norms for 15-yr-old boys (N=160).

characteristic of the sample in Aszód than of the two other groups ($p < .001$). Results for the Detachment factor suggest an increased degree of psychopathology for the boys in Aszód compared to the other two groups.

A comparison of the Eysenck personality measures in Hungary, Canada and Great Britain

An examination of the relationship between Eysenck's personality factors for the present sample are shown in Table 8.2, together with data reported for Canadian (Saklofske & Eysenck, 1983) English (Eysenck, 1981), and Hungarian (Kozéki & Eysenck, 1985) subjects. Only those correlations that have potential implication in the formation of antisocial behaviour, are shown. Although our data were based on the responses of 14–19-year-old teenagers; presenting various kinds of 'problems', it seems informative to see together the results for 'normal' samples and problem children from other countries. There is some degree of consistency in the pattern of correlations for the five groups. Canadian children show the highest relationship between P and Imp, N and Emp, and P and Emp. The Hungarian delinquent and technical school groups exhibited the smallest correlations between P and Emp and the correlation between N and Imp was weakest for the former groups who also had the highest correlation for Imp and Ven. It should be remembered that the

Table 8.2 Correlations between the Eysenck-factors for 7–15-year-old boys in Canada[1], Great Britain[2] and Hungary[3], and for boys between 14 and 19 years attending technical school or living in reform school

Eysenck-factors	7 to 15 year old boys*			14 to 19 year old boys**	
	Canadian N=542	British N=101	Hungarian N=573	technical school boys N=145	delinquent boys N=276
Psychoticism – Impulsiveness	.5	.31	.25	.20	.26
Extraversion – Venturesomeness	.59	.60	.54	.52	.51
Neuroticism – Empathy	.32	.12	.05	.11	.18
Psychoticism – Empathy	−.43	−.37	−.29	−.18	−.17
Neuroticism – Impulsiveness	.47	.39	.56	.29	.55
Impulsiveness – Venturesomeness	.17	N=663 .17	N=776 .20	.43	.20
Impulsiveness – Empathy	.00	.03	−.02	−.01	.05
Venturesomeness – Empathy	−.05	−.01	.04	−.05	.12

[1] Saklofske & Eysenck (1983).
[2] Eysenck (1981).
[3] Kozéki & Eysenck (1985).
* Junior Eysenck Personality Questionnaire and Junior Impulsiveness Inventory were used.
** Junior Eysenck Personality Questionnaire and Hungarian Eysenck Impulsiveness-Venturesomeness-Empathy Questionnaire (adult form) were used.

samples are not strictly comparable. For example, the Canadian subjects ranged in age from 8–15 years compared with the two adolescent samples of Hungarian subjects with an average age of approximately 15 years.

Analysis of smoking behaviour

For the analysis of smoking habits, we classified our subjects as non-smokers (0–4 cigarettes a day), light smokers (5–14 cigarettes a day), medium smokers (15–24 cigarettes a day) and heavy smokers (25 or more). We then compared our groups according to the degree of smoking and the data of this comparison are shown in Table 8.3.

The smoking habits of the two adolescent samples differed significantly with delinquent boys smoking the most. In Hungary, 52% of the adults between the ages of 20–40 are non-smokers, but only 13% of the delinquent boys are non-smokers. 51% of the Aszód subjects smoke about 1 packet of cigarettes a day and 8.7% of the delinquent teenagers smoke more than this although 27% are classified as light smokers.

For the technical school boys too, the situation is less favourable than the results for our adult male population: 48% are non-smokers, 33% are light smokers, and almost 1 in 5 of the subjects (18%) smoke 18 cigarettes a day on the average.

There were only 3 of the 17 psychological measures which revealed statistically significant differences between non-smokers, light smokers, and heavy smokers in our Aszód delinquent adolescent sample. Table 8.4 shows that significant differences

Table 8.3 Comparison of delinquent boys: technical Problem school boys and an adult male sample according to their smoking habits

Samples' average ages		Average number of cigarettes per day				
		Total sample	Non-smokers	Light smokers	Medium smokers	Heavy smokers
delinquent boys 16.03 yr (SD=1.02)	M	15.88	0.4	10.17	18.38	41.54
	SD	11.69	1.03	1.99	2.19	19.85
	N	276	35	75	142	24
	%	100	13	27	51	8.7
technical Problem school boys 16.24 yr (SD=0.99)	M	6.52	0.78	8.59	17.88	26.0
	SD	6.72	1.27	2.17	2.52	—
	N	141	68	46	26	1
	%	100	48	33	18	0.7
adult male sample 32.18 yr (SD=6.0)	M	6.03	0.11	8.69	17.58	27.5
	SD	8.94	0.54	2.53	2.50	4.14
	N	335	215	35	65	20
	%	100	64	11	19	5.97

Table 8.4 Statistically significant differences in the psychological measures between non-smokers and 'light' and 'heavy' smokers in the delinquent boys' sample

Psychological measures		Non-smokers N=35	Light smokers N=75	Heavy smokers N=24	*t* Tests
CRS-H commitment to running	M	43.4*	40.55	42.	*t*=1.725,
	SD	7.08	8.24	8.5	df=108, (*p* < .1)
HJEPQ Lie-factor	M	10.46	8.73*	12.21	*t*=3.114,
	SD	5.91	4.49	5.56	df=97, (*p* < .01)
IMD Impulsivity	M	21.49	22.29	23.92*	*t*=2.093,
	SD	4.46	3.47	4.26	df=57, (*p* < .05)

occurred beween non-smokers and light smokers on the CRS-H and L-factor measures, light smokers and heavy smokers on the L-factor and non-smokers and heavy smokers on the IMD scale of Impulsivity.

Non-smokers have a more favourable opinion about running, but light smokers appear to be less positive. Heavy smokers' responses may be in part explained by their high L scores but at the same time pupils in this group are more impulsive (IMD) than non-smokers.

The medium and high correlations between the psychological variables employed in the investigation of smoking behaviour of delinquent boys only are presented in Table 8.5. From the subgroups formed according to the degree of smoking, all the correlations are moderate to high for the 'medium smoker' group. The pattern of correlations emphasizes the variability between personality measures and the extent of smoking behaviour among delinquent boys.

An interaction analysis of smoking behaviour
In an earlier study of the relationship between Eysenck's personality factors and smoking, Parkes (1984) found that among extraverts, and subjects low in psychoticism, neuroticism was not related to smoking. However, among introverts and subjects high in psychoticism, the relationship between neuroticism and smoking was significant. Parkes's subjects were female student nurses (N=270), of whom 34.1% were smokers. These results indicated that an analysis of the interaction effects within Eysenck's three-dimensional personality model was necessary in order to understand the relationship between neuroticism and smoking reported in the literature.

We attempted to compare Parkes's data with only certain subgroups of our Hungarian samples; specifically light smokers (5–14 cigarettes per day) were selected for analysis at this time. Also, this is not so much an effort to compare adults and adolescents or 'normal' and delinquent subjects, but rather to examine the robustness of Parkes's interactive description across groups.

Table 8.5 Medium- and high correlations between psychological measures for the delinquent boys' sample

Psychological measures	Total sample N=276	Non-smokers N=35	Light smokers N=75	Medium smokers N=142	Heavy smokers N=24
Extraversion – Venturesomeness	.51	—	.51	.50	—
Neuroticism – Impulsiveness	.55	.72*	—	.55	.63
Neuroticism – A-Trait	.56	.62	—	.62*	—
Neuroticism – Somatic Anxiety	.47	—	.48	.46	—
Neuroticism — Psychic Anxiety	.45	—	.49	.45	—
Neuroticism – Muscle Tension	.50	—	.48	.55	—
A-Trait – A-State	.62*	.71*	.65*	.59	—
A-Trait – Somatic Anxiety	.47	—	.49	.51	—
Muscle Tension – Somatic Anxiety	.58	—	.60	.56	.66
Muscle Tension – Psychic Anxiety	.51	.62	—	.55	—

*$r \geq 0.5$, $p = 0.05$

The A-sector of Figure 8.1 describes Parkes's results, where the N-value of the 23.4% smoking introverts is higher than that of the 43.8% smoking extraverts. A similar trend was observed on N between high P smokers and non-smokers.

The B-sector presents the results for Hungarian men (Sipos et al., 1987) who completed the EPQ (Eysenck & Matolci, 1984) in Hungarian. Comparing non-smokers and light smokers we can see that N scores increased for Low E and Low P smokers but decreased slightly for high E and P smokers compared to non smokers.

In the C-Sector of Figure 8.1 are the results for our delinquent adolescent group based on the HJEPQ. In the D-sector, the results of the technical school boys's sample can be seen. It seems that with 14–19 year-old boys, whether they are classified as delinquent or are manifesting various problem behaviours, high P in those individuals smoking 5–14 cigarettes compared with non-smokers is associated with a decrease in N. At the same time, the data in the C-sector suggest that the N-scores of smokers in all of the other 3 personality groupings (Low E, High E, Low P) are significantly higher compared with non-smokers. In the D-sector of Figure 8.1, the N-value of introverted technical school boys in contrast to the results

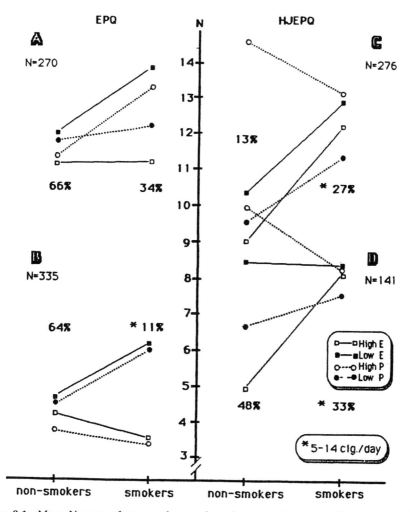

Figure 8.1 Mean N score of non-smokers and smokers in high and low E groups, and high and low P groups. For female student nurses ('A' according to Parkes, 1984); for adult male group ('B' according to Sipos *et al.* 1987); for institutionalized delinquent boys ('C') and for 'problem children' in a technical school ('D')

of all the other subgroupings, is the same for both smokers and non-smokers. N increased slightly for Low P smokers, increased for high E smokers but decreased in high P smokers.

The present results obtained from several Hungarian samples of 'light' smokers, support the need for interaction analyses but do not replicate Parkes's data. Further investigation of smoking behaviour and personality is warranted, both with delinquent and non-delinquent adolescents.

Discussion

The data presented in this study have permitted a comparison of Hungarian delinquent and 'problem' adolescents on various personality measures. As well these results were viewed together with data obtained from Hungarian normative studies and from other countries. Since there is much interest in Hungary about smoking behaviour in relation to personality and delinquency, an examination of these factors was undertaken here.

Delinquent boys in the Rehabilitation Institute of Aszód were considerably more anxious than either of the technical school boys or normative groups. This finding was upheld across the six anxiety measures employed in this investigation. Furthermore, delinquents reported the highest neuroticism scores on the HJEPQ, which, taken together with the anxiety results, supports the view that general emotionality or emotional instability is an important correlate of antisocial behaviour. Although the E and P scores were not significantly higher for the Aszód delinquent subjects, they did score higher on the HEIVQ Impulsiveness measure compared to the other two groups which is very much as expected from studies reported elsewhere (Eysenck, 1981). However, there was much less discrimination between groups when the IMD Impulsivity measure was employed.

Delinquents exhibited a more favourable opinion about running activity and it may be speculated that, together with their higher levels of impulsivity and high detachment scores, these boys may have greater difficulty adapting to the treatment setting and benefiting from the rehabilitation programs currently available at Aszód. Approximately 8% of the delinquent boys at Aszód could be classified according to Schalling's (1978) Impulsive Syndrome. Alternatively the detachment subgroup defined by high IMD Detachment scores and high P scores from the HJEPQ comprises approximately 16% of the Aszód population. Both of these groups require specially designed rehabilitation programs under close psychiatric supervision. Thus the various personality measures may be taken one at a time or in combination (i.e. representing a syndrome or 'group' classification) which may have greater potential for recognizing similarities but also individual differences within delinquent populations and between delinquent and non delinquent groups. Such information is crucial in the process leading from diagnosis to treatment. The recognition and measurement of individual differences within the delinquent population of Aszód will permit the careful and appropriate selection of treatment methods by the specially trained staff members. At the same time, it is necessary to continue our research investigations of the relationship between delinquency and personality and to determine which factors are predictive not only of delinquency but also treatment efficacy.

The data for smoking behaviour showed that 60% of delinquents in Aszód smoke more than 15 cigarettes a day. Only 13% of delinquents were non-smokers in contrast to 48% of problem boys attending technical school and 64% of the adult male sample. The personality differences between smokers and non-smokers in the delinquent sample showed only a few small differences. The heaviest smokers were slightly more impulsive and had higher HJEPQ Lie scores than non-smokers. However, the correlation between various psychological measures for delinquents classified according to smoking behaviour does reveal a variable pattern which may prove useful when combining data from different measures for the purposes of 'describing' the individual subject. For example, the correlation between neuroticism and impulsiveness within a delinquent sample is quite strong and considerably greater for non-smokers compared with light smokers but is moderate for medium smokers. Further research is required to sort out the interaction of smoking, personality and delinquency.

Parkes's active model was employed to examine the relationship of Eysenck's personality dimensions to smoking. Specifically, neuroticism scores of smokers and non-smokers, within delinquent and non delinquent samples were calculated for subjects who were high or low on E and P. N scores were lower for high P subjects who were smokers compared with non-smokers, especially in the delinquent and technical school boy groups whereas a reverse trend was observed for low P subjects. Introverted smokers were higher on N than non-smokers, except for the technical school boys, and high E delinquent and problem boys who smoke showed quite large increases in N compared with their non-smoking peers. These results reinforce the need to examine the interactive nature of personality dimensions in relation to smoking. Further, N scores show considerable variation between smokers and non-smokers as a function of personality but also according to classifications such as delinquent or 'problem children'. Thus, while delinquents tend to have, on average, higher N scores compared with non-delinquent groups in the Hungarian samples, individual differences based on a consideration of other personality dimensions and smoking behaviour are of importance when employing these data for the purpose of classification and development of treatment intervention strategies. Such interactive models hold considerable promise in further understanding and investigating the personality correlates of human behaviour, including smoking and delinquency.

Finally, the comparison of Hungarian, Canadian and British questionnaire data showed a high similarity in the pattern of correlations for the impulsivity, venturesomeness and empathy measures. Somewhat greater variation was noted in the correlations between these primary traits and Eysenck's three major personality dimensions although a trend was discernible with several exceptions. These findings add further support to the growing literature which has identified the E, N and P factors in a number of different countries and across various culturally different groups while showing that the degree and expression of such personality dimensions, as well as the questionnaire measurement of personality, may vary between countries. For example, extraversion can be thought of as a universal personality factor, but may show higher or lower levels in one country compared to another. Following this is the need to explore similarities and differences between clinically or otherwise defined groups of individuals (e.g. delinquents). It is necessary to confirm or determine the relationships between measures, especially when they form, singly or in combination with other measures, the data base for differential diagnosis and program planning. Continuing efforts to employ personality measures in our assessment work at the Aszód Institute in Hungary is continuing and our understanding of delinquent behaviour is increasing as we explore further both group and individual behaviour patterns and personality.

References

A Magyar Királyi Országos Javitó-Intézetek Ismertetése. (1899) (*Hungarian Royal State Reform Schools*) Kiadja a Magyar Királyi Igazságügyministerium. Budapest, Légrády Testvérek, 165.

Carmack, M.A. & Martens, R. (1979) Measuring commitment to running: a survey of runners' attitudes and mental states. *Journal of Sport Psychology*, **1**, 25–42.

Computest Programs (1983) *Microcomputer programs* for STAI-H, MCA/IV, IMD, HJEPQ, and HEIVEQ. Budapest, Metracomp.

Eysenck, H.J. (1980) *The causes and effects of smoking*, London, Maurice Temple Smith, 400.

Eysenck, H.J. (1983) A note on smoking, personality and reasons for smoking. *Psychological Medicine*, **13**, 447–8.

Eysenck, S.B.G. (1981) Impulsiveness and antisocial behaviour in children. *Current Psychological Research*, **1**, 31–7.

Eysenck, S.B.G. & Eysenck, H.J. (1977) The place of impulsiveness in a dimensional system of personality description. *British Journal of Social and Clinical Psychology*, **16**, 57–68.

Eysenck, S.B.G. & Eysenck, H.J. (1978) Impulsiveness and venturesomeness: their positions in a dimensional system of personality description. *Psychological Reports*, **43**, 1247–55.

Eysenck, S.B.G. & Matolcsi, Á, (1984) The Hungarian version of the Eysenck Personality Questionnaire: a comparative study of Hungarian and British adults. *Pszichológia*, **2**, 231–40.

EYSENCK, S.B.G., KÁLMÁNCHEY, M. & KOZÉKI, B. (1981) A comparative study of Hungarian and British children. *Pszichológia*, **2**, 213–41.

EZEKIEL, M. & FOX, K.A. (1970) *Korreláció és regresszió analizis*, Budapest, Közgazdasági és Jogi Könyvkiadó, 332.

KOZÉKI, B. (1984) Személyiségfejlesztés az iskolában. *Personality developing in the school*, Békéscsaba, Békés megyei Pedagógiai Intézet, 371.

KOZÉKI, B. & EYSENCK, S.B.G. (1985) The Hungarian version of the Impulsivity-Venturesomeness-Empathy Questionnaire. *Pszichológia*, **4**, 579–600.

MARTENS, R. (1977) *Sport Competition Anxiety Test*, Champaign, Ill., Human Kinetics, 111.

PARKES, K. (1984) Smoking and the Eysenck personality dimensions: an interactive model. *Psychological Medicine*, **14**, 825–34.

SACHS, M.L. & BUFFONE, G.W. (1984) *Running as Therapy*, Lincoln, NE, University of Nebraska Press, 339.

SAKLOFSKE, D.H. & EYSENCK, S.B.G. (1980) Personality and anti-social behaviour in delinquent and non delinquent boys. *Psychological Reports*, **47**, 1255–61.

SAKLOFSKE, D.H. & EYSENCK, S.B.G. (1983) Impulsiveness and venturesomeness in Canadian children. *Psychological Reports*, **52**, 147–52.

SCHALLING, D. (1978) Psychopathy-related personality variables and the psychophysiology of socialization. In R.D. Hare and D. Schalling (eds.) *Psychopathic Behaviour* (Approaches to Research), Chichester, Wiley, 86–106.

SIPOS, K. (1978) First examinations with the Hungarian version of the State-Trait Anxiety Inventory. In I. Dancs (ed.) *75 éves a Magyar Tudományos Akadémia Pszichológiai Intézete*. Budapest, MTA Pszicológiai Intézete, 141–51.

SIPOS, K. AND SIPOS, M. (1983) The Development and validation of the Hungarian form of the State-Trait Anxiety Inventory. In C.D. Spielberger and R. Diaz-Guerrero (eds.) *Cross-cultural Anxiety*, vol. 2, Washington DC, Hemisphere, 27–39.

SIPOS, K., VURA, M., ISTVÁNFI, M. & SIPOS, M. (1986) Relation of attitude toward running and running performance with psychological factors in secondary school pupils instructed by 'special physical education curriculum'. *A Testnevelési Fóiskola Közleményei*, **1**, 35–49.

SIPOS, K., ZSEMBERY, J., VURA, M., SIPOS, M. & JAKABHÁZY, L. (1987) Psychological examination in the selection of members of the jury and technical ambulance staff of the Formula-1 World Championship in Hungary. The VIIth *European Congress of Sports Psychology*. 14–19 September 1987, Bad Blankenburg (GDR).

SOSNOWSKI, T. AND WRZESNIEWSKI, K. (1986) Research with the Polish form of the State-Trait Anxiety Inventory. In C.D. Spielberger and R. Diaz-Guerrero (eds.) *Cross-cultural anxiety*, vol. 3, Washington, Hemisphere, 21–35.

SPIELBERGER, C.D. (1966) Theory and research on anxiety. In C.D. Spielberger, (ed.) *Anxiety and Behavior*, New York, Academic Press, 3–20.

SPIELBERGER, C.D. (1970) *Manual for the State-Trait Anxiety Inventory*, Palo Alto, CA, Consulting Psychologists Press, 24.

SPIELBERGER, C.D. (1980) *Preliminary professional manual for the Test Anxiety Inventory* ('Test Attitude Inventory') TAI, Palo Alto, CA, Consulting Psychologists Press, 12.

SPIELBERGER, C.D. & DIAZ-GUERRERO, R. (1976) *Cross-cultural anxiety*, vol. 1, Washington, Hemisphere, 195.

SPIELBERGER, C.D. & DIAZ-GUERRERO, R. (1983) *Cross-cultural anxiety*, vol. 2, Washington, Hemisphere, 218.

SPIELBERGER, C.D. & DIAZ-GUERRERO, R. (1986) *Cross-cultural anxiety*, vol. 3, Washington, Hemisphere, 167.

SPIELBERGER, C.D. & JACOBS, G.A. (1982) Personality and smoking behavior. *Journal of Personality Assessment*, **46**, 4, 396–403.

VURA, M. (1986) A complex study of the commitment to running and the running performance in connection with personality traits at 10–18-year-old pupils. Budapest, Lorand Eötvös University (*dissertation*), 99.

VURA, M., SIPOS, K. & SIPOS, M. (1982) Commitment to running. Contributing psychological anthropometrical and sport achievement factors. In T. Orlick, J.T. Partington & J.H. Salmela (eds.) *Mental training for coaches and athletes*, Ottawa, Ontario, Sport in Perspective Inc., and The Coaching Association of Canada, 117–18.

VURA, M., SIPOS, K. & SIPOS, M. (1983) A study on the psychological, anthropometrical and performance components of attitude toward running in elementary school pupils of 10–14 years. *A Testnevelési Föiskola Közleményei*, **1**, 69–83.

9 Introversion-extraversion perspectives in the subgrouping of conduct disorders in Israel

M. Margalit

Conduct disorders represent an important target for investigation, because of their frequency in childhood, persistent stability in longitudinal studies, and association with serious adolescent and adult psychopathology (Achenbach, 1982; Olweus, 1978; Schwartzman & Moskowitz, 1985). Physical aggression, non-compliance, destructiveness, verbal combativeness and negative relationships with peers and adults serve as a definition of conduct disorders. These characteristics emerge from studies of normal and clinical populations in different countries, across the span of childhood, from preschool age through adolescence (Achenbach & Edelbrock, 1978; Quay, 1983; Quay & Werry, 1979; Stewart, DeBlois, Meardon & Cummings, 1980).

The study of adjustment and competence patterns of conduct disordered boys in Israel (Margalit & Shulman, 1986) demonstrated that these boys represent a distinctive group, when compared to their control peers. On several aspects of social adjustment and academic competence, significant differences were noted, even at the earliest stages of academic experience. Their behaviour and learning style resembled, to a large extent, those of much younger children. The conduct disordered boys were described, with respect to school expectations and developmental tasks, as less mature than their peers. However, both groups of boys were described similarly with regard to their academic competence: creativity and curiosity, and academic achievements at school. The finding that academic achievements did not distinguish between the two groups of boys emphasized the notion that at the first stages of schooling (first to third grade), conduct disordered behavior cannot be attributed to academic failure, as suggested by several previous studies (Feshbach & Price, 1984; Kohn, 1968).

Greater differences were found between the conduct disordered and nonconduct disordered boys at the second (fourth through sixth grades) and third (seventh through ninth grades) stages of schooling. Academic achievements added to differentiation at these stages. Analysis of the results revealed a significant maturational change that occurred in the groups of boys without conduct disorders that was not evident in the conduct disordered group, suggesting a developmental arrest in the abilities for controlling and inhibiting behaviour.

The findings of this study can be incorporated into the broader framework of processes taking place in latency and adolescence. Developmental changes can be conceptualized as the growing ability for controlling and inhibiting behaviour, in which the verbal self-regulation component is of essential importance. The differences that were found in the three nonconduct disordered age groups reflected a growing ability for self-control and adjustment. In the conduct disordered group, prolonged and increased difficulties may be related to lower levels of the inhibitory processes.

Social status and peer interrelations of conduct disordered children were the focus of research interest. Intuitively, one would speculate the existence of significant peer problems. The results are equivocal, with some studies finding them to experience peer problems (Green, Forehand, Beck & Vosk, 1980), whereas others have actually

The author would like to acknowledge the editorial assistance of Johanna Klein.

found them to earn some degree of positive reputation and popularity (Olweus, 1978).

In order to develop an individualized approach to intervention and further study the inconsistent results regarding the social status of conduct disordered boys, several attempts have been made to identify different subgroups within this heterogeneous group. Ledingham (1981) distinguished between two groups of conduct disordered children. The group labeled as aggressive/withdrawn children had problems in distractibility and sustaining attention, finishing tasks, and delaying responses. The second group did not reveal attentional difficulties. In another study, Milich & Landau (1984) supported Ledingham's conceptualization of subtypes of conduct disordered children and demonstrated that the social status of the aggressive/ withdrawn group was lower than that of the pure aggressive group. They reported that the second group was significantly lower in solitary play, unlike the first group, and was observed as being more frequently engaged in both positive and negative interactions with peers.

The descriptions of the aggressive/withdrawn subgroup of conduct disordered children seem similar to Loney & Milich's (1982) and Stewart's (Stewart, Cummings, Singer & DeBlois, 1981), descriptions of the hyperactive/aggressive subgroup. For example, Ledingham (1981) has reported that the aggressive/withdrawn boys were distractible, had attentional problems, were unable to delay response, and were more reliant on others. These descriptions have been typically associated with hyperactivity. The Milich & Landau (1984) results provided additional evidence that there is a considerable overlap between these two groups of conduct-disordered boys, as the aggressive/withdrawn group had a higher mean hyperactivity score than the second subgroup.

Consistent with previous research (Coie, Dodge & Coppotelli, 1982; Ledingham, 1981; Loney & Milich, 1982), two distinct groups of conduct disordered children can be defined: an immature, disruptive, unpopular, and poorly self-controlled group, and a disruptive but popular, assertive and controlling group. Research to date has not addressed the introversion-extraversion characteristic. It may provide an additional perspective to the definition of subgroups within the conduct disorder syndrome, clarifying patterns of functioning and adjustment.

Eysenck & Eysenck (1964) described the extravert as a person who is sociable, needs people to talk to, and craves excitement. The introvert, on the other hand, is more reserved and distant toward other persons, does not like excitement, and takes matters of every day life with 'proper seriousness'. Eysenck proposed that molar behavioral differences between introverts and extraverts are the result of individual differences in the functioning of the brain's reticular activating system. He argued that introverts are chronically more highly aroused than are extraverts, given the same conditions of stimulation. Because the introvert's cortex must exercise more control over the primitive lower brain centres, the introvert exhibits more restrained, inhibited behaviour than does the extravert. Many of the behavioral differences may be attributed to systemic differences in pattern of self-regulation: both groups seek an optimal level of arousal, but this level is lower for the introvert.

Social situations often produce powerful arousal effects, and the introvert tends to be more aroused than the extravert. As a consequence, extraverts may seek out personal contacts, and are able to develop higher levels of intimacy, preventing the level of arousal from becoming too low. The introvert, in similar situations, may tend to avoid these contacts due to potential overarousal that may lead to loss of self control (Eysenck & Eysenck, 1985). Gray's (1972, 1973) modification of Eysenck's arousal theory has a special value for the study of intervention as related to conduct disorder subgroups. He argued that introverts have a more reactive septohippocampal system ('stop system'), whereas extraverts have more reactive medial forebrain bundles and hypothalamic areas ('go system'). As a consequence, extraverts are more oriented toward the pursuit of rewards, paying relatively little attention to potentially aversive consequences of such pursuits. Introverts, on the other hand, are more oriented toward avoiding punishment than toward gaining rewards.

Accepting the notion that introverts may differ from extraverts in the way they encode, process, and retrieve situational cues (Eysenck, 1977), it is possible that previous aversive social encounters may have been more vivid for introverts than for extraverts. Consequently, when introverts recall social encounters, estimates of frequent aversive encounters will be greater than for the extravert (Ferguson & Wells, 1980; Pryor & Kriss, 1977). Introverts do anticipate social encounters as less friendly, with more disagreements between themselves and others, than do extraverts (Cooper & Scalise, 1974; Graziano, Bernstein-Feldesman & Rahe, 1985).

These differences are important to the study of conduct disorder subgroups since social encounter expectations can contribute to a self-fulfilling prophecy system in which expectations are translated into social reality. When one expects a particular encounter to be unfriendly and not enjoyable, one's expectation and associated behaviour may actually elicit the behaviour that is feared (Snyder, Tanke & Berscheid, 1977). Introverts may be creating an unpleasant and unfriendly social environment for themselves through their own negative expectations. The low link found between the extraversion/introversion discrimination and conduct disorders (Eysenck, 1981; Saklofske, McKerracher & Eysenck, 1978) supports the attempt for subgrouping conduct disordered children. The aim of the present study was to investigate introvert vs. extravert conduct disordered boys (ICD-ECD), using Schaefer's model.

Schaefer (1981; Schaefer, Edgerton & Hunter, 1983, 1985) proposed a spherical model of academic competence and social adjustment that promotes an understanding of children's behaviour in school. Interest was focused on three major areas: (a) academic competence, (b) social adjustment, and (c) extraversion/introversion. Schaefer's model was selected for the present investigation because of its potential for facilitating a distinction between the introvert conduct-disordered (ICD) and extravert conduct-disordered (ECD) boys in their educational environment. These findings were expected to highlight the boys' specific difficulties, pinpointing different modes of intervention.

Method

Sample

The sample consisted of 114 conduct-disordered boys from 18 different schools in the Tel Aviv area. The boys were regular students of 62 first through ninth grade classrooms, with an age range of 7.0 to 15.4 years, M = 11.02, SD = 2.56. The proportion of girls from the original sample was small, therefore they were not included in the present study.

Two subgroups were identified using the Introversion-Extraversion score of the Classroom Behaviour Inventory (CBI) factors as a criterion. The introverted group (ICD) consisted of 52 boys whose scores were less than 3.00 on the criterion, and the extraverted group (ECD) consisted of 62 boys whose scores were greater than 4.00 on the criterion measure.

Instruments

Classroom Behaviour Inventory (CBI) (Schaefer & Edgerton, 1978). The Hebrew adaptation of the CBI consisted of 42 items describing typically observed child behaviour in classrooms. Teachers rate each behaviour on a four-point scale from 'not at all' (1) to 'very much' (4). The instrument yields scores on ten scales:

(1) Considerateness (e.g. 'Is agreeable and easy to get along with')
(2) Task Orientation (e.g. 'Works carefully and does his best.')
(3) Independence (e.g. 'Tries to figure things out for himself before he asks questions')
(4) Verbal Intelligence (e.g. 'Has a good fund of information for a child of his/her age')
(5) Creativity/Curiosity (e.g. 'Thinks up interesting things to do')
(6) Extraversion (e.g. 'Does not wait for others to approach him, but seeks others out.')
(7) Hostility (e.g. 'Gets angry quickly when others do not agree with him')
(8) Distractibility (e.g. 'Is quickly distracted by events in or outside the classroom')
(9) Dependence (e.g. 'Asks for help when it is not really needed')
(10) Introversion (e.g. 'Tends to withdraw and isolate himself when he is supposed to be working in a group')

Internal consistency reliabilities above .90 have been achieved for the Hebrew adaptation, similar to the original version (McKinney & Forman, 1982), but reliabilities vary from scale to scale; higher for the rating of Verbal Intelligence (.96) and lower for Introversion (.67). Schaefer reported internal reliabilities from moderate (.40) to high (.70) for the various scales across several studies.

Factor analysis of the Hebrew adaptation scales replicated the factor structure reported by Schaefer, validating the spherical model of the three main factors: Social Adjustment (Considerateness versus Hostility; Alpha = .95), Academic Competence (Verbal Intelligence and Creativity/Curiosity; Alpha = .96), and Extraversion versus Introversion (Alpha = .80). Two additional subscales show high loadings on some of the three factors: Task orientation versus Distractibility (Alpha = .94) and Independence versus Dependence (Alpha = .86).

Teacher Adjustment Ratings. This instrument provided three global ratings on a 5-step Likert-type scale highlighting Academic Achievement (from a low achiever to an excellent student), Social Status (very low status to very high status), and Conformity to school (disruptive and disobedient to behaves as expected). These three measures were based on the suggestions of ten teachers, who stressed the necessity for treating the ratings as separate measures of adjustment.

Conners Abbreviated Symptom Questionnaire (ASQ). The Hebrew adaptation of the ASQ was utilized to obtain an overall index of hyperactivity (Margalit, 1981). The scale has been frequently used for identifying hyperactive children and has proven to be one of the most valid and reliable instruments available (Sprague & Sleator, 1977). The interrater reliability and the validity were high for the Hebrew adaptation, as was the internal consistency score (alpha = .95). The scale consists of 10 items, each rated on a 0 to 3 severity index; scores range from 0 to 30. A score of 15, which is two standard deviations above the mean for normal children, has been suggested (Sprague & Sleator, 1977) as the cut-off score for the presence of hyperactive behaviour.

The Aggressive Behaviour Scale. This scale provided an overall index of aggression. It consists of 10 items, each rated on a 0 to 3 severity index. The items were selected from two lists of aggressive behaviour (Prinz, Connor & Wilson, 1981; Stewart *et al.*, 1980; Stewart & Leone, 1978) and composed the most appropriate description for the Israeli educational system, as judged by teachers and as reported elsewhere (Margalit, 1985). The alpha coefficient of internal consistency was .96.

Procedure

Teachers were asked to name (using only first names to protect confidentiality) up to two children in each class who had demonstrated pronounced conduct disorders at school for at least six months. The original sample included 219 male students with conduct disorders. Using the Introversion/Extraversion score as a criterion, and leaving a confidence interval of one standard deviation above and below the mean score, 52 boys were defined as demonstrating Introversion and conduct disorders (ICD) with a score smaller than 3.00, and 62 boys defined as demonstrating Extraversion and conduct disorders (ECD), with a score greater than 4.

Results

One-way Multivariate Analysis of Variance (MANOVA) was undertaken with Introversion/Extraversion status serving as the independent variable, and the subscales of CBI as the dependent variables. The MANOVA revealed a significant main effect between groups, F (8105) = 3.91, $p < .001$. Univariate analysis of variance were undertaken to examine the contribution of each dependent variable in differentiating between groups. Five of the eight subscales contributed to the significant difference: Creativity, Verbal Intelligence, Dependence, Independence and Considerateness. Three subscales did not reveal significant differences: Hostility, Distractibility and Task Orientation. The ECD boys were found to be more intelligent, creative and curious, independent and considerate than the ICD peers. Similar levels of hostility and distractibility were demonstrated in the two subgroups of conduct disordered boys. Means, standard deviations and F scores are presented in Table 9.1.

Table 9.1 Means, standard deviations and F scores of Introvert-Conduct Disordered and Extravert-Conduct Disordered boys

Variables	Introverts (N=52)		Extraverts (N=62)		F(1112)
	M	SD	M	SD	
			CBI		
Creativity	2.03	0.81	2.71	0.98	16.18**
V. Intelligence	2.26	1.06	2.93	1.07	11.01**
Independence	2.39	0.90	2.89	0.87	9.31**
Dependence	2.98	1.04	2.60	1.00	3.97*
Distractibility	4.02	0.87	4.07	0.73	0.11
Task Orientation	2.37	0.68	2.31	0.72	0.30
Hostility	3.80	0.92	4.04	0.83	2.09
Consideration	1.92	0.67	2.17	0.65	3.99*
			Global ratings		
Academic status	2.04	1.78	2.95	1.21	13.25**
Social status	2.04	0.85	3.68	0.84	103.30**
Conformity	1.98	0.97	2.07	0.89	0.24
			Self-control		
Hyperactivity	22.10	5.34	18.87	5.97	9.09**
Aggression	17.77	8.05	14.19	6.95	6.48**

$^* p < .05$, $^{**} p < .01$

One-Way Multivariate Analysis of Variance (MANOVA) was undertaken with the Introversion/Extraversion status serving as the independent variable, and the three global ratings as the dependent variables. The MANOVA revealed a significant main effect between groups, $F(3106) = 37.08$, $p < .001$. Univariate analysis of variance revealed that two out of the three ratings (academic and social status) contributed to the significant difference. Means, standard deviations and F scores are presented in Table 9.1. The ECD boys were rated by their teachers as being more successful in their studies, and more popular in their social interrelations. Similar levels of difficulties were demonstrated by the boys of the two groups in their conformity to classroom rules.

In order to investigate the self-control measures, a one-way MANOVA was performed with hyperactivity (ASQ scale) and aggressiveness (ABS) as the dependent measures. Although the main difficulty of the two groups lies in their self-control deficit, a significant main effect was revealed between the groups, $F(2,111) = 4.94$, $p < .01$. The two measures contributed to the significant difference. Means, standard deviations and F scores are presented on Table 9.1. The ICD boys were more hyperactive and more aggressive than their counterpart.

In order to further investigate the interrelations of variables in each group, two sets of Pearson correlations were performed (see Table 9.2).

Table 9.2 Correlation coefficients between CBI factors and self-control measures

Variables		Hyper.	Aggres.	1	2	3	4
			Introvert-Conduct Disordered boys				
Hyperactivity		—	.64**	-.04	-.29*	-.24	-.16
Aggression		.56**	—	.09	-.33*	-.13	-.02
(1)	Creativity/ V.Intelligence	-.33**	-.25*	—	-.11	-.57**	-.63**
(2)	Hostility/ Considerateness	-.51**	-.43**	.04	—	.20	.17
(3)	Dependence/ Independence	-.42**	-.43**	.62**	.05	—	.56**
(4)	Distractibility/ Task Orientation	-.46**	-.48**	.62**	.16	.66**	—
			Extravert-Conduct Disordered boys				

* $p < .05$, ** $p < .01$

The comparison of the correlation coefficients between CBI variables demonstrate a similar pattern, focusing attention on different patterns between the self control measures and the CBI variables. For the ECD boys, significant negative coefficients were found between the measures of self-control and four CBI measures. All the correlations of the ICD were low and insignificant, except those between the social interrelations factor and the self-control measures. Even in these interrelations, higher coefficients were evident for the ECD group than the ICD group. In both groups of conduct disordered boys, those found to be more aggressive and hyperactive were less able to develop positive social interactions. However, in the extraverted group, greater degrees of hyperactivity and aggression correspond with lower levels of intelligence, task orientation, and independence. The relations between variables in the introverted group were low and insignificant.

Discussion

The aim of the study was to define conduct-disordered subgroups, introducing the individual difference approach. The results demonstrated that the ECD and ICD boys represent two distinct subgroups with regard to their competence, adjustment and achievements. The ICD were characterized as hyperactive aggressive boys who were more dependent on others, and less considerate than the ECD. Their academic achievements and social status were lower than their counterpart, and they were described as less intelligent and less creative. The extraverted group was also disruptive, yet more popular, considerate and independent.

The results of the study support the previous subgrouping of conduct disordered children, adding the Introvert/Extravert perspective as presented in Table 9.3.

The immature, unpopular and poorly self-controlled conduct-disordered boys defined earlier as a hyperactive/aggressive group (Loney & Milich, 1982), or as an aggressive/withdrawn group (Ledingham, 1981) may be regarded as rather similar to the introverted conduct disordered (ICD) boys. The finding that the extraverted group reached higher levels of considerateness, though their levels of hostility were not different from their peers, is in line with Eysenck's notion that extraverts may seek out personal contacts, and are capable of developing intimacy (Eysenck, 1967). The introverts, on the other hand, may tend to avoid social encounters due to fear of overarousal and their tendency to anticipate aversive experience in social encounters.

An individualistic approach to intervention planning is needed in order to account for the differences within the conduct-disordered subgroups. The ECD boys seem to be more self-controlled and more popular. Their interest in excitement, social encounters, and pursuit of rewards (Gray, 1972) may serve as key concepts in planning effective intervention. Introverts' difficulties with excitement-provoking situations, immature and less controlled behaviour, and efforts to avoid punishment rather than gaining rewards should be considered in the planning. Group influence may be emphasized as the source of reinforcement for the first group, but not for the second one. Further studies are needed in order to investigate the different characteristics of the ICD and ECD boys, and the effects of different intervention approaches on developing self-control and reducing disruptive behaviour.

Differences between introverted and extraverted groups were emphasized, but the similarity between them should not be ignored. We are dealing with groups of boys who manifested hostility and low conformity in their social interrelations, and distractibility in their cognitive style. Interventional efforts should be focused on their hostility and their concentration difficulties. Only a comprehensive approach to intervention may promise a better future for these youngsters.

Table 9.3 Comparison of Conduct Disordered subgroupings

Aggressive/Withdrawn	Hyperactive/Aggressive	Introvert CD
Ledingham (1981); Milich & Landau (1984)	Loney & Milich (1982) Stewart *et al.* (1981)	
Unpopular and rejected	Anti-social, rejected	Lower social status
Less mature	Egocentric	Less considerate
Unable to delay responses	Reactivity	High aggressive score
High hyperactive score	High hyperactivity	High hyperactive score
More externally reliant	—	More dependent
Distractibility	Distractibility	—

References

ACHENBACH, T.M. (1982) *Developmental psychopathology*, New York: John Wiley & Sons.

ACHENBACH, T.M. & EDELBROCK, C.S. (1978) The classification of child psychopathology: a review and analysis of empirical efforts. *Psychological Bulletin*, **85**, 1275–301.

COIE, J.D., DODGE, K.A. & COPPOTELLI, H. (1982) Dimensions and types of social status. *Developmental Psychology*, **18**, 557–70.

COOPER, J. & SCALISE, C.J. (1974) Dissonance produced by deviations from life-styles. The interaction of Jungian typology and conformity. *Journal of Personality and Social Psychology*, **29**, 566–71.

EYSENCK, H.J. (1967) *The biological basis of personality*, Springfield: C.C. Thomas.

EYSENCK, H.J. (1977) Crime and personality, London: Routledge & Kegan, Paul.

EYSENCK, H.J. (1981) *A model for personality*, New York: Springer.

EYSENCK, H.J. & EYSENCK, M.W. (1985) *Personality and individual differences*, New York: Plenum Press.

EYSENCK, H.J. & EYSENCK, S.B.G. (1964) *Manual of the Eysenck Personality Inventory*. London: University of London Press.

FERGUSON, T.J. & WELLS, G.L. (1980) Priming of mediators in causal attribution. *Journal of Personality and Social Psychology*, **38**, 461–70.

FESHBACH, S. & PRICE, J. (1984) Cognitive competencies and aggressive behavior: a developmental study. *Aggressive Behavior*, **10**, 185–200.

GRAY, J. (1972) The psychophysical nature of introversion/extraversion: a modification of Eysenck's theory. In V.O. Nebylitsyn & J.A. Gray (eds.) *Biological basis of individual behavior* (182–205). London: Academic Press.

GRAY, J. (1973) Causal theories in personality and how to test them. In J.R. Royce (ed.) *Multivariate analysis and personality theory*, (216–45). London: Academic Press.

GRAZIANO, W.G., BERNSTEIN-FELDESMAN, A. & RAHE, D.F. (1985) Extraversion, social cognition, and the salience of aversiveness in social encounters. *Journal of Personality and Social Psychology*, **49** (4), 971–80.

GREEN, K.D., FOREHAND, R., BECK, S.J. & VOSK, B. (1980) An assessment of the relationship among measures of children's social competence and children's academic achievement. *Child Development*, **51**, 1149–56.

KOHN, M. (1968) *Competence and symptom factors in the preschool child*, New York: William Alanson White Institute.

LEDINGHAM, J. (1981) Developmental patterns of aggressive and withdrawn behaviour in childhood: a possible method for identifying preschizophrenics. *Journal of Abnormal Child Psychology*, **87**, 431–41.

LONEY, J. & MILICH, R. (1982) Hyperactivity, inattention and aggression in clinical practice. In M. Wolraich & D. Routh (eds.) *Advances in developmental and behavioral pediatrics* vol. 2, 113–47, Greenwich, Connecticut: JAI Press.

MARGALIT, M. (1981) Cultural differences in the hyperactive syndrome rated in the Conners Abbreviated Scale. *Journal of Learning Disabilities*, **14**, 330–1.

MARGALIT, M. (1985) Perceptions of parents' behavior, familial satisfaction and sense of coherence in hyperactive children. *Journal of School Psychology*, **23**, 355–64.

MARGALIT, M. & SHULMAN, S. (April 1986) *Social adjustment and academic competency of children with conduct disorders*. Manuscript presented at the CEC convention, New Orleans.

McKINNEY, J.D. & FORMAN, S.G. (1982) Classroom behaviour patterns of EMH, LD and EH students. *Journal of School Psychology*, **20** (4), 271–9.

MILICH, R. & LANDAU, S. (1984) A comparison of the social status and social behavior of aggressive and aggressive/withdrawn boys. *Journal of Abnormal Child Psychology*, **12** (2), 277–88.

OLWEUS, D. (1978) *Aggression in the schools*. New York: Wiley.

PRINZ, R., CONNOR, P. & WILSON, C. (1981) Hyperactive and aggressive behavior in childhood: intertwined dimensions. *Journal of Abnormal Child Psychology*, **9**, 191–202.

PRYOR, J.B. & KRISS, M. (1977) The cognitive dynamics of salience in the attribution process. *Journal of Personality and Social Psychology*, **35**, 49–55.

QUAY, H.C. (1983) A dimensional approach to behavior disorder: the revised behavior problem checklist. *School Psychological Review*, **12**, 244–9.

QUAY, H.C. & WERRY, J.S. (1979) *Psychopathological disorders of childhood* (2nd edn). New York: Wiley.

SAKLOFSKE, D.H., McKERRACHER, D.W. & EYSENCK, S.B.G. (1978) Eysenck's theory of criminality: a scale of criminal propensity as a measure of antisocial behavior. *Psychological Reports*, **43**, 683–6.

SCHAEFER, E.S. (1981) Development of adaptive behavior: conceptual models and family correlates. In M.J. Begad, H.C. Haywood & H.L. Barber (eds.) *Psychosocial influences in retarded performance*. vol. 1. *Issues and theories in development* (155–178). Baltimore: University Press.

SCHAEFER, E.S. & EDGERTON, M. (1978) *Classroom behavior inventory*. Unpublished manuscript. University of North Carolina at Chapel Hill.

SCHAEFER, E.S., EDGERTON, M. & HUNTER, W.M. (1983, August) *Unified model for academic competence, social adjustment and psychopathology*. Paper presented at the American Psychological Annual Meeting, Anaheim, CA.

SCHAEFER, E.S., EDGERTON, M. & HUNTER, W.M. (1985, April) *Spherical model integrating academic competence with social adjustment and psychopathology*. Paper presented at the Biennial Meeting of the Society for Research in Child Development, Toronto, Canada.

SCHWARTZMAN, A.E. & MOSKOWITZ, D.S. (1985, July) *The predictive validity of peer evaluation of behavior problems in childhood*. Paper presented at the Biennial meeting of the International Society for the Study of Behavioral Development, Tours, France.

SNYDER, M., TANKE, E.D. & BERSCHEID, E.S. (1977) Social perception and interpersonal behavior: on the self-fulfilling nature of social stereotypes. *Journal of Personality and Social Psychology*, **35**, 656–6.

SPRAGUE, R.L. & SLEATOR, E.K. (1977) Methylphenidate in hyperkinetic children: differences in dose effects on learning and social behavior. *Science*, **198**, 1274–6.

STEWART, M.A. DEBLOIS, C.S., MEARDON, J. & CUMMINGS, C. (1980) Aggressive conduct disorders of children. *Journal of Nervous and Mental Disease*, **168** (10), 604–10.

STEWART, M.A., CUMMINGS, C., SINGER, S. & DEBLOIS, C.S. (1981) The overlap between hyperactive and unsocialized aggressive children. *Journal of Child Psychology and Psychiatry*, **22**, 35–45.

STEWART, M.A. & LEONE, L. (1978) A family study of unsocialized aggressive boys. *Biological Psychiatry*, **13**, 107–17.

10 The fears of Italian children and adolescents

E. Sanavio

There are considerable individual differences in the type, number and intensity of fears experienced by children and adolescents. In spite of the importance of this subject, our knowledge of it is far from satisfactory. One American study specifically examining fears at three different age levels (11, 17 and 60+ years) suggests that, with increasing age, the dimensions along which fears are structured become more varied and complex (Russell, 1967). Another research investigation on the time-evolution of fears in 13–85-year-old subjects indicates that the diffusion of predominantly unrealistic fears is substantially constant at different ages, while realistic fears are more frequent in adolescents (Spiegler & Lambert, 1970).

Fear evaluations generally make use of several questionnaires more or less directly derived from the Fear Survey Schedule (Wolpe & Lang, 1964), a self-report inventory evaluating the intensity of reactions of anxiety and fear to a vast range of stimuli. Items prevalently describe unrealistic fears, since the inventory was developed mainly as an aid in initial exploration of adults' phobias. Beyond its original aims, the FSS has been extensively used in research on fears in normal subjects and administered to American, English, Irish, Israeli, Italian, Dutch and Venezuelan university students. We therefore have a large number of quantitative studies providing much information on the diffusion and characteristics of fears in the normal adult population (Arrindel, Emmelkamp & van der Ende, 1984). Knowledge of fears in adolescents is far more limited. Bamber's (1979) investigation of 1112 young people between 12 and 18 in Belfast, using the FSS-III, showed that:

Girls have both total scores and numbers of fears which are significantly higher than those of boys;

Fears tend to increase in both sexes in late adolescence;

The most important fears are connected with social situations, interpersonal relationships, and tissue damage;

Eleven fear factors are common to adolescents, independent of sex and type of education: (1) social rejection; (2) exposure in public; (3) tissue damage; (4) medical/dental treatment; (5) people with deformities; (6) small animals; (7) pets; (8) travelling; (9) stormy weather; (10) acrophobia; (11) social isolation.

A Fear Survey Schedule for Children has been derived from the FSS-III and administered to 9–12-year-olds (Scherer & Nakamura, 1968). In this age-range too, girls report greater fears than boys. The scale shows high internal consistency, correlates with the Taylor Manifest Anxiety Scale, and is structured into eight factors; however, the group studied was so small (99 subjects) that the factorial results may be lacking in validity. More recently, this schedule has also been revised and results show: (a) high internal consistency; (b) satisfactory score stability in time over one week; (c) positive correlations with the trait anxiety scores of the Spielberger State-Trait Anxiety Inventory for Children; (d) five factors, including the fear of failure and criticism; the unknown; injury and small animals; danger and death; medical fears; (e) systematically higher fear scores for girls; (f) a tendency for fears to diminish with increasing age, although statistical significance is not reached (Ollendick, 1983; Ollendick, Matson & Helsen, 1985).

As regards kindergarten and elementary-school children, one other version of the Children's Fear Survey Schedule may be administered aloud and contains items appropriate for younger subjects (Ryall & Dietiker, 1979). Fears were more intense in kindergarten and elementary-school girls than in boys, but age-related variations did not appear. Moreover, the children with the highest scorse were known to have problems connected with anxiety and fear.

In Italy two studies of adults' fears have used FSS-derived inventories. The first research study (Sanavio, 1986) employed 92 items, of which 54 are common to the FSS-III and 38 deal with fears encountered frequently in preliminary studies and mainly concerned with realistic threats to personal safety. As results showed the possibility of reducing the inventory to 58 items with five subscales, a second study (Sanavio, Bertolotti, Michielin, Vidotto & Zotti, 1986) was carried out, showing good internal consistency and temporal stability of the subscales, and supplying normative data for the Italian population. The two inventories were given to a total of 1700 normal subjects aged between 15 and 80 years, and to various clinically interesting groups: somatic and psychiatric in-patients and out-patients with depression, insomnia, single phobias, social phobias, and agoraphobia. Factorial analyses identified five main fear factors:

I   natural calamities, wars and situations of grave danger, or diseases which could compromise personal safety;
II   social events, particularly situations involving criticism and social rejection: the items loading this factor allow discrimination between patients with social phobias from others with phobic disturbances and from the other groups;
III   animals which, although not dangerous, are traditionally considered repellent and associated with dark or dirty places (e.g. mice, bats, insects);
IV   journeys and situations involving separation from familiar places or people: items offer excellent discriminatory power between agoraphobic and other types of patients;
V   blood, wounds, and medical/surgical procedures: these items arc not influenced by situational context and do not vary with the imminence of a surgical operation.

Women suffer more than men both from a higher number of fears and from their greater intensity. On all five subscales women's scores were statistically higher.

This paper reports three investigations carried out at different age levels, explores the main characteristics of Italian children's and adolescents' fears, and compares these results with similar studies from other countries.

Study 1

The primary aim of this study was to explore the fears of 11–15-year-olds using an inventory specially derived from the FSS (Italian version for adults). The secondary aim was to study the relation of fears with personality by using a well-known and widely-used questionnaire, the Eysenck Personality Questionnaire (EPQ). (Eysenck & Eysenck, 1975).

Subjects: 500 children between 11 and 15 years, 50 boys and 50 girls in each age-group were considered. All subjects were attending junior school of the first year of high school, and all were residing in north-eastern Italy.

Procedure: The fear inventory (Sanavio, 1984) used may be considered the Italian equivalent of the FSS-FC of Scherer & Nakamura (1968). The only differences are number of items (78), the contents of some of them, and the greater reference to realistic fears. Children were asked to choose between five fear possibilities and, in scoring, each item was assigned 0 (not at all), 1 (a little), 2 (a fair amount), 4 (much), and 5 (very much).

All subjects were contemporaneously given the Italian translation of the EPQ. As the Italian adaptation of the junior form was not available, the adult form was used, with only some very small changes (S.B.G. Eysenck, 1985).

Both questionnaires were completed anonymously by subjects subdivided into small groups, in one of their classrooms at school.

Results

Figure 10.1 shows total fear scores according to sex and age. Girls reported greater fears than boys, and scores tended to diminish with increasing age in both sexes. A two-way ANOVA on total scores showed the significant effects of sex ($F_{1490} = 31.9$, $p < .001$) and age ($F_{4490} = 5.2$, $p < .001$), but the interaction was not significant.

Internal consistency: Cronbach's alpha coefficient was .95.
Fears and EPQ: Correlation coefficients with the four EPQ scales were calculated, as follows:

N-scale (neuroticism)	.31	$p < .01$
E-scale (extraversion)	$-.13$	$p < .05$
P-scale (psychoticism)	$-.27$	$p < .01$
L-scale (lie)	.05	n.s.

Factorial structure: The method of principal components with iterations was used: 16 factors with eigenvalues greater than 1 were obtained and were Varimax-rotated. They may be summarized as follows:

(1)   catastrophic events (e.g. wars, nuclear explosions, earthquakes, fires);
(2)   travel and journeys using different means of transport;
(3)   repellent animals (worms, mice, bats);

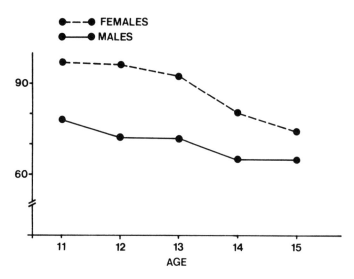

Figure 10.1   Total scores on Fear Inventory of Italian 11/15-year-olds, 50 boys and 50 girls in each age-group

(4) people with physical deformities or diseases;
(5) medical personnel (dentists, doctors) and procedures (injections);
(6) embarrassment due to nakedness and people of the opposite sex;
(7) traffic dangers (cars, crossing the road);
(8) often attractive but dangerous situations (high speeds, air or sea travel);
(9) stimuli linked to physical accidents (wounds, blood, screams);
(10) social disapproval (being made fun of, rejected by others, scolded);
(11) water (single item);
(12) dirt
(13) loneliness associated with the dark, thunder and lightning;
(14) dogs (single item);
(15) unknown people and places;
(16) speaking in front of friends (single item).

Discussion

With increasing age, fears decrease regularly in both boys and girls. A similar trend has been found in American children and adolescents (Ollendick *et al.*, 1985), but not in adolescents in Northern Ireland (Bamber, 1979).

Girls show higher fear scores than boys, and this has also been found in children, adolescents and adults in different countries. One explanation for this finding is that males have greater difficulty in admitting their fears and wish to appear in a favourable light, following the stereotype of courageous males and fearful females.

The correlation with the EPQ L-scale was almost nil and indicates the absence of dissimulation and of an attitude of social desirability in responses. On the EPI L-scale non-significant correlations with fear were found by both Farley & Mealiea (1971) in American college students and by Bamber (1979) in Northern Ireland students. Thus the difference in our scores between boys and girls also requires a different explanation than that of contamination of response by simulation and social desirability phenomena.

The negative correlation of the fear scale with the E-scale, although significant, was very low. This suggests the possibility of greater fear in introverts than in extraverts, and adds to results reported for Italian adults (Sanavio, 1986). Bamber (1979) found negligible correlations in three of his four groups of adolescents and nil correlations were also found in Canadian college students (Hannah, Storm & Caird,, 1965). However, the existence of our correlation, even such a low one, is easily comprehensible, since some items refer to interpersonal situations.

Fears correlate clearly with the N-scale, indicating that 11–15-year-olds with poor emotional stability tend to report more intense fears. This was also found in Bamber's sample of adolescents and has been observed in adult populations (Hannah *et al.*, 1965; Sanavio, 1986).

Of particular interest is the negative correlation between fears and scores on the EPQ P-scale. This indicates that subjects showing 'tough-minded', non-conformist and asocial behaviour tend to have few fears. We do not know if this relation has been found in other cultures, since earlier research was carried out with the MPI or EPI, both predecessors of the EPQ but lacking in a scale that measures the P dimension.

The junior version of the Fear Inventory shows very high internal consistency which is somewhat surprising in such a heterogeneous inventory. It may therefore be hypothesized that, beyond the specific reactions of fears described in the single items, the inventory measures a rather broad and general construct, connected to traits of anxiety and emotional instability. This hypothesis is supported by an examination of the factorial structure of responses. Although our analysis shows as many as 16 factors that explain 59.4% of the total variance, factor 1 alone accounts for 24%. This factorial analysis merely has an introductory aim, and the same multi-dimensional hypothesis is questionable. However, it does allow comparison with methodologically similar studies carried out in other countries. There are many similarities with the 11 factors common to Bamber's adolescents, which correspond to 11 of the 16 identified here and which clearly show basic agreement in the items loading those factors. The main difference is that in our study the main factor (24% of the variance) is composed of fears regarding catastrophes and realistic dangers, while in the Northern Ireland adolescents it was described by fears regarding criticism and social rejection. Bamber's study used the original form of the FSS-III and thus included very few items on realistic fears. One further difference is age. In the British study, subjects were between 12 and 18 years, and social fears may become pre-eminent with increasing age.

Study 2

The aim of this study was to examine the fears of subjects younger than those of Study 1. The sample of children studied here were between 7 and 12 years old. Extensive revision of the previously used inventory was necessary to make it more appropriate to subjects' age and for simpler administration. The response reliability of this version of the inventory was also examined by re-administering it one month later. In American 8–11 year-olds, test-retest reliability determined over a 3-month interval was .55 and over a 1-week interval was .82 (Ollendick, 1983). One-week reliability was also reported for 4–12-year-olds, to whom the CFSS had been administered aloud by the examiner: reliability values varied between .79 and .91 (Ryall & Dietiker, 1979).

Subjects: 600 children between 7 and 12 years, 50 boys and 50 girls in each age-group were considered. Subjects were chosen randomly for each year of age from registers of children attending elementary schools in Vicenza (a medium-sized town in the Venetian region of north-eastern Italy).

Procedure: All subjects completed a revised version of the fear inventory used in Study 1. Items were reduced to 50 and sometimes lexically modified in order to facilitate understanding. Subjects were asked to respond to three instead of five possibilities, so that scores were rated 1 (not at all), 2 (a little) and 3 (a lot). This revised form may be considered the Italian correspondent of the CFSS-R inventory (Ollendick, 1983).

The inventory was completed anonymously by subjects in small groups, in one of their classrooms at school.

Results

Figure 10.2 shows mean fear scores for the various age-groups. A two-way ANOVA shows the significant effect of sex with girls reporting more fears than boys (F_{1588} = 5.3, $p < .05$) and age where fears decrease with increasing age: (F_{5588} = 2.4, $p < .05$). A non-significant interaction was found between these factors.
Reliability: Cronbach's alpha coefficient was .93.

The inventory was re-administered to 280 subjects one month later and the test-retest correlation was .72. Substantially similar or slightly higher scores were found on retest: the second mean was 89.2 (SD = 17.4), not significantly higher than the means of 87.9 (SD = 14.3), obtained at the first testing.
Factorial analysis: Three separate factorial analyses were carried out on the male

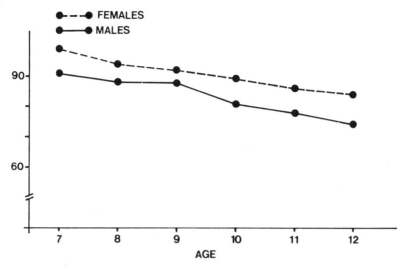

Figure 10.2 Total scores on Fear Inventory of Italian 7/12-year-olds, 50 boys and 50 girls in each age-group

and female subgroups and on both combined. The method of principal components with iterations was employed, with Varimax rotation. From the three groups, extraction procedures gave 17, 17 and 16 factors with eigenvalues higher than 1. However, these showed breaks after the first 4 or 5 factors, and continued extraction gave factors loaded by pairs of similar items or by single items. We therefore chose a four-factor solution which had shown substantial agreement in the three separate analyses. They were:

I   dirt and animals associated with dirt and the danger of infection, the main items are dirt, dead animals, and mice;
II   illnesses and medical procedures: main items are doctors, dentists, injections;
III   travel, crowds and noise: main items are travelling by train, cars, sudden noises;
IV   social criticism and disapproval: main items are being made fun of, being questioned at school, speaking in front of friends.

Discussion

As expected, in the 7–12 age-group girls report more fears than boys, diminishing with age in both sexes. In the two researches on American children of the same age, one (Ryall & Dietiker, 1979) found ample but not significant variations across grade levels; the other (Ollendick *et al.*, 1985) found a clearly decreasing though not significant trend. However, these were preliminary studies and as such the numbers of children in each sex- and age-group were less than ten.

Factorial analyses indicate four factors. Two correspond to similar factors in Ollendick's (1983) analysis: our factor II corresponds to 'medical fears' and factor IV to 'fear of failure and criticism'. A comparison with our Study 1 with 11–15-year-olds is also interesting. Factor II corresponds substantially to 5 (medical personnel and procedures) and factor IV to 10 (social disapproval). Factor I (fears connected with dirt and repellent animals) did not overlap except for some items which reached moderate loadings on the Ollendick factor 'fear of injury and small animals' and differed in overall significance. However, correspondence was clearer on two factors of our Study 1: 3 (repellent animals) and 12 (dirt). Factor III turned out to be heterogeneous and ambiguous to interpret. It contains items which in

Study 1 were distributed over three different factors: 2 (travel and separation), 7 (traffic dangers) and 9 (personal safety). There was no correspondence with the Ollendick analysis.

Inventory reliability appeared to be satisfactory. In particular, responses remained stable over time, at least after an interval of one month. Retest scores were very slightly higher but not statistically significant. After a similar interval, adult subjects show definite reductions in fear scores which, according to various studies, range between 5% and 14% of the initial scores (Arrindel *et al.*, 1984; Sanavio, 1986; Suinn, 1969; Tasto & Suinn, 1972).

Study 3

A third study was set up to investigate fears in late adolescence (16–19 years of age). The same fear inventory as that for adults was used, with quite a wide battery, for deeper understanding of the problem.

Subjects: There were 400 students, between 16 and 19 years old, with 50 boys and 50 girls in each age-group, attending higher-education institutes. All subjects were asked to participate on a voluntary basis, and anonymity was guaranteed.

Procedure: Each subject was given a sealed envelope containing a brief outline of the research aims and a folder holding the CBA–2.0 'Scale Primarie' series of questionnaires: (Bertolotti, Michielin, Sanavio, Simonetti, Vidotto & Zotti, 1985) to be completed and sent back by post.

The CBA–2.0 batteries contain the following:

Fear Inventory: the 58-item version for adults, described above (Sanavio, 1986);
Italian version of a reduced (48-item) form of the EPQ (Eysenck & Eysenck, 1975), specially translated and adapted for the battery:
Italian version of the Maudsley Obsessive-Compulsive Questionnaire (Hodgson & Rachman, 1977; Sanavio & Vidotto, 1985);
Italian version of the State-Trait Anxiety Inventory (Spielberger, Gorsuch & Lushene, 1970; Lazzari & Pancheri, 1980);
reduced (30-item) form of a Psychophysiological Questionnaire (Pancheri, Chiari & Michielin, 1985) on main psychophysiological disturbances;
a 24-item questionnaire on depression (Questionnaire D of Michielin, Bertolotti, Sanavio, Simonetti, Vidotto & Zotti, 1985), specially adapted for the battery.
an extensive autobiographical schedule containing a standardized form of subjects' psychological and psychosocial histories (for details, see Sanavio *et al.*, 1986).

Results

The description of total fear scores is shown in Figure 10.3. The ANOVA shows a significant effect for sex ($F_{1312} = 17.3$, $p < .001$), but not for age ($F_{3312} = 1.4$, n.s.), or the interaction of sex with age ($F_{3312} = .6$, n.s.).

Correlations with other questionnaires are shown in Table 10.1.

On the basis of total scores on the Fear Inventory, three subgroups were identified:

– 25 boys and 25 girls with the lowest scores in their respective groups;
– 25 boys and 25 girls with the highest scores;
– 25 boys and 25 girls with scores nearest the mean.

Subjects' case-histories and autobiographies are summarized in Table 10.2.

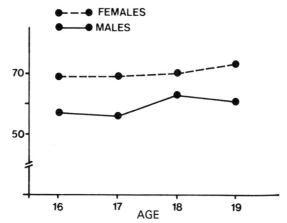

Figure 10.3 Total scores on Fear Inventory of Italian students between 16 and 19, 40 boys and 40 girls in each age-group

The CBA–2.0 program (Vidotto, Bertolotti, Michielin, Sanavio, Simonetti & Zotti, 1986) was used to correct answer-sheets. This program scores the questionnaires, gives a narrative interpretation, and indicates cases of clinical interest for further psychodiagnostic work. The percentages of subjects in each subgroup were 46% for the group with the highest scores, 19% for that with the lowest scores, and 8% for the intermediate group.

Table 10.1

Questionnaire & content	F	I	II	III	IV	V
EPQ – E (extraversion)	−.13	−.08	−.34	−.02	−.10	−.03
EPQ–N (neuroticism)	.39	.34	.36	.28	.40	.23
EPQ – P (psychoticism)	.04	.09	.11	.06	.04	.03
EPQ – L (lie)	−.10	−.06	−.12	−.10	−.07	−.11
MOCQ (obsessions/ compulsions)	.21	.24	.21	.14	.25	.12
QD (depression)	.27	.34	.04	.05	.31	.22
QPF (psychophysiol. disorders)	.31	.32	.28	.23	.28	.19
STAI-X1 (state-anxiety)	.12	.09	.09	.12	.15	.09
STAI-X2 (trait-anxiety)	.39	.31	.38	.42	.38	.32

$p < .01$ for coefficients higher than .18

Table 10.2

	Fear score		
	Low	Intermediate	High
Slight psychological problems	21%	9%	40%
Severe psychological problems	10%	4%	15%
Daily psychological obstacles	24%	18%	46%
Psychological/psychiatric examinations	8%	6%	31%
Psychotherapy	4%	1%	10%
Psychopharmacological treatments	8%	2%	12%
Psychiatric hospitalization	1%	0%	5%
Attempted suicide	0%	0%	4%
Occasional use of soft drugs	14%	16%	24%
Habitual use of soft drugs	8%	8%	10%
Occasional use of heavy drugs	7%	3%	6%
Habitual use of heavy drugs	6%	0%	4%
Frequent insomnia	9%	5%	26%
Habitual use of sleeping-pills	4%	2%	9%
Excessive use of alcohol	8%	2%	17%

Discussion

In the 16–19-year-old group too, the fact that girls have greater fears than boys of the same age was confirmed. The most interesting result was that the tendency of scores to decrease with age is halted at this age level.

The Fear Inventory showed three quite high correlations with the other questionnaires: with the EPQ N-scale, the trait scale of the Spielberger State-Trait Anxiety Inventory, and the Psychophysiological Questionnaire. It was shown that subjects with higher fears tend to show poor emotional stability, anxiety traits and enhanced psychophysiological reactivity. This triad of results is easily linked in the light of the Eysenckian personality theory and confirms the high correlation between fear and neuroticism found in the 11–15-year-old group.

Of particular interest are the data obtained from the autobiographies, which suggest strong coincidence between episodes and/or complaints of emotional instability and behavioral adaptation in adolescents with greater fears. However, having few fears is not synonymous with psychological well-being, since the group with the lowest fear scores also reported behavioral and psychiatric instability to a greater extent than the group with intermediate scores.

Conclusions

In Italian children and adolescents, fears are seen to become progressively less intense between the ages of 7 and 15, stabilizing after the age of 15.

It was also found that girls systematically show greater fears than boys over the whole age-group from 7 to 19, in agreement with results found in Italian adults, and in children, adolescents and adults of other nationalities. The usual interpretation is that women do not differ so much in experiencing fear, as in admitting that they do. The cultural pressure of the stereotype of the courageous man may act at two main levels: first, as a filter systematically attenuating subjects' verbal responses with respect to their effective perception and evaluation of fear: verbal responses are thus 'touched up' and made to conform to the expectations of the social group. Subjects' responses are thus expected to correlate with a lie-scale like that of the EPQ which does measure subjects' tendency to present themselves in a favourable light and conform to social expectations. However, the correlational analysis for our groups of both children and adolescents did not support this interpretation. The second hypothesis is that cultural pressure functions like a telescope used the wrong way, making observed objects tiny, so that subjects constantly underestimate their fears. Responses thus reflect effective beliefs or perceptions: however, it may be that the sex differences are not revealed in external evaluations, as psychophysiological recordings and behavioral observations are.

The same problems occur when attempting to explain the differences found with increasing age. Reduced fears may reflect 'effective' variations: development makes children gradually less vulnerable and more capable in the face of difficulties. However, it may also be hypothesized that reduction in fear evaluation is due to the pressure of common stereotypes which require that small children are likely to be fearful and which link the fact of growing up with less fear in daily situations.

These results lead to three main considerations in the study of fear. First, fear is multi-dimensional and shows both subjective and psychophysiological/behavioral features (Lang, 1968). Second, there is the problem of relationships between the subjective (cognitive) and 'objective' (psychophysiological/behavioral) aspects of fear, which do not necessarily overlap. There is then the question of the modalities along which the cognitive dimension of fear develops. Self-ratings offer a measure of beliefs and expectations. Occasional experiences, in which we evaluate the level of emotional activation experienced and the behavior shown, within the limits of what we may remember and what others said about us, definitely go towards forming subjective evaluations. Apart from the fact that self-ratings are sometimes different from external observation, in any case we form self-ratings only by means of a theory – both implicit and rudimentary – on what is meant by fear, what is regarded as an indicator of fear, the kinds of behaviour which are considered normal and which fearful, on our capacity for self-control in the face of fear, etc. The circularity of relations between the various components of fears is also evident in which subjects' beliefs, however determined, influence their behaviour on future occasions and their psychophysiological reactions.

It was observed that total scores on the Fear Inventory correlate with emotional instability and with anxiety traits and psychophysiological hyper-reactivity. Future research might examine whether, in children, a fear inventory may be an index of anxious characteristics more immediately comprehensible and more useful than commonly used psychodiagnostic tools. In the psychological assessment of children and adolescents, fears are considered only when they are so far-reaching and severe as to constitute phobias. Instead, early evaluation of children's and adolescents' fears is important for the prevention of the development of phobias and maladaptive phenomena. This seems particularly important in the case of fears regarding negative judgments and social rejection, which are common and which may prepare the ground for the social phobias and more severe disturbances often appearing in late adolescence (Marks, 1969). Another area of great interest is that of fears concerning solitude and separation from familiar places and persons: this problem was clearly identified by factorial analysis, and may be of possible importance in the etiology of agoraphobia.

Lastly, it is suggested that it would be relatively easy to improve current fear inventories. In this writer's opinion, it would be useful to offer a wider representation of realistic and common fears and to make some items less ambiguous by reformulating them in greater detail (e.g. 'staying alone at home for a couple of hours' instead of 'being alone').

References

ARRINDELL, W.A., EMMELKAMP, P.M.G. & VAN DER ENDE, J. (1984) Phobic dimensions: I. Reliability and generalizability across samples, gender and nations. *Advances in Behaviour Research and Therapy*, **6**, 207–54.

BAMBER, J.H. (1979) *The fears of adolescents*, London: Academic Press.

BERTOLOTTI, G., MICHIELIN, P., SANAVIO, E., SIMONETTI, G., VIDOTTO, G. & ZOTTI, A.M. (1985) *Cognitive Behavioural Assessment. Batteria CBA–2.0 Scale Primarie*. Firenze: Organizzazioni Speciali.

EYSENCK, H.J. & EYSENCK, S.B.G. (1975) *Manual of the Eysenck Personality Questionnaire*, Hodder & Stoughton, London.

EYSENCK, S.B.G. (1985) Confronti transculturali tra le personalita' di soggetti italiani continentali, siciliani e inglesi. *Bollettino di Psicologia Applicata*, **176**, 11–16.

FARLEY, F.H. & MEALIEA, W.L. (1971) Dissimulation and social desirability in the assessment of fears. *Behavior Therapy*, **2**, 101–2.

HANNAH, F., STORM, T. & CAIRD, W.K. (1965) Sex differences and relationships among neuroticism, extraversion and expressed fears. *Perceptual and Motor Skills*, **20**, 1214–16.

HODGSON, R. & RACHMAN, S. (1977) Obsessional-compulsive complaints. *Behaviour Research and Therapy*, **15**, 389–95.

LANG, P.J. (1968) Fear reduction and fear behavior: problems in treating a construct. In J.M. Schlien (ed.) *Research in psychotherapy*. Washington: American Psychological Association.

LAZZARI, R. & PANCHERI, P. (1980) *STAI, questionario di autovalutazione dell'ansia di stato e di tratto*, Firenze: Organizzazioni Speciali.

MARKS, I.M. (1969) *Fears and phobias*, London: Heinemann.

MICHIELIN, P., BERTOLOTTI, G., SANAVIO, E., SIMONETTI, G., VIDOTTO, G. & ZOTTI, A.M. (1985) *Questionario D*. Firenze: Organizzazioni Speciali.

OLLENDICK, T.H. (1983) Reliability and validity of the revised Fear Survey Schedule for Children (FSSC-R). *Behaviour Research and Therapy*, **21**, 685–92.

OLLENDICK, T.H., MATSON, J.L. & HELSEN, W.J. (1985) Fears in children and adolescents: normative data. *Behaviour Research and Therapy*, **23**, 465–67.

PANCHERI, P., CHIARI, G. & MICHIELIN, P. (1985) *Questionario Psicofisiologico, Forma ridotta*, Firenze: Organizzazioni Speciali.

RUSSELL, G.W. (1967) Human fears: a factor analytic study of three age levels. *Genetic Psychology Monographs*, **76**, 141–62.

RYALL, M.R. & DIETIKER, K.E. (1979) Reliability and clinical validity of the Children's Fear Survey Schedule. *Journal of Behavior Therapy and Experimental Psychiatry*, **10**, 303–9.

SANAVIO, E. (1984) La valutazione delle paure in eta' evolutiva: presentazione della forma 'bambini' dell'Inventario delle Paure. *Terapia del Comportamento*, **2**, 85–96.

SANAVIO, E. (1986) La valutazione della paure: presentazione della forma 'adulti' dell'Inventario delle Paure. *Bollettino di Psicologia Applicata*, **175**, 3–20.

SANAVIO, E. & VIDOTTO, G. (1985) The components of the Maudsley Obsessional-Compulsive Questionnaire. *Behaviour Research and Therapy*, **23**, 659–62.

SANAVIO, E., BERTOLOTTI, G., MICHIELIN, P., VIDOTTO, G. & ZOTTI, A.M. (1986) *CBA–2.0 Scale Primarie: Manuale. Una batteria a largo spettro per l'assessment psicologico*, Firenze: Organizzazioni Speciali, 1–234.

SCHERER, M.W. & NAKAMURA, C.Y. (1968) A Fear Survey Schedule for Children (FSS–FC): a factor-analytic comparison with manifest anxiety. *Behaviour Research and Therapy*, **6**, 173–82.

SPIEGLER, M.D. & LIEBERT, R.M. (1970) Some correlates of self-reported fear. *Psychological Reports*, **26**, 691–5.

SPIELBERGER, C.D., GORSUCH, R.L. & LUSHENE, R.E. (1970) *The State-Trait Anxiety Inventory. Test manual for form X*, Palo Alto: Consulting Psychologist Press.

SUINN, R.M. (1969) Changes in non-treated subjects over time: data on a fear survey schedule and the test anxiety scale. *Behaviour Research and Therapy*, **7**, 205–6.

TASTO, D.L. & SUINN, R.M. (1972) Fear survey schedule changes on total and factor scores due to non-treatment effects. *Behavior Therapy*, **3**, 275–8.

VIDOTTO, G., BERTOLOTTI, G., MICHIELIN, P., SANAVIO, E., SIMONETTI, G. & ZOTTI, A.M. (1986) *CBA–2.0 Scale Primarie. Libreria di CBA versione 2.0*, Firenze: Organizzazioni Speciali.

WOLPE, J. & LANG, P.L. (1964) A fear survey schedule for use in behavior therapy. *Behaviour Research and Therapy*, **2**, 27–30.

11 Cognitive abilities in Japanese children

S. Iwawaki

Introduction

People differ from one another and individual differences have influence on the probable occurrence of certain behaviours and the pattern of behavioural sequences. Systematic research on individual differences in personality and cognitive ability has existed for over a century. The major purpose of personality and ability measurement is to assess interindividual differences. Psychologists have produced a variety of important ideas and measures concerning the assessment of individual differences. The study of individual differences in children has focused on the evaluation of individual development. From a cross-cultural point of view, individualism is held to be psychologically more prominent in Western people than in their Oriental counterparts (Hofstede, 1980). People in an individualistic society emphasize ingenuity and originality of thought and the emphasis on individualism has direct and indirect effects on Western education (Christopher, 1984). Thus it is important for parents to understand the implication of their child's individuality (Lerner, 1986). In such circumstances promotion from grade to grade would be determined on a child's academic achievement. If this is the case, it is very important to assess the individual differences of each child objectively.

Japanese primary and secondary education is highly controlled by the Ministry of Education. School teachers have to follow the curriculum set by the Ministry of Education and all school children receive essentially the same material at the same pace. There is little grouping by ability and gifted children take the same course in the same classroom with borderline children. *Juku*, private tutorial schools, which children attend after regular school hours, give them the opportunity to understand materials given in the regular classroom. Japanese people assume that all children have the capacity to achieve an academic goal regardless of their ability differences if they do their best. Japan is a perfectible society (Smith, 1983). School children are urged to strive for perfection in taking an examination. The assumption that the perfectibility is attainable is also held by big companies and other groups. Furthermore, harmony of all members of a group is considered highly important in Japan. Children of a classroom are expected to conform and cooperate with others. The group pressures toward conformity is against personal qualities that would foster individualistic endeavour (US Study of Education in Japan, 1987). Many children who go abroad with their parents and then return to school in Japan have difficulties in adjusting their behaviour in the classroom and are often bullied by other children, because they cannot behave like their peers. A Japanese proverb says that the protruding stake is hammered down. Hutchinson, Arkoff & Weaver (1966) reported that Japanese-American students only gave few responses in class discussions at the University of Hawaii. The Japanese are brought up not to express their strong individuality in public and self-assertion is viewed as undesirable behaviour in the classroom.

As the US study of education in Japan (1987) reports, Japanese children do not receive individualized teaching and are promoted automatically to higher grades on the basis of egalitarianism, together with the principle that children should never be made to lose face. A symposium at the 1974 Annual meeting of the Japanese Educational Psychology Society discussed 'Tests and Education', and concluded that since norm-referenced tests deprive children of the right to be educated, educational tests must not be used in school. Some Japanese psychologists have criticized psychological tests as discrimination tools. Such a trend weakened research activities on individual differences, so few papers on children's individual differences have appeared in Japanese professional journals for the past decade.

Cognitive tests of Japanese children

The 1905 version of the Binet–Simon intelligence test was introduced in Japan in 1908. Kubo (1922) translated the Binet–Simon test into Japanese and gave it to Japanese children, introducing new items suitable to them. A non-verbal group test for 4th and 6th grade Japanese children was developed by Tanaka (1934). Since then, the Tanaka group test has been widely used for the assessment of Japanese children's intelligence and other psychologists have also conducted many studies of IQ and other tests.

After World War II, the US Educational Mission recommended that children's scores on standardised tests be placed on school record forms. New tests were constructed by educational psychologists and were put on sale by Japanese publishers in the 1950s, though tests developed by Japanese psychologists were based on Western intelligence models. A summary of Japanese work on IQ tests from 1908 to 1958 was provided by Osaka (1961). In the 1960s, many books on intelligence tests were published and articles on IQ tests appeared in academic journals and university bulletins. Since the early 1970s, however, professionals and non-psychologists have criticized IQ tests as imperfect instruments to measure cognitive ability and have suggested that the measurement of individual differences in school and employment infringes on human rights. Since then the interest of Japanese psychologists in IQ studies has waned, and articles on IQ tests rarely appeared in Japanese academic journals for the past decade. Since IQ researches in Japan were reviewed by Vernon (1982) and Iwawaki and Vernon (1987), detailed discussion on Japanese children's ability researches will be excluded here. However, Lynn's findings of the superiority of the intelligence of Japanese to American children should be referred to somewhat in detail because his studies hold important issues of methodology in IQ researches.

Lynn (1977) reported that the intelligence of the Japanese is superior to that of Americans, using the Japanese standardisations of the Wechsler scales. Mean Japanese IQs of 106 (Lynn, 1977) and 111 (Lynn, 1982) were expressed in relation to the American mean of 100. Lynn & Dziobon (1980) gave the American Primary Mental Abilities (PMA) Test and a Japanese group intelligence (Kyodai NX 9–15) test to a sample of 212 children (aged 9 and 10) in Northern Ireland. Using the data from the Northern Ireland sample, they converted the Japanese means on the Kyodai subtests to the corresponding IQs on the PMA. As a result, they found that the mean IQ of Japanese children aged about 10 years seems to be 109 in relation to the American mean IQ of 100. These findings were criticized on the basis of the methodological weakness for cross-cultural comparison. Stevenson and Azuma (1983) suggested that the Japanese sample for the standardisation of WISC–R in Japan was not representative of all Japanese children. As they pointed out, the Japanese version of the WISC–R used an urban biased sample in the standardisation which was the basic material in Lynn's studies. Many studies (e.g. Agarie & Ohnishi, 1964; Egawa, 1956; Nakajima, 1954; Ohira, 1962) conducted in the 1950s and 1960s found that the urban children were significantly superior on IQ tests. More recently, Sugimura (1980) showed significant differences in the Japanese version of the McCarthy Scales of Children's Abilities scores between rural and urban children. However, it is not conclusive that there are significant differences in mean IQ between Japanese urban and rural children. Hattori, Misawa, and Fujita (1982) found that there were no significant differences in mean IQ between rural and urban children, using the Japanese version of the Columbia Mental Maturity Scale.

In doing cross-cultural research, the sampling procedure is very important, but it is difficult in practice for researchers to get a representative sample of the population. Though college students are usually not representative of a culture, they are often employed as a sample for a cross-cultural study. The main reason is that college students are subjects who are easily obtainable for investigations. The cooperation of teachers is indispensable to conduct an investigation on children's abilities. It would be possible to do good sampling if all teachers were always willing to cooperate with psychologists for the purpose of research. Since there are school differences even in the same city and rural children in Japan get cognitive information due to the development of transportation and a remarkable increase in TV ownership, researchers should give careful consideration to the matter of sampling. Unfortunately, there seem to be no good guidebooks to teach good sampling for cross-cultural researches (Lonner & Berry, 1986).

Massive IQ gain in Japanese children

Flynn (1984) has suggested that the mean IQ of Americans has been rising over the period 1932 to 1978, using Stanford–Binet and Wechsler tests. Based on Japanese group IQ testing, several studies (e.g. Kaneko, 1971; Sano, 1974; Ushijima, 1961) have provided evidence of the massive gain of mean IQ scores over time. Ushijima (1961) administered the same IQ test to children (aged 9–15) in 1953 and to a comparable sample of children in 1960 and found that there was an IQ increase of 10 points. Kaneko (1971) and Sano (1974) also found increases similar to Ushijima's figure of 10 points. These findings from Japan were summarized by Lynn & Hampson (1986a) and Iwawaki & Vernon (1987). This IQ gain over time was also found in the USA and Britain (Flynn, 1982, 1984; Lynn & Hampson, 1986a). The Japanese gains were found to be the greatest of the three countries. Much yet remains to be solved on the causes of these remarkable gains of IQ scores over time.

The IQ estimates in Lynn's earlier study (Lynn, 1977) which suggested that intelligence of Japanese children is superior to that of their American counterparts should be adjusted for the dates of standardisation of the IQ used. Lynn adjusted the estimates of mean IQ in his later studies on Japanese IQ. Misawa, Motegi, Fujita & Hattori (1984) reported that the mean IQ for the Japanese sample was 113 in relation to the American mean IQ of 100, using the Japanese version of the Columbia Mental Maturity Scale (CMMS) which is a non-verbal test for young children. However, we should be careful how we interpret the mean IQ of Japanese children because the Japanese version of the CMMS was standardized ten years later than the standardization of the American version. It is worthy of note that the superiority of the intelligence of Japanese to American children occurred at the time when non-verbal tests were used for cross-national comparison.

Stevenson & Azuma (1983) suggested that it is not appropriate to make cross-national comparison of IQs with the omission of the verbal scale. Mean Japanese IQs of 106 (Lynn, 1977), 111 (Lynn, 1982), and 113 (Misawa *et al.*, 1984) were derived from non-verbal IQ tests only. There was no difference in overall mean IQ between Japanese and American children (Stevenson, Stigler, Lee, Lucker, Kitamuar

& Hsu, 1985). Thus the existing data present conflicting results. Lynn & Hampson (1986a) have suggested that the conflicting findings in Japanese intelligence lies in the distinctive pattern of intellectual ability among the Japanese. The proposal has been based on data obtained from the McCarthy Scale for Children's Abilities (Lynn & Hampson, 1986b) and the Wechsler Preschool and Primary Scale (Lynn & Hampson, 1987). In both studies, they found that Japanese children did not differ from white children in the United States on general intelligence (Spearman's *g*), obtained higher scores on the spatial primary, and scored lower on the group verbal factor. These findings are consistent with those of Stevenson *et al.* (1985). Many researchers have used tests with a spatial content which are supposed to be culture-fair. Non-verbal tests have often been used as a culture-fair instrument because these tests were supposed to avoid the translation problems of verbal tests. Several studies comparing the intelligence of Japanese children with that of American children have given high mean IQs for Japanese samples. These studies have usually used non-verbal tests with a strong spatial content. This suggests that Japanese children's superiority is dependent on spatial abilities. Lynn, Hampson & Iwawaki (1987) gave the abstract reasoning and space relations scales of the Differential Aptitude Test (DAT) to school children (13–15 years old) in the two Japanese schools: one was the secondary school in a fishing village and the other was in a dormitory town outside Tokyo. Since the Japanese data were collected 13 years later than the American standardisation data, Japanese mean IQs were adjusted for time lag. Thus the Japanese mean IQs based on the American mean of 100 (SD 15) were 104.5 for abstract reasoning and 114.0 for spatial ability. This result confirms the earlier studies showing that the Japanese score high on spatial ability. Findings of high spatial ability among American Orientals has been reviewed by Vernon (1982). Causation for high spatial ability among Oriental populations is unclear for the present, though some speculations may be possible.

The IQ gains over time on culture-fair tests and fluid intelligence tests were demonstrated by data from 14 nations by Flynn (1987) who suggested that the culture-fair tests do not measure intelligence and that inter-group IQ differences do not equate with those of intelligence. Major claims for the level of Japanese intelligence have been based on traditional IQ tests. Models of mental measurement employing IQ scores from traditional tests applied to different cultures have manifested themselves as inexact and inappropriate (Irvine & Berry, 1983). It is necessary to take a new approach to mental assessment. Many psychologists agree that a new approach to intelligence needs to bring together cognitive motivational, and social measures in scientific systems (Newstead, Irvine & Dann, 1986).

Cognitive styles

Witkin, Dyk, Faterson, Goodenough & Karp (1962) developed the concepts of cognitive style and psychological differentiation systematically. Witkin's work was mostly concerned with the contrast between field-independent and field-dependent cognitive styles and many cross-cultural studies (see Witkin & Berry, 1975) have tested the generalizability of Witkin's theory, using mainly the Rod and Frame Test (RPT) and the Embedded Figures Test (EFT). They emphasised that field-dependent people have a stronger tendency to conformity and affiliation. Werner (1979) reviewed several studies that were conducted in both Western and developing countries on psychological differentiation, and concluded that the more field-dependent cognitive style is widespread among autocratic societies which expect and encourage social conformity.

Japan is an autocratic and group-oriented culture in which people conform to group behaviour (DeVos, 1985; Morsbach, 1980). Since Japanese children are exposed to a socialisation which puts emphasis on psychological dependence on family and school, people may hypothesise that they would have high levels of field-dependent cognitive styles on the Children's Embedded Figure Test (CEFT). However, this hypothesis would be untenable since Japanese children are found to score well on spatial abilities tests. Hilger, Klett & Watson (1976) showed that a sample of 6-year-old Japanese boys scored significantly higher than did American boys of the same age, using the Harris revision of the Goodenough Draw-a-Man test which is related to the disembedding skills involved in psychological differentiation. Kojima (1978) tested 312 Japanese children (aged five to six) with a new simplified version of the EFT and found that the EFT did not correlate with one of the Wechsler subtests, Block Design, and that they were high scorers on his modified EFT. He suggested that though the EFT had usually been used without a time limit, field-independence might best be measured with speed tests. Using the original version of the EFT, Bagley, Iwawaki & Young (1983) tested English, Japanese and Jamaican children (aged 10 years old) and gave them a questionnaire for measuring perceived parental authoritarianism. The CEFT scores for Japanese children in both Japan and London were significantly higher than any of the non-Japanese groups. DeVos (1980) suggested that the Japanese would show conforming behaviour in school and elsewhere but develop a field-independent cognitive style. Bagley *et al.*'s findings support his suggestion. Means for parental authoritarianism of Japanese children were 10.7 in Japan and 10.6 in Japanese children in London. These means were close to those of the British children (10.9). The parental authoritarianism questionnaire showed no significant correlation with the CEFT scores in any of the groups, except Jamaican girls in rural Jamaica. The CEFT may be better interpreted as an ability test rather than a measure of socialised cognitive style, at least for Japanese children.

Another popular cognitive style is Kagan's reflectiveness-impulsiveness, which is assessed by the Matching Familiar Figures Test (MFFT) (Kagan, Rosman, Albert & Phillips, 1964). Hatano (1974) found that Japanese children made fewer errors and were more cautious and reflective before reaching decisions in comparison with their American white counterparts. This was confirmed by Salkind, Kojima & Zelniker (1978), who administered the MFFT to a number of American, Japanese and Israeli Children (aged 5 to 12 years). They showed that the Japanese children made fewest errors and that they became reflective two years earlier than did the other groups in cognitive development. Hatano & Inagaki (1976) also administered the MFFT, along with a tactual-visual matching test and two conceptual choice tests, to 51 Japanese children (aged 5–6 years). Reflective children on the MFFT showed longer latencies, and tended to spend some time seeking more information before they reached a decision. Furthermore, Hatano & Inagaki (1982) gave a questionnaire on four fictitious models (Reflective, Fast-Accurate, Impulsive, and Slow-Inaccurate) to 64 reflective and 58 impulsive fifth-graders and found that the reflective children rated the Fast-Accurate model brighter and the Slow-Inaccurate model more diligent than their impulsive counterparts.

Child-rearing practices play an important role in cognitive development. Forty-four Japanese children and 47 US children served as comparative samples in a longitudinal study (Hess, Holloway, Dickson & Price, 1984; Hess, Kashiwagi, Azuma, Price & Dickson, 1980; Kashiwagi & Azuma, 1981; Kashiwagi, Azuma & Miyake, 1982; Kashiwagi, Azuma, Miyake, Nagano, Hess & Holloway, 1984). A series of research investigations by Japanese and American groups revealed several family influences on children's achievement in school. Some Japanese children's behavioural characteristics reported by the mothers of 4-year-olds gave high correlations with cognitive measures obtained at 11–12 years. Negative correlations were found between impulsiveness and cognitive measures ($-.48$ for IQ and $-.46$ for school achievement ratings), and positive correlations were found between persistence and cognitive measures (.47 for IQ and .51 for school achievement ratings). In contrast, for American children these characteristics gave no significant correlations with any cognitive measures. The Japanese tend to be self-critical about their performance and sensitive to the criticism of outsiders (DeVos, 1985). The Azuma–Hess research group suggested that cognitive socialization in the Japanese family emphasizes obedience and conformity which are characteristics opposite to impulsiveness. Their findings also showed that the WISC-R intelligence test scores at age 11 were correlated more highly with non-verbal measures at age 4 than with other pre-school cognitive measures and that Japanese mothers required their child to perform well verbally less frequently than did their American counterparts. These may be related to the findings that the Japanese are strong on spatial abilities.

Conclusion

Individual difference research on Japanese children is not very active. Only a few papers on this topic have appeared in academic journals in Japan. Recently, the Japanese tend to emphasize egalitarianism in education regardless of the children's abilities rather than emphasizing equality of opportunity for receiving education according to the individual's abilities. This may be the reason why individual difference research has waned in Japan for the last decade.

Japanese children's scores on spatial ability tests are superior to those of American or British children, based on traditional tests developed in Western countries (mainly the United States). Japanese psychologists have used tests of cognitive abilities which were developed in Western countries or which were guided by the framework of cognitive ability theory constructed in the American tradition. Further research should make more efforts to understand the cognitive abilities of the Japanese people in the Japanese culture. Furthermore, it is necessary to construct a contemporary model that outgrows traditional intelligence theories and provides evidence for the generalisability of the model through cross-cultural researches.

References

AGARIE, Y. & OHNISHI, S. (1964) A study on regional differences in the structure of intelligence: comparisons of Okinawa and Kansai. *Japanese Journal of Educational Psychology*, **12**, 28–36.

BAGLEY, C., IWAWAKI, S. & YOUNG, L. (1983) Japanese children: group-oriented but not field dependent? In C. Bagley & G.K. Berma (eds.) *Multicultural childhood: education, ethnicity and cognitive styles*, 27–37. Aldershot, Hampshire: Gower.

CHRISTOPHER, R.C. (1984) *The Japanese mind*, London: Pan.

DEVOS, G. (1980) Ethnic adaptation and minority status. *Journal of Cross-Cultural Psychology*, **11**, 101–24.

DEVOS, G. (1985) Dimensions of the self in Japanese culture. In A.J. Marsella, G. DeVos & F.L. Hsu, (eds.) *Culture and self: Asian and Western perspectives* (141–84). New York: Tavistock.

EGAWA, R. (1956) Intellectual differences between rural children and city children: a factor analytic study. *Japanese Journal of Educational Psychology*, **4**, 102–9.

FLYNN, J.R. (1982) Lynn, the Japanese and environmentalism. *Bulletin of the British Psychological Society*, **35**, 409–13.

FLYNN, J.R. (1984) The mean IQ of Americans: massive gains 1932 to 1978. *Psychological Bulletin*, **95**, 29–51.

FLYNN, J.R. (1987) Massive IQ gains in 14 nations: what IQ tests really measure. *Psychological Bulletin*, **101**, (in press).

HATANO, G. (ED.) (1974) *Development of children and education* (Report No. 2), Tokyo: National Institute for Educational Research.

HATANO, G. & INAGAKI, K. (1976) Reflection-impulsivity in perceptual and conceptual matching tasks among kindergarten children. *Japanese Psychological Research*, **18**, 196–203.

HATANO, G. & INAGAKI, K. (1982) The cognitive style differences in the use of latency and the number of errors as cues for inferring personality characteristics. *Japanese Psychological Research*, **24**, 145–50.

HATTORI, K., MISAWA, G. & FUJITA, K. (1982) A comparison of item difficulty on the Columbia Mental Maturity Scale among Japanese and the United States children. *National Rehabilitation Center Research Bulletin*, **3**, 149–52.

HESS, R.D., HOLLOWAY, S.D. DICKSON, P.W. & PRICE, G.G. (1984) Maternal variables as predictors of children's school readiness and later achievement in vocabulary and mathematics in sixth grade. *Child Development*, **55**, 1902–12.

HESS, R.D., KASHIWAGI, K., AZUMA, H., PRICE, G.G. & DICKSON, W.P. (1980) Maternal expectations for mastery of developmental tasks in Japan and the United States. *International Journal of Psychology*, **15**, 259–71.

HILGER, M.I., KLETT, W.G. & WATSON, C.G. (1976) Performance of Ainu and Japanese six-year-olds on the Goodenough-Harris Drawing test. *Perceptual and Motor Skills*, **42**, 435–8.

HOFSTEDE, G. (1980) *Culture's consequences: international differences in work-related values*, Beverly Hills, CA: Sage Publications.

HUTCHINSON, S., ARKOFF, A. & WEAVER, H.B. (1966) Ethnic and sex factors in classroom responsiveness. *Journal of Social Psychology*, **69**, 321–5.

IRVINE, S.H. & BERRY, J.W. (eds.) (1983) *Human assessment and cultural factors*. New York: Plenum.

IWAWAKI, S. & VERNON, P.E. (1987) Japanese abilities and achievements. In S.H. Irvine & J.W. Berry (eds.) *Cultural context of human abilities*, New York: Cambridge University Press (in press).

KAGAN, J., ROSMAN, B.L., ALBERT, J. & PHILLIPS, W. (1964) Information processing in the child: significance of analytic and reflective attitudes. *Psychological Monographs*, **78** (578).

KANEKO, S. (1971) Changes in intelligence test performance during ten years. *Bulletin of Niigata University – Takata Branch*, **15**, 11–20.

KASHIWAGI, K. & AZUMA, H. (1981) Sex typing in the cognitive socialisation processes in Japan and the United States. *Japanese Journal of Psychology*, **52**, 296–300.

KASHIWAGI, K., AZUMA, H. & MIYAKE, K. (1982) Early maternal influence upon later cognitive development among Japanese children: a follow-up study. *Japanese Psychological Research*, **24**, 90–100.

KASHIWAGI, K., AZUMA, H., MIYAKE, K., NAGANO, S., HESS, R.D. & HOLLOWAY, S.D. (1984) Japan–US comparative study on early maternal influences upon cognitive development: a follow-up study. *Japanese Psychological Research*, **26**, 82–92.

KOJIMA, H. (1978) Assessment of field dependence in young children. *Perceptual and Motor Skills*, **46**, 479–92.

KUBO, Y. (1922) The revised and expanded Binet–Simon tests, applied to the Japanese children. *Journal of Genetic Psychology*, **29**, 187–94.

LERNER, R.N. (1986) *Concepts and theories of human development* (2nd ed.), New York: Random House.

LONNER, W.J. & BERRY, J.W. (1986) Sampling and surveying. In W.J. Lonner & J.W. Berry (eds.) *Field methods in cross-cultural research*, (85–110). Berry Hills, CA: Sage Publications.

LYNN, R. (1977) The intelligence of the Japanese. *Bulletin of the British Psychological Society*, **30**, 69–72.

LYNN, R. (1982) IQ in Japan and the United States shows a growing disparity. *Nature*, **297**, 222.

LYNN, R. & DZIOBON, J. (1980) On the intelligence of the Japanese and other mongoloid peoples. *Personality and Individual Differences*, **1**, 95–6.

LYNN, R. & HAMPSON, S. (1986a) The rise of national intelligence: evidence from Britain, Japan and the USA *Personality and Individual Differences*, **7**, 23–32.

LYNN, R. & HAMPSON, S. (1986b) Intellectual abilities of Japanese children: An assessment of $2\frac{1}{2}$–$8\frac{1}{2}$-year-olds derived from the McCarthy Scales of Children's Abilities. *Intelligence*, **10**, 41–58.

LYNN, R. & HAMPSON, S. (1987) Further evidence on the cognitive abilities of the Japanese: data from WPPSI. *International Journal of Behavioral Development*, **10**, 23–36.

LYNN, R., HAMPSON, S.L. & IWAWAKI, S. (1987) *Abstract reasoning and spatial abilities among American, British and Japanese adolescents*. (for submission)

MISAWA, G., MOTEGI, M., FUJITA, K. & HATTORI, K. (1984) A comparative study of intellectual abilities of Japanese and American children on the Columbia Mental Maturity Scale (CMMS). *Personality and Individual Differences*, **5**, 173–81.

MORSBACH, H. (1980) Major psychological factors influencing Japanese interpersonal relations. In N. Warren (ed.) *Studies in cross-cultural psychology*, vol. 2 (316–44). New York: Academic Press.

NAKAJIMA, T. (1954) Intellectual development of children and preadolescents in isolated villages. *Japanese Journal of Educational Psychology*, **2**, 211–16.

NEWSTEAD, S.E., IRVINE, S.H. & DANN, P.L. (eds.) (1986) *Human assessment: cognition and motivation*, Dordrecht: Martinus Nijhoff.

OHIRA, K. (1962) A study on the intelligence and the language proficiency of city and farm-village children. *Japanese Journal of Educational Psychology*, **10**, 107–12.

OSAKA, R. (1961) Intelligence tests in Japan. *Psychologia*, **4**, 218–34.

SALKIND, N.J., KOJIMA, H. & ZELNIKER, T. (1978) Cognitive tempo in American, Japanese and Israeli children. *Child Development*, **49**, 1024–7.

SANO, T. (1974) Change in intelligence test performance during eighteen years. *Japanese Journal of Educational Psychology*, **22**, 110–14.

SMITH, R.J. (1983) *Japanese society*, London: Cambridge University Press.

STEVENSON, H.W. & AZUMA, H. (1983) IQ in Japan and the United States. *Nature*, **306**, 291–2.

STEVENSON, H.W., STIGLER, J.W., LEE, S., LUCKER, G.W., KITAMURA, S. & HSU, C. (1985) Cognitive performance of Japanese, Chinese and American children. *Child Development*, **56**, 718–34.

SUGIMURA, T. (1980) Cognitive and motor abilities of young children in remote mountain areas and cities. *Japanese Journal of Educational Psychology*, **28**, 324–7.

TANAKA, K. (1934) A tentative scale for measuring general intelligence by non-language tests. *Japanese Journal of Psychology*, **9**, 62–5.

US STUDY OF EDUCATION IN JAPAN (1987) *Japanese education today*. Washington, DC: US Department of Education.

USHIJIMA, Y. (1961) Changes in IQ level. *Jido Shinri*, **15**, 629–35.

VERNON, P.E. (1982) *The abilities and achievements of Orientals in North America*, New York: Academic Press.

WERNER, E.E. (1979) *Cross-cultural child development: a view from the planet earth*. Belmont, California: Wadsworth.

WITKIN, H.A. & BERRY, J.W. (1975) Psychological differentiation in cross-cultural perspective. *Journal of Cross-Cultural Psychology*, **6**, 4–87.

WITKIN, H.A., DYK, R., FATERSON, W., GOODENOUGH, D. & KARP, S. (1962), *Psychological differentiation*, New York: Wiley.

12 The present status of juvenile delinquency problems in Korea

H.S. Lee

Introduction

In the last 50 years, juvenile delinquency has become a major concern to psychologists, criminologists and other applied scientists although Socrates discussed the problems of delinquency some 2500 years ago. In 1960, the Second United Nations Congress on the prevention of crime and treatment of offenders was held in London, England. After profitable and enthusiastic discussions, most of the participants agreed substantially on the seriousness of the problems posed by juvenile delinquency (Middendorff, 1960).

It is a well-known fact that crimes and juvenile delinquency problems are on the increase throughout the industrialized and urbanized countries of the world (Bloch & Geis, 1962). Since the Second World War, public concern about crime and juvenile delinquency has grown considerably in many European and Asian countries. Especially in technologically and economically advanced countries, juvenile delinquency problems are increasing at an alarming rate. This trend of an increase in juvenile delinquency is not limited to Europe and Asia, there being a similar trend in North America.

In this chapter, the present status of juvenile delinquency problems in Korea will be described including (1) a brief statement of the definition of delinquency, (2) some trends and statistics reflecting the kind and extent of juvenile crimes, and (3) an overview of the judicial treatment processes as it has evolved in recent years.

Definitions of juvenile delinquency

What is juvenile delinquency? Although it is of great interest and importance to psychologists, judges and applied scientists, there are no simple and clear definitions of it. The reason is that it has been defined from different points of view in different cultural and educational settings (Phillipson, 1971). Furthermore, professionals such as psychologists, sociologists, biologists, criminologists and even medical doctors each offered their own definitions based on their particular academic backgrounds. Consequently, there are many and varied definitions of juvenile delinquency.

Commonly, juvenile delinquency is understood as the failure of children and adolescents to meet certain obligations expected of them by the society in which they live (Cavan & Ferdinand, 1975). Owing to the present status of delinquency research, adoption of the legal definition of juvenile delinquency is almost mandatory for psychologists and behaviour scientists. The first juvenile delinquency law, passed by the State of Illinois in 1899, defined the delinquent as:

> A delinquent child is any male who under the age of 17 years, or any female who while under the age of 18 years, violates any law of this State; or is incorrigible or knowingly associates with thieves, vicious or immoral persons; or without just cause and without the consent of its parents, guardian or custodian, absents itself from its home or place of abode, or is growing up in idleness or crime; or knowingly frequents a house of ill repute; or knowingly frequents any police shop or place where any gambling device is operated; or

frequents any saloon or dram shops where liquors are sold; or patronizes or visits any police room or bucket shop; or wanders about the streets in the night time without being on any lawful business or lawful occupation; or habitually wanders about any railroad yards or tracks or jumps or attempts to jump onto any moving train; or enters any cars or engine without lawful authority; or uses vile, obscene, vulgar or indecent language in any school house; or is guilty of indecent or lascivious conduct (Huston, 1937).

The Children's Bureau (1972), a federal agency of the United States, also use a legal definition of delinquency as follows:

The juvenile delinquency cases are those referred to courts for acts defined in the statutes of the State as the violation of a state law or municipal ordinance by children or youth of juvenile court age, or for conduct so seriously antisocial as to interfere with the right of others or to menace the welfare of the delinquent himself or of the community. This broad definition of delinquency includes conduct which violates the law only when committed by children, e.g., ungovernable behaviour, and running away (US Department of Health, Education and Welfare, 1972, p. 7).

In Korea, juvenile delinquency is defined, in law, to include a juvenile (1) who is above the age of 14 and under 20 and has committed crimes, (2) who is above the age of 12 and under 14 and has contravened the criminal law and decrees, but who is exempted from criminal responsibility, (3) who habitually disobeys his guardians, (4) who leaves home without proper reasons, and (5) who associates with criminals, or immoral persons or who corrupts other persons' moral character (Chung, 1981).

The following are the main features or expressions of juvenile delinquency in Korea:

(1) theft; stealing
(2) rough and tumble crime; homicide, arson
(3) sex-related offences; forced rape
(4) group based offences; committed by more than two persons
(5) high frequency of offending in urban areas
(6) increasing number of younger offenders
(7) high frequency of juvenile delinquency behaviours without distinctive motives
(8) high rate of reconviction or recidivism (Chung, 1981).

The trend of juvenile delinquency problems in Korea

In order to identify, treat and prevent juvenile delinquency effectively, a national organization (Coordinating Committee of Youth governed by the Prime Minister) was founded in 1977. Before that, there was a small-scale specific committee, the Youth Guidance Committee, which was administered and governed by the Minister of Home Affairs. This shift to government level involvement indicates that juvenile delinquency is now regarded as one of the most serious problems in Korean society, just like in so many other countries.

Table 12.1 shows that from 1975 to 1984, a large number of juvenile criminals were placed under arrest. Arrested juvenile criminals in 1975 numbered 62 007, and increased steadily to 105 298 by 1984, constituting an increase of 69.82%. In the same period, the number of arrested male juvenile criminals increased from 57 508 to 99 805, a rate of increase of 73.55%, whereas arrested female juveniles increased from 4499 to 5493 or by 22.09%. It is quite clear that male criminals far outnumber female criminals and that the rate of delinquency increased at a greater rate for males than for females. Arrests of both male and female juveniles continue to increase in the 1980s.

Table 12.1 Total number of arrested Juvenile delinquents 1975–84*

Years \ Sex	Male	Female	Total
1975	57 508	4 499	62 007
1976	74 059	5 765	79 824
1977	77 739	5 991	83 730
1978	69 922	5 378	75 300
1979	74 639	4 601	79 240
1980	82 722	5 240	87 962
1981	82 976	5 960	88 936
1982	99 715	6 586	106 301
1983	96 803	6 285	103 088
1984	99 805	5 493	105 298

* Included special law offenders

From examination of the *Analysis of crimes*, published by the Office of Supreme Public Prosecutors, from 1975 to 1984, (1) violence offences (53.85%), (2) property offences (40.94%) and (3) barbarous criminal offences (5.21%) are clearly identified as the major juvenile delinquency problems in Korea. As the *Analysis of crimes* shows, the most serious aspect of juvenile delinquency in Korea has been violence offences since 1975. Among all arrested juvenile delinquents, 53.85% were for violence offences and from 1975 to 1984, the number of juvenile violence offenders increased by 64.42%.

From 1975 to 1984, the total number of arrested juvenile property offenders increased by 44.98%. This is a rather less marked increase than for other juvenile offenders during the same period. As far as property juvenile offenders are concerned, a greater increase was shown in the 1970s than the 1980s with the number of arrested property offenders gradually decreasing year by year from 1982 onward.

5.21% of delinquents who were under arrest during the last ten years were barbarous offenders. From 1975 to 1984, there was a marked increase equivalent to 141.18%. More details of changing trends of major juvenile criminals are shown in Table 12.2.

Major criminal offences

As Table 12.2 shows, juvenile violence offences consisted of injury, attack, blackmail and infringement of rules, the last being the most frequent. As far as infringement of rules are concerned, the number of arrested offenders increased by 74.23% from 1975 to 1982. From 1978 to 1984 the number of offenders arrested for blackmail increased by 83.14%. Comparing the number of blackmail offences between the 1970s and 1980s, there was an increase from the 1970s to the 1980s. From 1975 to 1984 there is no apparent change in the number of offenders arrested for injury except for the 1975 and 1982 period. The number of arrested attack offenders showed a gradual decrease in the 1980s in comparison with the 1970s. From 1975 to 1984 its number decreased by 20.70%.

Juvenile property offences consist of larceny, fraud and stolen goods. On the whole, the most frequent offences committed are larceny offences. As with other juvenile offences, from 1975 to 1982, there has been a considerable increase in the number of juvenile property offences. Larceny increased by 65.66% in the same period. From 1975 to 1980, the number of juveniles arrested for stolen property offences decreased by 23.76%. In 1975, only 1065 stolen property offenders were

Table 12.2   Sub-patterns of major juvenile offences 1975–84

Patterns of offences / Years	Violence offences					Barbarous offences					Total
	Injury	Attack	Infringement of rules	Blackmail	Sub-total	Homicide	Burglary	Forcible rape	Arson	Sub-total	
1975	972	802	26 433	194	28 401	81	1037	1100	55	2273	54 994
1976	1 190	874	32 394	195	34 653	60	982	1397	46	2485	69 703
1977	1 342	944	38 064	214	40 564	80	783	1702	49	2614	72 920
1978	1 345	820	34 010	172	36 347	64	716	1650	38	2468	62 275
1979	1 303	763	37 941	196	40 203	79	875	2093	45	3092	64 384
1980	1 278	683	39 763	290	42 014	88	1822	2278	28	4216	75 436
1981	1 203	655	35 935	271	38 064	86	1826	3152	59	5123	75 911
1982	1 611	786	46 053	301	48 751	93	1875	3642	53	5663	93 559
1983	1 444	673	42 824	297	45 238	103	1838	3360	57	5358	87 955
1984	1 483	636	44 262	315	46 696	79	2010	3342	51	5482	87 438

Patterns of offences / Years	Property offences				
	Larceny	Fraud	Stolen property	Others	Sub-total
1975	21 856	568	1 065	831	24 320
1976	29 572	670	1 316	1 007	32 565
1977	27 239	632	951	920	29 747
1978	21 131	618	838	873	23 460
1979	18 955	689	636	809	21 089
1980	26 929	714	812	721	29 206
1981	30 183	788	1 012	741	32 724
1982	36 183	949	1 192	821	39 145
1983	34 347	1 154	1 042	816	37 359
1984	31 834	1 773	920	733	35 260

arrested; this is a small number in comparison with other patterns of juvenile offenders in absolute terms, but there was a gradual increase from 1981 onward. As far as fraud is concerned, its rate of increase is far greater than any other type of offence. In 1975, only 568 fraud offenders were arrested, but by 1984 this had increased by 212.15%.

Juvenile barbarous offences include homicide, burglary, forcible rape and arson. In order of increasing frequency, they are forcible rape, burglary, homicide and arson. From 1975 to 1984, the number of forcible rapes showed a startling increase of 203.82%!

Between 1979 and 1980, the number of burglary offences increased by 108.22% and showed a steady increase until 1984. Offences of homicide and arson, however, have been only minor delinquency problems in Korea since 1975. Homicide offences showed a limited increase of 27.16% between 1975 and 1983, and since then have shown a considerable but gradual decrease. Arson offences remained steady and only a small number have been recorded since 1975.

To investigate the effect of age on delinquent behaviour, juvenile delinquents were divided into four groups: (1) under 14 years, (2) 14–15 years, (3) 16–17 years and (4) above 18 years. Without regard to the types of offences, the number of juvenile delinquents who were under 14 years old was considerably smaller compared to the number of delinquents who were above 18 years old (see Table 12.3).

Conduct disorder problems

As Table 12.4 shows, problems of conduct disorders are less serious than other juvenile delinquent behaviours in Korean society. To date, the most serious conduct disorder problems include: (1) smoking (21.57%), (2) drinking (17.85%), (3) fighting (14.34%) and (4) joining immoral groups (11.85%). From 1980 to 1984, juvenile smoking became the primary object of public attention as the most serious problem; of secondary importance is drinking. Together smoking, drinking, fighting and joining immoral groups account for 65.61% of the total number of conduct disorder problems. In this context, it is possible to hypothesize that juvenile smoking and drinking behaviours may be associated with other aspects of delinquency in Korea.

Student juvenile crimes

To obtain a more comprehensive understanding of the nature of juvenile delinquency, a broad division is made between (1) general juvenile crime and (2) student juvenile crime. As shown in Table 12.5, from 1975 onward, crimes committed by both general and student groups showed a gradual increase year by year. Moreover, the rate of student juvenile crime to general juvenile delinquency also showed a marked increase. In 1980, police arrested 26 615 student juvenile delinquents, which is equivalent to 30.26% of the total number of juvenile delinquents. From 1980 to 1983, the number of student juvenile delinquents to the total number of juvenile delinquents increased by 62.83%.

Further, student juvenile problems are compared with the total number of students in the same period. From 1975 to 1984, the total number of students increased by 68.42%. On the other hand, the total number of student criminals increased by 234.88%. As this figure indicates, student criminality far exceeds the increase in size of this group (Office of Supreme Public Prosecutor, 1975–84; Ministry of Education, 1975–84).

Table 12.6 shows that student juvenile delinquency also includes violence, property and barbarous offences. From 1975 to 1984, the number of violence and property offenders increased by 149.51% and 454.99% respectively, compared with a student

Table 12.3 Age distributions of major juvenile offences 1975–84

age / years	Under 14				14–15			
	Violence offences	Property offences	Barbarous offences	Sub-total	Violence offences	Property offences	Barbarous offences	Sub-total
1975	332	1 099	14	1 445	2 242	4 916	234	7 392
1976	296	1 855	22	2 173	2 508	6 792	226	9 526
1977	316	1 823	35	2 174	2 775	6 244	234	9 253
1978	314	1 357	23	1 694	2 571	4 985	287	7 843
1979	284	1 364	24	1 692	2 886	4 654	334	7 874
1980	278	1 970	44	2 292	3 505	7 666	566	11 737
1981	275	2 594	49	2 918	3 471	9 198	696	13 365
1982	368	2 840	50	3 258	4 784	11 177	744	16 705
1983	264	2 304	49	2 617	4 813	11 415	769	16 997
1984	344	1 534	38	1 916	4 813	10 527	743	16 083

age / years	16–17				above 18			
	Violence offences	Property offences	Barbarous offences	Sub-total	Violence offences	Property offences	Barbarous offences	Sub-total
1975	8 923	8 763	825	18 511	16 904	9 542	1 200	27 646
1976	11 212	11 620	922	23 754	20 637	12 298	1 315	34 250
1977	13 881	10 943	1 022	25 846	23 592	10 932	1 343	35 667
1978	12 055	8 381	1 053	21 489	21 407	8 737	1 105	31 249
1979	12 438	6 771	1 169	20 378	24 595	8 280	1 565	34 440
1980	13 480	9 701	1 626	24 807	24 751	9 869	1 990	36 610
1981	12 663	11 054	2 108	25 825	21 655	9 878	2 270	33 803
1982	16 971	13 439	2 348	32 758	26 628	11 689	2 521	40 838
1983	15 858	12 826	2 256	30 940	24 303	10 814	2 284	37 401
1984	15 829	11 836	2 268	29 933	25 710	11 363	2 433	39 506

Table 12.4 Patterns of conduct disorders 1980–4

Patterns of conduct disorders / Years	Illegal public entertainment	Drinking	Smoking	Fighting	Keeps bad company	Immoral sex relations	Illegal possession of weapons	Joining with misconduct groups	Possession of hallucinogens	Others	Total
1980	4 876	42 369	39 949	26 309	21 855	1 146	3 102	1 006	500	116 955	258 067
1981	3 529	38 923	43 811	26 371	21 685	795	2 055	425	357	79 422	217 373
1982	4 702	49 906	57 977	31 639	24 388	1 366	2 155	545	348	82 319	255 345
1983	4 678	53 797	69 137	33 791	29 761	1 117	1 842	530	328	87 623	282 604
1984	1 368	48 765	74 639	31 934	26 519	1 253	1 517	428	317	111 068	297 828

Table 12.5 General juvenile delinquency and students' juvenile delinquency 1980–4

Classification / Years	General juvenile delinquency	Students' juvenile delinquency	Ratio
1980	87 962	26 615	30.26
1981	88 936	32 383	36.41
1982	106 301	42 414	39.90
1983	103 088	43 338	42.04
1984	105 298	42 038	40.20

Table 12.6 Patterns of students' criminal offences 1975–84

Years \ Patterns of offences	Violence offences	Property offences	Barbarous offences	Others	Total
1975	8 124	2 464	124	1 841	12 553
	(64.7)	(19.6)	(1.0)	(14.7)	
1976	9 803	4 041	140	2 671	16 655
	(58.9)	(24.3)	(0.8)	(16.0)	
1977	11 197	4 475	99	2 657	18 428
	(60.8)	(24.3)	(0.5)	(14.4)	
1978	10 522	4 189	128	2 821	17 660
	(59.6)	(23.7)	(0.7)	(16.0)	
1979	12 609	4 638	154	3 162	20 563
	(61.3)	(22.6)	(0.7)	(15.4)	
1980	13 954	8 563	365	3 733	26 615
	(52.4)	(32.2)	(1.4)	(14.0)	
1981	15 201	11 134	372	5 675	32 383
	(46.9)	(34.4)	(1.1)	(17.5)	
1982	21 169	14 442	528	6 275	42 414
	(49.9)	(34.1)	(1.2)	(14.8)	
1983	19 959	15 213	487	7 679	43 338
	(46.1)	(35.1)	(1.1)	(17.7)	
1984	20 270	13 675	1 950	6 143	42 038
	(48.2)	(32.5)	(4.6)	(14.6)	

population increase of only 68.42%. This figure also points out that the increasing rate of violence and property offences exceeded the rate of increase of the population. Surprisingly, for ten years or so, barbarous offences showed more than a fifteen-fold increase.

As in the case of general juvenile delinquency, the majority of student juvenile problems occurred in the larger cities, and a negligible number occurred in small cities. On the whole, irrespective of regional conditions, student juvenile delinquency showed a gradual increase year by year. By 1980, the rate of student juvenile criminals to the total number of juvenile delinquents was 56.44%, then it increased to 60.96% in 1984. A lack of 'distinctive motives' is one of the features of student juvenile delinquency problems; they broke the law by chance, or impulsively. Very few student juvenile delinquents broke the law out of boredom, vanity or because of a grudge against someone (Office of Supreme Public Prosecutor, 1975–84).

Ability and school attainment of juvenile offenders

Levels of education
With an increase in the time spent in school, as Table 12.7 shows, the number of student offenders has increased steadily from 1975 to 1984. Over the same time period, the number of illiterate (from 2.4% to 0.8%) and primary school grade delinquents (from 42.8% to 12.7%) has decreased considerably year by year. In contrast the number of middle school grade (from 30.9% to 33.1%), high school grade (from 21.6% to 40.7%), and university and college level (from 1.3% to 3.5%) delinquents has increased gradually year by year.

Levels of intelligence
Regardless of the pattern of juvenile convictions, more than 40% of juvenile delinquents have an average level of IQ (89–111), whereas a negligible proportion

Table 12.7 Educational levels of juvenile criminals 1975–84

Years \ Levels of education	Illiterate	Primary school	Middle school	High school	University	Others	Total
1975	1 495	26 550	19 173	13 410	830	549	62 007
	(2.4)	(42.8)	(30.9)	(21.6)	(1.3)	(0.9)	
1976	1 985	33 068	23 256	17 200	871	3 444	79 824
	(2.5)	(41.4)	(29.1)	(21.5)	(1.1)	(4.3)	
1977	1 497	32 461	25 569	19 946	954	3 303	83 730
	(1.8)	(38.8)	(30.5)	(23.8)	(1.1)	(3.9)	
1978	1 121	24 293	24 302	19 864	943	4 777	75 300
	(1.5)	(32.3)	(32.3)	(26.4)	(1.3)	(6.3)	
1979	853	22 527	25 803	23 589	1 330	5 138	79 240
	(1.1)	(28.4)	(32.6)	(29.8)	(1.7)	(6.5)	
1980	816	24 720	29 254	27 812	1 644	3 716	87 962
	(0.9)	(28.1)	(33.3)	(31.6)	(1.9)	(4.2)	
1981	808	20 176	30 108	29 939	1 945	5 960	88 936
	(0.9)	(22.7)	(33.8)	(33.7)	(2.2)	(6.7)	
1982	768	19 621	36 222	39 806	2 962	6 922	106 301
	(0.7)	(18.5)	(34.1)	(37.4)	(2.8)	(6.5)	
1983	723	17 537	34 970	40 464	3 385	6 009	103 088
	(0.7)	(17.0)	(33.9)	(39.3)	(3.3)	(5.8)	
1984	794	13 314	34 623	42 609	3 690	9 548	105 298
	(0.8)	(12.7)	(33.1)	(40.7)	(3.5)	(9.1)	

of offences were committed by delinquents who have extremely high or low IQ levels (over 128 or under 69) (Institution of Juvenile Classification, 1980–1984).

Standard of living

The majority of juvenile crimes were committed by delinquents from lower class home backgrounds, although juvenile delinquents from middle and upper middle class home backgrounds also broke the law quite often. Quite recently, however, there has been a gradual change in the standard of living of juvenile delinquents in Korea. The number of juvenile delinquents from lower class home backgrounds has shown a gradual decrease since 1978, while the number from middle class home backgrounds has increased proportionately. In 1975, 92.5% of juvenile crimes were committed by delinquents from the lower class, whereas in 1984, this had decreased to 88.5%. In 1975, 7.1% of all juvenile crimes were committed by juvenile delinquents from the middle class, increasing to 11.0% in 1984. It is noteworthy that changes took place in the number of juvenile crimes by lower and middle class delinquents but not in upper class delinquents at all (Office of Supreme Public Prosecutors, 1975–1984).

Seasons

Throughout the seasons of the year, the frequency of juvenile crimes in Korea is constant except for winter (January–March). In summer (July–September, a relatively larger number of juvenile criminals were arrested than in winter (Office of Supreme Public Prosecutors, 1975–84).

Regions

The majority of juvenile crime occurs in the larger cities, increasing from 56.9% in 1980 to 63.7% in 1984. In the medium-sized cities, the number of juvenile offences exhibits a steady increase although its absolute number is less than that of the larger cities. In 1980, 10.2% of all juvenile delinquents arrested came from medium-sized cities, and this increased to 12.1% by 1984. On the other hand, in regions other than big and medium sized cities, delinquency arrests showed a gradual decrease; 33.0% in 1980 decreasing to 24.2% in 1984 (Office of Supreme Public Prosecutors, 1975–84).

This extensive set of statistics portrays the growing problem of juvenile delinquency. The next section of this chapter will focus on the various agencies and groups involved in the identification and treatment of juvenile delinquents.

Treatment officers

Priority is given to judicial guidance rather than punishment in the process of intervention and treatment for juvenile delinquency in Korea. An exception, however, is made in the case of delinquents who commit heinous crimes (e.g. habitual violence) and who do not show promise of responding to treatment or those who are too aggressive and unable to control their impulsiveness. They are subject to criminal punishment just like adult criminals.

As a rule, the police, the prosecutor and the judge are expected to treat juvenile delinquency with judicial guidance rather than criminal punishment. Different kinds of correctional institutions are available; the Institution of Juvenile Classification, the Institution of Juvenile Reformatory, and the Juvenile Prison. Moreover, in order to provide more intensive after-care for delinquents who have been discharged from different levels of correctional institutions, Institutions of Rehabilitative Protection and Protection Homes are operated in this country.

The police

According to the Juvenile Acts, the police are responsible for the prevention and treatment of juvenile delinquency problems. They are obligated to investigate the kinds and motives of crimes, the delinquents' personal affairs and environmental conditions, then send a report pertaining to the case to the prosecutor. The police are responsible for sending delinquents to the Juvenile Court or Juvenile Department of District Court.

The prosecutor

In order to maintain public peace and social order, the prosecutor is responsible for investigating crime, making sure that the court applies the law adequately, and advising offenders on the function of judicial guidance. In the process of treatment of juvenile delinquents, the prosecutor is obligated to investigate the delinquents' environmental conditions and personality characteristics, and has to make disposal decisions about delinquents, based on the results of their investigations. Those delinquents who are expected to need certain kinds of judicial protection, will be allocated to the most suitable institution. On the other hand, those who cannot be expected to reform or benefit from rehabilitation efforts will be punished just like adult criminals.

Korea operates a system of indictment suspension, which applies to those who have been judged in need of judicial guidance rather than punishment. To facilitate the successful operation of this system, the Minister of Justice or the Chief Prosecutor of the District Office of Prosecutors nominates suitably qualified persons to membership on a Civilian Judicial Guidance Committee. Qualifications are as follows: (1) full membership in the community, (2) public confidence from the community, (3) engagement in certain occupations and (4) interest in and commitment to the prevention and correction of juvenile delinquency. By 1982, members of this Committee numbered 4236. Of those delinquents who had their indictments suspended in 1984, only 128 of them (1.5%) were later reconvicted (Coordinating Committee of Youth, 1985).

The judge

The Juvenile Court is identified with the Family Court or the Juvenile Department of the District Court. There is a Juvenile/Family Court in Seoul and Juvenile Departments in seven District Courts in Korea. Here, the judge is responsible for investigating and examining the nature of the crime which was committed by the delinquents, and then has to decide whether to punish them or not based on investigators' reports. There are a limited number of qualified investigators associated with the Juvenile Court or the Juvenile Departments of the District Courts. The investigator has two functions; to (1) place the juvenile delinquent on probation and (2) conduct psychological and psychiatric investigations on juvenile delinquents and to present the available evidence to the judge. There are six different probational treatments that may be arranged in the Juvenile Court by the judge:

(1) place the juvenile concerned under the care and custody of his or her guardian or other eligible person;
(2) place the juvenile concerned with a temple, church and other organizations protecting juveniles;
(3) place the juvenile into hospital or other sanatorium;
(4) transfer the juvenile to the reform school;
(5) place the juvenile to Juvenile Reformatory;
(6) place the juvenile concerned under supervision.

Correctional agencies

Institution of Juvenile Classification

With the object of conducting scientific diagnosis and investigation, the Seoul Institution of Juvenile Classification was founded in 1977. Subsequently, three more Institutions, with the same purpose, were established in district areas. According to juvenile law, the institution has a mandate to classify and conduct the diagnostic assessment of juvenile delinquents. The Institution's specific functions are to: (1) make accurate judgements on the advisability of probation, (2) understand the motives of the delinquent behaviour and (3) detect the delinquents' behaviour at as early a stage as possible. In practice, the investigators use various psychological tests (intelligence, aptitude and interest tasks), in order to get more reliable and scientific evidence for diagnosis and investigation. At the same time, they carry out medical assessments, especially EEG to those suspected of having organic or neurological injury.

Institution of Juvenile Reformatory

As a rule, the Institution functions as an educational or correctional organization rather than as a part of the legal machinery. The Institution accommodates the juvenile delinquent who has been transferred from the Family Court or the Juvenile Department of the District Court for correctional or educational training. Programmes consist of not only fundamental educational programmes, but also vocational programmes to facilitate the social rehabilitation of the delinquent. The Institution of Juvenile Reformatory is divided into four groups depending on regional characteristics: (1) Institution for Formal Education Training, (2) Institution for Vocational Training, (3) Institution for Agricultural Management and (4) Comprehensive Institution.

In the early stages of classification, the instructor or therapist investigates their social backgrounds and personal affairs in order to collect reliable and objective data on the individual juvenile delinquent. They also consult the results of psychological tests and medical investigations to assist in the planning of educational programs. Whenever instructors or therapists feel that delinquents need to talk to their parents or guardian, they arrange this without hesitation. Results of the examination of each delinquent are referred immediately to the Treatment Committee at the Institution of Juvenile Reformatory.

The Treatment Committee allocates the individual delinquents into one of the following treatment plans after comprehensive examination of the test results and the nature of the delinquent's problems:

(1)   if the delinquents' problems are so mild that they are likely to reform, they are allocated a short term treatment programme (less than six months);
(2)   if the delinquents' problems seem more difficult to remediate, they are allocated to a mid-term treatment programme (more than six but less than twelve months);
(3)   if the delinquents' problems are so severe that there appears to be a small likelihood of solving them, they are allocated to a long term treatment programme (more than twelve months).

It is also possible to shorten the length of training programmes and arrange early discharge from the institution in order to encourage self control and self monitoring of behaviour by individual delinquents.

At the first stage of retraining, the instructor or therapist arranges the programmes so as to correct trainees' undesirable ways of living, and cultivate healthy living attitudes. They are encouraged to learn acceptable modes of behaviour and language as well as to become more aware of social attitudes, values and norms. To acquire desirable human relationship skills, the therapist encourages the youth to participate in informal or formal group activities, as well as recreational programmes. Upon recognising the need for specialist counselling services for the delinquent, the instructor or the therapists can arrange this without hesitation.

At the second stage of retraining, fundamental educational services are implemented. Individual delinquents are allocated to different classes depending on their previous educational backgrounds and school achievement. They are assigned to 33–38 hours per week of intensive classroom work.

At the third stage of retraining, special educational programmes are available to them. This is the preparatory stage for their return to society. To accomplish this purpose more effectively, priority is given to vocational training. Such an arrangement is believed to minimize the after-effects of institutionalization and to encourage social skills. Formal vocational education was first inaugurated for juvenile delinquents in Korea in 1973.

Juvenile prison

The Juvenile Prison was founded to separately accommodate the delinquent who is sentenced to penal servitude or imprisonment. The two Juvenile Prisons in Korea are located in Incheon and Kimcheon. The Incheon facility caters to male first offenders who are under the age of 20 years and were educated beyond the middle school level. On the other hand, the Kimcheon facility contains male recidivist offenders who are under 20 years of age and were educated below the primary school level. Unfortunately there is no equivalent to the Juvenile Prison for females in Korea. They are accommodated in the women's prisons with complete separation.

In the Juvenile Prison setting, priority is given to educational training and correctional activities rather than punishment as is the case for adult criminals. The incarcerated delinquent benefits from school subject courses and vocational training. For illiterates, this offers them the first opportunity to acquire formal education. On the other hand, it offers many delinquents the opportunity to continue their formal education from primary to high school level without the interruption which could otherwise be expected from imprisonment.

The juvenile prison provides the various examination classes for those who aim to achieve educational certification. They may earn different levels of educational qualifications depending on their learning ability and examination results. The youth in Juvenile Prison also benefit from guidance education and can acquire healthy living attitudes and ways of self-improvement.

After-care systems

In order to be effective in preventing re-offending or recidivism and in guiding the juvenile delinquent, wherever possible priority is given to social treatment rather than judicial intervention and treatment in institutional settings. To successfully achieve these objectives, two kinds of institutions were founded in Korea: The Institution of Rehabilitative Protection and The Protection Home.

The Institution of Rehabilitative Protection

The Institution of Rehabilitative Protection accommodates discharged delinquents from Juvenile Prison and The Institution of Juvenile Reformatory, or those whose indictments were suspended by the prosecutor. They are protected in different ways; by home placement, probation, employment guidance, vocational training, providing funding for rehabilitatin, and arranging to meet a socially benevolent person.

The Institution has ten district offices and by 1984, the Committee of Rehabilitative Protection numbered 5500 members in Korea. The Ministry of Justice operates a probation system for delinquents discharged from Juvenile Prison or the Juvenile Reformatory, who are at risk for offending. To prevent recidivism of juvenile delinquents, each member of the Committee of Rehabilitative Protection makes home visits, gives judicial guidance and helps discharged delinquents to improve their home environment and friendships.

Protection homes

The Protection Home is provided under the children's welfare law as one of the civilian level organizations. The Home accommodates those children who are expected to recommit juvenile crimes, to continue to behave immorally, or those discharged from the Juvenile or Family Court. To date, there are ten civilian level Protection Homes in Korea. The best known one is Seongji Vocational Guidance Home, which is located in Daedeokkoon, Choongcheongnamdo, in the middle regional part of the Republic of Korea.

Advocates for change in the treatment of juvenile delinquents

Although juvenile delinquency is, in part, a psychological problem, psychologists have only begun to study its causes scientifically. Neumeyer (1961) declared as follows: 'Statistics of juvenile crime is rather a description of traffic through juvenile courts and law enforcement agencies'. As mentioned in previous paragraphs, there is a lack of reasonable theoretical systems and research methodology when undertaking epidemiological studies of criminal and delinquent behaviour. Since juvenile delinquency in Korea is rising year by year, and is now posing an even greater threat to society than before, delinquency problems are receiving much more attention at governmental and civilian levels.

Coordinating Committee of Youth

In order to facilitate effective guidance, treatment and prevention of juvenile delinquency problems, a nationally authorized organisation, called the Coordinating Committee of Youth was founded in Korea. Even before 1977, there was a small scale committee, named the Youth Guidance Committee, which was administered by the Minister of Home Affairs.

The Coordinating Committee of Youth consists of a chairman, a vice-chairman and a limited number of members. As a rule, some state ministers and some socially important persons usually become members of the Committee. Unfortunately, no psychologists or behavioural science specialists sit on the Committee. The 3216 Local District Committees of the Coordinating Committee of Youth have four main aims:

(1) planning the fundamental strategy for guidance, training and protection of juveniles;
(2) coordinating the strategy of youth administrations;
(3) establishment and management of facilities for juveniles;
(4) planning and developing practices of cultivating the body and mind, guidance of and induction into civilian youth clubs.

Activities of civilian organizations for the rehabilitation and protection of juvenile delinquents

To date, there are more than 30 civilian level organizations involved in the rehabilitation and protection of juvenile delinquents, which are supported by some three million people (Cha, 1983). Specific aims of the organizations are as follows:

(1) the prevention of delinquent behaviour; considerable emphasis is placed on religious education to improve the mental states of individuals and to relieve mental tension and a sense of alienation. Individual delinquents are required to become involved and to participate in formal as well as informal group activities. To acquire fundamental knowledge and understand their family as well as the community and to cultivate citizenship, public lectures are made available to them;
(2) therapy of delinquents' problems; for the juvenile delinquent who has mild psychological problems, special counselling services are provided. On the other hand, the delinquent who has serious psychological problems is referred to behaviour therapists or psychiatrists as soon as possible.

A decade ago, a few criminologists in Korea actively crusaded to reform the treatment processes of juvenile delinquents (Kim, 1981). According to their opinions, juvenile delinquency should not necessarily be treated by judicial officers such as police, prosecutor and judge, because it is not a pure judicial problem in principle, but rather a definite psychological problem. They insisted that juvenile delinquents should be referred to behavioural scientists who emphasize probation, parole and rehabilitation rather than punishment.

Campaigns for reformation in judicial treatment processes

In addition to the previously mentioned campaigns, another group of criminologists carried out new campaigns for reform in the judicial treatment processes for juvenile delinquents (Kim, 1973). They also insisted that judicial officers such as the police, prosecutor and judge have to make large concessions to behavioural scientists. In practice, they put great store on ideas of correction and protection rather than punishment. It was recommended that the treatment of juvenile delinquency should recognize and include the following points:

(1) the priority of the prosecutor should be eliminated in the course of judgement;
(2) the extension of the Juvenile court and Family Court as a treatment agency;
(3) more scientific investigation and classificatory systems should be operated in the process of juvenile delinquency judgement;
(4) induction of a probation system in juvenile delinquency judgement;
(5) induction of more intensive educational and training programmes at the Juvenile Reformatory.

Summary

Korea has adopted laws or decrees with formal definitions of juvenile delinquency as follows: (1) those who are above the age of 14 and under 20 and commit crimes, (2) those who are above the age of 12 and under 14 who commit acts which are contrary to criminal laws and decrees, but are exempted from criminal responsibility, (3) those who habitually disobey the supervision of their guardians, and (4) those who leave home without proper reasons and (5) those who associate with criminals or immoral persons or habitually corrupt other persons' moral character.

According to the *Analysis of crimes*, which produces the most authoritative statistics of crimes in Korea, in recent years the number of juvenile delinquents has sharply increased, and their behaviours are 'rough in manner', group based, intellectualized and their average age is decreasing. From 1975 to 1984, the rate of juvenile delinquency increased by 69.82%, and the major Korean juvenile delinquency problems include: violence offences, property offences and barbarous offences. The standard of education of juvenile delinquents has risen and more than 40% of juvenile delinquents have an average IQ level of 89–111. The number of juvenile delinquents from middle class home backgrounds has shown a gradual increase since 1975. The frequency of juvenile crime is fairly constant except for winter, and the majority of offences occur in the larger cities.

Problems of conduct disorders are less serious in comparison to other delinquents' behaviours. Since 1980, juvenile smoking and drinking have become the object of public attention as one of the more serious social problems in Korea. Student juvenile crime increased greatly in recent years and frequently appears to be 'impulsive' acts.

In practice, priority is given to judicial guidance rather than punishment in the treatment of juvenile delinquency in Korea, so that special judicial processes are provided for some exceptional cases. There are different levels of correctional institutions: Institution of Juvenile Classification, Institution of Juvenile Reformatory,

Juvenile Prison and finally, to provide more intensive after-care to the delinquent who has been discharged from the different levels of correctional institutions, the Institution of Rehabilitative Protection and the Protection Home. These agencies and provisions are intended to meet the individual needs of delinquents in an effort to ensure their rehabilitation.

References

BLOCH, H.A. & GEIS, G. (1962) *Man, crime and society: the forms of criminal behaviour*. New York: Random House.

CAVAN, R.S. & FERDINAND, T.M. (1975) *Juvenile delinquency*. Philadelphia: J.P. Lippincott.

CHA, K.S. (1983) Juvenile delinquency and the judicious guidance. *Studies in Juvenile Delinquency*, **1**, 231.

CHUNG, T.K. (1981) *A Study on the prevention of recommitment of crimes in juvenile delinquency*. Seoul: Pupjosa.

COORDINATING COMMITTEE OF YOUTH (1985) *Annual reports of youth*. Seoul: Coordinating Committee of Youth, Office of Prime Minister.

HUSTON, W. (1937) *Social welfare laws of the forty-eight states*, Seattle, Washington: Wendell Huston.

Institution of Juvenile Classification (1984) *Classification of juvenile delinquency*. Seoul.

KIM, C.W. (1981) *Present status of juvenile delinquency in Korea: problems and strategies for juvenile delinquent behaviour*. Thesis collection, Ministry of Justice, Seoul, Korea.

KIM, C.D. (1973) A study on the treatment of juvenile delinquents in Korea. *Seoul Law Journal*, **14**, 5–36.

MAYS, J.B. (1963) *Crimes and social structure*, London: Faber.

MIDDENDORFF, W. (1960) *New forms of juvenile delinquency: their origin, prevention and treatment*, New York: United Nations, Department of Economic and Social Affairs.

MINISTRY OF EDUCATION (1975–85) *Statistics of education*. Seoul.

NEUMEYER, M.H. (1961) *Juvenile delinquency in modern society*, Princeton: D. Van Nostrand.

Office of Supreme Public Prosecutors. *Analysis of crimes*, Seoul: Office of Supreme Public Prosecutors, 1975–85.

PHILLIPSON, M. (1971) *Sociological aspects of crime and delinquency*, London: Routledge & Kegan Paul.

SOUTHERLAND, E.M. & CRESSEY, D.R. (1960) *Principle of criminology*, Philadelphia: J.B. Lippincott.

Training Institute (1985) *Reports on crimes*, Seoul: Training Institute, Ministry of Justice.

US Department of Health, Education and Welfare (1972) *Juvenile court statistics: 1971*, Washington, DC: Government Printing Offices.

13 Sex differences in psychosocial adjustment among Lithuanian schoolchildren

*A. Goštautas, A. Pakula &
L. Grinevičiene*

Introduction

Psychosocial adjustment is a complicated multivariate phenomenon reflecting the extent to which a balanced interaction between personality and the social environment can be achieved through processes of psychological regulation. The latter are believed to have a great impact upon the ill/health issue in psychosomatic medicine. Thus, such behavioural manifestations as type A behaviour, smoking, alcohol consumption and low physical activity have often been strongly related to a risk of developing ischemic heart disease. On the other hand, it has been documented that prevalence of both, risk factors and ischemic heart disease, are sex-related, and this may be partly a biological fact and partly be determined by differential socialization in childhood and adolescence. Therefore, in addition to biological sex differences, it might be reasonable to look for a clue to the problem in different psychosocial adjustability of males and females *in toto*. Following this line of reasoning, in nature versus nurture terms, the question should also be posed about the feasibility of effective intervention upon certain behavioural variables playing (presumably) a crucial role in psychosomatic medicine much earlier than the first signs of the disease become manifest. In this sense, studies of psychosocial adjustment in children and adolescents is a promising approach.

Below we present some of the evidence accumulated by us from 1976 to 1986 while studying various aspects of psychosocial adjustment in Lithuanian schoolchildren.

Since our target population was schoolchildren, a few words would be appropriate here in presenting the high school education system effective in Lithuania.

At the time of this study, the high school education in Lithuania envisaged 11 years of studies, eight of which were compulsory. The general tendency on the part of school authorities was to exert pressure on schoolchildren to induce them to leave high school after having finished compulsory education and to go to work or continue studying at a vocational school. The major concern of high schools at that crucial point would usually be to get rid of those schoolchildren considered by form monitors and teachers, to be 'incapable'. Usually, the decision about one's academic aptitudes would be based on a number of various objective and subjective criteria that essentially would boil down to the same concept of psychosocial adjustability. Albeit the majority of such dropouts can really be labeled as less adjusted at that point, the opposite might not be claimed for the continuers, who for a variety of causes usually represent a mixture of individuals with different degrees of psychosocial adjustment.

Sex differences of a self-concept

To get a better insight into the problems of psychosocial adjustment in children and adolescents, we employed two approaches, self-rating and expert rating. Since these approaches are predominantly believed to reflect inner psychological regulation processes and their outward-projected manifestations respectively, we were interested in finding out the personality features that might correlate with manifest behaviour patterns by which the degree of one's social adjustment is judged by society.

Polar adjectives

As one of the instruments for self-evaluation, a form with 164 original scales of Lithuanian polar adjectives reflecting various behavioural responses and psychological peculiarities of the subject was used, with 400 8th to 11th form pupils. In addition to two end-scale anchor words each scale had five unlabeled gradations.

Table 13.1 shows only those mean scores (± SEM) that significantly, $p < .05$, discriminated between sexes.

In general, boys more often than girls displayed a socially 'undesirable' self-concept. They were comparatively less good-hearted, more disregarding regulations, undisciplined, disobedient, dressing tastelessly, doing worse at school, non-diligent, hypocritical, untidy, niggardly, mocking, ruthless and cunning. Some qualities as presented by boys may be considered indicative of their greater emotional stability in comparison with girls; they accept their failures more easily, keep their temper better, are more manly, experienced, imperturbable and hard-boiled. Boys more often than girls present a self-concept characteristic of the adults' behaviour known as type A which is believed to be predisposing to the development of myocardial infarction; they are comparatively *more* eager for superiority, self-confident, challenging, inventive, dominating, aggressive, vindictive, cruel, planning, firm, resistive, resolute, competitive, strong and rough.

The profile of the girls' self-concept qualities significantly discriminating between sexes was shifted to labels as follows: merciful, gullible, shy, unpretentious, decent, open-hearted, doubtful, keeping to regulations, disciplined, elegant, good-hearted, doing well at school, homely, modest, proud, uninventive, peaceful, meticulous, submissive, feeling failures keenly, easily upset, feminine, sincere, naive, nervous, acting without a plan, dandy, reserved, agreeing, vacillating, noncompetitive, weak, honest, tender, generous, sympathetic, delicate, following orders and meek.

The EPQ and the EPI

The greater emotionality of girls was also confirmed by the greater rate of their positive answers to items 3, 20, 24, 32, 36, 40, 82 and 89 of the EPQ (see Table 13.2) belonging to the neuroticism scale, as well as to item 43 from the extraversion scale.

As shown in Table 13.2, boys significantly more often rated items 88 & 93 of the EPQ higher, thus suggesting their greater rigidity. Also, they were more active in making new friends (item 42-E).

A parallel study, involving the use of the EPI with 916 schoolgirls and 629 schoolboys of forms 7 to 11, showed sex differences significant at a $< .05$ level for all the scales, with girls scoring higher, on the Extraversion scale, 12.0 ± 3.1 vs. 11.4 ± 3.2, and on Neuroticism, 13.9 ± 4.1 vs. 11.1 ± 3.9. However, a tangible difference was found for the greater neuroticism in girls only.

Differences of psychosocial adjustment

Expert rating

In an attempt to find out the relationship between personality traits and psychosocial adjustment, schoolchildren were classified into groups based on the evidence from standardized interviews with their form monitors, classmates, and parents.

Form monitors, who served as the basic source of reference, were questioned in two stages. Firstly, they were asked to list their 'most negative' pupils and these were considered as the most maladjusted ones, group MM; then, again according to their own criteria, they listed the 'most positive', i.e. well-adjusted, pupils (group AA); next-to-the-most-positive (group A) and next-to-the-most-negative (group M) schoolchildren. The pupils that had not been mentioned at all were assigned by us to the intermediate group, group I, which actually represented a population norm. At the second stage, the form monitors were asked to characterize each of their pupils and to expose the reasoning why they had assigned a given subject to a given adjustment group.

In this way 675 schoolchildren (377 girls and 298 boys) of forms 7 through 11 were classified by their 24 form monitors as follows: 66 Ss (10%) went to group MM, 78 Ss (11%) to group M, 142 Ss (21%) to group A and 133 Ss (20%) to group AA. The remaining 256 Ss (38%) were considered as belonging to group I.

There were more boys, 31%, than girls, 14%, in the two maladjusted groups, MM and M. This difference was even more clear-cut if group MM only was considered, 17% versus 4% respectively. At the other extreme, in groups AA and A, girls dominated, even though not in such an evident manner, 40% versus 38%.

The behaviour characteristics on which form monitors most often based their judgements while classifying their pupils as well-adjusted (groups AA and A) or maladjusted (groups MM and M) are presented in Tables 13.3 and 13.4 respectively, with % prevalence and rank number data presented by sex.

In well-adjusted children and adolescents, form monitors would emphasize their doing well at school, dutifulness, academic abilities, social activeness, amicability (cf Table 13.3). Girls exceeded boys in such entities as social activeness, industriousness, participation in amateur talent activities, and tidiness. Boys were *more often* reported as well-read, authoritative and, somewhat unexpectedly, as affectionate, compassionate and polite as compared with girls.

As seen from Table 13.4, maladjusted boys and girls displayed certain differences in their characteristics as described by their form monitors. So, maladjusted boys were *more often* than maladjusted girls characterized as disobedient, undisciplined, lazy, agile, nervous, weak-willed and susceptible to evil influences; whereas girls were *more often* failing in schoolwork, abrupt, easily losing their temper.

The greater prevalence of behaviour patterns incompatible with the accepted school regulations in schoolboys was also indicated by a 'peer rating' conducted among the best of the class employing a list of 40 six-graded characteristics of maladjusted behaviour. Such an evaluation of the 9th form pupils, 860 girls and 579 boys, showed that as many as 36 out of the 40 characteristics were significantly ($p < .05$) more frequent for boys than girls.

Although the greater prevalence of maladjusted behaviour among boys, as against girls, is evident with either teachers' or peers' classification, this is generally not sufficient to infer a lower overall adjustability of boys, since such rating is usually based on social behaviour only and does not reflect the psychological adjustment level. For instance, a person suffering from loneliness or anxiety may be successfully masking his/her psychological maladjustment with socially desirable behaviour, consciously or not. The opposite may be true as well. Such possibilities should be allowed for when considering individual cases; however, in our instance, this could only have diminished the contrasts observed in the comparisons performed.

Self-rating using polar adjectives

To assess psychological aspects of adjustment in Lithuanian schoolchildren, the above-mentioned self-evaluation techniques employing 164 seven-graded scales of polar adjectives was used.

Table 13.1   Polar adjectives and mean scale scores (± SEM) significantly discriminating between sexes on self-rating in schoolchildren aged 12 through 18 years

		Schoolboys	Schoolgirls
(1)	Open-hearted — Devious	3.10 ± 1.3	2.70 ± 1.2
(3)	Active — Passive	3.23 ± 1.3	2.88 ± 1.4
(4)	Cunning — Gullible	4.11 ± 1.6	4.87 ± 1.5
(5)	Ambitious — Unpretentious	2.94 ± 1.3	2.52 ± 1.4
(14)	Attentive — Distracted	2.92 ± 1.4	2.53 ± 1.4
(15)	Doubtful — Decided	4.16 ± 1.6	3.50 ± 1.5
(18)	Disregarding regulations — Keeping to regulations	4.16 ± 1.6	4.86 ± 1.6
(23)	Preferring things — Preferring people	4.94 ± 1.6	5.34 ± 1.6
(24)	Courageous — Timid	2.81 ± 1.2	3.05 ± 1.2
(26)	Industrious — Lazy	2.66 ± 1.2	2.32 ± 1.1
(27)	Decent — Indecent	2.72 ± 1.3	1.95 ± 1.1
(28)	Shy — Impudent	3.28 ± 1.4	2.95 ± 1.5
(29)	Disciplined — Loose	3.19 ± 1.4	2.51 ± 1.2
(32)	Elegant — Tasteless	2.96 ± 1.2	2.37 ± 1.1
(33)	Good-hearted — Callous	2.41 ± 1.2	2.01 ± 1.0
(36)	Clever — Dull	2.50 ± 1.1	2.44 ± 1.1
(41)	Vivacious — Cold	3.07 ± 1.6	2.53 ± 1.5
(42)	Having pity for him/herself — Ruthless to him/herself	3.94 ± 1.7	3.55 ± 1.6
(43)	Doing well at school — Failing in schoolwork	3.53 ± 1.5	2.95 ± 1.4
(44)	Proud — Humble	3.20 ± 1.1	2.82 ± 1.2
(49)	Idealist — Materialist	3.71 ± 1.2	3.44 ± 1.2
(52)	Defiant — Homely	4.41 ± 1.5	4.94 ± 1.6
(53)	Imperative — Begging	4.02 ± 1.5	4.54 ± 1.6
(54)	Inventive — Uninventive	2.78 ± 1.2	3.40 ± 1.3
(57)	Faithful — Unfaithful	2.59 ± 1.3	2.2 ± 1.3
(58)	Bellicose — Peaceful	4.02 ± 1.9	4.74 ± 1.8
(60)	Modest — Boastful	2.90 ± 1.2	2.63 ± 1.3
(63)	Tending to group activities — Individualistic	2.87 ± 1.4	2.52 ± 1.3
(64)	Vindictive — Merciful	3.74 ± 1.8	4.52 ± 2.0
(67)	Meticulous — Unscrupulous	2.93 ± 1.3	2.50 ± 1.2
(69)	Militant — Submissive	3.13 ± 1.5	3.76 ± 1.6
(71)	Taking his/her failures easy — Feeling his/her failures keenly	4.05 ± 1.6	4.89 ± 1.8
(74)	Easily upset — Undisturbable	4.24 ± 1.6	3.34 ± 1.7
(81)	Polite — Cheeky	2.59 ± 1.2	2.34 ± 1.2

	Schoolboys	Schoolgirls
(83) Feminine — Masculine	5.89 ± 1.4	1.68 ± 1.1
(86) Sincere — Hypocritical	2.58 ± 1.2	2.12 ± 1.1
(88) Natural — Haughty	2.54 ± 1.3	2.21 ± 1.2
(89) Quick-witted — Slow-witted	2.65 ± 1.1	2.40 ± 1.1
(92) Naïve — Experienced	5.03 ± 1.2	4.37 ± 1.3
(93) Imperturbable — Nervous	4.27 ± 1.5	4.76 ± 1.5
(98) Self-confident — Hesitating	3.23 ± 1.6	5.20 ± 1.7
(100) Envious — Nonenvious	4.79 ± 1.6	5.20 ± 1.7
(111) Compliant — Evading	3.77 ± 1.7	3.37 ± 1.6
(112) Planning actions — Acting at random	2.60 ± 1.3	3.09 ± 1.5
(114) Dandy — Untidy	3.46 ± 1.0	2.94 ± 1.0
(116) Mocking — Reserved	4.04 ± 1.6	4.89 ± 1.5
(118) Objecting — Agreeing	3.58 ± 1.6	4.20 ± 1.5
(119) Resolute — Vacillating	2.96 ± 1.4	3.55 ± 1.6
(123) Serious — Frivolous	3.25 ± 1.4	2.86 ± 1.6
(124) Competitive — Noncompetitive	2.37 ± 1.2	2.92 ± 1.4
(125) Rational — Emotional	3.19 ± 1.5	3.59 ± 1.7
(130) Abrupt — Sluggish	2.75 ± 1.2	3.10 ± 1.2
(132) Strong — Weak	2.83 ± 1.2	3.57 ± 1.3
(133) Diligent — Lax	3.21 ± 1.2	2.76 ± 1.1
(134) Self-critical — Self-uncritical	3.02 ± 1.4	2.65 ± 1.4
(136) Honest — Fraudulent	2.90 ± 1.5	2.32 ± 1.2
(142) Rude — Tender	4.69 ± 1.3	5.35 ± 1.4
(143) Avaricious — Generous	5.00 ± 1.3	5.53 ± 1.2
(145) Neat — Messy	2.50 ± 1.2	2.14 ± 1.2
(146) Economical — Wasteful	3.30 ± 1.9	3.94 ± 2.0
(148) Straightforward — Guileful	3.74 ± 1.7	3.30 ± 1.6
(150) Sympathetic — Intolerant	2.10 ± 1.1	1.71 ± .9
(153) Hardened — Delicate	2.53 ± 1.1	2.90 ± 1.4
(154) Capricious — Undemanding	3.51 ± 1.3	3.19 ± 1.4
(157) Directing — Executing	3.80 ± 1.4	4.27 ± 1.6
(159) Imperious — Obedient	3.65 ± 1.4	4.07 ± 1.6
(161) Sociable — Recluse	2.71 ± 1.4	2.40 ± 1.3
(162) Cruel — Meek	4.63 ± 1.5	5.39 ± 1.4

Table 13.2   The EPQ items yielding largest differences between percent rates of schoolboys and schoolgirls answering to them positively

		Boys	Girls
(3)	Does your mood often go up and down?	49.5	70.8
(20)	Are your feelings easily hurt?	39.4	67.4
(24)	Do you often feel 'fed-up'?	31.7	43.8
(32)	Would you call yourself a nervous person?	38.2	55.5
(36)	Are you a worrier?	30.8	43.8
(40)	Do you worry about awful things that might happen?	50.0	69.4
(42)	Do you usually take the initiative in making new friends?	54.8	27.1
(43)	Can you easily understand the way people feel when they tell you their troubles?	70.2	85.4
(82)	Do you suffer from 'nerves'?	23.3	36.7
(88)	Do you sometimes like teasing animals?	64.1	39.3
(89)	Are you easily hurt when people find fault with you or the work you do?	46.1	63.1
(93)	Would you like other people to be afraid of you?	35.3	21.3

Table 13.5 gives the mean scale scores ($\pm$ SEMs) for a comparison between socially well-adjusted schoolboys (groups AA and A) and group I for age group 12 through 18 years. Only scales with mean scores differing at a level of $p < .05$ have been presented. Analogous data for schoolgirls are shown in Table 13.6.

Socially better-adjusted schoolboys had a self-concept with the trait profile statistically significantly shifted, with respect to the 'population norm' (group I),

Table 13.3   Characteristics most often used by form monitors in describing their well-adjusted pupils

	Schoolboys		Schoolgirls	
	Percent	Rank	Percent	Rank
Doing well at school	33	1	37	1
Dutiful	23	2	25	2
Talented	20	3	18	5
Polite	20	4	10	13
Socially active	17	5	22	3
Affectionate & compassionate	17	6	11	12
Sincere	16	7	14	7
Amicable	15	8	17	6
Authoritative	15	9	3	16
Industrious	14	10	20	4
Honest	13	11	14	8
Quiet & calm	13	12	14	9
Well-read	12	13	5	15
Good-hearted	9	14	13	11
Going in for amateur talent activities	7	15	14	10
Tidy	4	16	10	14

Table 13.4 Characteristics most often used by form monitors in describing their maladjusted pupils

	Schoolboys		Schoolgirls	
	Percent	Rank	Percent	Rank
Lazy	33	1	22	4
Disobedient, undisciplined	26	2	11	14
Weak-willed	24	3	12	13
Failing in schoolwork	22	4	31	1
Abrupt, easily losing his/her temper	22	5	27	2
Incompetent	21	6	24	3
Undutiful	19	7	17	7
Liar	18	8	21	5
Agile	18	9	11	15
Nervous	18	10	11	16
Conflicting	16	11	14	10
School-fleer	15	12	19	6
Susceptible to evil influences	15	13	10	17
Disliked by others	14	14	16	8
Reticent	14	15	16	9
Neglecting home assignments	14	16	14	11
Dishonest, cunning	12	17	13	12

towards qualities as follows: righteousness, academic abilities, progress in studies, creativity, correctness, nonconservatism, fast learning, being busy, activeness, comprehension, tact, optimism, originality, straight-forwardness and leadership. Well-adjusted schoolgirls significantly distinguished themselves from the 'normals' by quick orientation, progress in studies, pride, intellect, diligence and leadership.

Socially maladjusted boys were significantly more shifted, as compared with 'normals', towards such qualities as poor self-control, dissoluteness, distraction, impudence, flunking, hyperactiveness, lack of diligence, cruelty, and negligence (cf Table 13.7).

Socially maladjusted schoolgirls significantly more often had a self-concept of being *relatively more* feminine, masterly, sincere, reliable, tender, wasteful, sociable, daring, ambitious, courageous, elegant, enduring, creative, lively, failing in school-work, and *less* individualistic, envying and idealistic.

Time factor in psychosocial adjustment

Important issues in psychosocial adjustment studies in children and adolescents are, whether the very shift from one ontogenetic stage to another may tangibly affect behaviour patterns, and how much of an undesirable behaviour can be corrected by direct intervention on certain variables.

To assess the possibility of reasonable prediction of psychosocially adjusted or maladjusted behaviour throughout childhood and adolescence, we have carried out several studies.

Dropouts versus continuers
As stated earlier, one of the 'hard' endpoints reflecting the psychosocial maladjustment in Kaunas schoolchildren is their leaving high school just after the eight years of compulsory schooling. In one study, we checked a hypothesis that dropouts would

Table 13.5　Self-concept qualities significantly discriminating between socially well-adjusted schoolboys and their population norm in age group 12–18 years

	Well-adjusted	Populat. norm
(4) Cunning — Gullible	4.56 ± 1.3	3.86 ± 1.7
(20) Alert — Listless	2.20 ± 1.1	2.63 ± 1.2
(22) Disbalanced — Well-balanced	5.44 ± 1.4	4.84 ± 1.4
(23) Preferring things — Preferring people	5.33 ± 1.5	4.66 ± 1.6
(29) Disciplined — Loose	2.61 ± 1.1	3.09 ± 1.2
(36) Clever — Dull	2.11 ± .8	2.69 ± 1.2
(43) Doing well at school — Failing in schoolwork	2.49 ± 1.3	3.60 ± 1.2
(47) Well-educated — Ignorant	2.60 ± .9	3.00 ± 1.2
(62) Creative — Without ideas	2.62 ± 1.2	3.26 ± 1.3
(65) Correct — Ill-mannered	2.42 ± 1.0	2.93 ± 1.0
(66) Conservative — Experimenting	5.27 ± 1.3	4.48 ± 1.3
(73) Slow learner — Fast learner	5.52 ± 1.3	4.20 ± 1.7
(87) Indolent — Energetic	5.61 ± .9	4.85 ± 1.4
(88) Natural — Haughty	2.17 ± 1.0	2.62 ± 1.2
(89) Quick-witted — Slow-witted	2.23 ± .8	2.79 ± 1.1
(91) Tactful — Upstart	2.18 ± .9	2.79 ± 1.2
(94) Optimistic — Pessimistic	2.51 ± 1.2	3.22 ± 1.1
(95) Original — Banal	2.56 ± 1.0	3.07 ± 1.0
(99) Flattering — Upright	5.26 ± 1.0	4.70 ± 1.1
(103) Intelligent — Silly	2.11 ± 1.0	2.51 ± 1.!
(104) Simple — Sophisticated	2.38 ± 1.3	2.86 ± 1.3
(106) Having manifold interests — With limited interests	2.25 ± 1.0	2.64 ± 1.2
(133) Diligent — Lax	2.70 ± 1.1	3.20 ± 1.0
(142) Rude — Tender	5.09 ± 1.2	4.61 ± 1.4
(157) Directing — Executing	3.42 ± 1.3	4.03 ± 1.3

continue to present more problems of psychological adjustment as compared with continuers even after some time has passed.

To check for the continuity of the trend, 150 boys and 150 girls were sampled from the dropouts out of 753 schoolboys and 874 schoolgirls that had been studied two years ago while in the 8th form (at an age of 15); and a comparison of their mean scores on clinical scales of the MMPI was performed with respective values for the schoolchildren continuing high school education.

Table 13.8 shows the MMPI scales with mean scores higher for the dropouts. It can be seen that both boys and girls were characterized by increased mean scores on the same Pa, Pt, Sc, Ma, and At scales. Only boys displayed an increase in Hs, D, Pd, and Si, while only girl dropouts scored higher than continuers on the F scale.

Thus, the dropouts, in general, showed a significantly worse psychological adjustment even two years after leaving school. Our findings show that dropouts

Table 13.6 Self-concept qualities significantly discriminating between socially well-adjusted schoolgirls and their population norm in age group 12–18 years

		Well-adjusted	Populat. norm
(2)	Cautious — Daring	2.82 ± 1.6	3.66 ± 2.0
(4)	Cunning — Gullible	5.42 ± 1.5	4.74 ± 1.5
(5)	Ambitious — Unpretentious	2.08 ± 1.2	2.67 ± 1.4
(6)	Authoritative — Without authority	2.60 ± 1.2	3.19 ± 1.3
(23)	Preferring things — Preferring people	5.90 ± 1.3	5.21 ± 1.6
(27)	Decent — Indecent	1.64 ± .9	2.02 ± 1.1
(43)	Doing well at school — Failing in schoolwork	1.57 ± .8	3.00 ± 1.4
(44)	Proud — Humble	2.32 ± 1.1	2.90 ± 1.3
(47)	Well-educated — Ignorant	2.53 ± 1.1	3.07 ± 1.1
(54)	Inventive — Uninventive	2.96 ± 1.2	3.50 ± 1.3
(55)	Agile — Slow	3.32 ± 1.6	2.53 ± 1.6
(61)	Critical — Tolerant	2.96 ± 1.2	3.61 ± 1.6
(62)	Creative — Without ideas	2.64 ± 1.1	3.21 ± 1.3
(103)	Intelligent — Silly	1.92 ± 1.0	2.51 ± 1.1
(133)	Diligent — Lax	2.14 ± .8	2.83 ± 1.2
(157)	Directing — Executing	3.50 ± 1.6	4.32 ± 1.5

are basically at an increased risk of developing a psychosomatic illness due to a predisposing background of emotional tension, as well as suggesting a rather permanent character of the psychological basis underlying maladjustment.

Trend persistence in continuers
On the other hand, the more positive characteristics of continuers as compared with dropouts do not imply homogeneity of psychological adjustment levels among them.

To test the predictability of maladjusted behaviour in adolescents, we compared the MMPI profiles of 456 schoolgirls and 306 schoolboys as evaluated in the 8th form with their adjustment levels rated by their form monitors in the 11th form (at the age of 18). The hypothesis was, that schoolchildren with the worst MMPI profiles in the 8th form would tend to cluster, as assigned by independent form monitors, in worst-adjusted groups.

Indeed, a retrospective analysis supported this hypothesis. So, schoolchildren who were worst-adjusted in the 11th form had increased mean scores on a number of clinical MMPI scales while in the 8th form, as compared with adjusted pupils (cf Table 13.9). The maladjustment was associated with increased scores on F, Pd, Pa, Sc and Ma scales, and this was characteristic of either sex. Among maladjusted girls, the Hy and Pt scale scores were increased as well, even though not to a level of significance. There was no difference in mean At scores.

What do maladjustment predictors predict?
The data from the two above-mentioned studies show that the evidence of impaired adjustment revealed at an age of 15 years has quite a long-term predictive power for social behaviour problems in Lithuanian schoolchildren.

Table 13.7 Self-concept qualities significantly discriminating between socially maladjusted schoolboys and their population norm in age group 12–18 years

	Maladjusted	Populat. norm
(14) Attentive — Distracted	3.39 ± 1.4	2.81 ± 1.4
(21) Without self-control — Self-controlled	4.44 ± 1.6	5.19 ± 1.4
(27) Decent — Indecent	3.24 ± 1.4	2.62 ± 1.1
(28) Shy — Impudent	4.00 ± 1.6	2.97 ± 1.2
(29) Disciplined — Loose	3.87 ± 1.6	3.09 ± 1.2
(43) Doing well at school — Failing in schoolwork	4.42 ± 1.6	3.60 ± 1.2
(52) Defiant — Homely	3.94 ± 1.7	4.59 ± 1.4
(55) Agile — Slow	1.96 ± 1.2	2.58 ± 1.4
(58) Bellicose — Peaceful	3.37 ± 1.8	4.12 ± 2.1
(65) Correct — Ill-mannered	3.42 ± 1.2	2.93 ± 1.0
(67) Meticulous — Unscrupulous	3.37 ± 1.5	2.75 ± 1.2
(77) Wrangler — Yielder	2.73 ± 1.6	3.40 ± 1.8
(81) Polite — Cheeky	3.11 ± 1.5	2.51 ± 1.1
(91) Tactful — Upstart	3.38 ± 1.5	2.79 ± 1.2
(95) Original — Banal	2.65 ± 1.1	3.07 ± 1.0
(97) Principled — Conformist	3.20 ± 1.7	3.98 ± 1.7
(116) Mocking — Reserved	3.57 ± 1.7	4.14 ± 1.5
(118) Objecting — Agreeing	3.15 ± 1.6	3.83 ± 1.7
(122) Quiet — Rebellious	4.00 ± 2.0	3.26 ± 1.5
(126) Concentrated — Absent-minded	3.77 ± 1.4	3.23 ± 1.3
(133) Diligent — Lax	3.75 ± 1.3	3.18 ± 1.0
(135) Restrained — Hothead	3.26 ± 1.7	2.47 ± 1.2
(146) Economical — Wasteful	3.84 ± 2.1	3.12 ± 1.8
(147) Silent — Noisy	4.62 ± 1.9	3.98 ± 1.6
(154) Capricious — Undemanding	3.10 ± 1.3	3.61 ± 1.3
(162) Cruel — Meek	3.92 ± 1.6	4.80 ± 1.4

As far as specific predictors of maladjustment are concerned, we found, in a comparative study of 49 delinquent adolescent girls, that the latter had considerably increased mean scores on F (19.9 ± 6), Pd (26.6 ± 4), Pt (23.7 ± 8) and Sc (31.2 ± 9) scales. On the other hand, a group of adolescent girls followed up because of various mental problems scored lower on the same scales, as compared with delinquents: F, 16.8 ± 8; Pd, 21.2 ± 5; Pt, 18.8 ± 8; and Sc, 24.7 ± 11. This finding may be indicative of these scales being predominantly sensitive to the social adjustment entity.

In this context, of interest are some other results from an anamnestic analysis of case records of adolescents followed up because of mental problems. So, on the basis of the data on 30 items included in the routine case record, quite a notable

Table 13.8 MMPI scales with mean scores (mean ± SEM) for the high school dropouts higher than for the continuers two years after finishing the compulsory education

	Dropouts	Continuers
Boys		
Hs (Hypochondriasis)	9.5 ± 4	7.2 ± 4*
D(Depression)	28.2 ± 6	24.7 ± 4[ns]
Pd (Psychopathic deviate)	22.2 ± 4	19.7 ± 5[ns]
Pa (Paranoia)	14.2 ± 7	12.7 ± 4**
Pt (Psychasthenia)	19.2 ± 9	15.4 ± 7**
Sc (Schizophrenia)	24.3 ± 5	19.4 ± 9**
Ma (Hypomania)	18.3 ± 4	16.9 ± 5[ns]
Si (Social introversion)	33.4 ± 7	31.6 ± 7[ns]
At (Anxiety)	20.6 ± 7	17.4 ± 7**
Girls		
F (Validity)	12.8 ± 7	9.7 ± 5**
Pa (Paranoia)	14.2 ± 7	12.7 ± 4**
Pt (Psychasthenia)	19.2 ± 9	15.4 ± 7**
Sc (Schizophrenia)	23.2 ± 10	19.0 ± 9**
Ma (Hypomania)	18.1 ± 5	16.8 ± 5**
At (Anxiety)	21.5 ± 7	19.5 ± 8[ns]

[ns] nonsignificant, * $p < .05$, ** $p < .001$

section of them became socially deviant: 49.3% (378 out of the total 767 adolescents aged 14–18 years) in Kaunas and 31.8% (232/729) in Vilnius. Except for one case, which was girls from a boarding school for the crippled, boys were prevailing among the socially deviant Ss. from different institutional settings (high schools, specialized boarding schools, schools for mentally retarded). Among socially deviant high school students, boys accounted for as much as 76.7% in Kaunas and 72.6% in Vilnius.

An analysis of living conditions did not reveal any substantial difference between the socially deviant and the control adolescents with mental problems. On the other

Table 13.9 Relationship between a significantly ($p < .05$) increased MMPI scale profile in the 8th form and the maladjustment in the 11th form

	Maladjusted	Adjusted
Boys		
F (Faking)	11.7 ± 5	7.6 ± 4
Hy (Hysteria)	21.0 ± 6	18.3 ± 5
Pd (Psychopathic deviate)	21.5 ± 4	16.6 ± 4
Pa (Paranoia)	14.0 ± 5	10.6 ± 4
Pt (Psychasthenia)	17.0 ± 8	14.0 ± 6
Sc (Schizophrenia)	22.3 ± 10	15.3 ± 7
Ma (Hypomania)	18.6 ± 5	14.7 ± 4
Girls		
F (Faking)	12.0 ± 4	8.6 ± 5
Pd (Psychopathic deviate)	22.2 ± 4	18.5 ± 5
Pa (Paranoia)	14.4 ± 4	12.2 ± 4
Sc (Schizophrenia)	21.0 ± 8	17.6 ± 8
Ma (Hypomania)	20.1 ± 3	16.1 ± 4

Table 13.10   Significantly age-dependent qualities of a self-concept in a comparison between age groups 12–15 and 16–18 years

	12–15 years	16–18 years
Boys		
(5) Ambitious — Unpretentious	3.11 ± 1.4	2.67 ± 1.2
(10) Prudent — Impulsive	2.76 ± 1.2	3.25 ± 1.5
(17) In low spirits — In high spirits	5.07 ± 1.6	5.61 ± 1.2
(28) Shy — Impudent	3.07 ± 1.3	3.64 ± 1.5
(44) Proud — Humble	3.39 ± 1.1	2.85 ± 1.1
(47) Well-educated — Ignorant	3.27 ± 1.2	2.55 ± 1.1
(57) Faithful — Unfaithful	2.41 ± 1.1	2.91 ± 1.6
(61) Critical — Tolerant	3.49 ± 1.2	3.05 ± 1.3
(73) Slow learner — Fast learner	4.29 ± 1.8	5.07 ± 1.7
(77) Wrangler — Yielder	3.30 ± 1.7	2.72 ± 1.5
(97) Principled — Conformist	4.13 ± 1.7	3.02 ± 1.2
(99) Flattering — Straightforward	4.72 ± 1.3	5.17 ± 1.3
(106) Having manifold interests — With limited interests	2.76 ± 1.2	2.32 ± 1.3
(111) Compliant — Evading	3.58 ± 1.7	4.10 ± 1.7
(118) Objecting — Agreeing	3.76 ± 1.6	3.20 ± 1.5
(121) Exacting — Not exacting	3.27 ± 1.2	2.54 ± 1.0
(134) Self-critical — Self-uncritical	3.20 ± 1.4	2.75 ± 1.2
(138) Day dreamer — Realist	2.36 ± 1.4	3.64 ± 1.7
(146) Economical — Wasteful	3.09 ± 1.9	3.66 ± 1.8
(157) Directing — Executing	4.03 ± 1.3	3.39 ± 1.4

hand, it was found that the family life conditions might be of importance in determining socially deviant behaviour. Thus, socially deviant Ss. were more likely to come from families in which parents were separated (61.3% vs. 37.3% in controls) or divorced (16.9% vs. 7.4%). Also, they more often had a stepfather (11.6% vs. 3.4%) or lived separately from their parents (18.7% vs. 10.9%); their mother (9.9% vs. 1.8%) and father (24.3% vs. 15.2%) were alcohol consumers and used physical punishment of their children (10.7% vs. 2.9%).

To summarize, the psychosocial maladjustment in schoolchildren and the socially deviant behaviour in adolescents, both apparently mentally sane delinquents and social deviants from the contingent with mental problems, display a parallelism in the sense of increased mean scores on some clinical scales of the MMPI. Since socially deviant behaviour seems to correlate with certain conditions in adolescents' family life, one may expect that an intervention on those variables could be one clue to improving the psychosocial adjustment status among children and adolescents in general.

Age-dependent changes in self-concept
Interestingly, only mean scores on two out of the 164 scales of polar adjectives reflecting personality traits did change with age in both sex groups of schoolchildren.

		12–15 years	16–18 years
(159)	Imperious — Obedient	3.82 ± 1.4	3.35 ± 1.3
Girls			
(2)	Cautious — Daring	3.30 ± 2.0	4.05 ± 1.9
(3)	Active — Passive	2.63 ± 1.4	3.14 ± 1.4
(12)	Hot-tempered — Cold-tempered	2.94 ± 1.4	3.48 ± 1.5
(36)	Clever — Dull	2.59 ± 1.3	2.96 ± 1.1
(55)	Agile — Slow	2.36 ± 1.4	2.77 ± 1.7
(62)	Creative — Without ideas	2.90 ± 1.3	3.25 ± 1.3
(64)	Vindictive — Merciful	4.24 ± 1.9	4.81 ± 2.0
(71)	Takes her failures easy — Feels her failures keenly	4.63 ± 1.8	5.16 ± 1.7
(87)	Indolent — Energetic	4.75 ± 1.6	5.21 ± 1.4
(97)	Principled — Conformist	3.85 ± 1.7	3.18 ± 1.7
(110)	Confident — Nonconfident	2.28 ± 1.2	2.00 ± 1.1
(124)	Competitive — Noncompetitive	2.73 ± 1.3	3.12 ± 1.5
(129)	With adjustment problems — Easily adjusting herself	4.62 ± 1.7	5.09 ± 1.7
(138)	Day dreamer — Realist	2.38 ± 1.3	2.77 ± 1.6
(143)	Avaricious — Generous	5.33 ± 1.3	5.70 ± 1.1
(156)	Busy — Idle	2.70 ± 1.6	3.16 ± 1.7
(160)	Crybaby — Even-tempered	5.18 ± 1.6	5.57 ± 1.3
(162)	Cruel — Meek	5.19 ± 1.4	5.60 ± 1.3

They were items 97 and 138, showing an increase in principledness and realism with age.

All other age-sensitive personality traits were different for the two sex groups (see Table 13.10). Thus, schoolboys appear to become more ambitious, impulsive, impudent, arrogant, critical, prone to argue, principled, straight-forward, objecting, exacting, directing and imperious with age. All these characteristics are related to certain patterns of social behaviour the majority of which would traditionally be sex-typed as rather 'masculine'. On the other hand, many of the age-related changes in personality reflect the development of what might be called truth-seeking attitudes towards surrounding reality, so characteristic of teenagers. This is also indicated by their self-reported increasing realism (item 138) and self-criticism (item 134). Other age-dependent changes in self-concept qualities of Lithuanian schoolboys were less arrayed. With increasing age, schoolboys were more often in high spirits, better-educated, less faithful, learned more quickly, developed manifold interests, became more evading and wasteful.

Schoolgirls displayed significant changes in fewer 'truth-seeking' behaviour characteristics as compared with boys. Their psychological 'masculinization' with increasing age was limited by their becoming more daring, energetic, principled and even-tempered. However, at the same time they reported significantly more often about increased presumably 'feminine' characteristics such as becoming more passive, slow-moving, less creative, noncompetitive, idle, meek and generous. With increasing age, schoolgirls would also evaluate themselves as less clever, which can be explained as another result of their developing more realistic judgements (cf item 138).

The self-concept changes observed with age in both sexes could be accounted for by either natural and social sex-typing of behaviour or by the elimination of a (presumably 'the worse') part of the class after the compulsory schooling (see above) could substantially affect the distribution of certain personality traits by the end of high school education. Our data cannot directly provide a definite answer to this question; nevertheless, the finding of quite different patterns of qualities subject to changes with age in the two sex groups explicitly indicates that they should rather be ascribed to the first of the above-said mechanisms.

Smoking

A particular case of age-dependent behaviour is represented by smoking. Smoking habit is one of the manifestations of socially negative behaviour predominantly characteristic of boys. In this country, it can be viewed as an important clue to one's personality, since for some five years an impressive national-scale antismoking campaign has been going on aimed at developing negative attitudes towards smoking at community and national levels. In these circumstances, smoking therefore should be considered as a challenging act, especially in schoolchildren.

A large-scale survey of smoking prevalence involving the entire Kaunas schoolchildren population of 22 000 we conducted in 1986, revealed a clear-cut increase in smoking prevalence among both boys and girls, across the eight age groups studied (Table 13.11).

Table 13.11   Prevalence (percent) of smoking among Kaunas schoolchildren population of 22 000 as a function of age (the 1986 survey data)

	Form							
	4th	5th	6th	7th	8th	9th	10th	11th
Boys	2.4	2.9	5.4	14.9	26.4	35.4	52.2	61.1
Girls	0.1	0.2	0.9	3.9	8.0	12.5	24.4	32.6

The finding that smoking prevalence continues to rise even after a considerable group of schoolchildren who are most likely to have developed bad habits has left high school, i.e. following the compulsory education, is indicative of increasing acquisition by teenagers of certain sex-typed behaviours through modeling. The greater age-related changes in qualities associated with psychosocial adjustment among boys could be interpreted as due to a shift of their identification with increasing age from the mother model towards the father model, in order to become masculine; whereas girls with increasing age may simply continue identification with their primary model to a greater extent.

Conclusion

The evidence from our studies of sex differences among Lithuanian schoolchildren employing analyses of self-concept qualities, teacher, peer, and parents' rating, and some other techniques has shown that boys rather than girls are more apt to display behaviours incompatible with accepted social standards or school regulations.

So, a self-concept analysis of high school students has shown that 12 out of the 26 (14, 27, 28, 29, 43, 52, 58, 67, 116, 118, 133, 162 – see Table 13.7) polar adjective scales that significantly distinguished maladjusted boys from well-adjusted ones, also significantly distinguished boys from girls in general. Although in general characterized by a greater emotional instability, girls displayed a more positive self-concept than boys and behaved closer to the socially accepted behaviour patterns.

The evidence obtained has also some practical implications. Thus, amongst the sex-discriminating qualities reflecting psychosocial adjustment in children and adolescents there are quite a number that are pertinent to a type A behaviour. Their prevalence is greater in boys and has a tendency to increase with age. Since there are also distinct sex and age differences in smoking prevalence, another ischemic heart disease risk factor, one may suppose that the agents that mediate these differences in childhood and adolescence are responsible for the higher myocardial infarction incidence rate in males as compared with females as well.

The majority of behavioural manifestations considered important in psychosomatic medicine are socially conditioned, i.e. actually learned ones. This was indirectly suggested also by our study of delinquents and mentally handicapped social deviants, and is also partly true of maladjustment. Therefore it is our feeling that much could be done by starting active intervention on certain behavioural variables as early as in childhood or adolescence; especially if there is evidence of a trend, since both psychosocial maladjustment and adjustment seem to be predictable.

Incidentally, in Kaunas efforts are made to obtain non-medicinal correction of behaviour and psychosocial adjustment, to prevent the development of ischemic heart disease via eliminating or diminishing levels of such risk factors as increased blood pressure, type A behaviour, and smoking. However, our experience shows that this is a far more difficult task, for both a subject and a psychotherapist, when one has to deal with adult persons, with their consolidated stereotypes of wrong behaviour patterns. The incidence of ischemic heart disease and other chronic noncommunicable diseases could possibly be diminished by much earlier interventions.

14 Reading disability, behaviour problems and juvenile delinquency

R. McGee, D. Share, T.E. Moffitt, Sheila Williams & P.A. Silva

Historical background

Research on the relationship between educational difficulties and behavioural problems has had a relatively long history. Cyril Burt (1931) identified over 50% of a sample of some 200 young delinquents as educationally backward. About one in five were 'so utterly unable to read, spell or calculate as to appear classifiable as "educationally defective"' (p. 336). Fendrick & Bond (1936), reporting on a sample of 187 boys aged 16 to 19 years committed to the 'House of Refuge', Randall's Island in New York City, found that the average reading age of the group was just over 12 years compared with their average chronological age of nearly 18 years. In a study of 229 14 to 15 year olds in a treatment clinic attached to a New York City juvenile court, Harrower (1955) found that over 75% were retarded in reading by two or more years on a test of oral reading. Critchley (1968) observed that 60% of 12 to 17 year old boys in a London remand home were retarded in reading by two or more years, with 51% retarded by three or more years. This association between educational (primarily reading) failure and delinquency has been reported by more recent researchers (Broder, Dunivant, Smith & Sutton, 1981; Lewis, Shanok, Balla & Bard, 1980; Robbins, Beck, Pries, Jacobs & Smith, 1983; Wilgosh & Paitich, 1982).

Over the same period, the association between reading failure and other kinds of problem behaviours has been noted. Blanchard (1928) reviewed several clinical cases where reading disability was associated with reports of laziness, inattention, absent-mindedness and feelings of inferiority. Gates (1941), in a review of studies from the Teacher's College at Columbia University, identified a number of 'maladjustments' accompanying reading difficulties including restlessness, squirminess, irritability, withdrawal, truancy, aggression, defeatism and chronic worry. He estimated that three-quarters of all reading disabled children show some or all of these problems. Fabian (1955) reported high rates of reading failure in children from both child guidance clinics and the observation ward of a psychiatric hospital. In the Rutter, Tizard & Whitmore (1970) Isle of Wight study, a wide range of individual behaviour problems were significantly associated with reading retardation in boys and girls. There was also a strong relationship between psychiatric disorder involving antisocial symptoms and reading retardation. Two-fifths of those with antisocial disorder were severely retarded in reading compared with about one in twenty of the no-disorder control group. The co-existence of reading disability and maladjusted behaviours has continued to be reported (Bale, 1981; Davie, Butler & Goldstein, 1972; Gregory, 1965; McMichael, 1979; Stott, 1981; Sturge, 1982).

Which comes first?

The consistency of reports of an association between reading disability and various problem behaviours both over time and across different types of samples suggests that the relationship is robust. What is not clear is the nature of the relationship or 'what leads to what'. However, this is an important question because of its implications for intervention. If, for example, it is believed that behaviour problems are responsible for academic failure, then the behaviours themselves would be the appropriate targets for treatment. Such reasoning underlies the use of stimulant medication in the treatment of hyperactive children. If, on the other hand, the behaviour problems are a response to repeated academic failure, then intervention designed to increase academic success should attenuate the problem behaviour (see Cunningham & Barkley, 1978).

As summarised by Rutter *et al.* (1970), there are three main hypotheses concerning the relationship between reading disability and behaviour problems. Hypothesis A proposes that reading failure precedes the problem behaviour. The mechanism of this sequence may be as follows. Reading failure leads to a more general school failure. Poor reading is associated with poorer spelling and arithmetic (Rutter *et al.*, 1970) and writing skills (Share, Silva & Adler, 1986), so that all school subjects may ultimately suffer. School failure, in turn, results in loss of self-esteem and frustration; others may perceive the child as 'awkward' or 'stupid' which only serves to reinforce the negative self-image. This may lead to truancy to escape the adversity of the classroom and to the association with other children who are similarly hostile to school. Disruptive behaviour may be a function of frustration; the child's association with others who are prone to delinquency; and/or attempts to regain a measure of self-esteem from peers.

Hypothesis B suggests the reverse causal direction, namely that the problem behaviour precedes the reading disability. Bale (1981) reported a strong association between restless uncontrolled behaviour and poor reading while Sturge (1982) found that motor restlessness and poor concentration differentiated between reading disabled and non-disabled boys. It is possible, therefore, that inattentiveness and related hyperactive behaviours interfere with reading acquisition during early schooling.

Hypothesis C proposes that reading disability and behaviour problems are the result of some factor common to both. That is, the relationship between reading and behavioural difficulties is not directly causal, but rather mediated by some third variable. For example, a disadvantaged social environment could predispose the child to behavioural disorder and educational retardation. Indeed, there is good evidence that social disadvantage is related to both problem behaviour (Davie *et al.*, 1972; Silva, McGee, Thomas & Williams, 1982) and poor reading (Davie *et al.*, 1972; Rutter *et al.*, 1970; Williams & Silva, 1985).

Finally, it may be the case that some combination of the foregoing three hypotheses most accurately reflects the true state of affairs. Bale (1981) has proposed that inattentiveness and restless impulsive behaviour disrupts reading acquisition and predisposes the child to the later development of antisocial behaviour.

In choosing between these alternative hypotheses on the basis of available evidence, one is confronted with a number of methodological problems. As Chazan (1985) points out, there are definitional problems involving the measurement of poor reading performance. Some studies have identified reading disabled children as those at the lower end of the distribution of reading scores, while others have defined reading disability in terms of IQ, with attendant notions of under-achievement versus 'expected' reading levels. Yule, Rutter, Berger & Thompson (1974), for example, make the distinction between specific reading retardation and general reading backwardness. The former refers to reading disability where the level of reading is significantly below that predicted on the basis of age and IQ. General reading backwardness refers to a reading level below that expected of the average child but not significantly below that predicted by the child's age and IQ. It is unclear whether this distinction has implications for the association between reading and behavioural problems.

Conclusions based upon specially defined samples such as incarcerated or adjudicated delinquents or clinic-referred children may also be erroneous because of adjudication or referral bias. For example, Broder *et al.* (1981) in a study of some 1600, 12 to 15 year old boys found a small but significant *negative* relationship between learning disability and self-reported delinquency. That is, learning-disabled youths tended to report less delinquent activity than non-disabled youths. However, learning disability was *positively* related to adjudication status. This implies that in the United States at least, learning-disabled youths are differentially treated by the justice system. The high prevalence of reading disability among delinquent populations may simply be a reflection of differential judicial processes, rather than a causal association between reading disability and delinquency. Finally, and perhaps more importantly, the cross-sectional nature of much of the research precludes any disentanglement of cause and effect. Only longitudinal studies of reading and behaviour on samples drawn from the general population seem to hold any promise of providing an adequate test of the alternative hypotheses.

Longitudinal studies of reading and behaviour

Unfortunately, there are few longitudinal studies of the relationship between reading disabilities and behaviour problems during the early school years. McMichael (1979) studied 198 boys at school entry in Edinburgh, and subsequently after the first and second years schooling. Although antisocial behaviour at school entry predicted later reading disability, such behaviour was already associated with poor 'reading readiness' skills at school entry. There was no strong evidence for increased behaviour problems over time with reading disability. Stott (1981) reported a study of some 1300 Canadian children assessed at entry to kindergarten and at the end of their third school year. Early behaviour problems, particularly lethargy and hyperactivity predicted poorer subsequent reading and arithmetic skills. Furthermore, those identified as poor learners did not show any significant increase in problem behaviour over the first three years of schooling. These results suggest that early reading failure does not produce maladjustment, rather the reverse. Research by Chazan and colleagues (Chazan, 1985) also suggests that adjustment at school entry predicts later progress in reading and general school attainment.

Two studies have distinguished between specific reading retardation and general reading backwardness. Richman, Stevenson & Graham (1982) found that parental reports of problems when the child was aged 3 did not predict either type of reading disability. Furthermore, both types of reading disability were unrelated to parental reports of problem behaviours at age 8. Jorm, Share, Matthews & MacClean (1986), on the other hand, examined teacher reports of behaviour problems for a sample of Australian primary school children and found that backward readers identified at grade 2 had higher rates of problems at school entry and at the end of grades 1 and 2. These behaviour problems were primarily related to inattention and hyperactivity. Specific reading retarded children, however, did not differ significantly from the non-disabled children in terms of behaviour.

The above research suggests that if anything, behaviour problems are evident in backward readers at school entry and may precede the experience of reading failure. There was no evidence for any increase in behaviour problems over time, suggesting that either the behaviour problems have a causative role in producing the reading disability or that some common factor produces both. In the latter regard, Stott (1981) found that controlling for housing conditions of the children as an index of social disadvantage did not affect the relationship between problem behaviour and reading disability. The studies of Richman *et al.* and Jorm *et al.*, however, found no association between specific reading retardation and behaviour problems which conflicts with the cross-sectional studies of Rutter *et al.* (1970) and Sturge (1982).

Longitudinal studies of reading disability and juvenile delinquency

Is there any evidence to suggest that reading disability results in juvenile delinquency in adolescence? Once again, there are few longitudinal studies specifically examining this question. We could find only two studies investigating the predictive significance of reading performance *per se* for later delinquency. Wadsworth (1979) using data from the National Survey of Health and Development (1946 birth cohort) found that reading measures taken at age 8 significantly predicted officially recorded delinquent activity between ages 8 and 21 years. However, after the effects of social class and birth order were taken into acount there was no significant relationship between reading and delinquency. Maughan, Gray & Rutter (1985) report a follow-up to age 18 of those boys identified by Sturge (1982). Official records of delinquent acts were available for about two-thirds of the boys. Although rates of delinquency were higher for specific reading retarded boys (43%) than for normal readers (24%) the difference was not statistically significant, possibly due to small numbers in the groups.

There are several longitudinal studies which have focussed on more general school attainment or cognitive skills. Elliott & Voss (1974) studied delinquency and school drop-out rates in a population of over 2500 adolescents. A composite measure based upon achievement test scores, grade point averages and teacher evaluation of academic performance was used as a measure of academic achievement. Overall, their findings suggest that poor academic achievement is a better predictor of future police contact than of future delinquent activity, as measured by self-report. These results predate the conclusions reached by Broder *et al.* (1981) regarding learning disability and adjudication status. Ensminger, Kellam & Rubin (1983) investigated school and family predictors of delinquency in a ten year follow-up of over 1000 first grade children in a Chicago community (Woodlawn Project). It was found that teacher-rated learning disability did not predict self-reported delinquency for either teenage boys or girls, while low cognitive achievement in first grade significantly predicted later delinquency for girls only. Olweus (1983), in a longitudinal study of Swedish boys, found that low aggregate school grades at age 13 did not predict peer ratings of aggressive behaviours three years later. Similarly, poor grades at ages 9 and 11 years did not predict aggressive behaviour at age 13. Finally, Spreen (1981), has reported a prospective study of 203 'learning disabled' children evaluated between the ages of 8 to 12 years in a neuropsychological testing unit. They were followed-up some 4 to 12 years later and both self and parent reports of police contact, delinquent offences and penalties were obtained. A control group similar in age, sex and socioeconomic level was also interviewed. The learning-disabled children did not differ from the controls in terms of offences or police contact. They did, however, receive slightly more penalties and somewhat more severe penalties than controls.

Overall, the studies reviewed provide little evidence for an association between early reading/learning disability or poor school-achievement, and subsequent delinquent behaviour. The results of Broder *et al.* (1981), Elliott & Voss (1974) and Spreen (1981), on the other hand, indicate the potential source of bias that may arise from a reliance on official delinquency data in testing hypotheses relating to educational variables.

The Dunedin multidisciplinary health and development study

This is a longitudinal investigation of the health, development and behaviour of a large sample of New Zealand children born in Dunedin between 1 April 1972 and 31 March 1973. The children were first followed up at age 3 (N = 1037) and have subsequently been assessed every two years. The most recent assessment has been at age 13 (1985–1986). Details concerning the study and the sample have been described by McGee & Silva (1982).

From ages 7 to 13, reading ability has been assessed using the Burt Word Reading Test (Scottish Council for Research in Education, 1976). Parent and teacher reports of behaviour problems were first gathered at age 5 using the Rutter *et al.* (1970) Child Scales A and B, respectively. In the case of the teacher assessments, the questionnaire was completed during the child's first year at school. These scales provide a total score as an overall measure of problem behaviour and sub-scale scores for hyperactivity, aggressiveness and worry-fearfulness.[1] The longitudinal nature of the data provides an opportunity to examine the association between reading disability and problem behaviour. First, we summarise the results of a longitudinal analysis of data from age 5 to 11 years, for the boys (McGee, Williams, Share, Anderson & Silva, 1986). Second, we report hitherto unpublished results concerning two other aspects of this research. We examine the relationship between reading disability and behaviour problems in girls from 5 to 11 years. Also, we report the results of a follow-up of the reading disabled boys and girls at age 13, with an emphasis on juvenile delinquency and attitudes to schooling and education.

Reading disability and behaviour problems in Dunedin boys

McGee *et al.* (1986) examined reading performance in the Dunedin sample at ages 9 and 11, and identified 18 boys who were specific reading-retarded at both ages and 22 boys who were general reading backward. The distinction between these two types of reading disability was based upon Yule *et al.* (1974). These two groups were compared with the remaining boys in the sample (N = 436).

In terms of reading scores at ages 7, 9 and 11 years, there was no significant difference at each age between the specific reading-retarded and general reading backward boys. The overall means of the two combined groups of reading-disabled boys were 9.4, 22.5 and 35.0 at 7, 9 and 11, respectively. The overall means for the remaining boys in the sample were 28.3, 53.2 and 72.7. Statistical analysis using a regression adjustment procedure (Plewis, 1985)[2] indicated that not only did both groups of reading-disabled boys show a level of reading at age 7 well below that of the remaining boys, but they showed a significantly slower rate of increase in reading scores over time (particularly from 7 to 9).

Figure 14.1 (a and b) shows the group average total behaviour problem scores on the parent and teacher questionnaires respectively, from 5 to 11 years. The relationship between the reading disability and behaviour was stronger in the case of the teacher ratings (see Figure 14.1b). Both groups of reading-disabled boys had higher teacher-rated problem scores during their first year at school, particularly on the sub-scale measures of hyperactivity and aggressiveness. Subsequently, the general reading backward group showed a significant relative increase in the total problem scores from age 5 to 7 years, while the specific reading-retarded group showed a relative increase from 7 to 9 years. In both instances, the increase was evident on the hyperactivity sub-scale only, not the aggressiveness or worry-fearfulness measures.[3] The reading-disabled boys continued to show high levels of teacher-rated behaviour problems at age 11. For the parent ratings, no clear differences were present at age 5. However, the specific reading-retarded boys did show a relative increase in parent-rated problems (primarily aggressiveness) from age 5 to 7 and continued to show high levels of problems through to age 11. The general reading backward group did not differ significantly from the remainder of the sample at any age. Although significantly more of the reading-disabled boys had higher scores on an index of family adversity[4], the inclusion of family adversity as an explanatory variable in the analysis left the above effects unchanged.

These results indicate that for boys, both types of reading disability are associated with behaviour problems from the first year at school. This confirms similar findings reported by Chazan (1985), McMichael (1979) and Stott (1981). Subsequently, these behaviour problems, particularly teacher-rated hyperactivity and parent-rated aggressiveness, showed increases over time. This provides support for the Cunningham & Barkley (1978) hypothesis that repeated failure in academic tasks, in this instance reading failure and its consequences for school work, can generate hyperactive and disruptive behaviour in children. While parent reports of behaviour problems showed an overall decline between ages 9 and 11, teacher reports showed high levels of problem behaviours through to age 11.

Reading disability and behaviour problems in Dunedin girls

Reading disability is typically regarded as being more prevalent in boys because referrals for remediation are more often boys and epidemiological studies report marked sex differences in prevalence rates (Jorm, 1983; Rutter *et al.*, 1970; Silva, McGee & Williams, 1985). While this has been cited as evidence for the operation of sex-linked genetic effects, there are reasons for suspecting that this sex difference may be more apparent than real. First, reading-disabled boys may come to the notice of parents and teachers more often than similarly disabled girls because the

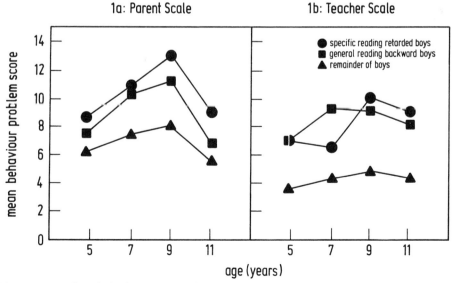

Figure 14.1 Mean behaviour problem scores for reading disabled boys from ages 5 to 11 (McGee *et al.* 1986). With kind permission, *Journal of Child Psychology and Psychiatry*, Pergamon Press

boys present more often as management problems. The results of the previous section suggest that such boys display hyperactive and aggressive behaviour. On the other hand, no researchers seemed to have looked at the behaviour of girls who cannot read. The second reason for the observed sex differences, particularly in epidemiological studies, may be that reading disability has been defined in terms of the distribution of reading scores for boys and girls combined (e.g. Rutter *et al.*, 1970; McGee *et al.*, 1986). In general, the average reading scores of girls are several points higher than that of boys. In addition, there is evidence to suggest that in predicting reading scores from IQ to identify specific reading retarded children, the regression equations of IQ on reading for boys and girls differ significantly (Share, Williams & Silva, 1987). The selection of reading-disabled children using total distribution of scores may be artificially biased towards identifying more boys because of these sex differences in the distributions of reading scores. A more appropriate procedure for identifying reading-disabled boys and girls would be to base the selection procedure upon the appropriate same-sex distribution.

To identify a group of reading-disabled girls, we decided to use a matching procedure whereby the reading levels of the girls would be matched to that of the reading-disabled boys from age 7 to 11. As there was no difference between specific reading-retarded and general reading backward boys on reading scores, the reading-disabled boys were combined into a single group (N = 40) and their reading performance relative to the remainder of the boys is shown in Figure 14.2. A group of 40 reading-disabled girls (IQ > 70) was chosen by examining the reading scores of those at the lower end of the distribution for girls (N = 447). Their reading performance relative to the remainder of the girls is also shown in Figure 14.2, and it can be seen from this figure that the profile of reading scores for the reading disabled girls mirrors that of the reading disabled boys. For example, by age 11 the

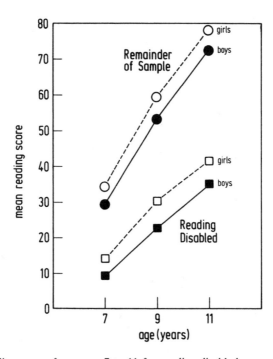

Figure 14.2 Reading scores from ages 7 to 11 for reading-disabled groups of boys and girls

reading-disabled boys were 1.9 standard deviation units lower in performance compared with the remaining boys; at this age, the reading-disabled girls were 1.8 standard deviations lower than the remaining girls.[5]

Figure 14.3 (a and b) shows the average total problem scores for the parent and teacher questionnaires from ages 5 to 11 years. Once again the results were analysed using a regression adjustment procedure. For the parent questionnaire there was no significant difference between the reading-disabled girls and the remainder of the girls at age 5, $F(1399) = 3.20$. $p > 0.05$. After adjusting for scores at age 5, there was no difference between the groups at age 7, $F(1398) = 1.86$, $p > 0.05$. However, there was differential relative change between ages 7 and 9 after adjusting for the earlier ages, $F(1397) = 10.98$, $p < 0.05$. In Figure 14.3a this is evident in the rise of total problem scores between 7 and 9 for the reading disabled girls. Analysis of the subscale scores for the parent questionnaire indicated that this differential increase between ages 7 and 9 was restricted to the aggressiveness measure. Between ages 9 and 11 years there was no subsequent differential change between the two groups of girls on the total problem score.

For the teacher questionnaire there was a significant difference between the reading disabled girls and the remaining girls at age 5, $F(1394) = 6.53$, $p < 0.05$, with reading disabled girls having higher behaviour problem ratings. At all subsequent ages, after adjusting for earlier age levels, there were no significant effects indicating no differential change between the groups after age 5. At age 5, analysis of the subscales indicated that the difference between the reading-disabled and remaining girls was evident only on the teacher ratings of hyperactivity. There were no differences on teacher ratings of aggressiveness and worry-fearfulness at age 5. As was the case with the reading-disabled boys, the inclusion of family adversity in the analysis did not significantly influence any of the above effects.

These results suggest a significant association between reading disability in girls and reports of behaviour problems. While there were similarities between reading-disabled boys and girls in terms of parent reports of problems, this was not the case for teacher report. The parents reported no differences between reading-disabled boys and girls and their non-disabled peers at age 5. Subsequently, there was an

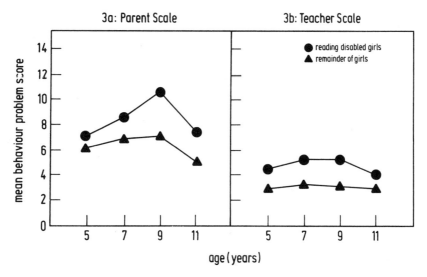

Figure 14.3 Mean behaviour problem scores for reading disabled girls from ages 5 to 11

increase in aggressive behaviour between 5 and 7 for the reading-disabled boys and between 7 and 9 for the reading-disabled girls. Teachers, on the other hand, reported no rise in behaviour problems over time for reading-disabled girls although such girls were rated as more hyperactive than their non-disabled peers during the first year of school. The latter finding suggests that teachers do not regard reading-disabled girls as particularly disruptive in the classroom and certainly not as disruptive as reading-disabled boys, a fact which may account for the under-identification of reading disability in girls.

Behaviour problems at age 3 and reading disability

The above results indicate that reading disability is associated with teacher reports of behaviour problems from the first year of schooling, i.e. during initial reading acquisition. It is still not clear, however, whether the behaviour problems preceded reading acquisition. The only other longitudinal evidence to draw from is that of Richman *et al.* (1982), who found that parent reported problems at age 3 were not predictive of reading disability at age 8. In the Dunedin sample, most children by age 5 had experienced being read to or had made some initial attempts to read on their own; 93% had attended a kindergarten or playcentre from about age $3\frac{1}{2}$ onwards. Consequently, a further test of the hypotheses relating to causal direction would be to examine whether behaviour problems were more prevalent in reading-disabled boys and girls prior to any pre-school experiences.

While detailed reports of problem behaviours were not collected from parents prior to age 5, there was no association between reading disability and parent report at the age 3 assessment of the child being 'very difficult to manage'. We identified a small group of 28 children at age 3 who were described as 'very difficult to manage' by the parent, and who showed behaviour problems during testing at the Unit (hyperactivity, aggressiveness or refusal to cooperate). Six of the reading-disabled children (3 boys and 3 girls) showed pervasive behaviour problems at age 3 compared with 22 of the non-disabled children, χ^2 (1df) = 4.60, $p < 0.05$. This suggests that early pervasive behaviour problems may precede reading disability in a small number of cases (7.5 per cent). However, most reading-disabled boys and girls showed no evidence of behaviour problems as measured at age 3.

Follow-up of the reading-disabled children at age 13

At the 13-year assessment, 6 boys and 4 girls who were reading-disabled were lost to follow-up owing to refusal to continue in the study or non-response to letters. Sixty-five were assessed at the Dunedin unit, while the remaining 5 were partially assessed by psychologists from the Department of Education. Teachers completed the Rutter Child Scale B once again, while parental report was obtained from the Revised Behaviour Problem Checklist or RBPC of Quay & Peterson (1983). Those adolescents attending the Dunedin unit completed a self-report of delinquency scale and information regarding their perceptions of school, schoolwork and career plans was obtained.

The reading-disabled boys and girls continued to show low levels of reading at age 13, with mean reading scores of 47.2 and 59.7 respectively. The mean scores for the remaining boys and girls were 84.8 and 89.2.[6] Both the reading-disabled boys and girls perceived themselves as below average in their reading, spelling, mathematics and general school work compared with the remaining adolescents. While about 28% of the non-disabled adolescents saw themselves as 'above average' in their schoolwork, none of the reading-disabled group perceived themselves as above average. On a general measure of 'attachment to school' in the sense of

Table 14.1 School leaving and reading disability at age 13

	Intended School Leaving			
	Form 5	Form 6	Form 7	Don't Know
Reading disabled	30%	27%	34%	9%
Remainder of sample	10%	25%	58%	7%

enjoyment, taking work seriously and so on (Fogelman, 1976), both reading-disabled boys and girls showed significantly lower attachment. Table 14.1 shows the form level at which the reading-disabled boys and girls intend to leave school. These results are shown for boys and girls combined as there were no sex differences. The overall association between reading disability and time of leaving school was significant with χ^2 (3df) = 27.53, $p < 0.05$. Three times as many reading disabled adolescents planned to leave school after the School Certificate examination at Form 5 or earlier compared with the remainder of the sample.

The mean total scores on the Rutter Child Scale B at age 13 are shown in Table 14.2. According to teacher report, the reading-disabled boys continued to show high levels of behaviour problems in the classroom. The reading-disabled girls, on the other hand, were not perceived by their teachers as showing behaviour problems. The reading disability × sex interaction was significant with F (1798) = 11.03, $p < 0.05$, and this interaction was evident for teacher rated hyperactivity and aggressiveness, not worry-fearfulness (see Table 14.2). The mean score of 8.5 for the reading-disabled boys at age 13 shows a level of behaviour problems equivalent to that reported at age 11 (see Figure 14.1b). By contrast, parent report at 13 indicated higher total behaviour problem scores for both reading-disabled boys and girls compared with their non-disabled peers, as shown in Table 14.2. The main effect for reading disability was significant with F (1825) = 35.90, $p < 0.05$, but there was no significant interaction. The reading-disabled boys and girls showed higher scores on the RBPC subscales of Attention-Problems, Anxiety-Withdrawal,

Table 14.2 Reading disability and teacher and parent reported behaviour problems at age 13

Measure	Reading Disabled		Sample Remainder	
	Boys	Girls	Boys	Girls
	N=34	N=36	N=394	N=367
Teacher Rutter:				
Total Score	8.5	3.1	3.8	2.4
Hyperactivity	3.5	0.8	1.4	0.7
Aggressiveness	3.7	0.7	1.2	0.6
Parent RBPC:				
Total	30.5	22.4	16.3	13.4
Attention Problems	9.5	6.6	4.3	3.0
Anxiety-Withdrawal	5.7	5.2	3.2	3.3
Conduct Disorder	9.5	7.2	6.0	5.0
Socialised Aggression	2.4	1.4	1.2	0.9

Conduct Disorder and Socialised Aggression. How these results relate to delinquent behaviour is considered in the following section.

Reading disability and juvenile delinquency

Degree of involvement in delinquent activity was assessed by information obtained from self, parent and teacher report. The self-report measure (see Moffitt, 1986) consisted of 58 delinquent behaviours presented on cards which the adolescent sorted according to whether or not they had ever committed the act described. Positive responses were followed by an interview clarifying the nature and circumstances of the delinquent behaviour. Each scale item was assigned a weighting reflecting its 'seriousness' as judged by professionals from the juvenile justice system, high school teachers and psychology undergraduates. Item weights were summed to produce a total score reflecting both frequency and seriousness of delinquent activity. In addition, each adolescent was asked about police contact involving some degree of official action.

Parent report of delinquent activity was based upon the Conduct Disorder and Socialised Aggression subscales of the RBPC. The former subscale represents a dimension of very aggressive, non-compliant, acting-out behaviour while the latter represents a dimension of acting-out and rejection of authority but with less aggressive behaviour and in the presence of strong bonds with others, e.g. a gang (Quay & Peterson, 1983). Parents were also asked about police contact with their son or daughter. Information on truanting was obtained from parent, teacher and adolescent self-report. The results for the delinquency measures are shown in Table 14.3.

Only the parent reported measures of Conduct Disorder and Socialised Aggression showed significant differences associated with reading disability, with $F(1825) = 13.41$ for the former scale and $F(1825) = 9.49$ for the latter, $p < 0.05$. Neither of the reading disability $\times$ sex interactions was significant. Reading-disabled boys and girls did not differ from their non-disabled peers on the measure of self-reported delinquency, with $F(1689) = 2.59$, $p > 0.05$. There was a significant sex difference in self-reported delinquency, $F(1689) = 40.93$, $p < 0.05$, but no significant reading disability $\times$ sex interaction. The reading disabled adolescents did not differ from the remainder of the sample on the measures of police contact or truanting. Examination of individual scale items relating to gang membership or delinquent

Table 14.3 Reading disability and delinquent behaviours at age 13

Measure	Reading Disabled		Sample Remainder	
	Boys	Girls	Boys	Girls
	N=34	N=36	N=394	N=367
Self-report Delinquency	8.3	6.8	4.9	3.3
Police Contact:				
Self-report	10%	6%	10%	3%
Parent-report	3%	0%	7%	2%
Truancy:				
Self-report	13%	13%	12%	6%
Parent-report	6%	0%	2%	1%
Teacher-report	6%	6%	8%	3%

behaviours in groups also revealed no significant differences between the reading-disabled adolescents and their peers, on both parent and self-report.

The measure showing the strongest difference between the reading-disabled and non-disabled adolescents was the RBPC subscale of Conduct Disorder. Examination of individual scale items indicated that the reading-disabled boys and girls were more often described as disruptive and annoying, negative and doing the opposite of what is requested, irritable, sulking, bragging, blaming others and to a lesser degree fighting, being disobedient and refusing to take directions. These behaviours are largely in agreement with the teacher ratings of the reading-disabled boys, namely, being more destructive, irritable, disobedient, bullying and not being liked as much as their peers. Teachers did not rate these boys as lying or stealing more than their non-disabled peers.

Overall, the findings suggest that reading-disabled boys and girls do not engage in more delinquent behaviour than those children reading at normal levels. Rather, they tended to be perceived as more oppositional and generally disobedient. As such, the results agree with those of Broder *et al.* (1981), Elliott & Voss (1974), Ensminger *et al.* (1983) and Spreen (1981) that learning-disabled children with low levels of school achievement do not engage in more juvenile delinquency than their non-disabled peers.

Concluding remarks

The evidence from the Dunedin study suggests a long-term association between reading disability and behaviour problems in both boys and girls. Furthermore, the results are consistent with the hypothesis that the behaviour problems of most of the reading-disabled children arose as a consequence of a failure to learn to read rather than vice-versa. Teachers, in contrast to parents, however, did not perceive reading-disabled girls as showing high levels of behaviour problems and for this reason such girls may remain a relatively underidentified group in need of remedial assistance. While reading disability in early adolescence was associated with poorer academic self-esteem and weaker attachment to school values, there was no evidence for an association with truanting or delinquent activity. Rather, reading-disabled children presented more of a general discipline problem for parents and teachers.

Follow-up studies of reading-disabled children suggest that their reading problems persist well into adolescence (Watson, Watson & Fredd, 1982). Unfortunately, there has been little longitudinal research following such children into adulthood. What evidence there is suggests that persistent reading disability results in poor school grades, early school leaving and restricted employment opportunities (Maughan *et al.*, 1985). As such, the consequence of reading failure during early schooling will follow the reading-disabled child through to secondary school and into the workforce.

Elsewhere we have argued that it is the child's academic difficulties rather than associated problem behaviour which should be given priority in any treatment programme (McGee & Share, 1987). What evidence there is suggests that remediation of reading difficulties does reduce levels of behaviour problems (Arnold, Barnebey, McManus, Smeltzer, Conrad, Winer & Desgranges, 1977). However, research directly investigating the academic and behavioural consequences of reading remediation for the reading disabled child is badly needed.

Notes

1. The hyperactivity measure consisted of the sum of the ratings for restlessness, squirminess and poor concentration/cannot settle. Aggressiveness was based upon the ratings for fighting,

bullying, irritability, not being liked, disobedience and destructiveness. Worry-fearfulness consisted of ratings for worry, fearfulness, being miserable, fussy and being solitary (see McGee, Williams, Bradshaw, Chapel, Robins & Silva, 1985).

2. Regression adjustment models examine the degree of relative change in scores at time $t + 1$ for two or more groups, if the groups were equated at time t. Such models allow for the testing of group differences at any one time, where the groups have been equated at all previous testing times. Plewis (1985) fully discusses the use of these models.

3. The difference in relative increases in hyperactivity between the specific reading-retarded and reading backward boys may be due to IQ differences between the two groups (means of 104 vs. 93 at age 5, respectively). However, we identified a group of boys (N = 83) with IQs at age 5 below 100 (means of 93.0) but with normal reading scores at 7, 9 and 11 years and contrasted them with the remainder of the sample of boys. This group, with the same mean IQ as the general reading backward boys, did not have higher behaviour problem scores than the remainder of the sample. This suggests that the behaviour problems of the general reading backward boys are not due to their lower IQ at school entry.

4. The family adversity index was based upon 5 year measures of low SES (semi-skilled/unskilled); large family size (4 or more children); parental separations or solo parenting; low maternal mental ability; poor maternal mental health; marriage counselling up to child's fifth year (see McGee *et al.*, 1986).

5. The identification of reading-disabled girls by 'matching' their reading levels over age with that of the boys ignores the distinction between concepts of specific reading retardation and general reading backwardness. Our more recent research has led us to believe that this distinction is not relevant to the issue of whether or not a child has a reading disability. That is, IQ does not provide any useful additional information in identifying reading disability; the main issue is whether or not the child can read satisfactorily (see Share, McGee, McKenzie, Williams & Silva, 1986; Share, McGee & Silva, 1987, for a discussion of this issue).

6. By age 13, the average reading scores of the reading-disabled boys and girls were below the average scores of the non-disabled boys and girls at age 9. While the scores of the latter two groups appear to be converging at age 13, this may be due to a ceiling effect on the Burt test.

Acknowledgements

The Dunedin Multidisciplinary Health and Development Research Unit is supported by the Medical Research Council of New Zealand and the Departments of Education and Health, and involves several departments of the University of Otago. Many of the data are gathered by voluntary workers from the Dunedin community. The authors are indebted to the many people whose contributions make this continuing study possible. Dr David L. Share was supported in this research by a Neil Hamilton Fairley Fellowship (National Health and Medical Research Council of Australia). Dr Terrie E. Moffitt was supported by USPHS Grant 1 R23 MY-39994-01 from the Antisocial and Violent Behaviour Branch of the United States National Institute for Mental Health.

References

ARNOLD, L.E., BARNEBEY, N., MCMANUS, J., SMELTZER, D.J., CONRAD, A., WINER, G. & DESGRANGES, L. (1977) Prevention by specific perceptual remediation for vulnerable first-graders. *Archives of General Psychiatry*, **24**, 1279–94.

BALE, P. (1981) Behaviour problems and their relationship to reading difficulty. *Journal of Research in Reading*, **4**, 123–35.

BLANCHARD, P. (1928) Reading disabilities in relation to maladjustment. *Mental Hygiene*, **12**, 772–88.

BRODER, P.K., DUNIVANT, N., SMITH, E.C. & SUTTON, L.P. (1981) Further observations on the link between learning disabilities and juvenile delinquency. *Journal of Educational Psychology*, **73**, 838–50.

BURT, C. (1931) *The young delinquent*, London: University of London Press.

CHAZAN, M. (1985) Behavioural aspects of educational difficulties. In D.D. Duane & C.K. Leong (eds.) *Understanding learning disabilities* (127–37) New York: Plenum Press.

COSTELLO, A., EDELBROCK, C., KALAS, R., KESSLER, M. & KLARIC, S.A. (1982) *Diagnostic Interview Schedule for Children (DISC)*. Written under contract to the National Institute of Mental Health.

CRITCHLEY, E.M.R. (1968) Reading retardation, dyslexia and delinquency. *British Journal of Psychiatry*, **115**, 1537–47.

CUNNINGHAM, C.E. & BARKLEY, R.A. (1978) The role of academic failure in hyperactive behaviour. *Journal of Learning Disabilities*, **11**, 15–21.

DAVIE, R., BUTLER, N. & GOLDSTEIN, H. (1972) *From birth to seven: a report from the National Child Development Study*. London: Longman.

ELLIOTT, D.S. & VOSS, H.L. (1974) *Delinquency and dropout*, Lexington: Lexington Books.

ENSMINGER, M.E., KELLAM, S.G. & RUBIN, B.R. (1983) School and family origins of delinquency: comparisons by sex. In K.T. Van Dusen and S.A. Mednick (eds.), *Prospective studies of crime and delinquency*. Boston: Kluwer Nijhoff.

FABIAN, A.A. (1955) Reading disability: an index of pathology. *American Journal of Orthopsychiatry*, **25**, 319–29.

FENDRICK, P. & BOND, G. (1936) Delinquency and reading. *Journal of Genetic Psychology*, **48**, 236–43.

FOGELMAN, K. (1976) *Britain's sixteen-year-olds*. London: National Children's Bureau.

GATES, A.I. (1941) The role of personality maladjustment in reading disability. *Journal of Genetic Psychology*, 59, 77–83.

GREGORY, R.E. (1965) Unsettledness, maladjustment and reading failure: a village study. *British Journal of Educational Psychology*, **35**, 63–8.

HARROWER, M. (1955) Who comes to court? *American Journal of Orthopsychiatry*, **25**, 15–25.

JORM, A.F. (1983) *The psychology of reading and spelling disabilities*. London: Routledge & Kegan Paul.

JORM, A.F., SHARE, D.L., MATTHEWS, R. & MACLEAN, R. (1986) Behaviour problems in specific reading-retarded and general reading backward children: a longitudinal study. *Journal of Child Psychology and Psychiatry*, **27**, 33–43.

LEWIS, D.O., SHANOK, S.S., BALLA, D.A. & BARD, B. (1980) Psychiatric correlates of severe reading disabilities in an incarcerated delinquent population. *Journal of the American Academy of Child Psychiatry*, **19**, 611–22.

MAUGHAN, B., GRAY, G. & RUTTER, M. (1985) Reading retardation and antisocial behaviour: a follow-up into employment. *Journal of Child Psychology and Psychiatry*, **26**, 741–58.

MCGEE, R. & SHARE, D.L. (1987) Attention deficit disorder – hyperactivity and academic failure: which comes first and what should be treated? In submission.

MCGEE, R. & SILVA, P.A. (1982) *A thousand New Zealand children: their health and development from birth to seven*, Special Report Series Number 8, Auckland: Medical Research Council of New Zealand.

MCGEE, R., WILLIAMS, S., BRADSHAW, J., CHAPEL, J.L., ROBINS, A. & SILVA, P.A. (1985) The Rutter Scale for completion by teachers: factor structure and relationships with cognitive abilities and family adversity for a sample of New Zealand children. *Journal of Child Psychology and Psychiatry*, **26**, 727–39.

MCGEE, R., WILLIAMS, S., SHARE, D.L., ANDERSON, J. & SILVA, P.A. (1986) The relationships between specific reading retardation, general reading backwardness and behavioural problems in a large sample of Dunedin boys. *Journal of Child Psychology and Psychiatry*, **27**, 597–610.

MCMICHAEL, P. (1979) The hen or the egg? Which comes first – antisocial emotional disorders or reading disability? *British Journal of Educational Psychology*, **49**, 226–38.

MOFFITT, T.E. (1986) Neuropsychology and self-reported early delinquency in an unselected birth cohort: a preliminary report from New Zealand. To appear in: *Biological investigations of antisocial behaviour* S.A. Mednick & T.E. Moffit (eds.) New York: Martinus Nijhoff.

OLWEUS, D. (1983) Low school achievement and aggressive behaviour in adolescent boys. In D. Magnusson & V.L. Allen (eds.) *Human development: an interactional perspective*. New York: Academic Press.

PLEWIS, I. (1985) *Analysing change: measurement and explanation using longitudinal data*, Chichester: Wiley & Sons.

QUAY, H.C. & PETERSON, D.R. (1983) *Interim manual for the revised behaviour problem checklist*, Miami: Authors.

RICHMAN, N., STEVENSON, J. & GRAHAM, P.J. (1982) *Pre-school to school: a behavioural study*, London: Academic Press.

ROBBINS, D.M., BECK, J.C., PRIES, R., JACOBS, D. & SMITH, C. (1983) Learning disability and neuropsychological impairment in adjudicated, unincarcerated male delinquents. *Journal of the American Academy of Child Psychiatry*, **22**, 40–6.

RUTTER, M., TIZARD, J. & WHITMORE, K. (1970) *Education, health and behaviour*. London: Longman.

Scottish Council for Research in Education (1976) *The Burt Word Reading Test – 1974 revision*, London: Hodder & Stoughton.

SHARE D.L., McGEE, R., McKENZIE, D., WILLIAMS, S. & SILVA, P.A. (1987) Further evidence relating to the distinction between specific reading retardation and general reading backwardness. *British Journal of Developmental Psychology*, **5**, 35–44.

SHARE, D.L., McGEE, R. & SILVA, P.A. (1987) IQ and reading progress: a test of the 'milk and jug' hypothesis. In submission.

SHARE, D.L., SILVA, P.A. & ADLER, C.J. (1986) Factors associated with reading plus spelling retardation and specific spelling retardation. *Developmental medicine and child neurology*, in press.

SHARE, D.L., WILLIAMS, S. & SILVA, P.A. (1987) Specific reading retardation: girls versus boys. In submission.

SILVA, P.A., McGEE, R., THOMAS, J. & WILLIAMS, S.M. (1982) A descriptive study of socio-economic status and child development in Dunedin five-year-olds. *New Zealand Journal of Educational Studies*, **17**, 21–32.

SILVA, P.A., McGEE, R. & WILLIAMS, S. (1985) Some characteristics of nine-year-old boys with general reading backwardness and specific reading retardation. *Journal of Child Psychology and Psychiatry*, **25**, 407–21.

SPREEN, O. (1981) The relationship between learning disability, neurological impairment and delinquency. *Journal of Nervous and Mental Disease*, **169**, 791–9.

STOTT, D.H. (1981) Behaviour disturbance and failure to learn: a study of cause and effect. *Educational Research*, **23**, 163–72.

STURGE, C. (1982) Reading retardation and antisocial behaviour. *Journal of Child Psychology and Psychiatry*, **23**, 21–31.

WADSWORTH, M. (1979) *Roots of delinquency*. Oxford: Martin Robertson.

WATSON, B.V., WATSON, C.S. & FREDD, R. (1982) Follow-up studies of specific reading disability. *Journal of the American Academy of Child Psychiatry*, **21**, 376–82.

WILGOSH, L. & PAITICH, D. (1982) Delinquency and learning disabilities: more evidence. *Journal of Learning Disabilities*, **15**, 278–9.

WILLIAMS, S.M. & SILVA, P.A. (1985) Some factors associated with reading ability: a longitudinal study. *Educational Research*, **27**, 159–68.

YULE, W., RUTTER, M., BERGER, M. & THOMPSON, J. (1974) Over and under-achievement in reading: distribution in the general population. *British Journal of Educational Psychology*, **44**, 1–12.

15 Child psychology and juvenile delinquency in Puerto Rican society

J.L. Porrata

Psychology and psychologically–related studies have been present in Puerto Rico since the latter part of the nineteenth century. However, it is mainly during the last 20 years that a greater development has taken place, as a function of the growth of local Academic Graduate Programs. Psychological paradigms from Europe and North America form the basis of Puertorican Psychology, although there is an effort to make contacts with other psychologists in Latin America, in order to further develop a Puertorican Psychology. There are five major areas of study: clinical, educational, industrial-organizational, community and general psychology. At the University of Puerto Rico, more than 500 theses have been completed, in the Caribbean Center for Advanced Studies, more than 100. Journals have been created such as the *Journal of the Psychological Association, Revista de Ciencias Sociales* of the University of Puerto Rico, and *Homines*, of the Interamerican University. The Association of Puertorican Psychologists was established in 1955, and since 1983 licensing laws exist for the provision of professional services.

The founding of a mental health organization by the government created a need for the development of the behavioral sciences in Puerto Rico. Trained personnel were needed to give services as well as to define clinical models that were directed to the specific needs of the population of Puerto Rico. In the development of such models, traditional ways of thinking are studied to devise action strategies. The goal of these models is to achieve social change (Quintero, 1971). Psychological values create an awareness and bring in a new morality; currently, topics such as the family are widely discussed both by the professional and the public. There is a growing awareness of the need for psychosocial models where the rights of everyone are respected (Trigo, 1984). Laws of confidentiality and for the protection of clinical patients' rights now exist in Puerto Rico.

A Puertorican historical and societal background

For many generations there has been a search for definitions and descriptions of the Puertorican personality; studies appeared from a historical and literary perspective, as well as from the social sciences perspective. Puertorican culture has its roots in an Indo-American, Spanish-European, African and North American background.

When Columbus discovered Puerto Rico, the Indian population lived in a Neolithic social organization (Alegría, 1969). Tasks, such as the rearing of children, were shared by the family and the community. With the Spanish conquest a more disciplinarian type of social organization emerged; the father as the *pater familia* exerted complete control over the family. Life followed a more hierarchical pattern. A growing African population, brought in to work as slaves, contributed a more matriarchal social organization. González (1983) has pointed out that the African contribution to Puertorican culture and society has not been fully explored and understood.

The economy of Puerto Rico through its history has been based on sugar and coffee production, which depended on the weather, the price of the crops in the international market and the rate of interest by the money lenders (Picó, 1981). Fatalism and depressive traits developed due to the uncertainties and periods of poverty of such an economic organization (Mintz, 1974). Geo-culturally, however, Puerto Rico, like the rest of the Caribbean islands, is a land of sun and lively music.

During the latter part of the 19th century liberal values of social organizations reached the island. For many, this culminated in the change of sovereignty, in 1898, from Spanish rule to North American rule. Ideas of liberty and democracy were welcomed in Puerto Rico from a society that had been through a revolution. The island's economic, religious and linguistic systems which were based on agriculture, Catholicism and Spanish customs were subjected to the capitalistic, Protestant and English influence of the United States.

Puertorican society became more complex since the emigration of many Puertoricans to the United States started; the trend in migration, however, reversed after the 1970s. Now two main types of Puertoricans have to be recognized: those raised in Puerto Rico and those raised in the United States, with many receiving various degrees of influences from both cultures (Izcoa, 1985). Some call this clash between cultures 'schizophrenia'; nevertheless Spanish predominates and is the language of daily life, business and education, and provides the basis for maintaining cultural stability. In the last 25 years there have been significant migrations to the island, especially of Dominicans and Cubans, who are slowly blending into the Puertorican mainstream.

The Puertorican socio-political evolution has been characterized by peaceful change in contrast to other countries of the Caribbean which have gone through revolution and civil wars. Self-government and democracy reached Puertoricans in the last part of this century. The island throughout its history has been under military governments. Puertoricans have learned to lead their lives by means of opportunism, possibly pretending to be docile, and not expressing fully how they felt (Pedreira, 1939; Márquez, 1962; Eysenck and Porrata, 1984).

With industrialism, education and democracy, Puertoricans have enjoyed a greater degree of welfare and security. These factors might have brought the population a greater trust and a feeling of being more in control of their lives than had traditionally been the case before. There is a belief that there is a political solution to the Puertoricans' problems. At present, individualism and consumerism in the island grows but family life has been eroding (Torres-Zayas, 1986).

Child psychology

The area of study which has generated most research is child psychology (Rivera-Ramos, 1985). Educational psychologists have followed the curriculum developed in institutions such as Harvard, New York and Temple University, and local institutions such as the University of Puerto Rico and the Interamerican University. Teaching and learning strategies have been developed from a learning, developmental and cognitive viewpoint.

Concepts such as national and moral development have also been studied. Puertorican children seem to lag behind in their formation of a national identity (Ortiz, 1973), while their morality tends to be conventional (Bravo, 1975). Due to the influence of two cultures, bilingual programs have emerged to prepare teachers in bilingual studies and techniques have been developed to teach English (Kavetsky, 1974).

In a recent study, adolescents born on the mainland of the USA of Puertorican parents show a similar self-concept and levels of aggression to those born in Puerto Rico. Time spent in the USA and Puerto Rico did not have an effect on the patterns of self-concept and aggression. A secondary finding was that older adolescents tended to be more aggressive (Alvárez, 1986).

In personality research, boys tend to have a more defined personality, while that of girls tends to be more diffused. Nevertheless boys score higher on psychoticism and extraversion while girls score higher on neuroticism and social desirability. Compared to British boys, Puertorican boys score significantly higher on social desirability, lower on neuroticism and there are no differences on psychoticism and extraversion. A version of the Eysenck Personality Questionnaire-Junior has been prepared for use with boys in Puerto Rico (Porrata & Eysenck, 1986), but responses by girls suggested the questionnaire was not appropriate for them in its present form.

In studies of aggression, the effects of television in the formation of violent responses point to no short term ill effects, but to a cathartic reaction of short term exposure to aggression in television (Purcell, 1973). In another study, television programs in Puerto Rico were found to present violence and sex in suggestive ways. There is, however, a recognition of the negative effects of long terms of exposure to violence in television (Canino, 1985).

Two studies were carried out on the relation of sex and level of aggression. No relation between the sex of the person and their response to aggression was found, but the level of provocation and the interpretation of it were found to be significantly related to sex (Vélez, 1973; Del Campo, 1982).

Evolution of the family

Child psychology must be seen in the framework of the family, of which children are the most vulnerable members. Puerto Rico has a problem of overpopulation; as early as the 1950s sterilization and the use of oral contraceptives were practised. This was also the time when industrialization flourished, while the sugar economy became less important. Many light industries appeared, employing women, while men lost their jobs in agriculture. Many men felt displaced from their position of economic and sexual mastery, as their wives started to earn money, while controlling and limiting their reproductive processes (Stykos, 1955). The traditional family organization started to disintegrate.

Divorce is very common in Puerto Rico, more than one-third of marriages ending in divorce. The reasons given for divorce according to Fernández & Muñoz (1986) by men are: that the wife belittled him and would not discuss her problems with him, but rather with her family; differences of ideas; infidelity; loss of love; impotence; the wife quarrelled too much; and loss of sexual interest by the wife. The women give as reasons for divorce that: husbands were unfaithful; alcohol abuse by husband; differences in values; physical and emotional abuse; the husbands were too possessive or jealous and did not help domestically. Women as they became economically and sexually liberated have decided to live on their own and the one parent family has become more common.

Many social and emotional problems observed in children such as juvenile delinquency have been attributed to broken homes (Kupperstein, 1974). Nevertheless, in a study on aggressive behaviour in children as an effect of the presence or absence of the mother in the home, no relationship was found between the mother being in the home and the level of aggression of the children (Martínez, 1975). Another study was conducted on the self-concept of children of divorced parents. No significant difference was found between the self-concept of children of divorced parents and non-divorced parents. However, it was found that boys of married parents said they resemble their father more than did boys of divorced parents; while girls of divorced parents said they resembled their mother more than did girls of married parents (González, 1977). A study was carried out on the acceptance and rejection of juvenile delinquents by their parents, delinquents being more often rejected by their parents (Alvárez, 1979).

Child rearing practices of the lower and the middle class have been compared.

Mothers of the lower classes tended to be more dominating, as perceived by themselves and their children. Children of middle class families tended to perceive their parents as more dominating than they perceived themselves (Cangino, 1969). A study of the discipline styles of mothers who worked in factories in a town of Puerto Rico, showed that there was a combination of authoritarian, lax passive and assertive methods of discipline, and that no single style predominated. Nevertheless 20% of the mothers had authoritarian inclinations which, in that group, could lead to mistreating the child (Del Valle, 1984). The problem of child abuse is being tackled in Puerto Rico and legislation has been passed making it a crime (Ley, 1975; 1980). Child rearing practices are advocated whereby the child can decide what is best for himself (Vidal, 1986).

Behavioral disorders and interventions

There are efforts underway to study autism, learning disabilities, drug abuse and other behavioral disorders in children. Behavior modification techniques have been successfully employed in the treatment of children's problems. Problems such as echolalia and temper tantrums have been treated using a social learning paradigm. The techniques used to modify inappropriate behaviors include extinction and positive reinforcement, the major emphasis being on eliciting positive responses (Porrata, 1979). School phobia is a disorder in which shaping techniques and family therapy is utilized.

Roca (1984) raises certain issues that must be addressed by a comprehensive theory of infantile autism: Why are there sex differences? Why are there chemical imbalances in the blood? Why the differences in intelligence, education and socioeconomic level between the parents of autistic children and other maladjusted children? In what form do the biological and psychological factors interact? What types of genetic mechanism can be hypothesized?

Autism has been studied from a communication theory framework (Rodríguez, 1987). Another trend in the study of autism includes the development of diagnostic criteria for this condition which includes adopted baselines for emotional cultural expressions (Sierra, 1978). Psychophysiological components of the autistic child reactivity pattern such as allergy, diet and immune response, is under current investigation at the University of Puerto Rico (Echegaray, 1987).

Hyperactivity is seen as a problem in some Puertorican children. It is characterized by impulsivity and distractibility (Colberg, González & Vargas, 1985), as measured by a children's scale developed by Bauermeister (1983). Causes of hyperactivity do not appear to be related to nutrition, as in Haiti, where malnutrition hinders biological growth. Nutrition in Puerto Rico is adequate, reaching the levels of developed countries. Rather, a major cause of hyperactivity in Puertorican children can be traced to the home environment. The need for social controls in many families causes instability in children which in turn affects their work in school, and is seen as a major cause of hyperactivity.

One of the most serious problems to Puerto Rico's youth is drug addiction. The drug most commonly abused is heroin and polydrug use is prevalent. A high percentage of crimes are committed by drug addicts, so the problem has been tackled from various fronts, from it being a police problem to a social and mental health one requiring psychotherapy. There is some effort being put into creating the cultural conditions for a drug-free society. The government of Puerto Rico has established a Department of Services Against Addiction to combat the problems of drug and alcohol abuse. The first goal of this program is to educate the community, especially school children and their parents on substance abuse. The second goal is to rehabilitate the addicts and substance abusers.

Centres are provided for the detoxification of addicts under medical supervision. Once the addict has been freed of drugs he can pass to an ambulatory program in which heroin is replaced by methadone, a non-intoxificating substitute, or to a resident program, where the drug-free addict is further rehabilitated within a therapeutic community. In both programs, individual and group psychotherapy is practised, employing techniques such as Reality Therapy (Glasser, 1975). With the help of the group, the addict tries to find answers to his problems as he assumes responsibility for his life. Confrontation techniques are sometimes used to sensitize the auto-absorbed personality. Addicts are assisted to see that drugs have a negative effect in their lives and in many cases, treatment is carried out by rehabilitated addicts under the supervision of professional staff.

One study of drug addicts that were in treatment showed that most had not finished high school and that the drug problem was related to criminality. Also, more than half were discontented with their treatment (Figueroa, 1979), further pointing to the difficulty of successfully treating individuals with substance abuse problems.

Psychiatric hospitalization programs are provided for children and adolescents who cannot be managed in the community. Adolescent patients who have a crisis, in many cases an intergenerational conflict, are taken care of in a residential program by an understanding group of professionals, who will look for resolution of the intergenerational gap, as well as providing an independent residence and vocational training opportunities. An approach is advocated where young people are not allowed to fall into the lifestyle or role leading to chronic maladjustment (Scheff, 1978).

Family therapy is practised as a way of treating children in their own surroundings. The models of Minuchin (1974), Haley (1976) and Watzlawick (1967) form the basis of the intervention strategies. The family system is studied as a total group; everyone is viewed as 'part of the functioning of the whole' (Bertalanffy, 1950). Many techniques (Minuchin, 1981) have been tried, such as describing the symptom, so that it becomes clear to the family in what way their behavior is maladaptive and if they wish they can change. Family councils have been used to establish communication channels between all members of the family (Popkin, 1983). Martínez (1986) points out that improvements in the 'identified patient' lead to the improvement of the whole family system. Batlle (1987) is studying the dynamics of psychosomatic families.

Cognitive and social development

An interest of the Puertorican psychologists is to encourage the development of abstract thought in its younger population by overcoming the intellectual and emotional blocks that hinder their progress. Puerto Rico has been an industrial state for the last forty years, and universal education was achieved during the last thirty years. There are many educational institutions from which the population benefit. Education is now seen by the general population as the way to advance socially and economically.

Nevertheless, compared to more advanced nations, Puertorican youth need to develop the skills and attitudes to deal with more complex systems. Culturally, the fears and taboos of an agricultural society must be left behind by a society which is reaching a post-industrial social organization. The problems of poverty might affect the academic performance of more than 20% of the school population and cultural deprivation has been a constant concern of teachers in the public school system. There are many children attending school who are only now in the first generation of literacy, because the parents are illiterate and cannot give effective help in school work.

There is a problem of school refusal, especially in rural areas (Tirado & Ríos, 1973). In a study of the role of the guidance counsellor with school refusers, the findings were that the students perceived the counsellors as agents of help, but would not go to them for counselling (Buitrago, 1986).

Seventeen per cent of the population are unemployed (Junta de Planificación, 1986), and this group is composed mainly of young people. Many social ills such as drug addiction are blamed on the idleness of parts of the population. The lack of motivation to study and work of many young people is thought to be because they have not developed self controls (Ramírez, 1987). Models of alienation are used to explain this phenomenon (López, 1981). Some see idleness as a problem of the utilization of time (Cirino, 1987). Puerto Rico, in contrast to more advanced nations, does not have the cultural activities to occupy large portions of its youth.

Much has been done in the last fifteen years to develop activities and community centres. Youth are served by these centres; work/study programs are also more readily available. More attention is being given to the special education student, especially the mentally retarded. A curriculum was developed stressing self help skills, socialization, perceptual-motor development, communication and functional academic skills (Valdés, 1978).

A course was devised to raise the self-esteem of talented students coming from low socio-economic backgrounds. The training consisted of the analysis of self-perception, physical perception, autoperception, self-disclosure patterns, self-acceptance, acceptance of others, perception of others, visualizing the perceptions of others and blocking irrational thoughts. The techniques consisted of short readings, cognitive reconstructing, feedback and reinforcement, assignments, simulation and visualizing of role. An experimental group counselled by this method showed a significant improvement in their self-esteem over that of a control group (Morales & Ruiz, 1984).

Porrata (1987) is currently preparing a course to instruct teachers as mental health agents, so that they can identify the mental health problems of their students and be better able to help the students cope with and manage their psychological predicaments.

Juvenile delinquency

Juvenile delinquency is a problem that should be approached from a neurological, sociological and psychological perspective. Neurological test data have been obtained from delinquent samples, but results do not reflect greater neurological abnormality in the delinquent population than the general population (Sánchez-Longo, 1975). The psychosocial conditions which give rise to delinquency problems have been researched. The cause of delinquency has been postulated to relate to the way certain groups have been socialized in the anomie of a society that is being industrialized (Rosario, 1976; Pacheco, 1980). The lower socio-economic classes are seen as being left behind in the push for upward mobility and, in their frustration, resort to crime (Toro-Calder, 1969). There is a tendency of the delinquent population to come from the lower socio-economic sectors, especially from public housing and slums in the metropolitan areas (Toro-Calder, 1971).

From a psychological perspective, studies show that delinquents present a very high incidence of analphabetism, early school leaving or truanting, mental retardation and emotional disorders, compared with the non-delinquent population (Kupperstein, 1974; Mangual, 1975; Bonet, 1977). A group of delinquents was compared to a group of non-delinquents and the delinquent sample showed three times more mental health problems than the non-delinquents (Ferracuti, Dinity & Acosta, 1976). The MMPI was given to a group of delinquents, and the results showed them to have a high degree of anti-social personality. It is argued that delinquency should be seen as one aspect of a mental health problem (Cruz-Martínez, 1986).

Currently a study is being conducted, using the Puerto Rican version of the Eysenck Personality Questionnaire which was given to a group of boys enrolled in a special education program and in juvenile custody programs. Results show a greater incidence of psychoticism and neuroticism in the students of the special education program from the population that was used to standardize the Questionnaire. Results from the delinquent population has not been received, but it is expected that they will also show a greater incidence of psychoticism than the general population (Porrata, 1987).

Studies were conducted on the conditions of the delinquent inmates in the industrial schools. Harsh conditions are described where the inmates resort to informal organizations to survive a barren and punitive environment (Palau & Ruiz, 1976). Tattoos are recourses in a search for activities, identity and as a message to society of their complaints and plight (Torres, 1978). More recently, pedagogical, social and psychological resources have been advocated to rehabilitate juvenile offenders. Hiraldo (1980) states that teachers in industrial schools assume the role of social facilitators in the resocializing of delinquents.

Conclusion

Certain directions emerge for child psychology in Puerto Rico. The challenges are to:

1. Continue to define what the characteristics of the Puertorican society are, so the 'forces' that determine and shape the behavior of Puertorican youth are identified.
2. Address the particular educational and cultural needs of Puertorican youth; such as the conflict of the Spanish and English cultures.
3. Redefine child rearing practices in line with the developing patterns of an evolving society and assist the process of social evolution of the Puertorican family.
4. Delineate strategies for the cognitive growth of the young population.
5. Participate in the rehabilitative efforts directed toward deviant and delinquent populations and devise treatment programs for these groups.

These challenges are currently being addressed and met, to a certain extent, by Puerto Rico's psychologists and behavioral scientists. The more completely they are met, the more Puertorican youth and society will benefit.

References

ALEGRÍA, RICARDO, E. (1969) *Descubrimiento, conquista y Colonización de Puerto Rico, 1493–1519*, Estudios Puertoriqueños, San Juan.

ALVÁREZ, A. (1979) *Las relaciones paterno-filiales y el comportamiento Desviado en los Menores Albergados en los centros de tratamiento social del area metropolitana de San Juan*, Tesis, UPR.

ALVÁREZ, L. (1986) *Adolescentes en EU de padres Puertorriqueños que Regresan: Relación entre su autoconcepto y nivel de Agresividad*. Tesis, UPR.

BATLLE, M. (1987) *Estudio Sobre Patrones de Familias Psicosomáticas*, Study in progress.

BAUERMEISTER, J.J. (1983) *Communicación Personal*. San Juan.

VON BERTALANFFY, L. (1950) An outline of general system theory. *British Journal of the Philosophy of Sciences*, **I** 134–65.

BONET, L.A. (1977) *Conducta Delictiva y Retardación Mental*, Tesis, UPR.

BRAVO, M. (1975) *El Desarrollo de Juicio Moral en Niños Puertorriqueños*, Unpublished thesis, UPR.

BUITRAGO, M. (1986) *Impacto del Programa de Orientación en el Problema de la Deserción Escolar en las Escuelas Superiores de P.R.* Tesis, UPR.

CANGINO, J. (1969) *Actitudes de las Madres Hacia la Disciplina en el Hogar: Comparación de la Percepción de las Madres Mismas en la Percepción de sus Hijos Adolescentes*, Tesis, UPR.

CANINO, G., BRAVO, M., RODRÍGUEZ, J. & RUBIO, M. (1985) Análisis de Contenido de la Televisión en Puerto Rico: Violencia, Sexo y Salud. *Homines, vol. 9, num. 122. Febrero-Diciembre.*

CIRINO-GERENA, G. (1987) *Estudio sobre el Tiempo Libre*, Unpublished paper.

COLBERG, C., GONZÁLEZ, L. & VARGAS, I. (1985) *Confiabilidad y Desarrollo de Normas para las Escuelas de Hiperactividad del Inventario de Comportamiento Escolar*, unpublished thesis.

CRUZ MARTÍNEZ, M. (1986) *Perfil Comparativo de Rasgos del Desorden de Personalidad Antisocial entre Jóvenes Delincuentes Primeros Ofensores y Reincidentes y Jóvenes No Delincuentes.* Tesis Centro Caribeño de Estudios Posgraduados.

DEL CAMPO, A. (1982) *Instigación Hacia la Agresión en Función del Sexo del Agresor y del Agredido, Nivel de la Provocación e Intentos de Interacción.* Tesis, UPR.

DEL VALLE, N.R. (1984) *Estilos Disciplinarios Usados por un Grupo de Madres que Trabajan en Fábricas del Municipio de Humacao*, Tesis, UPR.

ECHEGARAY, I. (1987) *Estudio de Niños Autistas*, Study under progress.

EYSENCK, S. & PORRATA, J. (1984) Un Estudio Transcultural de Personalidad: Puerto Rico e Inglaterra. *Revista Latinoamericana de Psicologia.*

FERNÁNDEZ, E. AND MUÑOZ, M. (1986) *Patrones de Divorcio en Puerto Rico.*

FERRACUTI, F., DINITY, S. & ACOSTA, E. (1976) *Delinquents and non-delinquents in the Puertorican slum culture*, Columbus, Ohio State University Press.

FIGUEROA, A. (1979) *Las Opiniones de los Adictos a Heroína Sobre el Tratamiento, Presión Legal y Abandono de Tratamiento.* Tesis, UPR.

GLASSER, W. (1975) *Reality therapy: a new approach to psychiatry*, Harper and Row, New York.

GONZÁLEZ, J.L. (1983) *El País de Cuatro Pisos*, Ediciones Huracán, Río Piedras, P.R.

GONZÁLEZ, Y. (1977) *Relación entre el Divorcio de los Padres y el Autoconcepto en Preadolescentes de 12 a 14 Años.* Tesis, UPR.

HALEY, J. (1976) *Problem-solving therapy.* Jossey-Bass, San Francisco.

HIRALDO, C. (1980) *La Educación y el Rol del Maestro en la Re-educación del Confinado Joven-Adulto.* Tesis, UPR.

IZCOA, A. (1985) Estudio Comparativo de la Imagen de Adolescentes Puertorriqueños: Immigrantes y no-emigrantes. *Homines*, vol. 9, num. 122, Febrero-Diciembre.

JUNTA DE PLANIFICACIÓN (1986) *Estadísticas sobre el Desempleo en Puerto Rico*, San Juan.

KAVETSKY, J. (1974) La Enseñanza del Inglés en Puerto Rico, *Revista del Colegio de Pedagogia*, UPR, vol. XXII, num. 122, Enero-Diciembre.

KOHLBERG, L. (1977) Implication of moral stages for adult education, *Religious Education*, **72**, 183–201.

KUPPERSTEIN, (1974) *Delincuencia Juvenil en Puerto Rico.* Centro de Investigaciones Sociales, UPR, Río Piedras.

Ley de Protección de Menores de Puerto Rico. Ley 1975, 1980.

LÓPEZ-GARRIGA, M. (1981) La Ideología del Trabajo y la Formación de la Conciencia: Notas para el desarrollo de un Objeto de Estudios, *Revista de Ciencias Sociales, vol. 23, num. 1–2.*

MANGUAL, N. (1975) *Delincuencia Juvenil*, Tesis, UPR.

MÁRQUEZ, R. (1977) *El Puertorriqueño Dócil: literatura y necesidad psicológica*, (1962) Editorial Antillana, Río Piedras.

MARTÍNEZ, M. (1975) *Conducta Agresiva en Niños como Efecto de la Ausencia ó Presencia de la Madre en el Hogar.* Tesis, UPR.

MARTÍNEZ-TABOAS, A. (1986) Terapia Sistemática de Familia, Evolución Crítica y Algunos Postulados. *Revista Latinoamericana de Psicólogia.* vol. 18, num. 1.

MINTZ, R. (1974) *Worker in the cane, a Puertorican life history*, Morton and Co., New York.

MINUCHIN, S. (1974) *Families and family therapy*, Harvard University Press, Cambridge.

MINUCHIN, S. & FISHMAN, C. (1981) *Family therapy techniques*, Harvard University Press, Cambridge.

MORALES, J. & RUIZ, M. (1984) El Efecto de la Orientación Grupal en el Autoconcepto de Estudiantes Talentosos Desventajados en los Económico y Social de una Escuela Metropolitana. *Revista Puertorriqueña de Psicólogia*, año 2, vol. 2, num. 2.

ORTIZ, R. (1973) *Teoría de Piaget sobre el Desarrollo de Conceptos de Nacionalidad y su*

Aplicabilidad a Niños de Padres Puertorriqueños Nacidos en Nueva York, Unpublished Thesis, UPR, Río Piedras.

PACHECO, A. (1980) Consideración Sobre la Criminalidad y la Violencia: Un Examen Critico del COncepto de Socialización. *Revista de Ciencias Sociales*, vol. XXII, Sept.–Dic. num. 3–4.

PALAU, A. & RUIZ, E. (1976) *En la Calle Estaba*. Ed. Universitaria, UPR.

PEDREIRA, A.S. (1970) *Insularismo* (1939) Obras Completas Instituto de Cultura Puertorriqueña.

PICÓ, F. (1981) *Amargo Café*, Edición Huracán, Río Piedras.

POPKIN, M., GARCÍA, E. & WOODWORK, H. (1983) *Active Parenting: leader's guide*. Active Parenting, Inc., Atlanta.

PORRATA, J.L. (1979) *Cómo Observar y Cambiar una Conducta Negativa*. Carta, Departamento de Instrucción Publica, Hato Rey.

PORRATA, J.L. & EYSENCK, S. (1986) *Un Estudio Transcultural de Personalidad: Niños Ingleses y Niños Puertorriqueños*. Unpublished study.

PORRATA, J.L. (1987) *Manual De Salud Mental Para Maestros*, en progreso.

PORRATA, J.L. (1987) *Estudio Sobre el Funcionamiento en el E.P.Q.-Jr. para Puerto Rico de Estudiantes de Educación Especial, Grupo de Transgresores y Muestra de Estandarización*, en progreso.

PURCELL GATEL, W. (1973) *Imitación de Conducta Agresiva en Niños y sus Implicaciones para la Televisión*. Unpublished thesis, UPR, Río Piedras.

QUINTERO ALFARO, A. (1971) Innovación y Cambios Educativos en las Ciudades con una Tecnología Menos Desarrollada. *Revista del Colegio de Pedagogia*, UPR, Río Piedras, vol. 212, num. 1, Enero-Diciembre.

RAMÍREZ, E. (1987) *Press Conference*, San Juan.

RIVERA-RAMOS, A.N. (1985) Investigaciones Psicológicas en Puerto Rico: limitaciones y alternativas. *Homines*, num. 3.

ROCA, I. (1984) La Etiología del Autismo Infantil: Biogenesis vs. Psicogenesis. Una Controversia que parece Resolverse. *Revista Puertorriqueña de Psicología*, año 2, vol. 2, num. 2.

RODRÍGUEZ, I. (1987) *Patrones de Comunicación en una Familia Autista*. Unpublished thesis, UPR, Río Piedras.

ROSARIO, C. (1976) Sobre el Concepto de Socialización en las Ciencias Sociales. *Revista de Ciencias Sociales*, **14**, 5–25.

SÁNCHEZ-LONGO, P. (1975) *Perfil de Características Sociales y Psicológicas de la Población Penal en Puerto Rico*. Universidad de Puerto Rico.

SCHEFF, T. (1978) *Being mentally ill: a sociological theory*, Aldine Publishing Co., Chicago.

SIERRA, S. (1978) *Patrones de Desarrollo del Niño Autista*. Unpublished thesis, UPR, Río Piedras, PR.

STYKOS, J. (1955) *Family and fertility in Puerto Rico. A study of the lower income group*, Columbia University Press, New York.

TIRADO, R. & RÍOS, A. (1973) La Deserción Escolar. *Revista de Pedagogía*, vol. 221, num. 2, Julio-Diciembre.

TORO-CALDER, J. (1969) *Bibliografía sobre Sociología de la Desviación Social y Glosario Criminológico*. Universidad de Puerto Rico, Centro de Investigaciones Sociales.

TORO-CALDER, J. (1971) *Estudio Sobre Intervenciones Policiales con Menores en la Ciudad Capital*. Informe Prevención de la Delincuencia Juvenil.

TORRES, M. (1978) *El Tatuaje de los Confinados en una Institución* Penal en P.R., Tesis, UPR.

TORRES-ZAYAS (1986) *Holocausto: La Familia Puertorriqueña de Hoy*. Ramallo Brothers Printing, Hato Rey.

TRIGO, G. (1984) El Rol del Ecuador en el Desarrollo de Valores. *Educación*, San Juan, Febrero.

VALDÉS, M. (1978) *Guía para la Enseñanza del Niño Retardado Adiestrable*. Departamento de Instrucción Pública, Hato Rey.

VÉLEZ, C. (1973) *Agresión en Función del Sexo del Agresor, Sexo del Agredido y Nivel de Provocación*. Tesis, UPR.

VIDAL, A. (1986) *Estudio Exploratorio de la Relación entre la Experiencia de Maltrato y el Desarrollo Intelectual y Visomotor de los Niños*. Unpublished thesis.

WATZLAWICK, P., BEVIN, J. & JACKSON, D. (1967) *Pragmatics of human communication*, W.W. Norton and Company, New York.

16 Some psychological features of children and youth in Romania

A. Bäban, P. Derevenco & A. Coaşan

Introductory elements

The psychology of children and of youth in all its aspects (cognitive, affective, motivational and personality development) have been a long-standing matter of interest for many researchers in Romania (Chircev, 1970; Cosmovici & Căluscher, 1985; Kulcsar, 1978; Radu, 1983; Schiopu, 1967; Zörge, 1980). It is not our intention to enlarge on this matter. Our aim, of a much more limited scope, is to describe briefly the way in which the endogenous and the exogenous factors determine the differentiating characteristics of the psychological development of the children and youth investigated in Romania.

The following lines deal in succession with the factors which characterize and influence the intellectual development, the affective and motivational aspects and, very succinctly, the adaptation to school-life of Romanian children. Our treatment of the matter is based on data gathered in the last few decades, very often through interdisciplinary studies in which, besides psychologists, there were applied medical doctors specialising in hygiene or in school medicine, and sociologists.

Mental development

Educators at all levels are showing an ever-increasing interest in all aspects of the development and growth of intelligence. Therefore intelligence testing is in current practice in this country. The results described here have been gathered after testing 10 236 children aged 4 months to 14 years. A sample of 2259 children aged 4 months to 36 months have been administered the Brunet–Lezine Test, by which such essential aspects of children's development as motor, cognitive, verbal and social functioning have been evaluated. In order to further underscore the role played by the environment in contributing to the child's overall development, the basic psychological aspects mentioned above have been studied in 1009 children in day-care centres (day-nurseries), in 936 children in nurseries with a five-and-a-half day a week programme (week nurseries), and in 314 children in foster homes (children's homes). (Foster homes in Romania are divided into 'cradle homes' housing children up to the age of 36 months and foster homes proper, housing children up to 6 years of age, although less frequently, to 18 years of age).

In the analysis of the data, we have considered the socioeconomic status of the children as reflected by the professions of the parents. Consequently, the children have been assigned to two groups; children of workers and those coming from families of 'intellectuals'. Our comparative results (see Table 16.1) show some clear trends for motor, cognitive, verbal and social development. Children in foster homes generally have the lowest developmental indices while the children in day-care centres have the highest values. After the age of 10 months, to the age of 36 months, the development differences, especially the motor and cognitive aspects, are in favour of the children in day-care centres as compared to week nursery children. Further, as expected, the rate of development is higher in children belonging to the

Table 16.1 Development trends for pre-school children grouped by age, care-taking setting, and socio-economic background

Age (months) / Origin	N	SCORES motricité $\bar{x}$	σ	cognitive $\bar{x}$	σ	verbal $\bar{x}$	σ	social $\bar{x}$	σ	TOTAL $\bar{x}$	σ
4-6 D.N.	76	4,4	2,2	2,2	1,4	0,9	0,6	1,5	0,7	9,0	4,2
W.N.	68	5,0	2,5	2,9	1,6	1,5	0,6	2,0	1,2	11,0	5,4
F.H.	60	4,5	3,1	3,1	1,8	1,3	1,0	1,9	1,5	10,4	6,2
7-9 D.N.	80	6,2	2,9	3,0	1,4	1,7	1,1	1,9	1,1	12,8	6,2
W.N.	49	5,6	2,9	2,5	1,4	1,9	0,8	2,2	1,0	12,3	5,5
F.H.	31	3,3	2,1	1,3	0,9	0,6	0,6	0,5	0,7	5,7	3,3
10-12 D.N.	104	4,9	2,2	3,4	1,8	2,2	1,1	1,5	0,9	11,7	5,1
W.N.	55	3,9	1,7	2,5	1,5	2,1	1,1	1,5	0,7	9,4	4,3
F.H.	42	2,1	1,8	1,3	1,3	0,1	0,3	0,1	0,3	3,8	2,7

Origin

Age (months)	D.N. N.	Levels of develop. A%	B%	C%	W.N. N.	Levels of develop A%	B%	C%	F.H. N.	Levels of develop. A%	B%	C%
15	81	41,3	50,1	8,6	68	29,6	49,9	20,5	40	-	5,0	95,0
18	86	37,2	53,4	9,3	76	15,7	78,1	6,3	42	-	11,5	88,5
21	67	53,7	41,8	4,5	65	46,2	50,0	3,8	45	-	8	92,0
24	72	64,2	31,4	1,4	89	63,2	31,6	5,2	64	4,2	12,5	83,3

Age (months) / Origin	Social level of parents I. N.	Levels of development A%	B%	C%	Social level of parents II N.	Levels of development A%	B%	C%	Level of significance P_A	P_B	P_C
27 D.N.	58	8,3	85,4	6,3	60	9,5	76,2	14,3	N.S.	N.S.	N.S.
W.N.	62	4,5	77,3	18,2	66	11,1	66,7	22,2			
30 D.N.	54	1,8	88,9	9,3	47	18,5	77,8	3,7	0,1	N.S.	N.S.
W.N.	77		70,6	29,4	61	11,1	77,8	11,1			
33 D.N.	63	30,0	67,5	2,5	60	43,7	56,3	-	N.S.	N.S.	N.S.
W.N.	51	22,2	77,8	-	44	37,5	62,5				
36 D.N.	42	9,1	59,1	31,8	59	6,9	69,0	24,1	N.S.	N.S.	N.S.
W.N.	41	10,0	50,0	40,0	64	-	40,0	60,0			

OBSERVATIONS TO TABLE:

day nurseries : D.N.   social level of parents: A: superior developm.
week nurseries : W.N.   I. = workers   B: mean development
foster homes : F.H.   II. = intellectuals   C: low development

intelligentsia reference group (Maier, 1983). These data support the importance of the environment and especially of the family environment, in determining the rate of psychological development of children aged 4 to 36 months.

A group of 1125 kindergarten children (aged 3 to 6 years) have been tested using the Goodenough test, the Coding (A) subtest of the Wechsler Intelligence Scale for Children, and the Raven Coloured Progressive Matrices Test to further describe the development of intelligence. At the same time the quality of the pronunciation of sounds in the native language (i.e. the accuracy of phoneme utterance in Romanian) has also been studieid on a comparative basis with children aged 3–7 years. The phonematic index reveals the percentage of correct phoneme utterance from a total of 28 phonemic sounds (Coaşan, 1977). The mental development, as well as the proficiency in utterance have been comparatively studied in children in foster homes and children in kindergartens.

The results (Table 16.2) show that: kindergarten children obtain higher scores on all intelligence measures and at all ages, as compared to those in foster homes. A comparison of children from kindergartens and foster homes again emphasizes the importance of the educational environment upon mental development at small ages. From a phonematic point of view, differences are observed in relation to age and also the care-taking setting. As Table 16.2 shows, children in foster homes have lower phoneme accuracy scores than children in regular (4-hour) programme kindergartens or even than children in extended (16-hour) programme kindergartens; no significant differences are noted between the latter two groups.

Mental development has been further studied in a sample of 1271 children (aged 5 to 11 years). Of special interest here is an examination of sex differences in

Table 16.2 Intelligence and phoneme scores of pre-school children grouped by age and care-taking setting

Origin	Age	Goodenaugh n	Goodenaugh $\bar{x}$	Goodenaugh σ	Cod. A. $\bar{x}$	Cod. A. σ	Raven $\bar{x}$	Raven σ
Foster homes	4	36	4,7	2,2				
	5	40	7,3	5,9	5,9	3,2		
	6	57	10,2	5,8	13,0	6,5	17,9	4,3
Kinder-garden	4	44	9,6	6,9				
	5	60	14,8	4,8	17,7	9,0		
	6	86	18,6	4,4	22,5	6,4	19,0	3,6

Phonematic index								
Foster homes			regular-hours kindergartens			extended hours Kindergartens		
Age	n	%	Age	n	%	Age	n	%
3	36	54,3	3	37	93,6	3	32	90,1
4	44	78,6	4	38	97,6	4	16	94,6
5	47	83,5	5	60	97,0	5	21	98,2
6	82	89,7	6	65	98,3	6	39	98,0
7	30	89,7	7	31	99,7	7	31	98,8

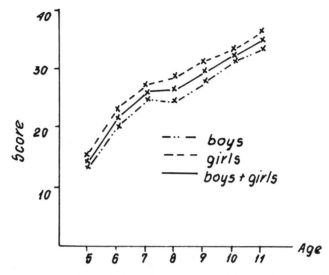

Figure 16.1 Dynamics of the evolution of scores obtained in the Goodenough test, on sex-differences

intelligence between the 636 boys and 635 girls. The results obtained by means of the Goodenough test (see Figure 16.1) show that girls scored consistently higher than boys at all ages (Coaşan, Săndulache, Man & Antal, 1973).

A group of 5581 school children (age 7 to 14 years) have been tested with the Gille Test and by The Raven Standard Progressive Matrices Test in order to further investigate the relationship between intelligence and environment. The children came from different social backgrounds. The results obtained by the Gille Test show that children coming from families of intellectuals have higher measured intelligence at all ages and grades examined here (see Table 16.3). This difference, which favours the children coming from an intellectual background, increases from one age group to the next.

Figure 16.2 displays results which compare the mental development, according to the Gille Test, of children aged 7 to 11 years from a town environment and from a countryside environment. The former category shows a certain degree of superiority compared to the latter. This discrepancy is maintained for the older age groups (11–14 years) according to scores from the Raven Standard Progressive Matrices Test as the graphic representation shows in Figure 16.2 (Coaşan, 1980).

The differences in mental development which are shown above gradually decrease in the following age groups (i.e. high-school students) while in College students there are no significant discrepancies with regard to measured intelligence. We are inclined to believe this to be the result of the educational efficiency of schooling as well as the selection that occurs as children and youth move up the educational ladder.

Differences in motivational and affective characteristics of children and adolescents

While some developmental processes, including cognition, fulfil specialized functions, the affective and motivational aspects are also important in determining general patterns of behaviour. Intelligence, for instance, is not an absolute 'psychic' value. Its efficiency is a function, in part, of all aspects of children's lives and especially affective and motivational characteristics of each individual. Along the ontogenetic

Table 16.3 Average values scored by the children in the Gille text on age groups, school-grade and socio-cultural background

school class	category	n.	7 years			8 years			9 years			10 years			11 years		
			n	x̄	σ	n	x̄	σ	n	x̄	σ	n	x̄	σ	n	x̄	σ
I.	A.	279	115	88,4	28,0	32	79,8	30,1									
	B.		94	109,4	30,5	28	103,6	26,6									
II.	A.	418				219	109,6	28,5	52	104,6	34,3						
	B.					122	132,2	26,8	25	128,6	28,4						
III.	A.	196							72	124,2	24,6	40	120,0	34,2			
	B.								63	148,9	20,9	23	145,0	26,7			
IV.	A.	437										186	140,3	22,4	112	137,6	26,5
	B.											88	154,4	25,1	51	164,3	21,0

Observation : Category A - workers ; B - intellectual

process, the child learns how to become 'a person' gaining, with each of his actions or experiences, new motives, new feelings and new interests. All these 'aspirations' bear the imprint of the socio-cultural habitat as well as the child's age and education. A neglect of these variables would lead to a one-sided simplification of the human being to only what he represents from the perspective of his intellectual growth and functioning.

Research on the role of affective and motivational factors as well as on their impact on conduct and on carrying out a successful activity has been a constant concern of Romanian psychologists (Golu, 1973; Roşca, 1943; Zörge, 1980).

Factors related to motivation and affective differences
Individual differences in motivational and affective development have been studied with regard to age, sex, socio-cultural and family environment on a group of 964

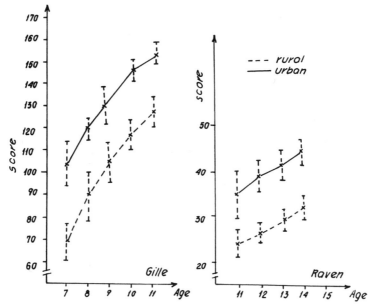

Figure 16.2 Raven and Gille test scores according to age and residential area (urban US rural)

schoolchildren, aged 10–18 years, with an Inventory of Valancies AC-Ref (this is a Romanian personality test) (Zörge, 1978). The results show that in 79% of the items of the inventory, the pattern of responses undergo considerable change from the age of 10 to the age of 18. This indicates that essential changes take place in the needs, interests and aspirations of children. At age 10, the first three priorities are need for dynamism and movement, need for relaxation and comfort and need for sociability, but at 18 years, the top priorities seem to be cultural interests and attraction for the opposite sex, while sociability is placed in a neutral zone. Besides age, sex is also a differentiating factor in the affective and motivational requirements all along the age-span of the group under study. The need for dynamic action and physical movement prevails in boys, together with a 'spirit for adventure' and risk-taking as well as a desire for the expression of self assertion through courage. Girls on the other hand, have greater preferences for activities that allow the expression of sociability as well as a predominant interest in the opposite sex and in cultural matters. These differences are quite clearcut in preadolescence, but less striking in children aged 17 to 18

The motivational and affective characteristics with regard to children's school performance are shown in Figure 16.3. These data indicate that students who are successful in school describe themselves as more interested in school, more assertive and autonomous and possessing greater intellectual aspirations and liking for intellectual activities.

The socio-cultural environment is also a good indicator of the motivational and affective status of the child. A difference in response to 55% of the items was observed in children coming from an urban environment as compared to those coming from rural settings. The latter group show a more accentuated tendency

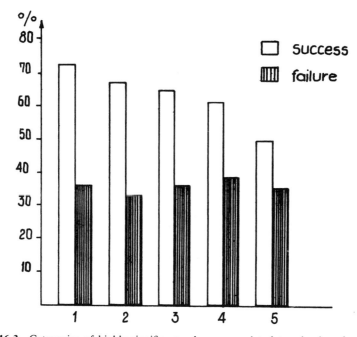

Figure 16.3 Categories of highly significant valences as related to school performances
1. school interests
2. intellectual aspiration
3. propensity to assert oneself
4. appreciation of intellectual qualities
5. autonomy vs dependance

towards sociability and cooperation, an increased response to social norms as well as higher motivation for practical activities, but a lower level of aspiration. A comparison between children coming from harmonious families, on the one hand, and children coming from broken families or foster homes on the other, shows significant differences. Those belonging to the latter group report decreased sociability, inferiority feelings, a special need for security as well as a lack of interest for school activities (Străjescu, 1986).

School motivation

School motivation is a result as well as a condition of the child's adaptation to the school curriculum. Some results from a longitudinal study of school motivation related to age and sex is shown in Table 16.4. A further analysis of the data showed a tendency to focus motivation upon certain subjects taught in school. Ranging agewise, a decrease in the intensity of the motivation for some of the subjects is noted as the child nears the age of 14. The decrease in motivation is at least partly related to the development of certain systems of motivational selectivity around the age of 14.

Table 16.4   School motivation of pupils (%)

Assessment Age	Sex	Motivation				
		Very high	High	Medium	Small	Very small
10–11	B	20.3	40.4	30.2	9.1	—
	G	39.2	30.5	25.3	5	—
12–13	B	25.4	44.2	25.1	5.3	—
	G	35.1	25.5	35.2	4.2	—
14–15	B	15.2	30.3	45.1	9.4	—
	G	5.7	60.4	25.4	8.5	—

A study of the motivation for school-work shows the occurrence of differences in direct correspondence to age. At the age of 11, affective criteria, which have a 'generalizing' character, are predominant (41.68%). Such motives refer to the quality of the subject that is taught (30.21%), a special liking for certain teachers (17.13%), or a personal skill (10.98%). Until the age of 14, these extrinsic motives are predominant (Neacşu, 1978; Potorac, 1978).

Motivation and interests

Another aspect of our research is an examination of children's interests in both the school curriculum and extracurricular activities. Particular patterns of interest have been noted between children and adolescents. Such differences have implications both for understanding the development of group and individual differences in motivation and interests, but also have practical applications for education/schooling.

Table 16.5 shows the rank order options selected by students, aged 11–14 years, for six categories of interests. In boys these interests are similar across categories all along the four years of the age under study. In girls there are fluctuations with

Table 16.5 Rank order of interests

Category of interests	Age (years)							
	11		12		13		14	
	B	G	B	G	B	G	B	G
Exact sciences	2	4	2	4	2	2	2	3
Humanities	4	2	4	3	4	3	4	2
Arts	6	1	6	1	6	1	6	1
Practical activities	3	6	3	6	3	6	3	6
Social matters	5	3	5	5	5	5	5	4
Sports	1	5	1	2	1	4	1	5

regard to the structuring and the stabilization of interests during the age of midschooling. In boys the interest for arts is very low and far below their main interest for sports. In girls all interests tend to become somewhat more stable towards the age of 13 or 14 (Rădulescu, 1980). Correlation coefficients calculated between the interests expressed for certain subjects studied at school and the average grades ($r = 0.54$ to 0.75) indicates an active and constructive pattern of school behaviour when the interests for knowledge acquisition are clearly delineated and relatively stable (Neacşu, 1978). Beside age and sex, the socio-cultural environment (town versus countryside) determines differences in the ontogenesis of interests (Cosmovici & Căluscher, 1985).

A further investigation of 672 adolescents reveals that the scope of their interests is considerably wider than that of preadolescents; a whole harmonious and rich constellation of interests and preoccupations is found to be oriented towards three large categories of problems: *I the wide world* (1 domestic and international political events; 2 historical events; 3 contemporary progress of science); *II philosophical issues* (1 the future of mankind, 2 the sense of life, 3 morals and religion); *III problems pertaining to the inner or personal world* (1 choosing one's future profession, 2 the assertion of one's personality, 3 the relationship between sexes). Viewed as a whole, the responses by this group do not confirm the views put forward by certain authors, according to which the contemporary, technical society narrows the scope of the adolescents' interests (Dumitrescu, 1980).

Professional aspirations, ideals and attitudes

The characterization of an open, active and prospective system of human personality is emphasized by the presence of desires, aspirations, ideals and purposes which guide or direct man's activity and conduct. All these form the content of the projective part of consciousness and underlie the expression and character of human behaviour. Projecting into a hypothetical future, professional aspirations and life ideals, by preadolescents and adolescents has been examined by a number of studies (Neacşu, 1978; Potorac, 1978). An analysis of Figure 16.4 illustrates some results based on Romanian studies. Children and adolescents recognize a wide variety of professional options which encompass different fields of economy and culture; more often aspire to professions which require academic instruction; most often express interest in industrial vocations; and show an inclination toward 'brilliant' professions (e.g. actors, pilots, navy officers, etc.). This tendency disappears around the age of 17 when options become more realistic; a professional preference does not appear to be decisive in preadolescents (the percentage of undecided subjects as well as fluctuations in choices are higher than in later adolescence).

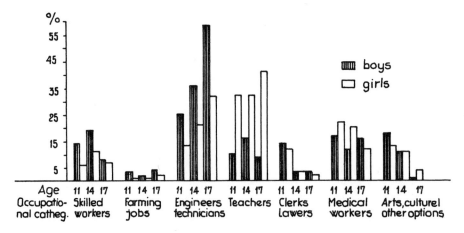

Figure 16.4   Occupational options

Professional aspirations of youth have also been studied by means of a comparison with the professions of the child's parents. These studies show a tendency to better one's professional status in comparison to that of one's parents. This general propensity for high professional aspiration exceeds, in many cases, the actual achievements and capabilities of the children and adolescents. Consequently, there seems to be a need for more educational guidance in order that the level and direction of schoolchildren's aspirations is based on a more accurate self-estimation of one's aptitudes and capabilities.

Even before adolescence, there occurs a slow but dynamic process moving from a state of passive and dependent socialization to the stage of an active and autonomous one. The building of a self and life ideal develops along three fundamental axes: the search for self identity; the need to identify; and the orientation towards socialization (Bazac, 1983). If, in preadolescents, the life ideal is first directed towards becoming 'a person' and secondly, towards gaining more extrinsic things such as fame and prestige, in adolescents the final orientation of the ideal changes. The results obtained from samples of adolescents ranging between 15–18 years are as follows: (1) personal happiness (22.39%); (2) sacrifice for a communal cause (19.64%); (3) intertwining personal interest with the general one (19.39%); (4) fulfilment of personality (15.71%); (5) prospects of chosen profession (14.71%); (6) desire to obtain fame (5.84%); (7) financial gains (2.32%). These results do not show a deep individualism, since the social aspects are predominant (Dumitrescu, 1980).

An active effort and concern for finding a life-model is reported by 81% of the adolescents under study. The hierarchy of the factors that influence life-model making is as follows: (1) family and close relatives; (2) school (including teachers); (3) personal life experience; (4) literature; (5) films; (6) friendships; (7) youth organizations; (8) t.v. and radio broadcasts. It is quite obvious that major influences in this formative process are determined by various social factors, however the person's own personality also has an impact. These data remind us that adolescence is an age of confrontations, of changes and decisions (Dumitrescu, 1980).

Attitude formation
As concerns attitude formation, motivation is considered both as a process and a product variable. Attitudes are influenced by socio-cultural factors and interpersonal or group relations. Schools and the educational systems have to take into account,

besides the development of intelligence and special skills, the attitudinal nucleus which ensures an open mind, prepared to take in knowledge.

Each developmental stage has its own 'eye' for receiving and evaluating the social, familial and school milieu as well as one's own personality (Radu, 1979). A study of attitudes toward school and towards learning in preadolescents may result in two general groupings of the subjects by the absence of an attitudinal system which generates either a conjectural, oscillating, uncommitted position, or a position of conventional compliance, or by the presence of an attitudinal system; in this case the schoolchildren conduct themselves either in accordance with the educational purpose and values, or they behave to the contrary (Nacşu, 1978).

It is generally considered that the child's attitude towards schooling is the synthetic expression of the dialectical relationship established between the child and school on one hand, and the attitude the child has with regard to himself, on the other. At an individual level, this means an ongoing reconsideration of one's own status. The comparative studies, drawn on various ages and on males and females with regard to the relationship between attitude and the image about oneself reveal some interesting findings. The attitude about oneself appears quite different at the age of 10 and 11 than at the age of 14 to 15. Subjects ranging between 10 and 11 years of age are inclined to consider themselvs as being very close to an optimum moral model; thus 83% of these subjects choose, out of ten positive moral criteria, 8 to 10 criteria as being pertinent to them. There is no significant difference between boys and girls at the ages of 10 to 13 but at 14 years, girls obtain higher scores in self-appreciation. In children of 11 years, the attitude about oneself is further characterized by a predominance of the physical as well as of the social selves. In adolescents of 17 years the attitude about self is concerned mostly with the spiritual and social selves, the physical self decreasing considerably especially in boys (Schiopu, Gîrboveanu & Onofrei, 1982).

The attitude of adolescents towards family and adults has been investigated on a group of 848 boys and girls, from town as well as rural environments. The question 'Where do you usually spend your spare time?' was answered as follows: 53.5% mostly in the family; 24% in the family and with school-mates; 22.5% mostly outside home. The second question 'Do the grown-up people around you hinder the assertion of your personality or do they offer you enough possibilities to assert it?' was answered as follows: 67.8% grown-up people are no hindrance; 20.8% sometimes are a hindrance; 8% yes, they definitely are a hindrance; and 0.7% remained undecided. No significant differences were noted in answers, considered by sex, or the social environment (urban or rural) of the subjects. The results of this survey do not reveal any strong tendency of the adolescents to evade their families, nor any tension of a general and compulsory nature, between parents or grown-ups and the children of this 'awkward' age; consequently there was little indication of any feeling of rebellion against one's family. This suggests that the affective ties between adolescents and their families are stronger than what the behaviour of adolescents shows. Family relationships remain an important factor in the system of environmental influences which concurrently form one's personality (Neacşu, 1978).

The study of moral attitudes as an expression of the person's integration of the acquired values and their manifestation within interpersonal relations, towards work and towards oneself allows for a description of certain characteristics which are relevant for a given age, sex or socio-cultural environment (Chircev, 1983; Dumitrescu, 1980; Spînoiu & Motescu, 1981). At the age of 9 or 10 years, children are still inclined to observe rules and requirements out of fear of punishment (akin to socio-moral immaturity). Towards the age of 14 or 15, the moral set of rules becomes internalized and the characteristic manifestations of the previous age diminish. However, it is noted that the moral knowledge of the adolescent is still rather poor, somewhat below the level of the intellectual development. There are no significant differences when it comes to the effects of urban or the rural environment, although adolescents coming from a rural environment are nonetheless slightly more responsive to moral norms. Differences between sexes and ages could be noted in the responses when the subjects were required to mention which moral category they cherished most. Girls, for instance, praised sincerity most, while boys' first choice went to industriousness and patriotism; at the age of 14 sincerity scored at the lowest pole while at the age of 18 it scored the highest.

The importance of teaching the children and the adolescents positive and active attitudes toward learning, work, moral norms, and so forth resides in the fact that, in accordance with their stability and importance, they become circumscribed within a person's character. The scope and the nature of motivation, as well as the configuration of the interests and of the attitude and the level of aspirations, all reflect the force, the dynamics and the evolution in the structuring of the child's personality. At the same time they also constitute an important way to estimate the efficiency of the instructive-educational process that is performed by family, school and society. The malfunctions that may appear in this respect have marring effects upon behaviour, ranging from the simplest misdemeanours all the way to delinquency.

Adaptation to school life

We shall end this paper with a brief note reflecting some of our research on school adaptation and factors which affect it. Many of the definitions of good mental health postulate adaptation to be a key-factor in it. Therefore we shall briefly approach the problem of how children adapt themselves to the environment by considering adaptation to school-life, the main form of social adaptation of their age. We have studied (Coaşan, 1980) the forms and the cause of inadequate adaptation to school-life at ages 6 to 11 years on 3462 subjects and have reached the conclusion that the proportion of children who experience adjustment difficulties is around 13.2%. Insignificant differences may appear from one age-group to another or from one form to the next, but they are to be found predominantly in the first form (age 6 to 7). Boys are noted to show non-adaptative characteristics more often than girls (62.1% in boys, 37.9% in girls). Figure 16.5 shows the most frequent forms of adaptation problems to school life. There is encouraging evidence to suggest that intervention with children of ages 6 to 7 years with instrumental problems can produce a significant decrease of this form of misadaptation; from a level of 17.2% in the first form schoolchildren to a level of 3% in the third form pupils.

A decrease in the frequency of some forms of school adjustment difficulties has been obtained through a systematic programme of physical exercise. Thus the sustained practice of physical exercises for one year has led to a reduction of 1.9% of children classed as maladapted; the practice of physical exercises for two years has led to a reduction of 2.9%, and a similar practice sustained for three years has led to a reduction of 5.1%. In the control groups, who did not practice physical exercises systematically, the modification of maladaptation manifestation varied both ways, the average reduction being only 1.4% (Antal, Timaru & Florea, 1967).

Taking morbidity as a tentative cause for school inadaptation we have found that in 11 000 schoolchildren aged 7 to 14 years who live in an area high in people afflicted with goitre, the frequency of school maladaptation was 11% to 16% higher than in the children of the control groups. Among 5900 children who had suffered from ailments like rheumatism, skull lesions, psychic disorders, TB, etc., the frequency of school maladaptation was 6% to 8% higher than in the control group (Antal, 1972; 1978).

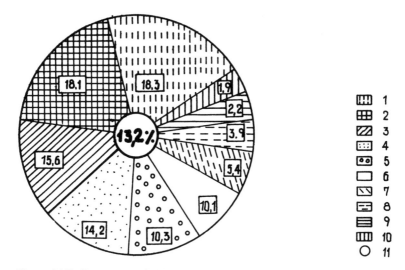

Figure 16.5 Percentage of different kinds of non-adaptative characteristics

1. specific learning disabilities
2. mental retardation
3. behavioural disorders
4. affective-motivational and volitive disorders
5. borderline intelligence
6. psychomotor instability
7. incapacity to cope with the demands attached to beginning school
8. slow rhythm of mental and motor activity
9. asthenia
10. other manifestations
11. the percentage of children with non-adaptative phenomena in the group of study

By studying the impact of overexertion on adaptation capacity, we have found that increases of 2 to 3 hours per day in the students' programme over the present average can result in some negative effects. Results for a sample of 16-year-olds showed a diminution of cognitive processes including attention and memory which was noted to alter depending on specific days of the week. At the same time, subjective symptoms of fatigue have been noted in 91.7% of the children in the experimental group (Antal, 1978).

Family atmosphere, as a tentative cause for maladaptation, and mental ill-health among children has been studied by means of a number of investigations. Some of our findings revealed that 81% of the maladapted children came from families in which parents apply inappropriate parenting methods or simply lack in authority. Forty-one per cent of the maladapted children suffered from indifference or rejection by the father and 24% from the same attitude/behaviour of their mothers. Furthermore, 72% suffered as a result of an autocratic and 'tyrannical' attitude of their parents, which was often accompanied by parental incompetence. A conflictual family atmosphere and flaws in the social-emotional climate of the family also contained 62% of maladjusted children and 20% came from broken families (divorce, separation, death, etc.) (Preda, 1981). Although these categories and numbers are certainly overlapping there is strong evidence that family factors can play a major and contributing role in the positive as well as negative psychological development of children.

In our country, the discovery and preventive actions as concerns school adaptation, are given special attention, with a view to ensuring a high level of health in children and youth. The amount of research as well as the various studies in this field in

Romania will attest to this (Antal, 1972; 1978a; 1978b; Antal, Timaru & Florea, 1967; Coaşan, 1980; Kulcsar, 1978; Radu, 1979).

Acknowledgement

Helpful suggestions by Dr Psychologist T. Kulcsar are gratefully acknowledged.

References

ANTAL, A. (1972) *Rev. Neuropsych. Infant* (Paris), **20**, 145–55.

ANTAL, A. (1978a) *School hygiene* (in Rom.) 2nd ed. Ed. Medicală, Bucharest.

ANTAL, A. (1978b) *Rev. Hyg. Med. Scol.* (Paris), **31**, 81–95.

ANTAL, A., TIMARU, I. & FLOREA, E. (1967) *Med. Educ. Phys. Sport (Paris)*, **41**, 145–9 & 150–5.

BAZAC, B. (1983) *Life ideals of adolescents* (in Rom.). Political Publ., Bucharest.

CHIRCEV, A. (1983) In I. Radu (ed.) *Developmental and educational psychology* (in Rom.). Academy of RSR, Bucharest.

CHIRCEV, A. (1970) *Psychology of children and adolescents* (in Rom.). Babeş Bolyai University Publ., Cluj-Napoca.

COAŞAN, A. (1977) *Revista de pedagogie*, **26**, 44–7.

COAŞAN, A. (1980) *School inadaption manifestations and prevention.* Doctoral thesis (in Rom.). Babeş Bolyai University, Cluj-Napoca.

COAŞAN, A., SĂNDULACHE, I., MAN., F. & ANTAL, A. (1973) *Igiena*, **22**, 737–44.

COSMOVICI, A. & CĂLUSCHER, A. (1985) *The adolescent and his leisure* (in Rom.). Junimea, Iasi.

DUMITRESCU, I. (1980) *Adolescents, their mental world and educational activity* (in Rom.). Serisul Romanesc, Craiova.

GOLU, P. (1973) *Revista de Psihologie*, **19**, 363–77.

KULCSAR, T. (1978) *Psychological factors of school success* (in Rom.). Didactic & Pedagogic Publ., Bucharest.

MAIER, A. (1983) In *Progress of Medical Sciences*, Cluj-Napoca, 21–23.

NEACŞU, I. (1978) *Motivation and learning* (in Rom.). Didactic & Pedagogic Publ., Bucharest.

POTORAC, E. (1978) Schoolchildren between endeavour and achievement (in Rom.). Didactic & Pedagogic Publ., Bucharest.

PREDA, V. (1981) *Prophilaxis of delinquency and social reintegration* (in Rom.). Scientific & Encyclopedic Pub., Bucharest.

RADU, I. (1979) In B. Zörge & I. Radu (eds.) *Researches in school psychology* (in Rom.). Didactic & Pedagogic Publ., Bucharest.

RADU, I. (ed.) (1983) *Developmental and educational psychology* (in Rom.). Academy of RSR, Bucharest.

RĂDULESCU, R.N. (1980) *Revista de Psihologie*, **26**, 229–47.

ROŞCA, AL. (1943) *Motivations of human actions (in Rom.). Psychological Institute of Cluj-Napoca University, Sibiu.

SCHIOPU, U. (1967) *Psychology of children* (in Rom.). Didactic & Pedagogic Publ. House, Bucharest.

SCHIOPU, U., GÎRBEVEANU, M. & ONOFREI, A. (1982) *Revista de Psihologie*, **28**, 19–29.

SPÎNOIU, D. & MOTESCU, M. (1981) In *Cognition of pupils' personality* (in Rom.). Didactic & Pedagogic Publ., Bucharest.

STRĂJESCU, A. (1986) *Revista de Psihologie*, **32**, 240–50.

ZÖRGE, B. (ed.) (1980) *Fundamental problems of psychology* (in Rom.). Academy of RSR, Bucharest.

ZÖRGE, B. (1978) *Rev. Roum. de Psychologie*, **22**, 141–53.

17 Individual differences and youth groups in Singapore

F.Y. Long & J.M. Elliott

Introduction

Singapore is an island Republic, founded as a British Colony in 1819 and independent since 1965. It was originally little more than a fishing village, and its present population of roughly 2.5m comprises immigrants and the descendants of immigrants since its founding. This immigrant stock has been extremely various (Table 17.1), resulting in a heterogeneous culture that creates certain real problems and challenges for the psychologist interested in individual differences. Not only are there three major ethnic groups, the Chinese, the Malays and the Indians, but these broad groupings (plus others) conceal a further series of both ethnic and linguistic divisions. Other differences, for example religious affiliations or educational background, may follow or cut across ethnic/linguistic groupings.

Mandarin, for example, is a dialect of Chinese. Traditionally the language of scholarship and administration in China, it has remained the official language of that country. It is also one of four official languages in Singapore. Despite its increasing use in daily life, as a result of education and government policies encouraging its use, many Singapore citizens of Chinese extraction still come from families speaking primarily Hokkien or other dialects, or English, or a combination of languages and dialects. Where partners in a marriage speak different mother dialects, they may resort to a third dialect or language to communicate. Children from dialect-speaking homes frequently grow up to use Mandarin or English more than their parents or grandparents did, and it is not uncommon to find quite marked differences across the generations in range of spoken languages. Singapore Chinese may have been educated to greatly varying degrees with either English or Mandarin as their first educated language, and may or may not be literate in the other. They may be Buddhists, Taoists, Christians of any of several denominations, or be agnostic; many retain a belief in ancestor worship and in Confucian ethical principles (the latter undergoing a revival of interest).

Similar lists could be generated for other major ethnic groupings in the country, and for the many minority groups. Singapore has four official languages, Malay, Mandarin, English and Tamil, and a bilingual policy (English plus another language) in education. It will be apparent, therefore, that the investigation of individual differences raises in a particularly acute form problems of psychological measurement in a plural society.

The investigator neglects these problems at his peril. For example Torrance, Wu, Gowan & Alliotti (1970) administered the Torrance Test of Creative Thinking to 'monolingual' and 'bilingual' children in Singapore. They concluded that monolingual children were more fluent and flexible, but less original and inventive, in their replies on the test items. However, the criterion of bilingualism was determined by the type of the school the children attended, not by assessment of the children themselves. Torrance *et al.* classed English stream pupils as 'bilingual' and Chinese and Malay stream schools were classed as 'monolingual'. Their classification was based on the nature of the language teaching in the school system as it then was,

Table 17.1   Ethnic and language/dialect groups in Singapore, 1980 Census of population. Note that the dialect (Chinese) or language given is not necessarily an indication of current linguistic competence, but of linguistic origins. Note also that dialects of Chinese, though sharing a very similar grammar and a single written form, are often very different in pronounciation and resemble separate languages rather than dialect variation of a single language (Newnham, 1971)

Ethnic Group	Dialect/language	Number	Percentage
Chinese	Hokkien	799 202	33.1
	Teochew	409 269	16.9
	Cantonese	305 956	12.7
	Hakka	137 438	5.7
	Hainanese	131 975	5.5
	Others	72 397	3.0
	All:	1 856 237	76.9
Malays	Malays	312 889	12.9
	Javanese	21 230	0.9
	Others	17 389	0.7
	All:	351 508	14.5
Indians	Tamils	98 772	4.1
	Malayalis	12 451	0.5
	Punjabis	12 025	0.5
	Others	31 384	1.3
	All:	154 632	6.4
Other groups	Europeans	23 169	1.0
	Eurasians	10 172	0.4
	Others	18 227	0.8
	All:	51 568	2.2
	Total:	2 413 945	100.00

Source: Khoo (nd), Census of population 1980, Singapore

but this may have had little relation to the actual linguistic capabilities of the individual subjects. Nor did it reflect the ethnic and cultural differences that tended to accompany the choice of school at that time. In short, the design was confounded and the conclusions of limited value.

In some cases a psychometric procedure may be applicable across a wide spectrum of cultural variation. The numerous cross-cultural studies of the Eysenck Personality Questionnaire suggest that it produces a similar factorial structure in a wide range of countries (Barrett & Eysenck, 1984). This structure was found in Singapore (Eysenck & Long, 1986), in a sample of 994 adults and 1028 children. The Eysenck and Long study confined itself to using subjects who could speak English and thus were by no means a quota sample. The results showed a high degree of similarity between the factors extracted from these samples and the corresponding factors in British samples. With the exception of the Lie scale, there was close agreement between the mean scores on each factor for adults in each country. Agreement for children was less marked, though the factors evidently corresponded, and social desirability items in particular were not always appropriate for both countries. In general, however, the study gave reason to think that personality traits as assessed by the EPQ and Junior EPQ were not different in the two countries, and that with some scoring modifications to omit less reliable and valid items, the scales could be employed locally.

The Eysenck & Long study is also one of the few to publish data from a large sample of subjects in Singapore. Apart from this study the present authors know of few cases where local norms have been developed. An exception is Cattell's 16 Personality Factors test (Form A), which has been normed on a sample of 2636 National Service entrants, but no analysis of the factor structure comparable with that of Eysenck & Long has been reported. The Wechsler scales (WAIS and WISC) and Raven's Standard Progressive Matrices are quite often used as an aid to assessing intellectual ability, but with limited unpublished local norms.

The net result is that for assessment of individual differences, psychometric instruments are sometimes used with highly specific local norms. They are sometimes used for guidance but with a heavy reliance on local knowledge and experience for interpretation. They are also sometimes used in research as a means of making comparisons between groups.

A situation where standardised psychological instruments are used outside their reference groups is clearly undesirable, but the practical solution is by no means self-evident. It can be argued that in a society as diverse as that of Singapore the notion of a national standardisation sample is impracticable on two grounds. The first ground is that a properly stratified and representative sample would be almost impossible to obtain in view of the number of potentially relevant variables that would have to be represented in the sample. These variables could in theory be specified, but in practice the sample would have to be enormous. This ground is essentially logistical. The second ground is theoretical and more serious. It is as follows.

The purpose of norms is to allow location of an individual on a known distribution. If this distribution is intended to be a national one, then in a heterogeneous society it consists in effect of a number of pooled distributions, the nature of which is unknown. An individual's score will then give his location relative to the superordinate distribution at the expense of precision regarding his location vis-à-vis what would be his own appropriate reference group. Scores obtained and standardised on a single distribution of this sort cannot then be used to investigate the differences between groups for which different norms might be appropriate. This problem is not new (e.g. Anastasi, 1982, ch.4), and it is recognised that in practice, many tests in their countries of origin are in effect using relatively restricted normative samples, but if different norms are sought for different groups in a country as diverse culturally as Singapore, then the problems of logistics outlined above become apparent again. The implication in a diverse nation is that the potential value of national norms lies mainly in the case where the test has high content validity and test scores are of value in their own right regardless of possible reasons for variation in scores. For attainment tests, for example, it is clearly valuable to have objective information about a standard achieved, and the question of norms for particular sub-groups arises only if one wishes to investigate or be informed of different levels of performance in members of such groups.

When the item content of the test allows the use of an external criterion of interest, superordinate standardisation procedures are also useful. Self-report measures of personality, such as the EPQ or the 16PF, rely upon external criteria of this kind. These tests and many others, however, additionally depend on assumptions about the interpretation of test items. One cannot assume the interpretation is the same for different groups of individuals. Other evidence, such as a shared factor structure, is important in justifying a decision to compare scores among different subgroups. If a 16PF questionnaire, for instance, is given to the members of several different reference groups, information can be obtained as to the size and direction of any group differences, and whether or not they differ statistically. However, the interpretation of these differences is quite another matter. Even the assumption of a common factor structure cannot be made unless specifically tested. At best, one can suggest that if the structure of personality is common to different groups then it is likely that the item loadings will be similar enough to allow some degree of interpretation in terms of personality structure. Even so, the norms for different groups might, if known, reveal large group differences. The extent to which these reflect real differences in the characteristic of interest, as opposed to apparent differences arising from differences in item interpretation is impossible to say.

This really amounts to a claim that the use of personality tests or other tests with an interpretive element is at best suggestive and at worst misleading. However, the perceived need for psychological assessment as an aid to enquiry is bound to lead to some use of test materials if this seems likely to be helpful. Indeed, the information may be worth having if it is all one has, so long as its limitations are appreciated. Two studies are offered below which try to show how some psychological assessments have been of value in investigating individual and group differences, despite the need for caution in interpretation. They also illustrate some of the practical difficulties with research of this sort. This work examined the social circumstances and individual characteristics of certain categories of youth in Singapore, with a view to explaining and predicting the type of social activity and group membership that an individual would be inclined to select.

Group affiliations in Singapore

The entire history and character of Singapore as a community of migrant origins would in the past have provided many reasons for expecting group membership to be important in the lives of individuals. The social history of pioneering days reveals the importance attached, first to kinship networks, and then to broader networks of linguistically and culturally connected individuals. These were the means by which individuals survived and established a foothold in an expanding and entrepreneurial trade-based society (see, for example, Purcell, 1964; Neville, 1969; Sandhu, 1969; Lee, 1978; Quahe, 1986).

Among the more obvious groupings were the Chinese clan associations, the 'hui-kuan' (provincial/dialect associations), the various trade and mercantile guilds and associations, and the Chinese secret societies, or Triad societies. Subsequently, the various religious groupings each with their place of worship and congregation also became important. Of all these, the Secret societies have attracted great interest. Originally formed in 1674 by the monks of the Shao-Lin Monastery, the Triad Society (Heaven, Earth and Man) was formed with the political objective of overthrowing the then ruling Manchu rulers of China (the Ching Dynasty) and restoring the defeated Ming Dynasty. However, with the end of the Dynasty and the republican revolution of 1913, this *raison d'être* vanished. The societies, however, persisted. They were in fact little more than protection rackets, but using a heavily mystical series of initiation rites. Indeed, some authorities dispute the political origins of the societies, tracing them instead to the early Han Dynasty (BC), and attributing their rise to the stratified society and rigidly bureaucratic system of government at the time (Ward, 1967).

On this view, the persistence of the secret societies in Singapore was partly explained by the tendency of the colonial administration to see them as a potentially benign means to control the Chinese population through the delegated authority of a 'Kapitan China', an individual reckoned as a leader or headman for the Chinese community and one able to settle disputes over local or indigenous matters. It may be noted though, that the first Protector of Chinese, William Pickering, was strongly of the view that the secret societies should be eradicated if the Chinese were to be either protected from exploitation or controlled and brought within the framework of the colonial laws, and this view came to prevail by 1870 (Lee, 1978; Ng, 1961).

The secretive and criminal character of these associations was better explained, according to other sources, by the character of Chinese society itself (Chew, 1975, Robertson, 1978). It was suggested that the desire to avoid official routes in the settling of disputes, and general dislike of any involvement with government, were a natural consequence of the frequently corrupt and feudal system of authority familiar to so many of these immigrants, most of whom were poor and had come to Singapore either as indentured labourers or simply to seek a better life than was possible in China. Moreover, some authors made specific allusion to what they assumed were particular Chinese characteristics, evidently making a dispositional attribution in doing so. Thus Robertson (1978) in a popular account thought that in 'recruiting members to their cause, or extorting payments, the Triads have three specifically Chinese characteristics working for them: innate secrecy, clannishness, and the ready acceptance of the fact that personal services should be paid for' (p. 7).

The problem posed by the existence of secret societies has preoccupied successive governments in the post-war period. Part of this concern has been a result of the involvement of young people in the societies. In 1979, a government-sponsored psychosocial study of secret society members was carried out, and revealed that the average age of first involvement with a secret society was 18 years. The first study reported below is based on the findings of that report.

Study 1: Psychological and social characteristics of secret society members in Singapore

Secret society members are the subject of provisions in the criminal law making membership of a secret society a criminal offence, and permitting preventive detention of suspected members and their release under police supervision orders. As of 31 December, 1979, 2415 secret society members were the subject of disposition under the criminal law, either serving sentences following conviction, or as a matter of preventive detention, or under police supervision orders. The files on these individuals formed the basis of an investigation into some demographic and sociological characteristics of secret society members.

Characteristics of 2415 secret society members:

1 *Sex*: All the subjects were male. There are very few recorded cases of women as members of secret societies.
2 *Age*: Ages ranged from 14 to 71, mean 27 years, sd 7.4. As already mentioned, however, the age at first involvement was on average 18 years.
3 *Ethnic group*: Predominantly ethnically Chinese, 89.6% as against a national figure of 72.9% taken from the census (males) for 1957. This is clearly significant ($\chi^2 = 496.6$ df 1, $p < .001$) and the only surprising feature is that there are any non-Chinese secret society members at all. The conclusion reached, as will be seen, was that for the most part these 'societies' have become simple criminal gangs. Members of such gangs are usually all of the same ethnic or dialect grouping, but the gangs need not be Chinese.
4 *Dialect group*: The lingua franca of Singapore is still to a considerable extent Hokkien dialect, and was even more so in earlier years. It is therefore unsurprising that Hokkien is overrepresented in the SS cases. Details of the

Table 17.2   Dialect origins among 2415 secret society members

Dialect	SS members %	Chinese pop. %
Hokkien	52.2	40.6
Teochew	21.3	22.5
Cantonese	10.3	18.9
Others	16.2	18.0
Total	100.0	100.0

($\chi^2 = 180.3$ df3, $p < .001$)

representation of the various main dialect groups are given in Table 17.2.

5   *Employment and social background*: On each of several indicators of socio-economic status secret society members are of lower status than the national average. They were apt to be unemployed (25%) at the time they came to the attention of the police; their income distribution showed a negative skew relative to the population as a whole. Education, though valued, was not obligatory at the time these men were of school age, and they had attained a substantially lower level of educational achievement by national standards of that period (73.2% had no post-primary education, compared to a national figure of 39.6%). Reasons for failing to continue school were overwhelmingly lack of interest (43%), examination failure (23.1%) and financial reasons (22.7%); the last may reflect either the inability to meet fees and expenses of education, or the greater felt need by the families to have the children in work at an early age. Interestingly, however, there was no evidence from the sample data (see below) of any failure due to intellectual limitations.

Sample of 131 individuals selected for further study

From the 2415 files discussed above, a representative sample of 131 convicted or suspected secret society members under detention or on police supervision orders was obtained. Individuals of various ranks within their societies were included in the sample at random in proportion to their frequency in the population on file. The sample comprised the following:

General Headman	5
Headman	31
Triad Master/Counsellor	15
Assistant Headman	8
Financier/Treasurer	1
Fighter	53
Member	9
Associate	9
	131

Scores on the following tests were obtained: Raven's Standard Progressive Matrices; Cattell's 16PF (Form A); and an Attitude/Socialisation questionnaire devised for the study, designed to examine allegedly peculiarly Chinese characteristics and to elicit attitudes to an involvement in Secret Society activities.

A sample of 153 Special Constables and Vigilante Corps recruits matched for age, ethnic group, sex, educational level, father's occupation (similar) and type of housing was used as a comparison group for the Attitude/Socialisation questionnaire. National Service norms were used for the 16PF scale, courtesy of the Ministry of Defence Personnel Research department.

Method

Group and individual testing was conducted under the supervision of the first author with the help of three other psychologists familiar with psychological testing in Mandarin and Chinese dialects. All instruments except Raven's Matrices were translated into Mandarin prior to administration, with 'blind' retranslation to English as a check on translation accuracy. All SS subjects were seen at police stations or in prisons, and all would thus have had a strong incentive to make socially desirable responses.

A further sample of 17 individual SS members were selected for in-depth interview. These were selected on the basis of ranks and personal background to give a wide range of variation within the sample. These interviews were helpful in interpreting the test results.

Results

Intellectual ability: Raven's Standard Progressive matrices raw scores were converted to IQ equivalents, using the percentile-based conversion given in the manual (Raven, 1956). This gave a mean IQ of 103.5, sd = 16.6. Suitable local norms for young adults are not available for the Matrices, but it seems reasonable to conclude that there is no evidence that intellectual deficiency (by this measure) characterised the secret society members.

Personality: the sten scores on the 16PF questionnaire for secret society members and national servicemen are given .in Table 17.3. Interpretation of the factors are problematic for reasons already discussed, but given the usual interpretations, there are unexpected differences between the two groups. Society members are less 'conscientious', but more 'submissive', 'shy', 'sensitive', 'imaginative' and 'forthright'

Table 17.3 Mean 16PF sten scores for secret society subjects

Factor		SS subjects		National servicemen	
A	Reserved/outgoing	5.5	(1.8)	5.9	(1.6)
B	Less/More intelligent	4.4	(1.9)	5.9	(1.7)*
C	Easily upset/emotionally stable	4.9	(1.8)	5.0	(1.4)
E	Humble/assertive	4.0	(1.8)	5.1	(1.6)*
F	Sober/happy go lucky	4.9	(1.8)	5.0	(1.6)
G	Expedient/conscientious	4.9	(1.8)	5.4	(1.2)*
H	Shy/venturesome	4.6	(1.5)	5.1	(2.0)*
I	Tough/tender minded	6.3	(1.8)	5.3	(1.8)*
L	Trusting/suspicious	5.0	(1.8)	5.2	(1.3)
M	Practical/imaginative	6.1	(1.5)	5.1	(1.5)*
N	Forthright/shrewd	4.4	(2.0)	5.9	(1.4)*
O	Self-assured/apprehensive	6.2	(1.7)	6.0	(1.7)
Q1	Conservative/experimenting	5.7	(1.8)	5.6	(1.6)
Q2	Group dependent/self-sufficient	6.0	(2.1)	5.6	(1.8)
Q3	Undisciplined/controlled	5.3	(1.8)	5.2	(1.3)
Q4	Relaxed/tense	5.6	(1.7)	5.3	(1.9)

* = $p < .05$

than the control subjects. This is an unexpected result. Membership of a secret society is itself an offence, but members are typically also convicted of a range of other offences (see Table 17.4). In the case of more senior members, more serious offences such as kidnapping were traditionally found. Nevertheless, insofar as secret society members differed from the control group they did so in personality dimensions many of which are the opposite of what one might expect.

At least three possible explanations suggest themselves. The first is that the interpretation of test items is different in Singapore to the extent that the instrument is simply not measuring its intended dimensions. The second is that the pressures to socially desirable responses led secret society respondents to depict themselves as submissive to authority. The third is that many members of the societies were actually inducted into membership as a result of a need for some degree of protection or association, and that in effect the societies comprised in large measure members who once initiated were bound by ties of obligation, but who were not in themselves adventurous, aggressive or tough-minded.

Table 17.4   Percentage secret society membership involvement in offences

Drug offences	37.6%
Housebreaking/theft/robbery	24.7%
Rioting/affray	23.2%
Homicide	18.4%
Armed Robbery	16.1%
Unlawful assembly	12.3%
Extortion/attempted extortion	11.3%
Causing Hurt	9.3%
Arms/explosives offences	7.4%
Rape/Kidnapping/Intimidation	5.2%
Other	35.0%

It is not easy to decide between these possibilities. The first is perhaps the least likely, in that even if great latitude in actual interpretation of results is allowed, it is difficult to see how such an anomalous result could have arisen. The second is much more probable, and cannot be ruled out; but the evidence from the remaining results actually suggests that the third possibility may in fact be correct. All the individuals studied were asked why they had originally joined their society, and also why they had continued to be involved as at the time of their conviction or supervision order. The results are given in Table 17.5, and it is clear that protection and association are prominent reasons for initial involvement, and that once involved, protection is the dominant reason for continued secret society association. 'Protection' in this context generally refers to protection from threats (e.g. from other societies, or from competitors for a job or trade). Note that few members claimed they were coerced into joining; many however were persuaded or felt they needed the protection offered, as judged by the interview protocols. The following extract from an in-depth interview protocol is typical of the circumstances under which older society members joined:

> A— joined as a member of the 'Chuen Tong' society of '18' group in 1947 at the age of 20. He was then working as a lorry attendant, sitting behind the cab and helping the driver to signal. The headman of Chuen Tong asked a fighter to approach A— to join the group for protection at a rate of $2.00 per month. As a member he did not participate in the gang's activities. He tried to avoid conflict with the law, but due to financial difficulties he had to rob to survive and maintain the family

Table 17.5 Reasons given for secret society involvement

Reason	First joining	At time of offence
Protection	20.9%	72.2%
Association	32.8%	18.8%
Financial gain	3.7%	3.5%
Thrills/adventure	18.8%	1.2%
Status	4.4%	0.9%
Forced to join	2.1%	0.7%
Other	17.3%	2.7%

On the other hand:

> G— first joined 'Sio Koon Tong' of '18' group in 1960 at the age of 16. He was influenced by his peer group of about 20 other youths, mostly school 'dropouts', living in the same area. Many were society members and he joined voluntarily in order to belong to the group. He joined as a 'fighter'. In 1966 he start to extort, rob and housebreak. As he put it, 'easy money, need not toil hard under the rain and sun for a paltry wage'.

Both the above scored at or below sten 3 on factor E (humble/assertive).

Chinese characteristics: Are there any attitudes which could be deemed peculiarly Chinese, and which are more noticeable among secret society membership? An attitude scale was devised for this study. It relied on content validation, and attempted to investigate 10 characteristics which some authors have suggested are so typical. These 10 characteristics are given in Table 17.6 with the mean score for each from the society and control subject groups. Of these characteristics, secrecy, group loyalty and political and social alienation might all have been reflecting reactions to detention or police supervision, but religious-mystical credulity and sense of obligation are not so readily accounted for in this way.

Other variables: A number of background variables were investigated by self-report for both the control and society groups. These were, the extent to which parents expected responsible behaviour, the extent to which the home was rule-oriented, the extent to which the parents sought to monitor their children's activities, and the nature of their reaction to disobedience. There was no detectable difference in the groups on these various self-report measures, except that corporal punishment appeared to be more prevalent in the secret society subjects' reports; in fact a small but significant rank order correlation exists between the extent of corporal punishment

Table 17.6 Mean scores from questionnaire on 'Chinese' characteristics

Characteristic	Subjects	Control	
Clannishness	6.7	6.4	
Face-saving	7.9	7.6	
Secrecy	8.4	9.3	$p < .05^*$
Revenge	6.2	5.9	
Sense of obligation	8.4	7.9	$p < .05$
Group loyalty	8.3	8.7	$p < .05$
Religious-mystical credulity	6.8	7.7	$p < .05$
Respect for the law	6.0	6.1	
Political alienation	7.2	6.7	$p < .05$
Social alienation	10.8	10.1	$p < .05$

* (*t*-tests. Regrettably, analysis of variance was not used at the time, and these data are not now available for re-analysis.)

in the home and frequency of criminal activities during the first year of involvement (Kendall's Tau = 0.106, $p < .02$).

An important further finding was that virtually none of the family members of secret society members had any criminal record (0.5%). A family background of criminal activities is not a feature of youths who joined secret societies. Yet the interview details bear strong witness to the role of social influence and circumstance in leading members to join. Less than 5% claimed they were forced to join. Overwhelmingly, they were introduced by childhood friends and neighbours (35.4%) or by fellow workers (21.6%), or even by recent friends or acquaintances (27.8%).

Conclusions from Study 1

The impression obtained from the 131 individuals studied in detail, and from the interview data, is that secret society members were not, for the most part, greatly different in personality or ability from other individuals of similar social background. Rather they were, if anything, even less aggressive and dominant personalities who entered into a criminal association for essentially practical reasons, such as a desire for companionship or protection from existing gangs, and who were led willingly into the association by friends or acquaintances. It is difficult to detect any psychological factors behind their decisions, and family background would appear to contribute very little to criminal involvement of this type. Rather, the persistence of a social attitude which favours a sense of obligation and which for historical reasons has seen associations of one kind or another as legitimate means of pursuing self-interest, coupled with the social pressure from friends and colleagues, seems to have sufficed in most cases to prompt entry to a society. The original political purposes behind the establishment of secret societies did not feature in the thinking of the members, and it seemed clear that the societies had become essentially criminal gangs involved in various organised rackets.

Study 2: Application of discriminant analysis to four groups of youths

The outcome of the study on secret society members suggested that individual psychosocial variables were unlikely to be clear predictors of group membership. However, the possibility that a combination of such variables might have predictive power deserves investigation. In view of the problems of valid psychological assessment discussed above, it seems reasonable to argue that a suitable research strategy is to endeavour to find empirical predictive measures which can be subsequently the subject of a degree of content analysis. A multivariate discriminant analysis based upon the measures used in study 1, and applied to a set of groups of interest, was therefore carried out as part of a broader investigation into the social and psychological background of four youth groups. These were motorcycle gangs, street-corner gangs, 'trendy' adolescents and People's Association young adults. The first three categories are officially viewed as undesirable; the fourth category represent a control group of individuals active in the People's Association, an association sponsored by government which offers a range of organised activities and facilities at local community centres.

Motorcycle gangs are loose associations of young adult motorcyclists who come periodically to the attention of the police for dangerous driving offences. In particular, these groups are apt to congregate for informal races on remote public highways in the small hours or late at night. A sample of 72 such individuals (all male but one) were interviewed in the aftermath of a police raid in one such race 'meeting'. The average age of this sample was 23.7 years, and 69 (96%) were ethnic Chinese.

Street-corner gangs are loosely organised groups of youths, the majority in National Service, or schooling, or employed, who frequent public places and appear to have few organised activities. Chinese gangs sometimes have secret society affiliations, which partly accounts for official interest in their activities, but many of the gangs comprise ethnic Malay youths. The majority of these youths have no criminal record. A sample of 71 such gang members (69 male) were interviewed, mainly following direct approaches in housing estates and eating houses. The average age of this sample was 19.7 years, all were male, and 54 (76%) were ethnic Malays.

'Trendy' adolescents are overwhelmingly Chinese and still schooling. Over 90% of the sample studied had reached at least secondary level education. These youths dress stylishly in modern and often distinctive 'punk' styles that are somewhat outlandish by the standards of Singapore. However, they would not attract much attention in any Western city, and in-depth interviews with a subsample suggested that they were interested simply in fashion and company, and frequented public shopping centres and fast food outlets simply as a pleasant way of passing the time of day. Complaints from the public about rowdy behaviour, or just a well-intentioned concern over the cultural values implied have prompted periodic expressions of concern in some official quarters, but these youngsters have typically no record of involvement in any kind of illegality. They appeared in this sample at least to be relatively innocuous if rather aimless and unconstructive in their general attitudes. That they should have attracted official attention at all is indicative of the fact that even in modern Asian societies, personal liberty in matters such as dress and conduct is not taken for granted to the extent that is regarded as normal in 'Western' countries. A sample of 79 young people were obtained by accidental sampling in public places. Forty were male, and 39 female. The average age was 15.6 years and all but four were Chinese.

People's Association young adults comprised a group of 92 interviewed at various community centres in Singapore. Fifty-four were male and 38 female. 73 were ethnic Chinese, 11 Malay, and eight were Indian. The average age was 22.8 years. Virtually all had secondary or higher education and were either in continuing education, employment, or National Service (men only). These subjects represented a group who in no way contravened public perceptions of desirability in young adults.

Summary of procedures

The subjects in each group were seen individually and the following information was sought:

Demographic details.
Raven's Standard Progressive Matrices scores.
16PF questionnaire profiles.
The attitude and socialisation scales used in study 1.

A second scale, constructed for the purpose of assessing social attitudes, incorporated three existing measures; the anomie scale of McClosky & Schaar, the alienation scale of Middleton, and the political alienation scale of Olsen (all reported in Robertson & Shaver, 1976).

Results

There were a total of 29 variables to consider in the results from this study, and a discriminant analysis was undertaken as the most appropriate method of discovering natural groupings among the individuals studied. The 'Discriminant' subprogram of the Statistical Package for the Social Sciences (SPSS) was used for this purpose. The analysis suggested that the variance in the data could be accounted for by three discriminant functions, which mainly involved personality variables. Taking the three greatest canonical correlation coefficients for each function, we obtain the following characterisations. The interpretation of these functions has to be extremely cautious for the reasons discussed in the introduction.

Function 1: PF 14, group dependent/self-sufficient (−0.544); PF 2 less intelligent/more intelligent (0.466); and PF 4, humble/assertive (0.30). This combination of self-sufficiency with lower intelligence (as assessed by the 16PF) and lower assertiveness tended to characterise the motorcycle gangs and the street-corner gangs alike, despite their typically contrasting Chinese and Malay composition respectively. This rather paradoxical low assertiveness was of course also found with secret society members in study 1.

Function 2: PF 5, sober/happy-go-lucky (0.645); PF 12, self-assured/apprehensive (0.328); and PF 9, trusting/suspicious (0.299). This somewhat odd combination of a carefree yet suspicious and apprehensive pattern of responses seems to pick out the adolescents. It nicely illustrates the real difficulty of knowing whether these responses – obtained by direct approach on a voluntary basis in suitable public places – reflect the circumstances under which data were gathered rather than anything valid about the personalities involved.

Function 3: PF 7, shy/venturesome (0.435); Parental monitoring (questionnaire) (0.373); and PF 8, tough/tender-minded (0.436). This does not clearly discriminate any single group.

Table 17.7 shows the ability of the three canonical discriminant functions to separate the groups. Discriminant analysis allows the prediction of group membership from individual scores. Table 17.8 shows that for 64.6% of cases the discriminant analysis correctly identified the individual's group membership.

Table 17.7   Canonical discriminant functions

Function	Eigen-value	Percent variance	Correlation	after function	Wilks lambda	Chi-square	df	p
1	0.632	52.4	0.622	0	0.374	271.5	72	< .001
2	0.420	34.8	0.544	1	0.610	136.3	46	< .001
3	0.154	12.8	0.366	2	0.866	39.6	22	< .01

Table 17.8   Accuracy of group membership predicted by discriminant analysis

Group		N	Predicted group membership			
			1	2	3	4
1	M-cycle gangs	72	40 (55.6%)	4	14	14
2	Trendy adolescents	56	10	34 (60.7%)	5	7
3	Street-corner gangs	71	14	5	46 (64.8%)	6
4	PA young adults	92	11	8	5	68 (73.9%)

Conclusions from study 2

The results of the above analysis do suggest that despite differences in age range, ethnic composition and self-report attitude and demographic variables, personality variables may be important in predicting the patterns of youth activity that appeal to individual young people. However, pending suitable validation studies, interpretation of specific personality variables is probably too speculative to be useful.

General conclusions

A rather tentative general conclusion from these studies is that secret society membership, though possibly associated with a surprisingly low score on scales purporting to assess adventurousness, tough-mindedness and assertiveness, is likely to have been in large measure a consequence of social pressures and influences given the nature of the social background of those who became members, and the circumstances of the 1940s and 50s. Contemporary youth groups, on the other hand, seem to be distinguished potentially at least by certain combinations of personality characteristics, but an accurate statement of the nature of these differences is frustrated by the absence of suitable validated and normed instruments for assessment. It is debatable to what extent this obstacle can be overcome in principle, and it may be necessary to settle for norms that do not do justice to the subcultural variation characteristic of Singapore society.

The first author has commented elsewhere (Long, 1987) that the absence of a university department of psychology in Singapore has virtually precluded an active programme of research of a high academic standard. 'Published work in established psychological journals by psychologists in Singapore based on on-going research activities in the country is rare' (p. 10). This situation may hopefully change with the start of an honours degree course in psychology at the National University of Singapore in 1986. However, a consequence of the absence of an academic focus for research in psychology has been a strong tendency for research to have an applied character. The studies reported here reflect that fact, as well as highlighting some of the difficulties in attempting research under these circumstances. Given that the public perception of psychology has always focussed on its professional and applied aspects (Long, *op. cit.*), this applied emphasis may be no bad thing if it allows the future development of the subject to avoid an emphasis on academic and theoretical concerns out of proportion to the scale of the practical matters where psychologists have a contribution to make. In the authors' opinion it is good that, although the outlook for local psychological research in all fields is probably better today than at any time previously, such research will be judged by its relevance for practical concerns as well as by its technical and academic merit.

Acknowledgements

The findings reported here were originally sought as part of government sponsored inquiries into aspects of youth in Singapore. Numerous individuals cooperated in obtaining this material, but we are especially grateful to Mr Ngiam Tee Liang, Department of Social Work, National University of Singapore; Dr Chiew Seen Kong, Department of Sociology, National University of Singapore; ASP Gilbert Tan, Police Operations Command; Senior ASP Ong Kian Min, formerly of Traffic Police; Dr Tan Chue Tin, formerly Consultant Psychiatrist, Woodbridge Hospital; Mr Loh Yan Poh, formerly Psychologist, Prisons Department, Ministry of Home Affairs; Mr See Khay Soh, formerly Psychologist, Ministry of Social Affairs; Mr Edmund

Wee, formerly psychologist, Personnel Research Department, Ministry of Defence; Dr Lim Yun Chin, Senior Registrar (psychiatry), Woodbridge Hospital; and Mrs Katherine Yip, psychologist and lecturer, Institute of Education.

References

ANASTASI, A. (1982) *Psychological testing* (5th ed), London, Collier Macmillan.

BARRETT, P. & EYSENCK, S.B.G. (1984) The assessment of personality factors across 25 countries. *Personality and Individual Differences*, **5**, 615–32.

CHEW, A. (1975) *Secret societies in Singapore: a legal and empirical study.* Unpublished LLM Thesis, University of Singapore.

EYSENCK, S.B.G. & LONG, F.Y. (1986) A CROSS-CULTURAL COMPARISON OF PERSONALITY IN ADULTS AND CHILDREN: SINGAPORE AND ENGLAND. *Journal of Personality & Social Psychology*, **50**, 124–30.

KHOO, C.K. (ND) *Census of population 1980 Singapore*, Release No. 2; Demographic Characteristics, Singapore, Department of Statistics.

LEE, P.P. (1978) *Chinese society in nineteenth-century Singapore*, Kuala Lumpur, Oxford University Press.

LONG, F.Y. (1987) Psychology in Singapore: its roots, contexts and growth. In G.H. Blowers & A.M. Turtle (eds.) *Psychology moving east: the status of Western psychology in Asia and Oceania*, Boulder, Westview Press, Inc.

NEWNHAM, R. (1971) *About Chinese*, Harmondsworth, Penguin.

NEVILLE, W. (1969) The distribution of population in the post-war period. In J.B. Ooi & H.D. Chiang (eds.) *Modern Singapore*, Singapore, University of Singapore.

NG, S.Y. (1961) The Chinese protectorate in Singapore. *Journal of Southeast Asian History*, **2**, no.1, 76–99.

PURCELL, V. (1964) *The Chinese in Southeast Asia* (2nd ed), London, Oxford University Press.

QUAHE, Y. (1986) *We remember.* Singapore, Landmark Books.

RAVEN, J.C. (1956) *Guide to using the Standard Progressive Matrices.* London, H.K. Lewis.

ROBERTSON, F. (1978) *Triangle of death: the inside story of the Triads – the Chinese Mafia*, London, Corgi Books.

ROBERTSON, J.P. & SHAVER, P.R. (1976) *Measures of social psychological attitudes.* Ann Arbor, The Institute for Social Research.

SANDHU, K.S. (1969) *Indians in Malaya*, Cambridge, Cambridge University Press.

TORRANCE, E.P., WU, J.-J., GOWAN, J.C. & ALLIOTTI, N.C. (1970) Creative functioning of monolingual and bilingual children in Singapore. *Journal of Educational Psychology*, **61**, 72–5.

WARD, B.E. (1967) Chinese secret societies. In N. McKenzie (ed.), *Secret societies*, London, Aldus Books Ltd.

18 Studies of the Lie scale with Spanish adolescents

N. Seisdedos

Introduction

One of the most common criticisms against questionnaire-type measures has been the possibility of the subject 'faking' his answers in order to give a deliberately good or bad impression of himself. The subject may answer the personality test questions having in mind his ideal 'self' or 'ego', or perhaps a more factual 'ego'. Much has been written about this variously named distortion, faking, or dissimulation.

To be fair, one should not necessarily consider this attitude to be a form of insincerity, lie or deliberate faking. It does not seem to us to be something necessarily negative from the subject's viewpoint to show his best 'ego', because, in some settings, that could be the way to adapt to the circumstances (e.g. in a personnel selection or clinical situation). It may be something like going to a rendezvous wearing one's best dress or suit, or after having paid a visit to the hairdresser. There are some praiseworthy aspects in this behaviour, although the psychologist would like to measure an individual with his 'normal dress'.

Nevertheless, it is well accepted that questionnaires, such as the Eysenck Personality Questionnaire (EPQ), provide a valid measure of some personality traits. Nias (1972) has suggested that, besides the fact that conditions of anonymity do not produce changes in personality scores as compared with name-signing conditions, there is also good evidence to indicate that under ordinary conditions subjects give relatively truthful answers about themselves.

It seems likely that under certain circumstances (e.g. when subjected to a job selection interview) many people will dissimulate, and even under ordinary experimental test conditions it also seems clear that some people will dissimulate. Then, knowing these facts, several different methods have been tried to define dissimulation behaviour, to measure it and, if possible, to correct the other measures for this faking. Originally, the main purpose was to measure the person's tendency to deceive using a number of personal questions 'which on the whole have rather widespread social approval, but which at the same time are rarely done' (Hartshorne & May, 1928). The measurement of this kind of lying has been pioneered by the authors of the Minnesota Multiphasic Personality Inventory (Dahlstrom & Welsh, 1960), and was introduced in the Eysencks' questionnaires: the Eysenck Personality Inventory (EPI), the Junior EPI and the two forms of the EPQ (Adults and Junior). In order to prepare a better Lie scale for the latter questionnaires, several studies were carried out attempting to establish the existence of one unitary dissimulation factor and its independence of the three main personality scales (Neuroticism, Extraversion and Psychoticism).

In the Spanish adaptation of these instruments, we attempted the same goals, translating the original items and elaborating new ones for this purpose (Sanchez Turet & Cuadras Avellana, 1972; Eysenck & Seisdedos, 1978; Eysenck, Escolar, Lobo & Seva-Diaz, 1982). The factorial and practical results have been well accepted by the Spanish users of the questionnaires.

However, before going further, we have to point out that in the Spanish adaptations of the L scale we have inverted the pole of the scores and named it as S (Sincerity);

that is to say, high S scores means the opposite of high L scores. This procedure was followed intentionally to avoid the Spanish deprecatory meaning of lie or dissimulation. Nevertheless, for the purpose of this chapter and English speaking readers, we have again inverted the scale and present the results as L measures.

Some hypotheses about the nature of the L scale

Several studies have pointed out that the L scale might have a situational meaning from the point of view of personality structure. Here, dealing with children and adolescents, we propose some tentative hypotheses about the influence of the subject's maturation and environment on the L scale (perhaps, readers can confirm or reject them with their own investigations; that will be welcome). For this purpose, we have reviewed several investigations and compared them with the L scale factorial structure and its relationships with other measures in Spanish subjects.

Dicken (1959) has suggested three possible and plausible reasons for high scoring on the L scale: deliberate 'faking', response in terms of an ideal self-concept rather than a candid self-appraisal and response in terms of an 'honest' but inaccurate and uninsightful self-assessment. Eysenck adds a fourth possibility, also suggested by Hartshorne & May (1928), that a genuine conformity to social rules or mores may result in elevated L scores. Another possibility is the subject's defensiveness. People differ in respect of this variable, and the degree of L depends partly on the stable individual personality structure, and partly on external motivational conditions.

An alternative hypothesis has been phrased in terms of another personality dimension or set of characteristics, independent of N, E and P, stressing such traits as conformity, orthodoxy and conservatism, whereby the high L scorer behaves in a more conforming way to the present social mores. That is to say, the high L scorer could be a conformist who puts himself in the best possible light to gain public approval.

Other researches (Michaelis & Eysenck, 1971) have demonstrated that the increase of motivational distortion is related to a higher negative correlation beween L and N; when the authors studied five groups with increasing drive to dissimulate and, therefore, of increasing percentages of liars (from 38% to 77%), the tetrachoric correlations between L and N become increasingly negative (from a non-significant $r = .07$ to a highly significant $r = -.58$), while correlations with E were not affected. This hypothesis was replicated in a relevant study by Furneaux & Lindhal (unpublished) at the Eysenck Laboratory of the Institute of Psychiatry, London. However, this general conclusion in fact became untenable after the also unpublished study of Dr L. Montag, Chief Psychologist to the Israeli Ministry of Health Medical Institute of Road Safety, using the EPQ results of 400 male subjects, mean age 25 years. In his very highly motivated group to do well on the personality test (in order to obtain a driving licence), the correlation between N and L was only $r = -.17$ (significant at the 0.01 level, but not as high as expected). Eysenck points out that the explanation probably lies in the variance of L or the threshold and ceiling effects of the motivational variable. That is to say, when the level of the motivation drive is very low or very high, there is not a large L variance (all the subjects of the group are similar in motivation to dissimulate), and the scatter diagram of the relationships between L and N is probably circular ($r = .00$), while in a middle motivated group the dissimulation variance is larger, and consequently more plausible for a significant correlation between the two variables.

Finally, we have to point out that Rie (1963) has reported some remarkable inconsistencies between different parts of a widely-used Lie scale, including negative correlations between one part of the scale and another. Nevertheless, Eysenck &

Eysenck (1970) have factor analysed 16 L items in a sample of 2500 children between 7 and 16 years, and in different age groups the outcome was a simple, strongly marked superfactor which loads appropriately on all items, and which can be identified confidently with lying or dissimulation. On the same line, we have analysed the 20 × 20 L item intercorrelation matrix of the Spanish EPQ-J version (with a sample of 265 8th grade children), and did not find any incongruencies at the item level (the results will be discussed later).

Our hypothesis about the nature of L is based on the motivation drive. Paraphrasing our Spanish philosopher Ortesa y Gasset who said, 'man is his self and his circumstances', this drive will function according to the individual personality as a whole and his environmental characteristics. That is to say, when answering a personality questionnaire the subject adapts himself to the surrounding demands with all his capabilities (knowledge, intelligence, experiences, etc.) and moods. 'Faking' could be an intelligent form of adaptation.

Spanish studies and results

One of the first findings derived from the Spanish factorial studies of the Eysencks' instruments adapted for use in Spain has been that, although the four factors, N, E, P and L, were orthogonal, some of the scales show significant interrelationships, mainly between P and L.

When the Spanish EPI adaptation was carried out (Sanchez & Cuadras, 1972), the L factor, with an average factor loading of 0.256, appeared after the two personality measures of N and E, and its discriminant value was better in males. The samples employed in this investigation were 200 adult males (mean age 33.7 years, standard deviation 12.6 years) and 200 adult females (mean age 36.2 years, standard deviation 14.5 years). The principal factor method and varimax solution were applied to the two sexes item correlation matrix. The L scale scores were negatively related to N and age. Some years later, with a sample of 263 8th grade adolescents we found a significant N-L correlation of $-.277$ ($p < .01$).

The Spanish EPQ Junior adaptation showed similar results (Eysenck & Seisdedos, 1978). Table 18.1 presents the comparative study of English and Spanish children. The L scale was negatively related to N and even more strongly to P. Besides the Spanish standardization data, other samples are included at the bottom of Table 18.1.

When the Spanish adaptation of the EPQ for adults was examined with 1030 subjects (Eysenck, Escolar, Lobo & Seva, 1982), the factor structure was very similar (see Table 18.2), although the L scale was now positively related to age (18 to over 50 years; male mean was 27.97 and female mean was 25.31). This scale had a reliability

Table 18.1 L relationships between the N, E and P scales (EPQ-J)

English		LN	LE	LP		Spanish		LN	LE	LP
1.751	M	$-.24^{**}$	.05	$-.41^{**}$	976	M	Norms	$-.26^{**}$	$.14^{**}$	$-.35^{**}$
1.636	F	$-.29^{**}$	.04	$-.35^{**}$	1.002	F	Norms	$-.28^{**}$	.04	$-.34^{**}$
					193	M+F	5 gr.	$-.23^{**}$		$-.33^{**}$
					347	M	5 gr.	$-.15^{**}$		$-.34^{**}$
					280	F	5 gr.	$-.24^{**}$		$-.17^{**}$

$^* p < .05$ $^{**} p < .01$

Table 18.2 L relationships between the N, E and P scales (EPQ-A)

English		LN	LE	LP	Spanish		LN	LE	LP
500	M	−.04	−.10*	−.23**	435	M	−.26**	−.14**	−.33**
500	F	−.15**	−.09*	−.19**	595	F	−.20**	−.12**	−.33**
					599	M	−.38**	−.23**	−.25**

* $p < .05$ ** $p < .01$

of 0.79 in males and 0.77 in females. One extra sample of 599 young adults in a selection procedure is included at the bottom of Table 18.2.

Recently, we have administered the EPQ-J to two representative samples of children, including 791 5th grade students (471 M + 320 F) and 1037 8th grade students (702 M + 335 F). Table 18.3 presents a condensed summary (males are above the diagonal) of the EPQ-J correlational structure, and all the basic statistics for the samples are very similar to the standardization results. At the bottom of Table 18.3 are the results of the mean differences analyses determined by Student 't' tests. The younger male children (5th grade) only show significantly higher P scores but the older males (8th grade), score higher on E and P and females on N and L.

Subjects were then classified into three groups according to their L scores, and the analysis was repeated with the high and low L groups. The results are given in Table 18.4. The L+ subjects of both age groups have lower N and P scores. The faking-dissimulation effects have not influenced the E score, suggesting that Spanish children are more concerned to 'hide' the instability and tough-minded aspects of their personality than their extraversion/introversion.

Another effect of controlling the L variable has been a change in the size of the Junior EPQ scale intercorrelations, mainly between N and P in both sexes of the 5th grades group and in the females of the 8th grade group. The highly significant

Table 18.3 EPQ-J results for two samples of Spanish children (males above the diagonal)

	5th grade				8th grade			
	N	E	P	L	N	E	P	L
N		−.10*	.33**	−.34**		−.09*	.24**	−.22**
E	−.20**		−.19**	.09	−.20**		−.11**	−.00
P	.34**	−.13*		−.34**	.30**	−.15**		−.37**
L	−.29**	.07	−.38**		−.26**	.04	−.35**	
	471 Males				702 Males			
Av.	10.33	19.00	3.01	9.61	10.39	17.76	3.55	9.07
S.d.	4.20	3.24	2.39	4.61	3.95	3.33	2.54	4.40
	320 Females				335 Females			
Av.	10.59	18.12	2.65	9.96	11.80	17.26	2.70	10.41
S.d.	4.13	3.04	2.35	4.53	3.99	3.26	2.15	4.78
t	0.85	0.52	2.10*	1.29	5.32**	2.29*	5.60**	4.32**

* $p < .05$ ** $p < .01$

Table 18.4 Pearson correlation of the EPQ-J scales and comparison of high (above the diagonal) and low L scores

	5th grade			8th grade		
	N	E	P	N	E	P
N		−.13*	.26**		−.12*	.27**
E	−.14*		−.21**	−.13**		−.08
P	.26**	−.17**		.09*	−.08	
		L+ (N=260)			L+ (N=345)	
Av.	8.78	18.37	1.84	9.92	17.55	2.30
S.d.	4.04	2.95	1.83	3.89	3.44	1.94
		L− (N=244)			L− (N=458)	
Av.	11.86	17.90	3.67	11.78	17.55	4.17
S.d.	4.01	3.23	2.63	4.00	3.31	2.61
t	8.56**	1.70	8.98**	6.61**	0.45	11.62**

** $p < .01$

$r = .303$ ($p < .01$) between N and P in 8th grade females of Table 18.3 fell to a non-significant $r = .093$ in Table 18.4.

Next we tried to go further and study both sexes of the 8th grade sample of students; the two sex groups were classified into five subgroups of increasing L raw scores (according to the L distribution of each sex). Table 18.5 shows the mean and standard deviation statistics and Pearson relationships. From the results we can see that the main effect of increasing the L score is a clear of the P score, which is not as clear for N scores, and the E variable shows a curvilinear effect between the points L3, L4 and L5 (very similar in both sexes). The Pearson correlation indices are more significant in the

Table 18.5 8th grade children with different and increasing L scores (L1 to L5, according to the L distribution of each sex, M and F)

Group	n	EPQ-N		EPQ-E		EPQ-L		Intercorrelations		
		Mean	SD	Mean	SD	Mean	SD	N-E	N-P	E-P
Males										
L1	217	11.41	4.09	17.81	3.31	4.73	2.87	−.21**	.16	−.05
L2	238	10.92	4.05	17.55	3.58	4.12	2.42	−.03	.17**	.04
L3	264	10.44	3.89	16.43	5.03	3.57	2.08	−.42**	.38**	−.42**
L4	159	10.95	3.74	14.57	5.18	3.25	2.00	−.40**	.23**	−.34**
L5	165	9.13	3.74	16.98	4.71	2.22	2.06	−.21**	.36**	−.32**
Females										
L1	83	12.65	3.98	17.53	3.79	3.99	2.58	−.44**	.22*	−.14
L2	98	12.89	3.79	17.62	3.32	2.87	1.70	−.23*	.08	−.10
L3	125	11.56	3.80	16.50	4.33	2.76	2.22	−.23*	.30**	−.42**
L4	89	11.62	3.29	15.46	5.13	3.04	1.73	−.27*	.35**	−.40**
L5	112	10.23	3.66	17.02	4.03	1.73	1.57	−.21*	.35**	−.13

* $p < .05$ ** $p < .01$

middle group (L3) and next over the middle (L4): Extraversion is negatively related to Neuroticism and Psychoticism, and Neuroticism is positively related to Psychoticism.

Although we have controlled for the influence of three possible variables, sex (separating both groups), age (studying a very homogeneous sample of 8th grade students) and dissimulation (different levels of L score), the Junior EPQ scales are not independent as were their dimensions in the Spanish adaptation factorial studies. And now, at this point of our studies, it is clear in the relationship of L and Psychoticism that both dimensions really have something in common. Figure 18.1 shows the fluctuations of the Neuroticism, Extraversion and Psychoticism levels when subjects were classified in five groups according to their L score; scale levels were previously calculated in S scores based, independently for each sex, on a mean of 50 and s.d. of 20.

Here, in the last paragraphs, could be one of the major factors underlying criticisms about the weakness of questionnaire-type tests. It would seem that the faking

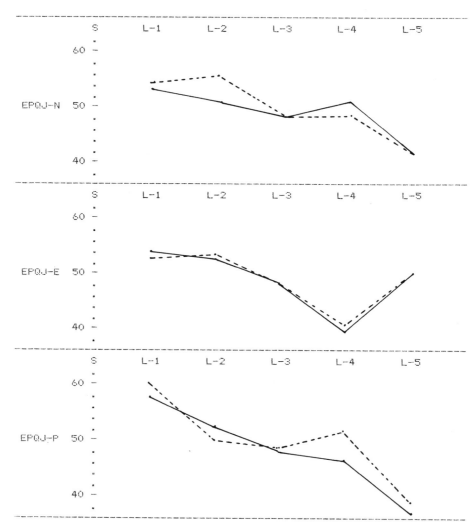

Figure 18.1 Diagrams of the EPQ–J scales fluctuations in five subsamples with increasing L raw score (males shown by a continuous line)

influence may not only change the size of the personality scale scores but also the personality structure relationships. This suggests that although the personality factors or variables are uncorrelated, the dimensions show some relationships when they are measured and the L influence is common to some measures. Hence, it would be wise to devise future research with a better control for L influences.

For the present, we have analysed the mean L scores of all the N-E-P cells for all subjects combined (1828 from 5th and 8th grades). First, in each variable we classified the subjects into three groups with approximately equal numbers of subjects and identified them with a sign, (+ = −), according to their high, middle or low score in the variable. Then we calculated the mean L score of the 27 possible comparison pairs in both sexes. Table 18.6 presents the average raw L score of the 12 extreme pairs (subjects neurotic-extraverted, neurotic-introverted, and so on). The highest and lowest extreme groups appear in this rank:

	Highest L scores			Lowest L scores	
N+P+	neurotic	toughminded	N−P−	controlled	tenderminded
E−P+	introverted	toughminded	E−P−	introverted	tenderminded
E+P+	extraverted	toughminded	E+P−	extraverted	tenderminded
N+E+	neurotic	extraverted	N+P−	neurotic	tenderminded

The highest Lie scores are found for the N+P+ group, and the lowest L scores for the N−P− group. That is to say, we have again arrived at a previously known fact, that the first reason for the L differences is P, and the second one is N. From these results one can also see that, although L was not related to E in previous data (see Tables 18.1–4), this scale can be influenced by L when it is associated with one of the other two (N or P).

Since Table 18.6 also presents the standard z scores, it can be seen that males, who tend to have lower L scores than females, also have more extreme low L scores, while females have more extreme high L scores; that is, the sexes differ in their extreme L scores.

Perhaps the best way to illustrate the data of Table 18.6 could be to draw a chart for each pair (NE, NP and EP), and introduce a diagonal in each quadrant with the size

Table 18.6 L scores of 12 extreme N E P pairs (140 M and 126 F)

Sex	N+E+	z	N+E−	z	N−E+	z	N−E−	z
M	8.76	−0.36	9.28	−0.25	11.64	0.27	11.64	0.28
F	8.91	−0.20	9.53	−0.28	11.00	0.25	10.81	0.21
Aver.		−0.28		−0.27		0.26		0.24

Sex	N+P+	z	N+P−	z	N−P+	z	N−P−	z
M	7.79	−0.58	11.83	0.32	10.43	0.01	12.81	0.53
F	7.21	−0.56	12.60	0.60	9.57	−0.06	12.60	0.60
Aver.		−0.57		0.46		−0.02		0.56

Sex	E+P+	z	E+P−	z	E−P+	z	E−P−	z
M	8.77	−0.36	12.18	0.39	8.42	−0.44	12.52	0.47
F	8.41	−0.30	12.60	0.60	8.28	−0.33	12.70	0.62
Aver.		−0.33		0.49		−0.38		0.55

z: deviation from the sex mean in standard deviation units

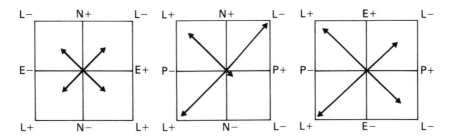

Figure 18.2   L tendency of pair N E P extreme groups

of the L 'z' deviation score of the group. In the first part of Figure 18.2, the L+ score is in the two quadrants of the N− pole, while in the second and third ones, it is in the two quadrants of the P− pole. Although N and P are significantly associated with L, the N−P+ group does not obtain an extreme L score, probably because the effects of the two scales are opposed.

In the next step, the focus of attention was on the wording and content of the 20 L questions. The Appendix shows the English translation of the Spanish items. In the standardisation process, two of the original questions (55 and 69) had unsatisfactory loadings and were substituted with better ones that had been included in the experimental version (they are written in brackets). As well, some minor changes were introduced in other items to adapt them for Spanish children to understand.

First, we examined the content of the L item pool and saw that the questions inquired about the children's behaviour in different settings (involving different persons or norms). Then we tentatively and subjectively classified the pool into three groups of L (GL) items; at the end of the Appendix are the item numbers of each group, and their content could be described as follows:

GL1 items are questions about norms/mores in relation to *other* children (e.g. 'Have you ever cheated at a game?').

GL2 questions are about norms/mores that apply to *adults* (e.g. 'Have you ever broken any rules at school?').

GL3 items ask about behaviour that applies to *abstract* rules (e.g. 'Do you throw waste paper on the floor when there is no waste paper basket handy?').

Next, we calculated and studied the three respective subscale scores in 265 8th grade children. Item 40 had an extreme mean and showed no discrimination. The results of the study (see first part of Table 18.8) showed that:

(a) Females obtain higher GL1 (Others) items, that is to say, they are more concerned than males about this type of relationship with their peers.
(b) Although non-significant for the males of this sample ($r = -.10$) and significant only at the 0.05 level for females ($r = -.23$), the main components of the negative N-L relationships are GL2 (Adults) items for males and GL3 (Abstract) questions for females.
(c) In both sexes, the least important component of the L-P correlation is the subscale GL3 containing items related to abstract norms.

The item intercorrelation matrix of these 20 items show positive relationships in the direction of the L scale consistency. Only a few indices are not significant, which does not confirm the inconsistencies reported by Rie (1963). Nevertheless, although it is not significant, we can see that the GL3 (Abstract) subscale changes the sign of its relationship with Extraversion in males and is the least correlated one for females.

Having these results in mind and omitting item 40, we factor analysed the remaining 19 items and arrived at an oblique principal factor matrix with four dimensions. Table 18.7 shows the factor loadings that surpass the 0.25 value. In fact, they are subfactors of L and were labelled FL1 (F from Factor and L from Lie) to FL4 and interpreted as follows:

FL1 – items that imply norms/mores related to *other* children.
FL2 – questions about rules of the *school* system.
FL3 – items about *abstract* norms, and
FL4 – conducts about norms/mores related to *adults*..

The respective subscale scores for the four L subfactors were then calculated in our sample of 265, 8th grade students. Table 18.8 presents the correlations between the three main personality scales and these subscales (as well as their relationships with the previous GL subscales). The main findings of this analysis are the following:

(a) NL: the main source of this correlation (a non-significant -0.11 in males and a -0.23, $p < .05$ in females) comes from the FL4 (Adults) subscale, in both sexes.

(b) EL: although, we had not previously found a significant relationship between these scales (-0.03 in males and -0.10 in females), the subscale FL1 (Others) is negatively related to E within the female group, and the sign of the FL3 (Abstract) relationship is changed in both sexes. Here we could see a possible faint clue to the inconsistencies reported by Rie (1963), because part of the L items (the FL3 ones) seem to behave differently.

(c) PL: both sexes show a different pattern when this L-P significant correlation (-0.38 in males and -0.35 in females, both with $p < .01$) is specified into four subscales. In males, the ranking of the effects is Adults, Others, School and

Table 18.7 Factor pattern for the 19 L items (N=265) (only loadings over 0.25)

Item	Others FL1	School FL2	Abstr. FL3	Adults FL4
L– 4	.50			
L– 8		.34		−.45
L–11	−.45	.55		
L–16	.73			
L–20				.59
L–24	−.42	−.29		
L–27	−.36		.29	
L–31			.72	
L–36		.39	.50	
L–43			.32	
L–47			.57	
L–51		.58		
L–55				.75
L–60		.45		
L–64	.29		−.26	.49
L–69	.70			
L–73	−.26		.63	
L–75	.49			
L–78		−.69		

Abstract, while in females it is Others. School, Adults and the effect of Abstract has decreased to the point of non-significance. That is to say, male children are more concerned about Adults items while the interests of the females are on Others items. In both sexes the least important components are the items related to Abstract norms.

Table 18.8 also shows the subscale number of items and their mean score for each sex group. Dividing each subscale mean by its number of items, one can see that females 'dissimulate' more on the Others GL items and that both sexes 'fake' higher on the Abstract FL3 questions. The subsamples are not large enough to generalize these conclusions (other studies and large samples are necessary to cross-validate them), but, from the point of view of psychological differences, they suggest that probably there are different components within the Lie dimension and both sexes differ in its manifestation.

L scale and other subject variables

Age

Original studies have shown that the L scale was related to age. Eysenck (1979) studied two samples of 600 adult males and 598 adult females and found a relationship of $r = .32$ $(p < .01)$. However, this pattern was inverted when the child population was tested. The 8 to 15-year-old children (N = 1978) of the Spanish EPQ-J standardization study showed a negative correlation between the L scale and age. The authors suggested that, probably, young children are more naive, conformist and less able to introspect. In our 5th and 8th grade children (N = 1851) of mainly 10 to 15 years olds, the 1191 males showed a significant negative L-age correlation $(r = -.12, p < .01)$, while for the 660 females the relationship was positive, although non-significant $(r = .04)$.

Table 18.8   L subscale relationships with EPQJ scales in both sexes

Subscales	Neuroticism		Extraversion		Psychoticism		Subsc. items	Means	
	M	F	M	F	M	F		M	F
Empirical									
GL1 Others	−.08	−.17	.02	−.13	−.35**	−.32**	8	2.56	3.29
GL2 Adults	−.13	−.19	.01	−.08	−.32**	−.38*	6	2.36	2.40
GL3 Abstr.	−.04	−.24*	−.11	−.01	−.24*	−.22**	6	2.39	2.24
Factorial									
FL1 Others	−.05	−.16	−.02	−.23*	−.29**	−.37**	6	1.89	2.59
FL2 School	−.04	−.08	−.10	−.09	−.24*	−.28**	4	1.35	1.40
FL3 Abstr.	−.04	−.09	.04	.14	−.22*	−.13	5	2.66	2.55
FL4 Adults	−.11*	−.23*	−.02	−.01	−.35**	−.21*	4	1.29	1.19

$^* p < .05$ $^{**} p < .01$

Bearing in mind the above results and data, particularly those of the subscales of the L scores, we could conclude that one of the reasons for the negative age relationship might be to do with maturation. As children grow older they become more concerned about the mores/norms/rules of the world around them which includes other children, adults, the school system and society in general. These developmental or maturational influences could follow the sequence whereby the young child, more dependent on adults, answers in the L direction and gets high L scores, (i.e. 'Yes, I do always do as I am told at once'). Later, when he becomes an adolescent, he is more independent, and perhaps more rebellious, and does not mind admitting 'No, I do not always wash my hands before a meal'. At this point, we have to remember that the female adolescent matures before the male, and in our 660 5th and 8th grade females the L-age relationship was different to that of the male group. This attitude is still true for young adults. However, as mature adults, they start to be more aware of the existing rules, try to adapt themselves to that world, and have to start to 'fake a civilized behaviour' and 'go to the hairdresser to look better'. These people are aware of their 'appearance' and normally say 'No. I have never said anything bad or nasty about anyone'.

Thus, it is suggested that young children and older adults may both obtain higher L scores on personality questionnaires such as the EPQ, although for different reasons. However, adolescents and young adults may be more rebellious with respect to society standards or simply more 'sincere' or honest with themselves.

Intelligence and interest

In relation to intelligence, previous studies with the MPI (Maudsley Personality Inventory) and the EPI tests have supported the hypothesis that there is a clear tendency for the L scale to be negatively related to intelligence, suggesting that bright children and adults are usually more 'sincere' when answering the questionnaire items. With a sample of 390 children the Eysencks (1976) found a -0.29 ($p < .01$) correlation between L and the Progressive Matrices, and report that it is typical of many others they have obtained in their work.

Saklofske (1985) studied Canadian children and did not obtain a significant relationship between the Junior EPQ L scale and the Sequential Simultaneous and Mental Processing Composite Scales of the Kaufman Assessment Battery for Children. Further, correlations between L and the K-ABC Achievement scale ($r = -.15$) and the Woodcock-Johnson Brief Scale Cluster ($r = -.14$) were found, but these did not reach the $p = .05$ level of significance. The Hungarian EPQ-J adaptation, (Eysenck, Kozeki & Kalmanchey, 1980) also showed a similar pattern: the L score did not go together with intelligence and academic achievement, was higher in children from two smaller settlements compared to children from two larger ones, and was higher in the low-status children groups than in the high-status ones.

The following results have been obtained with our Spanish samples. The EPI-L scores of 263 male 8th grade children only correlated significantly ($r = -.14$, $p = .05$) with the Verbal subtest of the Primary Mental Abilities scale. The EPQ-J L scale also shows negative relationships with the scores of the battery of SRA 'Tests of Educational Ability', by Thurstone, in our sample of 791 5th grade students, although only two of the indices are significant at the 0.05 level. The Dominoes test and five scores of the 'Differential Aptitude Tests' also correlated negatively with L in our sample of 1037 8th grade students, as reported in Table 18.9.

In our group of 265 8th grade children, abilities and preferences were also correlated with the 7 subscales derived from the EPQ-J Spanish L items. Results are shown in Table 18.10. L scores are nearly independent of abilities in males but

Table 18.9   L relationships with abilities

| Test | 5th grade | | Test | 8th grade | |
	471 M	320 F		702 M	335 F
TEA-Ver. Pictures	−.07	.06	Dominoes test	−.24**	−.21**
TEA-Word Grouping	−.06	−.05	DAT-Verbal Reasoning	−.20**	−.22**
TEA-Vocabulary	−.11*	.06	DAT-Abstract Reason.	−.16**	−.07
TEA-Language	−.11*	.03	DAT-Numerical Reason.	−.24**	−.18**
TEA-Reasoning	−.02	−.05	DAT-Space Relations	−.24**	−.15**
TEA-Quantitative	.06	−.06	DAT-Mechanical Reason.	−.14**	−.04
TEA-Total	−.04	−.03			
TEA-Non-Reading	−.05	−.01			

$* p < .05 ** p < .01$

not in females. Although there is a general tendency of all the subscales to be negatively related to abilities, the stronger relationships are in the female (F) group and with the Others (GL1 and FL1) and Adults (GL2) subscales. One explanation for this could be linked to the earlier social maturation of females. If that is so, by this process they become less rebellious, more conformist and prone to use their intelligence to better adapt to the adult mores.

The preference or interest variables had also been tested in the sample of 265 8th grade adolescents with the Kuder Preference Record Form C, and their results related to the L scale. Of the ten Kuder variables, the dissimulation scale only shows significant correlations with the three following preference areas: Persuasive (meeting and dealing with people, and promoting projects or things to sell), Musical (going to concerts, playing instruments, singing, or reading about music and musicians), and Clerical (doing office work that requires precision and accuracy). In an effort to understand the meaning of these relationships with L, the 7 L subscales were also correlated with the Kuder areas and the results are shown at the bottom of Table 18.10.

Antisocial behaviour

Another variable that has usually been suggested in relation to personality is adolescent antisocial behaviour, and in previous paragraphs we have used the rebelliousness construct as a possible variable to understand the functioning of the L scale in older children. Eysenck's early theory was that antisocial behaviour is causally related to extraversion and neuroticism, and he later extended this to include the psychoticism dimension of personality (Eysenck, 1970). If we applied Eysenck's theory to the content of previous paragraphs, it follows that children engaging in antisocial behaviour should also get different L scores.

Elsewhere, Saklofske (1977) reported significantly lower L scores for 10–11-year-old New Zealand boys who scored high on classroom misbehaviour compared to their well-behaved peers. These results were replicated for a sample of adolescent New Zealand boys by Saklofske & Eysenck (1980), although the difference between well-behaved school boys and a sample of delinquents was not statistically significant.

However, the same has been found to be true in a study of Spanish children described by Seisdedos (1982). Two experimental samples (N = 95 and 59) of

Table 18.10 L and subscales relationships with abilities and preferences

Test	L scale		Empirical subscales						Factorial subscales							
			Others		Adults		Abstr.		Others		School		Abstr.		Adult	
	M	F	M	F	M	F	M	F	M	F	M	F	M	F	M	F
Dominoes	-10	-15	-13	-19	-08	-22	-02	-05	01	-20	-05	-06	-17	-04	-05	-09
Word Grouping	-07	-22	-11	-21	-01	-26	-05	-06	-11	-21	-12	-14	02	-25	02	-12
Vocabulary	-11	-29	-15	-29	-03	-27	-09	-10	-08	-17	-14	-14	-05	-33	-06	-19
Language	-17	-30	-23	-30	-08	-31	-11	-09	-14	-22	-16	-16	-11	-35	-09	-19
Number Reasoning	-04	-29	-11	-25	05	-32	-02	-15	-10	-28	-09	-17	04	-20	06	-24
Letter Reasoning	-01	-18	-07	-11	05	-23	-02	-06	-04	-16	-12	-04	04	-09	10	-19
Reasoning	-04	-28	-14	-22	06	-33	-01	-13	-08	-27	-10	-13	-00	-18	09	-25
Quantity	-01	-24	-07	-25	05	-27	-00	-07	-02	-26	-06	-13	02	-22	06	-16
TEA-Total	-12	-34	-23	-31	-01	-37	-04	-12	-09	-30	-08	-17	-15	-31	-02	-24
Pers. Pref.	-27	-27	-21	-16	-25	-26	-20	-29	-25	-19	-09	-26	-14	-14	-29	-29
Musi. Pref.	-19	-15	-07	-07	-19	-16	-21	-20	-14	-07	-11	-18	-16	-09	-12	-08
Cler. Pref.	-11	-21	-17	-21	-05	-21	-04	-20	-10	-15	00	-14	-12	-15	-10	-23

Decimals omitted. $r = .17$ ($p = .05$) in 140 males; $r = .18$ ($p = .05$) in 126 females children with different grades of behaviour problems and a control group (N = 99 children), were used to develop a Spanish A–D questionnaire with two scales, Antisocial and Delinquent.* At the end of the study we classified all the children (N = 253) via the median of the A and D scales, and analysed EPQ-J scores of the extreme groups (95 A−D− children and 86 A+D+ subjects). The results are shown in table 18.11 and suggest that children with behaviour problems (higher in both A and D scales), were not only higher on the P scale, as was expected, but also more 'sincere' (L−). The L mean score of the A+D+ children is exceedingly low, perhaps because these subjects do not concern themselves with the 'conformist' rules of the surrounding world. The N and E scales have remained nearly unchanged, in contrast to Eysenck's theory.

Recently we have had a further opportunity of studying the A–D and EPI scores of 1076 Spanish children and young students (11 to 25 years old, mean = 14.92, s.d. = 2.55). They were not delinquents, but about half of them lived in suburbs of Madrid where there is a high index of juvenile delinquency. Table 18.12 shows the statistics of the five scale scores for the total sample, as well as for the two sexes and four age levels. The D (Delinquent acts) scale is very asymmetrical, because half of the subjects do not admit having done any, the D frequencies decrease very steeply when the scores increase and only a few subjects admit having committed more than four juvenile delinquent acts. In contrast, the A measure is very discriminating for this type of population, and males and older subjects obtain higher scores, which is also true for the D behaviours.

Table 18.11   Junior EPQ scores of Antisocial-Delinquent extreme groups

EPQ-J	A− D− N=95)		A+ D+ (N=86)		't' of the mean diff.
	Mean	SD	Mean	SD	
N	12.52	3.60	12.56	3.64	0.07
E	18.13	3.39	17.81	3.62	0.60
P	3.40	2.18	5.99	3.13	6.29**
L	9.30	3.71	2.07	3.82	5.60**

** $p < .01$

Table 18.12   A-D and EPI scores in total, sex and age groups

Group	N	A		D		EPI–N		EPI–E		EPI–L	
		Mean	SD	Mean	SD	Mean	SD	Mean	SD	Mean	SD
Total	1076	8.54	4.91	1.24	2.52	12.55	3.90	12.71	3.72	2.46	1.63
Sex											
Males	402	9.66	4.91	1.91	2.99	12.16	3.91	12.77	3.45	2.38	1.69
Females	604	7.85	4.80	0.73	1.93	12.82	3.92	12.67	3.91	2.44	1.58
Age											
11–13	291	7.47	4.82	0.94	2.22	12.23	3.79	12.21	3.69	2.74	1.69
14–15	422	8.78	4.81	1.27	2.58	12.34	3.91	12.85	3.67	2.41	1.59
16–17	286	9.21	4.93	1.43	2.73	13.13	3.90	13.12	3.72	2.30	1.61
18–25	71	8.89	5.18	1.45	2.56	12.61	4.49	12.20	4.06	2.28	1.62

The EPI scores are similar to the Spanish norms; females get higher N scores, and if older subjects have lower L scores (against our previous hypotheses and data) perhaps that is because they also are higher on A and D scales. In order to analyse this from the correlational point of view, we calculated the five scale intercorrelations for the same groups of Table 18.12, and results are given in Table 18.13.

These analyses suggest that the A and D scales are correlated (and indices are stronger in males and young subjects). Although the underlying variables are clearly distinct, they have something in common, sharing between 16% and 30% of the total variance in this sample. As in the experimental study of the A–D questionnaire and in contrast to Eysenck's theory, these types of behaviour (A and D) seem to be independent of neuroticism. However, Extraversion is positively related to both antisocial and delinquent variables, more strongly to the former. But, bearing in mind that the D–E relationship could be due to the A correlation with both variables, we calculated the D–E correlations partialling out the A influence and all the D–E column indices of Table 18.13 became statistically nonsignificant. We repeated the analysis with the A–E correlations partialling out the D influence, and the indices remained nearly unchanged. Hence, we conclude that only high A scorers tend to be more extraverted, but not high D subjects.

Higher A scorers are also more independent of society standards and obtain lower L scores. That has not proved to be true for the high D scorers; the small negative tendency that appears in the D–L column of Table 18.13 is probably due to the A common variance with D and L. The N–L indices are similar to those of Table 18.1 but not those of column E–L because the sign is inverted. Adult (see Table 18.2) extraverted subjects of this sample obtain lower L scores; the relationship being stronger for females and increasing with age until 17 years, perhaps because these older children score higher on A and D.

Finally, we were interested to know how the EPI personality scales function within the extreme Antisocial and Delinquent groups. All the subjects were classified via the median as higher (+) or lower (−) on the A and D variables, and the statistics for the four groups are given in Table 18.14. These results show that Neuroticism only increases a little from the well behaved subjects (A−D−, low on both variables) to the badly behaved ones (A+D+, high on both scales). However, the increase is statistically significant on Extraversion, as well as the decrease of the L scores between the two extreme groups. So, it seems reasonable to conclude that subjects high on misbehaviour are more extraverted and, at the same time, less conformist to the social standard norms. The EPI interrelationships are similar to those of Table 18.13, but as bad behaviour increases, the significance of the N–L and E–L indices decreases, that is to say, N and E scales are more independent of L for antisocial subjects. This could be a further indication that the L implications in Neuroticism and Extraversion are due more to environmental factors to which the subjects try to adapt than to a clear personality dimension.

Summary

In order to achieve a better understanding of the L construct, several investigations have been reviewed and their results compared with the factorial and empirical data of the Spanish adaptation of the Eysencks' questionnaires (EPI and the two Forms of the EPQ). Recent Spanish researches have also been mentioned and their data analysed from the point of view of the L implications.

The L influences on the main personality scales were controlled by sex and age and by reducing the L variability in order to study the Psychoticism, Neuroticism and Extraversion relationship with the dissimulation variable. It seems that Spanish children, independently of their sex and age, are motivated to 'hide' their socially

Table 18.13 A-D and EPI relationships in total, sex and age groups

Group	n	A-D	A-N	A-E	A-L	D-N	D-E	D-L	N-E	N-L	E-L
All	1076	.42**	.04	.33**	-.29**	-.04	.12**	-.06	.02	-.29**	-.20**
Sex											
Male	402	.49**	.08	.28**	-.32**	.07	.18*	-.09	.01	-.30**	-.16**
Female	605	.39**	.09	.46**	-.35**	.03	.23**	-.10*	.02	-.30**	-.25**
Age											
11-13	291	.55**	.11	.39**	-.27**	.02	.23**	-.06	.03	-.24**	-.10
14-15	425	.45**	.02	.28**	-.24**	-.07	.10*	-.06	-.01	-.31**	-.19**
16-17	286	.40**	-.05	.39**	-.35**	-.01	.17**	-.08	.00	-.28**	-.28**
18-25	71	.51**	.04	.25**	-.43**	.02	.24**	-.19	-.04	-.26*	-.14

* $p < .05$ ** $p < .01$

Table 18.14 Subjects with different Antisocial (A) & Delinquent (D) scores (classified via the median of each distribution)

Group	n	EPI-N		EPI-E		EPI-L		Intercorrelations		
		Mean	SD	Mean	SD	Mean	SD	N-E	N-L	E-L
A−D−	479	12.33	3.91	11.53	3.60	2.87	1.64	.02	-.32**	-.14**
A−D+	149	12.69	4.01	12.44	3.45	2.64	1.67	.03	-.22**	-.20*
A+D−	163	12.75	3.70	14.09	3.67	2.10	1.42	-.05	-.27**	-.17*
A+D+	286	12.89	3.96	14.03	3.42	1.88	1.47	-.08	-.24**	-.01

* $p < .05$ ** $p < .01$

unfavourable traits (mainly of the psychotic and unstable type). However, the L data analyses in relation to the other Junior EPQ scales, has shown that there is a curvilinear 'U' effect associated with the maturation process of the child until he is a mature adult. Younger children and adults (although for different reasons) are both more likely to obtain higher L scores, while the adolescent and the young adult are more 'sincere' in their answers to a personality questionnaire. When a very young child encounters a task of this type, he may 'fake' in order to adhere to the adults' norms (and that could be an intelligent and an adaptive behaviour). In the case of an adult who earns high L scores, it is his goal to avoid the P+ and N+ socially unfavourable aspects of his personality, or to show his best 'face' according to situational motivation (this also could be an intelligent behaviour of adaptation). On the other hand the independent and rebellious attitudes of adolescents and young adults lead them to be more 'sincere', unless they are in a special and high drive setting (e.g. looking for a job).

The L items were also analysed in order to develop comprehensible subscales which are related to the four personality scales, and also to other variables (abilities, preferences and antisocial behaviour). The results add some support to the above conclusions on the subjects' maturation process and on individual special circumstances.

Particular attention has been paid to antisocial behaviour which has been linked with the Psychoticism, Extraversion and L factors, but its earlier relationship with Neuroticism has not been supported by the results. If, in adolescents, this behaviour is a form of adaptation to the environment the L or faking behaviour is also consequently modified. The issue, although not conclusive, could be noteworthy for further researches.

References

ALLSOPP, J.F. & FELDMAN, M.P. (1974) Extraversion, Neuroticism, Psychoticism and Antisocial Behavior in schoolgirls. In Eysenck (1976), 505–511.

DAHLSTROM, W.G. & WELSH, G.S. (1960) *An MMPI handbook: a guide to use in clinical practice and research* Minneapolis: University of Minnesota Press.

DICKEN, C.F. (1959) Simulated patterns on the Edwards Personal Preference Schedule. *J. Appl. Psychol.*, **43**, 372–8.

EDWARDS, A.L. (1970) *The measurement of personality traits by scales and inventories*. New York: Holt, Rinehart and Winston.

EYSENCK, H.J. (1970) *Crime and personality*. London: Paladin.

EYSENCK, H.J. (1976) *The measurement of personality*. Lancaster: MTP Press Ltd.

EYSENCK, H.J. (1979) Personality factors in a random sample of the population. *Psychol. Reports*, **44**, 1023–7.

EYSENCK, H.J. & EYSENCK, S.B.G. (1976) *Psychoticism as a dimension of personality*. London: Hodder and Stoughton.

EYSENCK, H.J. & EYSENCK, S.B.G. (1978) *EPI. Cuestionario de personalidad*. Madrid: TEA Ediciones.

EYSENCK, H.J. & EYSENCK, S.B.G. (1978, 1982) *EPQ. Cuestionario de personalidad*. Madrid: TEA Ediciones.

EYSENCK, S.B.G., ESCOLAR, V., LOBO, A. & SEVA DIAZ, A. (1982) Diferencias transculturales de personalidad: España e Inglaterra. *Rev. Psic. y Psiquiatria Medica*, Barcelona, **5**, 283–93.

EYSENCK, S.B.G., KOZEKI, B. & KALMANCHEY, G.M. (1980) Cross-cultural comparison of personality: Hungarian children and English children. *Person. Indiv. Diff.*, **1**, 347–53.

EYSENCK, S.B.G. & SEISDEDOS, N. (1978) Un estudio internaciones de la personalidad. *Rev. Psic. Gral. y Apl.*, **XXXIII**, 151, 271–81.

EYSENCK, S.B.G. & EYSENCK, H.J. (1970) A factor-analytic study of the lie scale of the JEPI. *Personality*, **1**, 3–10.

GARCIA-HOZ ROSALES, V. (1977) *Los cuestionarios de personalidad en seleccion profesional: un estudio experimental del falseamiento*. Madrid: Univ. Fac. of Pedagogy, Doctoral Thesis (unpublished).

HARTSHORNE, H. & MAY, M.A. (1928) *Studies in deceit.* New York: MacMillan.

MICHAELIS, W. & EYSENCK, H.J. (1971) The determination of personality inventory factor patterns and intercorrelations by changes in real-life motivation. *J. Genet. Pychol.,* **118,** 223–34.

NIAS, D.K.B. (1972) A note on the effects of administration conditions upon personality scores in children. *J. Child Psychol. Psychiat.,* **13,** 115–19.

PEREZ, J., ORTET, G., PLA, S. & SIMO, S. (1986): Test-retest reliability of the Spanish version of the Junior Eysenck Personality Questionnaire. *Person. Indiv. Diff.,* **7,** no. 1, 117–18.

PRIETO ZAMORA, J.N. (1979) *Estructura multidimensional de la personalidad con datos Q (Estudio factorial con muestras españolas)* Madrid: Univ. Fac. of Psych., Doctoral Thesis (unpublished).

RIE, H.E. (1963) An explanatory study of the CMAS Lie Scale. *Child Dev.,* **34,** 1003–17.

SAKLOFSKE, D.H. (1977) Personality and behavior problems of school boys. *Psychological Reports,* **41,** 445–6.

SAKLOFSKE, D.H. (1985) The relationship between Eysenck's major personality dimensions and simultaneous and sequential processing in children. *Person. Indiv. Diff.,* **6,** 4, 429–33.

SAKLOFSKE, D.H. & EYSENCK, S.B.G. (1980) Personality and antisocial behavior in delinquent and non-delinquent boys. *Psychological Reports,* **47,** 1255–61.

SANCHEZ TURET, M. & CUADRAS AVELLANA, C. (1972) Adaptacion Española del Cuestionario EPI de Eysenck. Barcelona: *Anuario de Psicologia. Departamento de Psicologia de la Universidad,* **6,** *31–59.*

SEISDEDOS, N. (1979) Personalidad, adaptacion, inteligencia y entorno. *Rev. Psic. Gral. y Apl.,* **159,** 651–9.

SEISDEDOS, N. (1982) La coducta antisocial de los adolescentes. *Rev. Surgam.,* **336,** 11–17.

VALVERDE MOLINA, J.M. (1980) *El proceso de inadaptacion social en el adolescente.* Madrid: Univ. Fac. of Psyh., Doctoral Thesis (unpublished).

Appendix

Spanish L items of the EPQ-J
(In brackets: words or items that are not in the English version)

Item
(4) Were you ever greedy by helping yourself to more than your share of anything? (NO)
(8) Do you always do as you are told at once? (YES)
(11) Have you ever broken any rules at school? (NO)
(16) Did you ever take anything (even a pin or button) that belonged to some one else? (NO)
(20) Did you ever pretend you did not hear when some one was calling you? (NO)
(24) Do you always finish your homework before you play? (YES)
(27) When you hear children using bad language do you try to stop them? (YES)
(31) Do you always say you are sorry when you have been rude? (YES)
(36) Are you always quiet when older people are talking? (YES)
(40) Have you ever said anything bad or nasty about anyone? (NO)
(43) Do you generally pick up papers and rubbish others throw on the classroom floor? (YES)
(47) Do you always wash [your hands] before a meal? (YES)
(51) Are you always quiet in class, even when the teacher is out of the room? (YES)
(55) [Have you ever eaten more candys than you were allowed?] (NO)
(60) Do you always eat everything you are given at meals? (YES)
(64) Have you ever been cheeky to your parents? (NO)
(69) [Have you ever felt the wish to play truant?] (NO)
(73) Do you always share all the sweets [toys or things] you have? (YES)
(75) Have you ever cheated at a game? (NO)
(78) Do you throw waste paper on the floor when there is no waste paper basket handy? (NO)

Composition of different subscales of L classified:
(a)   By content:
GLI (Others)   Items 4, 16, 20, 27, 31, 40, 73, 75.
GL2 (Adults)   Items 8, 11, 24, 36, 51, 64.
GL3 (Abstract)   Items 43, 47, 55, 60, 69, 78.

(b)   By factorial analysis (item 40 was previously eliminated):
     FL1 (Others)   Items 4, 16, 24, 27, 69, 75.
     FL2 (School)   Items 11, 51, 60, 78.
     FL3 (Abstract)   Items 31, 36, 43, 47, 73.
     FL4 (Adults)   Items 8, 20, 55, 64.

Acknowledgement

We should like to thank J.F. Allsopp and M.P. Feldman who sent us their ASB and CC Questionnaires. These items and Spanish ones were factor analysed to define two clear dimensions: Antisocial (trivial and serious acts against the social norms) and Delinquent (acts that, being at the law borderline, could be punished in a court). The present version of the A–D Questionnaire contains the 20 best items of each factor.

19 A cross-cultural comparison of personality with special reference to Sri Lanka

K.M.H. Perera

Introduction

Character portrayal is beset with many stereotypes. Perhaps the mysticism of the East and the materialism of the West are mythical concepts. This also filters down to national and even racial levels. The stiff upper lip of the British and the bobbing courtesy of the Japanese, or the shrewd business acumen of the Jews and the warrior-like behaviour of the Gurkhas are but a few examples of such typologies. Personality, perhaps is best explained as the characteristic identity of an individual and in order to inject a degree of scientific objectivity various schemes have been proposed, for its assessment. Briefly then, they emanate from four basic models including trait psychology, psychodynamics, situationism and interaction. The trait model assumes that traits are the prime determinants of behaviour and serve as the basis for apparent stimulus-response consistency, a trait being a relatively stable feature of an individual. The psychodynamic theories assume that there is a basic core of personality. This becomes the predispositional basis for behaviour under given situations. While situationism regards the situation as the important aspect that determines the behaviour, the interaction model emphasises the importance of the person by situation interaction in personality.

Generally the trait model is considered to be dominant in this field. In order to make an assessment of personality using the trait model, the individual could be asked to report on his/her own characteristic behaviour by filling out a questionnaire (or an inventory). Although the Minnesota Multiphasic Personality Inventory (MMPI), was much in vogue earlier, more recently Cattell's 16 personality factor (PF) questionnaire and Eysenck's personality inventories have gained popularity. The Eysencks' personality questionnaires have been translated and validated for use in many different countries. Of particular relevance in this context is the translation of the adult version of the Eysenck Personality Questionnaire (EPQ) into Sinhala (Perera & Eysenck, 1984). In order to perform a comparative study of personality between Sri Lankan and British children, a junior version of the EPQ was translated into Sinhalese. (Sinhala is the language spoken by over 70% of the Sri Lankan people.) In the present material our attempts at developing the Sinhalese translation of the Junior EPQ will be presented and this will also be used as the basis for discussing some aspects of making cross-cultural comparisons of personality.

Materials and method

The questionnaire
The 97-item version of the Junior EPQ (Eysenck & Eysenck, 1975) was used for the translation. This personality questionnaire measures extraversion, neuroticism (or emotionality), psychoticism (or toughmindedness), and lying (or social desirability). It may, perhaps, be as well to describe these factors briefly. Extraverts are sociable, enjoy parties, have many friends, and need excitement. They are sensation-seekers and risk-takers, like practical jokes, and are lively and active. Conversely, introverts

are quiet, prefer reading to meeting people, have only few close friends, and usually avoid excitement. Children who score high on emotionality tend to be worriers, are often anxious, moody, and sometimes depressed; and they tend to overreact to stress, finding it difficult to calm down afterwards. Stable individuals, on the other hand, are usually quiet, even-tempered and unworried; they are slow to respond emotionally and recover their equipoise quickly after arousal. Toughminded girls and boys tend to be aggressive, hostile, and cold emotionally; they lack empathy, are insensitive to the feelings of others as well as their own, and are impulsive and egocentric. They are, however, often original and creative, tend to be unconventional, and have a liking for odd, unusual people and things. Finally, the lie score was originally regarded simply as a scale to detect faking, but has recently been recognized as a personality dimension of some intrinsic interest apart from faking. The social desirability aspect of the lie score is probably of greatest importance in cross-cultural projects because norms on this factor may reflect the degree of social permissiveness of the country or culture under observation and the degree of conformity of the child.

The Sri Lankan translation of the Junior EPQ

The translation followed a similar procedure to that adopted earlier with the adult EPQ (Perera & Eysenck, 1984). The main objective was to reproduce in Sinhala, as accurately as possible, the questions asked in English. The next aim was to find suitable Sinhalese equivalents of items where it was necessary; this happened only in a few instances. Finally the grammar was checked for gross irregularities. The translators were Sinhala speaking persons. Two of them had received their education in English and were trained in psychiatry and psychology respectively, one was a school teacher and the other was a professional Sinhalese scholar.

Translations, in general, pose problems and personality inventories in particular are associated with special difficulties in translating from one language to another. Primarily the *meaning* of the original question needs to be conveyed to the reader in the vernacular while accuracy of the translation is maintained. Finding suitable equivalents for some English words, adjectives especially (e.g. moody, lively), presented some difficulties. In those instances the concept was briefly explained rather than use glossary terms which are not well known by the average Sri Lankan child. Since water skiing was not known to these children, the original item stating that water skiing would be fun was substituted with an item dealing with motorcycle racing.

Back translations were performed in order to check on the validity of the translation. Ideally the process of translation and back translation should be performed several times until equivalence is reached. This was not undertaken since it was not cost-effective and impractical in the present instance. Another point worthy of mention is an obvious difference between spoken and written Sinhalese. Therefore, when the translation was performed we attempted to strike a balance between the use of colloquial and grammatical language.

Sample

The Junior EPQ was administered to 578 boys and 528 girls whose ages were 13.09 ± 1.32 and 13.47 ± 1.42 respectively. They were Sinhala speaking. They were all school children and comprised a mixed social strata; i.e. very rich, middle class, poor and working class. Children were selected from both the primary and secondary school grades on the basis of their age and also the availability of free time and access to the students. The schools were situated in the capital (Colombo), mid country (Kandy) and the Central Province (Anuradhapura) and their suburbs. Most subjects were from sexually segregated schools but some were from mixed schools.

School dropouts and delinquent children were not questioned, these constituting less than 20% of Sri Lankan children within this age.

Data analysis

The Sri Lankan data were analyzed in the same way as the British data. The product-moment correlations were factored by principal components method, rotated by direct oblimin taking the first four factors only for rotational purposes. A few brief comments are perhaps in place regarding the method of factor analysis adopted. The usual rules regarding factor analysis as an explanatory or theory-generating tool do not apply when it is used as a theory testing or confirmation method. In this instance, the necessary theory tested was that the same four factors of the EPQ will also be present in the Sri Lankan culture. This led to the decision to extract and rotate only four factors. Scree tests have always indicated the expected fall in eigenvalue contribution after the extraction of the four factors, and this leads to doublets and single item loading factors when further extraction is undertaken. These factors are of no psychological interest. 'Superfactors' are necessarily less homogeneous than primaries, hence very high loadings are not to be expected.

Results

The first thing to establish was whether the factors extracted were the same as those obtained with the English samples. This was achieved by means of factor comparisons following the method of Kaiser, Hunka & Bianchini (1969). It will be seen from Table 19.1 that these values are all high, in excess of 0.96, except that of Sri Lankan and British girls on N where the value is 0.93 which is still adequate. Eysenck & Eysenck (1969) have previously suggested that values in excess of 0.95 should be regarded as accepting that the factors are virtually identical.

Table 19.1   Factor comparisons on P, E, N and L between various groups

Factor comparison	P	E	N	L
Sri Lanka boys vs. British boys	0.97	0.96	0.98	0.99
Sri Lanka girls vs. British girls	0.99	0.97	0.93	0.98
Sri Lanka boys vs. Sri Lanka girls	0.96	0.98	0.99	0.98

The next step was to select scales for P,E,N,L, comprised of items with adequate loadings on the respective factors. The item loadings on the four factors for the Sri Lankan subjects, based on the items comprising the British scoring key, and others suitable for inclusion or substitution in the four scales, are given in the Appendices I–IV.

The results were encouraging. Only 5 out of a total of 17 psychoticism items failed to load as was the case for English children. Four substitute items, however, were available making the P scale 16 items in all. Similarly, 5 extraversion items out of 24 failed in Sri Lanka but 2 suitable items presented themselves for inclusion making the E scale a total of 21 items. While only one item out of a total of 20 on the N scale was weak enough to be omitted, there were 3 items worthy of inclusion thus making 22 items in all. Finally social desirability or the Lie scale had 2 items with poor loadings, but there was one item suitable for substitution. Thus the L scale had 19 items. In order to have uniform scales for both girls and boys only those items that loaded equally well for both sexes were retained. For example, item 13

'Are you rather lively' and item 17, 'Have you got many friends' were omitted from the E scale as they had lost their loadings for the boys. Another feature was that some items while losing their loadings on one scale gained entry to another; e.g. item 1, an extraversion item in the British scale, gained loadings for the psychoticism scale and was thus included in it for the Sinhala version.

Using the scoring key developed for the Sri Lankan children, reliabilities (alpha coefficients) and intercorrelations of the *scales* were calculated, as distinct from the *factors* which were compared (cf Table 19.1) by the method of factor comparisons and in which *all* loadings of each, entire factor are utilised. As shown in Table 19.2, reliabilities are reasonably high except for that for P in girls (.54) and possibly that for E for boys (.67). Intercorrelations, unfortunately, yield unusually high values for PN, PL and NL, the latter two suggesting a considerable involvement of the social desirability issue.

Table 19.2 Reliabilities (alpha coefficients) and intercorrelation of P, E, N and L

Reliabilities

	Boys	Girls
P	0.70	0.54
E	0.67	0.70
N	0.74	0.76
L	0.77	0.80

Intercorrelations

	Boys	Girls
PE	0.20	0.27
PN	0.37	0.37
PL	−0.41	−0.29
EN	0.05	−0.02
EL	−0.04	−0.01
NL	−0.33	−0.35

Table 19.3 gives the means and standard deviations of the scales for Sri Lankan boys and girls and these are all in line with other studies; boys scoring higher than girls on P, lower on N and L and no different on E.

In order to compare the personality structure described by the four scales, means on the personality scales for Sri Lankan and English children were studied. For this purpose only the items common to both English and Sri Lankan scoring keys were used in the calculation of the means. As shown in Table 19.4, Sri Lankan children had much higher social desirability scores than the British children, much lower neuroticism scores, and slightly lower extraversion scores. While the boys scored the same on psychoticism, Sri Lankan girls scored somewhat higher than their British counterparts on this personality dimension.

Discussion

Difficulties faced by an investigator making cross-cultural comparisons are legion. Nonetheless delineation of some of these problems will enable the researcher to

Table 19.3 Means ($\bar{x}$) and standard deviations (SD) on P, E, N and L for Sri Lankan children (N=578 and 528 for boys and girls respectively)

	Boys		Girls	
	$\bar{x}$	SD	$\bar{x}$	SD
P	4.47	2.77	3.95	2.10
E	14.49	3.42	14.22	3.43
N	6.51	3.85	7.04	4.00
L	12.63	3.85	13.54	3.87

perform such studies more effectively. The use of pencil and paper tests in the assessment of personality makes hard data available for statistical analysis. In the present study the statistics used have subsumed the underlying normality of the data distributions, and in most of the instances, it would seem that this assumption has not been blatantly violated. Furthermore the use of trait scores as employed in this investigation makes the assumption that the score obtained on the test and the degree to which that attribute is represented by that test is linearly related.

In order to make meaningful comparisons of personality across cultures, not only must the instrument used in the assessment be comparable but also some degree of equivalence of the sample are seen as pre-requisites. In the present study, for instance, school children have been selected, and selection procedures were similar in both the British and Sri Lankan studies. (Ideally of course an investigation carried out simultaneously in the different places needs to be performed). Also if national typologies are being contemplated, due regard must be given to the ethnic minorities when sampling strategies are being devised. Pitfalls of improper sampling have been adequately discussed elsewhere (Eysenck, 1953).

The use of factor analysis has been helpful in deriving scales for the four personality traits. It is encouraging to note that most items for the Sri Lankan scales corresponded with those for the British scales (Appendices I–IV). We, therefore, feel that these traits describe similar behaviours in both cultures. The involvement of the social desirability (Lie scale) element with P and N scales (cf Table 19.2) may cast some doubt on these scores. Perhaps some dissimulation took place. In order to actually estimate the influence of the L scale, regression techniques could be employed and they may be of use in future studies. Also the use of statistical techniques which do not make explicit assumption regarding the normality of the data distributions may be more appropriate.

Another interesting feature was the comparison of the results with those obtained in the adult cross-cultural study of Perera & Eysenck (1984). The lowest factor comparison value of 0.93 on the N factor for girls is not similarly low for women being 0.996. In fact none of the values for adults are below 0.977. A confident claim could, therefore, be lodged that the factors of P E N and L are identical in both countries.

Reliabilities, however, show some weakness in both adult and junior groups. While similar behaviours are probably being described in both countries (*vide supra*), more appropriate items to measure especially the P and E scales, could perhaps be found for Sri Lanka. The P reliability for boys (0.70) is considerably stronger than that for men (0.52) but on the other hand, the E reliability for boys (0.67) is marginally below that for males (0.72). Overall the reliabilities seem acceptable for the Junior EPQ in Sri Lanka, with some caution in the interpretation of the P results being suggested as far as the girls are concerned.

Table 19.4 Comparison of means (x̄) and standard deviations (SD) of Sri Lankan subjects and British subjects on scales of common items

	P		E		N		L		Age		n
	x̄	SD	x̄	SD	x̄	SD	x̄	SD	x̄	SD	
Sri Lankan boys	2.88	2.27	13.16	3.14	5.87	3.54	11.99	3.63	13.09	1.32	578
Sri Lankan girls	2.66	1.62	12.89	3.19	6.35	3.69	12.84	3.62	13.47	1.42	528
British boys	2.94	2.24	14.68	3.06	10.69	4.33	5.02	3.68	13.02	1.12	264
British girls	1.40	1.55	13.73	3.12	12.47	3.74	5.73	3.71	13.38	1.12	195
	P		E		N		L		Age		
Boys	NS		<.001		<.001		<.001		ns		
Girls	<.001		<.001		<.001		<.001		ns		

As a matter of interest, exactly the same results cross-culturally were obtained in the adult personality study. Sri Lankans scored twice as high as the British on the social desirability scale and significantly lower on the neuroticism scale. The N and L intercorrelations being high (−0.34 for males and −0.38 for females) the groups, therefore, probably dissimulated as did the children in this study. Similar results have been obtained in other cross-cultural comparisons from Hungary (Eysenck, Kozeki & Kalmanchey-Gellenne, 1980), Hong Kong (Eysenck & Chan, 1982) and Greece (Eysenck & Dimitriou, 1984). Our results were, however, dissimilar to results from several studies which were more similar to those obtained in the British studies. These studies emanated from Singapore (Long, 1973), New Zealand (Saklofske & Eysenck, 1978), Japan (Iwawaki, Eysenck & Eysenck, 1977) and Canada (Eysenck & Saklofske, 1983). The relatively high Lie score means (sometimes double that of the British) was the main difference seen in the studies from Sri Lanka, Hungary, Hong Kong and Greece. The suggestion made by Nyborg, Eysenck & Kroll (1982) was that the high Lie score means may be a reflection of the degree of permissiveness of that society. On the other hand one can not help but comment that this difference (the high L scores) occurred in the translated inventories in all instances with the exception of the Japanese. It was, however, not possible to evaluate the effects of translation, if any, on the size of the L score.

In this chapter some aspects of cross-cultural comparisons of personality have been described and certain constraints have been discussed. It is felt that this is an important area for investigation, since many factors that may impinge on the development of the individual's personality can be studied.

References

EYSENCK, H.J. (1953) *Uses and abuses of psychology* Middlesex: Penguin Books (1977 reprint, ch. 13).

EYSENCK, H.J. & EYSENCK, S.B.G. (1969) *Personality structure and measurement*, London: Routledge & Kegan Paul.

EYSENCK, H.J. & EYSENCK, S.B.G. (1975) *Manual of the Eysenck Personality Questionnaire (Junior & Adult)*, Kent: Hodder & Stoughton.

EYSENCK, S.B.G. & CHAN, J. (1982) A comparative study of personality in adults and children: Hong Kong versus England. *Personality and Individual Differences*, **3**, 153–60.

EYSENCK, S.B.G. & DIMITRIOU, E.C. (1984) Cross-cultural comparison of personality: Greek children and English children. *Social Behaviour and Personality*, **12**, 45–54.

EYSENCK, S.B.G., KOZEKI, B. & KALMANCHEY–GELLENNE, M. (1980) Cross-cultural comparison of personality: Hungarian children and English children. *Personality and Individual Differences*, **1**, 347–53.

EYSENCK, S.B.G. & SAKLOFSKE, D.H. (1983) A comparison of responses of Canadian and English children on the Junior Eysenck Personality Questionnaire. *Canadian Journal of Behavioral Sciences*, **15**, 121–30.

IWAWAKI, S., EYSENCK, S.B.G. & EYSENCK, H.J. (1977) Differences in personality between Japanese and English. *Journal of Social Psychology*, **102**, 27–33.

KAISER, H.J., HUNKA, S. & BIANCHINI, J. (1969) Relating factors between studies based upon different individuals. In H.J. Eysenck & S.B.G. Eysenck (eds.) *Personality structure and measurement*. London: Routledge & Kegan Paul.

LONG, F.Y. (1973) Some intelligence and personality data of Singapore medical students. *Singapore Medical Journal*, **14**, 34–6.

NYBORG, H., EYSENCK, S.B.G. & KROLL, N. (1982) Cross-cultural comparison of personality: Danish children and English children. *Scandinavian Journal of Psychology*, **15**, 291–7.

PERERA, K.M.H. & EYSENCK, S.B.G. (1984) A cross-cultural study of personality: Sri Lanka and England. *Journal of Cross-Cultural Psychology*, **15**, 353–71.

Saklofske, D.H. & Eysenck, S.B.G. (1978) Cross-cultural comparison of personality: New Zealand and English children. *Psychological Reports*, **42**, 1111–6.

Acknowledgements

I am grateful to Dr Sybil Eysenck for her help with the statistical analysis and the encouragement given throughout this project. I would also like to thank Mr Shamil Wanigaratne and Mrs Winitha de Silva for their active help with the data collection.

Appendix IA

Factor loadings for boys and girls on the P scale

	Boys: n = 578				Girls: n = 528			
	P	E	N	L	P	E	N	L
3	.46	−.15	−.02	−.05	.35	−.05	−.01	−.09
7	.43	.00	−.05	−.10	.36	.03	.18	−.06
12	.49	.07	−.02	−.16	.36	.01	.09	−.16
15	.39	.04	−.06	−.04	.30	.21	−.10	−.07
19	.43	.01	.01	−.33	.30	−.03	−.01	−.15
23	.28	−.06	.13	−.32	.21	.03	.13	−.22
−32	−.19	.26	.08	.20	−.14	.09	−.04	.08
34	.17	−.01	.25	−.26	.20	−.01	.24	−.09
37	.54	.19	−.17	−.05	−.08	.42	.11	−.16
41	.27	.01	.27	−.14	.33	.02	.17	−.18
45	.25	−.06	.29	−.22	.28	−.08	.04	−.18
49	.49	.20	−.21	−.06	−.09	.48	.05	−.14
53	.35	−.07	.09	−.13	.41	−.03	−.08	−.06
57	.05	.32	.07	−.08	.12	.28	.19	.17
61	.21	−.13	.23	.16	.14	.03	.33	−.02
−69	−.27	.32	.02	.25	−.29	.03	.09	.08
−81	−.14	.25	.16	.20	−.18	.11	.09	.09
1	.33	−.17	.08	−.02	.40	.02	−.06	.00
5	.37	−.01	.06	.18	.28	.06	.13	.16
35	.30	.24	.04	.00	.39	.35	.15	.09
65	.32	.22	.05	.08	.12	.16	.09	−.04

Note   P = Psychoticism, E = Extraversion, N = Neuroticism.
    L = Lie scale

Appendix IB

P Scale original items
(Underlined items were those omitted from the Sinhala scale)
Item
 (3) Do you enjoy hurting people you like?
 (7) Would you enjoy practical jokes that could sometimes really hurt people?
(12) Would you like other children to be afraid of you?
(15) Would you enjoy cutting up animals in Biology class?
(19) Do you sometimes like teasing animals?
(23) Do you seem to get into more quarrels and squabbles than most children?
(32) Would it upset you a lot to see a dog that has just been run over?
(34) Is there someone who is trying to get even with you for what they think you did to them?
(37) Do you rather enjoy teasing other children?
(41) Do you seem to get into a lot of fights?
(45) Are you in more trouble at school than most children?
(49) Do you like playing pranks on others?
(53) Is it sometimes rather fun to watch a gang tease or bully a small child?
(57) Would you like to go to the moon on your own?
(61) Are your parents unreasonably strict with you?
(69) Would you feel very sorry for an animal caught in a trap?
(81) Are you always specially careful with other people's things?

New items that were added
  (1) Do you like plenty of excitement going on around you?
  (5) Do you nearly always have a quick answer when people talk to you?
  (35) Do you think water skiing would be fun?[1]
  (65) Do you like some strong tasting medicines, like cough sweets?

Appendix IIA

Factor loadings for boys and girls on the E scale

	Boys: n = 578				Girls: n = 528			
	P	E	N	L	P	E	N	L
1	.33	−.17	.08	−.02	.40	.02	−.06	.00
5	.37	−.01	.06	.18	.28	.06	.13	.16
−9	.06	−.18	.18	.14	−.06	−.19	.28	.11
13	−.05	.10	.04	.26	.17	.31	−.13	.28
17	.14	.19	.10	.12	−.05	.32	−.10	.08
21	−.01	.34	.08	−.04	−.04	.29	−.03	−.14
26	−.00	.28	.09	−.03	−.06	.26	.00	−.06
30	.18	.26	.05	.15	.20	.39	.15	.31
35	.30	.24	.04	.00	.39	.35	.15	.09
39	.00	.21	−.13	.18	.02	.22	.05	.16
43	.03	.35	−.00	.11	−.00	.41	−.00	−.10
47	.09	.33	−.01	.08	−.02	.46	.00	.02
−51	−.00	−.44	.17	.00	.14	−.42	.23	.03
55	.21	.25	.12	−.26	.14	.38	.02	−.31
59	.06	.39	−.12	−.02	−.10	.36	−.09	−.16
63	.05	.49	.06	−.09	.05	.42	.09	−.02
67	.12	.41	−.16	.06	.08	.38	−.19	−.02
71	.19	.28	.26	−.07	.14	.12	.25	−.22
75	.19	.41	.05	−.00	.07	.48	.15	−.04
79	.04	.22	−.02	.30	.10	.23	−.16	.15
83	.03	.39	.01	−.09	.03	.38	.08	−.14
−87	.02	−.32	.25	.04	.16	−.28	.29	.06
93	.00	.29	−.12	.12	.05	.38	−.17	.21
96	.24	.39	.04	.00	.29	.41	.06	−.07
57	.05	.32	.07	−.08	.12	.28	.19	.17
90	−.10	.35	−.10	.16	.07	.31	−.26	.09

Note P = Psychoticism, E = Extraversion, N = Neuroticism, L = Lie scale

Appendix IIB

E Scale original items
(Underlined items were those omitted from the Sinhala scale)
Item
  (1) Do you like plenty of excitement going on around you?
  (5) Do you nearly always have a quick answer when people talk to you?
  (9) Would you rather be alone instead of meeting other children?
  (13) Are you rather lively?
  (17) Have you got many friends?
  (21) Would you like to explore an old haunted castle?
  (26) Do you like doing things where you have to act quickly?
  (30) Can you get a party going?
  (35) Do you think water skiing would be fun?
  (39) When you make new friends do you usually make the first move?
  (43) Do you like telling jokes or funny stories to your friends?
  (47) Have you many different hobbies and interests?

---

1 This item was translated as an item relating to motorcycle racing.

(51) Would you rather sit and watch than play at parties?
(55) Do you like doing things that are a bit frightening?
(59) Do you like mixing with other children?
(63) Would parachute jumping appeal to you?
(67) Can you let yourself go and enjoy yourself a lot at a lively party?
(71) Do you often make up your mind to do things suddenly?
(75) Do you enjoy diving or jumping in the sea or a pool?
(79) Do other people think of you as being very lively?
(83) Do you like going out a lot?
(87) Do you find it hard to really enjoy yourself at a lively party?
(93) Would you call yourself happy-go-lucky?
(96) Would you like to drive or ride on a fast motor bike?

New items that were added
(57) Would you like to go to the moon on your own?
(90) Are you usually happy and cheerful?

Appendix IIIA

Factor loadings for boys and girls on the N scale

| | Boys: n = 578 | | | | Girls: n = 528 | | | |
	P	E	N	L	P	E	N	L
2	.12	−.03	.33	−.00	.00	−.15	.43	−.02
6	.19	.05	.04	.01	.11	.08	.24	−.02
10	.11	.08	.25	−.04	−.10	.06	.53	.08
14	.16	.08	.29	−.28	−.00	.12	.19	−.32
18	−.03	.02	.47	.03	.14	−.01	.41	.03
22	.11	−.03	.29	.10	−.03	−.05	.36	.03
27	−.10	.19	.32	−.18	−.26	.05	.33	−.15
31	.06	.08	.26	−.15	−.06	.14	.29	−.11
36	−.01	−.13	.48	.09	.20	−.12	.39	.01
40	−.10	.16	.28	−.15	−.21	.08	.21	−.32
48	−.00	.04	.37	−.15	−.32	.04	.40	−.18
52	.05	−.14	.54	−.01	.05	−.18	.55	−.02
56	.17	−.09	.31	.06	.20	.01	.24	−.06
64	−.14	.08	.46	−.10	−.22	.13	.43	−.13
68	−.01	−.03	.46	−.07	−.20	.06	.53	−.12
72	.06	.10	.41	−.09	.07	−.05	.36	−.13
76	.14	.01	.40	.10	.05	−.01	.53	.17
80	.02	−.03	.53	.01	−.02	−.07	.56	.11
88	.04	.08	.39	.10	−.09	.14	.51	.08
94	.16	.14	.16	.14	.26	.20	.11	.03
44	.00	−.16	.33	.05	.14	−.23	.18	−.04
60	.18	−.13	.24	.20	.24	−.11	.30	.26
61	.21	−.13	.23	.16	.14	.03	.33	−.02

Note P = Psychoticism, E = Extraversion, N = Neuroticism, L = Lie Scale

Appendix IIIB

N Scale original items
(Underlined items were those omitted from the Sinhala scale)
Item
 (2) Are you moody?
 (6) Do you very easily feel bored?
(10) Do ideas run through your head so that you cannot sleep?
(14) Do lots of things annoy you?
(18) Do you ever feel 'just miserable' for no good reason?

(22) Do you often feel life is very dull?
(27) Do you worry about awful things that might happen?
(31) Are you easily hurt when people find fault with you or the work you do?
(36) Do you often feel tired for no good reason?
(40) Are you touchy about some things?
(48) Are your feelings rather easily hurt?
(52) Do you often feel fed-up?
(56) Do you sometimes get so restless that you cannot sit still in a chair for long?
(64) Do you worry for a long while if you feel you have made a fool of yourself?
(68) Do you sometimes feel life is just not worth living?
(72) Does your mind often wander off when you are doing some work?
(76) Do you find it hard to get to sleep at night because you are worrying about things?
(80) Do you often feel lonely?
(88) Do you sometimes feel specially cheerful and at other times sad without any good reason?
(94) Do you often need kind friends to cheer you up?

New items that were added
(44) Do you have 'dizzy turns'?
(60) Do you have many frightening dreams?
(61) Are your parents unreasonably strict with you?

Appendix IVA

Factor loadings for boys and girls on the L scale

| | Boys: n = 578 | | | | Girls: n = 528 | | | |
	P	E	N	L	P	E	N	L
−4	.06	.10	.31	−.20	.16	.09	.11	−.27
8	.31	.08	−.06	.33	.09	.04	.19	.37
−11	.04	.17	.22	−.41	.18	.00	.04	−.36
−16	−.05	.23	.21	−.48	.01	.11	.04	−.62
−20	−.05	.15	.27	−.42	−.04	.06	.12	−.51
24	−.02	.06	.01	.45	−.08	−.03	.08	.48
28	−.15	.10	.00	.28	−.16	.09	−.09	.21
33	−.14	.13	.04	.28	−.05	.18	.05	.33
38	.02	.00	−.01	.44	−.04	.04	.06	.46
−42	−.14	.24	.28	−.48	−.08	.12	.11	−.58
46	−.18	−.00	.24	.35	−.00	−.04	.01	.39
50	−.03	.13	.05	.35	−.13	.02	.18	.43
54	−.21	−.08	.11	.49	.09	−.17	.03	.58
58	.01	.15	.10	.26	−.04	.14	−.02	.11
66	.06	.09	.13	.17	.14	.05	.10	.22
−70	−.08	.08	.28	−.44	−.08	.14	.08	−.65
−77	.34	.06	.02	−.28	.11	−.03	.01	−.44
82	−.08	.10	.00	.32	−.10	.12	.04	.30
−86	.04	.17	.22	−.40	.12	.05	.05	−.40
−89	.12	.20	.02	−.47	.15	.08	−.04	−.57
−95	.03	.16	.06	.47	−.04	.10	.11	−.53

Note   P = Psychoticism, E = Extraversion, N = Neuroticism, L = Lie scale

Appendix IVB

L Scale original items
(Underlined items were those omitted from the Sinhala scale)
Item
(4) Were you ever greedy by helping yourself to more than your share of anything?
(8) Do you always do what you are told at once?
(11) Have you broken any rules at school?
(16) Did you ever steal anything (even a pin or button) that belonged to someone else?

(20) Did you ever pretend you did not hear when someone was calling you?
(24) Do you always finish your homework before you play?
(28) When you hear children using bad language do you try to stop them?
(33) Do you always say you are sorry when you have been rude?
(38) Are you always quiet when older people are talking?
(42) Have you ever said anything bad or nasty about anyone?
(46) Do you generally pick up papers and rubbish others throw on the classroom floor?
(50) Do you always wash before a meal?
(54) Are you always quiet in class, even when the teacher is out of the room?
(58) At prayers or assembly, do you always sing when the others are singing?
(66) Do you always eat everything you are given at meals?
(70) Have you ever been cheeky to your parents?
(77) Did you ever write or scribble in a school or library book?
(82) Do you always share all the sweets you have?
(86) Have you ever cheated at a game?
(89) Do you throw waste paper on the floor when there is no waste paper basket handy?

New item that was added
(95) Did you ever break or lose anything belonging to someone else?

20 Levels of delinquency in three cultures

J.A. Opolot

Introduction

As societies undergo social change and as urbanization increases, it affords opportunities for greater impersonality in social relations and gives rise to extensive social differentiation in social norms and values, many of which may be conducive to crime and delinquency. Urbanization and urbanism are supposed to afford greater freedom of action, more temptation for violation of the law and a general decline in social morals exerted through the family.

With the growth of Kampala as the capital city of Uganda, complex social problems have resulted – problems of accommodation, sanitation, health, welfare, education and crime, to name but a few. Created in people are new aspirations, hopes and desires which have led to inevitable and regrettable consequences. These promises, dreams and desires have a very strong appeal to people of either sex, young and old who have experienced economic, political and social frustration in rural areas. This appears to have led over a number of years to a constant flow of people from rural areas of every part of Uganda into Kampala at an alarming rate. Especially is this the case with school leavers of both primary and secondary levels who have had an unsettling school education. These adolescents are unable to continue with their schooling or settle down in their rural areas but would rather come to Kampala in search of employment. This migration into Kampala has therefore precipitated and complicated the situation. At the receiving end, however, neither the government nor any other agency has ever made any arrangements as to how such a large number of new migrants into Kampala can be absorbed and integrated into the new urban environment. On the contrary, these adolescents lack the necessary guidance and assistance on how they can meet their needs and aspirations in the new environment. In short, they are left to their own devices in their effort to become integrated into the new environment. As a result, the incidence of crime and delinquency has been on a steady increase. Over a period of 25 years now, crimes against property, all types of theft, violence and so on have been rising in Kampala with a fair degree of sophistication and innovation.

The young offenders of these crimes are usually sent by courts either to remand homes or approved schools in the country. About 5% of these committed youngsters are found to be in need of care, protection and control in civil proceedings. The government, through courts of law, believes that the basic objectives of this type of treatment for juvenile delinquents are re-adjustment and social re-education in preparation for his return to the community. An interpretation of this objective would be that approved schools or remand homes attempt to modify attitudes, or other personality characteristics found to be typical of the youngsters committed to these institutions in the direction of those characteristics common to children in the community at large. A measure of the effectiveness of these institutions would be the demonstration both of such changes, and of a relationship between the degree of such modification and any subsequent reconviction after leaving an institutional setting.

Before one can, however, evaluate the effectiveness of approved school training or the remand homes, it is necessary to have a valid instrument that is able to differentiate between delinquents and non-delinquents or between 'levels' of delinquency. Such an instrument already exists – the Jesness Inventory (Jesness, 1962, 1963, 1966), which was constructed as a result of the large-scale research programme undertaken by the California Youth Authority.

General description of the Jesness inventory

The Inventory consists of 155 items to which the subject is asked to respond 'true' or 'false'. The criteria for the selection of items were:

(a) discriminatory power between delinquents and non-delinquents, and
(b) covering a wide range of attitude and sentiment about self and others to provide the basis of a personality typology meaningful for use with both delinquents and non-delinquents (Jesness, 1963).

The items included in the Inventory were not selected on the basis of any particular theory of personality of delinquency. They were written by Jesness to reflect the results of a number of studies and a variety of theoretical standpoints, which appeared to indicate the attitudinal characteristics which discriminate between children who have been dealt with by the legal system for delinquent behaviour and those who have not.

The Inventory was constructed to provide scores on ten subscales. Three of the sub-scales (Social Maladjustment, Value Orientation and Immaturity) were developed from an item analysis using appropriately selected criterion groups. The remaining seven subscales were derived from a cluster analysis. A prediction score, the Asocial Index, based on a discriminant function analysis using scores from all ten subscales, was also developed.

Jesness (1963) defined the subscales as follows:

(1) '*Social Maladjustment* (63 items) refers to a set of attitudes associated with unfulfilled needs as defined by the extent to which an individual shares the attitudes of persons who demonstrate inability to meet, in socially approved ways, the demands of their environment;
(2) *Value Orientation* (39 items) refers to a tendency to hold values characteristic of persons in the lower social classes;
(3) *Immaturity* (45 items) refers to the tendency to display attitudes and perceptions of self and others which are usual for persons of a younger age;
(4) *Autism* (28 items) refers to a tendency in thinking and perceiving to distort reality according to one's personal desires or needs;
(5) *Alienation* (26 items) refers to the presence of distrust and estrangement in a person's attitudes towards others, especially toward persons representing authority;
(6) *Manifest Aggression* (31 items) refers to an awareness of unpleasant feelings especially of anger or frustration, a tendency to react readily with emotion, and perceived discomfort concerning the presence and control of these feelings;
(7) *Withdrawal* (24 items) involves a perceived lack of satisfaction with self and others and a tendency toward passive escape or isolation from others;
(8) *Social Anxiety* (24 items) is defined as the perceived emotional discomfort associated with interpersonal relationships;
(9) *Repression* (15 items) refers to the exclusion from conscious awareness of feelings and emotions which the individual normally would be expected to experience, or his failure to label these emotions;
(10) *Denial* (20 items) refers to the failure to acknowledge unpleasant events or aspects of reality normally encountered in daily living;
(11) *Asocialization*, as measured by the *Asocial* Index, refers to a generalized disposition to resolve problems in social and personal adjustment in ways ordinarily regarded as showing a disregard for social customs or rules.' (pp. 8–9)

Some of the items in the Inventory contribute to scores on more than one subscale, so that 315 responses are scored. There is most item overlap between the Social Maladjustment, Value Orientation and Immaturity subscales; 16 items scored in the same direction appear in both the Social Maladjustment and Value Orientation subscales, and 9 in the former and the Immaturity subscale.

The intercorrelations between the subscale scores for the Californian standardization samples, both delinquents and non-delinquents, are presented in Appendix A together with the intercorrelations for a sample of English and Ugandan delinquents.

The reliability of the Inventory

Jesness (1963) reported split-half reliability coefficients for each Inventory subscale ranging from 0.88 (Social Maladjustment) to 0.62 (Withdrawal). Test-retest coefficients, after an eight-month interval, range from 0.79 (Social Maladjustment, Value Orientation) to 0.40 (Alienation). As the Inventory was devised to measure change of attitude following rehabilitative treatment, the test-retest coefficients are difficult to evaluate because, as Jesness says, 'the ideal compromise between stability and sensitivity remains a matter of judgement'.

Research studies of the Inventory

The claim that the Jesness Inventory provides a sensitive and valid measure of deviant personality has led to many cross-cultural studies. In Britain, for instance, several investigators have used the Inventory and sufficient data have been generated to enable at least a tentative evaluation of its usefulness in a British setting. Fisher (1967), for example, administered the Inventory to 203 English borstal boys. Their scores were compared with those of American institutionalized boys of the same 16–18-year-old age group. It was found that the English sample tended to be described by test scores as more socially maladjusted but at the same time more inhibited against acting out in socially unacceptable ways than the American sample. Fisher's (1967) explanation for the observed differences between the American and English delinquents was that the two samples of subjects had different test-taking sets probably attributable to cultural differences. It was evident that the differences in test-taking techniques were related to a relatively pronounced acquiescent response set among the English borstal boys.

Davies (1967) used the Jesness Inventory as part of a Home Office Research Unit investigation into the problems presented by 507 male probationers from eight different areas in England. Attention was given to isolating stresses in the offenders' social environment and relating these factors to personality assessments. Davies commented favourably on the practicality of using the Inventory with probation groups and made comparisons with previous studies. He cautioned that the Jesness T-score equivalents should not be used in view of certain response differences evident in the British probationer sample and that scores on the Immaturity subscale should also be treated with caution. It was noted that seven of the subscales behaved very similarly in England and America, and that five of these plus two others also discriminated satisfactorily between English samples of differing degrees of delinquency.

Mott (1969) evaluated the Inventory for use with English approved-school boys in the hope that it would be an important adjunct to present assessment procedures. In general, Mott (1969) found that those subscales, which had discriminated between the American delinquents and non-delinquents, also satisfactorily discriminated between the comparable English samples. Detailed comparisons with previous studies were made and the tendency for all English samples to score higher on the Immaturity and Alienation subscales was noted.

Her results did not, however, confirm the acquiescent response set explanation of the American–English differences (Fisher, 1967). In a follow-up study, Mott (1973) found no association between the Inventory subscale scores and reconviction in her samples of delinquent school boys.

Vallence & Forrest (1971) administered the Inventory to 174 approved-school and 306 day-school boys in the West of Scotland. Their results also revealed that the Inventory discriminated significantly between these two samples of approved and non-delinquent school boys.

Saunders & Davies (1976) reported a study done in England which examined the validity of the Jesness Inventory. Evidence was reported that some of the subscales of the Inventory satisfactorily differentiated between various levels of delinquency. Also it was reported that some of the subscales are able to predict from a group of offenders those who are destined to continue their delinquent dispositions. These authors conclude by saying that the scales purporting to measure social maladjustment, manifest aggression, value orientation, and alienation are related to the concept of 'deviant personality'; and that the recidivist is more likely to be unsocialized, aggressive, anti-authority, and unempathic as measured by the Inventory.

Statement of the problem

The present paper will therefore present evidence that some of the subscales of the Jesness Inventory are able to differentiate between different levels of delinquency with an Ugandan sample. The paper will also compare the Ugandan results with those previously reported with American and English samples.

The samples

The Californian standardization sample
The delinquent sample (Jesness, 1963) consisted of 970 boys ranging in age from eight to eighteen, drawn from California Youth Authority Reception Centres and two training schools. There were 59 boys aged ten and under, with a minimum of 100 boys in each subsequent age sample.

The non-delinquent sample consisted of 1075 boys in the same age range and with the same minimum sample number at each age. These boys attended state schools and most of them lived in lower-class urban areas.

The English sample
The delinquent sample (Mott, 1969) consisted of 208 consecutive admissions of 13–16-year-old boys to one classifying approved-school during the period December 1965 to March 1966.

The non-delinquent sample consisted of 162 boys in the same age range attending a comprehensive school. No selection criteria other than age were used to collect this sample.

The Ugandan sample
The delinquent sample consisted of 167 boys admitted to Kapingiriza Approved School near Kampala. Their ages ranged from 13 to 16 years old and they had been in the school for no less than six months.

The non-delinquent sample consisted of 190 boys in the same age range attending a secondary school near Kampala city.

The number of boys at each age level for each sample is given in Table 20.1.

Table 20.1   Composition of standardisation samples

Age	Ugandan Samples		English Samples		California Samples	
	Delinquent	Non-delinquent	Delinquent	Non-delinquent	Delinquent	Non-delinquent
13	45	52	50	57	102	115
14	49	53	54	40	115	102
15	40	43	53	33	135	123
16	33	42	51	32	130	129

The administration of the inventory

The Jesness Inventory was administered to groups of Ugandan boys in each school by their teachers. The first two items were read aloud as demonstration items. Slow or dull boys were usually helped by the teacher by having difficult items read aloud to them and it was occasionally necessary to explain the meaning of some words. Such assistance, however, was kept to a minimum.

Results

Data on the Ugandan samples are presented followed by a comparison of data on Ugandan, English (Mott, 1969) and American (Jesness, 1963) delinquents. Data on the 'Asocial Index' were not available for the Ugandan sample and so will not be presented here. The mean scores on the ten Jesness scales for Ugandan samples of delinquent and non-delinquent boys are presented in Table 20.2

It will be seen from Table 20.2 that Social Maladjustment, Value Orientation, Autism and Repression subscales clearly discriminate the two Ugandan groups ($p < .01$) across all age groups. The Withdrawal, Denial and Immaturity subscales do almost as well, failing only at the age levels 13, 14 and 15 respectively.

The Alienation, Manifest Aggression and Social Anxiety subscales do not significantly distinguish Ugandan delinquents from non-delinquents across all ages. In all the subscales, delinquents scored higher than non-delinquents, except on the Denial subscale where this trend was reversed.

The mean scores of the Ugandan delinquent group were then compared with those of the English and American delinquents. Patterns of differences between the subscale mean scores of these groups appear in Tables 20.3–20.12.

Discussion

The Jesness Inventory is unique in that it was designed to classify delinquents and disturbed adolescents, with the aim of using the typology for evaluating the effects of types of treatment on different types of offenders. Its development 'came as a consequence of the apparent lack of an adequate structured test already available which would be sensitive to change, yet stable enough to provide a measure of personality types' (Jesness, 1966, p. 3). The Social Maladjustment, Value Orientation and Immaturity subscales in the Jesness Inventory were empirically derived as a result of an item analysis of the responses of appropriate criterion samples. These subscales may, therefore, be considered to have been validated by this method of construction.

Table 20.2 Means and standard deviations of Ugandan delinquents and non-delinquents on sub-scales of the Jesness Personality Inventory by age

Scale	Age	Delinquents		Non-delinquents		Comparison of means	
		Mean	SD	Mean	SD		
(1) Social maladjustment	13	32.00	6.41	27.30	5.45	t=3.858	p<.01
	14	30.25	5.56	21.30	6.21	t=7.679	p<.01
	15	29.50	5.12	20.35	6.07	t=7.522	p<.01
	16	27.54	5.54	18.62	4.83	t=7.319	p<.01
(2) Value Orientation	13	23.75	6.61	16.60	5.23	t=5.844	p<.01
	14	22.25	7.08	14.85	4.49	t=6.247	p<.01
	15	21.45	5.41	13.45	6.54	t=6.089	p<.01
	16	19.75	6.06	12.93	5.74	t=4.951	p<.01
(3) Immaturity	13	22.15	4.84	17.60	5.79	t=4.215	p<.01
	14	23.25	5.09	21.00	4.26	t=2.411	p<.05
	15	20.43	4.22	19.60	3.10	t=1.015	ns
	16	23.50	6.91	17.30	4.60	t=4.440	p<.01
(4) Autism	13	15.25	3.61	9.60	4.97	t=6.461	p<.01
	14	14.20	3.09	11.30	3.95	t=4.146	p<.01
	15	14.00	3.21	10.60	3.54	t=4.589	p<.01
	16	14.50	3.24	9.00	3.14	t=7.397	p<.01
(5) Alienation	13	16.25	3.51	10.60	4.46	t=8.881	p<.01
	14	12.25	4.06	11.54	5.44	t=0.751	ns
	15	15.00	5.89	13.00	5.56	t=1.588	ns
	16	15.50	3.92	10.30	4.51	t=5.335	p<.01
(6) Manifest aggression	13	17.25	4.14	16.25	5.73	t=0.994	ns
	14	18.75	3.06	15.30	6.74	t=3.370	p<.01
	15	16.12	5.89	14.75	4.46	t=0.867	ns
	16	16.50	4.94	14.95	5.32	t=1.304	ns
(7) Withdrawal	13	14.05	4.41	13.25	3.09	t=1.019	ns
	14	13.75	3.34	11.60	4.97	t=2.581	p<.05
	15	14.25	2.25	11.25	3.75	t=4.454	p<.01
	16	13.00	3.75	10.95	3.44	t=2.437	p<.05
(8) Social anxiety	13	14.55	3.04	13.30	3.46	t=1.894	ns
	14	14.00	3.99	13.60	3.74	t=0.521	ns
	15	13.50	3.63	11.00	2.63	t=3.570	p<.01
	16	15.25	2.95	13.00	3.94	t=2.827	p<.01
(9) Repression	13	8.75	3.41	5.30	2.07	t=5.910	p<.01
	14	10.50	4.87	6.30	2.03	t=5.604	p<.01
	15	6.75	2.92	5.00	1.14	t=3.547	p<.01
	16	5.59	2.34	4.30	1.64	t=2.690	p<.01
(10) Denial	13	8.55	3.94	10.30	3.51	t=2.240	p<.05
	14	10.25	3.98	11.30	3.72	t=1.308	ns
	15	7.50	2.72	9.30	3.14	t=2.797	p<.01
	16	8.15	2.09	10.25	3.26	t=3.383	p<.01

Table 20.3   Means and standard deviations of delinquent samples on social maladjustment

	Samples					
	Ugandan		English		American	
Age	Mean	SD	Mean	SD	Mean	SD
13	32.00	6.41	30.88	5.88	28.68	6.68
14	30.25	5.56	29.16	6.05	29.23	7.66
15	29.50	5.12	28.09	6.14	26.55	6.80
16	27.54	5.54	27.04	5.51	25.72	7.09

Table 20.4   Means and standard deviations of delinquent samples on value orientation

	Samples					
	Ugandan		English		American	
Age	Mean	SD	Mean	SD	Mean	SD
13	23.75	6.61	19.74	6.28	18.74	6.91
14	22.25	7.08	17.68	5.41	18.64	7.35
15	21.45	5.41	17.54	6.14	15.93	7.56
16	19.75	6.06	17.31	6.26	15.35	7.34

Table 20.5   Means and standard deviations of delinquent samples on immaturity

	Samples					
	Ugandan		English		American	
Age	Mean	SD	Mean	SD	Mean	SD
13	22.15	4.84	18.46	3.96	14.83	4.39
14	23.25	5.09	16.78	3.54	14.60	4.78
15	20.43	4.22	15.30	3.96	13.19	4.47
16	23.50	6.91	15.19	4.69	12.14	3.84

Table 20.6   Means and standard deviations of delinquent samples on autism

	Samples					
	Ugandan		English		American	
Age	Mean	SD	Mean	SD	Mean	SD
13	15.25	3.61	9.82	3.88	9.42	3.89
14	14.20	3.09	8.81	3.44	9.43	4.86
15	14.00	3.21	7.68	3.18	7.17	4.29
16	13.50	3.24	7.57	3.47	6.86	3.64

Table 20.7 Means and standard deviations of delinquent samples on alienation

	Samples					
	Ugandan		English		American	
Age	Mean	SD	Mean	SD	Mean	SD
13	16.25	3.51	11.76	4.93	9.77	4.69
14	12.25	4.06	10.31	4.36	9.58	4.75
15	15.00	5.89	10.53	4.46	8.39	5.26
16	14.50	3.92	9.98	4.34	7.95	4.93

Table 20.8 Means and standard deviations of delinquent samples on manifest aggression

	Samples					
	Ugandan		English		American	
Age	Mean	SD	Mean	SD	Mean	SD
13	17.25	4.14	15.56	4.84	17.16	5.50
14	18.75	3.06	13.64	5.17	17.10	6.17
15	16.12	5.89	14.40	5.68	15.38	6.86
16	16.50	4.94	14.55	5.30	13.96	5.83

Table 20.9 Means and standard deviations of delinquent samples on withdrawal

	Samples					
	Ugandan		English		American	
Age	Mean	SD	Mean	SD	Mean	SD
13	14.05	4.41	13.68	3.21	13.54	3.63
14	13.75	3.34	13.51	2.87	12.63	3.62
15	14.25	2.25	12.94	3.60	12.53	3.71
16	13.00	3.75	13.08	3.19	12.91	3.71

Table 20.10 Means and standard deviations of delinquents on social anxiety

	Samples					
	Ugandan		English		American	
Age	Mean	SD	Mean	SD	Mean	SD
13	14.55	3.04	14.96	3.48	14.30	4.06
14	14.00	3.99	14.61	4.03	13.83	3.89
15	13.50	3.63	14.24	3.92	13.28	4.36
16	15.25	2.95	14.12	3.68	13.71	3.83

Table 20.11   Means and standard deviations of delinquent samples on repression

	Samples					
Age	Ugandan		English		American	
	Mean	SD	Mean	SD	Mean	SD
13	8.75	3.41	5.94	2.77	4.04	2.83
14	10.50	4.87	4.96	2.64	4.30	2.90
15	6.75	2.92	5.23	2.84	3.74	2.58
16	5.59	2.34	4.94	2.41	3.68	2.48

Table 20.12   Means and standard deviations of delinquent samples on denial

	Samples					
Age	Ugandan		English		American	
	Mean	SD	Mean	SD	Mean	SD
13	8.55	3.94	10.84	2.50	11.37	3.52
14	10.25	3.98	10.87	2.81	12.08	3.64
15	7.50	2.72	10.51	3.50	12.20	3.73
16	8.15	2.09	10.76	3.74	12.34	3.70

The remaining seven subscales: Autism, Alienation, Manifest Aggression, Withdrawal, Social Anxiety, Repression and Denial, were derived from a cluster analysis, but some subjective judgement was used to produce apparently clinically meaningful scales. Less, therefore, is known about the significance of scores on these subscales. Let us discuss the results on each scale in turn.

The empirical subscales

(1)   Social Maladjustment
Jesness (1966, p. 28) defined this subscale as measuring 'the extent to which the individual shares attitudes expressed by persons who show an inability to meet, in socially approved ways, the demands of living', and suggested that the criterion group of delinquents has 'presumably demonstrated this inability'.

The Ugandan delinquents scored significantly higher than the comparable nondelinquents at every age level on this subscale, thus confirming the American (Jesness, 1966) and the English (Mott, 1969) findings. No significant differences were found between the mean Social Maladjustment scores of the English and the American delinquents at any age whereas the scores of Ugandan delinquents were found to be consistently higher than the comparable English and American delinquents at all ages in the range tested.

Jesness's (1966) results indicate a tendency for the delinquent scores on this subscale to decline with age. A similar tendency was shown by the present Ugandan delinquent sample and the English group (Mott, 1969). Davies (1967) and Fisher (1967) also reported a decrease in scores with age for their samples. Thus, there is evidence to suggest that scores on the social maladjustment subscale discriminate between groups of differing degrees of delinquency.

(2) Value Orientation

The items in this subscale were constructed to 'tap the main themes of lower class culture, including the trouble, luck and thrill motives, the fear of failure, the gang orientation, the toughness ethic, and the desire for early or premature adulthood' (Jesness, 1966, p. 32). Jesness devised this subscale with the intention of measuring 'the extent to which an individual holds values characteristic of lower class culture' (Jesness, 1966, p. 32). He found a significant relationship between scores on this subscale and the socioeconomic status of his samples assessed by paternal occupation

Highly significant differences were found between the mean scores of the Ugandan delinquents and non-delinquents at all ages on this subscale, with the delinquent groups scoring higher. There were also significant differences between the scores obtained by the Ugandan delinquents and the comparable English and American delinquents, with the Ugandan delinquents scoring higher at each age level.

No significant differences, however, were found between the mean scores of the English and American delinquents at any age level on this subscale. Davies (1967) also reported no significant differences between the scores of his probation sample and the comparable American delinquents.

(3) Immaturity

The Immaturity subscale measures 'the extent to which the individual fails to show those responses, attitudes, points of view and perceptions which are usual and expected for his age level' (Jesness, 1966, p. 38). Jesness considered that it was reasonable to attempt to develop a measure of this characteristic because the concept of maturity is commonly used by persons working in the field of delinquency to describe boys who are neither highly delinquent nor highly disturbed. Further, evidence of increased maturity, however defined, is frequently used to describe a satisfactory response to treatment. Jesness reported a consistent tendency, not always statistically significant, for the American delinquents at all ages to score higher than the comparable non-delinquent groups, that is, to be more 'immature'.

The present Ugandan delinquent group scored consistently and significantly higher, at all ages, than the comparable English and American groups. The scores of the Ugandan delinquent group resemble very closely those of American delinquents two years younger as does the English delinquent group. Fisher (1967) and Davies (1967) have reported similar results for older borstal inmates and probationers. These results, therefore, suggest a cultural difference in the expectations of the appropriate attitudes, etc., at particular ages, between the three populations from which the Ugandan, English and American samples were drawn.

In spite of the differences in the level of scores obtained by the Ugandan groups, scores on this subscale were found to discriminate significantly between the delinquent and non-delinquent groups at all ages in the range tested, except at age 15; with, however, the delinquents scoring higher.

The cluster subscales

(4) Autism

Jesness (1966) defined this subscale as measuring 'the tendency for the individual's thinking to be regulated unduly by personal needs' (p. 41) with a 'strong tendency toward unrealistic self-evaluation and concern over bizarre thoughts' (p. 40).

The Ugandan delinquents scored significantly higher than the non-delinquents at all ages in the range tested. Thus, this subscale clearly discriminated the present two Ugandan groups. Significant differences in mean scores were also found between the Ugandan and the English and American delinquents, with the Ugandan delinquents scoring higher at each age level.

No difference in mean scores, however, were found between the English and the American delinquent groups at any age level. This finding gives support to Davies's (1967) report where no difference between the scores of the probationers and the American delinquent was found. While Fisher's (1967) sample of 16-year-old borstal inmates scored significantly higher than the comparable American delinquents their score did not differ from that of the 16-year-old approved school boys.

(5) Alienation

According to Jesness (1966), the items in this subscale refer to the presence of distrust and estrangement in relationships with others, especially with authority figures (p. 42). Jesness found that the American delinquents scored significantly higher on this subscale than non-delinquents at all ages, and considered that this was in line with descriptions of delinquents as manifesting rebelliousness and distrust of authority (p. 43).

Scores on this subscale discriminate significantly between the Ugandan delinquents and non-delinquents at ages 13 and 16, thus confirming Jesness's (1966) general finding that delinquents score higher than non-delinquents.

The Ugandan delinquents scored significantly higher than the English or American delinquents at all ages in the range tested. These differences provide some evidence for suggesting that scores on this sub-scale distinguish between samples of differing degrees of delinquency. These consistent differences between the Ugandan and the English and American delinquents from the age of 13 and older suggest a further cultural difference between the three populations from which the delinquent groups were drawn.

(6) Manifest Aggression

Jesness (1966) found that this subscale contained items which 'suggest angry, aggressive feelings' (p. 44) with the high scoring individual being 'aware of, and made uncomfortable by his feelings of anger and hostility' (p. 44). He emphasises that he uses the term 'manifest aggression' to indicate 'simply perception of unpleasant feelings' (p. 45) and not overt aggressive behaviour. As he found that scores on this subscale and the Alienation subscale were highly intercorrelated (p. 58) he suggested that overt aggressive behaviour, if indicated at all from the Inventory scores, might be shown by individuals who scored highly on both these subscales. He reported that his delinquent groups tended to score higher on the Manifest Aggression subscale than the non-delinquent groups.

Scores on this subscale did not discriminate between the Ugandan delinquents and non-delinquents except at age 14. Similarly, the subscale did not discriminate between the Ugandan delinquents and the English delinquents at any age except at age 14. With the Ugandan and American delinquents, the subscale discriminated between them only at ages 14 and 16. These differences may again be related to differences in the degree of delinquency of the three groups.

(7) Withdrawal

Jesness (1966) describes withdrawal as 'a tendency to resolve a lack of satisfaction with self and others by passive escape or isolation from others (p. 47). This suggests the term 'dysthymia' as used by Eysenck (1961), referring to a combination of withdrawal and depression. Jesness (1966) found differences between his delinquents and non-delinquent groups with the delinquent tending to give higher scores. This finding is confirmed with the present results of the Ugandan samples.

Scores on this subscale revealed no significant differences between the Ugandan, the English and the American delinquents at any age except at age 15.

(8) Social Anxiety

This subscale contains items which 'point to emotional discomfort associated with interpersonal relationships' (Jesness, 1966, p. 49). Jesness found no differences between his delinquent and non-delinquent samples at any age. The present Ugandan sample results confirms this finding except for ages 15 and 16 where the delinquents were found to be scoring significantly higher than the non-delinquents.

No differences, however, were found between the scores of the Ugandan and the English delinquents, and the English and the American delinquents at any age level. Similarly, no differences were found between the Ugandan and the American delinquents at any age level except at age 16.

(9) Repression

Jesness (1966) observed that the items in this subscale referred to 'the exclusion from conscious awareness of, or a failure to label, feelings ordinarily experienced' (p. 52). He reported generally higher scores for the delinquent groups, but there were no significant differences between the American delinquents and non-delinquents. This finding is contrary to the present finding with Ugandan groups where the delinquents score significantly higher scores than non-delinquents.

Compared with the English delinquent group, the Ugandan delinquents scored significantly higher than the American delinquents at all ages in the range tested. Similar results were observed between the Ugandan and English delinquents at all age levels except at age 16.

(10) Denial

The items in this subscale deal with the 'suppression of critical judgement and the avoidance of unpleasant thoughts about interpersonal relationships' (Jesness, 1966, p. 54). This is the only subscale in the Inventory where the American delinquent groups scored lower than the non-delinquent groups. This tendency was also observed among the Ugandan groups. The subscale discriminated between the Ugandan delinquents and non-delinquents at all ages in the range tested except at age 14. Both the English and American delinquents scored significantly higher than the comparable Ugandan delinquents except for the Ugandan versus the English group at age 14 where, although the English delinquents still scored higher, the difference in mean scores was not statistically significant.

Conclusion

The present report has offered evidence that some of the subscales of the Jesness Inventory are able to differentiate between different levels of delinquency across cultures. At the same time, it should be noted that quite high correlations were obtained between several of the subscales, suggesting some overlap or commonality in the constructs being measured by this instrument. Thus caution is required when viewing the results of a single subscale in isolation from the others. Secondly, the Inventory has demonstrated its value and relevance in a Ugandan setting. No radical alteration in scale construction seems to be necessary. Future work will be concerned with administering the Inventory to samples of other age levels similar to those of Jesness (1966) groups in order to provide norms for Ugandan delinquents.

Thirdly, the validity of the Inventory in the Ugandan setting should be established especially regarding the ability of the instrument to predict from a group of offenders those who are destined to continue their delinquent careers.

References

DAVIES, M. (1967) *The use of the Jesness Inventory on a sample of British probationers* London: HMSO.

EYSENCK, H.J. (ed.) (1961) *Handbook of abnormal psychology* New York: Basic Books.

FISHER, R.M. (1967) Acquiescent response set: the Jesness Inventory and implications for the use of 'foreign' psychological tests. *British Journal of Social and Clinical Psychology*, **6**, 1–10.

JESNESS, C.F. (1962) *The Jesness Inventory: development and validation. Research Report* no. 29. Sacramento: California Youth Authority.

JESNESS, C.F. (1963) *Re-development and revalidation of the Jesness Inventory, Research Report* no. 35. Sacramento: California Youth Authority.

JESNESS, C.F. (1966) *Manual of the Jesness Inventory*. Palo Alto: Consulting Psychologists Press.

MOTT, J. (1969) *The Jesness Inventory: application to approved school boys*, London: HMSO.

MOTT, J. (1973) Relationship between scores on the Jesness Inventory and reconviction for approved school boys. *Community School Gazette*, **14**, 212–14.

SAUNDERS, G.R. & DAVIES, M.B. (1976) The validity of the Jesness Inventory with British delinquents. *British Journal of Social and Clinical Psychology*, **15**, 33–9.

VALLENCE, R.C. & FORREST, A.R. (1971) A study of the Jesness Personality Inventory with Scottish children. *British Journal of Educational Psychology*, **41**, 338–44.

Appendix

Jesness inventory subscale inter-correlations*

Subscales	V.O.	Imm.	Aut.	Alien.	Agg.	Withd.	Soc. Anx.	Rep.	Den.
Social Maladjustment	0.78	0.38	0.71	0.66	0.65	0.48	0.18	0.13	-0.51
	0.75	0.30	0.71	0.59	0.65	0.53	0.31	-0.00	-0.48
	0.73	0.33	0.69	0.68	0.66	0.59	0.26	0.12	-0.55
Value Orientation		0.30	0.72	0.81	0.83	0.43	0.14	-0.02	-0.70
		0.26	0.65	0.75	0.81	0.46	0.24	-0.08	-0.65
		0.34	0.80	0.69	0.84	0.44	0.28	-0.06	-0.66
Immaturity			0.48	0.35	0.14	0.25	0.06	0.59	-0.14
			0.41	0.26	0.00	0.21	-0.30	0.63	-0.01
			0.45	0.36	0.11	0.24	0.05	0.62	-0.13
Autism				0.58	0.63	0.38	0.14	0.09	-0.54
				0.47	0.57	0.42	0.19	0.07	-0.50
				0.60	0.55	0.45	0.15	0.08	-0.53
Alienation					0.58	0.24	-0.15	0.06	-0.57
					0.53	0.20	-0.14	0.00	-0.46
					0.56	0.23	-0.18	0.01	-0.55
Manifest Aggression						0.38	0.25	-0.18	-0.66
						0.39	0.26	-0.18	-0.59
						0.40	0.27	-0.17	-0.64
Withdrawal							0.51	0.03	-0.59
							0.49	0.04	-0.56
							0.53	0.04	-0.60
Social Anxiety								-0.16	-0.33
								-0.18	-0.44
								-0.15	-0.45
Repression									0.18
									0.19
									0.21
Denial									

* Upper row – correlations for 1888 Californian male delinquents and non-delinquents aged 10 to 18 (Jesness, 1963).
Middle row – correlations for the second sample of 287 approved school boys aged 13 to 16 (Mott. 1969).
Lower row – correlations for Ugandan sample of 167 approved school boys aged 13 to 16.

21 The competence to be a child witness: an individual differences perspective

K.K. Singh

Introduction

Legal standards for the competence of child witnesses vary substantially among jurisdictions and are undergoing rapid reform and refinements in statutes and case law (Quinn, 1986). Until recent years it had been commonly assumed that compared with adults, children notice less, omit more, forget faster, confuse imagination and perception in their recollections and are more susceptible to suggestion (Varendonck, 1911; Stern, 1939; Rourke, 1957; Trankell, 1972). These traditional assumptions are of considerable importance when they are translated into legal practice but there is little empirical evidence to support them (Goodman, 1984; Johnson & Foley, 1984).

Concern about a child's competence to be a witness has become especially important because of the increasing involvement of children in the courtroom. Davies, Flin & Baxter (1986) suggest that this trend is due to a number of interrelated factors:

(1) Police have more formal involvement in domestic disputes involving violence in which children are often the principal witnesses.
(2) There is growing concern about cases of child sexual abuse and in such cases the child may be both the victim and the sole witness.
(3) Children are the most frequent victims of road accidents, where there are often no other witnesses.
(4) Civil law is increasingly concerned with the protection of children's rights, e.g. in divorce proceedings.

This chapter examines ways in which interrogator biases can influence the reports of child witnesses. The approach adopted to this topic will be from an 'individual differences' perspective in which the factors that determine why individuals respond differently to leading questions are considered. This approach is distinguished from the 'experimental' approach which examines differences in the conditions under which leading questions are likely to affect witnesses' reports (e.g. Schooler & Loftus, 1987).

Factors affecting witness competence

The position of the child witness in England and Wales is governed by the Children and Young Person's Act of 1933 (s. 38), whereby children under 12 years are admonished to tell the truth while those over 14 years take the oath. Between these ages the judge may exercise discretion regarding the form of evidence. However, there is divided opinion about the competence of children's testimony, as Yarmey & Jones (1983) recently demonstrated. They obtained views from psychologist experts, lawyers and the general public (i.e. potential jurors) concerning matters of evidence and their attitudes toward the evidence supplied by an 8-year-old. The only group to show a clear opinion were the 'experts', i.e. psychologists specialising in witness testimony, who generally believed that the child could be easily manipulated (even though there is no empirical evidence for this view). The lawyers and laymen were split with opinion polarising between those who were likely to accept the child's statement and those expressing outright scepticism. In England and Wales judges have a duty to warn juries that there are risks in convicting a defendant on the basis of the testimony of a child when the testimony is uncorroborated by other evidence.

Some measure of competence is required in order to testify, not only at the time of the witnessed event but also at the time of the trial. The child must therefore be able to organise the experience cognitively and to differentiate it from his or her own thoughts or fantasies. The ability to record and communicate a memory may also require a consistent vocabulary of objects and behaviour, and the child must also maintain these skills under psychological stress and pressure, real or perceived from adult authority figures. The level of his or her suggestibility, in particular will be an important factor. Dent (1978) reported several cases in which child witnesses were led to give erroneous accounts, and she has shown that current police methods of questioning, for example, are not ideal. Dent (1982) also notes that relatively little attention in police training has been paid to the ways in which their interviews are conducted, and clearly, the manner and style of questioning is crucial in obtaining a testimony. Even prior to the interrogation witnesses will differ in a variety of ways that may influence how they respond to the interview, although Bevan and Lidstone (1985) point out that, 'English law has never formally recognised that the modern practice of in-custody interrogation is psychologically rather than physically oriented' (p. 224).

For most people being detained in a police station for questioning is highly stressful. Children may be particularly vulnerable to the three kinds of stress that Irving and Hilgendorf (1980) describe as follows: (i) unfamiliarity with the environment, police procedures and rights; (ii) isolation and confinement away from family and friends; and (iii) submission to authority which may lead the person to obey instructions and suggestions which would commonly be rejected.

Experimental studies of witness testimony

There are a great variety of situations in which witnesses may be questioned about their recollections. They are asked not only to recall events and recognise people but also to describe the persons they have seen. Such verbal descriptions are often an essential part of criminal investigations, and individuals vary widely in their abilities to perceive and recall complex events accurately and in their tendencies to accept misleading suggestions. Nevertheless, the high face validity of eyewitness testimony, for example, exerts a powerful influence in court cases, particularly when it is confidently presented in court, and this can be despite contradictory forensic evidence or even alternative and conflicting eyewitness testimony (Tata, 1983).

The Devlin Report on evidence of identification in criminal cases (1976) called for further research into 'establishing ways in which the insights of psychologists could be brought to bear on the conduct of identification parades and the practice of courts in all matters relating to evidence of identification' (p. 73).

Psychological studies of testimony have focused predominantly on the 'capacity' of witnesses to report complex events. Much of the experimental research has concentrated on studying the ability of witnesses to report accurately and completely a complex event, by presenting them with pictures, slides, films, stories, or 'real' events (e.g. a staged assault), and subsequently questioning them about irrelevant and peripheral details of the event presented. In these experiments 'many investigators produced evidence of marked inaccuracies in . . . (the) . . . recording of details' (Loftus, 1979, p. 29). However, these were not studies of real police interviews with witnesses to real crimes; and the question of the relative merits of the validity of analogue versus applied or clinical research is a complex one (Wells, 1978; Yuille, 1980; Shepherd, Ellis and Davies, 1982). As Undeutsch (1984) points out:

before jumping from these findings to conclusions regarding the worthlessness of eyewitness testimony in real-life criminal proceedings, one has to take into account that the percentage of the correct answers is far more a function of the capacity of the experimenter to invent countless questions about tiny details than of the capacity of the eyewitness to report accurately an important event. The alleged 'evidence of marked inaccuracies in the recording of details' is only an artifact produced by the design of the experiments. (p. 52)

The experimentalists often treat people as if they all behave in the same way and often forget that the performance of the 'average subject' is a convenient summary statement reflecting very few of the actual performances.

It is important to determine whether there are factors within an individual that relate to how good (or bad) a witness that individual will be and an individual differences approach takes account of the fact that people come into a situation with varying backgrounds and abilities.

Research on children's testimony

Since the early research of Stern (1939) most studies have concentrated on factors contributing to the accuracy of recall (e.g. Loftus & Palmer, 1974; Loftus & Loftus, 1980; Shepherd *et al.*, 1982). These factors and processes are all interrelated but can usefully be divided into a number of areas.

Developmental studies of memory (see reviews by Brown, 1979; Chi, 1983; Mandler, 1983), generally divide the memory process into three stages – acquisition, retention and retrieval of information. Memory can fail because of a breakdown at any of these stages (Loftus & Davies, 1984).

Studies in the literature have investigated purposeful remembering and show that younger children do not deal with memory tasks in a strategic manner by making use of rehearsal, mental imagery or linkages based on common categories. These strategies undergo development between five and ten years of age (Brown, 1979). Nor do children have the relevant prior knowledge to help them interpret events coherently so that they can later report them accurately. However, this may not always be a disadvantage as it could also make children less suggestible, because they will not process events as efficiently and so not be as influenced by them. For example, children who are expert chess players can reproduce from memory the positions of pieces at a given stage of play better than adult novices (Chi, 1983). Similarly, the child who is 'Mad on cars' may prove to be a superior witness concerning a getaway vehicle than his less knowledgeable adult counterpart to whom all cars are 'minis' or 'family saloons' (Davies *et al.*, 1986).

It is also assumed in much of the literature that children notice less than adults even though developmental studies show age changes in the salience of dimensions, such as from colour to form in vision, and from nonsemantic to semantic categories in the use of language (Wright & Vliestra, 1975). It is therefore unclear whether children do in fact notice less. Neisser (1979) has shown that younger children are often better than adults at reporting events that are irrelevant to some ongoing activity (e.g. what people wore or incidental pieces of conversation) and these 'irrelevant' events are sometimes the potentially relevant pieces of information in the courtroom. Another assumption is that forgetting occurs more rapidly in younger children but the evidence does not support this either (Johnson & Foley, 1984) and, while some studies have used lengthy recall intervals (e.g. 28 days in Brown and Scott, 1971) available research has not tested possible developmental differences in recall over periods of months, which is a more common demand in court cases.

The child's competence to testify will also depend on his cognitive and moral development. For example, if a child has difficulty in understanding time as independent of distance and speed he may have difficulty in describing the chronology of events. Similarly, there is little correlation between age and honesty (Burton,

1976) and asking the child to tell the meaning of 'truth', 'oath' or 'God' probably reveals more about the child's intellectual development than about his propensity to tell the truth (Melton, 1981). Therefore, appropriate questioning techniques are necessary to bridge the gap between what the child knows and what he or she can tell. The understanding of the oath is probably unimportant although immature moral development may only be a major factor when the child confuses the suggestions of an adult authority figure with the truth.

It is well established in the experimental studies by Loftus (1979; 1984) that the wording of a question will affect the answer given, and that misleading information introduced in earlier questions will affect answers to later questions. Thus, 'it is no longer a matter of proving that children are suggestible but rather of trying to quantify how much more suggestible, if at all, child witnesses are compared to their adult counterparts.' (Davies et al., 1986, p. 89) However, there are very few developmental studies which have compared children and adults under equivalent circumstances, and even fewer studies have attempted to simulate the conditions of a real-life criminal incident, or investigated methods for obtaining the most accurate and least trauma-inducing testimony from children (during pretrial and trial stages).

One of the more realistic studies was that of Marin, Holmes, Guth & Kovac (1979). They examined the ability of groups of subjects from 5 to 22 years to report on a live incident they witnessed involving an angry confrontation between two experimenters and a confederate. Within half an hour each subject-witness was asked to provide a free recall account of the incident, answer a questionnaire and attempt to identify the confederate in a photo line-up. They found that younger subjects were able to provide accurate accounts of the events they had witnessed, although the information was sparse and incomplete. Performance improved steadily with age, with the 22-year-olds recalling five times as much as the 5-year-olds, but the effects due to age were attenuated when the results of the questionnaire were included; no statistical difference was then found between childrens' and adults' reports. They also concluded that children were no less affected by a leading question than adults. As Davies *et al.* (1986) point out one must first consider a 'number of significant qualifications (before) accepting the optimistic view emerging from this study' (p. 90). First, in testimony situations we rarely know all the factors at the outset and so it would not be obvious what questions to ask, and as Dent & Stephenson (1979) illustrate, there is as much art in knowing what questions to ask as in framing such questions in a nonsuggestive manner. Secondly, the interviewer probably had less authority in the eyes of a child than would a lawyer asking what seem to be threatening, challenging questions in the imposing setting of a courtroom. There is little empirical data on the child's perception of the trial setting (Grisso, 1982). Thirdly, the Marin *et al.* (1979) study only used two leading questions, whereas more would be likely during cross-examination (Goodman, 1984).

A more representative study of suggestive questioning was undertaken by Cohen & Harnik (1980), who showed a film of a handbag snatching incident to a group of children aged 9 and 12 years and to adults. They subsequently answered a questionnaire in which half the questions were conventional (e.g. 'what was the young woman carrying when she entered the bus?') and half were leading (e.g. the young woman was carrying a newspaper when she entered the bus wasn't she?' when the woman had been carrying a shopping bag). A week later a follow-up multiple-choice test was administered. In contrast to Marin *et al.* (1979) accuracy on both conventional and leading questions was poorer among 9-year-olds, and although all subjects had a tendency to incorporate erroneous facts into their memory the trend was more marked among the 9-year-olds.

Cohen & Harnik's (1980) investigation involved more complex and open-ended questions than that of Marin *et al.* (1979). This may explain their finding of lower accuracy and greater susceptibility to leading questions among the younger children.

However, another study by Duncan, Whitney & Kunen (1982) provides conflicting results, indicating that children are no more suggestible than adults.

The available studies are therefore inconclusive and there is probably no single factor that can explain the discrepant findings. Age alone does not account for the difference in suggestibility between adults and children and it is more likely that it is the interaction between age and a number of other factors that is important. These other factors may include the use of mental imagery, rehearsal and semantic organisation to increase memory skills as well as attitudes, beliefs and expectations which form part of their general cognitive set. To date, views on children's testimony have not sufficiently taken into account the multi-faceted view of memory and other cognitive factors that influence suggestibility; and investigators have not systematically explored the possibility that children's testimony may be more credible in some instances than in others. The current status of research on suggestibility has revealed a few useful pointers but still has a long way to go. There is clearly a need to substantiate and extend the existing findings and to explore how other variables contribute to or mitigate against age trends in suggestibility. The study of these age trends is important since witnesses of all ages are continually called upon by the legal system, and if children are to play a more active part in the legal process, adequate assessment of their competence and credibility is essential.

Interrogative suggestibility

A pioneering single case study by Gudjonsson & Gunn (1982) recently established a precedent at the Old Bailey or Central Criminal Court in London. The case involved a young mentally handicapped woman who claimed to have been sexually assaulted by a group of youths. The Director of Public Prosecutions asked for an assessment of her degree of subnormality and for an opinion on the likely reliability of her testimony and in particular her level of suggestibility, including her readiness to respond to leading questions. The results showed that she was only susceptible to suggestive questions about facts of which she was unsure, but when she was certain or clear in her recall, she was consistent in her replies and could not be made to alter them through leading or suggestible questions. This information was of considerable help to the jury who were thus assisted in assessing her performance under gentle but thorough cross-examination by counsel.

Although it may be erroneous to draw parallels between children and the mentally handicapped, it is obviously important to discover whether recall in children can be adversely affected by the nature of questioning and in particular, the degree of suggestive influence such questioning poses. This will have important implications for the witness as well as the interrogated suspect. However, most tests of suggestibility are primarily concerned with hypnotic susceptibility rather than interrogative situations (Gudjonsson, 1987) and the few studies that have investigated interrogative suggestibility have generally involved complicated experimental procedures in laboratory settings that are not easily replicated (e.g. Powers, Andriks & Loftus, 1979; Cohen & Harnik, 1980). In addition, the early literature (e.g. Muscio, 1915) drew no clear distinction between 'suggestion', which relates to a 'stimulus property' (e.g. a hint, an idea or a cue), and 'suggestibility' which relates to the tendency of an individual to respond in a particular way. Gudjonsson (1984a) recognised these limitations and he demonstrated that interrogative suggestibility appears to be a special type of suggestibility:

> the major problem facing the clinical psychologist when asked to give an opinion on a defendant's susceptibility to suggestive influences has been the lack of a suitable objective psychometric instrument for quantitatively measuring interrogative suggestibility (p. 56)

For this reason Gudjonsson (1984b) constructed a suggestibility scale to assess an individual's response not only to 'leading questions' but also to 'negative feedback' instructions, as he considered that both aspects were directly relevant to the questioning of witnesses and suspects during police interrogation.

Within an interrogation context post-event information can be incorporated into individual testimony in at least two distinct ways. First, the questions asked may be loaded with suggestion and misleading cues; and secondly, the instructions given may be suggestive and misleading. The former type of suggestibility is commonly referred to in the literature in terms of so-called 'leading questions' (e.g. Burtt, 1948; Loftus, 1979; Powers *et al.*, 1979). However, the second type of suggestibility which relates to the extent to which individuals' replies can be shifted by interrogative pressure has been largely neglected in previous research, although it is clearly highly relevant to an interrogation context.

The Gudjonsson Suggestibility Scale and theoretical model

The Gudjonsson Suggestibility Scale (GSS) is intended to measure the extent to which the subject 'yields' to leading questions; and the degree to which he or she can be made to 'shift' elements of his or her previous answer in response to critical feedback or interpersonal pressure. It therefore has conceptual roots both in legal notions of interrogation variables relevant for considering voluntariness of confessions and psychological notions of individual differences in susceptibility to suggestion.

A considerable amount of work has been carried out on the validity of the GSS and its theoretical components. This has subsequently allowed Gudjonsson to propose a detailed definition of interrogative suggestibility (Gudjonsson & Clark, 1986). It is defined as:

> The extent to which, within a closed social interaction people come to accept messages communicated during formal questioning, as the result of which their subsequent behavioural response is affected.

Gudjonsson & Clark (1986) illustrate that the definition contains five interrelated components: (i) the nature of the social interaction; (ii) a questioning procedure; (iii) a suggestive stimulus question; (iv) some form of acceptance of the stimulus message; and (v) a behavioural response.

These components are discussed more fully by Gudjonsson & Clark (1986) who also present a theoretical model of interrogative suggestibility which relates to the 'process whereby people come to accept uninformed and incorrect premises and expectations during police interrogation, resulting in inaccurate testimony' (p. 84).

Empirical evidence has also shown that interrogative suggestibility is not related to other types of suggestibility (Gudjonsson, 1987). The questions are primarily concerned with past experiences and events, memory recollections and knowledge states, whereas traditional types of suggestibility are almost extensively concerned with the motor and sensory experiences of the immediate situation. Therefore, rather than examining specific experimental conditions that affect suggestibility, Gudjonsson and his colleagues have primarily examined individual differences in susceptibility to an interrogator's leading questions (e.g. Gudjonsson, 1984a; Gudjonsson & Lister, 1984; Singh & Gudjonsson, 1984). The interrogative suggestibility model recognises 'general situational expectations' and 'coping strategies' as the person enters the 'serious questioning' phase of interrogation, and it integrates 'leading question' and feedback aspects of suggestibility as variants of a single underlying model.

Gudjonsson & Clark (1986) suggest that even prior to the interrogation witnesses differ in a variety of ways that will have a bearing on how they respond to the interview. First, witnesses differ in their general cognitive set, i.e. their expectations about the interrogation. This set, according to Haward (1963), can be affected by a large number of variables, which lead people to see what they expect, desire or need to see and so will be affected also by past interrogation experiences, attitudes towards the police, expectations, motives, beliefs, etc. Gudjonsson & Singh (1984a), for example, demonstrated that delinquent boys who were familiar with police procedures were likely to have a different cognitive set to that of the unfamiliar person. For example, the person who has a hostile and negative attitude towards the police or authority figures in general, may have a cognitive set that is affected by the expectation of negative contingencies. Likewise, a witness who is strongly motivated to help the police with their enquiries is likely to perceive and view the police interrogation differently from a suspect who wishes to conceal his or her involvement in a crime. Secondly, the model predicts that witnesses differ in the coping resources upon which they can draw during interrogation. The coping resources that witnesses use will depend in part on their general cognitive and personality characteristics. Some variables that are of particular interest to interrogative suggestibility are those related to memory ability, intellectual functioning, self-concept, hostility, attitude to authority and field dependence, as they will contribute to the coping resources that the witness employs.

In the case of 'field orientation', for example, which is one of the most extensively studied cognitive styles (Witkin, Oltman, Raskin & Carps, 1971), field-independent people are more likely to be successful in situations that require logical and critical analysis than field-dependent people, who are more dependent on an external frame of reference (Witkin & Goodenough, 1977). Field-independent people are also prone to express anger and hostility directly against others, whilst field-dependent people express such feelings indirectly.

Gudjonsson & Clark's (1986) theoretical model, implies that field-orientation may influence the general coping strategies which the witness adopts when confronted with predicaments in the police interrogation. The specific cognitive set and coping resources determine the general coping strategies with which witnesses enter the interrogation. Gudjonsson & Clark (1986) list a number of strategies that may be broadly classified as either suggestible (willing to accept the interrogators premises) or resistant (unwilling to accept these premises).

As the interrogation progresses the witness's changing appraisal of the situation may affect his general coping strategies. Three factors are critical to this appraisal: (1) *Uncertainty* (if the interrogator asks questions about details that the witness is unsure about, the witness may be more disposed to accept the interrogators premises); (2) *Interpersonal Trust* (the witness is more likely to accept the premises of a trusted interrogator); and (3) *Expectation* (witnesses may produce responses because they believe that a particular response is appropriate).

The final factor that determines the interrogative suggestibility of an individual is feedback, and individuals will differ in terms of how they respond to positive and negative feedback. For example, in response to negative feedback (criticism) one individual may become suspicious that he is being tricked and may become angry and even more resistant, whilst another person may experience a reduction in self-esteem that leads him to doubt his own recollections and rely on the cues of the interrogator. In general, however, negative feedback (and to a lesser degree positive feedback) are thought to make individuals more likely to accept the interrogator's premises.

The model therefore contains a number of testable theoretical and practical implications which may further our understanding of the processes involved in producing erroneous testimony, and may aid identification of the circumstances under which people are potentially vulnerable.

Interrogative suggestibility in children and adolescents

There are considerable opportunities for exploring these individual differences with respect to influential cognitive and personality factors, and particularly with respect to differences between adults and children. Sah (1973) has suggested that as children grow older they develop greater independence of thought and learn to rely on their own judgement when dealing with difficulties and ambiguities. In general it is assumed that the reliability of childrens' memory during testimony will not be problematic if direct, simple questions are used, but if the child has difficulty in free recall this may make him or her more subject to leading questions (Melton, 1981). However, the attempts to investigate these assumptions by Marin *et al.* (1979) and Cohen and Harnik (1980), for example, have as already demonstrated produced discrepant findings.

Recent research by the author partly support these conclusions (Singh, 1986). Adolescents have been relatively neglected in studies concerning the reliability of recall and suggestibility although they are a particularly relevant group because juveniles and young adults contribute disproportionately to the figures of those cautioned and charged by the police (Farrington & Bennett, 1981; Rutter & Giller, 1983; West, 1985).

Singh's (1986) results reveal that adolescent boys are no more likely to respond to (mis)leading questions than young adults when memory factors are controlled for. However, the results go further: they also show that the adolescent boys were significantly more prone to respond to negative feedback (criticism) so that their answers to questions were easily altered by pressure. In other words, adolescents may be particularly susceptible to cues provided by adults and authority figures, and their answers can be easily altered by interpersonal pressure.

In a previous study, (Gudjonsson & Singh, 1984b) delinquent adolescent boys' responses on the Gudjonsson Suggestibility Scale were variable and polarised, and several of the boys were found to be strongly resistant to suggestive pressure. In fact, four of the boys became verbally aggressive after the negative feedback had been given and they had to be gently persuaded to continue with the test. It was felt that this was related to their delinquent backgrounds, which made them more likely to have a 'resistant' cognitive set. This was supported by the finding that the number of their previous criminal convictions was significantly related to the extent to which they resisted interpersonal pressure during interrogation. Since susceptibility to suggestions proffered by 'interrogators' in the form of cued instructions and negative feedback (criticism) has been shown by Gudjonsson (1984b) to be an important part of individual testimony, and there is evidence that negative feedback may actually increase suggestibility (Kelman, 1950; Tata, 1983), these results have important implications for police interrogation procedures. In particular, they indicate that young delinquent boys may be prone to give untrustworthy testimony when they have been criticised and pressured by interrogators.

Gudjonsson's (1983) research with adults and Singh's (1986) study with adolescents also showed that the subjects who were most suggestible during the experiment tended to be of lower intelligence and have poorer memory recall. Furthermore, although intelligence and memory recall were clearly related to suggestibility, some of the subjects with high IQ and memory scores were also quite suggestible, and conversely, some subjects with low IQ and memory scores were not highly suggestible. The individual differences in other cognitive and personality factors, according to Gudjonsson & Clark's (1986) model may therefore have affected how interrogation influenced witnesses' reports. This point is particularly important to bear in mind, since Gudjonsson & Gunn (1982) showed that even when subjects are highly suggestible, they may give a reasonably reliable account of basic facts that they clearly remember.

Conclusions

Gudjonsson & Clark's (1986) model 'represents a formidable attempt to make sense of a multi-faceted problem' (Schooler & Loftus, 1987). Clearly, more research is needed in this area, and a useful direction would be to investigate further the cognitive and personality individual differences that contribute to interrogative suggestibility. There is already much research in the experimental literature on the influence of post-event suggestions and the cognitive mechanisms that may mediate them (see Loftus, 1979 for reviews). It would be of interest to integrate more fully this experimental work with Gudjonsson & Clark's (1986) contribution to the study of interrogative suggestibility.

Acknowledgement

I am grateful to Dr Gisli H. Gudjonsson for his helpful comments on the manuscript.

References

BEVAN, V. & LIDSTONE, K. (1985) *Guide to the Police and Criminal Evidence Act 1984*, London: Butterworths.

BROWN, A.L. (1979) Theories of memory and the problems of development: activity growth and knowledge. In F. Craik and L. Cernack (eds.) *Levels of processing*. Hillsdale NJ: Erlbaum.

BROWN, A.L. & SCOTT, M.S. (1971) Recognition memory for pictures in preschool children. *Journal of Experimental Child Psychology*, **11**, 401–2.

BURTON, R.V. (1976) Honesty and dishonesty. In T. Lickona (ed.) *Moral development and behaviour: theory, research and social issues*. New York: Holt, Rinehart and Winston.

BURTT, H.E. (1948) *Applied psychology*. New York: Prentice Hall, 291–321.

CHI, M.T.H. (1983) *Trends in memory development*, Basel, Switzerland: Karger.

COHEN, R.L. & HARNIK, H. (1980) The susceptibility of child witnesses to suggestion: an empirical study. *Law and Human Behaviour*, **4**, 201–10.

DAVIES, G., FLIN, R. & BAXTER, J. (1986) The child witness. *The Howard Journal*, **25**, 81–99.

DENT, H.R. (1978) Interviewing child witnesses. In M.M. Gruneberg, P.E. Morris & R.N. Sykes (eds.) *Practical aspects of memory*. London: Academic Press.

DENT, H.R. (1982) The effects of interviewing strategies on the results of interviews with child witnesses. In A. Trankell (ed.) *Reconstructing the past*, Stockholm, Sweden: Norstedt and Soners Forlag, 279–98.

DENT, H.R. (1986) An experimental study of the effectiveness of different techniques of questioning mentally handicapped child witnesses. *British Journal of Clinical Psychology*, **25**, 13–17.

DENT, H.R. & STEPHENSON, G.M. (1979) An experimental study of the effectiveness of different techniques of questioning child witnesses. *British Journal of Social and Clinical Psychology*, **18**, 41–51.

DEVLIN, Rt. Hon. Lord (1976) *Report to the Secretary of State for the Home Department of the Departmental Committee on Evidence of Identification in Criminal Cases*. London: HMSO.

DUNCAN, E.M., WHITNEY, P. & KUNEN, S. (1982) Integration of visual and verbal information in children's memories. *Child Development* **53**, 1215–23.

FARRINGTON, D.P. & BENNETT, T. (1981) Police cautioning of juveniles in London. *British Journal of Criminology*, **21**, 123–35.

GOODMAN, G.S. (1984) Children's testimony in historical perspective. *Journal of Social Issues*, **40**, 9–31.

GRISSO, T. (1982) Lawyers and child clients: a call for research. In J.S. Henning (ed.) *The rights of children: legal and psychological perspectives*. Springfield, Illinois: C.C. Thomas.

GUDJONSSON, G.H. (1983) Suggestibility, intelligence, memory recall and personality: an experimental study. *British Journal of Psychiatry*, **142**, 35–7.

GUDJONSSON, G.H. (1984a) Interrogative suggestibility: comparison between 'false confessors' and 'deniers' in criminal trials *Medical Science and Law*, **24**, 56–60.

GUDJONSSON, G.H. (1984b) A new scale of interrogative suggestibility *Personality and Individual Differences*, **5**, 303–14.

GUDJONSSON, G.H. (1987) Historical background to suggestibility: how interrogative suggestibility differs from other types of suggestibility, *Personality and Individual Differences*, **8**, 347–355.

GUDJONSSON, G.H. & CLARK, N.K. (1986) Suggestibility in police interrogation: a social psychological model. *Social Behaviour*, **1**, 84–104.

GUDJONSSON, G.H. & GUNN, J. (1982) The competence and reliability of a witness in a criminal court: a case report. *British Journal of Psychiatry*, **141**, 624–7.

GUDJONSSON, G.H. & LISTER, S. (1984) Interrogative suggestibility and its relationship with self-esteem and control. *Journal of the Forensic Science Society*, **24**, 99–110.

GUDJONSSON, G.H. & SINGH, K.K. (1984a) Interrogative suggestibility and delinquent boys: an empirical validation study. *Personality and Individual Differences*, **5**, 425–30.

GUDJONSSON, G.H. & SINGH, K.K. (1984b) The relationship between criminal conviction and interrogative suggestibility among delinquent boys. *Journal of Adolescence*, **7**, 29–34.

HAWARD, L.R.C. (1963) The reliability of corroborated police evidence in a case of 'Flagrante Delicto'. *Journal of the Forensic Science Society*, **3**, 71–8.

IRVING, B. & HILGENDORF, L. (1980) *Police interrogation: the psychological approach*. Royal Commission on Criminal Procedure Research Study No. 1. London: HMSO.

JOHNSON, M.K. & FOLEY, M.A. (1984) Differentiating fact from fantasy: the reliability of children's memory. *Journal of Social Issues*, **40**, 33–50.

KELMAN, H.C. (1950) Effects of success and failure on 'suggestibility' in the autokinetic situation. *Journal of Abnormal and Social Psychology*, **45**, 267–85.

LOFTUS, E.F. (1979) *Eyewitness testimony*. London: Harvard Univ. Press.

LOFTUS, E.F. (1984) Expert testimony on the eyewitness. In G.L. Wells and E.F. Loftus (eds.) *Eyewitness testimony: psychological perspectives*. Cambridge University Press.

LOFTUS, E.F. & DAVIES, G.M. (1984) Distortions in the memory of children. *Journal of Social Issues*, **40**, 51–67.

LOFTUS, E.F. & PALMER, J.C. (1974) Reconstruction of automobile destruction: an example of the interaction between language and memory. *Journal of Verbal Learning and Verbal Behaviour*, **13**, 585–9.

LOFTUS, E.F. & LOFTUS, G.R. (1980) On the permanence of stored information in the human brain. *American Psychologist*, **35**, 409–20.

MANDLER, J.M. (1983) Representation. In J.H. Flavell and E.M. Markham (eds.) *Handbook of child psychology*, vol. 3, New York: Wiley, 420.

MARIN, B.V., HOLMES, D.L., GUTH, M. & KOVAC, P. (1979) The potential of children as eyewitnesses: a comparison of children and adults on eyewitness tasks. *Law and Human Behaviour*, **3**, 295–306.

MELTON, G.B. (1981) Children's competency to testify. *Law and Human Behaviour*, **5**, 73–85.

MUSCIO, B. (1915) The influence of the form of a question. *British Journal of Psychology*, **8**, 351–386.

NEISSER, U. (1979) The control of sensitive pick-up in selective looking. In A.D. Pick (ed.) *Perception and its development*, Hillsdale NJ: Erlbaum, 201–19.

POWERS, P.A., ANDRIKS, J.L. & LOFTUS, E.F. (1979) Eyewitness accounts of females and males. *Journal of Applied Psychology*, **64**, 339 17.

QUINN, K.M. (1986) Competency to be a witness: a major child forensic issue. *Bull. Am. Acad. Psychiat. Law*, **14**, 311–21.

ROURKE, F.L. (1957) Psychological rsearch on problems of testimony. *Journal of Social Issues*, **13**, 50–59.

RUTTER, M. & GILLER, H. (1983) *Juvenile delinquency: trends and perspectives*, Harmondsworth: Penguin.

SAH, A.P. (1973) Perceptual suggestibility as a function of age, sex and education. *Indian Journal of Experimental Psychology*, **7**, 21–5.

SCHOOLER, J.W. & LOFTUS, E.F. (1987) Individual differences and experimentation: complimentary approaches to interrogative suggestibility, *Social Behaviour*, **2**, 105–12.

SHEPHERD, J.W., ELLIS, H.D. & DAVIES, G.M. (1982) *Identification evidence: a psychological evaluation*, Aberdeen University Press.

SINGH, K.K. (1986) *Interrogative suggestibility among adolescent boys and its relationship with cognitive set, delinquency and age*. M.Phil., University of London.

SINGH, K.K. & GUDJONSSON, G.H. (1984) Interrogative suggestibility delayed memory and self-concept. *Personality and Individual Differences*, **5**, 203–9.

STERN, W. (1939) The psychology of testimony. *Journal of Abnormal Social Psychology*, **34**, 3–20.

TATA, P.R. (1983) *Some effects of stress and feedback on interrogative suggestibility*. M.Phil., University of London.

TRANKELL, A. (1972) *Reliability of evidence*, London: Beckmans.

UNDEUTSCH, U. (1984) Courtroom evaluation of eyewitness testimony. *International Review of Applied Psychology*, **33**, 51–67.

VARENDONCK, J. (1911) Psychological research on problems of testimony. Reported in F.L. Rourke (1959) *op. cit.*

WELLS, G.L. (1978) Applied eyewitness testimony research: system variables and estimator variables. *Journal of Personality and Social Psychology*, **36**, 1546–57.

WEST, D. (1985) Delinquency. In M. Rutter and L. Hersov (eds.) *Child and adolescent psychiatry* (2nd edn), Oxford: Blackwell.

WITKIN, H.A., OLTMAN, P.K., RASKIN, E. & CARPS, S.A. (1971) *A manual for the Embodied Figures Test*, Palo Alto, Ca: Consulting Psychologists.

WITKIN, H.A. & GOODENOUGH, D.R. (1977) Field-dependency and interpersonal behaviour. *Psychological Bulletin*, **24**, 661–89.

WRIGHT, J.C. & VLIESTRA, A.G. (1975) The development of selective attention: from perceptual exploration to logical search. In H.W. Reese (ed.) *Advances in child development and behaviour*, vol. 10, New York: Academic Press, 195–239.

YARMEY, D. & JONES, H. (1983) Is the study of eyewitness identification a matter of common sense? In S. Lloyd-Bostock and B.R. Clifford (eds.) *Evaluating eyewitness evidence*, Chichester: Wiley.

YUILLE, J. (1980) A critical examination of the psychological and practical implications of eyewitness research. *Law and Human Behaviour*, **4**, 335–45.

22 Understanding IQ differences between groups: deaf children as a natural experiment in the nature-nurture debate

J.P. Braden

Many racial and social class groups have different IQ distributions. This finding has been reported over time and in a variety of settings. Although the IQ differences between North American blacks, whites and Asians are well-documented, IQ differences have also been noted between social class groups in Europe (Burt, 1957), Kalahari Bushmen of Africa and Westerners (Reuning, 1972), and a variety of other groups (e.g. Court, 1972, 1974, 1976). The finding that groups differ in IQ is no longer in doubt. However, the reason for the differences in IQ between groups is still hotly debated.

The explanations of IQ differences between groups can be broken down into three general categories. The first is that the differences are not real; i.e. the various IQ distributions are an artifact of test construction or bias in the test content. This position has been repudiated in the professional literature (e.g. Jensen, 1980), although it still enjoys some popularity in the popular press. The second explanation of IQ differences between groups cites environmental factors that differ between groups. Environmentally-based arguments have been called the 'nurture' side of the debate, because they propose that the nurturing experiences encountered in the lifetime of an individual promote or inhibit the development of intellectual skills measured by IQ tests. Nurture explanations point out that most minority groups experience significant environmental disadvantages, and that most majority groups enjoy environmental advantages. These circumstances lead to the superior IQs of majority groups relative to minority groups, according to the nurture agreement.

The third category of explanations cites hereditary factors as the cause of IQ differences between groups. The genetic endowment of various social and racial groups is proposed to be different, due to the selection factors at work in the various groups. Environmental factors are acknowledged to be a necessary condition for the development of intelligence, but the nature argument proposes that even if environmental advantages were held constant between groups, the groups would still exhibit different IQ distributions.

Unfortunately, what appears to be a relatively logical and straightforward debate between nature and nurture positions has become Pandora's Box. The major problem for both sides of the debate is the confounding of environmental and hereditary factors. The two methods for addressing the confound are natural experiment manipulations that move a genotype to a different environment (e.g. studies of separated twins), and data manipulation that statistically removes the variation due to recognized environmental factors from the obtained distributions.

A review of the findings from each of these methods for ferreting out the relative contributions of nature and nurture factors is beyond the scope of this chapter. What is important is that the debate has lost its original logic. Questionable experimental practices such as Cyril Burt's fabrication of twin data (Jensen, 1974) and Leon Kamin's remarkably biased critiques of adoption studies (see Loehlin, Lindzey & Spuhler, 1975, Appendix H) have the unfortunate effect of casting doubt on the experimental evidence. Likewise, the complexity of statistical manipulations of data (e.g. pseudo-age cohorts) overwhelm even the well-educated reader. Statistical manipulations also smack of charlatanism, because they create results that are removed from reality by a series of numerical transformations. Taken together, the shadow cast on experimental data and increasingly complex statistical procedures have muddled the nature-nurture debate to the point where it is widely regarded as a scientific blind alley.

A group that has experienced environmental deprivation similar to minority groups, but that has the genotypic endowment of majority groups, could restore the logical character of the nature-nurture debate. If such a group could be found, one could test the hypothesis that IQ differences between groups are due to environment (i.e. the IQ distribution would be similar to disadvantaged minority groups) or test the hypothesis that group IQ distributions are unaffected by environmental factors (i.e. the distribution would be similar to majority groups). Ethics prevent researchers from arbitrarily manipulating environmental factors in order to create a group that would have a majority genotype and deprived environment. Occasionally, however, these factors are accidentally manipulated. A researcher can take advantage of this 'natural experiment' by studying the groups to test nature-nurture hypotheses.

Congenitally deaf children offer a natural experiment condition in which children with majority genotypes experience profound environmental deprivation. The study of deaf children may be used to restore a logical character to the nature-nurture debate regarding the causes of IQ differences between groups. This argument is developed in two stages: (a) the environmental circumstances of deaf children are reviewed; and (b) deaf children's performance on intellectual tasks is reviewed to determine which side of the debate is supported or refuted. Finally, the implications of these findings for future studies of individual differences between groups are discussed.

Deaf children as a natural experiment

Deaf children have long been considered to be a natural experiment condition in which children are deprived of language (Furth, 1964; Vernon, 1968). Consequently, deaf children's performance on intellectual tests is used to reveal insights into the development of thought and intelligent behaviour. Recent studies of deaf children and adults complicate this experimental paradigm in two ways: (a) deaf children differ from unimpaired controls on many more indices than language exposure alone; and (b) there are three distinct subgroups of deaf children that each differ from the other. The confounding factors, and the distinctions between subgroups of deaf children, are discussed in the following sections.

Confounding factors

Deaf children differ from unimpaired cohorts in six major ways: (a) genetic endowment; (b) medical trauma; (c) language exposure; (d) auditory deprivation; (e) familial factors; and (f) social factors. Deaf children experience deficits, or a disadvantage, in each of these areas relative to unimpaired majority and minority children.

Genetic endowment
Approximately 47% of deaf children in North America are estimated to be deaf due to recessive genetic causes (Rose, Conneally & Nance, 1977). This appears to contradict the assumption that deaf children and majority children have similar

genotypes. The contradiction is not as damaging as it might appear. This is because most hearing parents are unaware of their defective genes, and therefore mate without regard to this characteristic (Rose *et al.*, 1977), producing a sample of deaf children that is random with respect to all genes except those that passed on the deafness to the child. There is no evidence linking polygenetic intelligence to hereditary deafness, although there are major gene syndromes that produce deafness in conjunction with other physical anomalies (Konigsmark & Gorlin, 1976). If deaf children with other handicaps are excluded from study, the pool of deaf children should be a random, representative sample of the gene pool with the exception of the genes involved in hereditary deafness. This exception may prove to be a significant caveat, as will be shown later.

Medical trauma

If 47% of North American deaf children are deaf due to genetic causes, the remaining 53% may be assumed to be deaf due to medical trauma (Rose *et al.*, 1977). The medical trauma experienced by deaf children was so severe it caused a major handicap (deafness). Not surprisingly, deaf children also have a high incidence of other handicaps due to the trauma that caused their hearing impairment (Ewing, 1957; Schein, 1975). It has also been proposed that there are many deaf children with mild handicaps (e.g. minimal brain damage) that are difficult to diagnose (Conrad & Weiskrantz, 1981). Therefore, even if multi-handicapped deaf children are excluded from research samples, it is likely that the remaining subjects exhibit a high incidence of mild medical defects relative to unimpaired peers.

Language exposure

Congenitally, profoundly deaf children are deprived of language from birth, and are therefore subjects in this 'natural experiment'. Consequently, adventitiously deaf children, and those with moderate hearing losses, are here excluded from consideration. However, deaf children in this study are not simply deprived of language. Deaf children are exposed to some language, but their exposure differs from unimpaired cohorts in four ways. First, most deaf children are denied access to language until they fail to speak, and even then their language exposure tends to be intermittent and severely limited relative to other children (Bellugi, 1972; Mindel & Vernon, 1971). Second, the language system that deaf children use and acquire is a restricted, nonstandard form of the dominant language (Cokeley & Gawlick, 1975; Siple, 1978). Third, deaf children are forced to use visual-motor means for decoding and encoding information (Bellugi, 1972). Fourth, speechreading and artificial sign systems are incompatible with visual processing and motor encoding demands (Parnasis & Samar, 1982). In short, deaf children do have some exposure to language, but their exposure is quantitatively restricted and qualitatively different from the language experiences of unimpaired peers.

Auditory deprivation

Despite the fact that it is deaf children's lack of access to auditory stimulation that creates a natural experiment condition, the effects of auditory deprivation *per se* are often overlooked as a confounding factor in comparisons between deaf subjects and unimpaired subjects. It has been hypothesized that a lack of access to sound qualitatively changes the structure of deaf children's intelligence (Myklebust, 1960). There is no evidence to support the notion that nonverbal IQ structures differ between deaf and hearing children (Braden, 1985a, 1985b), but deaf children encode and recall information differently and less efficiently than hearing peers (Tomlinson-Keasy & Kelly, 1978).

Familial factors

The parents of deaf children typically experience grief and anger over their child's disability (Altshuler, 1974). The presence of a disabled child in the family alters family dynamics in ways that inhibit the ability of the family to meet intrinsic and extrinsic demands (Hannah & Midlarsky, 1985). The net effect of parental anguish, and altered family dynamics may be a punitive, authoritarian and nonsupportive environment for deaf children (Mindel & Vernon, 1971 Schlesinger & Meadow, 1972; Stinson, 1974). The only advantage a deaf child may have is greater parental attention, but this parental attention is typically focused on the disability, not the child (Altshuler, 1974). In terms of systems theory (Bell, 1975) the child's impairment threatens the family system and thus increases the likelihood that the child will become the 'identified patient' within a dysfunctional family. All of these factors combine to place the deaf child at a disadvantage relative to unimpaired cohorts in family settings.

Social factors

A high proportion of deaf children reside in low socioeconomic status (SES) homes (Anderson & Sisco, 1977; Karchmer, Rawlings, Trybus, Wolk & Milone, 1979). Within public schools, deaf children are frequently the target of teacher prejudice (Blood & Blood, 1982) and peer ostracism (Vandell, Anderson, Ehrhart & Wilson, 1982). Because they are often placed in schools where there are few other deaf children (Trybus & Karchmer, 1977), deaf children lack associations with other deaf children. Deaf members of a dominant racial group have a social advantage in distal encounters (i.e. contacts that do not involve talking). Proximal encounters reveal that the deaf person is not 'normal', which typically elicits discriminatory behaviour directed toward the deaf person (Jacobs, 1974). Deaf members of racial minorities are at a disadvantage in both distal and proximal encounters.

In summary, deaf children are subjected to a natural experiment condition that confounds a number of variables. However, deprivation on each variable is not constant between subgroups of deaf children. These subgroups are discussed in the following section.

Three subgroups of deaf children

Not all deaf children experience similar levels of deprivation on the six deprivation factors (i.e. genetic, medical, linguistic, auditory, familial, and social factors). In fact, deaf children may be divided into three distinct subgroups on the basis of these factors.

Nongenetically deaf children

These children are deaf due to medical trauma. Genetically, they are representative of unimpaired peers. Otherwise, they experience severe medical trauma, linguistic and auditory deprivation, and negative family and social environments.

Genetically deaf children

These children have an atypical genetic endowment, but may be assumed to be free from the handicaps associated with medical trauma (Conrad & Weiskrantz, 1981). Unfortunately, it is difficult to identify these children. Because their deafness is due to recessive genes, these children are frequently misdiagnosed as deaf due to medical trauma, or the cause of their deafness is diagnosed as 'unknown' (Rose *et al.*, 1977). The presence of a deaf sibling is often used to identify these children, because it is extremely unlikely that two siblings would be deaf due to nongenetic causes (Conrad & Weiskrantz, 1981; Rose *et al.*, 1977). Deaf children with hearing parents and deaf siblings (HP/DS) may therefore be used to estimate the performance of genetically deaf children. However, HP/DS enjoy a slight benefit on language, familial, and social factors relative to other genetically deaf children because they have a hearing impaired sibling.

Deaf children of deaf parents

Only those deaf children with two hearing parents have been discussed, yet 3% of the school-aged deaf children in North America and England have two deaf parents (Conrad & Weiskrantz, 1981; Karchmer, Trybus & Paquin, 1977). Deaf children of deaf parents (DP) differ from deaf children of hearing parents (HP) on all factors except auditory deprivation. Genetically, 100% of DP may be considered to be deaf due to genetic causes, with the majority of the genes acting in a dominant fashion (Rose *et al.*, 1977). Unlike HP, the genetic root of DP deafness plays a significant role in the mating behaviour of the parents, because deaf adults intermarry. It is not known what assortative mating factors may affect DP genes.

The environmental deprivation endured by DP is less severe than the circumstances confronting HP. DP are relatively free from medical trauma. Deaf parents do not suffer from guilt or altered family dynamics as a result of their child's deafness (Meadow, 1968, 1969), although they may be less attentive and nurturing than unimpaired parents (Galenson, Miller, Kaplan & Rothstein, 1979). Deaf families are similar to ethnic minority groups in that they are low SES and use a different language. DP have the advantages of growing up within a family where deafness is 'normal' (Meadow, 1968), and greater access to deaf peers in home and school (Karchmer *et al.*, 1977), but they are targets of discrimination in proximal encounters with unimpaired people. Most importantly, North American DP naturally acquire American Sign Language (ASL) from their parents. ASL is not a form of the dominant language; rather, it is a language in its own right (Bellugi, 1972; Siple, 1978) that conforms to the processing demands of the visual-motor channel (Frishberg, 1975; Parnasis & Samar, 1982). In fact, DP tend to use language earlier than HP and unimpaired peers (McIntire, 1977).

The relative standing of deaf children, and North American blacks and whites, may be compared on the variables in the natural experiment. Situations in which a particular group enjoys an advantage are marked with a '+'. Disadvantages are shown with a '−', and unknown judgments are shown with a '?'. The results of the comparisons appear in Table 22.1. Although the sum of the weights may overlook the relative importance of some factors, deaf children clearly experience a disadvantage relative to majority and minority groups. Therefore, they offer an appropriate paradigm for comparing nature vs. nurture effects on IQ differences between groups.

Intellectual performance of deaf children

Verbal intelligence

Deaf children score far below average on items with verbal content (Furth, 1964; Hiskey, 1966; Vernon, 1968). Furthermore, deaf children score in the low average to retarded range on nonverbal items that require extensive verbal directions (Hiskey, 1966; Vernon & Brown, 1964). Scholastic achievement tests also show deaf children performing one to two standard deviations below unimpaired peers on verbally-loaded subtests (Karchmer & Trybus, 1977). Although deaf children of deaf parents score slightly higher than other deaf children on verbal tests (Meadow, 1969; Stuckless & Birch, 1966), they still place well below-average in comparison to unimpaired peers.

Table 22.1   Estimated environmental deprivation of HP, DP, HP/DS, and unimpaired North American white and blacks

Environmental factors	Groups				
	HP	DP	HP/DS	Whites	Blacks
Normal genotype	53% + 47% −	−	−	+	+
Auditory stimulation	−	−	−	+	+
Language factors:					
Early exposure	−	+	−	+	+
Accessibility	−	+	−	+	+
Standard Dialect	−	−	−	+	−
Common modality	−	−	−	+	+
Language-modality congruence	−	+	−	+	+
Normal medical history	47% + 53% −	+	+	+	+
Familial factors:					
Acceptance of child	−	+	−	+	+
Nurturance of child	−	?	−	+	+
Normal dynamics	−	+	−	+	+
Social factors:					
SES	−	−	−	+	−
In-group acceptance	−	+	−	+	+
Out-group acceptance	−	−	−	+	−
Distal contacts	+	+	+	+	−
Proximal contacts	−	−	−	+	−
Sum of weights assigned to environmental factors	−12	1	−12	16	6

The low performance of deaf children on verbal tests does not necessarily reflect low intellectual abilities. Deaf children do poorly on verbal tests because they never acquire vocal language. Consequently, test items are unfamiliar and do not tap their intellectual abilities. The average North American and British deaf student, with twelve or more years of education, is functionally illiterate (Ewing, 1957; Karchmer & Trybus, 1977; Wrightstone, Aranow & Moskowitz, 1963). Because verbal items do not provide an accurate assessment of deaf children's intelligence, researchers usually avoid using verbal measures with deaf subjects (Sullivan & Vernon, 1979).

Verbal tests measure different constructs in deaf children than are measured in hearing children. Factor analyses of test batteries including verbal, nonverbal, and demographic data show verbal subtests correlate with the severity of the child's hearing loss and tend not to correlate with nonverbal subtests (Farrant, 1964; Hine, 1970). Also, deaf children tend to demonstrate average nonverbal IQs, but these same children have verbal IQs in the retarded range (Vernon, 1968). These data suggest that verbal items tap the severity of language deprivation, not the intelligence, of deaf children.

However, it may be possible to assess deaf children's verbal reasoning with carefully constructed items. Deaf children place in the average range on reasoning subtests of the WISC-R Verbal Scale (Wechsler, 1974), when the items are presented in speech and sign to insure comprehension (Miller, 1984). The fact that modification of vocabulary items does not improve deaf children's scores suggests their reasoning abilities may be sound, but they lack verbal fluency. Verbal fluency and verbal reasoning abilities have not been adequately separated in an intelligence test, so the construct validity of the fluency-reasoning dichotomy is unsupported. Deaf children's poor verbal scores may be due to a lack of verbal fluency, or may be due to poor verbal reasoning abilities. The fact that deaf children lack verbal fluency clouds the interpretation of deaf children's below-average verbal IQs.

Nonverbal intelligence

Deaf children score well within the average range on nonverbal IQ measures (Vernon, 1968). In fact, a meta-analysis of deaf children's nonverbal IQs yields a total effect size (*ES*) less than one-sixth of a standard deviation below the normative mean of 100 (*ES* = -0.1632), based on a sample size of 6661 deaf children of hearing parents (Braden, 1986). Qualitative descriptions of deaf children's nonverbal intelligence also place within the average to low-average range (Braden, 1986; Furth, 1964). Therefore, deaf children have average to slightly below-average nonverbal intelligence.

Surprisingly, the *ES* derived from published research probably overestimates deaf children's nonverbal IQ deficit. There are two reasons for the overestimation. The first reason is poor test administration. Often, a hodge-podge of pantomime, gestures, speech and signs are used by examiners who are unfamiliar with deafness (Sullivan & Vernon, 1979; Vernon & Brown, 1964). When tests are carefully administered, deaf children show no deficit in nonverbal IQ (Sullivan, 1982; Ray, 1982). The second reason for overestimation is publication bias. In order for an article to be accepted for publication, it must typically report a 'significant' result (Bangert-Drowns, Kulik & Kulik, 1984). Consequently, studies reporting no difference between deaf children and unimpaired controls are less likely to be published because they do not show significant differences between groups. Therefore, test administration and publication bias probably exaggerate the negative *ES* for deaf children's nonverbal IQs.

Nonverbal intelligence tests demonstrate similar factor composition for both deaf children and hearing children (Braden, 1984, 1985a). Nonverbal IQ tests also maintain psychometric consistency in deaf samples (Braden, 1985b). Distributions of nonverbal IQ derived from deaf children often have larger variances than unimpaired peers (Braden, 1986), but the shape of their distribution is essentially normal (Ewing, 1957; Evans, 1980). In short, nonverbal IQ tests measure similar constructs, with similar accuracy, in deaf children and in unimpaired children.

Implications for IQ differences between groups

Deaf children's low verbal IQs, and their poor scholastic achievement, suggests environment plays a major role in the development of verbal skills. Deaf children score much lower on verbal tests than North American black children. Whereas deaf children's verbal reasoning is better than their verbal fluency, the opposite is true for black children. Black children do better on items assessing previously learned information than they do on items requiring verbal reasoning (Jensen & Reynolds, 1982). The lack of data regarding deaf children's verbal reasoning skills precludes a direct comparison of reasoning abilities between black children and deaf children, but it is clear deaf children score much lower than blacks on verbal fluency tests.

The finding that deaf children have nonverbal IQs within the average range stands in stark contrast to the below-average IQs of North American blacks. Black children and adults have a mean nonverbal IQ approximately one standard deviation (SD) below North American whites (Chastain & Reynolds, 1984; Jensen & Reynolds, 1982; Loehlin *et al.*, 1975). The WISC-R Performance IQ means of normative samples of black, white, and deaf children illustrate this finding. The mean for each sample is subtracted from the arbitrary value of 100, and divided by the SD of the sample, to provide effect size estimates for whites, blacks, and deaf children (standardization data reported in Anderson & Sisco, 1977, and Jensen & Reynolds, 1982). The results are presented in Figure 22.1.

Interpreting the data

The pattern of verbal test results supports the environmentalist camp. The facts that deaf children's verbal skills are lower than black children's verbal skills, and that minority children are lower than majority children, support the environmental deprivation hypothesis. There can be little doubt that environmental factors play a major role in the acquisition of culturally-specific skills, such as academic achievement and verbal fluency.

On the other hand, nobody has seriously challenged the proposition that environment influences acquisition of culturally-specific skills. The real challenge is discovering whether environmental factors play a major role in shaping native intellectual abilities. Do the environmental factors that are known to differ between

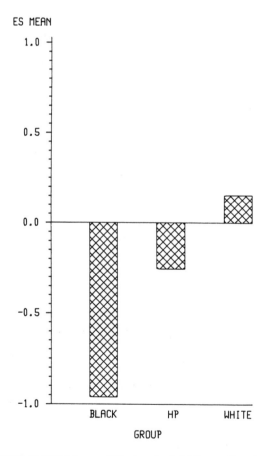

Figure 22.1 The WISC–R PIQ Means of blacks, deaf children of hearing parents (HP), and whites expressed as effect sizes

groups lead to IQ differences between groups? Or are the IQ differences between groups due to other (genetic) factors?

The fact that deaf children's mean nonverbal IQ is average provides convincing evidence that environmental deprivation has little effect on native intellectual ability. In other words, the environmental differences between groups cannot account for the IQ differences between groups. The fact that deaf children's mean nonverbal IQ is superior to the minority mean, and equal to the majority mean, is inconsistent with environmental explanations of the IQ differences between groups.

These data offer three other reasons supporting the nature side of the debate. First, the effect size reported for deaf children is well within the range predicted by heritability estimates for effect sizes due to environmental variation (e.g. Jensen, 1972). Second, the data support the proposition that environment behaves as a threshold variable with regard to genotypic intelligence (Vernon, 1968). Once a minimum threshold of environmental stimulation is provided, there is little additional effect on phenotypic intelligence. Deaf children's average phenotypic intelligence suggests the environmental threshold does not include many social factors treasured by the nurture camp. Third, the data support the construct validity of IQ tests. The similar psychometric properties for whites, blacks, and deaf children, and deaf children's profile of average nonverbal IQ and depressed verbal performance, refute the notion that IQ tests measure nothing more than familiarity with culturally-specific information (e.g. Mercer, 1979; Williams, 1974).

A recap of the natural experiment paradigm is in order. The value of deaf children as a natural experiment condition lies in the fact that deaf children are a random genetic sample that has been exposed to severe deprivation across a variety of environmental factors. The power of the experiment is built on a framework of empirical evidence and supported by a solid rational foundation. The results of this natural experiment provide a convincing refutation of the nurture argument that explains IQ differences between groups in terms of environmental factors. This refutation is accomplished without resorting to twin studies, complex statistical manipulations of data, or other potentially confusing methods. The data also appear to conform to a priori predictions from the nature camp. It would be tempting to conclude that the nature side of the debate has won the day, and all that is left to do is to clean up a few details such as separating verbal reasoning from verbal fluency when testing deaf children.

The conclusion that the nature side has won is wrong – or at the very least, premature. There are a number of anomalies in the data that contradict hereditarian explanations of IQ differences between groups. These anomolous findings have implications for understanding genetic and environmental effects on intelligence.

Anomalous findings

The anomalies in the data are found in the studies of subgroups of deaf children, i.e. deaf children of deaf parents (DP) and deaf children of hearing parents with deaf siblings (HP/DS). The mean nonverbal IQ of DP is significantly above average. The $ES = 0.8076$, based on seven studies (total N = 346), is higher than unimpaired majority children (Braden, 1986). Furthermore, the mean nonverbal IQ for HP/DS is also above average ($ES = 0.6308$). There are only three studies that report HP/DS IQs (total N = 84), so this ES is less reliable than the other ES estimates for deaf and unimpaired samples.

DP are also superior to unimpaired controls on non-normative tests, such as NeoPiagetian analyses of innate capacity and reaction time experiments. DP surpass HP and match unimpaired peers on Piagetian tasks (Furth, 1964). However, a NeoPiagetian analysis of task performance shows the apparent similarity between

DP and unimpaired peers stems from different attributes. DP have greater capacity for processing information than do unimpaired controls, although they tend to lack efficient, learned schema to solve problems (Springer 1978). DP have smaller Reaction Times (RTs) than HP and unimpaired cohorts, and HP and unimpaired controls do not differ on RT. DP also exhibit smaller movement times (MTs) than HP and unimpaired controls (Braden, in press). Although there are no studies of HP/DS using NeoPiagetian nor RT tasks, the evidence from normative and non-normative intellectual measures suggests genetically deaf children are superior to HP and unimpaired cohorts.

These findings have prompted the hypothesis that genetic deafness is biologically linked to superior intelligence (Kusche, Greenberg & Garfield, 1983). This hypothesis looks appealing, but it raises more questions than it answers. First, the hypothesis is merely a tautology. To propose genetically deaf children have superior IQs because of genetics is like saying black children have below-average IQs because they are the victims of discrimination. Second, there is no evidence linking genetic deafness to polygenetic intelligence. However, genetic deafness is associated with mental retardation in some major gene syndromes (Konigsmark & Gorlin, 1976), which does not support a superior IQ-genetic deafness link.

Paradoxically, if it is true that genetic deafness and intelligence are related, the small effect size reported for HP poses a problem for hereditarian explanations of IQ differences between groups. The reason is as follows. The overall ES reported for HP is the sum of two effect sizes – the ES for the 47% of HP who are genetically deaf plus the ES for the 53% of HP who are nongenetically deaf. If the overall ES = -0.1632, and the HP/DS ES = 0.6302 for the ES estimate of HP who are genetically deaf, the nongenetically HP ES = -0.8674. Therefore, the random genetic sample of HP would have a mean nonverbal IQ nearly one s.d. below the value predicted by genetic theories! Rather than supporting the nature argument, the effect size of nongenetically deaf HP could be used to argue the nurture side of the debate, because it is similar to ESs for minority groups.

The DP and HP/DS data are also anomalous for environmental explanations of IQ differences between groups. Both groups of genetically deaf children suffer environmental deprivation more severe than that endured by racial or social class minority groups, yet their nonverbal IQs are superior to the privileged, unimpaired majority. It might be argued that sign language use and exposure compensates for the environmental deprivation. Both DP and HP/DS have deaf family members, and could therefore be expected to sign more than other HP. However, it should also be true that black deaf children should have similar nonverbal IQs to white deaf children, due to the compensating benefits of sign language. The fact that black deaf children's nonverbal intellectual performance is about one s.d. below white deaf children (Bowe, 1974; Clegg & White, 1966; Hurley, Hirshoren, Kavale & Hunt, 1978; Kaltsounis, 1971) contradicts the sign language compensation theory.

The HP/DS and DP data present a problem for both genetic and environmental explanations of IQ differences between groups. The anomalies raise many questions. Are HP/DS superior to HP and unimpaired peers on Piagetian, NeoPiagetian, and RT tasks? How do black deaf children and white deaf children perform on non-normative intellectual tasks? Can pedigree studies link genetic deafness to polygenic intelligence? Is the HP nonverbal IQ distribution bimodal, conforming to different means for genetic and nongenetic deaf children? These are just a few of the intriguing questions raised by the study of HP, HP/DS, and DP groups.

Conclusions

Deaf children provide a remarkable natural experiment condition for separating the effects of environment and genotype from IQ differences between groups. The results of this natural experiment lead to two conclusions. First, the linguistic, medical, familial and social disadvantages experienced by deaf and minority children severely depress verbal IQs and achievement, especially for deaf children. Second, these same environmental factors exert a barely noticeable effect on the nonverbal IQ of deaf children, and so, by logical implication, they do not explain the low nonverbal IQs of disadvantaged minority children. These data seriously jeopardize the nurture position on IQ differences between groups.

The results of this natural experiment provides the nature camp with a Pyrrhic victory. Many questions are raised by the performance of DP and HP/DS groups. Clear support for hereditarian explanations of IQ differences between groups becomes less clear and even something of a liability on closer examination.

Of course, the real value to be derived from studies of deaf children's nonverbal IQs are just these sorts of problematic findings. These data certainly cannot be accounted for by current environmental theories, but these data may prompt rethinking of environmental models. The specification of heretofore unidentified factors or interactions could open new fields for research. Deaf children, and their various subgroups, offer fertile ground for growing new ideas and pruning current theories. The freedom from statistical manipulations of data, and the empirically-supported logic of the natural experiment condition, provide the means to return the nature-nurture debate to a rational, scientific enterprise. The return to rational inquiry could only further our understanding of individual differences between groups.

References

ALTSHULER, K.Z. (1974) The social and psychological development of the deaf child: problems and treatment. In P.J. Fine (ed.) *Deafness in infancy and early childhood*, New York: Medcom.

ANDERSON, R.J. & SISCO, F.H. (1977) *Standardization of the WISC-R Performance Scale for deaf children*. (Office of Demographic Studies Publication Series T, No. 1), Washington, DC: Gallaudet College.

BANGERT-DROWNS, R.L., KULIK, J.A., & KULIK, C.L.C. (1984, August) *The influence of study features on outcomes of educational research*. Paper presented at the annual meeting of the American Psychological Association, Toronto.

BELL, J.E. (1975) *Family therapy*, New York: Aronson.

BELLUGI, U. (1972) Studies in sign language. In T. O'Rourke (ed.) *Psycholinguistics and total communication: a state of the art*, Silver Springs, MD: American Annals of the Deaf.

BLOOD, I.M. & BLOOD, G.W. (1982) Classroom teacher's impressions of hearing impaired and deaf children. *Perceptual and Motor Skills*, **54**, 877–8.

BOWE, F. (1974) Deafness and ethnic minorities. In J.D. Schein (ed.) *Education and rehabilitation of deaf persons with other disabilities*, New York: New York University, Deafness Research and Training Center, School of Education (ERIC Document Reproduction Service No. ED 091 908).

BRADEN, J.P. (1984) The factorial similarity of the WISC-R Performance Scale in deaf and hearing samples. *Journal of Personality and Individual Differences*, **5**, 403–9.

BRADEN, J.P. (1985a) The structure of nonverbal intelligence in deaf and hearing subjects. *American Annals of the Deaf*, **131**, 496–501.

BRADEN, J.P. (1985b) WISC-R deaf norms reconsidered. *Journal of School Psychology*, **23**, 375–82.

BRADEN, J.P. (1986) *Deaf children's nonverbal IQs: implications for group differences*. Manuscript submitted for publication.

BRADEN, J.P. (in press) An explanation of the superior performance IQs of deaf children of deaf parents. *American Annals of the Deaf*.

BURT, C. (1957) The distribution of intelligence. *British Journal of Psychology*, **48**, 161–75.

CHASTAIN, R.L. & REYNOLDS, C.R. (1984, August) *An analysis of WAIS-R performance by sample stratification variables used during standardization*. Paper presented at the Annual Convention of the American Psychological Association, Toronto, Canada (ERIC Document Reproduction Service No. ED 249 409).

CLEGG, S.J. & WHITE, W.F. (1966) Assessment of general intelligence of negro deaf children in a public residential school for the deaf. *Journal of Clinical Psychology*, 22, 93–4.

COKELY, D & GAWLICK, R. (1975) Childrenese as pidgin. *Sign Language Studies*, 5, 72–81.

CONRAD, R. & WEISKRANTZ, B.C. (1981) On the cognitive ability of deaf children with deaf parents. *American Annals of the Deaf*, 126, 995–1003.

COURT, J.H. (1972, 1974, 1976) *Researcher's bibliography for Raven's Progressive Matrices and Mill Hill Vocabulary Scales (3 eds. and supplements)*, Adelaide, South Australia: Flinders University.

EVANS, L. (1980) WISC Performance Scale and Coloured Progressive Matrices with deaf children. *British Journal of Educational Psychology*, 50, 216–22.

EWING, A.W.G. (1957) *Educational guidance and the deaf child*, Manchester, UK: Manchester University Press.

FARRANT, R.H. (1964) The intellective abilities of deaf and hearing children compared by factor analyses. *American Annals of the Deaf*, 109, 306–25.

FRISHBERG, N. (1975) Arbitrariness and iconicity: historical change in American Sign Language. *Language*, 51, 696–719.

FURTH, H.G. (1964) Research with the deaf: implications for language and cognition. *Psychological Bulletin*, 62, 251–67.

GALENSON, E., MILLER, R., KAPLAN, E. & ROTHSTEIN, A (1979) 'Assessment of Development in the deaf child. *J.AM.ACAD Child Psychiatry*, 18, (1) 128–42.

GOSS, R.N. (1970) Language used by mothers of deaf children and mothers of hearing children. *American Annals of the Deaf*, 115, 93–6.

HANNAH, M.E. & MIDLARSKY, E. (1985) Siblings of the handicapped: a literature review for the school psychologist. *School Psychology Review*, 14, 510–20.

HINE, W.D. (1970) The abilities of partially hearing children. *British Journal of Educational Psychology*, 40, 171–8.

HISKEY, M.S. (1966) *Hiskey – Nebraska Test of Learning Aptitude*, Lincoln, NB: College View Printers.

HURLEY, O.L., HIRSHOREN, A., KAVALE, K. & HUNT, J.T. (1978) Intercorrelations among tests of general mental ability and achievement for black and white deaf children. *Perceptual and Motor Skills*, 46, 1107–13.

JACOBS, L. (1974) *A deaf adult speaks out*, Washington, DC: Gallaudet College Press.

JENSEN, A.R. (1972) Interpretation of heritability. *American Psychologist*, 27, 973–5.

JENSEN, A.R. (1974) Kinship correlations reported by Sir Cyril Burt. *Behavior Genetics*, 4 (1), 1–28.

JENSEN, A.R. (1980) *Bias in mental testing*, New York: Free Press.

JENSEN, A.R. (1985) The nature of the black–white difference on various psychometric tests. *Behavioral and Brain Sciences*, 8, 193–263.

JENSEN, A.R. & REYNOLDS, C.R. (1982) Race, social class and ability patterns on the WISC-R. *Personality and Individual Differences*, 3, 423–8.

KALTSOUNIS, B. (1971) Differences in creative thinking of black and white deaf children. *Perceptual and Motor Skills*, 32, 243–8.

KARCHMER, M.A., RAWLINGS, B.W., TRYBUS, R.J., WOLK, S. & MILONE, M.N. (1979) *Educationally significant characteristics of hearing-impaired students in Texas, 1977–78* (Office of Demographic Studies Services C, No. 4), Washington, DC: Gallaudet College, Office of Demographic Studies.

KARCHMER, M.A. & TRYBUS, R.J. (1977) *Who are the deaf children in 'mainstream' programs?* (Office of Demographic Studies Series R, No. 4), Washington, DC: Gallaudet College, Office of Demographic Studies.

KARCHMER, M.A., TRYBUS, R.J. & PAQUIN, M.M. (1977, APRIL) *Early manual communication, parental hearing status, and the academic achievement of deaf students*. Paper presented at the Annual Meeting of the American Educational Research Association, Montreal, Canada.

KONIGSMARK, B.W. & GORLIN, R.J. (1976) *Genetic and metabolic deafness*, Philadelphia, PA: Saunders.

KUSCHE, C.A., GREENBERG, M.T. & GARFIELD, T.S. (1983) Nonverbal intelligence and verbal achievement in deaf adolescents: an examination of heredity and environment. *American Annals of the Deaf*, 128, 458–66.

LOEHLIN, J.C., LINDZEY, G. & SPUHLER, J.N. (1975) *Race differences in intelligence*, San Francisco: Freeman.

McINTIRE, M.L. (1977) Acquisition of American Sign Language hand configurations. *Sign Language Studies*, 16, 247–66.

MEADOW, K.P. (1968) Early manual communication in relation to the deaf child's intellectual, social and communicative functioning. *American Annals of the Deaf*, **113**, 29–41.

MEADOW, K.P. (1969) Self-image, family climate, and deafness. *Social Forces*, **47**, 428–38.

MERCER, J.R. (1979) In defence of racially and culturally non-discriminatory assessment. *School Psychology Digest*, **8**, 89–115.

MILLER, M.S. (1984, June) *Experimental use of signed presentations of the verbal scale of the WISC-R with profoundly deaf children: a preliminary report.* Paper presented at the International Symposium on Cognition, Education and Deafness, Washington, DC. (ERIC Document No. 247 727).

MINDEL, E.D. & VERNON, M. (1971) *They grow in silence: the deaf child and his family*, Silver Springs, MD: National Association of the Deaf.

MYKLEBUST, H.R. (1960) *The psychology of deafness: sensory deprivation, learning, and adjustment*, New York: Grune & Stratton.

PARNASIS, I. & SAMAR, V.J. (1982) Visual perception of verbal information by deaf people. In D. Sims, G. Waiter & R. Whitehead (eds.) *Deafness and communication: assessment and training* (53–71), Baltimore: Williams and Wilkins.

RAY, S. (1982) Adapting the WISC-R for deaf children. *Diagnostique*, **7**, 147–57.

REUNING, H. (1972) Psychological studies of Kalahari Bushmen. In L.J. Cronbach & P.J.D. Drenth (eds.) *Mental tests and cultural adaptation*, (171–81), The Hague: Mouton.

ROSE, S.P., CONNEALLY, P.M. & NANCE, W.E. (1977) Genetic analysis of childhood deafness. In F.H. Bess (ed.) *Childhood deafness: causation, assessment, and management* (19–35), New York: Grune & Stratton.

SCHEIN, J.D. (1975) Deaf students with other disabilities. *American Annals of the Deaf*, **120**, 92–9.

SCHLESINGER, H.S. & MEADOW, K.P. (1972). *Sound and sign: childhood deafness and mental health*, Berkeley: University of California Press.

SIPLE, P. (1978) Linguistic and psychological properties of American Sign Language: an overview. In P. Siple (ed.) *Uunderstanding language through sign language research* (3–23), New York: Academic Press.

SISCO, F.H. & ANDERSON, R.J. (1980) Deaf children's performance on the WISC-R relative to hearing status of parents and child-rearing experiences. *American Annals of the Deaf*, **125**, 923–30.

SPRINGER, S.A. (1978) A study of the performance of deaf and hearing subjects on Piagetian and NeoPiagetian tasks. *Dissertation Abstracts International*, **438**, 5618B.

STINSON, M.S. (1974) Relations between maternal reinforcement and help and the achievement motive in normal-hearing and hearing-impaired sons. *Developmental Psychology*, **10**, 348–53.

STUCKLESS, E.R. & BIRCH, J.W. (1966) The influence of early manual communication on the linguistic development of deaf children. *American Annals of the Deaf*, **111**, 452–60, 499–504.

SULLIVAN, P.M. (1982) Administration modifications on the WISC-R Performance Scale with different categories of deaf children. *American Annals of the Deaf*, **127**, 780–8.

SULLIVAN, P.M. & VERNON, M. (1979) Psychological assessment of hearing impaired children. *School Psychology Digest*, **8**, 271–90.

TOMLINSON-KEASEY, C. & KELLY, R.R. (1978) The deaf child's symbolic world. *American Annals of the Deaf*, 123, 452–8.

TRYBUS, R.J. & KARCHMER, M.A. (1977) School achievement scores of hearing-impaired children: national data of achievement status and growth patterns. *American Annals of the Deaf*, **122**, 62–9.

VANDELL, D.L., ANDERSON, L.D., EHRHART, G. & WILSON, K.S. (1982) Integrating hearing and deaf preschoolers: an attempt to enhance hearing children's interactions with deaf peers. *Child Development*, **53**, 1354–63.

VERNON, M. (1968) Fifty years of research on the intelligence of deaf and hard of hearing children: A review of literature and discussion of implications. *Journal of Rehabilitation of the deaf*, **1** (4), 1–12.

VERNON, M. & BROWN, D.W. (1964) A guide to psychological tests and testing procedures in the evaluation of deaf and hard-of-hearing children. *Journal of Speech and Hearing Disorders*, **29**, 414–23.

WECHSLER, D. (1974) *Wechsler Intelligence Scale for Children – revised*, New York: Psychological Corporation.

WILLIAMS, R.L. (1974) Scientific racism and IQ: the silent mugging of the black community. *Psychology Today*, May, 32–41.

WRIGHTSTONE, J., ARANOW, M. & MOSKOWITZ, S. (1963) Developing reading test norms for deaf children. *American Annals of the Deaf*, **108**, 311–16.

23 Extraversion/introversion and reward/ punishment

C.V. Collard

Personality dimension of individual differences

A dimension is a defined aspect of personality conceptualized as a line on which individuals can be ranked according to the degree to which they possess and/or exhibit a particular personality trait as measured by a specific testing device. The opposing ends of this continuum scale represent the extremes of the measured personality characteristic. These extremes are referred to as the high end and the low end to indicate degrees of the trait and it should not be evaluated that a higher or lower degree of a given personality trait is better or worse. The dimension or continuum is usually visualized on a horizontal plane to connote parity rather than inferiority/superiority of the specific personality characteristic.

In his discussion of Extraverts and Introverts, Wakefield (1979) points out that there is no 'best' place on the extraversion/introversion dimension and that both 'strengths and weaknesses' can be attributed to persons who fall any place along the continuum. He further states that though persons who exhibit high degrees of extraversion or introversion are placed at the opposite ends of the dimension, 'most people are somewhere between these two extremes'. He illustrates this point with the following graphic figure.

Though technically there is no 'best' place on the dimension, the mid-range does represent the normative tendency and would be considered by most to be the more 'normal'. Those who fall into this mid-range between the extremes of extraversion and introversion are referred to as ambiverts. Persons who exhibit behaviours of extreme extraversion and extreme introversion would characteristically be considered as exhibiting 'abnormal' behaviour patterns.

The extraversion/introversion dimension ranks persons according to the degree of sociability and impulsivity they display. Eysenck & Eysenck (1975) give a more detailed description of these two dominant elements of extraversion/introversion:

> The typical extravert is sociable, likes parties, has many friends, needs to have people to talk to, and does not like reading or studying by himself. He craves excitement, takes chances, often sticks his neck out, acts on the spur of the moment and is generally an impulsive individual. He is fond of practical jokes, always has a ready answer, and generally likes change. He is carefree, easy-going, optimistic, and likes to 'laugh and be merry'. He prefers to keep moving and doing things, tends to be aggressive, and to lose his temper quickly. His feelings are not kept under tight control, and he is not always a reliable person.
>
> The typical introvert is a quiet, retiring sort of person, introspective, fond of books rather than people; he is reserved and distant except to intimate friends. He tends to plan ahead, 'looks before he leaps', and distrusts the impulse of the moment. He does not like excitement, takes matters of everyday life with proper seriousness, and likes a well-ordered mode of life. He keeps his feelings under close control, seldom behaves in an aggressive manner, and does not lose his temper easily. He is reliable, somewhat pessimistic, and places great value on ethical standards.

Predictive value of personality dimension

The essence of science and the degree to which a science is accorded validity (and subsequent prestige) rests on the science's ability to accurately predict. The sciences

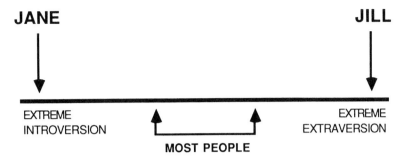

Figure 23.1 Extraversion-introversion dimension (from Wakefield, 1979)

of human behaviour are not exempt from this rule. The power of scientific prediction lies in the capacity to foretell future behaviour from information acquired through observations of past performance of a subject under given circumstances. The behavioral sciences facilitate the predictive process by combining complex behavioral responses into single categories. In this sense, Extraversion represents a category just as Introversion represents another category. It is simpler and more efficient to avoid the complex enumeration of traits such as 'sociable', 'impulsive', 'craves excitement', 'takes chances', 'loud', or 'outgoing', by categorizing them under the single complex set or category of 'extraversion'.

Prediction, then, is based on the tendency of humans to repeatedly exhibit a given category of behavioral responses under similar circumstances. That is, a person who gives extravertive responses in a given situation will predictably, at a future time, give similar responses under similar circumstances. The power of prediction is limited and extraneous variables may intervene in circumstances which are similar but not identical. Nevertheless, the probability is extremely high that an extravert will give extraverted responses in most circumstances most of the time.

Sociability and impulsivity

Eysenck has pointed to degrees of sociability and impulsivity as two characteristic differences that mark the extreme extravert and the extreme introvert. The extraverted individual displays the higher degree of sociability in typical interaction patterns. The extravert likes people, likes being with people and likes working with people. Conversely, the introvert cares less for the company of others, often feels awkward and shy in social situations, frequently possesses fewer social skills than the extravert and prefers to work in occupations not involving people, and given the chance, prefers to work alone.

The extravert displays impulsivity by speaking impulsively whatever 'comes into his head'. This tendency makes him appear outgoing but may also make him appear rude. The introvert tends to mull over an idea and to carefully consider his words prior to expressing them; exemplifying the person who counts to ten before speaking. In most instances, the true introvert is more likely to count to ten and then keep quiet. This characteristic may make the introvert appear to be shy and withdrawn in one social situation or polite and respectfully courteous under another circumstance.

These same characteristics are apparent in the occupational setting. The extravert displays sociability by preferring to work with others and shows impulsivity by working rapidly to finish a given task, yet more easily manages interruptions in his work. The extravert's reward for speedy accomplishment is more frequent breaks between tasks and increased opportunity to vary types of tasks. The introvert prefers solitary work, works meticulously slowly and deliberately giving greater attention to detail, is prone to make fewer errors, finds interruptions to be annoying, and has a longer attention span in persevering at a single task. The introvert's inclination to achieve accuracy and to 'do the job right' stems from the desire to avoid the punishment of condemnation for a sloppy performance.

The reward/punishment differential

The motivational differences between extraverts who are motivated to seek rewards and introverts who are motivated to avoid punishment has been noted by Gray (1973). Knowledge of the motivational efficacy of the carrot and goad principle is as old as written history (surely Eve was an extravert being prompted to action by the promise of reward). Gray has refined that ancient principle in his application of reward and punishment to degrees of extraversion/introversion and neuroticism. Essentially, Gray's theory asserts that extraverts will respond more readily to reward while introverts react primarily to punishment. In detailed elaboration, however, this essence contains many conditional subtleties. Though the extravert will react positively to an achieved reward and an introvert will react positively to an applied punishment, both extraverts and introverts perceive rewards and punishment in terms of ongoing or future realizations. The extravert is motivated to gain the *promised* reward; the introvert is motivated to avoid the *threatened* punishment. In this sense, over-application of the principle tends to lessen the intended effects, dampening the motivational qualities of reward and punishment. Since the extravert is motivated by opportunity to gain reward, too much rewarding reinforcement tends to create a sating effect on the extravert's desire to achieve. Contrariwise, since the introvert is motivated by a need to avoid punishment, too many threats or actual enforcement of the negative reinforcement places the introvert in the position of being unable to avoid punishment, he becomes immobilized and the motivational effect of punishment is decreased.

The motivating effects of rewards and punishment are not mutually exclusive; an extravert does not wish to be punished and will react to negative reinforcement. Similarly, an introvert wants to be rewarded and is motivated by positive reinforcement. The two influencing factors here are: (1) the tendency of the extravert or introvert to perform more satisfactorily in the face of either rewards or punishment and (2) the degree of extraversion or introversion in a given personality. Gray is clear on this second point. Considered on the extraversion/introversion continuum previously described, Gray's principle would apply according to where a person would rate on that dimension. The nearer a person scales toward the extraverted end of the continuum, the greater sensitivity would that person have toward promises of reward. Likewise, a person closer to the introversion end would display greater sensitivity toward threats of punishment.

The practical applications of Gray's theory are obvious. Socializing agents can now more effectively apply the carrot/goad principle in socializing human behavioral responses. It becomes apparent that it would be a waste of time to try to motivate an extravert with threats of dire punishment and would prove equally unsuccessful to attempt to entice an introvert with visions of sugarplums. To exact the highest level of performance from individuals, motivators must encourage the extravert with potential rewards and prompt the introvert with judicial use of punitive threats.

Neuroticism and reward/punishment

Gray's theory concerning sensitivity to signals of reward and punishment not only explains individual differences in extraversion and introversion but also deals with the neuroticism dimension. Just as extraversion and introversion can be viewed on a continuum scale, so, too, can individuals be evaluated on a continuum of stability and neuroticism. Then this personality dimension can be combined with degrees of extraversion/introversion to explain individual differences in sensitivity to reward and punishment.

The degree of neuroticism heightens an individual's sensitivity to reward or punishment. The introvert is already sensitive to punishment but the introvert who displays high neuroticism becomes more sensitive to *both* reward and punishment with the greatest increase in sensitivity being toward punishment. That is, the neurotic introvert becomes more concerned with reward but is even more anxious about punishment than the low neuroticism introvert. As neuroticism increases, the extravert (already sensitive to reward) becomes more sensitive to *both* reward and punishment; with higher increases in reward sensitivity. Though extraverts and introverts increase in sensitivity to reward and punishment as neuroticism increases, each has the highest increase of sensitivity to that trait commonly attributed to extraversion or introversion. The following Figure (23.2) of Gray's model illustrates the relationship of neuroticism and extraversion/introversion to reward and punishment.

Neuroticism and socialization

Whereas the application of Gray's theory relating to extraversion/introversion and reward/punishment has been directed primarily to social issues, the addition of the

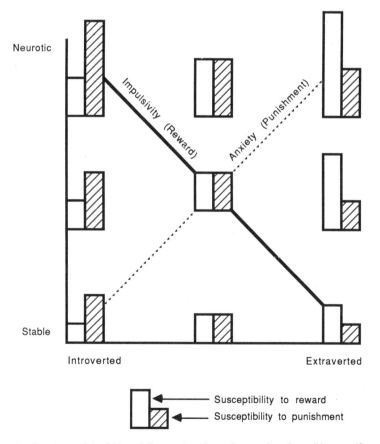

Figure 23.2 Gray's model of N and E as a function of reward and punishment (from Gray, 1973)

neuroticism dimension lends further applicability. Considered in terms of socialization, Gray's theory shows that since the high neuroticism introvert has greater sensitivity to threats of punishment, that individual would be more susceptible to high internalization of social norms to the point of over-socialization and, thus, display the neurotic tendencies of Durkheim's Altruistic Type. The High Neuroticism-High Extraversion individual, being more sensitive to reward, would be less prone to strong internalization of social norms and less likely to become rigidly socialized, resultantly displaying maladaptive behaviours characteristic of Durkheim's (1951) Egoistic Type.

A further effect of the neurotic/extraversion/introversion dimensions is evident in social control. High Neurotic individuals are usually more responsive to control techniques than Low N (stable) individuals. Whether reward or punishment are the control factors, the over-socialized individual will respond readily and may tend to become over-controlled, while under-socialized individuals may show little or no response to control measures. Consequently, the Low N (stable) individual may necessitate the use of rigid control and severe disciplinary measures (Wakefield, 1979).

Summarization of Gray's theory

Gray postulates a theory of individual difference concerning neuroticism, extraversion/introversion and sensitivity to signals of reward and punishment. Extraverts are motivated primarily by positive reinforcement; the opportunity to obtain rewards. Introverts are motivated primarily by negative reinforcement; the desire to avoid punishment. These traits are enhanced by the degree of neuroticism in the individual.

Reward/punishment examined in a laboratory setting

Drawing upon the works of Eysenck & Gray, B.S. Gupta (1976) designed a laboratory experiment to examine the relationship existing between extraversion and types of reinforcement (positive/reward and negative/punishment) in verbal operant conditioning. Gupta hypothesized that extraverts would be more effectively motivated by positive reinforcement while introverts would display more responsive behaviour to negative reinforcement.

Subjects in the experiment were eighty male college students selected on the basis of extraversion scores from the Eysenck Maudsley Personality Inventory (EMPI). The extraversion scores of the selected subjects ranged from high extraversion (E+ = 39+) to lower extraversion (E− = 15−) indicating introversion.

Implementing Taffel's (1955) sentence completion technique, Gupta used 100 3 × 5 index cards as stimulus material. On each card there was placed a single neutral verb in the past tense. Below the verb were typed five pronouns; I, We, You, He and They. The subject was required to formulate 100 sentences using the verbs printed on the cards. A further stipulation was that each sentence must begin with one of the five pronouns. The student subjects were divided into four groups, each group corresponding to one of the four reinforcement conditions.

The experiment was controlled in three stages:

(1)   First twenty cards. No reinforcement. Observation of frequency of subject's use of personal pronouns 'I' and 'We' to determine operant level.
(2)   Next sixty cards. Reinforcement given when subject used either pronoun 'I' or 'We'. Positive reinforcements applied were (a) the word 'Good' spoken in a non-stimulating monotone; (b) buzzer sounded. The negative reinforcements applied were (a) the word 'bad' spoken in a non-stimulating monotone; (b) mild electric shock applied to the right index finger.

(3) Last twenty cards. No reinforcement. Observation of frequency of the use of pronouns 'I' and 'We' as a quantitative measure of the conditioned response.

Gupta determined final scores, which he called 'inflexion ratios', by first subtracting the operant score (frequency of I/We responses in the first 20 cards) from the test score (frequency of I/We responses in the last 20 cards) to achieve the conditioning score. Each conditioning score was then divided by the corresponding operant score.

Example: test score = 9
operant score = 6

$$9 \atop -6 \over 3 = \text{conditioning score}$$

$$\frac{\text{conditioning score} = 3}{\text{operant score} = 6} = .5 = \text{inflexion ratio}$$

Results of the Gupta experiment

The results of Gupta's (1976) experiment showed that subjects who were given positive reinforcement ('good' or buzzer) for I/We responses in the Conditioning phase had higher mean inflexion ratios, indicating that those subjects gave more frequent I/We responses in the Test phase. Subjects who were given punishment ('bad' or electric shock) for I/We responses in the Conditioning phase had lower mean inflexion ratios, indicating that those subjects gave fewer I/We responses in the Test phase. The subsequent conclusion is that there is a positive correlation between extraversion and types of reinforcement.

In the analysis of response differential between extraverted and introverted subjects, Gupta found evidence to support Gray's theory that extraverts condition more easily to rewarding reinforcement while introverts are conditioned more readily by punishing stimuli. In addition, Gupta's experiment also supported Eysenck's supposition that introverts are more susceptible to conditioning than extraverts as shown in Figure 23.3.

An interesting sidelight to Gupta's experiment was observed. Gupta used two experimenters. Though all the subjects were male, one experimenter was male and the other was female. One aspect of the experiment indicated that extraverts were more responsive to positive reinforcement from the female. When the word 'good' was vocalized by the female the young male extraverts showed a more significant response differential than when the word was spoken by the male experimenter. Gupta concluded that apparently the encouraging word from the female was sufficiently rewarding while it appeared probable that more explicit reward was required from the male. This is a strong sexual response indicator. On the strength of this finding, Gupta commented, 'The strength of conditioning is to a certain extent determined by an individual's subjective attitude towards the person who administers the reinforcement' (Gupta, 1976). He adds that not only is the nature of reinforcement important for verbal operant conditioning but that also the sex of the experimenter is a significant factor.

Practical application of reward/punishment

We have examined the principles of Eysenck (1967) and Gray (1973) regarding extraversion and modes of reinforcement, and reviewed Gupta's (1976) experimental design testing those principles. Another noteworthy consideration is Wakefield's (1979) practical application of those principles to the field of education. Wakefield maintains that achievement in the elementary classroom can be improved by applying differential modes of reinforcement to extraverts and introverts. Extraverts should

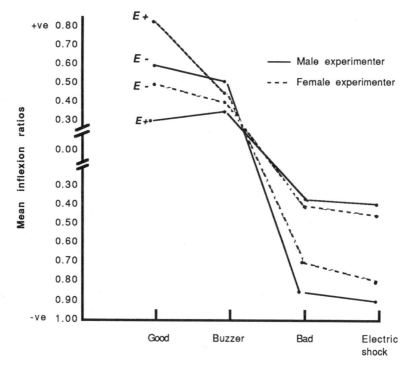

Figure 23.3 Mean inflexion ratios, showing relationship between extraversion and modes of reinforcement (from Gupta, 1976)

be rewarded with extensive praise and consistently encouraged by reminders of potential rewards commensurate with competent performance. Introverts, on the other hand, should be judicially exposed to threats of punishment and made continually aware of the negative sanctions resulting from unsatisfactory performance. According to Wakefield, both extraverts and introverts will benefit from the differential application of these techniques and their academic performances will be enhanced.

In an effort to test Wakefield's concepts, McCord and Wakefield (1981) designed a field study to examine the relationship between extraversion, teacher-presented reward-punishment and arithmetic performance by pupils of public elementary schools. Their underlying assumption was that individuals who share common categorical characteristics (i.e. degrees of extraversion) tend to display dissimilar behaviour patterns when subjected to different modes of reinforcement such as rewarding or punitive measures. Their hypothesis was that: (1) introverts would have better arithmetic achievement than extraverts when exposed to higher levels of teacher-presented punishment in the classroom, and (2) a reversal would occur in which extraverts would achieve arithmetic advantages in classroom situations where teacher-presented reward was prevalent. Extraversion/introversion of students was measured by the Junior Eysenck Personality Questionnaire (JEPQ). The subjects chosen for the study were 101 fourth and fifth graders from 5 classes in a California public elementary school. Distribution by sex was approximately equal.

The researchers first field task was to determine the extent of teacher-presented reward and teacher-presented punishment exhibited by participating teachers. This was accomplished by observing and recording each incident of teacher-presented reward or punishment on four different occasions. Incidents of reward or punishment from the separate observations were totalled and a mean established. The five classes were then rank-ordered on the basis of the mean scores of teacher-presented reward or punishment. The ratio of mean teacher-presented reward to punishment determined a relative index of the degree of teacher-presented reward and punishment for each teacher.

It should be noted from Table 23.1 that teacher-presented reward was more predominant in every classroom. This represents a bias in the study regarding the relationship between teacher-presented punishment and introversion. Therefore, because teacher-presented punishing was not prevalent in any of the observed classrooms, the study could not demonstrate whether introverts gained higher arithmetic achievement as a result of teacher-presented punishment.

Following the establishment of the relative index of teacher-presented reward and punishment, the students of the selected classroom were given the JEPQ to determine extraversion-introversion tendencies. The students were then given an arithmetic pretest adapted from the California Test Bureau's 'Diagnostic Tests and Self Help in Arithmetic' (1955), as a control for pre-study arithmetic ability. An arithmetic post test was administered after 8 weeks of observation to determine effects of reward/punishment conditioning.

Table 23.1 Means and ratios of teacher-presented punishments per 45 minute period (from McCord & Wakefield, 1981)

Classroom	Rewards (Mean)	Punishments (Mean)	Rewards Punishments (Ratio)
1	53.50	5.25	10.19:1
2	52.00	7.75	6.71:1
3	45.25	11.00	4.11:1
4	39.00	16.50	2.37:1
5	22.75	22.50	1.01:1

Results of the McCord & Wakefields study

The McCord & Wakefield study was a successful application of the Eysenck (1967) and Gray (1973) theories in that it did show a positive relationship between degrees of extraversion and reward/punishment reinforcement. Further, those researchers state that not only does the relationship exist but that the relationship may not be established exclusively on teacher-presentation of reward or punishment; 'Instead, it appears that the interaction may be based on relative differences between the use of reward-punishment'. (McCord & Wakefield, 1981). That is, extraverts do meet expectations of higher achievement than introverts in classrooms where there is a predominance of teacher-presented reward, but when the gap between reward and punishment predomination narrows, introverts have a greater achievement advantage. (See Figure 23.4)

Psychoticism and Neuroticism are additional factors in the extraversion and reward/punishment relationship. Psychoticism, often referred to as 'tough-mindedness', describes people who are solitary, non-empathetic, insensitive, aggressive and hostile. McCord & Wakefield (1981) found that extraverts who were low on psychoticism gained the greatest advantage from high rewarding teachers and introverts who were low on psychoticism profited the least. This is an effect of extreme differences. As a result of these findings, McCord & Wakefield concluded that for those students

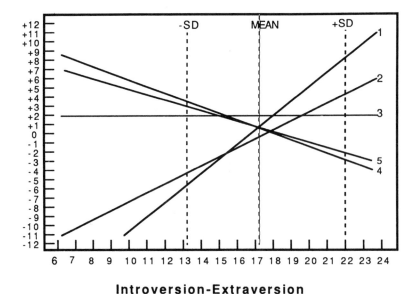

Introversion-Extraversion

Figure 23.4 Regressions of residual arithmetic achievement on introversion-extraversion for different ratios of reward to punishment (from McCord and Wakefield, 1981)

who were low on psychoticism, extraverts achieved more with high rewarding teachers while introverts performed better with teachers who stressed punishment. Furthermore, punishment was more effective for all high psychoticism students except for those who scored high on extraversion and low on neuroticism. For this latter group, reward was more effective.

Implications of the McCord & Wakefield study

The implications of the McCord & Wakefield study are that the differential use of positive and negative reinforcement in relationship to extraversion has practical applicability in education. Optimal individual achievement can be accomplished by the teacher's knowledge of the extent of a student's extraversion and the appropriate use of reward or punishment in relationship to that student.

Though the application of these principles concerning individual differences has exciting potentiality, implementation is limited and the process should not be construed as a pedagogical panacea. Wakefield (1979) cautions that the relationship between extraversion and reward/punishment is not clear and that the effectiveness of exploiting that relationship may lie in judicial use of reward and punishment. He declares that the efficacy of the process is not in a polarized totality of exclusivity of only rewards for extraverts and only punishment for introverts but, rather, in a compatible balance of both reward and punishment for all students.

Based on the supposition that 'introverts achieve more in the relatively less rewarding/more punishing classrooms, and extraverts in the relatively higher reward/lower punishment classrooms', McCord & Wakefield (1981) draw from their study three possible scenarios for optimizing classroom achievement in arithmetic:

> First, students could be assigned to arithmetic classes based on their personality scores and the extent of teacher-presented reward-punishment in each class. Secondly, the classroom teacher could alter the presentation of reward-punishment based on the characteristics of each pupil. Lastly, the child might be encouraged to alter his characteristics in order to be effective regardless of the extent of teacher-presented reward-punishment.

Given the relatively stable character of personality, the third alternative lacks the potential of the other suggestions for utilizing the knowledge gained through this study. Nevertheless, it must be included as one aspect of the definitive evaluation of possibilities. The possibilities extant for the utilization of the extraversion/reward/punishment relationship are not limited to the teaching of arithmetic or to the elementary schools, but has applicability for many academic areas and for varied age cohorts.

The Ketcham study

The usefulness of the extraversion/reward/punishment relationship in differing academic realms is demonstrated in Ketcham's (1980) study of reading achievement as a function of extraversion and teacher-presented reinforcement and punishment. Drawing on Eysenck's (1967) theory that introverts condition more rapidly than extraverts, and Gray's (1973) theory on extraversion and modes of reinforcement, Ketcham designed a study to test the practical implementation of those theories to reading achievement in the classroom.

Ketcham showed especial interest in arousal as a factor in conditioning. The Eysenck theory postulates that introverts condition more rapidly than extraverts because introverts have a higher level of arousal which allows them to associate relationships between stimuli and responses and to transform these perceived stimuli into conditioned responses faster than extraverts. There is a point, however, when this advantageous capability of introverts begins to work to their disadvantage. Beyond an optimal level of arousal, increased anxiety slows the learning process for introverts. In this situation the extravert, who is less prone to anxiety, will condition more rapidly than the introvert. Wakefield describes this relationship between arousal and conditioning as an inverted 'U' (see Figure 23.5).

Though Ketcham used the Eysenck formulation to anchor her study, the primary emphasis was on Gray's theory regarding extraversion and sensitivity to conditioning stimuli. Ketcham's study hypothesis was drawn from Gray's (1973) statement that sensitivity to signals of reward increases and sensitivity to signals of punishment decreases at higher levels of extraversion. Her twofold hypothesis was: (1) that extraverts would have better reading achievements than introverts when the teacher primarily used positive reinforcement, and (2) introverts would have better reading achievement than extraverts when the teacher primarily used negative reinforcement and punishment.

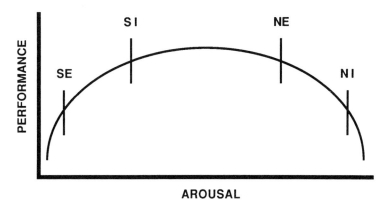

Figure 23.5 Arousal-Performance for Four Personality Combinations; stable extraverts (SE), stable introverts (SI), neurotic extraverts (NE), and neurotic introverts (NI) (from Wakefield, 1979)

Ketcham selected as subjects for the study 62 elementary level pupils from three fourth, fifth, and sixth grade combination classrooms at a California public school. She used the Junior Eysenck Personality Questionnaire to measure extraversion. Form S of the Comprehensive Test of Basic Skills (CTBS) was administered as a pretest to determine reading ability. After 6 weeks, Form T of the CTBS was given to determine reading improvement. Reward or punishment behaviour of the teachers was established by observing and recording each incident of reinforcement during reading sessions and a ratio of mean teacher-presented rewarding to mean teacher-presented punishment was established based on the collected data. Teachers were rank-ordered according to this ratio. See Table 23.2.

Table 23.2 Means and ratios of teacher-presented reinforcement and punishment. (from Ketcham, 1980)

Teacher	No. of Reinforcers (MEAN)	No. of Punishments (MEAN)	Reinforcement to Punishment (RATIO)
1	12.33	10.67	1.16/1
2	18.00	2.00	9/1
3	28.33	1.67	17/1

Results of the Ketcham study

One of the difficulties with studies of this nature has been that most teachers are reward-oriented and in a typical classroom few teachers use negative consequences primarily. Ketcham's study was no exception in this regard. None of her observed teachers predominantly used punishment as a mode of responding to children's behaviour. Consequently, her second hypothesis, that introverts will display higher reading achievement than extraverts in classrooms where teachers predominantly used punishment could not be substantiated.

However, the results of the study did support her first hypothesis that extraverts would have better reading performance than introverts in classrooms where teachers predominantly used rewards as reinforcement. These results were also consistent with Gray's theory that, 'As we move in a direction from introvert to extravert, sensitivity to reward increases and sensitivity to punishment decreases' (Buss & Poley, 1976). This is graphically illustrated in Figure 23.6. As indicated, introverts had better performance in the classroom where the ratio of reward to punishment was lowest. Conversely, extraverts had better performance in the classroom where the ratio of reward to punishment was highest. Ketcham (1980) states:

> The balance point, or cutoff, above which reinforcement is most effective and below which punishment is most effective was found to be slightly above the mean of extraversion. This suggests that those scoring near the mean (ambiverts) as well as those scoring below the mean (introverts) are more sensitive to punishing conditions.

Prognosis for the future

As currently defined, the mission of society is to care for the needs of the people both as a collectivity and as individuals. Too frequently, in the past, the needs of

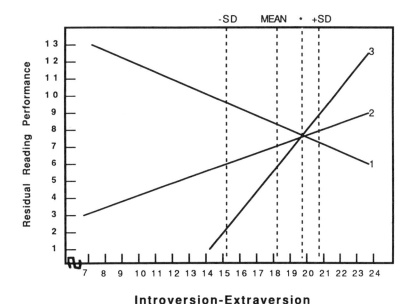

Figure 23.6 Regressions of extraversion on residual reading performance for lowest (1) to highest (3) ratios of reinforcement to punishment (from Ketcham, 1980)
*Balance point above which reinforcement is most effective and below which punishment is most effective.

the individual were subordinated to the needs of the community. More recently, researchers have come to examine closely individual differences and the effects of societal influence on differing personalities, realizing that that which benefits the individual also benefits the society as a whole.

The theories, principles, and studies cited here have emphasized the importance of individual differences in regard to extraversion and modes of reinforcement. There is still much to be considered in the clarification of those concepts. Sex and age are key variables which need to be examined in relationship to levels of extraversion and the effects those variables have on reinforcement techniques. There is need to explore the wide range of applicability for individual difference theories such as those of Eysenck and Gray. Future studies on extraversion and reinforcement need to devise methods to confirm the introvert/punishment relationship by overcoming the reluctance of authority figures to predominantly use negative consequences or by conducting studies in areas where negative reinforcement is the prevailing mode of responding to behaviours. Finally, and perhaps most importantly, the concepts of individual differences and modes of reinforcement need to be accepted and commonly utilized as widespread techniques for maximising individual achievement and optimizing employment of society's human resources.

References

Buss, A.R. & Poley, W. (1976) *Individual differences: traits and factors*, New York: Garden Press, Inc.

Durkheim, E. (1951) *Suicide*, New York: The Free Press.

Eysenck, H.J. (1967) *The biological basis of personality*, Springfield, Ill.: Charles C. Thomas.

Eysenck, H.J. & Eysenck, S.B.G. (1975) *Manual: Eysenck Personality Questionnaire*, San Diego: Educational and Industrial Testing Service.

Gray, J.A. (1973) Causal theories of personality and how to test them. In J.R. Royce (ed.) *Multivariate analysis and psychological theory*, New York: Academic press.

GUPTA, B.S. (1976) Extraversion and reinforcement in verbal operant conditioning. *British Journal of Psychology*, **67**, 47–52.

KETCHAM, K. (1980) *Reading achievement as a function of extraversion and teacher-presented reinforcement and punishment*. Unpublished master's thesis, California State University, Stanislaus.

McCORD, R. & WAKEFIELD, J.A., JR. (1981) Arithmetic achievement as a function of introversion-extraversion and teacher-presented reward and punishment. *Personality and Individual Differences*, **2**, 145–52.

TAFFEL, C. (1955) Anxiety and the conditioning of verbal behavior. *Journal of Abnormal Social Psychology*, **51**, 496–501.

WAKEFIELD, J.A., JR. (1979) *Using personality to individualize instruction*, San Diego: Educational and Industrial Testing Service.

24 Personality and health in children and adolescents

R.N. Jamison & J.J. Vasterling

Health traditionally has been equated with absence of disease or injury. In the past, most illnesses were seen as having a specific medical cause and were treated with prescribed remedies. However, advances in medical treatment have drastically reduced acute illnesses as well as increased the life span of individuals with chronic physical conditions. This has been particularly noticeable in the treatment of children and adolescents. For instance, antibiotics now enable children with cystic fibrosis to live well into adulthood. The discovery of insulin permits children with insulin-dependent diabetes to maintain a reasonable life expectancy. Progress in chemotherapy and radiological treatments has also significantly reduced the number of childhood deaths resulting from cancer.

The gradual shift in medical focus away from treatment of acute illness and toward management of chronic illness has resulted in an increased interest in how psychological factors influence health. New areas of research called 'behavioural medicine' and 'healthy psychology' have emerged and studies on how psychological attitudes and pre-dispositional personality factors influence health have increasingly appeared in the medical literature.

There have been generally two theoretical approaches in examining the psychological factors influencing health and disease. First has been the emphasis on environmental factors of *life events*. These events may include daily stressors, loss of a loved one, or lack of sufficient emotional support. This approach emphasizes that environmental influences or the negative appraisal of these influences may adversely affect health. A second emphasis is on *personality characteristics* which mediate health outcome. This includes individual factors which predispose each person to engage in unhealthy behaviour. Factors such as emotional states, perception of risk, impulsivity and coping strategies are included in this approach.

To date, there has been no unified personality theory which addresses health and health behaviours in children and adolescents. Eysenck's personality dimensions of Psychoticism, Extraversion, and Neuroticism are, however, of particular value in examining how individual differences determine health. Psychoticism has been equated with poor risk perception, poor emotional control and 'tough-mindedness', a quality more often found in males than females. Individuals with this trait often indulge in 'sensation-seeking arousal jags' without thinking of the dangers involved (Eysenck & Eysenck, 1975). Extraversion is highly correlated with sociability. Individuals who are extraverted tend to crave excitement and are prone toward engaging in smoking, drinking and sexual behaviours. They act impulsively and this often leads to frequent accidents. Neuroticism, which is associated with anxiety and strong emotional reactions, has been linked to a number of physical illnesses. Individuals with this trait tend to worry about most things and maintain a constant state of physical arousal. All of these personality dimensions have been linked to health status and contribute in influencing wellness.

Of course, it would be difficult to examine personality characteristics without assessing the influence of environmental factors. Often these factors interact in contributing to the outcome of one's health. For instance, those individuals who are constantly exposed to carcinogenic substances would be at greater risk to contract cancer, but it has been argued that predispositional personality factors may also play an important role in influencing the onset of disease (Eysenck, 1985). Thus, it would be artificial to totally exclude one or the other. The emphasis of this review, however, is to examine the evidence for or against personality factors in influencing health in children and adolescents. Because there have been many different personality traits investigated, for consistency we will attempt to relate findings in the literature to Eysenck's personality traits. More specifically, the hypothesis that children and adolescents who are high on the traits of psychoticism, extraversion or neuroticism are prone toward health problems will be investigated.

It is important initially to mention some of the methodological problems which are encountered when reviewing the literature on health and personality in children. First, a great many studies cited in the literature are based on clinical observation. Although studies of this kind can help to identify testable hypotheses, they cannot be regarded as reliable sources of evidence in supporting a given hypothesis. Thus, to conclude, based on a few case studies, that children with diabetes are depressed and emotionally maladjusted does not prove that this is generally true for diabetic children. Second, in those studies in which control groups were used, the groups were often poorly matched and unrepresentative of the unhealthy group. This invariably leads to misrepresentation of the data and invalidates any generalization to the overall population. A third difficulty encountered in our review was distinguishing between health and health behaviours. Although much of the literature seems concerned with behaviours which influence health, often the relationship between health and health behaviour is undefined and correlational at best. For the purpose of this chapter, health refers to the physical absence of disease or ailment, while health behaviours refer to activities which either help to prevent illness or place certain individuals at risk for physical illness. A fourth major problem with all studies of this nature is the difficulty of obtaining prospective information. Most studies are retrospective in nature which makes the identification of predispositional, contributing factors only conjectural. Finally, because childhood covers only a limited time period, few studies have targeted this age group in examining how personality influences health. In this chapter, we will attempt to review the present literature, and examine the evidence that personality factors influence illness and health behaviours in children and adolescents. In particular, we will examine personality correlates of specific chronic diseases including asthma, diabetes and cancer as well as correlates of general health and adjustment to illness. In addition, we will review the relevant literature on important health related risk factors, including smoking and substance abuse, and other risk factors, in children and in adolescents.

Chronic illness

Asthma

The psychosocial dimension of bronchial asthma has been a focus of interest in a number of studies. Based on clinical observations, it has been theorized that the asthmatic patient shows a distinctive personality pattern. In the past, asthmatics have been described as overanxious, lacking in self-confidence, emotionally dependent and somatically preoccupied (Neuhaus, 1958). Most studies, however, base their conclusions on anecdotal observations. There have been relatively few controlled studies and no prospective studies cited in the literature.

Some empirical support of asthmatic personality characteristics was reported by Sharma & Nandkumar (1980). They compared 25 asthmatics with 25 healthy controls based on findings from the Rorschach, the Eysenck Personality Inventory and the

Sentence Completion Test. They concluded that the asthmatic patients were significantly higher in neuroticism and dependency and lower in self-confidence. This population included adolescents as well as adults. Likewise, Kim, Ferrara & Chess (1980) compared 12 asthmatics with 12 non-asthmatic children between the ages of 3 and 7. They found that asthmatic children had lower adaptability, less persistence and a tendency to withdraw compared with healthy children. These findings were based on parental ratings of their child's temperament.

In another study, Newhaus (1958) matched 34 asthmatic children with 34 children with cardiac illness and 34 healthy controls between the ages of 8 and 14 and examined the results of a series of subjective personality tests. Also, 25 siblings of the asthmatic children were compared with 24 siblings of the heart disease patients. He found the asthmatic patients to be significantly higher in neuroticism and dependency and lower in self-confidence than the other two groups of children. No differences, however, were found between the asthmatic children and their healthy siblings or between the two physically ill groups on any other personality characteristics. He concluded that physically ill children display a deviant emotional pattern but that no distinctive personality characteristics emerged for the asthmatic children. Similarly, Jones, Kinsman, Schum & Resnikoff (1976) and Rosenthal, Aitken & Zeally (1973) found no differences on matched groups of asthmatic and healthy children using the MMPI and the Cattell Sixteen PF. Tavormina, Kastner, Slater & Watt (1976) also showed no significant differences between 19 asthmatics and matched controls between the ages of 5 and 9 on personality tests including the Junior Eysenck Personality Questionnaire (JEPQ). Thus, although there have been some findings that asthmatic children show higher neuroticism traits compared with non-asthmatic children, little consistent evidence is available to support an 'asthmatic' personality. Of interest is a finding by Dirks, Schraa & Robinson (1982) that asthmatic adolescents who are anxious, dependent and emotionally depressed tend to mislabel a non-airway obstruction symptom as an asthmatic attack. Thus, personality factors tend to influence the child's perception of the severity of the illness.

Diabetes

There has been considerable interest in identifying a specific personality type in children with diabetes mellitus. Adolescents with diabetes have been found to have higher levels of anxiety and depression, lower self-concepts and poorer interpersonal relations than non-diabetic controls (Gross, Delcher, Snitzer, Bianchi & Epstein, 1984). Dunbar, Wolfe & Rioch (1936) initially described the diabetic person as weak, irritable, dependent, explosive, subject to mood swings and prone to changes in behaviour. Most of the studies in support of these characteristics have been inconclusive and generally have been retrospective in nature. Of 26 studies which have been frequently cited, 12 showed significant differences between diabetic and non-diabetic samples on psychological functioning while 16 showed no differences (Dunn & Turtle, 1981; Johnson, 1980). No significant differences on personality between diabetic and non-diabetic adolescents were consistently reported in these studies while significant differences emerged between groups for adults. Most of these studies also showed evidence of clinical depression in diabetic adults while only one study reported depression in adolescents (Sullivan, 1979). This tends to support the notion that individual characteristics tend not to antedate the onset of diabetes but rather are a result of having the disease for a number of years.

In another study examining personality differences between adolescents, Kellerman, Zeltzer, Ellenberg, Dash & Rigler (1980) compared 349 healthy adolescents with 168 adolescents with various chronic diseases on trait anxiety, self-esteem and health locus of control. These diseases included diabetes, cancer, cystic fibrosis, coronary heart disease, hypertension and rheumatoid arthritis. Overall, no differences emerged between the healthy or ill groups. Similar results were reported by Sullivan (1979), Gross et al. (1984) and Zeltzer, Kellerman, Ellenberg, Dash & Rigler (1980). Most of these studies were designed to investigate how adolescents adjust to their disease and little attention was paid to pre-dispositional personality factors. Using the Hamburg Neuroticism and Extraversion Scale (Buggle & Baumgartel, 1973) and the Children's Personality Questionnaire, Steinhausen (1981) compared diabetic, hemophiliac and physically handicapped children with matched controls. While physically handicapped children were found to be less extraverted than the children in the matched control, no difference on any of the personality scales were noted between the diabetic and non-diabetic children. Overall, there appears to be minimal support for the notion of a predisposing diabetic personality.

Cancer

There have been a number of studies which have linked personality traits of extraversion with cancer diagnosis in adults (Eysenck, 1985; Cooper & Metcalfe, 1963), but little has been reported in the literature regarding cancer and personality in children. Hatcher, Guest, Stewart, Stewart, Trussell, Cerel & Cates (1986) report that teenage girls who have been sexually active with three or more partners before age 20 are at high risk for cervical cancer. This would place extraverted girls at greater risk for this type of cancer. To date, however, no study has attempted to determine a consistent link between personality traits and cancer in children.

General health

A well-designed prospective study in which children were followed until adulthood found that teenage personality traits did predict adult health. Bayer, Whissell-Buechy & Honzik (1980) examined early health and personality data of urban children from the Berkley Guidance Study from birth to age 42 and the Oakland Growth Studies from 11 to 50 years of age. In total, 458 children were involved in the analysis. Factor scores from the California Personality Inventory and the California Q Sort showed that children and adolescents who were calm, controlled, dependable, sympathetic, likeable, satisfied with self and not rebellious or irritable tended to be in better physical health when they were adults. Many of these factors are in keeping with the traits of stability, introversion, and tender-mindedness (three traits which are on the opposite end of the continuum to neuroticism, extraversion and psychoticism). Similarly, Vaillant (1979) found that those individuals who coped best with stress during their adolescent years were less likely to have major physical illnesses after 40 years.

Adaptation and adjustment to illness

There has been much evidence to suggest that individual personality differences influence health status in *adapting* to chronic illness. Diabetics with poor insulin control have been found to be highly extraverted (Steinhausen, 1981). This is in keeping with Eysenck's theory that due to greater conditionability introverted diabetics are better able to learn methods to insure clinical control over their blood sugar. Thus, extraverted children may be at risk for complications related to their diabetes (Steinhausen, 1981). Murawski, Chazan, Balodimos & Ryan (1970) and Cochran, Marble & Galloway (1979) support this by reporting that the long term complications from diabetes are related to failure of diabetic adolescents to maintain careful control of their blood sugar levels. The implication is that individuals who are tough-minded and extraverted would be less inclined to adapt to the rigors of self-management. They would resist periods of bedrest and would be less likely to keep accurate records and follow detailed dietary instructions. They would also not perceive the risks of future complications. On the other hand, introverted patients would tend to be more compliant and adjust to a life of routine and control. In support of this theory, a number of studies have found that personality does influence compliance with treatment of cancer in adolescents (Blotcky, Conatser, Cohen & Klopovich, 1985; Jamison, Lewis & Burish, 1986a). Thus, although the evidence is inconsistent that personality factors contribute to the development of chronic illness in children, personality factors do seem consistently to influence adjustment to chronic disease.

Little empirical evidence has emerged to support the presence of psychopathology in children with chronic diseases such as diabetes, cancer, cystic fibrosis and cardiovascular disease. Comparing randomized groups of chronically ill adolescents with healthy controls, Kellerman *et al.* (1980) found little evidence of differences on measures of anxiety, self-esteem and locus of control. They concluded that chronically ill adolescents should not be considered to inevitably exhibit psychopathology. Jamison, Lewis & Burish (1986b) also found no differences on self-image between adolescents with cancer and healthy peers. Similar findings were reported by Zeltzer *et al.* (1980). These findings suggest that children generally are able to cope with a chronic disease as they do with any disruptive life stress without resulting in clinical psychopathology. Thus, these studies were unable to address the extent to which personality factors influence the onset of the disease.

Up to this point, we have reviewed the evidence relating personality to health. We will now focus on how personality influences health behaviours or risk factors. Smoking and substance abuse will be examined since these are important predictors of future health. Also, other risk factors including attributes leading to cardiovascular disease will be reviewed.

Risk factors

Smoking

Cigarette smoking has been documented as being one of the most significant risk factors associated with a number of serious chronic illnesses including cancer (Armstrong & Doll, 1974), stroke (Kannel, 1971), and heart disease (Report of the Inter-Society Commission for Heart Disease Resources, 1972). In fact, the annual cost of health damage related to cigarette smoking has been estimated to be as high as 27 billion dollars (Lichtenstein, 1982). It has been reported that people commonly start smoking during adolescence (McKennell, 1969). The results of one study (McKennell & Thomas, 1969) indicated that 70% of the adolescents who smoked more than one cigarette became regular smokers and continued to smoke for at least 40 years. Therefore, because the early onset of smoking often is associated with a lifetime of smoking, and regular smoking behaviour often is associated with the development of chronic disease, adolescent smoking may be a powerful predictor of subsequent health problems.

A considerable amount of published research has attempted to link personality to adolescent smoking behaviour. Although there have been a variety of attributes linked with early smoking onset, adolescent smokers typically seem to display a pattern of behaviours that are closely related to the Psychoticism and/or Extraversion dimensions of Eysenck's Personality Scales (Eysenck & Eysenck, 1969).

The majority of studies that have been conducted are retrospective in nature. Most frequently, a group of adolescents were given a personality questionnaire and were questioned about their smoking habits. Typically, the relationship between high and low levels of smoking and personality dimensions was then assessed. For example, Jamison (1979) administered the Junior Eysenck Personality Questionnaire (Eysenck & Eysenck, 1975) to 1282 school children between 13 and 16 years of age. Smoking behaviour was measured through three items of the Antisocial Behaviour Questionnaire (Allsopp & Feldman, 1976): 'Smoking during school hours', 'Buying cigarettes to smoke yourself', and 'Smoking cigarettes'. Results indicated that there was a significant positive relationship between both Psychoticism and Extraversion and the smoking items. Interestingly, these correlations tended to be stronger for girls than for boys.

Other retrospective reports have shown adolescent smoking behaviour to be positively correlated with a variety of personality attributes that are thought to be related to psychoticism and extraversion. For example, using a shortened version of Jackson's (1968) Personality Research Form, Labouvie & McGee (1986) found that adolescents that smoked heavily and abused substances frequently scored higher on Affiliation, Autonomy, Exhibition, Impulsivity and Play (attributes related to Eysenck's Extraversion dimension) than did 'light users'. Conversely, light cigarette and substance users scored higher on Harm-avoidance (an attribute more likely to be found among 'Introverts'). In contrast to Jamison (1979), the correlation tended to be stronger for boys than for girls among adolescents 12 to 18 years of age. Sex differences disappeared among subjects older than 18 years. Other related traits which have been found to be positively associated with early smoking behaviour include interpersonal aggression (Brook, Whitman & Gordon, 1981), antisocial behaviour (Reitsma-Street, Offord & Finch, 1985), and sensation-seeking (von Knorring & Oreland, 1985).

In addition to retrospective reports, there have been several prospective, longitudinal studies which found a relationship between both psychoticism and extraversion and early smoking behaviour. For example, Seltzer & Oechsli (1985) administered a battery of psychological and cognitive tests to 1127 nine to eleven year old children in San Francisco, California, presumably prior to the acquisition of any smoking behaviour. At ages 15 to 17, the children were again interviewed, and were questioned about their smoking habits. The results indicated that at ages 9 to 11, adolescents who subsequently smoked regularly at ages 15 to 17 tended to show significantly more extraversion, psychoticism, anger, and restless sleep than adolescents who were classified as nonsmokers at ages 15 to 17. In addition, smokers tended to display more type A or 'coronary-prone' behaviours (e.g. competitiveness, hostility) than did nonsmokers. Thus, this and other prospective studies (e.g. Kellam, Ensminger & Simon, 1980; Stewart & Livson, 1966) have shown that extraverted and psychotic personality attributes are often present before smoking behaviour is initiated by adolescents. This suggests that these attributes are not merely correlated with smoking behaviour, but may be predisposing factors.

In addition to associations between both psychoticism and extraversion and adolescent smoking behaviour, which have received the strongest empirical support, there are several other associations between early smoking behaviour and personality that have received modest empirical support. Among those attributes which have been positively associated with smoking behaviour are depression (Malkin & Allen, 1980), orality, social confidence, and acceptance to ambiguity (Veldman & Brown, 1969). Personality dimensions which have been negatively correlated with adolescent smoking include Eysenck's Lie dimension (von Knorring & Oreland, 1985), self-esteem and motivation (Veldman & Brown, 1969), and cognitive ability (von Knorring & Oreland, 1985).

Overall, then, it appears that adolescent smokers are likely to be outgoing, impulsive, irresponsible, sensation-seeking, aggressive, and hostile individuals, whereas nonsmokers more often tend to be nonrebellious, responsible, and cautious.

Studies with adults (Eysenck, 1980) have shown that both cigarette smoking and the personality traits of extraversion and lack of neuroticism are associated with the development of lung cancer. Thus, extraverted adolescents who smoke may be at greater risk for future health problems. Although there may be other attributes which are associated with adolescent smoking (e.g. degree of truthfulness, depression, and cognitive ability) there has been less empirical support for those associations.

Substance abuse

Substance abuse, which includes both excessive alcohol and drug consumption, is regarded as an important risk factor for a number of health-related problems, including digestive disorders, cirrhosis of the liver, fetal alcohol syndrome, hepatitis, some forms of cancer, impaired cognitive functioning (Taylor, 1986), and death from overdose (Siegel, Hinson, Krank & McCully, 1982). Moreover, the heavy use of substances often puts one at greater risk for accident-prone behaviour. It is estimated, for example, that as many as 68% of the annual highway fatalities can be attributed to drinking and driving (Taylor, 1986). Unfortunately, substance abuse is not limited to adults, but appears to be quite common among adolescents. Because adolescent substance abuse is such a prevalent and health-threatening problem, many researchers have investigated the potential origins of substance abuse among adolescents. In general, these investigations have provided considerable evidence that, in addition to environmental and social factors, personality may be a strong predictor of substance abuse.

Although the majority of the studies that have assessed the relationship between adolescent substance abuse and personality factors have not directly measured the personality dimensions of the EPQ, a review of the literature reveals that personality attributes most frequently found to be associated with adolescent substance abuse are consistent with Eysenck's concept of Psychoticism and are related, to a lesser degree, with the Extraversion dimension. The most common of these attributes includes psychiatric symptoms, antisocial tendencies, aggressiveness, and impulsivity.

Several studies have found a relationship between psychiatric symptoms and/or antisocial tendencies and adolescent substance abuse. In one retrospective study (Sutker, Moan, Goist & Allain, 1984), 97% of a sample of 60 adolescents with an exaggerated drug use pattern met the criteria for one of three MMPI profiles that were considered indicative of psychopathology. The adolescents in this study were 18 years of age or younger and were recruited from a substance abuse treatment program. The substances included alcohol, marijuana, tranquilizers, barbiturates, stimulants, LSD and other hallucinogens. Adolescents classified in Profile I (47%) exhibited primary elevations of scales Pd and Ma, suggesting marked antisocial characteristics; adolescents classified in Profile II (30%) exhibited marked elevations on scales Sc, Ma, Pd and Pt, higher elevations on scale F, and lower scores on scale K, a profile closely associated with the DSM-III (APA, 1980) classification of Borderline Personality Disorder; and, finally, adolescents classified in Profile III (20%) exhibited elevations in Pd and Sc, representing a combination of antisocial and borderline features with marked emotional distress. Although the overall extent of substance use did not differ significantly between groups, adolescents classified in Profile I (suggesting marked antisocial tendencies) reported a heavier involvement with a greater variety of substances than did the other adolescents.

Kellam, Ensminger & Simon (1980) conducted a prospective study in which they measured several psychological variables in all of the 1966–7 first graders of a poor, black, Chicago neighbourhood. The population was then reassessed 10 years later for drug and alcohol use. In general, at the 10 year follow-up, the adolescents tended to use beer or wine, hard liquor, and marijuana or hashish more frequently than psychedelics, amphetamines, barbiturates, tranquilizers, opiates, cocaine, inhalants and cough syrup or codeine. One major finding of the study was that teenage antisocial behaviour was strongly related to substance use for both males and females.

Another important finding of this study was that aggressiveness tended to be highly correlated with substance usage. They found that males who were aggressive in first grade used hard liquor, beer or wine, and marijuana more frequently as teenagers than did males who were non-aggressive in first grade. Interestingly, antisocial behaviour mediated this relationship in that aggressive males used beer or wine and marijuana less often if they became less antisocial as teenagers and more often if they became more antisocial. The high correlation between aggressiveness and adolescent substance use is consistent with the results of a number of other studies that have found a strong positive relationship between aggressiveness and degree of alcohol use in adolescents (see Braucht, Brakarsh, Follinstad & Berry, 1973 for a review).

The final attribute which has been strongly and consistently associated with adolescent substance abuse is impulsivity. Several studies have linked impulsivity to adolescent alcohol use (see Braucht et al., 1973) as well as to the use of illegal drugs. For example, Holroyd & Kahn (1974) administered the Personality Research Form (Jackson, 1968) to a random sample of 160 university students. Each student was interviewed about his or her use of illicit psychotropic drugs. The data indicated that 34% of the sample did not use illicit drugs, 66% used marijuana, 28% used amphetamines, 17% used barbiturates, 27% used hallucinogens, and 15% used opiates. The investigators found that male nonusers scored significantly lower on measures of impulsivity than did subjects in the moderate and heavy user groups, which did not differ from each other on impulsivity scores. This finding, however, was not replicated for females.

In a more recent study, Labouvie & McGee (1986) reported similar results. Also using the Personality Research Form (1968) to assess personality attributes, the investigators found that among a random sample of 882 adolescents, subjects that abused substances (alcohol, marijuana and cocaine) frequently scored higher on measures of impulsivity than subjects who were light users. Much like the findings of Holroyd & Kahn (1974), the results of this study indicated that the relationship between personality and substance abuse was much stronger for males than for females in adolescents 12 to 18 years of age. However, these differences disappeared among subjects older than 18.

Other attributes found to be positively associated with adolescent substance abuse that are related to Eysenck's concepts of Psychoticism and Extraversion but for which there is only modest empirical support include immaturity, insecurity, irresponsibility (Braucht et al., 1973), autonomy, exhibition, and play (Labouvie & McGee, 1986). Attributes which have been found to be negatively associated with adolescent substance abuse include achievement, harm-avoidance (Holroyd & Kahn, 1974; Labouvie & McGee, 1986), and shyness (Kellam et al., 1980).

In summary, adolescent substance abusers tend to display psychotic and extraverted personality characteristics, especially psychiatric symptoms, antisocial tendencies, aggressiveness, and impulsivity. Generally, there does not seem to be any consistent or strong relationship between personality factors and specific substances. The data does, however, imply that there may be some sex differences, with substance abuse being more strongly related to personality factors among males than among females.

Other risks

There has been much research on the coronary-prone 'type A' individual who is described as competitive-aggressive, impatient, restless, tense and who feels under constant time pressure (Jenkins, 1971). These individuals have been shown to be at risk for cardiovascular disease. Siegal (1984) showed how anger in adolescents can accurately predict physical and psychological measures of cardiovascular risk. Adolescents who become angry were found to be type A and overweight. They tended to report more frequent negative life events and lower self-esteem, and had smoked more often than their non-angry peers. It cannot be determined from Siegal's study, however, whether anger preceeded or was a consequence of factors associated with coronary heart disease.

In reviewing the literature on cardiovascular disease in children, Nora (1980) argued that there was a strong genetic basis for predicting risks of myocardial infarction. He related this to abnormalities of lipids and lipoproteins in the blood. He also implied that personality factors which interfere with compliance and diet and exercise can increase risk of ischemia heart disease.

There have also been studies which have related delinquency with accident-proneness in children and adolescents. In a matched study between delinquent and non-delinquent children, Lewis & Shanok (1977) observed that delinquent children had significantly more accidents, hospital contacts and injuries when comparing hospital records from their date of birth. Jamison (1980) further found that delinquent children tended to mis-perceive risk and were more inclined to take part in activities which were dangerous and unhealthy. In summary, from these studies there is some evidence that children who are stable, tender-minded and controlled tend to remain in better health while children who are anxious, impulsive and mis-perceive risk show evidence of being at greater risk for poor health.

Summary

This chapter attempted to investigate the relationship between personality traits and health in children and adolescents. From the studies reviewed on personality and chronic disease in children, there is no clear evidence that certain personality types are predisposed toward early onset asthma, diabetes, cancer or heart disease. There is some suggestion that neuroticism is implicated in asthmatics while extraversion and psychoticism are linked to cancer and cardiovascular disease. These findings have yet to be adequately replicated. The studies do strongly suggest, however, that personality significantly contributes to how children and adolescents adjust to their disease. Although chronic diseases do not necessarily lead to psychopathology, individuals who are anxious, impulsive and lacking in risk perception are at risk for health problems related to their disease. Likewise, those children who are emotionally stable, compliant and aware of the risks involved with their disease have a greater chance of avoiding the complications associated with their illness. Consistent with personality studies in adults, children who show traits of psychoticism and extraversion are prone toward engaging in behaviours (e.g. accident proneness, smoking and substance abuse) which could put them at high risk for developing future health problems.

The preceding attempt to review the literature on health and personality in children and adolescents highlights the many gaps of knowledge in this field. Many studies suffer from methodological problems and what is known must be pieced together from a number of different sources. An attempt to increase our understanding of the contribution personality plays in health and health behaviour must be an ongoing process for which thorough analysis has yet to be completed. The introduction of testable personality theories, the incorporation of reliable, standardized psychometric measures as well as a need to address a variety of methodological issues are perhaps the most important tasks facing investigators in this area. Observational studies can not determine the etiology of an illness by testing identified patients whose health problems have already existed. Prospective, longitudinal studies are needed to adequately assess the contribution personality plays in the future health of children and adolescents. Determining predisposing factors which impact health and illness in children and adolescents is within the domains of psychology and behavioral medicine. These disciplines are now called to develop personality theories which address health-related factors and to implement rigorous ways to assess these factors.

References

ALLSOPP, J.F. & FELDMAN, M.P. (1976) Personality and antisocial behavior in school boys: item analysis of questionnaire measures. *Br. J. Criminal.*, **16**, 337–51.

AMERICAN PSYCHIATRIC ASSOCIATION (1980) *Diagnostic and statistical manual of mental disorders* (3rd ed.), Washington, DC: Author.

ARMSTRONG, B. & DOLL, R. (1974) Bladder cancer mortality in England and Wales in relation to cigarette smoking and saccharin consumption. *Br. J. Preven. Socio. Med.*, **28**, 233–40.

BAYER, L.M., WHISSELL-BUECHY, D. & HONZIK, M.P. (1980) Adolescent health and personality. *J. Adoles. Health Care*, **1**, 101–7.

BLOTCKY, A.D., CONATSER, C., COHEN, D.G. & KLOPOVICH, P. (1985) Psychosocial characteristics of adolescents who refuse cancer treatment. *J. Consult. Clin. Psychol.*, **53**, 729–31.

BRAUCHT, G.N., BRAKARSH, D., FOLLINGSTAD, D. & BERRY, K.L. (1973) Deviant drug use in adolescence: a review of psychosocial correlates. *Psychol. Bull.*, **79**, 92–106.

BROOK, J.S., WHITMAN, A. & GORDON, A.S. (1981) Maternal and personality determinants of adolescent smoking behavior. *J. Gene. Psychol.*, **139**, 185–93.

BUGGLE, F., & BAUMGARTEL, F. (1973) *Hamburger Neurotizismus Extraversionsskala für Kinder und Jugendliche* (HANES-KJ) Göttingen: Hogrefe.

COCHRAN, H., MARBLE, A. & GALLOWAY, J. (1979) Factors in the survival of patients with insulin-requiring diabetes for 50 years. *Diabetes Care*, **2**, 363–8.

COOPER, A. & METCALFE, M. (1963) Cancer and extraversion. *Br. Med. J.*, **11**, 18–19.

DIRKS, J.F., SCHRAA, J.C. & ROBINSON, S.K. (1982) Patient mislabeling of symptoms: implications for patient-physician communication and medical outcome. *Inter. J. Psychia. Med.*, **12**, 15–27.

DUNBAR, H.F., WOLFE, T.P. & RIOCH, J.M. (1936) Psychiatric aspects of medical problems. *Am. J. Psychia.*, **93**, 649–79.

DUNN, S.M. & TURTLE, J.R. (1981) The myth of the diabetic personality. *Diabetes Care*, **4**, 640–6.

EYSENCK, H.J. (1985) Personality, cancer and cardiovascular disease: a causal analysis. *Person. Individ. Diff.*, **6**, 535–56.

EYSENCK, H.J. (1980) *The causes and effects of smoking*, London: Maurice Temple Smith.

EYSENCK, H.J. & EYSENCK, S.B.G. (1969) *Personality, structure and measurement*, London: Routledge & Kegan Paul.

EYSENCK, H.J. & EYSENCK, S.B.G. (1975) *Manual of the Eysenck Personality Questionnaire: Junior and Adult*, London: Hodder and Stoughton.

FERRARI, M. (1984) Chronic illness: psychological effects on siblings. I. Chronically ill boys. *J. Child Psychol. Psychia.*, **25**, 459–76.

GROSS, A.M., DELCHER, M.K., SNITZER, K., BIANCHI, B. & EPSTEIN, S. (1984) Personality variables and metabolic control in children with diabetes. *J. Gene. Psychol.*, **146**, 19–26.

HATCHER, R.A., GUEST, F., STEWART, F., STEWART, G.K., TRUSSELL, J., CEREL, S. & CATES, W. (1986) *Contraceptive technology 1986–1987* (13th ed.) New York: Irvington Publishers.

HOLROYD, K. & KAHN, M. (1974) Personality factors in student drug use. *J. Consult. Clin. Psychol.*, **42**, 236–43.

JACKSON, D.N. (1968) *Personality Research Form*. Goshen, NY: Research Psychologists Press.

JAMISON, R.N. (1979) Cigarette smoking and personality in male and female adolescents. *Psychol. Report*, **44**, 842.

JAMISON, R.N. (1980) Psychoticism, deviancy and perception of risk in normal children. *Person. Indiv. Diff.*, **1**, 87–91.

JAMISON, R.N., LEWIS, S. & BURISH, T.G. (1986a) Cooperation with treatment in adolescent cancer patients. *J. Adoles. Health*, **7**, 162–7.

JAMISON, R.N., LEWIS, S. & BURISH, T.G. (1986b) Psychological impact of cancer on adolescents: self-image, locus of control, perception of illness and knowledge of cancer. *J. Chron. Dis.*, **39**, 609–17.

JENKINS, C.D. (1971) Psychological and social precursors of coronary disease. *New Eng. J. Med.*, **294**, 987–94.

JOHNSON, S.B. (1980) Psychosocial factors in juvenile diabetes: a review. *J. Behav. Med.*, **3**, 95–116.

JONES, N.F., KINSMAN, R.A., SCHUM, R. & RESNIKOFF, P. (1976) Personality profiles in asthma. *J. Clin. Psychol.*, **32**, 285–91.

KANNEL, W.B. (1971) Current status of the epidemiology of brain infarction associated with occlusive arterial disease. *Stroke*, **2**, 295–318.

KELLAM, S.G., ENSMINGER, M.E. & SIMON, M.B. (1980) Mental health in first grade and teenage drug, alcohol, and cigarette use. *Drug Alcohol Depend.*, **5**, 273–304.

KELLERMAN, J., ZELTZER, L., ELLENBERG, L., DASH, J. & RIGLER, D. (1980) Psychological effects of illness in adolescents. I. Anxiety, self-esteem, and perception of control. *J. Pediat.*, **97**, 126–31.

KIM, S.D., FERRARA, A. & CHESS, S. (1980) Temperament of asthmatic children. *J. Pediat.*, **97**, 483–6.

LABOUVIE, E.W. & McGEE, C.R. (1986) Relation of personality to alcohol and drug use in adolescence. *J. Consult. Clin. Psychol.*, **54**, 289–93.

LEWIS, D.O. & SHANOK, S.S. (1977) Medical histories of delinquent and non-delinquent children: an epidemiological study. *Am. J. Psychia.*, **134**, 1020–5.

LICHTENSTEIN, E. (1982) The smoking problem: a behavioral perspective. *J. Consult. Clin. Psychol.*, **50**, 804–19.

MALKIN, S.A. & ALLEN, D.L. (1980) Differential characteristics of adolescent smokers and non-smokers. *J. Family Pract.*, **10**, 437–40.

McKENNELL, A. (1969) Implications for health education of social influences on smoking. *Am. J. Public Health*, **59**, 1998–2004.

McKENNELL, A.D. & THOMAS, R.K. (1969) Adults' and adolescents' smoking habits and attitudes. (*Government Social Survey*). HMSO, London.

MURAWSKI, B.J., CHAZAN, B.I., BALODIMOS, M.C. & RYAN, J.R. (1970) Personality patterns in patients with diabetes mellitus of long duration. *Diabetes*, **19**, 259–63.

NEUHAUS, E.D. (1958) A personality study of asthmatic and cardiac children. *Psychosom. Med.*, **3**, 181–6.

NORA, J.J. (1980) Identifying the child at risk for coronary disease as an adult: a strategy for prevention. *J. Pediat.*, **97**, 706–14.

REITSMA-STREET, M., OFFORD, D.R. & FINCH, T. (1985) Pairs of same-sexed siblings discordant for antisocial behaviour. *Br. J. Psychia.*, **146**, 415–23.

REPORT OF THE INTER-SOCIETY COMMISSION FOR HEART DISEASE RESOURCES (1972) Primary prevention of the atherosclerotic diseases. *Circulation*, **42**, 1–44.

ROSENTHAL, S.V., AITKEN, R.C.B. & ZEALLY, A.K. (1973) The Cattell 'sixteen personality factors' (16PF) personality profile of asthmatics. *J. Psychosom. Res.*, **17**, 9.

SELTZER, C.C. & OECHSLI, F.W. (1985) Psychosocial characteristics of adolescent smokers before they started smoking: evidence of self-selection. *J. Chron. Disorders*, **38**, 17–26.

SHARMA, S. & NANDKUMAR, V.K. (1980) Personality structure and adjustment pattern in bronchial asthma. *Acta Psychiat. Scand.*, **61**, 81–8.

SIEGAL, J.M. (1984) Anger and cardiovascular risk in adolescents. *Health Psychol.*, **3**, 293–313.

SIEGEL, S., HINSON, R.E., KRANK, M.D. & McCULLY, J. (1982) Heroin 'overdose' death: Contribution of drug-associated environmental cues. *Science*, **216**, 436–7.

STEINHAUSEN, H.C. (1981) Chronically ill and handicapped children and adolescents: personality studies in relation to disease. *J. Abnorm. Child Psychol.*, **9**, 291–7.

STEWART, L. AND LIVSON, N. (1966) Smoking and rebelliousness: a longitudinal study from childhood to maturity. *J. Consult. Clin. Psychol.*, **33**. 109–19.

SULLIVAN, B.J. (1979) Adjustment in diabetic adolescent girls; II. Adjustment, self-esteem, and depression in diabetic adolescent girls. *Psychosom. Med.*, **41**, 127–38.

SUTKER, P.B., MOAN, C.E., GOIST, K.C. JR. & ALLAIN, A.N. (1984) MMPI subtypes and antisocial behaviors in adolescent alcohol and drug abusers. *Drug Alcohol Depend.*, **13**, 235–44.

TAVORMINA, J.B., KASTNER, L.S., SLATER, P.M. & WATT, S.L. (1976) Chronically ill children: a psychologically and emotionally deviant population? *J. Abnorm. Child Psychol.*, **4**, 99–110.

TAYLOR, S.E. (1986) *Health psychol.* New York: Random House.

VAILLANT, G.E. (1979) Natural history of male psychological health: effects of mental health on physical health, *N. Eng. J. Med.*, **301**, 1249–54.

VELDMAN, D.J. & BROWN, O.H. (1969) Personality and performance characteristics associated with cigarette smoking among college freshmen. *J. Consult. Clin. Psychol.*, **33**, 109–19.

VON KNORRING, L. & ORELAND, L. (1985) Personality traits and platelet monoamine oxidase in tobacco smokers. *Psychol. Med.*, **15**, 327–34.

ZELTZER, L., KELLERMAN, J., ELLENBERG, L., DASH, J. & RIGLER, D. (1980) Psychological effects of illness in adolescence. II. Impact of illness in adolescents-crucial issues and coping styles. *J. Pediat.*, **97**, 132–8.

25 Black–white differences in American children's patterns of information processing independent of overall ability differences

C.R. Reynolds, V.L. Willson & J.A. Hickman

The disparity of about one standard deviation (SD) between the mean scores of American blacks and their white counterparts on standardized tests of intelligence has been considered a well established fact in differential psychology (e.g. see Jensen, 1980; Reynolds & Brown, 1984a). The reasons for the difference are much debated and thus far unresolved (e.g. Reynolds & Brown, 1984b). Explanations range from claims that all race differences on intelligence tests are due simply to the cultural bias of the test developers and environmental differences between blacks and whites (by such persons as Asa Hilliard and George Albee among others), to Harrington's (1984) claim that race differences are an artifact of the psychometric methods of item selection, to contentions by Arthur Jensen, Richard Herrnstein, and others that the differences are not only valid but due for the most part (about 80%) to genetic differences between blacks and whites. The nature-nurture controversy is unlikely to be resolved to the satisfaction of the experimentalist since humans can neither be randomly assigned to mating conditions nor the offspring randomly to conditions of rearing. However the criticism of classical methods of psychometrics leveled by Harrington (1984) seems to be ineffectual in explaining minority-majority differences in standardized tests scores (Hickman & Reynolds, 1986)

A next step toward understanding the phenomenon of black-white differences in intelligence, and one which we (and others, e.g. Jensen & Reynolds, 1982) believe must precede additional causal theorizing, is to describe precisely how blacks and whites differ in patterns of intellectual ability. Most of the existing research on black-white differences (and other racial differences in ability) in abilities, particularly research with intelligence measures, examines principally the overall or summary IQ as exemplified by the Full Scale IQ of the Wechsler series of tests, also by far the most studied of intelligence scales in this regard. Current research (Burns & Reynolds, in press; Jensen & Reynolds, 1982; Reynolds & Jensen, 1983) has begun to address more precise questions, to wit: In which abilities, factors, contents, or formal features of intelligence tests do Whites and Blacks differ the most and the least? Are racial differences homogeneous across item types designed to measure sometimes subtle distinctions among abilities? Or, are racial differences heterogeneous such that the direction and magnitude of differences cannot be predicted independent of the component parts of a composite IQ?

At least since the seminal study of Lesser, Fifer, & Clark (1965), psychologists who study individual differences have been aware that racial and ethnic groups differ from one another more or less, on the average, on some mental tests than on others. A battery of various tests then will show different mean profiles, profiles with different elevations and different shapes, representing common measured abilities for various groups. Lesser et al. (1965) administered tests of verbal, general reasoning, number, and spatial abilities to children ages 6 to 8 years from Chinese, Jewish,

Puerto Rican, and Black racial groupings (but all living in New York City). The four groups showed distinctly different patterns of ability on these measures. Racial grouping was clearly related to the pattern or shape of the profile, however, a more striking finding was that high and low socioeconomic status (SES) groups within each racial category showed almost identical patterns of ability – but differences in the relative elevation of their profiles. SES, in the Lesser *et al.* study, was related to overall level of ability while ethnicity was related more closely to the pattern of abilities expressed.

Surprisingly, very few such studies have been conducted. A comprehensive review of the individual differences literature (Willerman, 1979) cites only seven studies of this nature. In a subsequent critique of efforts until that time, Jensen (1980, pp. 729–36) elaborated a number of methodological problems inherent to such studies, as of the Lesser *et al.* (1965) genre, making the psychological and the psychometric interpretation of the manifest differences in ability profiles highly ambiguous.

The most serious ambiguities of early research (1965–81) result from the fact that the groups may have actually differed on only one or a very few independent factors of ability, and, because the various subtasks or component parts of the battery have different factor loadings on these few factors (i.e. are differentially correlated with any latent general factors), it could cause the groups to differ from one another to varying degrees on each of a large number of tests. As an example, if two groups differed only on Spearman's '*g*' (the general intelligence factor), but differed on *no* other abilities, and if the two groups were compared on a number of ability tests each of which had a different correlation with *g*, the groups would show marked differences in their profiles across the various tasks, but purely as an artifact of the differential relationship of each specific ability to *g*.

The groups would also show differences if the *g* loadings were the same for all of the subtasks but the various tasks differed substantially in their respective reliability coefficients. the reliabilities of the subtasks would be directly related to the magnitudes of the group differences when these are expressed in standard score units.

Several studies (see review in Jensen, 1980, as well as specific studies by Jensen & Reynolds, 1982, and Reynolds & Jensen, 1983) have shown that the magnitude of the average difference between blacks and whites on various tests is substantially related to the test's *g* loading (i.e. the test's correlation with a first principal component or first principal factor from factor analyses of an intercorrelation matrix including the test in question). Such findings confirm the methodological or statistical problems previously noted and are also in accordance with Spearman's (1927) hypothesis that Black-White differences on mental tests reflects mainly a difference in *g* rather than any other more narrow or specific abilities that might be present. Do Blacks and Whites differ in any abilities other than *g*?

This question truly addresses only phenotypic differences in specific abilities and attempts to answer this question can but investigate the existence and character of phenotypic ability differences between Blacks and Whites, independent of the cause of the differences (except of course for a rejection of the cultural test bias hypothesis of Black-White differences as explained in Reynolds, 1982), asking specifically whether there are population differences in abilities other than *g*. Such a question is of interest for clinical as well as theoretical reasons.

If there are true differences in *patterns* of abilities, as suggested in prior work, it could mean that the composite IQ or other summary score derived from a number of component parts, such as with the popular Wechsler scales or the Kaufman Assessment Battery for Children (K-ABC), is not composed of equal parts for Blacks and Whites and that different weighting systems might be needed to service IQs for different racial groupings were the effect a substantial one.

Three fairly recent studies have examined patterns of race differences for Blacks and Whites on the Wechsler Intelligence Scale for Children – Revised (WISC-R; Wechsler, 1974). Vance, Hawkins & McGee (1979), in a study of Black-White differences in subscale patterns on the WISC-R, reported that Blacks earn their highest level of performance on the verbal subtests of this battery, a finding in sharp contrast to the common clinical mythology of the US, which holds that Blacks are relatively disadvantaged on verbal as contrasted with nonverbal tests. Although their sample was nonrepresentative of the Black and White population of the USA, the findings of Vance *et al.* is consistent with numerous other studies using more sophisticated sampling techniques (e.g. Reynolds & Gutkin, 1981). However, these studies have failed to take account of the relative *g* loadings of verbal and nonverbal tasks. If nonverbal tasks are simply more *g* loaded than verbal tasks and the groups differ principally on *g*, then such profiles are nothing more than statistical artifacts.

Two more recent studies controlled for this problem, each using a different method however. Using the standardization sample from the WISC-R consisting of 1870 White and 305 Black children ages 6 to $16\frac{1}{2}$ years, drawn in a stratified random sampling of the USA population, Jensen & Reynolds (1982) used two statistical methods to assess specific ability differences between the two groups. The first method uses the partial point-biserial correlation. It is possible to express a difference between two nominally designated groups on any variable as the correlation between group membership and performance. In the case of Black-White differences on the WISC-R, the point-biserial *r* between race (where Black is coded 0 and White is coded 1) and performance on each WISC-R subtest is calculated. The point-biserial *r* between race and the WISC-R Full Scale IQ is also determined. To assess any differences between racial groupings that may be present *and* that are unrelated to *g*, the partial point-biserial *r* is next calculated, using the *r* between race and Full Scale IQ as the partialling statistic, thus controlling for differential relationships with *g*. (The WISC-R Full Scale IQ is not a perfect match to the battery's *g*-factor but is considered adequate as a control as the correlation of Full Scale IQ with *g* is about .96 to .98). Use of the partialling technique reduces the differences overall considerably, removing all variance attributable to differences in general ability. This is tantamount to equating the two groups on overall IQ but allows the use of randomly selected samples. Following this procedure, Jensen & Reynolds (1982) reported that differences remained on six of the 12 subtests of the WISC-R. The remaining differences favoured Whites on Block Design, Object Assembly, Comprehension, the Mazes and favoured Blacks on Arithmetic and Digit Span. The partial *r* for Vocabulary, believed by many to be one of the most culturally biased of all subtests (against Blacks) showed a partial *r* of 0.00!

The pattern of subtest differences then shows the largest differences, independent of overall ability, to favour Whites on tests that involve spatial and constructional skills (with the exception of Comprehension, a measure of social reasoning in meaningful contexts) . The tests that favour Blacks involve auditory sequential memory. Clearly differences in specific abilities exist independent of *g*, however, as Jensen & Reynolds (1982) show, *g* contributes nearly 4 times as much to distinguishing between the races as do the specific subtests.

As a second approach to the same question, and using the same stratified random sample, Jensen & Reynolds (1982) conducted a hierarchical factor analysis of the intercorrelations of the 12 WISC-R subtests, first extracting *g* from the matrix. An orthogonal solution extracting three factors was then determined. Any racial differences on these three factors would be independent of *g* since they were taken from the residual matrix from which *g* had been extracted. When the WISC-R is subjected to factor analysis, three factors are the common result; these factors are traditionally regarded as Verbal Comprehension, Perceptual Organization and Freedom-from-Distractibility (the latter also being called a memory factor). When

Blacks and Whites are compared on these hierarchically-determined and orthogonalized factors, Blacks score highest on the third or Memory factor while Whites score higher, but less so, on the remaining two factors. These results affirm findings from the individual subtest analyses.

Reynolds & Jensen (1983) took a different approach to the same question and compared groups of Blacks and Whites carefully matched for age, sex, and Full Scale IQ. A total of 250 exact matches were obtained and performance on the various subtests of the WISC-R contrasted via a series of ANOVAS (following a multivariate analysis of variance which yielded a highly significant F). The Verbal, Performance, and Full Scale IQs of these groups differed by less than one point each attesting to the accuracy of the matching procedure. Results of this series of analyses were for the most part consistent with the findings of Jensen & Reynolds (1982). Whites significantly exceeded the performance of Blacks on the subtests of Comprehension, Object Assembly, Mazes, and Picture Arrangement. Blacks outscored Whites on the subtests of Arithmetic, Digit Span, and Coding. A factor analysis was also done with this group using the Jensen & Reynolds (1982) technique and comparisons made on the factor scores thereby derived. In this analysis, Blacks exceeded Whites on the third factor, the so called memory or Freedom-from-Distractibility factor, and Whites outscored Blacks on the Performance or Perceptual Organization factor.

Results with the newer statistical procedures support the general conclusion of past studies that there are reliable differences between Blacks and Whites in cognitive abilities other than *g*. The patterns revealed by those methods are inconsistent with the specific patterns found in earlier work by Lesser *et al.* (1965) and Vance *et al.* (1979) among others. Jensen & Reynolds (1982) and Reynolds & Jensen (1983) both support the findings of a Black spatial deficit, superiority of Blacks on short-term memory related tasks, and essentially equivalent verbal performance, all, of course, when *g* is controlled.

To extend these findings, which have thus far been restricted to the Wechsler Scales, new or at least different measures of intelligence must be assessed using the newer methodologies. The recently published Kaufman Assessment Battery for Children (K-ABC; Kaufman & Kaufman, 1983) seems an excellent candidate for a next step for a variety of reasons: it contains several novel intellectual tasks not appearing on other batteries; it was designed from a heuristic model of information processing; it compares favorably to such standards as the WISC-R in its reliability and validity evidence; it was standardized using large, stratified random samples of Blacks and Whites taken from the USA at large and, Jensen (1984) has noted that the K-ABC presents an unusual circumstance with regard to Black-White differences (to be reviewed below).

The present study was intended to extend and assess the findings of Jensen & Reynolds (1982) and Reynolds & Jensen (1983) with additional tasks from the K-ABC and with a distinct and even larger sample. Because of the way the K-ABC was developed (not all subtests are administered at every age), it is also possible to take a preliminary look at age effects.

Method

Subjects

Children for the study included 807 Black and 1569 White children (total N = 2376) tested during the standardization of the K-ABC. The standardization sample proper was stratified on the basis of age (from $2\frac{1}{2}$ years to $12\frac{1}{2}$ years), sex, geographic region of residence within the USA, community size, parent educational level and public school placement (regular education or a variety of special education or handicapping conditions.) The sample used in the present study has an overrepresentation of Blacks, but this was desirable for purposes of the research; the additional Black children were taken from children assessed during the K-ABC standardization for the purpose of developing additional sociocultural norms (see Kaufman & Kaufman, 1983, for a full explanation). These are still only 17 Black children at ages 2 years 6 months to 2 years 11 months but thereafter Black children represent from 30 to 35% of the total N by age. Children were grouped by age into six groups (shown in Table 25.2) according to the subtests administered at each age. More detail regarding the sample and its selection can be found in Kaufman & Kaufman (1983) and in Kamphaus & Reynolds (1987).

Instrumentation

The K-ABC is an individually administered psychological test of intelligence and achievement based on Kaufman & Kaufman's interpretation and integration of the theories of Luria, Sperry & Neisser and related workers. It is normed for use with children aged $2\frac{1}{2}$ years to $12\frac{1}{2}$ years. The K-ABC provides four global or summary scales, a Sequential Processing Scale, a Simultaneous Processing Scale, a Mental Processing Composite (a linear combination of the two preceding scales) and an Achievement Scale. A Nonverbal Scale can also be calculated. Each global score yields an age-corrected deviation scaled score scaled to a mean of 100 and a standard deviation (SD) of 15.

Sixteen subtests go into making up these global scales; not all are administered to each age group. The 10 subtests of the Mental Processing Scale yield standard scores with a mean of 10 and an SD of 3. Achievement subtests (6) yield standard scores with means of 100 and SDs of 15. A description of the scales and their subtests follows:

Mental processing subtests
SEQUENTIAL PROCESSING SCALE
Hand Movements (ages $2\frac{1}{2}$ years–$12\frac{1}{2}$ years). Imitating a sequence of hand movements precisely as demonstrated by the examiner.
Number Recall (ages $2\frac{1}{2}$–$12\frac{1}{2}$ years). Repeating a series of digits (forward only) in the same sequence as the examiner.
Word Order (ages 4–$12\frac{1}{2}$ yrs). Touching a series of silhouetted pictures in the same sequence as named by the examiner with the introduction of color interference for later items.
SIMULTANEOUS PROCESSING SCALE
Magic Window (ages $2\frac{1}{2}$–4 yrs) Identifying a picture exposed by moving it past a narrow slit or window so that only parts of it are available at any one time.
Face Recognition (ages $2\frac{1}{2}$–4 yrs). Selecting a previously exposed picture of a face from a multiperson photo.
Gestalt Closure (ages $2\frac{1}{2}$–$12\frac{1}{2}$ yrs). Naming an object in a partially completed inkblot style drawing.
Triangles (ages 4–$12\frac{1}{2}$ yrs). Assembling triangles to match a model.
Matrix Analogies (ages 5–$12\frac{1}{2}$ yrs). Selecting a picture or a design to complete a visual analogy.
Spatial Memory (ages 5–$12\frac{1}{2}$ yrs). Recalling the placement of objects briefly exposed.
Photo Series (ages 6–$12\frac{1}{2}$ yrs). Placing photographs of an event into chronological order.
ACHIEVEMENT SCALE
Expressive Vocabulary (ages $2\frac{1}{2}$–4 yrs). Naming objects in photographs.
Faces & Places (ages $2\frac{1}{2}$–$12\frac{1}{2}$ yrs). Naming a famous person, place, or object.

Arithmetic (ages 3–12½ yrs). Answering arithmetic questions given orally but with illustrations also presented.

Riddles (ages 3–12½ yrs). Naming an object from a list of its characteristics.

Reading/Decoding (ages 5–12½ yrs). Naming letters and calling words.

Reading/Understanding (ages 7–12½ yrs). Performing written instructions.

Reliability of the global scales is typically in the .90s and individual subtests have reliabilities in the .60 to .90 range, comparing favorably with other individually administered tests like the WISC-R. The K-ABC Mental Processing Composite (MPC) and the WISC-R Full Scale IQ correlate about .70 (Kaufman & Kaufman, 1983).

Simultaneous processing on the K-ABC is defined as the child's ability mentally to integrate input simultaneously to solve a problem correctly, that is to synthesize input, or to 'see the whole' of the picture. Sequential processing refers to the child's ability to arrange input into a serial order where each stimulus is related to the preceding one, establishing a form of serial interdependence necessary for analysis and leading to the correct solution to a problem. The K-ABC Achievement Scale measures skills designed to complement the intelligence scales and attempts to estimate a child's success in Knowledge acquisition through the application of sequential and simultaneous processing strategies. The Achievement Scale measures verbal concept formation, vocabulary, general information, reading, and basic arithmetic skills.

Procedure

To assess Black-White differences in ability patterns, as expressed in the K-ABC, two methods were used. First, partial point-biserial correlations were calculated at each age between race and subtest score, partialling the relationship between race and total test score, the MPC, the K-ABC's analog to the Wechsler Full Scale IQ. As with the WISC-R, this overall summary score is not a perfect measure of *g*, but it is highly correlated and serves as a reasonable approximation (Kaufman & Kaufman, 1983; Kamphaus & Reynolds, 1987, ch. 3). In computing the partial *r*s, Black was coded 0 and White 1, meaning that negative correlations indicate higher performance by Blacks and positive correlations higher performance by Whites.

The Schmid-Leiman hierarchical factor analysis was also performed as described in Jensen & Reynolds (1982). The general factor was first extracted from the matrix of intercorrelations of all of the 16 K-ABC subtests and three factors, Sequential, Simultaneous, and Achievement, then taken from the residual matrix.

Results and discussion

If one simply examines the K-ABC without partialling or otherwise controlling for *g*, then Whites outperform Blacks at a statistically significant level on all subtests and global scales except Number Recall, traditionally Blacks' best task on tests of mental ability. Even so, the results of such a simple comparison produces controversial findings that should be reviewed prior to pursuing results of the present work. Table 25.1 shows the global score comparisons for the K-ABC scales for Blacks and for Whites from the standardization and sociocultural norms groups. The PPVT-R scores of the same sample of more than 2300 children is shown for comparison purposes. As is readily apparent, the differences on the K-ABC variables are sharply reduced from the typical 15 points or so found for the last 75 years of research in individual differences. Sampling error and other attempts to explain this reduction remain

Table 25.1 Black-white differences on the K-ABC for children in the standardization sample

	Blacks	Whites	Difference
Sequential processing	98.2	101.2	+3.0
Simultaneous processing	93.8	102.3	+8.5
Mental processing composite	95.0	102.0	+7.0
Achievement scale	93.8	102.7	+8.9
PPVT-R	84.6	99.6	+15.0

inadequate (Kamphaus & Reynolds, 1987). Following a thorough analysis of this phenomenon in which he partially explains the reduction in Black-White score differences on the K-ABC, Jensen (1984) was forced to conclude that the remaining variance (in the reduction) was the major puzzle of the K-ABC.

Since the level of differences in the performance of Blacks and Whites is reduced on the K-ABC, it becomes even more intriguing to view the pattern of differences to see whether it is affected. Table 25.2 shows the partial point-biserial correlations; significant correlations indicate a reliable Black-White difference as noted earlier.

Once *g* is partialled, the profile changes dramatically from the constant higher performance by Whites. In Table 25.2 Blacks can be seen to outperform Whites on 2 of the 3 Sequential Processing tasks, Number Recall and Word Order. On Hand Movements, a visually presented sequential memory task, Whites score higher but only at the highest age level, age 7 to 12½ years. It is tempting to rely upon a short-term memory explanation of these results as has been popular for similar findings on the WISC-R, however this is not a good fit to the data.

Looking further, we see that the most important remaining trends in Table 25.2 are for Whites to score higher on Spatial Memory (at 2 of 3 age levels) and photo series (at both age levels where it is administered), both Simultaneous processing scale tasks, and one (Spatial Memory) having memory demands. Of the five short-term memory tasks on the K-ABC, Blacks score higher on two, Whites score higher on two, and on the other, Face Recognition, given only at three age levels, Whites score higher at one age level (3–0 to 3–11). A simple memory versus reasoning explanation thus fails. These subtests do differ substantially in their loading on *g* which could account for the observed pattern except that any effects due to total test score, used to approximate *g*, have been removed by the partialling procedure. A cognitive processing explanation seems to fare better and may be consistent with prior WISC-R data as well.

Number Recall and Word order, Blacks' highest scores, are clearly sequential information processing tasks (see, for example, reviews of all K-ABC factor analyses in Kamphaus & Reynolds, 1987, ch. 3). Hand Movements seem an oddity at first since it is on the Sequential Scale, is a short-term memory task and Whites score highest on Hand Movements in contrast to the other sequential tasks. However, examination of the K-ABC factor structure provides a ready explanation. There is no Black-White difference on Hand Movements prior to age 7–0 years. At these ages, Hand Movements has nearly equivalent loadings on the K-ABC sequential and simultaneous factors. At the upper age levels, where Whites score higher, Hand Movement's loading changes and it actually loads more highly, if only slightly so, on the simultaneous factor. Face Recognition is clearly a simultaneous processing task at early ages.

An alternative interpretation, and an equally viable one to 'memory' or 'distractibility' for the triad that makes up the WISC-R third factor (Arithmetic, Digit Span and Coding) is that it measures sequential processing (Kamphaus &

Table 25.2 Partial point-biserial correlations between race (black-white) and performance on individual subtests of the K-ABC, controlling for general intelligence

Scale and subtests	Partial Correlations[a] Ages					
	2-6 to 2-11 N=99	3-0 to 3-11 N=250	4-0 to 4-11 N=258	5-0 to 5-11 N=248	6-0 to 6-11 N=217	7-0 to 12-11 N=1304
Sequential scale						
Hand movements	.12	-.04	.01	-.04	.04	.10**
Number recall	-.25**	-.21**	-.17**	-.16**	-.15*	-.19***
Word order	—	—	-.02	.02	-.13*	-.15***
Simultaneous scale						
Magic window	-.01	.05	.04	—	—	—
Face recognition	.04	.14*	.00	—	—	—
Gestalt closure	.07	.03	.13*	.00	-.03	.03
Triangles	—	—	.10	-.00	.08	.12**
Matrix analogies	—	—	—	-.02	-.13*	.03
Spatial memory	—	—	—	.20**	.16*	.04
Photo series	—	—	—	—	.43**	.08*
Achievement scale						
Expressive vocabulary	.15 (-.13)	.28** (.10)	.24** (.14*)	.10 (.04)	-.06 (-.13*)	.03 (-.18**)
Faces & places	.30** (.15)	.28** (.09)	.07 (-.11)	.13* (.08)	.04 (.04)	.23** (.16**)
Arithmetic	—	.06 (-.20**)	.12 (-.05)	.33** (.31**)	.34** (.39**)	.27** (.19**)
Riddles	—	.26** (.04)	.21** (.09)	-.09 (.28**)	-.17** (.29**)	.07 (-.14**)
Reading/decoding	—	—	—	—	—	.15* (-.01)
Reading/understanding	—	—	—	—	—	

[a] (+) indicates higher white score and (−) indicates higher black performance.

[b] Values in parentheses are partialed for total achievement while remaining values are partialed against the mental processing composite.

* p ≤ .05, ** p ≤ .01. Significance levels change as a function of changes in sample size. Ns for each coefficient may vary slightly from the column heading due to missing data on a specific variable.

Reynolds, 1987; Kaufman, 1979). Object Assembly, Mazes, and Block Design from the WISC-R, tasks on which Whites excel, are very good measures of simultaneous processing. Such a processing distinction may help organize thinking about patterns of differences between Blacks and Whites. Other evidence points in this direction as well.

Results of the follow-up Schmid-Leiman Hierarchical analysis show that when *g* is partialled from the initial correlation matrix of K-ABC subtests, Blacks score higher on the sequential factor and Whites score higher on the simultaneous factor. This interpretation also receives support from results with the K-ABC Achievement Scale. Riddles, a subtest on which Whites outscores Blacks at every age, even when *g* has been partialled, loads most highly on the simultaneous factor of the K-ABC. Other findings on the Achievement Scale are more sporadic and await elaboration in future analyses, but lean in the anticipated direction. Reading/Decoding, a 'Black strength', is more dependent upon sequential processing while Arithmetic loads more highly on the sequential factor at age 3 years, where Blacks score highest but is more aligned with the simultaneous scale at the uppermost age where Whites score higher.

As in previous studies (e.g. Jensen & Reynolds, 1982; Reynolds & Jensen, 1983), the residual differences, after removing *g*, are relatively small. Nevertheless, it is clear that there are differential profiles of ability (independent of overall ability level) between Blacks and Whites. This would support the weak form of the Spearman Hypothesis, stating that Blacks and Whites differ principally on *g* but also exhibit smaller differences on the specific aptitudes that make up the total of human intelligence. The mental processing distinctions offered by the K-ABC to explain the residual differences in Black-White ability profiles appears to be a viable one, however, other explanations exist, most notably those of Jensen (1984). Research into these data are continuing as we pit alternative hypotheses against one another and gather additional data in attempting to define the nature of Black-White differences in specific mental skills and patterns of ability.

References

BURNS, C.W. & REYNOLDS, C.R. (in press) Sex differences in sequential and simultaneous processing independent of 'g'. *Journal of School Psychology*.

HARRINGTON, G.M. (1984) An experimental model of bias in mental testing. In C.R. Reynolds & R.T. Brown (eds.), *Perspectives on bias in mental testing*, New York: Plenum.

HICKMAN, J.A. & REYNOLDS, C.R. (1986) Are race differences in mental test scores an artifact of psychometric methods? A test of Harrington's experimental model. *Journal of Special Education*, **20**, 409–30.

JENSEN, A.R. (1980) *Bias in mental testing*, New York: The Free Press.

JENSEN, A.R. (1984) The nature of the black-white difference on the K-ABC and its implications for future intelligence tests. *Journal of Special Education*, **3**, 377–408.

JENSEN, A.R. & REYNOLDS, C.R. (1982) Race, social class and ability patterns on the WISC-R. *Personality and Individual Differences*, **3**, 423–38.

KAMPHAUS, R.W. & REYNOLDS, C.R. (1987) *Clinical and research applications of the K-ABC*, Circle Pines, MN: American Guidance Service.

KAUFMAN, A.S. (1979) *Intelligent testing with the WISC-R*, New York: Wiley – Interscience.

KAUFMAN, A.S. & KAUFMAN, N.L. (1983) *Kaufman assessment battery for children*, Circle Pines, MN: American Guidance Service.

LESSER, G.S., FIFER, G. & CLARK, D.H. (1965) Mental abilities of children from different social-class and cultural groups. *Monographs of the Society for Research in Child Development*, **30** (4).

REYNOLDS, C.R. (1982) The problem of bias in psychological assessment. In C.R. Reynolds & T.B. Gutkin (eds.), *The handbook of school psychology*, New York: John Wiley & Sons.

REYNOLDS, C.R. & BROWN, R.T. (1984a) Bias in mental testing: an introduction to the issues.

In C.R. Reynolds & R.T. Brown (eds.), *Perspectives on bias in mental testing*, New York: Plenum.

REYNOLDS, C.R. & BROWN, R.T. (1984b) *Perspectives on bias in mental testing*, New York: Plenum.

REYNOLDS, C.R. & GUTKIN, T.B. (1981) A multivariate comparison of the intellectual performance of blacks and whites matched on four demographic variables. *Personality and Individual Differences*, **2**, 175–80.

REYNOLDS, C.R. & JENSEN, A.R. (1983) WISC-R subscale patterns of abilities of blacks and whites matched on full scale IQ. *Journal of Educational Psychology*, **75**, 207–14.

REYNOLDS, C.R. & WILLSON, V.L. (1984) *Factorial consistency of simultaneous and sequential cognitive processing for whites and blacks ages 3 to 12½*. Paper presented to the annual meeting of the National Council on Measurement in Education, New Orleans, April.

SPEARMAN, C. (1927) *The abilities of man*, New York: MacMillan.

VANCE, H.B., HAWKINS, N. & McGEE, H. (1979) A preliminary study of black and white differences on the revised Wechsler Intelligence Scale for Children. *Journal of Clinical Psychology*, **35**, 815–19.

WECHSLER, D. (1974) *Wechsler intelligence scale for children – revised*, San Antonio: The Psychological Corporation.

WILLERMAN, L. (1979) *The psychology of individual and group differences*, San Francisco: W.H. Freeman.

26 Cross-cultural perspectives in the assessment of individual differences: methodological and conceptual issues

Y.L. Hanin

The main goal of this chapter is to examine some of the methodological and conceptual aspects of the problem of cross-cultural assessment of individual differences, based on experimental studies and clinical work with students, school children, young athletes and others. First, a standard strategy (algorithm) for the development and validation of equivalent forms of any personality and/or social psychological self-evaluation scale or inventory will be described. Then, selective experimental and normative data obtained in several studies conducted during the last 12 years will be presented. These studies substantiate the validity of the Russian forms of such well known personality scales and inventories as Spielberger's STAI (Spielberger, Gorsuch & Lushene, 1970), H.J. and S.B.G. Eysenck's (1975) EPQ, McCrosky's (1970) PRCA, Nideffer's (1983) TAIS, Martens's (1977) SCAT and Crowne and Marlowe's (1960) SDS. After discussing procedures to construct and apply valid and reliable equivalent forms of various inventories, some important conceptual aspects relevant to the assessment of individual differences using, as an example, the theory of 'zones of optimal functioning' (e.g. Hanin, 1978; 1985), will be examined and practical implications suggested.

Methodological problems in the assessment of individual differences

The first problem encountered in studies involving the assessment of individual differences under conditions of varying or different socio-cultural milieus is the task of developing reliable and valid equivalent scales. There is a wide range of different attitudes towards the application of personality inventories and scales from other countries among Soviet psychologists, ranging from uncritical and enthusiastic acceptance of a particular instrument to blind rejection of its use. Also encountered are cases of the application of tests or their parts without a thorough preliminary acquaintance with both the theoretical background and rationale underlying a particular scale, and the socio-cultural acceptability of the content and format of the items. Until quite recently the whole process of 'scale adaptation' to new socio-cultural conditions was practically limited to a simple translation of the text into Russian without any experimental substantiation of its equivalence to the original scale. Psychometric characteristics of the scale and/or normative data were, as a rule, absent.

Recent developments and research in this field in our country (e.g. Y.L. Hanin, V.S. Magun, M.P. Miroshnikov, A.A. Semenov) as well as abroad (e.g. S. Sharma, K. Sipos, C.D. Spielberger) offer promising strategies for the development of equivalent scales enabling cross-cultural comparisons in the assessment of individual psychological and social psychological differences. This work has emphasized the application of a standard strategy (algorithm) of adaptation providing for systematic control of the quality of the development of a particular inventory or scale at any stage of its construction (e.g. Hanin, 1977a; Lichko, 1976). This standard algorithm includes the following steps:

(1)   Becoming fundamentally familiar with the rationale and theoretical background of the scale;
(2)   Preparation of the preliminary translation of the text of the original scale into Russian (or any other language) following three steps:
   (a) translation of the text of the scale into Russian keeping the psychological content of the items maximally exact;
   (b) evaluation of the adequacy of this preliminary Russian language translation with the assistance of professional psychologists and interpreters with a good command of the spoken language of the original scale (sometimes a 'blind' back translation of the scale and direct contact with its author is most valuable);[1]
   (c) a pilot administration of the preliminary form of the scale to determine the first reactions of the subjects to the scale items, their format and instructions.
(3)   Experimental evaluation of the equivalence of the Russian form of the scale by:
   (a) having bilingual subjects respond to the scale in both languages;
   (b) using language samples for both male and female subjects of particular age groups;
   (c) calculating psychometric characteristics of the new scale (means, standard deviations, inter-item correlations, test-retests, evaluations, indices of concurrent validity of the scale, and finally norms).
(4)   Preparation of the scale manual, conducting further relevant research, and compilation of a bibliography of publications using the adapted scale.

Using this briefly described standard strategy, several experimental studies were undertaken to develop the Russian forms of some of the most important foreign language scales and inventories for the assessment of individual differences in both children and adults. These include Spielberger's State-Trait Anxiety Inventory (STAI), McCrosky's Personal Report of Communication Apprehension (PRCA), Martens's Sport Competition Anxiety Test (SCAT) and Eysenck's Personality Questionnaire (EPQ). Nideffer's Test of Attentional and Interpersonal Style and Marlowe and Crowne's Social Desirability Scale have been adapted for use in the USSR although these forms are mainly used with adults.

As detailed reviews of these experimental studies are reported elsewhere (e.g. Hanin, 1978, 1985, 1986), we shall briefly present only some of the normative data for several of the scales, particularly in reference to children and adolescents although some adult studies will be noted. This will be followed by a discussion of how to overcome some of the limitations of standard instructions of the tests and a description of the concepts of retrospective and prospective assessments.

State-Trait-Anxiety-Inventory (Spielberger, 1966; Spielberger *et al.*, 1970; Spielberger & Sharma, 1976). The findings on the development and validation of the Russian form of the STAI reported by Hanin (1976) and Hanin & Spielberger (1983) demonstrate the equivalence of the scale to the original, its reliability and validity. A-State and A-Trait were observed to vary among samples of students, athletes, musicians, ballet dancers and others (e.g. Hanin, 1977b; Hanin & Bulanova, 1979). On the whole, mean level of anxiety, both state and trait, is comparable to various samples tested in the USA, Hungary, India and other countries. Trait anxiety was consistently higher in practically all the female samples, which is also similar to the findings obtained in other countries.

A Russian form of the STAI for children was also developed. The level of A-St. and A-Tr. of 4–6 form school children (boys and girls aged 9–13) was also comparable to their American counterparts tested by Spielberger and his co-workers. Specifically, boys' A-St. level was in the range of 30.1–31.8 points, and A-Tr. was respectively 36.3–37.3 points. Comparable findings were obtained in testing girls of the same age: A-St. = 30.3 – 30.6 points and A-Tr. = 37.3 – 38.1 points.

Personal Report of Communication Apprehension (McCrosky, 1970) Mean level of communication trait anxiety (PRCA) in a sample of 94 male and 100 female students was quite similar to the American sample (M = 70.83, s.d. = 9.68 in males and M = 72.71, s.d. = 9.53 in females). As expected, no significant correlations between the PRCA and A-Tr. (on Spielberger's scale) and sport competition trait anxiety measured by Martens's (1977) SCAT were found. Only in the female sample was there a significant correlation between the PRCA and SCAT ($r = .56$, $p < .01$).

Sport Competition Anxiety Test (Martens, 1977) This scale is well suited for testing subjects from 10 years old. Mean level of competition trait anxiety in a male sample of 100 subjects was 18.77, s.d. = 4.46 and in a female sample was 21.45, s.d. = 3.50 ($t = 2.57$, $p < .01$). Moderate correlations, significant at the .01 level, between SCAT and A.Tr. were found in samples of 43 males ($r = .50$) and 42 female students ($r = .45$). In a study of 15–16 year old athletes attending a special sports school, moderate and significant ($p < .05$) correlations between SCAT and A.Tr. were found in 56 boys ($r = .32$) and 39 girls ($r = .39$). These data show a relative independence of the two parameters which is in line with the findings of Martens.

Eysenck Personality Questionnaire (H.J. Eysenck & S.B.G. Eysenck, 1975). This personality inventory was adapted into Russian using a sample of 402 subjects (184 males and 218 females). Means and standard deviations for psychoticism, neuroticism, extraversion and social desirability (a lie scale) are comparable with those obtained in English samples. However, in our studies of younger student samples, psychoticism and neuroticism levels were somewhat higher. Also, the lie scale level was consistently higher in the female than in the male sample ($t = 4.7$, $p < .01$). It will be necessary to also adapt the Junior EPQ into Russian in order to examine further the personality of younger adolescents and children.

The above data illustrates one part of the work involved in the development of reliable and valid personality and social psychological scales suitable for cross-cultural studies and represents an important but nevertheless only a first step in the assessment of individual differences, mostly at the *group* level. Another promising perspective is related to the possibility of modifying the standard test instructions and the procedures of their administration (e.g. Allen, 1970; Bucky, Spielberger & Bale, 1972). This could be done by orienting the subjects to assess their emotional or other experience in the context of, what might be called 'space-temporal dynamics'.

The point is that almost any test administration, by its instructions to the subjects, emphasizes 'actual' or 'present moment' assessments. The usual response format to personality test items (e.g. yes–no, true–false, agree–disagree) also implies, even for situational scales that significant time periods in one's past and/or future are missing from the analysis. As well, social psychological factors operating in the immediate environment of the subject and/or in the activity of tasks she/he is performing are usually also ignored. This is a serious limitation in a description of individual differences and especially for the assessment of situational variables affecting one's level of performance in real life activity. One of the possible ways to overcome this limitation is to introduce, additionally to standard test instructions, new 'time and environment-specific' instructions enabling:

(a) retrospective, actual (current), and predictive (anticipated) self-evaluations orienting the subject to assess his/her past, present and future experience;

(b)   a close 'connection' of the assessment to the particular conditions of the subject's physical and social-cultural milieu and/or the task at hand.

This approach will be illustrated by the assessment of individual differences in A-State and A-Trait using modified instructions to Spielberger's STAI.

Retrospective and prospective test administrations

Several studies were conducted to assess individual differences in the emotional reactions of participants in various sports activities (Hanin, 1978). For those purposes, the most adequate scale turned out to be Spielberger's STAI enabling the measurement of two distinct and closely related dimensions: state anxiety – a situational emotional reaction to various stressors, and trait anxiety – a relatively stable personality disposition, a tendency to react with elevated levels of A-St. in situations of threat to one's self-esteem.

Following Spielberger's definition of state anxiety as a temporal cross-section in the emotional life-stream of man's experience represented in one's subjective feelings of tension, apprehension, concern, and nervousness accompanied by manifested activation of the autonomic nervous system (Spielberger et al., 1970), it was decided that the following concepts be distinguished:

(a)   retrospectively assessed A-St. – a self-evaluation of one's emotional reaction in a particular situation in the past. A new modified instruction asks the subject to assess 'how he felt in this particular situation at a definite moment in the past';

(b)   predicted or anticipated A-St. – an assessment of one's anticipated emotional reaction in a particular situation at a definite moment in the future which asks 'how do you think you will feel just before the contest, (exam, blind date, etc.) in a week from now?';

(c)   performance A-St. in the past, present or future – an emotional reaction felt while performing a task ('activity A-St.') is assessed by asking a subject to evaluate 'how he felt/feels/will feel during his performance of a particular task?';

(d)   communication A-St. in the past, present, future – an emotional reaction felt during communication with a particular individual (e.g. a colleague, subordinate, boss etc.) reflecting *interpersonal* situational anxiety (A-St.$_{int}$) or a group of persons describing *intragroup* situational anxiety (A-St.$_{gr}$) assessed by questions such as 'how did/do/will you feel in this particular group?';

(e)   optimal A-St. – situational anxiety accompanying the best personal performance at a particular task (A-St.$_{opt}$) assessed in a series of real-life situations (current A-St. of best individual performances) or retrospectively ('How did you feel performing your best on this particular task?'.

As evidenced by our research and clinical work with top Soviet athletes including young divers, rowers, volley-ball players, weight-lifters as well as ballet dancers and musicians (e.g. Cratty & Hanin, 1980; Hanin & Kolovarsky, 1977; Rushall, 1983), it is more productive to assess not just the level of individual optimum A-St., but, what we call 'individual zones of optimal functioning' (ZOF). The upper and lower boundaries of the ZOF are established, for example, for individual athletes by adding and subtracting four points to their optimal prestart A-St. levels, which corresponds approximately to one-half the average standard deviation of observed precontest A-St. scores in more than 200 athletes. Thus, if the retrospective prestart optimal A-St. score was 53, as measured by the STAI, the ZOF range would be 49 to 57, with the lower and upper zones being 49–53 and 53–57, respectively (Hanin, 1986, pp. 46–64).

A-St. optimal and ZOF are strictly individual matters and, depending on one's level of professional expertise, situational readiness for the task at hand, as well as past emotional experience, could be relatively low, moderate, or high. In other words, a person can do his/her best when experiencing no anxiety at all (psychological comfort), or moderate anxiety, or an extremely high level of situational anxiety. ZOF theory also stipulates that individual zones of optimum functioning are different for different tasks (sport events, for instance), conditions of performance (in training versus competition) and level of proficiency (skills).

The above concepts were validated in several experimental studies involving hundreds of top athletes, students, ballet dancers and musicians. Additionally, from the cross-cultural perspective, very interesting experimental data were obtained by Bill Morgan and his co-workers (Morgan & Ellickson, 1987) at the Sport Psychology Laboratory at the Wisconsin University confirming our theoretical and empirical findings on a sample of American athletes.

The concepts of time-specific (retrospectively assessed and predicted) anxiety turned out to be valid not only for situational A-St., but also for the assessment of trait anxiety. For instance, in a study of 70 freshman students, their A-Trait, using STAI, was measured in two ways: (a) actual A-Tr. at the time of testing, and (b) anticipated A-Tr. by the end of their studies in the college (in 3.5 years or 7 semesters). Upon graduation from the college each subject again completed the STAI assessing one's actual A-Tr. (predicted 3.5 years ago) and his/her A-Tr. (retrospectively) at the freshman year. The correspondence of these assessments offers additional proof of the validity of retrospective and anticipated measures of anxiety and opens up some new perspectives in the application of time-specific evaluations of individual differences in the dynamics of a person's life cycle. As well, case studies involving retrospective self assessments show the 'productivity' of a dynamic view of individual differences in the perception of one's behaviour and emotional experience during a relatively large period of time.

And finally, as an illustration of the assessment of communication anxiety, Table 26.1 reports the findings of a comparative study of intragroup A-St. in adolescent samples of technical school pupils, 'difficult' pupils and delinquents, while in the company of one's school classmates, friends, and families. As expected, the highest level of intragroup anxiety was found in the presence of study groups and especially among delinquents.

Table 26.1 Intragroup state anxiety in three samples of adolescents

Samples	N		Intragroup state anxiety			X_r^2
			1	2	3*	
Technical school pupils	31	M	40.10	31.66	31.6	70.59
		SD	7.72	8.01	5.56	p<.001
"Difficult" pupils	21	M	39.14	33.50	34.50	8.6
		SD	8.77	7.41	7.69	n.s.
Delinquents	59	M	49.66	33.47	31.45	58.6
		SD	10.04	9.3	8.6	p<.001

* 1 – A-state in a study group/one's class
  2 – A-state in a company of one's friends
  3 – A-state at home in one's family
X_r^2 – significance of differences as determined by Friedman's two-way analysis of variance by ranks

Conceptual issues in the assessment of individual differences

Both research and clinical studies of the optimum levels of A-St. in individual athletes (male and female, adult and youth) in various sports events gave us some ground for the contention that, in the assessment of individual differences, irrespective of the scales and/or inventories used, it is very important to clarify some of the principal conceptual issues. First of all, the ZOF conception illustrates the importance and usefulness of making a clear distinction between situational and relatively stable aspects of the parameters under study. In this case, A-Tr. and A-St. should be considered 'in unity', with state anxiety representing a concrete situational manifestation of trait anxiety. This is a bridge connecting the 'general' and the 'particular' at the level of the 'singular'. Assessing A-St., for example, we assess a situational manifestation of trait anxiety under very definite conditions with the emphasis on the intensity and process characteristics while performing a task in a specified environment. On the other hand, a trait could be conceived of as a generalized probability characteristic based on past experience with implications for future (anticipated) behaviour patterns, i.e. the probability of certain emotional reactions to some environmental cues, task demands, etc. By assessing individual differences along time-environment parameters (vectors) we, in fact, fill in 'the vacuum devoid of any social elements' (Vallerand, 1983).

The second point is also well represented in our ZOF theory and in the management of unfavorable prestart emotional states of athletes. It is concerned with the necessity of sharpening the distinction between *interindividual* and *intraindividual* comparisons. Almost all normative data for personality tests provided by researchers are, in fact, interindividual scores of intersubject differences at a group and/or intergroup (intersample) level. Interindividual scores are aimed at answering the question of the degree that one group of persons is different from or similar to another. On the other hand intraindividual or within-individual assessments are oriented to principally different aspects of measurement, to determine the most favourable conditions 'for a particular individual to do his/her best' (Mischel, 1977). Only intraindividual assessments provide the bases for offering psychological help to a particular individual or a group at a definite moment in one's life cycle. Re-orientation to intraindividual assessments requires more flexible test instructions, the collection of normative data for a particular individual, and the application of specific scales and instruments (e.g. grid techniques in the measurement of intrapersonal space, Slater, 1976) of which our psychologists are just beginning to become familiar.

Conclusion

Several methodological and conceptual issues in the cross-cultural study of individuality were examined in this chapter. From the data presented above, it is evident that the assessment of individual differences can be further improved by the introduction of a standard strategy for the adaptation and validation of the most sophisticated scales and inventories in current use by psychologists throughout the world. Another productive approach in the assessment of individual differences consists of modifications of standard instructions to incorporate also 'time-environment' dimensions of the situation given to intraindividual dynamics in the study of people in varying life situations. Finally, cross-cultural studies of individual differences require better international cooperation in the development of equivalent and parallel forms of the most promising scales and inventories, observational techniques and projective tests. Joint projects involving psychologists from different countries interested in the study of individual differences (and similarities) especially in children and adolescents could be an exciting road to both professional and 'humane' progress in the field.

References

ALLEN, G.J. (1970) Effect of three conditions of administration on trait and state measures of anxiety. *Journal of Consulting and Clinical Psychology*, **34**, 355–9.

BUCKY, S.F., SPIELBERGER, C.D. & BALE, R.M. (1972) Effect of instructions on measures of state and trait anxiety in flight students. *Journal of Applied Psychology*, **56**, 275–6.

CRATTY, B.J. & HANIN, Y.L. (1980) *The athlete in the sports team: social psychological guidelines for coaches and athletes*, Denver, Co.: Love Publishing Company.

CROWNE, D.P. & MARLOWE, D. (1960) *The approval motive: studies in evaluative dependence*, New York: Wiley.

EYSENCK, H.J. & EYSENCK, S.B.G. (1975) *Manual of the Eysenck Personality Questionnaire*, London: Hodder and Stoughton.

HANIN, Y.L. (1976) *A short manual for application of the Spielberger's STAI*, Leningrad: LNIIFK (in Russian).

HANIN, Y.L. (1977a) The standard strategy for adaptation of verbal scales and tests from other languages. In Y.Y. Kisselev (ed.) *Psychological problems of pre-competition preparation of athletes*, Leningrad: LNIIFK (in Russian).

HANIN, Y.L. (1977b) On the immediate assessment of personality's state anxiety in a group. *Theory and Practice of Physical Culture*, **8**, 8–11 (in Russian).

HANIN, Y.L. (1978) The study of anxiety in sports. *The Questions of Psychology*, **6**, 94–106 (in Russian). Reprinted in W.F. Straub (ed.), *Sport psychology: an analysis of athlete behavior*, (236–49), New York: Movement Publications.

HANIN, Y.L. (1985) Personality and social psychological inventories in the applied research: Problems and perspectives. In *Social psychology and public service*, (163–77), Moscow: Nauka Publishers (in Russian).

HANIN, Y.L. (1986) State-trait anxiety research on sports in the USSR. In C.D. Spielberger & R. Diaz-Guerrero (eds.) *Cross-cultural anxiety*, (vol. 3, 45–64), Washington: Hemisphere Publishing Corporation.

HANIN, Y.L. & BULANOVA, G.V. (1979) Anxiety state of undergraduates in study and sports groups. *Theory and Practice of Physical Culture*, **4**, 45–7 (in Russian).

HANIN, Y.L. & KOLOVARSKY, P.B. (1977) On the assessment and regulation of psychological states of ballet dancers before the important gala performances, concerts and competitions. In *Professional teaching of choreography and psychological differences of adolescents*, (37–43), Perm. (in Russian).

HANIN, Y.L. & SPIELBERGER, C.D. (1983) The development and validation of the Russian form of the State-Trait Anxiety Inventory. In C.D. Spielberger & R. Diaz-Guerrero (eds.) *Cross-cultural anxiety* (vol. 2, 15–26), Washington: Hemisphere Publishing Corporation.

LICHKO, A.E. (1976) The main principles of scale construction, procedure of its administration and scoring the results. In *Pathocharacterological inventory for adolescents and experience of its practical application*. (5–30), Leningrad: V.M. Bekhterev Psychoneurological Institute (in Russian).

MARTENS, R. (1977) *Sport Competition Anxiety Test*. Champaign, IL.: Human Kinetics, 1977.

McCROSKY, J.C. (1970) Measures of communcation-bound anxiety. *Speech Monographs*, **30**, 269–77.

MISCHEL, W. (1977) On the future of personality measurement. *American Psychologist*, **32**, 246–54.

MORGAN, W.P. & ELLICKSON, K.A. (1987, in press) Health, anxiety and performance. In C.D. Spielberger & D. Hackfort (eds.) *Anxiety in sport: international perspectives*, FEPSAC.

NIDEFFER, R.M. (1983) Identifying and developing optimal levels of arousal in sports. In Y.L.Hanin (ed.) *Stress and anxiety in sport (189–204)*, Moscow: Physical Culture and Sport Publishers (in Russian).

RUSHALL, B.S. (1983) Assessment of stress-tolerance in top athletes. In Y.L. Hanin (ed.) *Stress and anxiety in sport* (125–35), Moscow: Physical Culture and Sport Publishers (in Russian).

SLATER, P. (ed.), (1976) *Explorations of intrapersonal space: the measurement of intrapersonal space by grid techniques*, (vol. 1), London: Wiley.

SPIELBERGER, C.D. (1966) Theory and research on anxiety. In C.D. Spielberger (ed.) *Anxiety and behavior*, New York: Academic press.

SPIELBERGER, C.D. & DIAZ-GUERRERO, R. (eds.) (1983) *Cross-cultural anxiety*, (vol. 2), Washington: Hemisphere Publishing Corporation.

SPIELBERGER, C.D., GORSUCH, R.L. & LUSHENE, R.E. (1970) *Manual for the State-Trait Anxiety Inventory*, Palo Alto, CA: Consulting Psychologists.

SPIELBERGER, C.D. & SHARMA, S. (1976) Cross-cultural measurement of anxiety. In C.D. Spielberger & R. Diaz-Guerrero (eds.) *Cross-cultural anxiety*, (vol. 1), Washington: Hemisphere Publishing Corporation.

VALLERAND, R.J. (1983) On emotion in sport: theoretical and social psychological perspectives. *Journal of Sport Psychology*, **5**, 197–215.

27 Personality correlates of faking personality tests: a cross-cultural perspective

P. Šipka

Introduction

Various strategies aimed at reducing the tendency to fake personality tests of the true/false format have been suggested, and are still being developed. Some of them, like the 'bogus pipeline' (Johnes & Sigall, 1971) or 'randomized response technique' (Warner, 1965) have received wide attention and were judged as ingenious. Whatever the merits of these techniques, their practical limitations are serious and numerous. That makes the so-called 'lie scales', built into personality questionnaires, useful instruments of bias detection. Although the former may possibly have better prospects, traditional lie scales are still at an advantage, if not for other reasons, then due to the fact that they are contained in widely used inventories of long standing (e.g. MMPI), and/or are supported by powerful theories (e.g. Eysenck's theory of personality). For that reason we focused our attention on the problem of dissimulation as measured by such scales. In this study, as well as in general, we particularly concentrated on the Lie scale from the Eysenck Personality Questionnaire (EPQ; Eysenck & Eysenck, 1975). Our choice was influenced by the fact that the latter is the only personality test in Yugoslavia which has passed a rigorous cross-national standardization, for both the adult (Lojk, Eysenck & Eysenck, 1979) and the children's population (Eysenck & Šipka, 1981).

Psychometric aspects: the dual nature of the EPQ-L scale

The EPQ-L (Lie or Social Desirability) scale, together with the other scales of the EPQ, measuring neuroticism (N), extraversion (E) and psychoticism (P), has undergone successive and successful trials of testing and purification. A factor analysis of the latest version of both the Adult and the Junior form of L gave satisfactory results, indicating a single, strongly marked factor, which was confidently identified as lying or dissimulation (Eysenck & Eysenck, 1976). The internal consistency of L was relatively high, loadings being very similar from one age to another. The scale was relatively independent from other EPQ dimensions.

The psychometric qualities of L have been confirmed in numerous studies on various national/cultural samples. However, interpretation of the L results faced some difficulties, revealing its complex nature. The authors of the EPQ (Eysenck & Eysenck, 1975) accepted Dicken's (Dicken, 1959) three different 'possible and plausible' reasons for the emergence of high L scores: (1) deliberate faking, with intent to deceive the user; (2) responding in terms of ideal self-concept; (3) 'honest', but inaccurate, and uninsightful self-assessment. To this they added a fourth possible cause: 'genuine conformity to social norms and mores'.

Discussing this and other interpretations in the light of the findings available at the time, Eysenck & Eysenck (1976) suggested an explanation based on sensitivity of the scale to circumstantial factors provoking different degrees of motivation to dissimulate. Under conditions of high subjects' motivation to present themselves in a desirable light, as for example in the selection situation, L results may serve as an index of dissimulation. This situation can be judged by common-sense evaluation (as to whether interests to fake good exist), but is also psychometrically identifiable by high L means and a high LN correlation. The authors cautioned that the relationship between factors generating distortion and L scores are complex, and that all three rather than just one of the conditions should be fulfilled in order to justify the conclusion of the presence of dissimulation.

On the other hand, when there is no external pressure to dissimulate, as in anonymous administration, L results should be considered to be a reflection of personality. The authors did not identify this personality dimension with the widely accepted concept of 'defensiveness' (after equating the resistance to requests for disclosure with the level of motivation to dissimulate), but rather speculated about conservatism, orthodoxy and conformity, finally deciding on the last as the most suitable to cover the research data discussed.

The interpretation of the Junior EPQ-L was slightly different. Eysenck, Nias & Eysenck (1971) mentioned three causes that can contribute to the elevation of L means: intentional faking, 'insightfulness' as a dimension of personality, and 'conventionality, an attitude to account for sex differences, namely the tendency that girls have higher L results. Elsewhere Sybil Eysenck (Eysenck, 1965) used the term social immaturity to label the insight-denial dimension in children.

It should be added that the complex, basically dual nature of lie scales does not seem to be specific to the EPQ-L. Discussing the validity of the MMPI 'validity scales' (L, F and K), King-Ellison Good and Brantner (1974) argued that the two levels of meaning of these scales are the chief difficulty in their interpretation. The results obtained could be considered as an indicator of the subject's 'test-taking competency or attitude', and at the same time as an 'aspect of personality'. Similar warnings about dual interpretation and the possible misuse of lie-scale scores can also be encountered in manuals for other personality tests.

Psychological background: two components of favorable self-presentation

The tendency of unrealistically positive self-evaluation in personality testing attracted the attention of some authors beyond the test-makers and psychometritians. More recent contributions are referring to this tendency as a phenomenon of 'favorable self-presentation'.

Two components of favorable self-presentation and two lines of research attempts may be differentiated, one of which addresses the person's image with regard to oneself, and the other with regard to an 'external audience'. The dichotomy clearly parallels the dual nature of lie scales, i.e. the difference between intentional faking and unrealistically positive but genuine self-description. In the more recent literature (Paulhus, 1984; Roth, Snyder & Lynn, 1986), the former mainly relies on the construct of self-deception, while the latter most frequently uses the concept of impression management (Edwards, 1957; Schlenker, 1980). The purpose of this study dictates a closer look only at self-deception as the component of self-presentation.

Self-deception as a concept, in fact, comes from Freud. The traditional psychoanalytic view of defence mechanisms is based on the protective role of the defence (e.g. Fenichel, 1945). The defences (denial, repression, rationalization, etc.) are activated in order to limit the pain provoked by threatening forces, which is done through preventing unacceptable impulses from reaching the consciousness to be associated with the self. The conscious self becomes distorted in the cognitive sense, but remains stable, being thus protected from harmful stimuli.

The self-deception theory (Gur & Sackeim, 1979) has been built on this better part of the psychoanalytic tradition, extrapolating at the same time from the theory of cognitive dissonance. The theory offers a similar explanation for the phenomenon of distorted self-evaluations. Self-deception is defined as a process in which personal motives decide on which of two contradictory beliefs will reach awareness. More recently the formulation was extended (Sackeim, 1983), also to cover those instances of information distortion that happen in the absence of threat. Unlike psychoanalysts, the author also maintains that no distinction can be made between the repression of negative and the exaggeration of positive information.

The construct of egotism (Frankel & Snyder, 1978), recently developed into 'excuse making theory' (Snyder, 1985; Snyder, Higgins & Stucky, 1983), is similar in nature. Here, the stress is put on minimizing responsibility for bad performance so as to protect self-esteem. The authors hold that similar excuse making processes are engaged in both self- and other-deception. The two mechanisms are viewed as frequently amalgamated and inseparable.

Some personality theoreticians have also capitalized on defence mechanisms. Byrne (1964) has further developed the ideas of previous researchers regarding repressing-sensitizing as a dimension of personality. Repressing involves avoidance of anxiety-arousing stimuli, while sensitizing consists in attempts to reduce anxiety by approaching and controlling these stimuli. There is some evidence that repressors tend to overcontrol their self-report when answering personality questionnaires like the MMPI (e.g. Megargee & Mendelsohn, 1964). Applying the concept of repressing-sensitizing to the explanation of personality test behaviour would be more justifiable if some findings (e.g. Gray, 1971) had not questioned the uniqueness of the dimension, revealing its similarity to personality traits (like extraversion-introversion and optimism-pessimism) of already acknowledged theoretical status. Besides, Byrne's R-S (repression-sensitization) scale was found to overlap considerably with anxiety scales (Bell & Byrne, 1978), which led Sackeim (1983) to claim that it was primarily a measure of psychopathology, and only indirectly of self-deception.

It should be added that the role of self-deception in producing 'non-content-based responding' on personality tests was not unknown to psychometrically oriented authors (e.g. Anastasi, 1961). Meehl & Hathaway (1946) pointed out that the tendency of self-deception was of greater importance in affecting scores than were extensively studied conscious distortions.

Cross-cultural perspective

The difficulties related to the meaning and use of lie scales not only limit the valid measurement of personality, but additionally restrict cross-cultural comparison in the field. Interest in this sort of research was revived in the past decade (e.g. Spielberger & Diaz-Guerrero, 1976; Lynn, 1981). Systematic comparative studies gradually pushed 'playful, one-shot, atheoretical' (Jahoda, 1980) comparisons of various national samples into the background. Finally, a method of cross-cultural comparison of personality has been developed (Eysenck & Eysenck, 1982). Due to the high replicability of factors proposed in their dimensional theory, Eysenck and Eysenck paved the way toward a 'universal' theory of personality. Findings obtained by means of the EPQ turned out to be in surprisingly good accord with national differences, estimated by some entirely different (social and behavioral) variables (e.g. Lynn, 1971).

Nevertheless, certain difficulties still make further research necessary. Among the most important of these seems to be the problem of large cross-national differences in L means, which arouse doubt as to the validity of the results and calls for a correction. However, it seems that simple correction is not justifiable even inside one culture, i.e. standardization population (e.g. Orvik, 1972; Rahim, 1984; Šipka, 1984). On the other hand, accepting non-corrected EPQ results may lead to generalizations that could be questioned. A recent comparison of EPQ results obtained on an impressive number (25) of national samples (Barrett & Eysenck, 1984) offered a picture of national (dis)similarities that is, at least where Yugoslav results are concerned, difficult to incorporate into the existing body of knowledge built on anthropological, historical and sociological studies. Regardless of the correction, we wonder if the use of 'social desirability' (L) as one of the dimensions of personality (together with P, E and N) is warranted in cross-cultural comparison, until the nature of the L is satisfactorily explained, since national samples differ on many grounds (cultural, political, economical), all of them presumably reflected in personality self-description.

The dilemmas briefly outlined above have aroused our interest in the problem of dissimulation in general, and the EPQ-L scale in particular. This interest was reinforced by the finding that Yugoslav samples regularly score very high on L. The major part of this research has been done in the selection context, as being the most productive of dissimulation.

A strong tendency of responding in a socially desirable way, as expressed on the EPQ-L scale, has been registered in Yugoslavia on various samples and age groups. In our meta-analysis of EPQ findings on Yugoslav samples (ref. note 17) it was found that L means vary on a broad range, depending on the nature of the samples and the aim of the testing, but remain high even in 'rigorous anonymous' or 'post-dispatched' administration, never approaching English standardization data.

On the other hand, interscale LN correlations, which would be the other symptom of dissimulation, sometimes reach values pointing to orthogonality and therefore suggest the absence of deliberate faking. In a study of 14-year-old boys in a selection (entrance examination) situation, designed to test this relationship (Šipka, 1984), it was found that two main indicators of faking are not in good accord, and that only L results are sensitive to situation-induced motivation to dissimulate. The other EPQ scales remained basically uninfluenced by the pressure. It looks like a phenomenon that may be labeled a 'suspect effect'. Lack of decent family upbringing, lying and cheating – the manifest content of L items – are perceived as more important than other weaknesses and are less likely to be admitted by children. The children, being in a position of 'suspects' and trying to prove their 'innocence', are more willing to acknowledge their numerous bad behaviours and features (e.g. on the P scale) than 'crime' itself (contained in L items). We are faced here with a possibility of a false alarm: high L results may suggest dissimulation and the need for correction (or dismissal of the data), while other scales of the EPQ may actually give valid results. On the basis of these results, we speculated on utilizing the positive, 'buffer' role of L under certain circumstances.

In another study, on adolescents (Šipka, 1980) it was found that the factor structure of the EPQ changes when dissimulation is excessive, but not in the same way as previously established by Michaelis & Eysenck (1971). In that study a tendency appeared which was similar to Vernon's 'self-halo', and which resulted in the forming of a general pathological factor, resembling Guilford's Emotional Health. The items from the P and N scale were clustered not on a qualitative basis, but rather according to their similar pathological probability. We attributed this tendency to individual differences in readiness 'to acknowledge one's personal foibles to a certain limit'. The results question the use of personality tests in selection on ethical grounds, and also point to the phenomenon of 'role faking' i.e. answering the EPQ in accordance with perceived selection criteria, a finding which was replicated in a recent study (ref. note 19). In the selection situation, the subjects who gauge the school they are trying to enter as preparing them for a 'male' profession tend to have higher scores on P, considerably lowering only their N results. This finding further complicates the relations among the indices of dissimulation, and questions unidimensionality of the construct 'social desirability'.

No doubt, dissimulation can be reduced by using various non-standard, e.g. 'honesty' instructions (warning the subjects of the presence of a lie scale; Power, 1968; Eysenck, Eysenck & Shaw, 1974). A Yugoslav experience confirmed the effectiveness of this technique. By using such instructions, Žužul, Petz, Vizek-Vidović and Mihovilović (1984) obtained EPQ means for P, N, and L in the selection and 'research' situation that did not differ significantly. However, the respective factor structures were quite different both from each other and from the standardization solution. It seems that the effects of honesty instructions on other EPQ scales still remain to be determined. An extension of this technique based on a sort of training of how not to dissimulate, together with feedback information about success (Levin & Montag, 1987), yielded promising results, but might be time-consuming.

The Yugoslav research on dissimulation using the EPQ did not, however, address the crux of our present interest: what is the origin of excessive dissimulation in our subjects? Is it intentional or attributable to some other factors? Does it stem from personality specificities or social circumstances including different attitudes toward testing? The answer to these questions is to be found in future studies, at least some of which have to be cross-cultural *and* experimental at the same time.

The purpose of the present study was threefold:

(1)   To develop an index of individual 'fakability' by separating intentional (instrumental) faking from the total lie score variance by determining the discrepancy in individual results from two administrations differing in the amount of external pressure to dissimulate;

(2)   To demonstrate the validity of such an index, by relating the results to a measure of experimental and real-life lying and cheating; and

(3)   To establish the personality correlates of both instrumental and unintentional dissimulative behaviour, by relating the two isolated components to a set of personality and cognitive variables.

It was assumed that two situations differing in motivation to dissimulate may be approximated by the selection and postselection anonymous testing of the same subjects, provided that the time span between two applications is sufficient to annul the effects of remembering. It was decided for this time span to be three months.

Study 1

Method

Procedure

The subjects were male freshmen, their age ranging from 18 to 20 years, who lived in a state dormitory and were preparing for a career in the state administration. They completed the EPQ in the course of regular entrance examinations. The Ss were led to believe that the EPQ was one of the selection instruments, although no such claim was explicitly expressed.

Three months later, the Ss (N = 247) completed the same questionnaire during the laboratory classes in psychology. The instruction was designed for standard anonymous administration. Test sheets were marked so as to be matched with Ss' EPQ selection results following the procedure suggested by Mužić (1977).

About three months afterwards the Ss (N = 181) participated in the following experiment. First, they answered a 20-item test of 'verbal intelligence'. The test consisted of a list of 20 words of foreign, mainly Latin origin, that have vague meaning but are frequently used and misused in public life. Five different definitions were offered for every term. The Ss were supposed to choose one of them using a response system having a facility to express a total frequency of every response. After answering each item, Ss received correct feedback about the solution and false feedback about their group achievement as expressed by the percentage of correct answers in the group: each time, 30% was added to their total score in order to minimize the subjective value of the individual results, and, consequently, to facilitate cheating behaviour. The Ss then registered their results by putting signs + or − on the sheets with their names.

After completing the test, Ss were asked to count their total scores 'since the responder does not memorize the data and the experimenter wished to save his time, by not doing this clerical job'. (The responder actually does not have the facility of permanent registration and that was already known to the Ss from previous testings, but a simple procedure of recording was developed for the purpose of this experiment.) The total procedure was designed to allow cheating in a simple way and at a low risk, since the places where Ss were working were separated by permanent partitions, allowing a high degree of privacy. Cheating was equally possible during the examination and afterwards, by simply changing signs − into +. No hints that Ss had discovered the experimenter's deception were registered.

Following the experiment, judgments of real-life cheating and lying behaviour were called for. It should be noted here that the groups tested, their size varying from 26 to 32, comprised the Ss that not only attended lectures, but also lived together in a dormitory. They were told that this part of the experiment (with them in the role of perceivers) was anonymous. Regarding the information to be gathered, it was pointed out that nobody but the experimenter would have access to the data. They were assured of the confidentiality of the procedure by citing a relevant paragraph from the Code of the Psychological Association.

The Ss were then asked to identify up to 5 students from the group they consider to be most: (1) honest; (2) prone to boasting; (3) prone to innocent, noninstrumental lying; (4) prone to instrumental lying and cheating. Every attribute was operationalized in a few sentences. Some subjects protested not to be able to answer the last question. They were reassured of the solely scientific purpose of the study and (without insisting) encouraged to try. Debriefing was done when all subjects completed the experiment.

Data processing

Descriptive statistics and t-tests for correlated data, obtained in the selection and 'anonymous' testing, were calculated for all EPQ scales using the programs by Cohen & Holliday (1982). The discrepancy score as an index of instrumental faking was expressed by the single difference between L scores obtained for an individual in two testings.

The difference between actual and reported score was used as an index of classroom cheating. Ss having zero and negative differences (N = 75) were classified as noncheaters, and those with maximal differences (4–12; N = 57) as cheaters. The same procedure was employed in identifying extreme groups in peer judgments. The *t*-test program for independent samples by Cohen & Holliday (1982) was used for calculating differences between the extreme groups.

Results and discussion

The results obtained in the two testing situations (Table 27.1) reveal slight but significant differences in responding for all the scales. The differences are in the predicted direction, except perhaps for E, which is known to be resistant to factors provoking dissimulation. The largest difference was obtained on L, which was expected on the basis of previous findings, obtained in selection studies on both English (Michaelis & Eysenck, 1971) and Yugoslav populations (Šipka, 1980). In

Table 27.1 EPQ results in two testing situations compared to standardization data

| | L | | P | | E | | N | |
	M	S	M	S	M	S	M	S
Selection situation	13.51	(4.19)	4.90	(2.37)	15.30	(3.20)	7.30	(4.19)
Anonymous administration	12.60	(4.40)	5.38	(2.74)	14.90	(3.45)	7.68	(4.71)
t-test (correlated data)	4.049**		−2.709**		3.422**		−1.721*	
Yugoslav reference group	11.18	(5.51)	5.52	(3.31)	12.80	(5.36)	7.62	(4.98)
English reference age group	6.05	(3.80)	4.63	(3.27)	14.46	(4.27)	10.69	(5.08)

** $p<.01$; * $p<.05$
English standardization data are from Eysenck & Eysenck (1975); males: age 16 to 19; N=540.
Yugoslav data are from Miharija & Subota (ref. note 14); high school boys; N=2653.

spite of some evidence of dissimulation, correlations between L and other EPQ scales did not change in postselection testing (Table 27.2).

Classroom cheating seems to be related to lie scores obtained in both testing situations (Table 27.3). Cheaters and noncheaters differ not only in the selection but also in anonymous testing L results, indicating that, even in this situation, a part of the variance can be ascribed to deliberate faking. However, the two groups do not differ in the discrepancy index.

At first sight, the results support the hypothesis about the validity of L as a measure of lying. The lack of a significant relationship between discrepancy scores and cheating may be explained in terms of the 'ceiling effect': L scores were so inflated by dissimulation in both situations, that too little of the variance was left to be separated and related to other variables. However, there is no dramatic

Table 27.2 Correlations among EPQ scales in two testing situations

	LP	LE	LN	PN	EN	PE
Selection situation	−.43	−.10	−.31	.21	−.23	.02
'Anonymous' administration	−.43	−.08	−.31	.30	−.22	.00

Table 27.3 L results of high and low scorers in cheating

| | | Selection | | Anonymous | | Discrepancy score | |
		M	S	M	S	M	S
Low scorers	(N=75)	12.18	3.88	11.84	4.41	−0.07	3.88
High scorers	(N=57)	14.30	4.29	13.53	4.55	−0.77	3.57
		$t = 2.77$**		$t = 2.01$*		$t = 1.12$	

** $p<.01$; * $p<.05$

difference between the L mean of our subjects and the standardization data obtained for their age group, nor can one observe any obvious difference on other EPQ scales. Furthermore, the LN and LP correlations did not change even minimally in postselection administration. Finally, the two extreme groups selected on the basis of cheating results do not differ on the discrepancy score, which is intended to measure instrumental faking in a more rigorous way. It seems that the difference in L means obtained for the two administrations are insufficient 'proof' of outright, conscious, instrumental lying of our subjects, i.e. of widespread attempts to 'beat the test' in selection. An explanation that calls upon the 'need for approval' is more plausible, since this variable is also appropriate to explain students' classroom cheating behaviour, especially when detection is viewed as unlikely, and the situation jeopardizes self-esteem.

No significant relationship could be found between peer judgments of various aspects of real-life dishonest behaviour and L and its derivative (discrepancy score*) in either the selection, or the anonymous testing situation (Table 27.4). Bearing in mind that our subjects were in close social interaction, living and studying together for more than six months, we take their judgments as relatively valid, and accept this finding as reasonably firm evidence that L results have little to do with real-life cheating and lying behaviour. When viewed in the light of pioneering work by Hartshorne & May (1928) the results obtained might be considered unexpected, but

Table 27.4 L results of extreme groups selected on the basis of peer judgments

		Selection		Anonymous		Discrepancy score	
		M	S	M	S	M	S
Honest behaviour							
Low scorers	(N=67)	13.00	3.79	12.91	4.63	−0.09	3.63
High scorers	(N=60)	13.27	4.30	12.75	4.25	−0.52	3.53
		$t = 0.37$		$t = 0.20$		$t = 0.67$	
Boasting							
Low scorers	(N=76)	13.43	4.25	13.05	4.59	−0.38	3.95
High scorers	(N=57)	13.39	4.11	12.84	4.58	−0.55	3.13
		$t = 0.06$		$t = 0.26$		$t = 0.29$	
Innocent lying							
Low scorers	(N=80)	13.60	4.24	13.29	4.55	−0.27	3.80
High scorers	(N=56)	12.57	4.01	12.09	4.60	−0.44	3.21
		$t = 1.44$		$t = 1.50$		$t = 0.30$	
Instrumental lying							
Low scorers	(N=86)	13.50	4.03	12.60	4.53	−0.71	2.99
High scorers	(N=49)	13.57	4.14	12.61	4.56	−0.63	3.05
		$t = 0.10$		$t = 0.01$		$t = 0.16$	

** $p<.01$; * $p<.05$

---

* Discrepancy scores as an index of instrumental faking may undoubtedly be further psychometrically refined, but we failed to develop any measure resulting in a significant relationship to either classroom or real-life cheating; this problem is discussed in some detail in Šipka *et al.* (ref. note 19).

they are fully consistent with the more recent findings of O'Hagan & Edmunds (1982), who also failed to demonstrate the correlation between L scores and (teachers') judgments of actual lying.

Thus, our attempt to isolate a 'deceptive' part of the L variance failed and we further concentrated on the problem of personality correlates of dissimulation by treating L scores in two subsequent studies as a unidimensional concept. The results of this study clearly indicated that a deception variance, even if it exists, is too small to be the generator of the inflation of L results, commonly observed in the Yugoslav population.

Study 2

Method

Subjects
The subjects (N = 340) participating in the study were drawn from the same population as in the previous experiment. The experimenter was a male psychologist, known to the Ss as a person responsible for personnel selection and psychological counselling.

Procedure
The tests were administered to groups of 25 to 33 Ss in the course of laboratory classes in psychology. In order to avoid the work becoming tedious the tests were given in four sessions, each lasting 45 minutes. The testing was done in ordinary sheet-signed conditions.

Variables
The explanatory set of 41 variables consisted of a 'short' form of the MMPI (MMPI–201, 8 scales, ref. note 7), Freiburg Personality Inventory (FPI, 11, ref. note 4), Emotion Profile Index (EPI, 8, ref. note 3), Eysenck Personality Questionnaire (EPQ, 3, ref. note 13), Locus of Suicidality Scale (LS*, 3, ref. note 20), Life Style Questionnaire (LSQ, 3, ref. note 17) and Somatic Self Scale (PSC, 4, ref. note 16).

The dependent variables were lie scales from the EPQ, MMPI and FPI. Regression analysis was also performed on control scales from the MMPI (K and F) and the EPI (Bias), so that the results could be compared.

Data processing
Multiple step-wise regression analysis was performed separately for each control and lie scale as a dependent variable. The set of independent variables remained the same in each analysis and did not include other control or lie scales. Testing of the significance of successive increments was performed at a confidence level $p < 0.01$.

Results and discussion

Regression analysis (Table 27.5) resulted in high multiple regression coefficients (R) in predicting all control and lie scales. Only four to seven variables were needed to raise the coefficients to values ranging from R = .613 to R = .941. It is noticeable that control scales have higher Rs, mainly with variables from the test they belong to, which was predicted, since they partly share items. Lie scales, on the other hand, tended to have correlates out of a narrow 'pathological space' of personality. This is particularly characteristic of the EPQ-L which, at the same time, has the greatest number of correlates, and the lowest R. Either this scale is less saturated with pathological contents than others, or some other factors out of the space covered by explanatory variables participate more to its variance.

Generally, variables measuring aggressiveness tend to be most involved in regression equations. High ranks and/or regression coefficients can also be observed for emotional instability, including neuroticism and depressiveness. Interestingly but not surprisingly, the MMPI scale measuring hysterical tendencies surfaced in three batteries, each time with positive beta-weights. It is also worth mentioning that some scales, highly saturated with pathological content (e.g. MMPI-Sh, MMPI-Pa), are not among the best predictors of lie scale scores. In summary, tendermindedness, emotional stability, and hysterical tendencies make up the pattern of most frequent and/or salient predictors of lie scale scores.

Any attempt to account for the results of a correlational study using pathological personality tendencies and social desirability variables cannot avoid the question, stated many times in the literature (e.g. Sarason, 1972), querying the meaning of the correlations obtained, since pathological content and undesirability are inevitably confounded in an inventory. Trying to avoid this pitfall, we decided on separate regression analyses for pathological and normal personality dimensions, so as to provide at least partial uniformity in the social desirability of the explanatory variables. Besides, although there are restrictions in interpreting multiple regression results, these are not as discouraging as when using simple correlations. In multiple correlations, at least a part of the desirability variance is suppressed by the effects of intercorrelations of independent variables. As a result, the pattern of regression coefficients differs considerably from that obtained for simple correlations, which is partly visible from the data presented in Table 27.5.*

On the basis of these arguments, we suggest that the results may be accepted not as an index of social (un)desirability of explanatory variables, but rather as a provisional list of pathological personality tendencies influencing dissimulative behaviour. As one can see from Table 27.5, this list in fact ends with the MMPI-Hy scale, which, in normals (and, accordingly in our subjects) is primarily a measure of the tendency to present oneself in the light of social success, 'moral' and 'sense of well-being' (King-Ellison Good & Brantner, 1974). Otherwise, what we call lying or dissimulation is related to personal adjustment.

Study 3

Method

Subjects
The Ss (N = 292) were drawn from the same population as in the previous study. The procedure of testing and data processing was also the same.

Variables
The explanatory set of 36 variables consisted in a battery of nine cognitive tests comparing Domino (ref. note 5), TBK (ref. note 8), DAT (3 subtests, ref. note 1), TSU (ref. note 11), TRL (ref. note 9), BTI (subtests OB and AII, ref. note 6), and 27 personality tests comprising Cattell's Sixteen PF (16 scales, ref. note 10), Barron's Ego Strength Scale (ref. note 2). Eysenck's Extraversion, Authoritarianism and

---

* Due to restricted space available, all simple correlations are not presented here; they are given in a canonical analysis of the same data (ref. note 20) that resulted in findings consistent with the ones presented in this report.

Table 27.5 The results of multiple regression analysis: pathological tendencies

Control scales

Step	Test-dimension	β	R	r
Dependant variable: PIE–B I A S				
(1)	PIE–Destruction	−.593	.874	−.87
(2)	PIE–Incorporation	.574	.911	.79
(3)	PIE–Noncontrol	.546	.926	−.04
(4)	PIE–Self-protection	.375	.941	.56
Dependant variable: MMPI–F				
(1)	MMPI–Pa	.170	.687	.69
(2)	FPI–Neuroticism	.096	.751	.64
(3)	MMPI–Hy	.160	.787	.63
(4)	MMPI–Sh	.140	.799	.66
(5)	FPI–Depressiveness	.095	.811	.66
Dependant variable: MMPI–K				
(1)	FPI–Emot. lability	−.374	.763	−.76
(2)	MMPI–Pt	.346	.821	−.03
(3)	MMPI–D	−.290	.844	−.47
(4)	MMPI–Hy	.460	.862	.12
(5)	FPI–Neuroticism	−.262	.884	−.53

Lie scales

Step	Test-dimension	β	R	r
Dependant variable: FPI–L				
(1)	FPI–Emot. lability	−.251	.668	.67
(2)	FPI–Sp. aggressiveness	−.309	.723	.65
(3)	MMPI–Hy	.108	.733	.10
(4)	LSQ–Going out	−.384	.740	.15
Dependant variable: MMPI–L				
(1)	FPI–Sp. aggressiveness	−.256	.624	−.63
(2)	FPI–Depressiveness	−.139	.679	−.59
(3)	MMPI–Hy	.116	.702	−.05
(4)	FPI–Re. aggressiveness	−.086	.710	−.51
Dependant variable: EPQ–L				
(1)	FPI–SP. aggressiveness	−.465	.467	−.47
(2)	LSQ–Going out	−.864	.515	−.25
(3)	EPQ–P	−.394	.554	−.36
(4)	MMPI–Sh	.169	.548	−.02
(5)	PSC–Condition	.089	.596	.23
(6)	FPI–Controllability	.162	.605	.22
(7)	LSQ–Learning	.194	.613	.26

Conservatism (ref. note 15), Mental Rigidity Scale R-2 (ref. note 15), Levenson's IPC Locus of Control Scale (3 scales, ref. note 12) sociometric indices IZK and SSK, as well as Professional Motivation Scale ISS (ref. note 11).

The dependent variables were the EPQ-L scale, the MMPI K and L which were built into Baron's scale for the purpose of this study, and MOT-L (a domestic lie scale built into a questionnaire of professional motivation). The last was used instead of the Plutchick's Bias and the MMPI-F scale that could not be administered separately from the tests in which they are incorporated.

Results and discussion

Multiple correlation coefficients (Table 27.6), ranging from $r = .555$ to $r = .669$, show that in this study lie and control scales share less variance with the independent variables than in the preceding study, a finding that could have been expected, considering the lower social desirability of tests involved in this analysis. Having this in mind, we may even argue that coeffiecients obtained are surprisingly high. Although the correlations among lie and control scales are relatively low, never exceeding $r = .50$, no systematic differences in the profiles of their best-predictor batteries could be claimed. Generally, the results suggest that the basic social attitudes (rigid acceptance of social values, authoritarianism and conservatism), positively weighted, and ergic tension (Q4), with negative weights, are dominant correlates of dissimulation. The cognitive tests also have substantive (negative) contributions in prediction, especially those among them which are measures of general reasoning.

The results are consistent with previous findings that dissimulation is related to overconformism (e.g. Powell, 1977) and low intelligence (Eysenck *et al.*, 1971; Miharija & Sobota, ref. note 1; but for nonsignificant or opposite findings see Saklofske, 1985; Kalmanchey & Kozeki, 1983). Together with low ergic tension, which is the most salient personality predictor, they make a triad of 'symptoms' which, in the light of the present dichotomy of favourable self-presentation, indicate that self-deception rather than impression management governs individual differences in lie scale scores.

General discussion

The findings and arguments set out in our three studies can now be summarized. In study 1 we failed to demonstrate unequivocally the existence of deceptive variance in the lie scale scores of our subjects. Although, as stated many times in the literature, one can never falsify a null hypothesis, it is our opinion that the procedure used (based on the comparison of the lie results observed in two situations differing extremely in the motivation to dissimulate) should have demonstrated instrumental faking, had this component been an important part of the lie score's variance. In terms of dimensions of favourable self-presentation, it can be argued that self-deception predominantly shapes individual differences in dissimulation.

The present results are consistent with our previous finding (Šipka, 1980) that dissimulation of our subjects is resistant to experimental manipulation. Unless further research demonstrates the opposite, we have no choice but to conclude that a personality dimension generates L scores, *regardless* of the level of motivation to dissimulate. The rationale for this conclusion is simple enough: if it 'changes' it is a motive, if not it is a personality trait.

In the regression analysis performed in studies 2 and 3, we obtained some additional support for this argument. The findings indicate that personal and social

Table 27.6 The results of multiple regression analysis: intelligence, personality and attitudes

Step	Test-dimension	β	R	r	Step	Test-dimension	β	R	r
Dependant variable: MMPI–K					Dependant variable: MMPI–L				
(1)	16 PF–Q4	-.161	.510	-.51	(1)	16 PF–Q4	-.123	.457	-.46
(2)	Barron's ego	.312	.601	.48	(2)	Domino	-.163	.560	-.36
(3)	16 PF–N	.207	.631	.30	(3)	Authoritarianism	.108	.598	-.02
(4)	16 PF–H	.096	.659	.43	(4)	Conservatism	-.057	.617	.22
(5)	DAT–M	-.051	.669	-.10	(5)	IPC–I	-.100	.637	-.12
					(6)	ISS	.032	.654	.24
					(7)	16 PF–Q3	.094	.664	.40
Dependant variable: MOT–L					Dependant variable: EPQ–L				
(1)	Rigidity	.112	.401	.40	(1)	Rigidity	.060	.359	.36
(2)	DAT–B	-.413	.493	-.40	(2)	16 PF–Q4	-.210	.465	-.35
(3)	ISS	.209	.568	.23	(3)	16 PF–F	-.196	.519	-.27
(4)	16 PF–G	.335	.584	.30	(4)	DAT–B	-.113	.543	-.31
(5)	Conservatism	.234	.598	.36	(5)	16 PF–Q2	-.144	.555	-.19
(6)	DAT–M	-.137	.607	-.28					
(7)	16 PF–C	.315	.616	.27					
(8)	16 PF–I	.441	.625	-.01					
(9)	16 PF–M	.297	.634	-.14					

(over)adjustment, as described by non-agressiveness, emotional stability, hysterical tendencies, low ergic tension, rigid social attitudes and lack of general ability, form the pattern of salient personality correlates of lie scale results.

In speculating about the single dimension which might be in the background of this set of features, one can offer a lot of possible labels, all of which can easily be challenged. It seems to us that 'self-satisfaction' may be an appropriate term to cover the pattern. More important than mere nomination, is the impression that self-deception rather than other-deception could be a behavioural product of this 'type' of personality.

It is worth trying to discuss the findings in cross-cultural perspective, i.e. in the light of commonly observed high lie score means in Yugoslav children and adolescents, since this tendency is expressed in many other particularly non-Western societies (Barrett & S. Eysenck, 1984). Some authors argue that it is not generally appropriate to use questionnaires in developing countries. Liggett (1983) suggested that 'transparent questions are inviting for conscious concealment and deception' and those 'enquiring into sensitive personal issues, such as family planning, provoke anxiety and unconscious defensive concealment'.

We do not believe that Liggett's experience should be related to either our subjects or the personality tests we used. This does not mean that we deny the importance of the purpose of testing and the perception of the experimenter as factors influencing test results. We found that positive attitudes toward psychology, were related to high L EPQ results (ref. note 3). This finding was explained in terms of the 'evaluation apprehension' hypothesis (Rosenberg, 1965): those subjects who perceive psychology as an important discipline are prone to 'please' the experimenter (being the psychologist) with socially desirable responding. There are some reasons to believe that this tendency is more strongly expressed in developing countries.

There are some authors (e.g. O'Hagan & Edmunds, 1982) who allow for the possibility that high lie scorers do not fake but sincerely accept and conform to social rules and regulations. It is possible that patriarchal, oppressive nurturing practices, still present in many rural and less educated families in Yugoslavia, result in behaviour which adheres more firmly to social rules. The common foibles contained in the lie scale items do not necessarily have to apply to the children and adolescents of such families. One can predict that outside of the Western industrialized ambiance more overconforming children do exist.

The difference in permissiveness in the school atmosphere and society in general has already been used to explain cross-cultural differences in Junior EPQ-L results (e.g. Eysenck, Kozeki & Kalmanchey, 1980; Eysenck & Saklofske, 1983). The present and previous findings allow us to hypothesize an even deeper relationship of L results with the social milieu. The authors of the EPQ themselves found that L was the only EPQ scale governed by the environmental factor labelled E2 (Eaves & Eysenck, 1974). There is some evidence that social factors operate to an even greater extent in shaping individual differences in lie scores in a country such as Yugoslavia. On a very large representative sample Miharija & Sobota (ref. note 1) found L, more than any other EPQ scale, to be (negatively) related to educational level of the father, school achievement, and size of the place of residence. Very similar results were obtained in neighbouring Hungary (Kalmanchey & Kozeki, 1983).

Thus, the results of the two 'inside-cultural' studies resulted in the findings that may be viewed as contributions to the permissiveness hypothesis. Accepting this hypothesis does not necessarily contradict the explanation we offered for L inflation of our subjects. Putting the two explanations together suggests a new hypothesis that non-permissiveness, self-deception and self-satisfaction are interrelated. We take the liberty of claiming that this hypothesis makes sense and deserves to be tested.

Conclusion

The initial philosophy of the use of lie scales as diagnostic and correction tools was simple and elegant. Personally threatening but universally true statements are used to catch people lying when denying them. Yet, as many times before in the history of psychology, a clear and distinct construct turned out to be a complex one. Looking closer into what lies behind lie scale scores revealed a variety of sources, some of them being culturally mediated. Lying itself is the least found among them.

The results of the present study indicate that a facet of personality which is neither a lying habit nor a need to impress others, but rather a learned, mistaken (self-deceiving, self-satisfactory) but genuine self-perception can be tentatively considered a latent factor generating high lie scale scores, regardless of environmental factors provoking dissimulation. Our future studies will be oriented toward testing this hypothesis.

What is comforting for personality test users, and the EPQ authors, is the phenomenon that these misperceptions hardly influence the global personality self-evaluation, if at all. But at the same time an upsetting fact is that the corrective function of the lie scale is not operative in a country such as Yugoslavia, in spite of high L means of our subjects and relatively high LN correlations. The results of the present study suggest that the correction is not justifiable, since significant correlations of L with N could simply be the genuine relationship between two personality dimensions: self-deception is known to be 'good for mental health' and its negative relationship with neuroticism is far from unexpected. We suggest that there is also no need to pay special attention to high L means in interpreting other EPQ results obtained in cross-cultural studies. In the final instance, this is also a sort of correction.

References

ANASTASI, A. (1961) *Psychological testing*, New York: Macmillan.
BARRETT, P. & EYSENCK, S.B.G. (1984) The assessment of personality factors across 25 countries. *Person. individ. Diff.*, **5**, 615–32.
BELL, P.A. & BYRNE, D. (1978) Repression-sensitization. In H. London and J.E. Exner (eds.) *Dimensions of personality*, (449–85), New York: Wiley.
BYRNE, D. (1964) Repression-sensitization as a dimension of personality. In B. Maher (ed.) *Progress in experimental personality research*, (169–220), New York: Academic Press.
COHEN, L. & HOLLIDAY, M. (1982) *Statistics for social scientists*, London: Harper and Row.
CROWNE, D.P. & MARLOWE, D. (1960) A new scale of social desirability independent of psychopathology. *J. consult. Psychol.*, **24**, 349–54.
DICKEN, C.F. (1959) Simulated patterns on the Edwards Personal Preference Schedule. *J. appl. Psychol.*, **43**, 372–8.
EAVES, L.J. & EYSENCK, H.J. (1974) Genetics and development of social attitudes. *Nature*, **249**, no. 5454, 288–9.
EDWARDS, A.L. (1957) *The social desirability variable in personality assessment and research*, New York: Dryden Press.
EYSENCK, H.J. & EYSENCK, S.B.G. (1975) Manual of the EPQ (Personality Questionnaire), London: Hodder & Stoughton Educational; San Diego: Educational and Industrial Testing Service.
EYSENCK, J. & EYSENCK, S.B.G. (1976) *Psychoticism as a dimension of personality*, London: Hodder & Stoughton.
EYSENCK, H.J. & EYSENCK, S.B.G. (1982) Recent advances in the cross-cultural study of personality. In C.D Spielberger and J.N. Butcher (eds.), *Advances in personality assessment*, vol. 2, Hillsdale, N.J.: Erlbaum.
EYSENCK, S.B.G. (1965) A new scale for personality measurement in children. *Br. J. educ. Psychol.*, **35**, 362–7.

EYSENCK, S.B.G., EYSENCK, H.J. & SHAW, L. (1974) The modification of personality and lie scale scores by special 'honesty' instructions. *Br. J. soc. clin. Psychol.*, **13**, 41–50.

EYSENCK, S.B.G., KOZEKI, B. & KALMANCHEY, G.M. (1980) Cross-cultural comparison of personality: Hungarian children and English children. *Person. individ. Diff.*, **1**, 347–53.

EYSENCK, S.B.G., NIAS, D.K.B. & EYSENCK, H.J. (1971) The interpretation of Children's Lie Scale scores. *Br. J. educ. Psychol.*, **41**, 23–31.

EYSENCK, S.B.G. & SAKLOFSKE, D.H. (1983) A comparison of responses of Canadian and English children on the Junior Eysenck Personality Questionnaire. *Canad. J. behav. Sci.*, **15**, 121–30.

EYSENCK, S.B.G. & ŠIPKA, P. (1981) Cross-cultural comparison of personality: Yugoslav children and English children. *Primjenjena psihologija*, **2**, 175–80.

FENICHEL, O. (1945) *The psychoanalytic theory of neurosis*, New York: Norton.

FRANKEL, A. & SNYDER, M.L. (1978) Poor performance following unsolvable problems: learned helplessness or egotism? *J. pers. soc. Psychol.*, **36**, 1415–24.

GRAY, J. (1971) *The psychology of fear and stress*, New York: McGraw-Hill.

GUR, R.C. & SACKEIM, H.A. (1979) Self-deception: a concept in search of a phenomenon. *J. Pers. soc. Psychol.*, **37**, 147–69.

HARTSHORNE, H. & MAY, M.A. (1928) *Studies in deceit*, New York: Macmillan.

JACKOBSON, L.I., KELLOGG, R.W., CAUCE, A.M. & SLAVIN, R.E. (1977) A multidimensional social desirability inventory. *Bull. Psychonom. Societ.*, **9**, 109–10.

JAHODA, G. (1980) Cross-cultural comparisons. In M.H. Bornstein, *Comparative methods in psychology*, (105–48), Hillsdale, N.J.: Lawrence Erlbaum.

JOHNES, E.E. & SIGALL, H. (1971) The bogus pipeline: a new paradigm for measuring affect and attitude. *Psychol. Bull.*, **76**, 349–64.

KALMANCHEY, G.A. & KOZEKI, B. (1983) Relation of personality dimensions to social and intellectual factors in children. *Person. individ. Diff.*, **4**, 237–43.

KING-ELLISON GOOD, P. & BRANTNER, J.P. (1974) *A practical guide to the MMPI*, London: Oxford University Press.

LAUNGANI, P. (1985) National differences in personality: India and England. *Person. individ. Diff.*, **6**, 217–21.

LEVIN, J. & MONTAG, I. (1987) The effect of testing instructions for handling social desirability on the Eysenck Personality Questionnaire. *Person. individ. Diff.*, **8**, 163–7.

LIGGETT, J. (1983) Some practical problems of assessment in developing countries. In F. Blackler (ed.) *Social psychology and developing countries*, New York: Wiley.

LOJK, L., EYSENCK, S.B.G. & EYSENCK, H.J. (1979) National differences in personality: Yugoslavia and England. *Br. J. Psychol.*, **70**, 381–7.

LYNN, R. (1971) *Personality and national character*, London: Pergamon.

LYNN, R. (1981) Cross-cultural differences in neuroticism, extraversion and psychoticism. In R. Lynn (ed.) *Dimensions of personality*, (263–86), London: Pergamon.

MEEHL, P.E. & HATHAWAY, S.R. (1946) The K factor as a suppressor variable in the MMPI. *J. Appl. Psychol.* **30**, 525–64.

MEGARGEE, E.I. & MENDELSOHN, G. (1964) A cross-validation of twelve MMPI indices of hostility and control. *J. abnorm. soc. Psychol.* **65**, 431–8.

MICHAELIS, W. & EYSENCK, H.J. (1971) The determination of personality inventory factor patterns and intercorrelations by changes in real-life motivation. *J. genet. Psychol.*, **118**, 223–34.

MUŽIĆ, V. (1977) *Metodologija pedagoškog istraživanja.* (Methods of research in education). Sarajevo: Svjetlost.

O'HAGAN, F.J. & EDMUNDS, G. (1982) Teachers' observations on pupil's untruthfulness in relation to the 'Lie' scale. *Person. individ. Diff.*, **3**, 335–8.

ORVIK, J.M. (1972) Social desirability for the individual, his group and society. *Multivar. Behav. Res.*, 3–31.

PAULHUS, D.L. (1984) Two-component models of socially desirable responding. *J. Pers. soc. Psychol.*, **46**, 598–609.

POWELL, G.E. (1977) Psychoticism and social deviancy in children. *Adv. Behav. Res. Ther.*, **1**, 27–56.

POWER, R.P. (1968) Simulation of stable and neurotic personalities by subjects warned of the presence of Lie Scales in inventories. *Br. J. Psychol.*, **59**, 105–9.

RAHIM, M.A. (1984) Social desirability response set and the Eysenck Personality Inventory. *J. Psychol.*, **116**, 149–53.

ROSENBERG, M.J. (1965) When dissonance fails: on eliminating evaluation apprehension from attitude measurement. *J. Pers. soc. Psychol.*, **1**, 28–42.

ROTH, D.L., SNYDER, C.R. & LYNN, M.P. (1986) Dimensions of favorable self-presentation. *J. Pers. soc. Psychol.*, **51**, 867–74.

SACKEIM, H.A. (1983) Self-deception, self-esteem and depression: the adaptive value of lying to oneself. In J. Masling (ed.) *Empirical studies of psychoanalytic theories*, (101–57), Hillsdale, NJ: Erlbaum.

SAKLOFSKE, D.H. (1985) The relationship between Eysenck's major personality dimensions and simultaneous and sequential processing in children. *Person. individ. Diff.*, **6**, 429–33.

SARASON, I.G. (1972) *Personality: an objective approach*, New York: Wiley.

SCHLENKER, B.R. (1980) Impression management: the Self-concept, social identity, and interpersonal relations. Monterey: Brooks/Cole.

ŠIPKA, P. (1980) Disimulacija u selekcionom kontekstu i faktorska struktura testa ličnosti EPQ (Dissimulation in the selection context and factor structure of the EPQ). *Psihologija*, **4**, 127–34.

ŠIPKA, P. (1984) *Distorzija rezultata na Junior EPQ, disimulcija i motivacija za disimulaciju: o jednoj novoj funkciji skala laži.* (Distortion of the results on the Junior EPQ, dissimulation, and the motivation to dissimulate: about a new function of the lie scales). VII Kongres psihologa SFRJ, Druga knjiga priopćenja, Zagreb: SDP SFRJ.

SNYDER, C.R. (1985) The excuse: an amazing grace. In B.R. Schlenker (ed.) *Self and identity: presentation of self in social life*, (235–60), New York: McGraw-Hill.

SNYDER, C.R., HIGGINS, R.L. & STUCKY, R.J. (1983) *Excuses: masquerades in search for grace*, New York: Wiley.

SPIELBERGER, C. & DIAZ-GUERRERO, R. (1976) *Cross-national anxiety*, London: Wiley.

WARNER, S.L. (1965) Randomized response: a survey technique for eliminating evasive answer bias. *J. Am. Stat. Assoc.*, **60**, 63–9.

ŽUŽUL, M., PETZ, 'B., VIZEK-VIDOVIĆ, V. & MIHOVILOVIĆ, M. (1984) Usporedba rezultata i faktorskih struktura dobivenih primjenom Eysencko-ova upitnika (EPQ) u selekcijskoj i istraživačkoj situaciji. (A comparison of the results and factor structures obtained by application of the EPQ in the selection and research situation). *Čovek i zanimanje*, 16–22.

Reference Notes

1. AHTIK V., ZAJEC, M. & POTOČNIK, Ž. *Priručnik za bateriju testova sposobnosti DAT*, Zavod SRS PD, Ljubljana, 1975.

2. BARRON, F. *Psychotherapy as a special case of personal interaction: prediction of its course.* Unpublished doctoral dissertation. University of California, Berkeley, 1950.

3. BAŠKOVEC-MILINKOVIĆ, A., BELE-POTOČNIK, Ž., HRUŠEVAR, B. & ROJŠEK, J. *Profil indeks emocija*, Zavod SRS PD, Ljubljana, 1979.

4. BELE-POTOČNIK, Ž., HRUŠEVAR, B., KRIZMANIĆ, M. & TUŠEK, M. *Frajburški upitnik ličnosti*, Zavod SRS PD, Ljubljana, 1981.

5. BELE-POTOČNIK, Ž., & ONIČ-NOVAK, H. *Test Domino 'D-48'*, Zavod SRS PD, Ljubljana, 1978.

6. BELE-POTOČNIK, Ž. AND ZAJEC, M. *Baterija testova sposobnosti BTI*, Zavod SRS PD, Ljubljana, 1972.

7. BIRO, M. & BERGER, J. *Praktikum za primenu i interpretaciju MMPI*, Savez društava psihologa SRS, Beograd, 1985.

8. BUJAS, Z. *B-Serija*, Republički zavod za zapošljavanje SRH, Zagreb, 1970.

9. DOLINAR, A. *Test rezonovanja likova TRL*, Zavod SRS PD, Ljubljana, 1971.

10. IGNJATOVIĆ, I. *Šesnaest faktora ličnosti – forma A; eksperimentalno izdanje*, Institut KKI, Beograd, 1962.

11. KOSTIĆ, P. *Uticaj osobina ličnosti na uspešnost u obavljanju rukovedećih uloga* (The influence of personality characteristics on success in performing leader's role), Magistarski rad, Filozofski fakultet, Beograd, 1984.

12. KRAMPEN, G. *IPC-Frageboten zu Kontrollüberzeugungen*, Verlag für Psychologie, Göttingen, 1971.

13. LOJK, L. *Eysenckov upitnik ličnosti*, Zavod SRS PD, Ljubljana, 1979.

14. MIHARIJA, Ž. & SOBOTA, I. *Standardizacija Eysenckovog upitnika EPQ za učenike završnih razreda srednjeg obrazovanja u SR Hrvatskoj.* (A standardization of EPQ for the pupils in final years of secondary education in Croatia), RSIZZ, Zagreb, 1982.

15. MOMIROVIĆ, K. & IGNJATOVIĆ, I. Struktura konativnih faktora. *Psihologija*, 3–4, 1977.

16. MRAZEK, J. Die Verkörperung des Selbst: Ergebnisse der Psychologie heute-Unfrage, *Psychologie Heute*, 2, 1984.
17. ŠIPKA, P. *Ličnost jugoslovena opisana testom ličnosti EPQ*. (The personality of the Yugoslavs as described by the Eysenck Personality Questionnaire). Manuscript submitted for publication, 1986.
18. ŠIPKA, P. & KOSTIĆ, P. *Ličnost, prikrivanje ličnih slabosti i stavovi prema psihologiji* (Personality, faking personality tests and attitudes toward psychology). In preparation.
19. ŠIPKA, P., KOSTIĆ, P., KOSANOVIĆ, B. & LOVRE, M. *Evaluacija eksterne valjanosti EPQ-L skale*. (An evaluation of external validity of the EPQ-L scale). In preparation.
20. ŠIPKA, P., *Kanoničke korelacije grupe kontrolnih i skala laži sa skupom testova ličnosti*. (Canonical correlations of a group of control and lie scales with a set of personality tests). Manuscript submitted for publication, 1987.

Index